CULINARIA
SPAIN
SPANISH SPECIALTIES

CULINARIA
SPAIN

MARION TRUTTER
EDITOR

GÜNTER BEER
PHOTOGRAPHY

PETER FEIERABEND
ART DIRECTOR

MICHAEL DITTER
COORDINATION AND LAYOUT

Culinaria
KÖNEMANN

ABBREVIATIONS AND QUANTITIES

1 oz	= 1 ounce = 28 grams
1 lb	= 1 pound = 16 ounces
1 cup	= 8 ounces **(note on right)
1 cup	= 8 fluid ounces = 250 milliliters (liquids)
2 cups	= 1 pint (liquids)
8 pints	= 4 quarts = 1 gallon (liquids)
1 g	= 1 gram = ⅟₁₀₀₀ kilogram
1 kg	= 1 kilogram = 1000 grams = 2¼ lb
1 l	= 1 liter = 1000 milliliters (ml) = approx. 34 fluid ounces
125 milliliters (ml) = approx. 8 tablespoons	
1 tbsp	= 1 level tablespoon = 15–20 g **(note on right) = 15 milliliters (liquids)
1 tsp	= 1 level teaspoon = 3–5 g **(note on right) = 5 ml (liquids)

Topics which appear on pages with a colored background relate to Spain as a whole. Exception: the introductory pages of each chapter deal with a particular region.

■ ■ ■

© 2004 KÖNEMANN*, an imprint of
Tandem Verlag GmbH, Königswinter

Concept:	Günter Beer, Ludwig Könemann, Marion Trutter
Editing:	Marion Trutter
Travel organization (photography) and photographic assistance:	Markus Bassler, Barcelona
Food Stylists:	Frank Schauhoff, Cologne Tonina Oliver, Llucmajor Patrik Jarös, Munich Stephan Krauth, Cologne (titles)
Maps:	Astrid Fischer-Leitl, Munich
Recipe editor:	Ingeborg Pils, Munich

Original title: *Culinaria España – Spanische Spezialitäten*
ISBN 3-8331-1050-3

© 2004 for the English edition
KÖNEMANN*, an imprint of Tandem Verlag GmbH,
Königswinter

Translation from German:	Mo Croasdale, Karen Green, David Hefford, Michele McMeekin, Judith Phillips, Elaine Richards, Janet Richmond.
Editing and Typesetting:	First Edition Translations, Cambridge, UK.
Project Coordination:	Bettina Kaufmann and Nadja Bremse

*KÖNEMANN is a registered trademark of Tandem Verlag GmbH
The usage rights for images attributed to Könemann Verlagsgesellschaft mbH,
Cologne in the picture credits lie with Tandem Verlag GmbH, Königswinter.

Printed in EU

ISBN 3-8331-1140-2

10 9 8 7 6 5 4 3 2 1
X IX VIII VII VI V IV III II I

Where measurements of dry ingredients are given in spoons, this always refers to the prepared ingredient as described in the wording following, e.g. 1 tbsp chopped onions BUT: 1 onion, peeled and chopped.
** The weight of dry ingredients varies significantly depending on the density factor; e.g. 1 cup flour weighs less than 1 cup butter.
Quantities in recipes have been rounded up or down for convenience, where appropriate. Metric conversions may therefore not correspond exactly. It is important to use either American or metric measurements within a recipe.

Quantities in recipes
Recipes serve 4 people, unless stated otherwise.
Exception: Recipes for drinks (quantities given per person).

Contents

"A country's cuisine is its landscape in a cooking pot," said the Catalan writer Josep Pla (1897-1981). That glance inside the cooking pot reveals more than just a country's geography. To savor a nation's culinary customs is to experience the unfolding of an entire culture. Like tasting a fine wine, it takes time and patience, and a readiness to discover some hitherto unfamiliar subtleties. Spain is much loved for its sun-drenched countryside and white beaches, but that very fact can be a disadvantage. Reality is reduced to a set of unrelated clichés, and that applies to Spanish culture and cuisine alike: paella and octopus, red wine and sangría so dominate our images of Spanish cuisine that no room remains for new discoveries.

This book aims to awaken the reader's appetite for Spain's variety, the countless facets of nature, culture, and cuisine which it offers. The great range of climate is a sure sign that this country has more than just one unified culinary tradition: the cool, damp northwest produces a very different harvest from the constantly mild Mediterranean or the sparse plateau of central Spain, with its searingly hot summers and icy winters.

Many peoples conquered or settled these lands in the course of history and left their mark; their passage can be traced even today in the flavors of Spain: Romans, Jews, Arabs, travelers returning from the New World, and those passing through on a pilgrimage to the shrine in Santiago de Compostela. All these different groups introduced goods, ideas, and customs to the Iberian Peninsula. A country of such variety, which has produced such different groups of people as the Andalusians and the Aragonese, Catalans and Canary Islanders, Basques and Madrileños, has of course also developed a complex cuisine. This comes not so much from the variation in tastes as from the fact that a mountain shepherd in the Pyrenees, for example, needs warming food, while a plantation worker in the Levante will prefer lighter fare.

Spanish cuisine has always been faithful to these roots, relying on what the earth produces. In milder regions, this produce was always light; in the mountains, robust; never contrived or using "imported" ingredients.

The decision to base the choice of recipes mainly on the traditional cuisines of the various regions was therefore an obvious one. This is not to say that there are clear-cut distinctions between the cuisines of adjacent areas. Similarities in geography, in the historic relationships of certain areas, or resulting from long years of mutual influence, have often created resemblances between neighboring cuisines. We have set out, however, to highlight the most strikingly characteristic specialties alongside the common heritage.

This book invites its readers to a world of enjoyment. Follow as it beckons and take a culinary journey through Spain. The way to the heart is said to be the stomach, but the heart may find far more than food. Eating is a pleasure of the senses, and can appeal to sight as well as taste, and to the emotions and the mind as well.

Marion Trutter

CATALUÑA

WALTER TAUBER

CATALONIA

In the mountains and forests of their homeland, the Catalans find the produce from which culinary miracles are created: an abundance of mushrooms and magnificent game.

Spontaneous, complex, and contradictory – the country and cuisine of the Catalans is like the character of the people themselves. Catalonia is a small nation pursuing independence within a united Europe. For a long time this region lay at the heart of a kingdom stretching as far as Sicily, Naples, and Sardinia, and its ships dominated trade in the Mediterranean in the name of the Crown of Aragon. But for much of its history, Catalonia was felt to lie at the edge of Europe: it constituted the westernmost borderland of the Carolingians, and a rampart against the onslaught of the Arabs. The country was repeatedly swept by invaders, from the Romans, Goths, and Arabs to the troops of the king of Castile. This mild region attracted settlers: French, Italian, and above all Andalusian, people from the south

of Spain. Constantly open to the world, Catalonia has adopted outside influences with enthusiasm and turned the blending of cultures into an art. Yet it has continued to hold its own roots, its language, and its customs, in high regard. The country derives its variety still more from its geography than its history: a harsh mountain region with rushing torrents in the north and fairly dry plains in the south, subjected to the continental climate of the Castilian plateau. At its edge laps the shining Mediterranean. Rugged as the coast may often be, the sea soothes the wild country; it provides riches and serves as a link with the world beyond. The cuisine reflects the varied characteristics of the land and people; the Catalans have always put the influences from other regions to good use, and the mixture simmering in their

cooking pots is varied indeed. There we find, for example, the playfulness of Provence and Valencia's baroque, together with the robustness of the Catalan hinterland. *Mar i muntanya* (sea and mountain) is the Catalan phrase given to the remarkable combinations of fish and meat which illustrate so strikingly their talent for creating a blend of the diverse. *Seny* (common sense) is another characteristic typical of the Catalans, and one they are especially proud of. This balance tempers their flights of fancy. Catalonia is the land which played host to the rise of banditry and anarchy, but where good sense, thrift and skill in determining how to act are respected to this day as fundamental virtues. Against such a background, a dish of chicken with shrimp stands to reason, surely?

Santiago de Compostela
Vitoria-Gasteiz
Cataluña
León
Pamplona
Girona
Valladolid
Zaragoza
Lleida
Madrid
Barcelona
Tarragona
Toledo
Palma de Mallorca
Valencia
Mérida
Ciudad Real
Murcia
Sevilla
Granada

Opposite: The magic of Catalonia owes much to its mix of mountains and water. The land rises to a height of some 9800 feet (3000 meters) above the Mediterranean.

THE BOQUERIA: BARCELONA'S CORNUCOPIA

La Pepa del atún is over 90 years old: "I shall die here in the Boquería," she affirms, wielding her sharp knife with the same skill as she has for decades past. Josepa Albiol – her full name – sells tuna and superintends the stallholders in Barcelona's most beautiful market. The Mercat de Sant Josep, known as La Boquería, is a treasure trove. Remarkable people like Pepa are just whom one finds on a trip around this market. They are the city's finest product. The history behind the place is fascinating:

There used to be a market near the present site on the popular promenade Las Ramblas when the city ended here. Farmers used to sell their wares at the city gates. The name *Boquería* is said to come from an old Catalan expression meaning "place where goat meat is sold." As the city grew in the 18th century, the city walls came down and the former river bed, the *rambla*, became a street, the people maintained their market, now conveniently situated among the houses where they lived.

The ironwork covered market was not erected until the 19th century. Looking back, the way this came about is a strange tale: Juan Alvarez Mendizábal was a former insurgent who had become convinced of the virtues of liberalism during his exile in London. He returned to Spain in 1835, becoming finance minister under Queen Isabel II. He was able at a stroke to solve both the crown's financial problems and the lack of space in the densely populated city of Barcelona: he dispossessed the Church by law and sold off its vast estates. Anarchists had in the past burned down some monasteries; now the law was finishing the job. The cramped inner city acquired a number of open squares and the Boquería market, on the site of two former monastic establishments. There was once a street named after Mendizábal, but the dictator, Franco, who was favorably disposed to the Church, later renamed it; the Bar Mendizábal still stands here, however, as a reminder of the man who introduced such a radical form of modern town planning.

The Boquería today sells everything the culinary heart could desire. The buyer in search of fresh fish will find the freshest of catches in infinite range and variety: for example, *pescado de roca* such as gurnard and brown sea scorpion from Rosas, and *gambas* (shrimp) from Arenys and Cambrils. A multitude of different types of sausage from Vic are on sale, Pyrenean cheese, mountains of fruit from Lleida and vegetables from Maresme, the coastal area northeast of Barcelona. In the fall, when the mushroom-hunters bring their wares to town, the displays gleam golden brown with these treasures. Chefs from the area's best restaurants of course trawl this small paradise for the produce required to create Catalonia's varied cuisine.

Above: In Barcelona, a good place to buy quality fruit and vegetables, fresh daily, is the Boquería market. The best way is to compare produce and prices.

Right: Shoppers stream in from Las Ramblas to the Mercat de Sant Josep, known as the Boquería. The ironwork covered market dates from the 19th century.

CULINARY CATALAN

Incredible as it may seem to some in Madrid, there are regions of Spain where people speak a different language from that spoken in the capital. The Catalan, Basque, and Galician languages have official status alongside Spanish. Today, *Català* is spoken by six million people, from Roussillon in France and the small state of Andorra down as far as Alicante, and on the Balearic islands. As long as a thousand years ago an independent dukedom developed in the western outskirts of the Carolingian Empire. For many years the Catalans dwelt in the heart of the kingdom of Aragon, which included Valencia, the Balearic Islands, Sardinia, and Sicily. The crown only passed to Castile when the counts of Barcelona died out in the 15th century. Since then, Catalonia has been "Spain's eternal problem," in the words of the philosopher Ortega y Gasset. People here feel a greater tie with Provence than Castile; their language is midway between Provençal and Spanish, with a rich literature that dates back to the first written records in the 13th century.

The first Spanish cookbooks come from Catalonia and were written in Catalan. The manuscript *Libre de Sent Soví* appeared in 1324, one of the first culinary manuals in Europe. It contains not only instructions on culinary techniques, but also an extensive collection of Catalan recipes. The first printed Catalan cookbook appeared some two hundred years later, around 1520; this was the *Libre del coch* by Rupert de Nola, which also contained many recipes from Italy, Provence, and Dalmatia, anticipating the "Mediterranean cuisine" so popular today.

Nowhere in Barcelona is the seafood as fresh as in the Boquería. This is where the best chefs – like Jean-Louis Neichel – buy their ingredients.

It is no more than a few steps from sea to market. Naturally the fish in Barcelona's loveliest market is fresh every day, and the catch is all sold that same day.

Many stallholders in the Boquería market have had the same stall for decades and know their customers personally.

TOMATO BREAD

The Catalans' simplest dish has something of a symbolic significance for them, and brings back fond memories: the deliciousness of that tomato bread that their mothers prepared for them when they came home from school. The well-loved *pa amb tomàquet* (bread with tomato, Spanish *pan con tomate*) is so much part of Catalan everyday life that people tend to think of it as an ancient tradition. In fact, the tomato was introduced from America, and only became common in Catalan cooking in the 18th century. The magnificent combination of tomato with bread and olive oil probably only came about in the mid-19th century.

The basic ingredient for tomato bread is the large, round country loaf, *pa de pagès*. It should have a firm texture, and beneath its brown baked crust it keeps fresh and moist for a day or two. The best tomatoes to use are small, deep red, and, above all, very ripe and juicy. Any well-ordered Catalan greengrocery store will have separate displays of salad tomatoes and bread tomatoes. *Pa amb tomàquet* is quite unlike a tomato sandwich. The way to make it is to cut a tomato in half and rub it over the slice of bread. A few drops of the best cold-pressed olive oil, followed by a scattering of salt, and it is ready.

Tomato bread is either eaten just as it is, or with cheese, smoked ham, or one of the many regional types of sausage. It also goes well with Spanish tortilla or meat cooked on a charcoal grill. The bread is sometimes toasted before rubbing with tomato. This tastes particularly good when combined with preserved sardines from the coastal village of L'Escala (*anxoves de l'Escala*).

Restaurants that like to observe tradition bring the bread and tomatoes to the table separately to allow guests to prepare their own tomato bread. Others specialize in *llesques de pa* (slices of bread); these consist of tomato bread with a host of different ingredients – from plain ham to *esclivada*, roast vegetables served cold with virgin olive oil. The possibilities for *pa amb tomàquet* are seemingly endless, despite its simple nature.

OLIVE OIL FROM CATALONIA

Catalonia accounts for only about five percent of the olive oil produced in Spain, but its output includes oils of the highest quality, including four of the 17 Spanish olive oils with a protected declaration of origin (*Denominaciones de Origen, D.O.*): Siurana, Les Garrigues, Aceite de Baix Ebre-Montsià, and Aceite de Terra Alta.

The most important variety of olive in Catalonia is the Arbequina, which is small and green if picked young, and violet-black if left on the tree until ripe. The green ones have a delicious fruity aroma, and are often served as tapas. Cold-pressed Siurana and les Garrigues olive oil contains 90 percent Arbequina olives. It has a very low acidity, 0.5 percent maximum. The oil has a greenish tinge, from young fruit, and has a slightly bitter but fruity bouquet. Riper fruit yields a yellow oil with an almost exotic fruit aroma, ideal for *alioli* and mayonnaise.

Nearly forgotten olive varieties, such as Morruda (Morrut) and Farga are used for the more recent oils originating in Baix Ebre-Montsià and Terra Alta, though here oil of a golden yellow tinge dominates, made of the Empeltre variety which is also grown in the neighboring region of Aragón.

Pa amb tomàquet tastes best using hearty country bread. Toast the bread lightly before spreading with the filling.

Slice a very ripe tomato in half across the middle, and rub the flesh generously onto the bread.

The perfect finishing touch to the flavor of Catalan tomato bread is cold-pressed olive oil.

The art of alioli

How could such a brutal human being invent such a fine dish? It is the Roman emperor Nero, loathed as the man who burned Rome, who is credited with inventing the combination of garlic and olive oil now known in Spain as *ajaceite* or *alioli*, and so basic to Spanish cuisine. Today, this creamy garlic mixture is especially popular with the Catalans, and the name comes from the Catalan words *all* (garlic) and *oli* (oil). True *alioli* (the Catalan word is pronounced *all-ee-ohlee*) consists only of these two ingredients, plus a pinch of salt, and nothing else. The garlic is pounded with a wooden pestle and the oil added to the mortar very gradually. The addition of egg used to be frowned on, but now, almost everyone uses a little. The test of the cook's skill is to be able to turn the mortar upside down with the finished *alioli* inside, without any of it falling out. Not many people manage that! *Alioli* is served as a piquant sauce to accompany a whole variety of fish and rice dishes, and also with broiled meat as well as vegetables.

To make real *alioli* you will need garlic, olive oil, salt, and a little patience, since the garlic sauce is traditionally prepared using a mortar and pestle. A little egg yolk is usually added these days to bind the sauce, and a food processor can be used when making larger quantities.

ALIOLI

Original version:
3 large cloves of garlic, coarsely chopped
¼–½ tsp salt
½–1 cup/125–250 ml olive oil
Lemon juice to taste

Pound the garlic and salt to an even consistency, using a mortar and pestle. Then add the olive oil drop by drop at first, increasing to a thin stream and stirring constantly until a thick paste is formed. Add lemon juice to taste.

Modern imitation:
3 large cloves of garlic, coarsely chopped
½ tsp salt
1-2 egg yolks
1 cup/250 ml olive oil
Lemon juice to taste

Cut up the garlic and pound it with salt to an even paste, using a mortar and pestle. Stir in the egg yolk. Then add the olive oil drop by drop at first, increasing to a thin stream and working it in by stirring constantly. Flavor with lemon juice to taste and serve cold. A balloon or hand whisk may be used to stir in the oil if preferred.

Peel the fresh cloves of garlic and slice them coarsely into a mortar.

Pound the garlic and salt to a thick, smooth paste. There should be no remaining lumps.

Now add the egg yolk. Stir it in carefully, until the ingredients are thoroughly mixed.

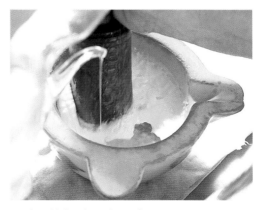

Lastly, add the olive oil in a thin stream, stirring to create a thick, smooth *alioli* sauce.

CALÇOTADA

There is an art to eating this specialty, which takes a little practice: tip the head back and open the mouth wide, then hold the long white stalk high above you and bring it down between the teeth. A napkin should be tied around the neck before commencing, and this will soon be smeared with blackish trickles. A roof tile serves as a plate. The ancient ritual of the *calçotada*, the great green onion feast, attracts thousands of devotees every year and has acquired an essential place in the economy of an entire region.

The countryman Xat de Benaiges, from Valls in the province of Tarragona, was the first to grill green onions over a flaming fire instead of a steady glow, about a hundred years ago. It is not recorded whether this was a stroke of genius or a mistake with the fire. Thrift being a Catalan virtue, Xat peeled off the blackened outer layer of the green onion and duly invented the *calçot*, now popular with locals and tourists alike.

The word *calçot* comes from the Catalan *calçar* (to support), because the young green onions are earthed up to blanch them as they grow, just like celery or asparagus. It takes almost a year from planting to harvest of the green onions. The seedlings are planted out in February, then dug up and divided in July and replanted. Harvesting starts in November and continues until Easter; the original *calçotada* season of February to March has been extended as a result of its success. Annual production today is about 20 million *calçots*, and accounts for about a third of the income of farmers in the region.

Many restaurants too depend for their existence on the green onion, for up to 300,000 people a year make their way to the region to eat *calçots*. The green onions are grilled in advance and wrapped in newspaper to keep in the heat. This makes them tender inside. Using a roof tile as a plate also helps to keep them hot. Eaters hold the green onion in their fingers, peel away the smoke-blackened outside, and dip the delicacy in *salbitxada*, a piquant sauce of almonds, tomatoes, garlic, special hot peppers called *bitxos*, vinegar, and oil (recipe opposite).

The high spot of the season is the *calçotada* held in Valls on the last Sunday in January. In a massive eating contest, masters of the art stuff over 200 green onions (about 6½ pounds, or 3 kilograms) into their mouths in 45 minutes.

Calçots, the small, flavorsome green onions from the Valls area, are ceremonially grilled on a flaming barbecue (background) and then eaten in traditional style from a baked terra cotta roof tile, dipping the green onions in *salbitxada*, a piquant almond and tomato sauce.

1 Elbow grease is needed when making *salbitxada*: first pound the roasted almonds in a mortar.
2 The piquancy is provided by small, red, hot peppers (*bitxos*). Remove the seeds and chop the flesh.
3 Plenty of fresh garlic is needed. Peel the garlic cloves and chop them finely.

4 Pound the almonds, peppers, and garlic to a thick paste.
5 Transfer to a larger bowl and add the diced tomatoes, chopped parsley, and vinegar.
6 Add the olive oil slowly, stirring all the ingredients together with a balloon whisk to create a thick sauce.

SALBITXADA
Sauce for *calçots*

2 tbsp blanched almonds
2 bitxo peppers
(alternatively hot red chili peppers)
6 cloves of garlic
2 ripe tomatoes, skinned and diced
1 tbsp chopped parsley
1 tbsp red wine vinegar
½ cup/125 ml olive oil
Salt and pepper

Heat a dry skillet and toast the almonds in this. Then crush them coarsely using a mortar and pestle.
Slit open the peppers with a small, sharp knife, deseed them and chop the flesh coarsely. Peel the garlic and chop coarsely.
Pound the almonds, peppers, and garlic to a paste in the mortar and then transfer to a slightly larger bowl. Add the tomatoes, parsley, and vinegar.
Then pour in the olive oil gradually in a thin stream, working the ingredients to a thick, even sauce using a balloon whisk.
Season with salt and pepper.
Tip: It is quicker to prepare this fine piquant sauce using a food processor, though the traditional way is with a mortar and pestle.
Salbitxada is the accompaniment to *calçotada*.

POPULAR SPANISH SAUCES

Romesco: Sauce made of tomatoes, almonds and/or hazelnuts, garlic, hot peppers, olive oil, and either stock or vinegar. Served with fish or seafood, also with *calçots*.
Picada: Sauce base consisting of roasted almonds, hazelnuts or pine nuts with garlic, parsley, and olive oil, pounded together in a mortar.
Sofrito (sofregit): Thick sauce of olive oil, onions, garlic, and tomatoes.
Samfaina: Catalan relation of ratatouille, made with garlic, onions, eggplants, zucchini, tomatoes, bell peppers, and olive oil. To make a sauce, the mixture is cooked for longer in liquid.
Alioli: An olive oil and garlic sauce (sometimes with egg) to go with fish or meat (see page 17).
Salsa mahonesa: Mayonnaise made with oil, salt, and egg, and frequently lemon juice (see page 68).
Salsa española: "Spanish sauce" made of onion, carrot, and leek with bacon or lard, meat or bones (usually beef or veal), and herbs, tomatoes, or wine as wished.
Salsa vinagreta: Vinaigrette made from vinegar, oil, onions, and herbs, often with chopped hard-cooked egg, capers, gherkins, or sardine fillets.
Salsa de tomate: Tomato sauce.
Salsa marinera: Sauce made of onions, parsley, fish stock, and wine.
Salsa verde: Garlic, parsley, and olive oil, often with a little white wine or egg yolk.
Salsa bechamel: Béchamel sauce of butter, flour, and milk.
Salsa Aurora: Béchamel sauce with tomatoes.

Angler fish (monkfish)

Lophius piscatorius is beyond doubt one of the oddest creatures in the Atlantic and Mediterranean. A reddish-colored fish up to 6½ feet (2 meters) long, the angler fish (*rape*) has an exceptionally large head, behind which the body is reduced to a thick tail. It is caught in coastal waters with a sandy or muddy bed, where it lies patiently waiting for something to swim by. This it senses with antennae, and the huge open mouth snaps shut around the unsuspecting prey. It has six spines to ward off enemies, as if its appearance were not enough. No wonder the Spaniards give it the disparaging alternative name *rata de mar* (sea rat), the Italians *rana pescatrice* (fishing frog), and the Portuguese *peixe sapo* (frog fish). In English, its

other name is monkfish. Its place in the kitchen was discovered by the Catalans, and its use spread from there throughout Spain. There are those who still regard its flavor as uninteresting, but its firm, aromatic flesh, skillfully prepared, can be the basis for some magnificent creations. Fishmongers seldom display the fish's ugly head, which can at best be used for soup. Apart from this, the only part of the head end of value to Catalans is the cheeks, which are a specialty. The liver is used to make sauce. The tail end, one third of the fish, is the most important part. The skin is leathery, without scales, and is pulled off like skinning a rabbit. Such skeleton as it has is made of cartilage, instead of the usual fish bones. The flesh is yielding but firm, has a consistency rather like shellfish, and is sliced for cooking. It lends itself to broiling on a skewer with chunks of tomato, bell pepper, and onion. It is found in fine one-pot dishes throughout Spain, or cooked on a griddle (*rape a la*

plancha). *Sopa de rape* (monkfish soup) is a typical dish from Barcelona. *Suquet*, a one-pot fish dish from the Costa Brava, would be unthinkable without it. The writer Manuel Vázquez Montalbán would enthuse about a dish of *mar i cel* (sea and sky), a wonderful combination of fish, rabbit, and sausage, which he tasted in Estartit. Monkfish can be used in stews with vegetables or potatoes, is delicious served with mushrooms, with *alioli* or with *romesco* sauce made of garlic, tomatoes, hot peppers, and almonds; it can even be cooked in breadcrumbs. It is increasingly sold as *rape a la langosta* or *rape alangostado* (monkfish in langouste style), because of its texture. For this, the flesh is held in a langouste or spiny lobster shape with string, and then boiled. A monkfish liver pâté is made in Northern Catalonia (as the Catalans call Roussillon, the region ceded to France 300 years ago).

Preparing a whole monkfish

Begin by cutting through the leathery skin along the center of the back.

Holding the skin of the head in both hands, loosen it and pull backward toward the tail.

Now turn the fish over onto its back and loosen the skin of the underside. The skin here is paler.

Remove the skin completely. It can be slippery, so holding it with a dish cloth helps maintain a grip.

Remove any remaining pieces of skin or other flaws with a sharp knife.

Cut away and discard the mouth, using a sharp knife aided by a hammer.

Separate the head and tail sections of the fish. The head can be used for soup or fish meal.

Cut the fine flesh of the tail section into steaks or bite-size pieces as needed.

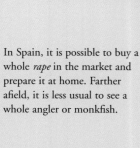

In Spain, it is possible to buy a whole *rape* in the market and prepare it at home. Farther afield, it is less usual to see a whole angler or monkfish.

The portions of monkfish tail can now be fried, steamed, or broiled. In Catalonia, they may also be used to make fine soups or else stews.

RAPE A LA MARINERA
Monkfish mariner style
(Photograph above)

4 monkfish steaks, 7 oz/200 g each
Salt and pepper
3 tbsp olive oil
Flour
1 small onion, finely chopped
1 tbsp blanched almonds
3 cloves of garlic, sliced finely
1 dried red chili pepper, deseeded and finely
chopped
1 bunch of parsley, chopped
1 slice of lightly toasted white bread
½ cup/125 ml white wine
1 cup/250 ml fish stock
4 langoustines, boiled

Preheat the oven to 345 °F/175 °C. Rinse the fish steaks and pat dry. Season with salt and pepper and leave to absorb the flavor. Heat the olive oil. Toss the fish steaks in flour to coat, and brown them on both sides in the oil. Transfer to an ovensafe dish. Sweat the onion in the remaining oil until transparent. Add the almonds, garlic, and chili, and fry. Stir in the parsley and bread. Pour on the white wine and bring to a boil. Blend to a purée in a food processor or similar. Add the fish stock and quickly reheat to boiling point. Pour this sauce over the fish steaks, and bake in the preheated oven for 10 to 15 minutes until cooked.
Arrange the fish steaks on a warmed platter to serve, with the sauce and the boiled langoustines.

SALPICON DE RAPE Y MARISCOS
Monkfish salad with seafood

10 ½ oz/300 g monkfish, boiled and flaked
7 oz/200 g small octopus, boiled
7 oz/200 g boiled and shelled shrimp
7 oz/200 g boiled and shelled mussels
1 green and 1 red bell pepper, cored and diced
2 small, firm tomatoes, diced
1 onion, finely chopped
2 tbsp sherry vinegar
1 tbsp lemon juice
Salt and pepper
6 tbsp olive oil

Carefully and thoroughly mix together all the fish, seafood, and vegetable ingredients in a bowl. To make the dressing, mix together the vinegar, lemon juice, salt, pepper, and olive oil. Pour the dressing over the salad ingredients and stir to ensure all are coated in dressing. Leave to infuse for about 30 minutes before serving.

Bacalao con samfaina –
Dried cod with vegetables

Dorada con verdura al horno –
Baked gilt head bream with vegetables

Suquet de peix –
Catalan fish stew

FISH A LA CATALANA

BACALAO CON SAMFAINA
Dried cod with vegetables
(Photograph opposite, above left)

Generous 1 lb/500 g dried cod, with bones and
skin removed
3 tbsp flour
1 cup/250 ml olive oil
2 onions, finely chopped
4 cloves of garlic, chopped
1 green and 1 red bell pepper, cored and diced
2 eggplants, diced
2 zucchini, diced
2 ripe tomatoes, skinned and diced
Salt and pepper
A pinch of sugar

Cut the dried cod into pieces and soak it for 24
hours, changing the water at least twice.
Remove the pieces of fish from the water, pat
dry, and toss in flour. Brown in olive oil, then
lift them out and drain them on paper towels.
Fry the onions, garlic, and bell peppers lightly
in the same oil, then add the eggplants and
zucchini. Fry all these together briefly. Add the
tomatoes and then pour on a little water. Season
with salt, pepper, and sugar. Cook the
vegetables for 10 minutes.
Add the pieces of fish, as well as a little more
water if needed. Cook the fish in the vegetables
until done.

SUQUET DE PEIX
Catalan fish stew
(Photograph opposite, bottom left)

14 oz/400 g monkfish
14 oz/400 g gilt head bream
Scant ½ cup/100 ml olive oil
8 oz/250 g ready-prepared small octopus
Generous 1 lb/500 g mussels, washed and
cleaned
2 onions, finely chopped
2 large, ripe tomatoes (beef tomatoes), skinned
and diced
2 cups/500 ml white wine
Salt and pepper
3 cloves of garlic
2 tbsp chopped parsley
1 tbsp ground almonds
A few threads of saffron

Preheat the oven to 345 °F/175 °C. Rinse and
clean the fish, pat dry and cut into pieces.
Heat the olive oil in a deep skillet and brown the
fish pieces. Transfer them to a large-diameter
ovensafe casserole. Fry the octopus in the oil until

Thousands of fishermen operating out of Mediterranean
ports bring in a daily supply of fresh fish for the kitchens
of Catalonia, where fish is an essential ingredient.

golden, and scatter over the fish. Fry the mussels
in the skillet until they open (discard any which
were already open when raw, or which fail to open
when cooked). Transfer to the casserole.
Sweat the onions in the cooking juices in the skillet
until transparent. Add the tomatoes and sweat
these too. Pour on the white wine and 1 cup of
water. Season with salt and pepper and cook these
ingredients together for a short while to blend.
Pound the garlic, parsley, and almonds together
with a mortar and pestle and blend in the saffron
threads. Stir this mixture into the vegetables in
the skillet. Bring to a boil, and pour the vegetable
mixture over the ingredients in the ovensafe
casserole. Place in the preheated oven for 5 to 10
minutes to cook together and absorb flavors.
Variation: This fish stew can be made using
various different types of fish, mussels, shrimp, or
langoustine and turned into a veritable feast. The
amount of liquid can be reduced if wished.

DORADA CON VERDURA AL HORNO
Baked gilt head bream with vegetables
(Photograph opposite, right)

1 gilt head bream (about 2 ½ lbs/1.2 kg weight)
(alternatively grouper or bass), ready prepared
Salt and pepper
1 tbsp chopped herbs, e.g. parsley, thyme,
tarragon
Butter to grease casserole
2 onions, thinly sliced
4 potatoes, thinly sliced
10 ½ oz/300 g fresh spinach, blanched
2 large carrots, thinly sliced
2 cloves of garlic, finely chopped
Scant ½ cup/100 ml olive oil
4 ripe tomatoes, skinned and diced
½ cup/125 ml white wine

Preheat the oven to 390 °F/200 °C. Rinse the
fish to clean it and pat dry. Score the skin in
several places with a sharp knife. Rub the fish
inside and out with salt, pepper, and chopped
herbs. Leave to absorb flavors for 15 minutes.
Grease an ovenproof casserole dish and line it
with the sliced onion and potato. Arrange the
spinach on top of them, then the carrots.
Scatter on the garlic and place the fish on the
bed of vegetables. Pour the olive oil all over.
Cover with aluminum foil and bake in the
preheated oven for about 15 minutes.
Take the casserole out of the oven and remove
the foil. Add the tomatoes and, lastly, the white
wine. Return to the oven to finish cooking
uncovered for about 10 minutes. Test before
serving, to ensure the food is fully cooked.

Fresh eel *(anguila)* is delivered to the fish market daily. In Catalan cuisine, as in Valencian, it is popularly cooked with
garlic and peppers *(allipebre)*. Other popular recipes for eel include eel cooked with white beans and tomatoes, eel
baked with almonds and wine, or soaked and broiled eel.

SHRIMP

On nights when the moon is full, the shrimp catch is said to be especially large. Then, when the fishermen set out to trawl along the Mediterranean coast with their nets, there is a good chance of landing a few hundredweight of shrimp – pink, gray-green, flecked, and transparent ones – next morning back in port.

It would be too simple just to speak of "shrimp" in Spain. A host of different terms exists to describe all the various types, as well as the ways of preparing them, and the choice is huge. Connoisseurs of *mariscos* (Spanish seafood) love to conjure with the names and the variety.

All types of shrimp have certain features in common: a long, narrow body, five pairs of legs, and long antennae with which they sense the approach of food or danger. Unlike the langoustine (*cigala*, which goes by various names, such as Danish or Norway lobster, Dublin Bay prawn and scampi), shrimp have no claws. Only a few of the 2000 to 3000 varieties of shrimp known today are used in the kitchen. In Spain, the smaller types are generally called *gambas*, and the larger ones *langostinos* – though exceptions to this rule may quite possibly appear on menus.

Opinions vary as to the place which produces the best shrimp, and local preferences or sheer regional and local patriotism inevitably have a role here. In Catalonia, the most famous are shrimp from Arenys; in Valencia, *gambas* from

Denia and *langostinos* from Vinaròs. To the Andalusians, the best are *gambas* from Garrucha and *langostinos* from Sanlúcar de Barrameda.

There are 35 ports in Catalonia, from Llançà in the north to Deltebre at the mouth of the Ebro river, sending the rich harvest of the Mediterranean to market. The fishermen of each port believe their produce to be the best, though the only type to have received the recognition of a quality mark from the regional government so far is the striped or tiger shrimp from the Ebro delta, whose Latin name is *Penaeus kerathurus*. The particular pattern of currents around the river mouth is said to ensure an especially good catch. This type of shrimp is recognized by its prominent black eyes and its yellowish gray flesh with darker horizontal stripes (which account for the name "tiger" shrimp). The flesh becomes pink when it is being cooked.

The most commonly found shrimp, *gamba roja (Aristeus antennatus)* is the one which the French call *crevette rouge*, and the Italians, *gambero*. It is normally between ½ inch and just under ⅔ inch (15-18 centimeters) long, occasionally more, and lives on muddy sea beds at a depth of 650-3300 feet (200-1000 meters). Its head is a reddish flesh-pink. The slightly smaller *gamba blanca (Parapenaeus longirostris)* is referred to as the ocean shrimp in England and France. It has all but disappeared from Catalonia; those which reach the market here are caught off the shores of Africa. This *gamba* looks like the larger *langostinos* and is often

GAMBAS AL AJILLO
Garlic shrimp

1 lb 5 oz/600 g shrimp tails, shelled and prepared
1 cup/250 ml olive oil
6 cloves of garlic, finely sliced
2 dried red chili peppers, cored and finely chopped
Salt

Warm four individual earthenware dishes ready for serving. Heat the olive oil in a suitable earthenware casserole or skillet, and add the garlic and chili peppers. Add the shrimp as soon as the garlic has colored slightly; sprinkle with salt and fry. Serve the fried shrimp immediately, along with the garlic and oil, in the earthenware dishes.

given the name *gamba llangostinera*.

Another *gamba* quite common in Catalonia is *Plesionika adwarsii*. It is roundish and has a delicate pink color. It contains eggs all year round, and is popularly called the *carrabiner* (policeman), possibly for that reason, as some folk craftily say. Other, more exotic types which sometimes appear on Spanish menus include *camarón* (Camaron) and *quisquilla* (sand shrimp), which Spanish fishermen catch far from their country's shores.

With this rich and varied range of shrimp varieties, the use of *gambas* and *langostinos* is universal. They are eaten alone as tapas, usually fried on a griddle with olive oil and a little sea salt, or prepared *al ajillo* with garlic (see recipe), or used as an ingredient in a salad or first course, broiled or served in breadcrumbs, in a paella, in soups and stews or in an elegant dish with other types of fish and seafood. The Catalans have become experts in exploiting the possibilities of this delicious *fruit de mer*.

Left: Freshly caught shrimps need little elaborate preparation. Here they are simply fried on a hot griddle *(plancha)* and sprinkled with sea salt.

How to tell if shrimp and langoustines are really fresh

It is important to look carefully at the heads of *gambas* or *langostinos* before cooking them, even if you do not intend to eat this part. For those who know what to look for, the heads provide the clue as to whether the shellfish is fresh: the older the shellfish, the darker the head. It also becomes softer with age, and contracts a little inside its hard casing. Only when the shellfish is fresh are the long antennae intact; once the creatures have been frozen and then thawed, the antennae break off. As a last resort, there is the smell, but by the time your nose tells you that a shellfish is not fresh, it is too late.

Background photograph: Most shrimp are of a rather pale-looking gray when raw. It is only the heating process that gives them their bright pink color.

ROMESCO DE LANGOSTINOS
Tiger shrimp with Romesco sauce

12–16 tiger shrimp (alternatively, prawns)
Scant ½ cup/100 ml olive oil
½ cup/75 g blanched almonds
3 cloves of garlic, sliced
1 small onion, finely chopped
2 dried red chili peppers, cored and finely chopped
3 ripe beef tomatoes, skinned and diced
1 bay leaf
1 slice lightly toasted white bread
1 tbsp chopped parsley
Salt and pepper
2 tbsp sherry vinegar

Fry the tiger shrimp or prawns lightly in the olive oil to cook. Remove and set aside. Fry the almonds and garlic in the oil until golden. Lift them out with a slotted spoon. Sweat the onion in the oil until transparent. Add the chili peppers and tomatoes, and stir to mix. Add the bay leaf and cook these ingredients briefly together on a high heat. Pound the almonds, garlic, bread, and parsley with a mortar and pestle. Add this to the tomatoes, and pour on a little water. Season with salt, pepper, and sherry vinegar. Place the tiger shrimp or prawns in the finished sauce, and leave to infuse for 5 minutes.

1 To peel a cooked shrimp or langoustine, begin by holding it between the thumb and forefinger of each hand.
2 Twist slightly to remove the head. It should come off cleanly; make sure all the edible flesh is left behind on the body section.
3 Now break open the hard body shell from the underside, teasing it open with your fingers.

4 If the shrimp are to be used for garnish, the tail may be left on when the rest of the shell is removed.
5 If the shrimp are to be used in a sauce or eaten straightaway, the whole of the shell is removed, body and tail.
6 The fine flesh is ready to eat. The heads and peeled-off shells can be used to make stock.

Mountain and sea blend to create an inspiring sight where the foothills of the Pyrenees run down to the Mediterranean (background). It is no coincidence that such a region should have given birth to a cuisine which so magnificently combines meat and poultry with fish and seafood – the produce of earth and sea (above).

SEA AND MOUNTAIN

"The magic triangle" is the name given to the Empordà, the area which lies between the Cap de Creus, the Costa Brava, and Girona, by those acquainted with this region. This is the land where the *tramontana* blows down from the Pyrenees, a constant, harsh north wind which is said to drive a person mad – or to create genius, as, for example, the surrealist painter Salvador Dalí. Imagination is certainly ever present in this rich and varied area. Legend has it that the marriage of a shepherd with a siren gave birth to the Empordà. The region's geography lends some truth to the tale, for its whole character – and its cuisine – is determined by the mountains, above all the mighty peak of Canigó which lies to the north, and the sea which lashes wildly against its southern shores.

Mar i muntanya (sea and mountain) is the Catalan expression for regional recipes combining fish or seafood with meat or poultry. In the big, strongly built, stone farmhouses which characterize the region, the *masies*, a unique culinary tradition, marked by its use of highly varied produce, developed. These ingredients are not at all exotic in themselves; the art lies in how they are combined. There is chicken with shrimp *(gambas)*, for example, or rabbit with *langostinos*. As long ago as Roman times, the Catalans have been open to novel influences. They gladly welcomed refined ideas from Renaissance Italy, and just as eagerly received the unfamiliar produce arriving from the newly discovered Americas. In Catalonia, chocolate made its appearance not as a dessert, but as a basic ingredient in *mar i muntanya* cuisine.

POLLO CON LANGOSTA
Chicken with spiny lobster

1 chicken, weighing about 2 ½ lbs/1.2 kg
Salt and pepper
Scant ½ cup/100 ml olive oil
1 large onion, finely chopped
2 ripe beef tomatoes, skinned and diced
½ cup/125 ml sweet white wine
1 cup/250 ml chicken stock
1 bay leaf
2 cloves of garlic, chopped
1 tbsp ground almonds
A few threads of saffron
⅓ cup/40 g grated dark cooking chocolate
1 tbsp breadcrumbs
1 tbsp chopped parsley
Generous 1 tbsp brandy
2 spiny lobsters, boiled

Rinse and clean the chicken thoroughly and dry it. Divide it into portions and rub each one with salt and pepper. Heat 4 tbsp olive oil in a large pot and brown the chicken pieces on all sides on a high heat. Reduce to low heat. Add the onion and sweat until transparent. Add the tomatoes and cook all together briefly. Pour on the white wine and chicken stock, and add the bay leaf. Bring to a boil and cook for 15 minutes on a medium heat.

Using a mortar and pestle, pound together the garlic, ground almonds, saffron, chocolate, breadcrumbs, parsley, brandy, and the remaining olive oil until they form a thick paste. Stir this into the cooking liquid to create the sauce. Halve the spiny lobsters and add to the other ingredients in the pot. Simmer gently in the sauce for 10 minutes. Season with salt and pepper before serving.

PATACÓ TARRAGONÍ
Tuna fish stew with snails

½ cup/125 ml olive oil
1 large onion, chopped
2 ripe beef tomatoes, skinned and diced
4 medium potatoes, diced
2 zucchini, sliced
½ cup/125 ml sherry or Rancio wine
1 cup/250 ml fish stock
Salt and pepper
1 tsp powdered mild paprika
A pinch of powdered hot paprika
1 bay leaf
2 cloves
Generous 1 lb/500 g tuna fillet, cut into bite-size pieces
Generous 1 lb/500 g medium-size snails, ready prepared
4 cloves of garlic, chopped
1 tbsp roasted almonds
A few threads of saffron
1 tbsp chopped parsley

Heat the olive oil in a deep skillet or pot. Sweat the onion until transparent. Add the tomatoes and potatoes, and cook lightly. Stir in the zucchini. Pour on the sherry and fish stock, and season with the salt, paprika, bay leaf, and cloves. Cover and simmer on a low heat for about 15 minutes.

Add the tuna and snails, with additional water if needed. Replace the lid, and simmer on a low heat for another 15 minutes until cooked.

Meanwhile pound the garlic, almonds, saffron, parsley, and 1 tbsp of the cooking liquid to a thick paste, using a mortar and pestle. Stir into the cooking liquid shortly before serving, to create the sauce.

Cannelloni & Co.

Catalonia is the only part of the Iberian peninsula where pasta has really become established. Only here was the local cuisine able to create new dishes using it. Pasta had originated in China, and Marco Polo introduced it to Italy. It was the Arabs who brought it from there to Spain, and noodles were consequently well known in Catalonia in the Middle Ages. They are mentioned in 14th century manuscripts dealing with culinary matters; these contain recipes for Arab *alatria* and for *fideos*, a word for noodles which has survived to this day.

The kingdom which constituted the Crown of Aragon, and once included Sardinia, Sicily, and Naples, created close contacts between its Italian possessions and the metropolis of Barcelona. It was, however, the Swiss and Italians in the 19th century who secured a firm place for pasta in Catalonia. Swiss clock and watchmakers who had come to work in the area are said to have had little liking for Spanish inns, and to have opened their own eating places during that period. It is at least certain that Swiss and Italian cooking was then the best in the country. The Café Suizo in Barcelona was for many years held to be the finest in the city. Along with a taste for Verdi operas, there spread at that time the liking for fine *canalones*. These stuffed rolls of pasta have since become so much a part of local cuisine that they are thought of as the traditional Catalan fare for the Feast of St. Stephen, celebrated on December 26, (known in Britain as Boxing Day).

CANALONES A LA CATALANA
Cannelloni Catalan style
(Photograph above, left)

½ cup/125 ml olive oil
2 ¼ cups/250 g ground beef and pork (mixed)
1 boneless chicken breast, cut into cubes
7 oz/200 g chicken livers, cut small
1 onion, finely chopped
1 leek, sliced into thin rings
2 tbsp breadcrumbs
Salt and pepper
3 ½ tbsp/50 g butter
½ cup/60 g flour
2 cups/500 ml stock
2 cups/500 ml milk
1 tsp thyme
1 tbsp chopped parsley
A pinch of ground nutmeg
14 oz/400 g cannelloni, ready to use
Butter for greasing
1 cup/100 g grated cheese

Preheat the oven to 390 °F/200 °C. Heat the oil in a deep skillet and brown the ground meat, chicken breast meat, chicken liver, onion, and leek. Remove from the heat. Stir in the breadcrumbs and season with salt and pepper. Melt the butter in a pan and blend in the flour; cook until the mixture takes on a pale yellow appearance. Add the stock and the milk, stirring constantly to blend thoroughly. When the mixture is smooth, bring it to a boil and place on a very low heat for 10 minutes to thicken. Season the béchamel sauce with thyme, parsley, nutmeg, salt, and pepper.

Fill the cannelloni with the meat mixture (this can best be done using a piping bag with a wide tip). Place the filled cannelloni side by side in a buttered ovensafe dish. Pour on the béchamel sauce and sprinkle with grated cheese. Bake in the preheated oven for about 25 minutes. Bring to the table in the baking dish.

Fideus a l'estil de Lleida
Noodles Lleida style
(Photograph center)

4 small pork chops or pork ribs
2 tbsp olive oil
2 onions, finely chopped
3 cloves of garlic, finely chopped
7 oz/200 g Butifarra *sausage or sausage meat*
3 ripe beef tomatoes, skinned and diced
1 cup/250 ml meat stock
9 oz/250 g fideos, *alternatively short vermicelli*
(soup noodles)
1 tsp mild powdered paprika
Salt and pepper

Fry the pork on both sides in the oil in a deep skillet or heatsafe earthenware pot. Lift out the meat, and sweat the onions and garlic in the oil until transparent. Mix in and brown the sausage meat. Add the tomatoes and cook together

briefly. Pour on the stock and continue to cook to make the sauce. Stir the noodles into the sauce and add the pork and paprika. Add enough boiling water to ensure that all the ingredients are well covered, and cook until the noodles are *al dente*. Season with salt and pepper before serving.

Arròs amb conill
Rice with rabbit
(Photograph right)

1 rabbit with liver, ready prepared
Scant ½ cup/100 ml olive oil
Salt and pepper
1 onion, finely chopped
2 cloves of garlic, chopped
4 large ripe tomatoes, skinned and diced
A few saffron threads
2 young artichokes, washed and halved
Generous 1 ⅔ cups/250 g shelled fresh peas
1 cup/200 g medium-grain rice
1 tbsp chopped parsley

Rinse and clean the rabbit; then pat dry and cut into pieces. Heat two-thirds of the olive oil in a pot and fry the rabbit until golden. Season with salt and pepper. Lift the rabbit pieces out of the oil and set aside. Sweat the onion and garlic in the frying oil until transparent. Add the tomatoes and cook together briefly. Put the rabbit back in the pot, pour on 6 cups of water, and stir in the saffron. Bring to a boil, cover and simmer for 20 minutes. Then add the rice, peas, and artichokes, and simmer for another 20 minutes until cooked.

Meanwhile fry the rabbit liver in the rest of the oil. Using a mortar and pestle, pound the fried liver, oil, and parsley together to make a coarse paste. Five minutes before the end of the cooking time, mix the liver paste with the ingredients in the pot. Season to taste with salt and pepper before serving.

The Ebro delta –
An oasis of simple delights

In spring, when the ricefields are under water, the Ebro delta glistens like a mirror. The round-grained variety *japónica* is the main type grown here. It is especially suitable for Catalan rice dishes. The area is also well known as a place to hunt wild duck. No visit here would be complete without tasting a meal of delicate roast duck in one of the eating places in the region. All that is needed to explore the Ebro delta is a shallow-draft rowing boat and plenty of time. Traveling down the last few miles of Spain's largest river before it reaches the sea, or negotiating the canals which crisscross the area, is to enter another world: lulled by the lazy splash of the water and the rustle of the wind in the reeds, hearing the distant crashing of the waves and the wings

of wild duck rising into the air above. This miracle of nature was unknown to the Romans, as the delta had hardly developed at all in their time. The mighty waters of the Ebro carried

down rocks and silt from the Pyrenees, however, depositing them at the river mouth, so that the flat land came to extend far into the Mediterranean within a remarkably short time in geological terms. The conservation area as it is today covers some 30 square miles (nearly 8000 hectares), and is a paradise for bird-lovers. In the waters stand pink flamingos, searching for crabs. Fishermen and farmers are still the main human inhabitants of this area, and the rank growth of vacation homes has not yet invaded this picturesque corner.

TRUFFLE MARKETS

The truffle belongs to the same class of fungi as the morel, the ascomycetes. Most other edible fungi come into the mushroom class. Three commercially important types of truffle are collected in Catalonia; these are the black *Tuber melanosporum* (the famous Périgord truffle), *Tuber brunale*, which is also black in color, and the white summer truffle *Tuber aestivum*. The white truffle of Piedmont *(Tuber magnatum)*, has never been found in Spain. During the season (December to March) truffles are bought and sold at special markets for high prices. The most important of these markets in Catalonia are those at Olot in the province of Girona, Vic and Centelles in the province of Barcelona, and Solsona in Lleida. Markets devoted to this noble fungus also exist in the neighboring provinces of Huesca (in Graus and Benasque), Teruel (Mora de Rubielos), and Castellón (Morella). Truffles are also found in the Castilian provinces of Cuenca (Tragacete, Valdemorillo de la Sierra, and Cañada del Hoyo), Guadalajara (Molina de Aragón and Peralejos de las Truchas), and Soria (Navaleno).

Truffles are considered to be the jewels of the forests. The truffle hunters of Catalonia set out on the trail of the noble truffle during the winter months and their finds fetch astoundingly high prices at market. Their neighbors in France have a particular love of truffles, but Spanish cooks too are full of ideas for using them in the kitchen. They produce imaginative creations such as fish or seafood with truffles, a salad featuring poultry with truffle vinaigrette, and cannelloni with truffles.

Truffle hunters would be lost without their dogs. They always set out together into the woods, since the truffles grow underground and are quite difficult to locate.

The human partner identifies a spot where eyesight and intelligence suggest the truffles might be found. Now the dog sniffs out the aroma with its fine sense of smell.

The faithful dog has found a truffle, but unlike truffle-hunting pigs, it has no desire to eat it. The hunter gives the dog a reward for its success.

TRUFFLES

All a truffle hunter needs is a good dog, a small, pointed shovel, a warm jacket, a reliable pair of boots, and expert knowledge. To a far greater extent than hunting for those species of mushroom, called *bolets* (Spanish *setas*), which grow above ground, the search for those most expensive of fungi, the subterranean truffles, requires knowledge and skill. The best terrain for truffles is a sunny slope at an altitude of 1000–5000 feet (300-1500 meters), with a calcareous soil and an annual rainfall of 12–35 inches (300–900 millimeters). They grow in a symbiotic relationship with hazel, holm oak, and oak trees. The soil should be loose-textured, and is usually bare; the truffle growing some 6–12 inches (15–30 centimeters) below ground takes away a great deal of moisture, and destroys small plants like weedkiller, so that little grass grows beneath trees that have truffles.

The *tofonaire* (truffle hunter) sets out to roam through the mountains between December and March, accompanied by a highly trained dog which is sent on ahead. A well-trained truffle hound can cost the equivalent of some $3000, but does not have to be any particular breed. The dog can scent a truffle from a distance of up to 330 feet (100 meters). It scratches at the ground over the spot, and is rewarded with a biscuit. The dog has no desire to eat the truffle itself, unlike the pigs which were once used for this task, but were hard to control because of their greed. For the dog, truffle hunting is just a game.

When the faithful dog has located a truffle, the *tofonaire* cautiously digs away the earth with the shovel, until it is possible to reach in and lift out the truffle by hand. The earth is then replaced layer by layer just as it was, with the soil that had been uppermost still on top. It is important not to trample down the earth over the site, because truffles need loose soil. In two years' time, as the expert knows, another find may be made on this spot. Despite their care, truffle hunting is becoming ever more difficult. Old hands place the main blame on the availability of orange butane gas cylinders. One truffle hunter says:

In the old days, people used to collect firewood in the forest and cleaned up the forest floor. Now, everyone cooks with gas. The forest is full of brushwood, and the sun never reaches the soil. Truffles need warmth to grow.

No one knows precisely how large the total Spanish truffle yield is. Estimates place it somewhere between 33 and 44 tons (30-40 tonnes). Up to 90 percent of this amount is exported to France, which consumes well over half the world harvest of truffles.

In Spanish cuisine, truffles are used almost exclusively in Catalonia. The word that they have long been an almost unaffordably expensive and scarce commodity has however been received and understood in Castile. An entrepreneur in Soria has made a bold attempt to ease the shortage; he has planted a 1700 acre (680 hectare) site with holm oaks whose roots have been inoculated with truffle spores. It remains to be seen whether the dream of producing a truffle at a democratic price will be fulfilled.

SUPREMA DE MERLUZA CON TRUFA
Medallions of hake with truffles
(Large photograph below)

8 medallions of hake, 3 ½ oz/100 g each
Salt and pepper
3 tbsp olive oil
1 carrot, cut into julienne strips
1 zucchini, cut into julienne strips
1 leek, cut into thin strips
1 tomato, skinned and diced
2 tbsp sherry vinegar
2 tbsp butter
1 black truffle, peeled and finely sliced
1–2 tbsp pine nuts (optional)

Rinse and clean the hake, pat dry and season with salt and pepper. Leave to infuse for 5 minutes.

Heat the olive oil in a large skillet and fry the fish on a low heat for about 5 minutes on each side. Lift out the fish and keep hot.

Sauté the vegetables for a few minutes in the frying oil and juices. Deglaze with the sherry vinegar.

Melt the butter in a second frying pan and lightly fry the slices of truffle.

Arrange the fish on individual plates with the vegetables and truffle slices to serve. Garnish with pine nuts as liked.

The truffle inspires great creativity among Catalan cooks. Works of art such as this salad with chicken and shrimp are the result.

Right: The fine flavor of black truffles harmonizes wonderfully with fresh fish. An example is hake with truffle and vegetables, shown here.

The mushroom hunter sets out with a wicker basket, a knife, and a sound fund of knowledge. The experts know where to find which edible variety.

GOURMET TYPES OF MILK CAP

"A moist, intense aroma of intimate delicacy, a little bitter, wonderfully earthy and vital." In these words the acknowledged king of Spanish gastronomy, Néstor Luján, described the flavor of a freshly harvested *rovelló*, an edible milk cap mushroom praised in Europe for its flavor. The Catalans wax poetic about this best loved of all mushrooms, and almost every individual claims to know just which hillside in just which pine forest is home to the best of the species. There are in fact two species of *Lactarius* or milk cap which are good to eat: the saffron milk cap, *Lactarius deliciosus*, which goes under the name *pinetell* in Girona, and the gourmet *Lactarius sanguifluus*, which is more "delicious." These two types of *rovelló* (Spanish *níscalo*) grow amid moss in dense pine forests. Standing on a short stem, the cap is thick and fleshy, yellow to orange in color, and measures up to almost five inches (12 centimeters) across. A tree nursery in Arbúcies (Girona) has for some years been selling pine trees injected with *rovelló* spores, making it possible to grow one's own. The Catalans eat the *rovelló* in a range of ways: in a simple salad as *tapas*, with *butifarra* sausage, in meat and game dishes, with fish or seafood.

Saffron milk cap *(níscalo, rovelló):* The Spanish name includes two types of this mushroom, the most popular edible mushroom in Catalonia.

Golden-hued treasures from the forest

The French ethnologist Claude Lévi-Strauss once wrote that the gastronomic culture of the Catalan people in their use of mushrooms was an essential factor of their identity. Why that should be remains a subject of discussion. The explanation offered by the writer Manuel Vázquez Montalbán is that the Catalans have always practiced a cuisine based on foraging, that is, the art of simply collecting and making use of what nature provides. Perhaps the Catalans yearn for the prehistoric days of hunter-gathering, before agriculture appeared to tame and enclose the natural produce of the land. The arrival of agriculture did after all spell the end of freedom, and in a country whose history is marked by long periods of anarchy, freedom retains considerable relative importance to this day.

Foraging for mushrooms is something of a religion, and has its own liturgy, a playful honoring of nature. Whatever the fun involved, however, it demands skill and knowledge. The "Pope" of mushroom hunters, Vicenç Serrano, has laid down its set of "Ten Commandments," and every wise mushroom hunter who knows what he or she is about keeps faithfully to them. In the Pyrenees and in Berguedà, the solitary delight of the *boletaire* (mushroom hunter) is handed down from generation to generation. People have set off into the woods with their baskets and knives since time immemorial; it is considered a crime among the initiated to pull up mushrooms. The locations where good mushrooms are to be found are strongly guarded family secrets, and the business of looking for mushrooms is taken so seriously that *boletaires* in the province of Girona refer to it quite literally as a mushroom "hunt." Vicenç Serrano lists 15 first-class mushrooms, 38 very good ones and 43 quite reasonably edible ones to be found in his country. The French, on the other hand, despite their gastronomic prowess, use only a limited number of mushroom varieties; in the interior of Spain, in León for example, mushrooms were fed to pigs until very recent times.

In Catalonia, however, the eating of mushrooms has all the qualities of a fine opera: exuberant, varied, and sensual. The simplest method of cooking is to broil them, ideally straightaway on returning from a mushroom foray at the forest edge. Other popular methods of preparation are to marinate them, fry or stew them, or to stir them with egg to make a *tortilla*. They are a popular ingredient in the noodle paella *fideuà*.

Opposite: The edible morel *(colmenilla, múrgola)* has a distinctive honeycombed cap. It is very flavorsome, but must be cooked; it is inedible when raw.

Russula cyanoxantha *(carbonera, llora)*: Very good to eat. Colors range from blue-violet to brown to greenish. Suitable for many different cooking methods.

Cep, Penny bun *(boleto, cep, cèpe* left) and the dark-capped variety, **Steinpilz** *(boleto negro)*: Very good to eat; has a slightly nutty flavor. Good for stewing or frying. Often dried.

Chanterelle *(rebozuelo, rossinyol)*: Tasty edible mushroom. Can be cooked in a large number of ways, but is difficult to digest.

Tricholoma *(negrilla, fredolic)*: This edible *tricholoma* is good to eat. Has a slight mealy aroma. Good in dishes using a variety of mushrooms.

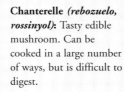

Honey Fungus *(armilaria color de miel)*: The young caps are very tasty. If cooked long enough, their slight bitterness disappears.

Wood Blewit, amethyst agaric *(pie azul, pimpinella morada)*: Good to eat; has a strong characteristic flavor. Especially good when young. Should not be eaten raw.

White truffle *(Choiromyces meandriformis)*: Good for flavor, not as fine as the true white truffle *(Tuber magnatum)*. Inedible when raw.

St. George's mushroom *(seta de primavera, moixernó, perretxiku) (Tricholoma gambosum)*: Very good to eat; especially popular in the Basque country. Has a fine, mealy aroma. Very good stewed.

Oyster cap *(seta de cardo, orellana)*: Very good to eat. Grows on tree stumps and trunks. The flavor is mild.

Tricholoma *(capuchina, fredolic gros)*: Larger than *negrilla* above. Found in pine forests. Very good to eat.

Parasol *(parasol, apagallums)*: Very good eating. Caps good for frying; stems rather tough. Should not be eaten raw.

Horn of Plenty *(trompeta de los muertos)*: Good to eat, despite its Spanish name ("trumpet of death"). Often used dried.

CATALAN STEWS OF MEAT, VEGETABLES, AND MUSHROOMS

MANOS DE CERDO RELENAS
Stuffed pig trotters (Main photograph)

2 pig trotters, generous 1 lb/500 g each
1 onion, studded with 1 bay leaf and 2 cloves
Salt
5 black peppercorns
1 bunch of soup vegetables and herbs (celery, carrot, leek, parsley)
3½ cups/400 g mixed ground meat
3½ oz/100 g air-dried ham, diced
2 eggs
2 tbsp breadcrumbs
Pepper
1 tbsp truffle oil
6 slices of fat, unsmoked bacon
5 tbsp olive oil
1 onion, chopped
2 cloves of garlic, chopped
8 oz/250 g ripe tomatoes, skinned and diced
1 cup/250 ml white wine
1 tbsp blanched almonds
1 tbsp pine nuts
1 tbsp chopped parsley
8 oz/250 g forest mushrooms, cleaned and cut into pieces

Rinse and clean the pig trotters thoroughly, scraping them with a knife. Place in a deep pot with the studded onion, salt, peppercorns, soup vegetables, and herbs, and a generous quantity of water. Bring to a boil and cook on a medium heat for about 2 hours. Take the pig trotters out of the cooking liquid; cool and lift carefully off the bone. Strain the cooking liquid and set aside.
To make the filling, mix together the ground meat, diced ham, eggs, and breadcrumbs. Season with salt, pepper, and truffle oil. Stuff the boned pig trotters with this mixture. Wrap a slice of bacon around each and secure in place with thread, to ensure that it keeps its shape.
Heat the olive oil in a large pot suitable for stewing or braising. Brown the trotters on all sides. Add the onions and garlic and fry together briefly. Add the tomatoes. Pour on the white wine and 2 cups/500 ml of the cooking liquid. Cover and cook on a low heat for about 1 hour.
Pound the almonds, pine nuts, parsley, and 2 tbsp cooking liquid using a mortar and pestle. Add to the sauce, along with the mushrooms. Cook for 10 minutes. Lift the trotters out of the sauce and remove the bacon. Place the trotters on a warmed serving dish. Taste the sauce and adjust the seasoning with salt and pepper. Pour the sauce over the trotters and serve.

SETAS CON GARBANZOS
Mushrooms with chickpeas

1¼ cups/250 g dried chickpeas
2 cups/500 ml meat stock
Salt and pepper
Scant ½ cup/100 ml olive oil
1 onion, finely chopped
4 cloves of garlic, finely sliced
8 oz/250 g forest mushrooms, cleaned and cut into pieces
2 tbsp chopped parsley

Soak the chickpeas in water overnight. Then drain them and bring them to a boil in the stock. Season with salt and pepper and simmer for 30 minutes.
Heat the olive oil in a deep skillet. Fry the onions and garlic until golden. Add the mushrooms and fry for a few minutes, stirring. Add these ingredients to the chickpeas and mix. Cook for another 15 minutes, adding more water if needed. Season with salt and pepper. Sprinkle with chopped parsley before serving.

SETAS CON CARACOLES
Mushrooms with snails

48 ready-prepared, medium-size Spanish snails
1 onion, studded with 1 bay leaf and 2 cloves
Salt
5 black peppercorns
4½ oz/125 g smoked bacon, diced
2 tbsp olive oil
1 small onion, finely chopped
4 cloves of garlic
8 oz/250 g mixed forest mushrooms, cleaned and cut into pieces
1 cup/250 ml white wine
1 cup/250 ml stock

Preheat the oven to 430 °F/220 °C. Clean the snails thoroughly, rinsing under running cold water. Bring 4 cups/1 liter of water to a boil, with the studded onion, 1 tsp salt, and the peppercorns. Add the snails and boil for 30 minutes. Pour off the water and drain the snails. Heat the bacon in a heatsafe casserole until the fat runs. Sweat the onion and garlic with the bacon until transparent, then add the mushrooms and stew a little. Stir in the white wine and stock, and add the snails. Transfer the casserole to the preheated oven and cook for about 10 minutes. Bring to the table in the casserole.

Pig trotters are delicious stuffed. Once the stuffing is inside, they are wrapped in bacon (background photograph), stewed with tomatoes and finally served with mixed forest mushrooms (above).

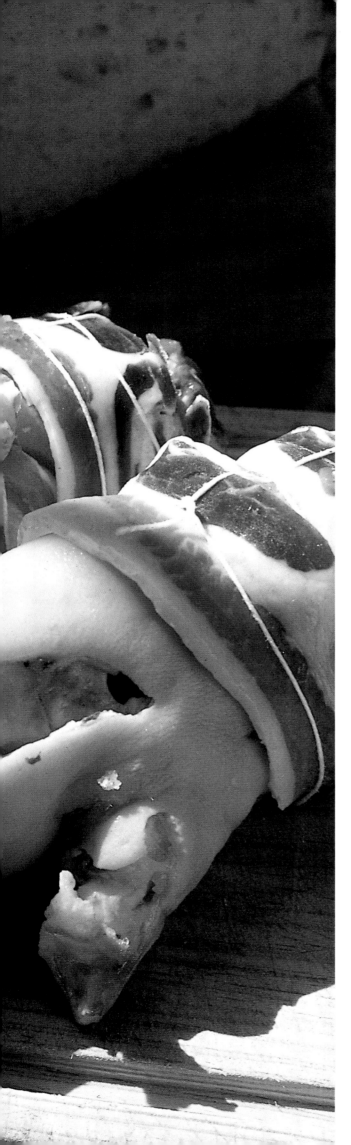

PERDICES CON COLES
Cabbage roulades with partridge
(Photograph above)

4 boned partridge breasts
Salt and pepper
3 tbsp olive oil
5 oz/150 g smoked bacon
1 onion, finely chopped
1 carrot, diced
1 leek, thinly sliced
1 ripe tomato, skinned and diced
2 Butifarra sausages or 5 oz/150 g sausage meat
2 tbsp flour
1 cup/250 ml chicken stock
1 cup/250 ml white wine
8 large boiled white cabbage leaves (whole)
Flour for coating
2 eggs, beaten
2 tbsp lard
1 clove of garlic, chopped
1 tbsp chopped parsley
2 tbsp roasted pine nuts

Halve the partridge breasts and rub them with salt and pepper. Heat 2 tbsp of oil in a casserole and brown the partridge breasts on both sides. Add the vegetables, mix and cook together on a low heat for 15 minutes until done.

Meanwhile fry the sausages in the rest of the oil in a deep skillet. When they are cooked, lay them on top of the vegetables. Blend the flour into the oil used for frying, and cook this roux until it takes on a pale yellow color. Stir in the chicken stock and white wine and blend thoroughly. Cook on a low heat for 10 minutes to thicken, stirring as necessary.

Remove the partridge breasts and sausages from the pot and let cool a little. Slice the sausages and return them to the pot. Blend the contents of the pot to a puree using a hand blender. Stir in the wine sauce and cook together over a low heat.

Wrap the partridge breasts in the cabbage leaves. Coat them in flour and then in beaten egg. Heat the lard in a skillet and fry them until golden. Remove and drain on paper towels to absorb excess fat before serving.

Pound the garlic, parsley, and pine nuts with 2 tbsp of the sauce, using a mortar and pestle. Stir this mixture into the sauce and season with salt and pepper. Place the partridge breast roulades in the sauce and leave to absorb flavors for about 5 minutes.

Curd cheese

The problem with *mató* is the problem of Babel: linguistic confusion reigns. Apart from this particular well-loved curd cheese, there are two other dairy products in Catalonia which are often sold under the name of *mató*. The three types, *mató*, *brossat*, and *recuit*, are however clearly distinct from one another.

Mató began with the itinerant life and economy practiced by the goatherds in the interior of Catalonia. The goatherds once used to travel from market to market, and would sell the milk straight from the animal. They would complete milking her later, and then make the next day's unsalted curd cheese. A rennet of vegetable origin *(herbacol)* was added to make the milk coagulate. Industrial producers today use pasteurized milk and animal rennet. They also increasingly use cow's milk, or a mixture of cow's and goat's milk. *Mató* has a slightly granular consistency, and the cheese is always shaped like an upturned bowl, with the mark of the ceramic mold or the weave of the linen impressed on its surface.

The *mató* of Montserrat has been renowned for as long as anyone can remember; the area around Vic also produces *mató* of the highest quality. Similar curd cheese from goat's milk can still be found in the Rioja (*Queso Camerano*, see page 151) and in Murcia (*Queso fresco de Murcia*). All these are eaten with honey as a dessert (in Catalonia under the name of *mel i mató*). It is also frequently eaten with fresh or stewed fruit, or with nuts.

Brossat is in effect a by-product of the cheese-making process – for example, where cheese producers are making cheeses such as Serrat or Vall d'Aran. *Brossat* is made from the whey, using heat and acid to curdle the dissolved whey proteins and separate them out in solid form. This white soft cheese is called *brull* in southern Catalonia. It is usually eaten fresh as a dessert as well, and is therefore often confused with *mató*.

Recuit (quark; *requesón* in Spanish) is basically simply coagulated milk. It used once to be made of sheep's milk only, but the milk used today is cow's milk, or a mixture of cow's and sheep's milk. The milk is first heated to boiling point over a *bain-marie*, and then left to cool down. Animal rennet or fermented herbs are used to curdle it, and the cheese is soon ready. It is usually sold in small earthenware pots. Recuit is softer and creamier than *mató*. Despite the difference, it is often served as a dessert under the name of *mel i mató*. In contrast to *mató*, however, its use in Spanish cooking extends far beyond simply combining it with honey, fruit, or nuts. One popular use is to spread it on a cake or pastry tart; or it may be made into a whipped sweet cream dessert, to be eaten on its own or with fruit. It is also used to fill cream puffs *(buñuelos)* or small turnovers *(empanadillas)*. In recent years, creative cooks have found a new role for these various soft cheeses. They are being used as a delicious, easily digested base for a number of elegant desserts which are to be found gracing the tables of the best restaurants.

Mató, the fine, unsalted Catalonian curd cheese made from goat's milk

Catalan cheese

If the cheese encountered in restaurants or the pitiful display in the average supermarket could be considered a fair guide, Catalonia would hardly be judged a place to visit for its cheeses. Appearances can be deceptive. Rich treasures await the visitor's discovery in this region. Recently, more and more cheese producers have been reviving ancient Catalan traditions. Goats are still the mainstay of cheese production in Catalonia. An example of the revival and renewal of tradition is provided by a group of young people from the cities who moved to the village of Clúa in the province of Lleida in 1978. There, they produce the dazzlingly white, creamy goat cheese *Montsec*. Another name for this cheese is *Cendrat*, ("with ash"), the reason being that the cheese is rubbed with ash during the ripening process. The flavorsome goat cheese *formatge d'oli amb herbes de musser*, which is preserved in herbs with oil, is a tempting product from the Cerdanya valley; from Berguedá comes the *Bauma*, another goat cheese. A gray-blue rind of penicillin mold (*Penicillin*

Montsec / Cendrat

glaucum) conceals the snowy white *Garrotxa*, which was once made in ancient earthenware pots in the rural district of that name. It is butter-soft and melts in the mouth, with a delightful aftertaste of hazelnuts. *Tupí* is a spreading cheese with an aggressive, piquant flavor. It comes from the Pyrenees, and is made and is sold in an earthenware pot (today it may also be found in a plastic one). *Tupí a la Ratafia de Muntanyola* is made of goat's milk with the addition of a fine fruit liqueur; it tastes particularly delicious on freshly made toast. *Tupí* is usually made from sheep's milk, as is the large Catalan raw milk cheese, *Serrat*, which is made the length of the Pyrenees. Beneath a straw yellow rind it is compact, white or off-white inside, and leaves a marked aftertaste of sheep's milk on the tongue. The rich, compact, and slightly smoky cheese *Vall d'Aran* is made from raw cow's milk, and comes from the valley of the same name. Even cheeses which were originally only made by goatherds and shepherds, such as *Garrotxa* and *Serrat*, are now available made from cow's milk. *Tou del Tilders* comes from the area around Pallars, as does *Serrat Roi*. There is a fine cow's milk cheese from the district of Garrotxa called *La Dama Blanca*, and in Cabrerès the cheese to look out for is *Moli de l'Alzine*.

The goat's milk curd cheese *mató* provides a light, easily digested dessert. The traditional combination is with honey and nuts; but its faintly bitter, delicate flavor harmonizes wonderfully with fresh fruit (above). Other possible accompaniments to enjoy with authentic *mató* are dried fruit or jam, or perhaps a dash of aniseed brandy.

Opposite: Goats are easily content, well able to live in dry regions or at some altitude. Goat's milk is used to make the curd cheese *mató*.

CREMA CATALANA
Catalan cream

1 cup/200 g sugar
4 egg yolks
1 tbsp cornstarch
1 stick of cinnamon
Grated rind of ½ lemon
2 cups/500 ml milk

Beat together the egg yolks and ¾ cup/150 g sugar in a pot until blended and frothy. Add the cinnamon and lemon rind, and pour on the milk. Slowly heat the mixture, stirring constantly, until it begins to thicken and the resistance can be felt. Remove from the heat. Remove the cinnamon stick, and divide the cream between 4 individual heatsafe dishes. Cool and place in the refrigerator.

Before serving this dessert, scatter the remaining sugar over the surface of each portion. Preheat the broiler. Place the dishes under the broiler until the sugar topping begins to caramelize. Serve immediately.

CREMA CATALANA

A dessert of this type may not seem unique – other nations claim to have known a similar one as far back as memory can reach – yet it occupies an important place in Catalan cuisine. The people of Catalonia call it *crema catalana* or *crema de Sant Josep* (St. Joseph's cream), and regard it as one of their most outstanding traditional dishes. The French equivalent, *crème brûlée*, can be found all over France today. However, it does not feature among the dishes offered by the doyen of French cuisine, Escoffier, in the early part of the 20th century. It may then be that the origin of this fine dessert does indeed lie in Catalonia.

Tradition gives the role of preparing this delicious cream to the grandmother or maiden aunts living as part of the family. It is made on March 19, St. Joseph's Day. For many families this is still something of an annual ritual, and they eat *crema catalana* on no other day. It is served in small, shallow earthenware dishes, to withstand the heat of browning the sugar. This is done with an iron specially designed for the purpose and heated in the fire. The sweet cream is also popular as a filling for apples. Genuine *crema catalana* is not found today outside good restaurants; a ready-made, powdered version is available instead.

NUTS AND FRUIT

Hazelnuts were known in Catalonia as long ago as the Stone Age. In Catholic Spain, the bush was dedicated to the Virgin Mary, because she is said to have sheltered from a storm under a hazel. It enjoys special favor as a result, so the saying goes. Folklore tells that lightning never strikes a hazel, which also offers protection from all manner of reptiles. Reus in the province of Tarragona is the modern center of hazelnut production.

Farmers here cultivate this fine crop over an area of around 50,000 acres (more than 20,000 hectares). Severe competition from Turkey means, however, that many give up each year. A mark of quality recognized by the EU (D.O) now exists, indicating the efforts being made to halt the trend toward domination of the market by cheap imported produce.

Catalans like to end a copious meal with a simple dessert: *postre de músic*. It consists of dried fruit and nuts: hazelnuts, almonds, pine nuts, dried figs, and raisins. A sweet wine accompanies this, drunk from the pointed communal drinking vessel called a *porrón*. The juice of the grape is poured straight into the mouth from the long spout.

A great range of different fruits is served in Catalonia; over 40 percent of the land area under cultivation is devoted to fruit-growing. Driving through the plain of Lleida is a delight, above all in spring. The chain of the Pyrenees gleams white as a backdrop; in the foreground stretches a tapestry of blossom. Apples, pears, peaches, and apricots are grown across an area of some 100,000 acres (40,000 hectares), with total production in the region of 1,100,000 tons (1,000,000 tonnes) a year. Apart from Lleida, the traditional fruit-growing area, there is production mainly in Penedès and in the hinterland of the Costa Brava. The velvety peaches of Pinyana (Lleida), and Penedès, apples from Girona and the Pla d'Urgell (Lleida) and cherries from the Baix Llobregat (Barcelona) are each distinguished by a seal of quality. On the Baix Llobregat, the plain south of Barcelona, under threat from the encroachments of the metropolis, vegetables are grown, and water melons and figs are produced by the ton.

Collecting wild strawberries in the Pyrenees is popular among the Catalans, though these fruits are gradually becoming rare. Today, they are often replaced as a dessert fruit by *maduixes*, strawberries grown in the glasshouses of the Maresme, the "Riviera" which lies north of Barcelona.

Hazelnut   Pine nut

Walnut

Magical desserts can be made from curd or cream cheese and fruit. Here, *mató* is layered with a confection of fruit; pears or quinces may be chosen.

A modern way to serve strawberries is with Cava or white wine and a hint of lemon. They also taste glorious unadorned or with whipped cream.

Pears in red wine: a simple but elegant dessert which will crown any meal in style.

A traditional heated iron with a spiral shape is used to brown the top of authentic *crema catalana* (above and opposite). The layer of sugar is transformed by this into a thin, hard glaze (right) which shatters when the dessert is eaten.

A CALENDAR OF SWEET CONFECTIONS

The progression of times and seasons through the year is not only marked by the feast days of the Church; in Catalonia, that path is paved with sugar. The late writer-cook and gourmet Manuel Vázquez Montalbán, who died in 2003, counted 50 days in the year for which there is a special and uniquely characteristic sweet cake or pastry. There seems to be a strange contradiction in the fact that while restaurants offer a range of last courses limited to ice cream or creamed desserts (and even *crema catalana* has become a rarity), the cake shops *(pastisserias)* display a profusion of tempting goodies. The first specialty cake shop in Barcelona was opened in 1382; Paris had to wait until 1608. The basis of Catalan cakes and confectionery is provided by the fine hazelnuts and almonds which the region produces, as well as flour, sugar, and eggs. There are six main categories of the confectioner's art today. These are *coques*, cakes made from yeast dough and baked in large, shallow pans, *tortells*, which are fine cake rings, *bunyols*, small doughnuts, also made with yeast dough, *galetes*, cookies, and *coquinyols*, which are cookies with hazelnuts. Finally in the sweet category, there are the Catalan desserts made with milk.

For centuries, the rhythm by which each sweetmeat in turn appeared in the course of the year was set by the Church, which controlled all aspects of Spanish life. The legacy of those days is the succession of sweet delights which Catalans enjoy to this day, as they crunch their way through the calendar. Innumerable local variations on the basic recipes exist; each village and each old-established family in the country claims to produce an utterly unique version.

The feast days of the Church dictate the cake or pastry eaten in any particular season (right). This calendar is observed by Catalan cake shops (above).

Christmas – Turrón de Navidad:
It is hard to imagine Christmas in Spain without this traditional almond nougat. Whatever dispute there may be between Catalans and Valencians over which of them invented this fine candy, the two regions are without equal in consuming it! (See page 382 f.)

Epiphany – Tortell de Reis: The "cake of the Kings," made to celebrate Epiphany is ring-shaped. It is decorated with candied fruits, and has an almond filling. It also contains a surprise. This used to be a bean, but nowadays it is usually a small plastic figure. The finder of the figure is allowed to wear the crown for the day.

January 17 – Tortell de Sant Antoni Abat: The "cake of St. Anthony" is filled with marzipan. It is often baked with an animal figure inside, because St. Antoni Abat is the patron saint of animals. People observe the day with a pilgrimage to one of the churches dedicated to this saint, where horses, dogs, and cats are blessed.

Carnival – Coca de llardons: This cake is made from a sweet yeast dough with pork cracklings. It is substantial and rich enough to provide a solid foundation for long nights spent celebrating over the carnival season. The cracklings used are usually genuine fresh ones, since carnival falls at the time of year when the pig is slaughtered.

Good Friday – Bunyols de quaresma: These are Lenten doughnuts: deep-fried ring doughnuts, made from a yeast dough and liberally scattered with superfine or confectioners' sugar before eating. In Empordà, they are made in the form of puffs, rather than rings, with a creamy filling or real dairy cream inside.

Easter Monday – Mona de Pasqua: The Easter ring is made from yeast dough, this time decorated with hard-cooked eggs. Godparents traditionally present their godchild with a *mona* every year, until the child reaches his or her first communion. Each year there is one more egg in the decoration.

All Saints – Panellets de Tots Sants: The whole of Catalonia bakes these small round or oval cakes for the feast day of All Saints on November 1. They are made of marzipan, almonds, and pine nuts. The range is constantly increasing; variations include versions with coffee, chestnut, egg yolk, chocolate, and hazelnuts.

St. John's Eve – Coca de Sant Joan: Midsummer (Feast of St. John, June 24) is celebrated with a public festival and fireworks. The event would not be the same without a "St. John's Cake," a large yeast-dough cake with candied fruits. According to taste, confectioners' cream or dairy cream are added.

The building housing the winery and cellars was designed for Codorníu by the modernist architect and artist Josep Puig i Cadafalch, and was completed in 1915. King Juan Carlos declared the bodega a national monument in 1976.

The owners of Bodegas Codorníu live in a beautiful estate at the same site as the winery, surrounded by the vineyards which produce the grapes for their famous Cava. This wine is stored in nearly 20 miles (30 kilometers) of galleried cellars beneath the buildings of the winery.

Codorníu can thus boast the distinction of being the largest bodega in the world.

CAVA

1872 was the year when Josep Raventós Fatjó of the estate Can Codorníu uncorked his first bottle of wine made by the *méthode champenoise*. Wine produced by this method is fermented and matured in the bottle. It is not a new method, however: the French Benedictine monk Dom Pierre Pérignon, cellarer of the monastery of Hautvilliers, developed the process of bottle fermentation as early as the 17th century. Raventós was so excited by the sparkling elixir he had produced that he had a cool cellar *(cava)* dug on his estate in Sant Sadurní d'Anoia, to provide suitable conditions for making sparkling wine. He then devoted himself to its production. His son, Manuel, introduced the first 864 bottles of this Spanish sparkling wine to the market in 1879. A special, exclusive drink, it met with success in the highest ranks of society; the Catalan family Raventós was soon supplying the royal household in Madrid. The elegant, *art nouveau* building which houses the winery and cellars in Sant Sadurní d'Anoia gives some idea of how glorious this rise to success was. Today, it attracts thousands of visitors every year. The popularity of sparkling wine attracted others into the production of sparkling wine by methods other than the traditional one. The label *Champán de Cava* ("Cellar champagne") was introduced to distinguish the better quality sparkling wines from modest fizz, and the better brands bore this label. The name *Champán* disappeared from the label when Spain joined the European Community, and France requested that its use be forbidden; from then on, the wine was known simply as *Cava*. It has brought prosperity to the region of Penedès, south of Barcelona.

Today in this hotly contested market, there are 270 smaller wine-producers, as well as the giant Codorníu and its fast-expanding rival Freixenet. In 1977, there were 65 of these producers. Around 6850 growers produce the grapes for Cava annually on approximately 79,000 acres (32,000 hectares). The quality of the wine derives from three native varieties: Xarello (Catalan: Xarel.lo), which provides strength and color, Macabeo, which lends delicacy and elegance, and Parellada, which ensures its aroma. Recently, more expensive, single-variety Cavas made from the Chardonnay grape have appeared on the market.

QUALITY DESIGNATIONS FOR CAVA

Legislation specifically concerned with this issue has been in place since November 1991, together with a controlling council. The purpose of both is to ensure that a consistent standard of quality is maintained for Cava. The European Community has also recognized the declaration of origin "Cava." Outside Catalonia, only a small number of producers in Alava, La Rioja, Badajoz, Valencia, Navarra, and Zaragoza are so far included in this. The distinguishing mark of genuine Cava, apart from the name, is a four-pointed star on the base of the cork. There are six official types of Cava, graded according to their residual sugar content. The alcoholic content ranges from 10.8 to 12.8 degrees. The six types are:
• *Extra Brut* (0-6 grams of sugar per liter)
• *Brut* (0-15 grams per liter)
• *Extra Seco* (12-20 grams per liter)
• *Seco* (17-35 grams per liter)
• *Semi-Seco* (33-50 grams per liter)
• *Dulce* (more than 50 grams per liter)
The designation *Brut Nature* for Cavas with under 3 grams of sugar per liter is no longer officially permitted. An increasing number of firms are now bringing vintage Cava *(Cava vintage)* onto the market – that is, Cava from a particular year.

All Spanish sparkling wine described as Cava must be made by the traditional method of bottle fermentation *(método tradicional* or *méthode champenoise)*. The principle is a simple one: to acquire its "sparkle," a sparkling wine has to undergo a second fermentation process. To make this happen, a mixture of yeast and sugar *(licor de tirajo)* is added to the original wine, and it is bottled. The bottles must then lie in a cool cellar for at least nine months. During this period, the yeasts convert the sugar into carbon dioxide. The yeast residue, or lees, is removed at the end of the maturation period. Depending on the type of Cava being made, sweetness and flavor are regulated by adding sugar and wine *(licor de expedición,* or *dosage)*. The bottles are then corked, sealed, and labeled, and dispatched to be sold.

Cava need not fear the comparison with champagne; nonetheless, consumption figures in Spain are quite low: an annual two bottles per head. As a comparison, the annual consumption of sparkling wine in Germany is seven bottles. On the international scene, however, the Catalans advance from success to success: since the 1970s, Cava has become a strong competitor for champagne and German sparkling wine on the basis of its price-performance ratio.

Increasing automation, with the invention of the *girasol* for riddling the bottles by machine instead of by hand, gave the Spanish version a still greater price advantage, and brought a breakthrough for the Catalans in the 1980s. Annual production today is well over 200 million bottles, of which more than half are exported. Thies, Cava has caught up with French champagne.

The fine marc, Marc de Cava, has only begun to make a name for itself beyond the borders of Catalonia in the last few years. This is the brandy made from the last pressing of the Cava grapes. Years of maturing in oak barrels, as happens in many Cava cellars, usually gives it a golden color and pronounced mildness. With its aroma of dried fruits, Marc de Cava is winning increasing numbers of friends as a fine *digestif*. It is best drunk ice cold – but not, of course, with ice cubes.

These ancient vaults are home to the Codorníu museum, which documents over 100 years of Cava tradition in Sant Sadurní d'Anoia, near Barcelona.

The *licor de expedición* is added to Cava toward the end of the bottle fermentation process. It is a mixture of wine and sugar, and gives the Cava its final nuances of flavor.

Below: In many cellars producing Cava, the task of riddling the bottles, *remuage*, is still done by hand. It is still performed this way at Codorníu, where the first Cava was made.

The systematic process of turning the bottles causes the yeast residue to collect in the neck. The neck is frozen to force the sediment out.

TOP CAVAS

Agustí Torelló: **Kripta**. Extra brut, with good volume and fine yeast. Complex woodland, earthy notes.

Can Feixes: **Huguet Brut Nature.** Extra brut, with an elegant note. Complex, with pronounced length.

Can Ràfols dels Caus: **Gran Caus.** Extra brut; slender, with a fine dryness in the fruit, and delicate bubbles.

Castellblanch: **Gran Castell.** Extra brut; light, with good maturity and notes of dried fruits.

Cavas Castillo de Perelada: **Castillo de Perelada Chardonnay:** Extra brut, with a steeliness, and elegance.

Jaume Giró i Giró: **Jaume Giró i Giró Extra Brut.** Fully mature. Powerful, subtle, and long.

Cavas Ferret: **Ezequiel Ferret.** Extra brut; soft and balanced, with a fine dry finish.

Cavas Hill: **Brut de Brut.** Extra brut; supple, with mature fruit. Persistent, with good body.

Llopart Cava: **Brut Leopardi.** Extra brut; floral bouquet, fresh. Notes of almonds.

Cavas Recaredo: **Recaredo Brut Nature.** Extra brut; very traditional. Full, with emphasis on body.

Caves Ramón Canals Canals: **R. Canals Canals Brut Nature.** Powerful, mature, rather exotic fruit.

Gramona: **Tres Lustros.** Extra brut; fine ripeness. Very balanced; differentiated in the mouth.

Segura Viudas: **Brut Vintage.** Brut; fine bubbles. Elegant notes of yeast contact. Fine dryness and prolonged finish.

Coll de Juny: **Dama.** Brut; fully matured and defined fruit (melon). Complex, round, and long.

Covides: **Duc de Foix.** Brut; pronounced yeast, well matured, soft, and supple.

Freixenet: **Brut Barroco.** Extra brut; medium bubbles. Flamboyant, exotic, and rich in nuances; has depth.

Joan Raventós Rosell **Brut Reserva Heretat.** Brut; crystal-clear structure, elegant and dry.

Juve & Camps: **Gran Juve & Camps.** Brut; mature and dominant in character. Very balanced; distinguished.

Parxet: **Brut Nature,** Extra brut; floral nose and fine bubbles. Elegant, powerful, with bite.

Roger Goulart: **Brut de Brut.** Extra brut; glorious balance. Powerful, with pronounced length.

Cavas Rovellats: **Rovellats Brut Nature Chardonnay.** Extra brut; flowery bouquet, structure, and length.

Robert J. Mur: **Robert J. Mur Brut Nature.** Extra brut; medium bubbles. Well matured and elegant.

Jané Ventura: **Jané Ventura Brut Nature.** Extra brut; subtle and elegant, with fine bubbles and pleasant acidity.

Codorníu: **Anna de Codorníu.** Brut; fine citrus notes and elegant structure.

Wine-producing areas

D.O. Penedès

This, the most famous wine-producing area in Catalonia, is characterized by innovation and the constant quest for quality. Vineyards occupy more than 64,250 acres (26,000 hectares) from the shores of the Mediterranean to altitudes of 3300 feet (1000 meters). The grape varieties grown are mainly Macabeo, Xarel.lo, Parellada, and Chardonnay, and these produce light white wines with a delicate, fruity aroma. The reds are velvety, matured in oak barrels, and made mainly from Cabernet Sauvignon, Ull de Llebre (Tempranillo), Merlot, Garnacha, and Cariñena. Today, however, the region's winemakers are increasingly experimenting with new varieties, such as Pinot Noir or Sauvignon Blanc.

D.O. Priorat

The loose slate soils of this mountainous region probably produce the most impressive musts from the Garnacha grape in all Spain. Some of the red wines of Priorat (or Priorato, as Spaniards from other regions call this Catalan area) are among the best in the world. These wines are dense and deeply colored, with great structure. They are positively bursting with fruit. The classic reds are made from Garnacha and Cariñena grapes, and sometimes exhibit a restrained sweetness reminiscent of raisins. The new generation of reds, which aroused a degree of furore over past years, are vinified from Cabernet Sauvignon, Merlot, and Syrah, as well as the two traditional varieties. *Vins rancis (rancios)* are dry white wines, mainly based on the Garnacha Blanca, which are matured for a long period in a large wooden vat, so developing oxidative notes.

D.O. Tarragona

As long ago as the days of the Roman Empire, the Roman historian Pliny praised the wines of this area; he called them some of the best in the Empire, and vintages from here were shipped to its capital, Rome itself. Today, the main wines produced in this area are soft, balanced, yet powerful whites made from Macabeo, Xarel.lo, and Parellada. The rosés have a cherry color and fruity freshness. The red wines combine the aroma and power of the Garnacha with the body and color of the Cariñena grape.

D.O. Empordà-Costa Brava

The Greeks discovered the excellent soils of this area, situated on the shores of the Mediterranean, and Catalonia's most northerly wine-producing region. Its best-known wines are its fruity rosés and its sweet Garnacha dessert wines. The light, cheerful *Empordà Novell*, sold as early as mid-November each year, is excellent. The red, barrel-aged Crianzas and Reservas develop a powerful bouquet.

D.O. Costers del Segre

The province of Lleida produces a number of very different wines, owing to its range of soils and climate. The area of Raïmat, in which grow European grape varieties (Sauvignon, Cabernet, Merlot, and Pinot Noir), as well as in Les Garrigues and Vall de Riu Corb, is characterized by a very dry, even harsh climate. Costers del Segre produces red wines with

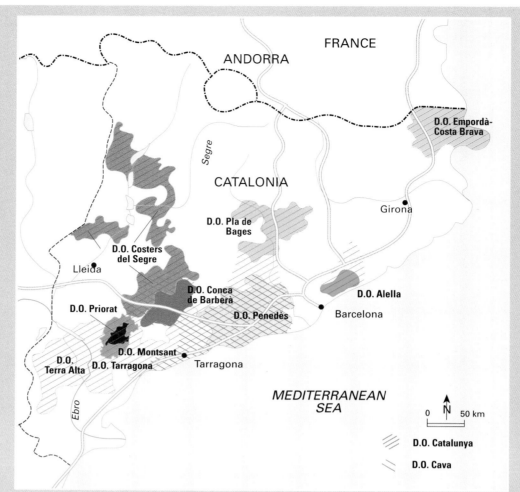

alcohol levels up to 13.5 degrees. The *varietals* in particular, single-variety wines made from Pinot Noir or Cabernet Sauvignon, are outstanding.

D.O. Conca de Barberà

The monks of Santa Maria de Poblet and the Knights Templar of Barberà de la Conca brought the grape to this region back in the Middle Ages. The young white wines produced here today from the Macabeo and Parellada varieties and, most recently, from the Chardonnay grape, are soft and pleasing. The rosés are made from the local variety Trepat. Good red wines are made not only from Ull de Llebre (Tempranillo), but have recently also been made from Sauvignon and Merlot.

D.O. Terra Alta

In this remote corner of Catalonia, almost on the border with Valencia, more and more modern and fruity - but also powerful - white wines are produced using the classic variety Garnacha Blanca. The reds are full and ripe. The local climate enables first-class *rancios* to be produced. These are old, golden colored white wines, which have been aged either in oak vats, or – a specialty of the region – in the open, in full sun.

D.O. Alella

Even centuries ago, wines from Alella enjoyed a good reputation, favored by the prelates of the cathedral in Barcelona. The most important grape varieties today are Pansá Blanca (Xarel.lo), Chardonnay as well as Ull de Llebre (Tempranillo) and Garnacha. The traditional

white Alella is partly made into single variety wine and has a light and fragrent aroma.

D.O. Pla de Bages

This region was created D.O., protected area, in 1997 and produces mainly young, fruity whites and pleasant red wines, made of international varieties. The local variety, Picapoll, is most worthy of notice. It produces harmonious white wines with lovely notes of melon and aniseed. There are only few acres of Picapoll vines in the whole of Spain, and the major part of these is in Pla de Bages.

D.O. Montsant

This small region surrounding the small town of Falset used to pertain to D.O. Tarragona but awarded its own D.O. status in 2001. The cultivation region is in close proximity to the Priorat, but the red wines produced here are not quite as powerful and mineral as those of his famous neighbor. The typical blends of Garnacha, Cariñena, Cabernet Sauvignon, and Syrah offer good-quality wines.

D.O. Catalunya

This ara of protected declaration of orgin (D.O.), recognized in 2001, covers many of the established traditional winegrowing areas of Catalonia. The D.O. seat helps many wine producers making simple wines blended from several grape varieties to market these in other territorres, too: more than 50% of these wines is exported.

VITICULTURE

Wine is as old as the civilization of the Mediterranean itself. Could it have been the Phoenicians who first brought the grape to Spain? It is certainly true that the Greeks of Ampurias drank the juice of the grape, and Roman colonial society promoted the cultivation of vines and the making of fine wine in the lands which today are Catalonia. Such was the winemakers' success that large quantities of wine were soon being supplied to the capital of the Empire in Rome.

Wine requires not only the right soils and climate, but also a society with both purchasing power and taste. This means that the history of wine in Catalonia has reflected the course of European history. Viticulture was unable to survive under the onslaught of the Goths and Vandals from the north, or of the Arabs from the south. In the Middle Ages, however, vines reappeared, despite the depredations of pirates which had destroyed the best vineyard land within reach of the coast. Monks were the only people at that point in history who had either the time or the knowledge to make fine wines. They came from Burgundy and the Rhine, bringing the art of winemaking to Catalonia. The powerful Knights Templar also planted vineyards for themselves.

Catalonia rose to become a trading power in the period up to the 14th century. Her ships brought Malvasía wine from Greece and the Vernaccia grape from the Cinque Terre, from La Spezia. This was the grape variety used at that time to make wine for the Popes. In Catalonia, it became the Garnatxa (Spanish: Garnacha); today, however, it is regarded as a native variety. The plague, politics, and greed for profit then intervened, bringing a long period of paralysis for viticulture in Catalonia. Then, in the 18th century, exports to America brought a revival of the Catalan wine trade. In its wake followed the cork and glass industries; even shipbuilding became soundly established.

The most important European development of this era, however, was one which passed Catalonia by: in 1758, the Marquis de Pombal created the first protected declaration of origin (D.O.) in Alto Douro, Portugal. While quality became the prime concern in other places, the Catalans continued to pursue quantity. Constantly rising exports had brought a sense of intoxication, but there was to be a rude awakening; in 1872, phylloxera reached the region of Alt Empordà. Viticulture became a thing of the past. The vineyards were replanted with improved varieties of phylloxera-resistant vines from America. At last, during this period of replanting, producers who cared about quality began to emerge, like Josep and Manuel Raventós of Codorníu.

Mineral water

In 1880, a doctor by the name of Modest Furest i Roca decided to buy a plot of land with a spring in Caldes de Malavella (Girona). Several reasons lay behind this purchase: local folk wisdom, archeological finds, since Roman walls had been discovered, and an interest in natural cures. The water emerged from the earth at a temperature of 140 °F (60 °C). Analysis revealed that it had a high mineral content. Furest opened a bottling plant in late 1889, and the water went on sale soon afterward, initially in drugstores. At that time, the name Vichy meant mineral springs and baths in general, so Furest adopted the name of the French health resort, to which he added the regional name, calling his spring Vichy Catalán. The name, fortunately for him, was registered in 1890, before the French did the same. Following some decades of legal wrangles, the firm has been allowed to retain its trademark.

The water rises from a depth of some 6600 feet (2000 meters), and emerges through three separate fissures. Today, each of the three has a bottling plant: Vichy Catalán, Malavella, and San Narciso. Although the three springs rise from a common source, each has its own quite different mineral content and flavor, because each passes through different rocks on its way to the surface. The mineral water at Caldes is not only used for drinking; the Romans had bathed at these springs (which they called, in so many words, "good water"). At the end of the 19th century, Dr. Furest set about the building of the baths, the spa itself. He did this with the financial help of some *Indianos*, citizens of the region who had made their fortune in the colonies, mainly Cuba. The spa continues to this day to attract visitors both young and old. The main aspect of the business is, however, the sales of bottled water.

Health-giving water gushes from the springs in Caldes de Malavella (above). It is bottled for sale, and has brought fame to the spa of Vichy Catalán (right).

Famous varieties of mineral water from Spain

Vichy Catalán
from Caldes de Malavella
(Girona, Catalonia)

Fontdor
from San Hilari Sacalm
(Girona, Catalonia)

Fontemilla
from Sigüenza (Guadalajara, Castile-La Mancha)

Font Vella
from San Hilari Sacalm
(Girona, Catalonia)

Agua de Mondariz
from Mondariz Balneario
(Pontevedra, Galicia)

Bezoya
from Ortigosa del Monte
(Segovia, Castile-Leon)

Fuensanta
from Balneario de
Fuensanta, Nava (Asturias)

Lanjarón
from Lanjarón/Alpujarras
(Granada, Andalusia)

Insalus
from Lizartza (Guipúzcoa,
Basque Country)

Viladrau
from Viladrau (Girona,
Catalonia)

Benassal from Balneario
Font d'en Segures, Benassal
(Castellón, Valencia)

Font del Regás
from Arbúcies (Girona,
Catalonia)

Solán de Cabras
from Beteta (Cuenca,
Castile-La Mancha)

Les Creus from
Maçanet de Cabrenys
(Girona, Catalonia)

Vilajuïga
from Vilajuiga (Girona,
Catalonia)

Valle de Cardó
from Benifallet
(Tarragona, Catalonia)

ISLAS BALEARES

Balearic Islands

Balearic Island farmers have good cause to smile: they bring in several harvests a year. Eggplants, bell peppers, and tomatoes destined for local markets are allowed to ripen fully.

Baleares – the images which come to mind at the mention of the Balearic Islands are many and contradictory. Wild nights of disco-dancing by the fashionable crowd of Ibiza on the one hand; the almost tangible, reflective silence of a bicycle ride through Formentera on the other. Untamed nature still exerts its charm along the rugged coast of Minorca, where quiet coves lie among jagged cliffs, despite all the encroachments of tourism. In Majorca the beaches may indeed be packed with endless rows of tourists, frying in the sun; other people take pleasure in the lonely, stone-strewn paths of the island's Sierra de Tramuntana, wild and enchanting country, where the scent of lavender, thyme, and other plants fills the air.

The history of this archipelago is as rich as its geography. The name comes from the Baliarides, fierce warriors, armed with slingshots, who went to war with Hannibal against Rome. The Phoenician rule over the islands was succeeded by the might of Rome. Later came the Vandals, after them, Byzantium, which gave way to the Arabs, and the Moors were driven out in the 13th century by the king of Aragon. The Balearic Islands have been firmly linked with Catalonia since that time. The native languages of the people, known as mallorqui, are variants dialect of the Catalan.

The Balearic Islands offer such a unique range of landscape and culture within a small area that they might be called a continent in miniature. Successive invaders did not destroy what they found, but tended it, adding new features of their own. The olive trees are centuries old, and bear abundant fruit. Viticulture goes back to the Romans; the Arabs bequeathed a wealth of knowledge about the care of figs and almonds. There have been periods of poverty, and the experience has made the islanders into masters of the art of making imaginative use of what they have. Cabbage soup, a pauper's dish, has been refined by this skill into a true specialty, in which even master chefs take pleasure today. Is anyone troubled by the thought that air-dried ham cannot be made where there is too much moisture in the air? Not at all: the people found other ways of preserving the meat, and produced the notable red *sobrasada* sausage, which is so popular.

The cuisine of the Balearics is that of the local market: the food on the stalls is the dish of the day. The secret of cooking with the islands' bounty is to keep it "fresh and simple." The sea views, the almond blossom in winter, or the vast stretches of vegetable plantations – provide the perfect introduction to the hidden culinary wonders of the Balearic Islands.

The sea is never far away wherever you go on the Balearic Islands. The hills rise out of the water, as here on Majorca, largest of the islands.

VEGETABLES

"We have all we need here," said a countryman from Majorca. Drawing on the produce of his vegetable garden, he stated the principle that sums up the history of the Balearic Islands and the philosophy of its inhabitants: "Other peoples have been coming to the islands throughout history to conquer us. But we lack nothing. That is in our nature. Maybe that is what makes us so patient."

Having all they need is especially important to the islanders when it comes to vegetables; they are prepared to pay a price for them at market. Home-grown vegetables often cost twice as much as imports from the mainland. But the inhabitants believe in the quality of their produce. "The soil here has a lot of lime," says Pedro Quetglas from the islands' agricultural ministry. "It limits the plants' uptake of minerals. And we often have shortages of water. That sometimes makes our vegetables a bit smaller, but all the more tasty." The opinion of the plant expert is endorsed by the islands' top cooks, who are happy to sacrifice size for good flavor. The small, succulent, purple artichokes are a good example.

The weekly markets on the islands exist mainly to provide for the inhabitants' everyday needs. Today, they also sell all manner of souvenirs for tourists.

On the Balearic Islands, small, aromatic tomatoes and round, hot peppers are often hung out on the walls of houses to dry.

Left: Many families grow vegetables in their own gardens. Peppers and other vegetables are grown commercially as well, of course.

The climate of the Balearics is so mild that many farmers are able to harvest three crops of potatoes a year. The king of the vegetables is the tomato, however, here as almost all over the world. More than 2400 acres (1000 hectares) of the islands are given over to growing tomatoes. The small, dark-colored tomatoes called *tomàtigues de ramellet* are worthy of particular note. These are braided together into bundles and hung up to dry in the open air in Majorca. On Ibiza, they are hung up individually by their long stems. This means that there are always tomatoes available to use in sauces or to rub onto hearty country bread.

Consumers benefit from the short distances on the islands. Fruit and vegetables here can be picked when ripe and transported straight to the weekly markets. Almost every village on the islands has its market, selling vegetables, ham and sausage, cheese, and inexpensive clothing. The connoisseur will find the finest produce in the covered market of the capital, Palma. There, in the spacious building of the Mercat Olivar, the agricultural splendors of the island are spread out: dazzlingly white onions, much in demand for the summer salad *trempó*, fleshy tomatoes, bright green and red hot peppers. There is cabbage of every variety, and, in the place of honor, eggplant *(berenjana)*, much to the fore in island recipes, such as those for the baked dish called *tumbet*, and for a number of different stuffed versions. This vegetable, one of the nightshade family, was brought from India to North Africa by the Arabs. The Moors then brought it with them to Spain.

The islands have several remarkable dining customs which are historical in origin; one concerns the cucumber. The British once ruled over Minorca, and it was they who introduced the cucumber, among other things. Freedom-loving islanders on the neighboring island of Majorca therefore shun the cucumber. There are said to be people there who refuse even to sit at a table on which a cucumber has been seen to rest.

TUMBET
Eggplant bake
(Photograph left)

3 eggplants
Salt
1 cup/250 ml olive oil
4 potatoes, thinly sliced
2 large zucchini, sliced
4 cloves of garlic, chopped
2 lbs/1 kg ripe tomatoes, skinned and diced
Pepper, a pinch of sugar

VARIATIONS ON THE OLIVE THEME

The olive is the most important of the three trees cultivated since the time of the Ancients, ranking before the almond and the fig. The gnarled old trees of the Balearic Islands are said by locals to date back to the Romans. Most of the terraces were laid out in the 16th century, and the majority of the islands' 24,700 acres (10,000 hectares) of olive groves lie in the Sierra de Tramuntana on Majorca. Olives are mainly pressed simply for the growers' own use, although the Sóller cooperative does produce a quality olive oil.

Olives produced to be eaten, on the other hand, enjoy great popularity. The green fruits are harvested at the end of September. They are preserved in brine, either whole *(senceres)* or cut *(trencades)*, and flavored with fennel, lemon peel, and capsicums. Cut, the olives need to be used quickly; the whole ones keep for about six months. The first *pansides*, slightly wrinkled and brown, fall off the trees in late October. They are prepared with oil, salt, garlic, and bay, and used immediately. The *negres* (black olives) are harvested in November. These are preserved in brine with whatever flavoring is wanted: soaked for two months in *aigosal* (water with salt), with bay or with lemon and garlic. Large wooden spoons with holes are used to scoop the olives out of the brine.

Slice the eggplants and lay the slices in a large strainer. Sprinkle them with salt, and leave them to drain for 1 hour.

Heat the olive oil in a deep skillet. Fry the slices of potato until golden brown. Transfer them to a casserole and sprinkle with salt. Fry the eggplants lightly in the oil; then drain them and arrange on top of the potato. Finally, lightly fry the zucchini in the oil, and place these on top of the eggplants. Season lightly with salt. Keep the vegetables hot.

Pour away all but a little of the frying oil. Fry the garlic in the remaining oil until golden. Add the diced tomato, and begin to cook lightly, stirring. Press the sauce through a sieve, or purée it with a hand blender. Season it with salt, pepper, and sugar.

Transfer the vegetables to a serving dish, and pour the sauce over them. *Tumbet* can be served hot or cold.

Black pigs have been indigenous to the islands for thousands of years. They live in meadows and open woodland, and provide excellent meat for *sobrasada* and other specialties.

The Balearic Islands' sausage, *sobrasada*, has a distinctive red color and spicy flavor. This comes from the hot paprika used in them. It is traditionally made from the islands' round peppers.

THE IMPORTANCE OF THE PIG

When the French writer, George Sand, and the composer, Frédéric Chopin, came to Majorca, their journey was a comfortable one – a fact which they owed to the island's pigs. A ban, imposed around that time because of swine fever, had been lifted shortly before the journey took place. The government of the island had purchased a ferry to facilitate the export of the pigs, and this boat of course had decks for two-legged passengers traveling to and from the mainland. The strong-willed Frenchwoman nonetheless felt the inconvenience of having a herd of pigs on board. She describes them in her writings sometimes as "dirty and wild," at other times as "the loveliest animals in the world."

These animals have been indigenous in the Balearic Islands for 7000 years, and have always been an important source of protein there. The local variety is known as *porc negre* (or *porcella negra*), black pig, because of its black skin and long, black bristles. The animals grow to about 2 feet 7 inches (80 centimeters) in height, and weigh around 330 pounds (150 kilograms). They usually roam freely in the olive groves and woods – which greatly startled the British journalist, Gordon West, back in the 1920s, when he wrote that a horde of slender, black pigs chased him through the woods, which felt somewhat threatening. Later, he was able to laugh at his absurd panic just as heartily as the farmer who "rescued" him.

Now as before, the attitude to the pig is ambiguous. It is valuable, yet despised. Carlos Garrido remarks in his book *Mallorca Mágica* that the pig is "a totem of Majorca." Since the time of the Ancients, a link has been seen between the pig and the moon. In times past, it was only permissible to slaughter a pig during the period when the moon was waxing.

The black pigs of the Balearics are fed on beans, carob, alfalfa grass, acorns, and figs. The figs in particular give the meat a special, almost sweet flavor. This comes most to the fore in the red "national" *sobrasada* sausage.

The day when the pig was slaughtered (*Sa matança*) used to be the high spot of the year. The butcher arrived to dispatch the pig, which had been fattened for a year. An army of neighbors and relations stood by, ready to spend the whole day chopping meat, stirring sausagemeat, and filling sausages. Those families who still follow the tradition usually

Opposite: The slaughter of the family pig is one of the major events of the year in villages of the Balearic Islands. The neighbors arrive to help the butcher.

The occasion when the pig is slaughtered does not merely provide people with fresh pork and homemade sausages. It is a communal meeting time. Friends, relatives, and neighbors gather, exchange the latest news, and drink a bottle or two of wine.

keep two pigs: one provides them with meat for the year, and the other is sold to a professional pork butcher. "It has to be done quickly," says a farmer from Fornalutx, "because the surviving pig pines after the other has been slaughtered, and can lose several pounds in weight."

Sobrasada

The famous national sausage of the Balearic Islands, *sobrasada* (Balearic *sobrassada*) – the name is said to have originated in Sicily – came into existence essentially as a compromise with the weather. The air of the islands has too much humidity for ham to be air-dried. However, the climate and the local type of capsicum, used to preserve the meat, do allow a unique, soft-textured sausage to be made. It can be eaten uncooked, spread on slices of bread, or cooked in various ways.

The meat of the black Balearic pig used to be chopped, pressed, and stirred by hand. Now modern sausage producers use a machine to first grind the meat, then hot paprika, salt, and black pepper are added. The sausagemeat is thoroughly stirred, again using a machine, and left to rest for an hour in a refrigerated store-room. Simple machines are then used to fill the sausage skins, and the ends tied with string. The sausages used to be dried in cellars after this, for a period of about 12 to 15 weeks. This caused a greenish layer of mold to form on the outside. It is completely harmless, but tends to discourage many consumers. Modern sausage producers have drying rooms which enable the drying process to be completed in seven weeks, in conditions of constant temperature and humidity.

The traditional *sobrasada* must be made from the meat of black pigs, and have a diameter of at least 4.5 centimeters (roughly 1¾ inches). Today, cheaper versions made of pork from white pigs, or from a mixture, exist alongside *sobrasada* made of *porc negre*. Only if the label says *Sobrasada de Mallorca de Cerdo Negro*, is the sausage made entirely with pork from black Balearic pigs.

THE SPINY LOBSTER

During the flight from the burning city of Troy, Palinurus steered the ship of the hero, Aeneas, with great skill through the darkness of the night. The voyage proved too much, however, even for this experienced mariner, and he fell asleep. His punishment was to be thrown overboard. He was washed up on the shore, still alive, but found no escape, for he was killed by the people of the Lucani. This legend was later to inspire zoologists to give the name *Palinurus* to a spiny creature which lives on the sea bed; this is the scientific name of the langouste or spiny lobster. *Palinurus* has now become the culinary king of the seas.

There are two main species found in the Mediterranean. The European spiny lobster *(Palinurus elephas)* has a purple-reddish shell and protective spines. It grows to a length of up to 20 inches (50 centimeters), weighs from 14 to 21 ounces (400-600 grams) and lives on rocky ground. It lives on sea urchins, small squid and octopus, and mussels – a diet which accounts for its delicious flavor.

The Portuguese or Mauritanian species *(Palinurus mauretanicus)* lives at depths of up to 1000 feet (300 meters), mostly around the coasts of North Africa. It reaches a length of up to 30 inches (75 centimeters), has a paler shell,

Spiny lobsters frequent the rocky shores of the Balearic Islands, where they feed on small marine creatures. This gives them their fine flavor.

The fishermen let down lobster pots to catch the spiny lobster. If they catch any which are smaller than 19 centimeters (7½ inches), they must release them.

of a lilac to greenish color, and faintly pink flesh. Its food is mainly dead fish, so its meat does not have such a pronounced shellfish flavor.

Today, strict regulations exist to protect spiny lobster: none are allowed to be caught off the Balearic Islands from September to March 1. During the rest of the year, those less than 19 centimeters (7½ inches) in length must be spared and put back. In the absence of a wild catch, farmed spiny lobster can be eaten, though they do not have as much flavor.

Lobster pots are used to trap and catch the spiny lobster on the sea bed. Balearic fishermen catch about 140 tons (125 tonnes) a year, and fishing for spiny lobster has become a specialty of Minorca in particular. The rugged north coast, primarily the deep bay of Cala Fornells, became famous for its *caldereta de langosta*. This spiny lobster dish is certainly worth the trip. Connoisseurs say that the ingredients must always include at least one female, because they have more flavor, and in the spring, they contain roe.

CALDERETA DE LANGOSTA
Stew of spiny lobster (Photograph below, left)

2 large spiny lobsters, boiled
Scant ½ cup/100 ml olive oil
5 shallots, finely chopped
3 cloves of garlic, finely chopped
Generous 1 lb/500 g ripe tomatoes, skinned and diced
2 cups/500 ml fish stock
1 bay leaf
1 bouquet garni bunch of herbs (parsley, thyme, tarragon)
3 tbsp/40 ml brandy
Salt and pepper
A pinch of sugar
4 thin slices of white bread
2 tbsp chopped parsley

Break open the spiny lobsters and cut them into portions. Heat the olive oil in a pot. Lightly fry the shallots and garlic until golden. Add the tomatoes, and cook gently for a few moments. Pour on the fish stock, stirring sufficiently to take up the flavorings from the bottom of the casserole. Add the bay leaf, bunch of herbs, brandy, and salt and pepper. Cook on a medium heat until the cooking liquid thickens. Then remove the herbs and bay leaf, put the portions of spiny lobster into the pot, and heat through thoroughly, but without letting it boil again. Adjust seasoning with salt, pepper, and sugar. Toast the bread lightly in a toaster, and place a slice in each of 4 large, individual soup dishes. Divide the spiny lobster, with the accompanying stew from the pot, between the dishes. Sprinkle with parsley, and serve immediately.

This stew of spiny lobster *caldereta de langosta* is a specialty of the island of Minorca (the island's name means "small"). The spiny lobster catch on Minorca is far greater than on Majorca (the "large" island). Even the Spanish royal family regularly makes the boat trip to the bay of Cala Fornells on the north coast of Minorca, to enjoy this dish.

A fully grown spiny lobster is the pride of a Balearic fisherman. When fresh, the creatures lash vigorously with their tails when lifted up. Less fresh ones do not react as strongly.

El Chiringuito –
THE BEACH SHACK

It was a very modest refreshment shack; they called it the "shrimp." Barely a dozen wooden supports, baked by the sun, roofed over with reeds. Behind, the shack itself, its door painted indigo blue, its zinc-sheeted counter, the water pump, the constantly dripping faucet, the barrels, the bottles, and the Coca-Cola crates with their crushed ice. Around, the big flower pots with red and white geraniums, and the broad, deep green leaves of hydrangeas. The "shrimp" – more than modest; in truth, it was wretchedly poor. Yet no other shack attracted more custom. It lay at the edge of the square, at the entrance to the pine wood. It had its own peculiar quality: perhaps the drip-drip of the water, perhaps the blue and green of its shadow, or the sighing of the wind in the pines. No one exactly knew. The "shrimp" filled with noisy, Sunday folk, their skin flushed pink with sunburn, unused to the sun. They sat at wooden tables beneath its roof of reeds, and pulled their cans of this and that from their picnic bags. They ordered wine, beer, and Coca-Cola; often ordered tomatoes, green salad, and olives, and, to finish, coffee, brandy, or anisette. After they had departed on the seven o'clock bus, it seemed that the air, the breeze which stirred the sand, still bore the echo of their laughter and fun.

(From: Ana María Matute, *The Rescue,* 1967)

Fish dishes

Arros a la marinera
Rice soup mariner style

Generous 2 lbs/1 kg fish trimmings
1 onion, studded with 1 bay leaf and 2 cloves
4 cloves of garlic
4 stalks of parsley
Salt
5 black peppercorns
Generous 8 oz/250 g small squid, ready prepared
1 onion, finely chopped
½ cup/125 ml olive oil
1¼ cups/200 g rice (medium-grain)
2 ripe tomatoes, skinned and diced
½ tsp mild paprika
1 hot red chili pepper, cored and finely chopped
A few threads of saffron
Generous 1 lb/500 g mixed cockles (heart clams)
and mussels (or similar), washed and thoroughly
cleaned (and any beards removed)
Generous 1 lb/500 g fish fillets (e.g. monkfish;
cod), cut into portions
8 shrimp
4 portions of langoustine

Place the fish trimmings, onion, garlic, parsley, salt, and peppercorns in a pot with a generous 3 US pints/1.5 liters of water. Bring to a boil, cover and simmer for 1 hour. Strain the stock and set aside. Cut the squid into small pieces. Brown them lightly in olive oil in a large pot with the chopped onion, until golden. Add the rice and turn it in the oil over the heat for a few moments. Mix in the tomatoes and pour on the fish stock. Season with paprika, chopped chili, and saffron. Boil for 15 minutes. Then add the cockles, mussels, portions of fish, shrimp, and langoustines. Cook the fish and seafood in the soup until done.

Burrida de ratjada
Skate with almonds

Generous 2 lbs/1 kg skate, cut into thick slices
Salt
Juice of 1 lemon
2 cloves of garlic, chopped
2 tbsp white breadcrumbs
½ cup/50 g ground almonds
1 tbsp chopped parsley
4 tbsp olive oil
2 large ripe tomatoes, skinned and diced
½ cup/125 ml fish stock
2 eggs
1 tbsp flaked almonds

Just as in ancient times, fish is air-dried on the Balearic Islands. Skate *(raya)* is one of the types of dried fish which is much appreciated here. The "wings" are in fact highly developed pectoral fins.

Preheat the oven to 350 °F/175 °C. Wash and dry the slices of fish, and sprinkle with salt and lemon juice. Leave to infuse for 10 minutes. Pound the garlic with the breadcrumbs, ground almonds, parsley, and 2 tbsp of the olive oil until a thick paste is formed.

Cook the tomatoes gently for a few moments in the rest of the olive oil. Pour on the fish stock and stir in the garlic paste. Bring to a boil; then remove from the heat and stir in the eggs.

Place the fish in a casserole and pour over the sauce. Bake in the preheated oven for about 20 minutes, until cooked. Sprinkle with the flaked almonds and serve in the casserole.

Mero al forn
Baked grouper fish
(Photograph above, right)

1 grouper, about 2 lbs/1 kg, ready prepared
(alternatively bream)
Salt and pepper
Olive oil
14 oz/400 g mangold, rinsed and cleaned
2 onions, coarsely cut
4 cloves of garlic, chopped
3-4/300 g small tomatoes, quartered
1 cup/250 ml vegetable stock
Lemon slices to garnish

Preheat the oven to 350 °F/175 °C. Rinse and clean the fish and pat dry. Rub inside and out with salt and pepper. Grease an ovensafe casserole with olive oil and put in the mangold. Arrange half the onions on this. Lay the fish on top, then add the remaining onions, the garlic, and the tomatoes. Pour on the stock and sprinkle the fish with a little olive oil. Bake in the preheated oven for about 30 minutes, and test whether the fish is cooked; adjust time as necessary. Serve in the casserole, garnished with slices of lemon.

Sepia amb trempó
Squid with summer salad
(Photograph below, right)

1½ lbs/750 g squid, ready prepared
Generous 1 lb/500 g tomatoes, cut into pieces
2 bell peppers (red or green), cut into pieces
2 onions, coarsely chopped
2 tbsp red wine vinegar
Salt and pepper
½ cup/125 ml olive oil
1 clove of garlic, finely chopped

Many types of fish can be baked whole with mangold, tomatoes, onions, and garlic. Grouper is one. This method gives the fish a succulent aroma.

Squid with summer salad *(sepia amb trempó)* is a light, healthy snack for a hot day. This delicate dish is also very quick to prepare.

Cut the squid into small pieces. Place the tomatoes, bell peppers, and onions in a bowl. Stir together the vinegar, salt, pepper, and 4 tbsp of the olive oil to make a dressing. Pour this over the salad ingredients, and turn them until thoroughly coated.

Heat the rest of the oil in a skillet. Fry the squid and garlic until golden. Scatter them over the salad while still hot. Mix carefully and serve immediately.

Meals with meat

Escaldums
Braised turkey with almonds
(Photograph below, left)

Generous 1 lb/500 g turkey breast
3 tbsp olive oil
1 large onion, finely chopped
1 clove of garlic, chopped
2 tbsp chopped almonds
1 bay leaf
2 tomatoes, skinned and diced
1 cup/250 ml white wine
1 cup/250 ml chicken or turkey stock
Salt and pepper

Cut the turkey breast into chunks. Heat the olive oil in a pot and brown the meat on all sides. Lift out of the pot and set aside.
Cook the onion and garlic lightly in the oil until they become translucent. Stir in the almonds and fry briefly. Add the bay leaf and tomatoes. Pour on the white wine and stock to deglaze. Replace the turkey pieces in the pot. Season to taste with salt and pepper, cover, and simmer on a medium heat for about 30 minutes, until cooked.

Conejo en salsa de almendras
Rabbit in almond sauce
(Photograph below, right)

1 rabbit, ready prepared and cut into portions
Salt and pepper
½ cup/125 ml olive oil, or 4½ oz/125 g lard
2 onions, chopped
5 cloves of garlic, chopped
1 tbsp flour
Generous 8 oz/250 g tomatoes, skinned and diced
1 cup/250 ml white wine
1 cup/100 g ground almonds
2 sprigs of thyme
1 bay leaf
1 tbsp flaked almonds (or matchstick slivers)

Season the pieces of rabbit with salt and pepper. Heat the oil or fat in a pot and brown the rabbit lightly on all sides. Add the onions and garlic, and fry together briefly. Sprinkle with the flour, add the tomatoes, and mix. Pour on the white wine and 1 cup/250 ml of water. Add the ground almonds, thyme, and bay leaf, and season with salt and pepper. Cover and cook on a medium heat for about 45 minutes, stirring occasionally. Before serving, remove the thyme and bay leaf. Sprinkle the rabbit with slivers or flakes of almond.

Arros brut
"Dirty rice"

½ hare with liver
1 pigeon, ready prepared
½ cup/125 ml olive oil
About 10 oz/300 g pork ribs, cut into pieces
Salt and pepper
7 oz/200 g wild mushrooms, washed, cleaned and cut into pieces
1 onion, finely chopped
2 cloves of garlic, chopped
4 large, ripe tomatoes, skinned and diced
1 cup/100 g fresh, young fava beans (shelled)
1¼ cups/200 g rice (medium-grain)
2 Spanish blood sausages, sliced
1 tbsp chopped parsley

Cut the hare into sections and quarter the pigeon. Heat two-thirds of the olive oil in a pot and brown the pieces of hare and pigeon and the pork ribs until golden. Season with salt and pepper. Lift out the pieces of meat and set aside. Fry the mushrooms briefly in the oil and set aside.
Cook the onion and garlic in the frying oil until translucent, add the tomatoes and cook briefly. Now return the meat to the pot and pour on a generous 3 US pints/1.5 liters of water. Heat, cover and then simmer for 20 minutes.

Add the beans and the rice, and cook for another 20 minutes. The rice should remain moist, so add more water if needed. Halfway through the cooking time, add the mushrooms and slices of sausage.

Meanwhile, fry the liver in the remaining oil. Pound the cooked liver in a mortar and pestle with the oil and the parsley. Stir this mixture into the ingredients in the pot, 5 minutes before the end of the cooking time. Season with salt and pepper before serving.

CODORNICES CON HIGOS
Quail with figs
(Photograph right)

4 quail, ready prepared
Salt and pepper
1 tbsp butter
1 bouquet garni bunch of herbs (e.g. thyme, rosemary, and oregano)
1-2 bay leaves
2 small onions, finely chopped
1 tbsp flour
6-8 fresh figs, peeled
Generous ¾ cup/200 ml white wine
1 tbsp grated semisweet chocolate

Preheat the oven to 465 °F/240 °C. Rinse and clean the quail and pat dry. Rub them with salt and pepper, and tie in shape with string.

Grease a casserole with butter. Place the quail, bunch of herbs, bay leaf, and onions in the casserole. Sprinkle the quail with flour. Cook them in the preheated oven for about 10 minutes, until the flour has browned. Turn them over and add the figs. Pour on the white wine and then stir in the chocolate. Reduce the oven temperature to 350 °F/175 °C, and continue cooking for another 10 minutes. Serve in the casserole.

COSTILLAS DE CORDERO CON AJOS FRITOS
Lamb cutlets with fried garlic
(Photograph right)

8 lamb cutlets, weighing about 3½ oz/100 g each
Salt and pepper
Scant ⅔ cup/150 ml olive oil
20 cloves of garlic

Rinse and clean the lamb cutlets and pat dry. Season with salt and pepper.

Heat the olive oil in a large iron skillet and fry the cloves of garlic until golden. Transfer to another container and keep hot. Fry the cutlets on both sides in the oil. Arrange on a serving dish with the garlic and serve very hot.

The slightly gamey flavor of quail harmonizes beautifully with the fruit of the Balearic Islands. The birds can be cooked with fresh figs, as here. Equally good alternatives are dried figs, dried apricots, fresh grapes or raisins. Mediterranean herbs intensify the flavor.

A simple, yet delicious dish: tender cutlets of lamb with fried whole cloves of garlic. The meat should still be slightly pink in the middle when cooked.

Coca

In the 14th century, the Franciscan friar, Eiximenis, wrote with humor and horror of a fat, greedy cook, who was so fond of the Balearic flat bread or "cake," *coca*, that she dunked it in all the dishes, and ended by choking. Bread is a staple food, and this is taken seriously on the Balearic Islands. Here, baking is seen as an important skill, and *coca* is regular fare. There are all sorts of variations: with yeast and without, with egg and without. The base can be wafer-thin or voluptuously well risen. The filling spread on it varies across the range: vegetables, as a first course, sardines, as a main course, or a sweet filling, as a dessert.

Coca
Yeast dough base

For the dough:
1¼ cakes/20 g compressed yeast
A pinch of sugar
4½ cups/500 g flour
1 tsp salt
2 tbsp olive oil
2 tbsp white wine
Flour for dusting work surface
Butter for greasing baking pan

Coca amb pebres is made with red bell peppers and onions. Extra flavor is provided by adding plenty of garlic.

Coca amb trempó uses the popular summer salad of bell peppers, tomatoes, and onions as its filling.

Roll out the yeast dough and use to line a large, flat baking pan. Pierce with holes and leave to prove.

Brush the dough with a blend of oil and herbs before baking, depending on the filling and flavor required.

One of the most popular versions is *coca d'espinacs*, with spinach, raisins, and pine nuts.

The delicious spinach *coca* can include tomatoes (here) or with fish (main photograph).

Stir the yeast into a little lukewarm water with a pinch of sugar. Sift the flour into a large bowl and make a well in the center; then pour in the yeast. Sprinkle with flour and leave for 15 minutes. Add the olive oil, white wine, and 1 cup/250 ml water, and knead to a smooth dough. Put in a warm place to prove until doubled in size.

Knead the dough once more, then roll it out to a rectangular shape on a floured surface. Use it to line a greased large, flat baking pan. Pierce the dough all over with a fork or roller. Prove again. Preheat the oven to 390 °F/200 °C. Spread the base with the chosen filling before baking. Whatever filling is used, the *coca* is baked for about 25 to 30 minutes in the preheated oven.

Coca d'espinacs
Coca with spinach
(Photograph left)

Filling:
Generous 2 lbs/1 kg spinach
Salt
⅓ cup/40 g pine nuts
⅓ cup/50 g raisins, soaked in water
Salt and pepper
Scant ½ cup/100 ml olive oil

Rinse and sort the spinach, and blanch it in a little salted water. Pour off the water and drain the spinach thoroughly; then spread it over the dough base. Scatter the pine nuts and raisins on top, season with salt and pepper, and sprinkle with the olive oil before baking as described above.
Variations: Pieces of tomato or fish (tuna, bream, cod) can be arranged on top (main photograph).

Coca amb trempó
Coca with summer vegetables
(Photograph far left, below)

Filling:
Generous 1 lb/500 g red and green bell peppers, cut into strips
Generous 1 lb/500 g onions, chopped
Generous 1 lb/500 g tomatoes, skinned and diced
Salt and pepper
3 tbsp chopped parsley
Scant ½ cup/100 ml olive oil

Scatter the bell peppers, onions, and tomatoes over the dough base. Season with salt and pepper. Sprinkle with parsley and also with olive oil before baking. Bake as described above.

Coca amb pinxes
Coca with sardines

Filling:
Generous 1 lb/500 g fresh sardines, ready prepared and with bones removed
3 cloves of garlic, finely chopped
2 shallots, finely chopped
1 bunch of parsley, chopped
Scant ½ cup/100 ml olive oil
½ tsp mild paprika
Salt and pepper

Lay the sardines on the dough base. Mix the remaining ingredients together thoroughly and scatter across the top. Then bake as described above.

Coca con sobrasada is easy to make: arrange the sausage over the dough base (above) – and then bake (right).

Hearty country fare

Sopes mallorquines
One-pot vegetable dish with cabbage
(Photograph bottom of page)

1 small white cabbage (alternatively, savoy cabbage)
2 young artichokes
Generous 8 oz/250 g asparagus
½ cauliflower
Generous 8 oz/250 g green beans
½ cup/125 ml olive oil
1 onion, chopped
2 cloves of garlic, chopped
2 tomatoes, skinned and diced
Salt and pepper
½ tsp hot paprika, ½ tsp mild paprika
2 tbsp chopped parsley
8 oz/250 g day-old dry white bread, thinly sliced

Rinse and clean the cabbage, artichokes, asparagus, cauliflower, and beans. Separate the cauliflower into florets and cut the vegetables into small pieces. Heat the olive oil in a pot. Fry the onion and garlic gently until translucent. Add the other vegetables and the tomatoes. Pour on 4 cups/1 liter of water and season with salt, pepper, paprika, and parsley. Bring to a boil, cover, and cook for about 20 minutes. Preheat the oven to 390 °F/200 °C. Line an earthenware casserole with the slices of bread. Transfer the vegetables to this casserole using a slotted spoon. Pour on the cooking liquid. Place the casserole in the oven for 5 minutes to allow the bread to absorb the liquid. Serve in the casserole.

Frit mallorquì
Majorcan fry
(Photograph left)

Generous 1 lb/500 g potatoes
2 carrots
1 red and 1 green bell pepper
Scant ½ cup/100 ml olive oil
1 onion, chopped
5 cloves of garlic
2 tomatoes, skinned and diced
1½ lbs/750 g pork or lamb offal, cut into thin strips
Salt, a pinch of cinnamon

Rinse and clean the potatoes, carrots, and bell peppers. Peel the potatoes and carrots, and core the bell peppers. Cut them all into strips of roughly equal size. Heat the oil in a deep skillet. Fry the onion and garlic gently until translucent. Add the potatoes and fry for a short while. Stir in the carrots, bell peppers, and tomatoes, and fry until done. Transfer them to another container and keep hot. Brown the offal in the frying oil. Pour on 1 cup/250 ml water, season with salt, and cook for a while. When almost done, add the vegetables and stir together for a few minutes and finish cooking. Season with salt and cinnamon.

Huevos al modo de Soller
Fried eggs Sóller style

1 leek, sliced into thin rings
1 large carrot, sliced into rings
1¾ cups/250 g fresh, shelled peas
2 tbsp olive oil
1 cup/250 ml milk
½ cup/125 ml meat stock
Salt and pepper
8 slices of sobrasada (alternatively, paprika sausage)
8 eggs

Venture just a couple of miles from the shore, and you will still discover the rural life of Majorca (above). It is by no means necessarily poor (main photograph).

Fry the vegetables briefly in 1 tbsp olive oil. Add the milk and meat stock, season with salt and pepper, and simmer for 20 minutes. Then purée with a hand blender and keep hot. Fry the slices of sausage on both sides in the rest of the oil. Lift them out, and fry the eggs. Arrange 2 slices of sausage on each warmed plate, with 2 fried eggs per person on top. Pour on the sauce. Serve immediately.

CARACOLES CON SOBRASADA
Snails with *sabrasada*
(Photograph left)

1 onion, finely chopped
2 cloves of garlic, finely chopped
3 tbsp olive oil
4 tomatoes, skinned and diced
5 oz/150 g air-dried ham, cut into thin strips
Salt and pepper
1 tsp sugar
½ tsp hot paprika
1 cup/250 ml white wine
7 oz/200 g sobrasada (alternatively paprika sausage) diced
4 tsp/20 ml brandy
48 small to medium-size snails, boiled

Cook the onion and garlic gently in the olive oil in a flameproof casserole until translucent. Add the tomatoes and ham, and season with salt, pepper, sugar, and paprika. Pour on the white wine. Cook for 20 minutes. Then add the sausage and brandy, and simmer for a few more minutes. Adjust seasoning with salt, pepper, and paprika. Add the cooked snails and heat them through thoroughly in the sauce, but without boiling. Serve in the casserole.

Two traditional ingredients are combined in this hearty feast of snails and *sobrasada* sausage. It is a classic of rural cuisine, and often served as tapas.

Mayonnaise

Discussion over salsa *mahonesa* rages at times as fiercely as a religious war. The islanders of Minorca are utterly convinced that it was invented there, though it has since become popular world-wide. When the French took Minorca from the British in 1756, their finest conquest was this creamy combination of egg and olive oil. A local chef is said to have created the sauce under the direction of the French military leader Richelieu, but historians have found documents dating back to the 16th century which mention mayonnaise. It is highly probable that wherever olive oil existed, a simple preparation of oil and egg came about – particularly in the Mediterranean region, where *alioli* (oil and garlic) is made (see page 17).

The ingredients are simply olive oil, egg yolk, a pinch of salt, and a little vinegar or lemon juice. An easy wrist movement and care when beating in the oil are the only secrets of preparation. *Mahonesa* comes in many variations, with salad, fish or vegetables, colored pink with tomato, or flavored with garlic. There is just one rule: that it should come straight from the kitchen to the table, bypassing a sojourn in the refrigerator.

Salsa mahonesa
Mayonnaise
(Photograph below)

2 egg yolks
1 tsp lemon juice or wine vinegar
1¼ cups/300 ml olive oil
Salt

Whisk the egg yolks well, using a balloon whisk, electric whisk, blender, or food mixer. Add a few drops of lemon juice or vinegar. Now begin to add the olive oil, no more than a few drops at first, increasing to a thin stream, and stirring constantly. When the mayonnaise has thickened, adjust the flavoring by adding salt and vinegar or lemon juice.

Ensaladilla rusa
Russian salad
(Photograph above)

1 large boiled potato
1 14 oz/400 g green beans (canned)
1 14 oz/400 g peas (canned)
1 14 oz/400 g carrots (canned)
4 ½ oz/125 g button mushrooms (canned)
Mayonnaise (made using recipe above)

Russian Salad *(ensaladilla rusa)*

In Spain, this recipe would probably use fresh vegetables but canned are a good alternative. Dice the potato fairly small. Drain the canned vegetables thoroughly. Place all in a salad bowl. Pour the mayonnaise over the vegetables and mix well. Serve as soon as possible, and keep refrigerated while waiting.

Like all dishes made with mayonnaise, *ensaladilla rusa* should be refrigerated and not kept longer than a couple of days.

Fresh eggs, olive oil, and salt are the main ingredients of mayonnaise, plus vinegar or lemon juice.

The first step is to whisk the egg yolks – with a hand whisk, blender, or food mixer, depending on the quantity.

A few drops of lemon juice or vinegar are added at this stage, before the oil.

Now add the oil slowly, in a very thin stream, whisking. This stage demands skill.

Minorcan cheese

The charm of Minorca lies in its rough grass and woodland, and its abrupt cliffs. This land is hardly suited to intensive agriculture, but has been known since ancient times for its cattle. The Greek seafarers called it *Meloussa*, "the cattle-rearing land." In the 18th century, the British engineer John Armstrong wrote the first history and geography of the island, which was for a short time under British rule. According to Armstrong, in 1741 there were 60,000 sheep, 20,000 goats, 6000 head of cattle, and 4000 pigs here. He proudly stated that the Italians even preferred the island's cheese to their own Parmesan.

In the 19th century, the British encouraged the keeping of cows and the production of cow's milk cheese. There are still a few dozen cows of the local Minorcan variety, but it is now mainly the highly productive Friesians that have spread on this, the second largest of the Balearic islands. Their milk is used to produce the famous *Mahón* cheese, which now officially bears the name *Queso Mahón-Menorca*. Until a couple of decades ago, this cheese was made entirely by hand. Between September and June, the women on the *fincas*, the farms, worked to process the milk twice a day. Instead of the rennin used today, they used herbs, and the cheeses were shaped in cotton cloths. A week later, the fresh, slightly sour cheese (*queso fresco* or *tierno*) was ready to eat, or to use in baking, for example as a filling for cakes.

Modernization and the hygiene requirements of the European Union have brought great changes to traditional cheesemaking. Unpasteurized fresh (curd) cheese is forbidden. However, a cooperative is successfully trying to maintain tradition. Raw milk cheese of the highest quality is being made under conditions of strict hygiene. The cheese has retained its traditional shape, square with rounded edges, as it is still wrapped in cloth for pressing.

Queso Mahón-Menorca exists in a semi-matured variety (*semicurado*, matured for at least two months) and as a fully mature cheese (*curado*, matured for six to ten months). Finally, there is the thoroughly hardened *añejo*, which spends a whole year developing its deep, tart flavor. Some of the cheeses are rubbed over, when one month old, with butter or olive oil and powdered paprika as an additional means of preserving them. *Mahón* cheese made with pasteurized milk may however be sold following a short maturation period ranging from 20 to 60 days maximum.

Mahón cheese is made with pure cow's milk. It is sometimes further preserved with oil and paprika.

Very mature *Queso Mahón-Menorca* develops an intense flavor. It is excellent when eaten as tapas.

Rosemary *(romero)* **:** Partners game, lamb, and pork. Also good in sauces, stuffings, and preserves.

Thyme *(tomillo)***:** Partners fish, meat, braised dishes, and summer vegetables. Also olive marinades.

Fennel *(hinojo)***:** Especially good with fish, lamb, and hearty stews. Its seeds are mainly used for tea and marinades.

Parsley *(perejil)***:** Goes well with soups, salads, and vegetables and meat of all sorts.

Majoram *(mejorana)***:** Partners game and lamb, good for stuffings and with some types of vegetable.

Oregano *(orégano)***:** Good with legumes, meat, game, and poultry, as well as organ meat and vegetables.

Basil *(albahaca)***:** Partners tomatoes and other vegetables, also salads, fish, and meat.

Bay *(laurel)***:** Used in marinades, cooking liquid, and for preserving. Also rice, fish, and meat dishes.

Herbs

The country folk of the Balearic Islands have a custom, when things are going badly at home or in business, of going outside their house and turning to the left, where a few evergreen plants can be seen. In summer, the plants bear bright yellow blossom. The plant is rue. The despairing local kneels down and asks for "health, happiness, and riches." Rue grows widely in southern Europe, and in the Balearics it is credited with magic powers. *Herba de bruixa* (witches' herb) is its popular name, *ruda* the Spanish, and it is said to give protection against ghosts and magic. It is always planted to the left of the yard, where the negative aspects of life are said to be located, and if it grows well, evil will stay away from the family. Woe betide if it withers; then, harm may come. Rue is used as a medicinal herb, to treat stomach ache and tapeworm.

Grasses of all kinds acquire special meaning in a sparse environment, whether this involves magic powers or medicinal uses. In the first century B.C., Pliny praised a drink made from a hundred herbs, which was used to treat all

Opposite (background): Peppermint *(menta)* is mainly used as a tea; the better-known Spanish mint *(hierbabuena)* for marinades and cocktails.

Rue *(ruda)* grows wild on the islands. Good fortune comes to those who have its yellow blossoms in their own yards.

Lamb encrusted with herbs is popular in Mediterranean countries, especially with summer vegetables.

kinds of illness. This must surely be the origin of *hierbas*, the Balearic herb liqueurs (see page 73). Later, Arab traders from the Moorish kingdom of al-Andalus brought spices: cloves, cinnamon, nutmeg, and pepper. The Moorish cooks also knew how to use the herbs which grew wild in the meadows: basil, rosemary, and thyme, of course, the most widely used herbs on the islands to this day. Bay is indispensable to a Spanish cook, and it is hard to imagine cooking without parsley. The Arabs loved to use mint in meat dishes; one of its Spanish names is *hierbabuena* ("good herb"). Interestingly, this use of mint survived longer in Britain than in Spain, where it is mainly used to make mint tea. Fennel, nettle, camomile, and linden blossom are all still used medicinally today for a variety of conditions.

The fragrant harvest is dried either by laying the herbs between sheets of newspaper or by hanging them up in loose bunches (see photograph below) with the leaves still on their stems. Dried herbs are sealed in dark, airtight glass jars or metal containers and stored in a cool place. They need to be used within a year. Herbs can also be frozen: they are blanched by immersing briefly in boiling water, then drained and frozen in batches. For use in cooking, the frozen herbs can be added directly to the dishes of your choice for added flavor and convenience.

GIN

In 1713, Colonel Richard Kane became Her Royal Britannic Majesty's governor on the island of Minorca. He ruled the island ably and caringly from its capital, Mahón. He was, it is true, succeeded by others in the colonial overlord mold, greedy and authoritarian, but even they were unable to unravel entirely the bonds forged by Kane, and some British traditions survive to the present day. Islanders still serve tea on a *tibord* ("tea board" or tray) and like to eat a *bifi* (beef) for lunch.

The best known British legacy on Minorca is without doubt its gin. The only ingredients permitted under the strict regulations for Mahón gin are juniper berries, water, and "ethyl alcohol of agricultural origin." On the Balearic island, however, the alcohol is usually distilled from grapes, rather than grain, as in the Dutch and British equivalents.

The juniper bush (which has the botanic name *Juniperus communis*) was burned as a fumigant by the Ancient Egyptians. In medieval Europe, juniper was set alight in fields and meadows to afford protection to cattle and crops. Still today, some native North Americans regard it as one of the most important plants used in religious rituals and ceremonies.

Juniper grows wild on the Balearic Islands, but the berries for Minorcan gin come mainly from the Pyrenees or eastern Spain.

Distillation is to this day required to be carried out in copper stills *(alquitara)*, like those introduced to Spain by the Arabs back in history. The still is heated by a woodburning stove, and the coiled condenser is cooled with cold water.

As a drink, gin has been widespread in the community since the 19th century. It has a strength of between 38 and 43 percent. Taken neat on an empty stomach, it has served as a shock breakfast to mariners and farmers alike. In the Balearic Islands, popular mixed drinks using gin are *pomades* (gin with lemonade) and *pallofes* (gin with soda water and lemon peel). These are drunk particularly at the feast of St. John in the town of Ciutadella. Mahón gin can be bought in tall, earthenware bottles in the Dutch style, or in the British broad, squat glass bottles.

Tourists from Britain are often surprised to find their national drink being made on this small Mediterranean island.

Though the concept and the technique are imported, Minorcan gin has long since been a homegrown island specialty. The Arabs introduced copper stills; the British, the practice of distilling an alcoholic beverage from juniper berries. Gin is still made in small distilleries (below) and is usually sold in earthenware bottles (right).

Gin is made from juniper berries. Drinkers reason therefore that gin has health-giving properties.

The copper stills are heated with wood, as prescription decrees for true Minorcan gin.

LIQUEURS

Palo began as a medicinal drink; today, it is a specialty enjoyed by connoisseurs. Majorca once had extensive marshes. These produced plagues of mosquitoes, and with them, malaria, which was a fatal disease. Peruvian bark *(Chinchona)* was introduced to the Balearic Islands in the 16th or 17th century, brought to Spain by the Countess of Chinchón. Both then and now, Peruvian bark and the quinine derived from it have been one of the most important treatments for malaria. Health-giving as it was, the extract of Peruvian bark and gentian tasted fairly unspeakable. The islanders soon began to improve the alcoholic extract by adding a variety of ingredients: sugar, cinnamon, nutmeg, and carob were the basic ones, with an anise spirit to make the whole into a liqueur. The Majorcans have become enthusiastic consumers of this liqueur – even though it is health-giving!

The general success of palo owes much to a disaster which happened at the end of the 19th century: phylloxera destroyed the vines, and the herb liqueur replaced wine on the domestic market. Today, various producers make a great range of palo, which derives its dark color from caramelized sugar and carob. It has an alcoholic strength of between 22 and 38 degrees, and is matured in oak barrels for at least a year, to develop depth of flavor. There is a palo for every time of day and every taste, for drinking as an apéritif or with dessert: sweet, semi-dry, and dry. It can also be used to flavor desserts and other sweet foods, like cakes and pastries.

For centuries, Majorcans have made their pale green hierbas liqueur, using up to 25 different herbs, such as mint, hyssop, rosemary, absinth, lavender, and myrtle. It is based on an anis spirit, which may be sweet or dry; this is mixed with herb extract. Orange and lemon flavors are often added. Hierbas are usually taken as a *digestif.* Frigola, bitters made from the leaves and flowers of thyme, comes from Ibiza. A bottle of this elixir, containing a piece of thyme, is a popular souvenir gift to bring home from the island. This liqueur is reddish or orange in color, and drunk mainly as a *digestif.* It is also popular as a filling for hand-made chocolates.

There is a long tradition of liqueurs with fine herbs on the Balearic Islands.

CAROB – A LITTLE-KNOWN FRUIT

The nutritional value of the locust bean or carob *(algarroba)* was known back in biblical times. John the Baptist is reported to have lived on these pods during his time in the desert. They belong to the family of legumes, and the bean pods are up to 8 inches (20 centimeters) long. In ancient times, the Greeks, Arabs, and Phoenicians used the seeds to weigh out gold and diamonds, because these miracles of nature seem designed to serve as a natural unit of measurement: every seed weighs 0.18 grams (six thousandths of an ounce). This later became the unit of weight, 1 carat, defined as 0.2 grams (equivalent to 3 grains avoirdupois). The word carat comes from the tree's Latin name, *Ceratonia siliqua.*

The carob then declined in significance for some hundreds of years. On the Balearic Islands and on the Spanish Mediterranean coast, the fruits were usually used to feed the pigs – pearls before swine. A substitute for coffee was made from them during times of hardship; besides that, carob is and has always been an important ingredient in the Majorcan palo liqueur. Apart from these uses, it is only in recent years that carob has regained status, mainly as a substitute for sugar and for cocoa. Its high sugar content, up to 45 percent, gives it a sweetish flavor, and it contains hardly any fat, unlike its rival the cocoa bean. On the other hand, it does contain more minerals than cocoa – calcium and iron, for example. It is considered beneficial for the digestion. Carob bean gum is a useful thickening agent, and is used as such especially in natural food products, often as a substitute for chocolate.

Ensaïmada

Majorcans sometimes wax positively philosophical on the subject of their favorite cake, the *ensaïmada*. There is endless matter for debate; the origins of these characteristic, yeast-based coiled cakes lie far back in the mists of time. Did they begin as large *ensaïmadas*, the ones that can feed a family, and shrink over time to produce the individual cake? Or did the reverse happen: did one person's breakfast expand to become the massive spiral some 20 inches (half a meter) across?

Some people believe that the *ensaïmada* is Jewish in origin, although, today, it is made with lard *(saím)*. Others link it with an Arab dessert which was called *bulemes dolces*. The first group counter that the Jews had a cake called *bulema*. Whichever is true, it was certainly Middle Eastern (and originally made without pork fat). This ingredient would have been introduced later, when the consumption of pork products was imposed by the Church, as part of contemporary attempts to drive out Jews and Arabs.

Ensaïmada spread gradually over the last hundred years, until they attained their present position of dominance on the breakfast tables of Majorca. At first, they were plain, without any filling; many varieties have since appeared: fillings such as *cabello de ángel* ("angels' hair," a type of pumpkin preserve), cream, or almond nougat *(turrón)*.

The *ensaïmada* has become something of a Majorcan trademark. Government sources on the Balearics estimate that each flight that leaves Palma airport in the direction of the mainland carries about 40 *ensaïmadas*. This informal export spreads them in ever-widening circles across Europe: travelers arriving from Majorca are instantly recognizable, heading through airports with broad, round cardboard boxes, whose contents go straight into the oven on arrival home. An *ensaïmada* tastes twice as good if quickly reheated before eating.

Right: Freshly baked *ensaïmadas* can be found today on breakfast tables across Spain. These light, coiled, yeast-based specialties originally came from Majorca.

Ensaïmada

4½ cups/500 g flour
⅛ cup/75 g sugar
1 tsp salt
2⅛ cakes/40 g compressed yeast
Generous 1 cup/250 ml lukewarm milk
2 tbsp olive oil
2 eggs
Flour for dusting work surface
7 oz/200 g melted lard
Oil for greasing baking sheet

Sift the flour into a large bowl with the sugar and salt. Make a well in the center. Dissolve the yeast in the warm milk and pour into this hollow. Sprinkle it with flour and leave to stand for 15 minutes. Beat the olive oil and eggs together lightly, add to the flour, and knead to a smooth dough. Leave to rise in a warm place until doubled in size. Knead the dough again. Roll it out extremely thinly on a floured surface, to form a long, narrow rectangle. Spread it with lard. Starting at one of the long sides of the rectangle, roll up the dough. Leave it to rise for 1 hour. Then coil the dough. Place it on a greased baking sheet and cover with an inverted mixing bowl, first brushed with oil so that it will not stick to the dough when it rises. Leave to rise overnight. Preheat the oven to 390 °F/200 °C, and bake for about 1 hour, until golden.

Variations: 2 strips of rolled-up dough may be braided together, then coiled into a round. Another alternative is to make several separate, small coils.

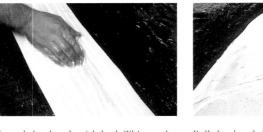

A yeast dough forms the basis for any *ensaïmada*. Knead it well, and let rise until it doubles in volume.

After rising, knead the dough again. Roll it out very thinly with a rolling pin.

Spread the dough with lard. This can be done with a tool or with the hands.

Pull the dough into position, to make it easier to roll up. Start rolling from one of the long sides.

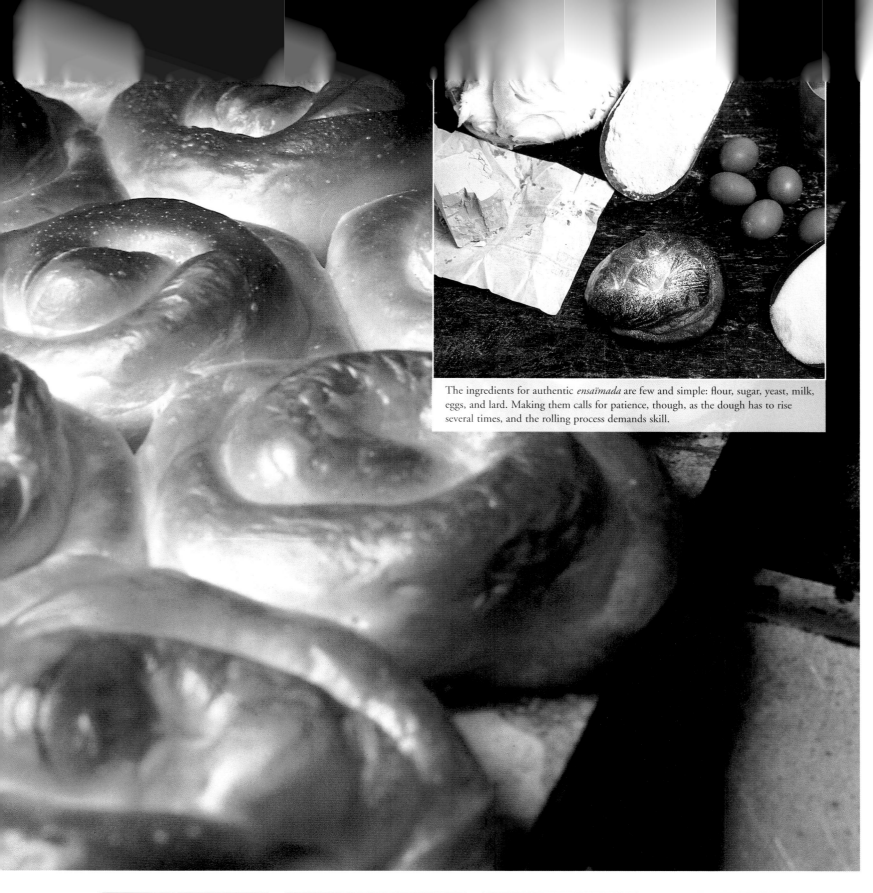

The ingredients for authentic *ensaïmada* are few and simple: flour, sugar, yeast, milk, eggs, and lard. Making them calls for patience, though, as the dough has to rise several times, and the rolling process demands skill.

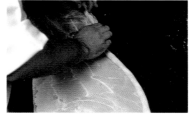

Roll the dough bit by bit, working from one long side to the other. Aim to make the roll as even as possible.

Care is needed at first, but as the roll grows thicker, the process becomes easier. It almost rolls itself.

The dough must be left to rest again. Then at last, it can be shaped into the characteristic coil.

Coil the dough loosely, ensuring there is enough room for it to rise again. It will puff up considerably.

Binissalem (backround) is one of two winegrowing areas on the Balearic Islands so far to be recognized officially with a protected declaration of origin (D.O.).

High-alcohol reds are the main wines produced at Binissalem. Half the grapes used are the native Majorcan variety, Manto Negro.

ISLAND-WINE

As long ago as the first century before Christ, Pliny was praising the wines of Majorca. Its mild climate meant that vines continued to be grown through the centuries which followed their introduction by the Romans – though this was only on Majorca, the largest of the Balearics. Continuing to the present day, Ibiza produces only a small amount of table wine, and Minorca has just some 7 acres (3 hectares) given over to vines.

The wine-producers of Majorca were able to maintain a steady increase in production until the end of the 19th century, because the phylloxera louse had attacked and devastated first the vines of France, then those of Spain, creating an insatiable demand in the European market. However, in 1891, phylloxera reached the island. Growers were forced to begin all over again. Viticulture re-established itself slowly, and simple table wine was the only type available for some time.

A change has taken place over the last few decades. The area around Binissalem in particular has calcareous soils, mild temperatures under the protection of the mountains, hot summers and low rainfall, which combine to provide excellent conditions for growth, and to enable the production of first class wines. Since 1991, producers growing wine on approximately 1235 acres (500 hectares) have enjoyed the status of an officially recognized vineyard area, the protected declaration of origin D.O. Binissalem-Mallorca. The best wines were produced in 1994, and have already been judged "historic."

The red wines of this D.O. have to contain 50 percent Manto Negro, a grape variety native to Majorca, which accounts for three-quarters of the grapes harvested. These grapes are large and very dark in color, and have a very high sugar content, which lends itself to producing strong wines. Further varieties are Tempranillo, a grape widely grown in Spain, Cabernet Sauvignon, which is allowed to make up 30 percent, and the varieties Monastrell and Callet. The white wines account for barely a fifth of the harvestin barissalam, and are made mainly from the local variety Moll (or Prensal Blanc), although Parellada, Macabeo, and a little Chardonnay are also used.

The twelve producers of the D.O. are in the enviable position of having no problem in finding a market. On the contrary: the demand for their wines on the island is so great that hardly any of the 1.5 million liters produced remains available for export. Most of the wines are fairly strong, with an alcoholic content of 11.5-14 percent, of marked character, and a particularly intense color. They are concentrated, but balanced, and suitable for laying down. *Crianza* wines from this winegrowing area must be matured for at least two years, of which six months must be in oak barrels.

In the east of Majorca, still on the central plain of the island, lies the winegrowing area **D.O. Plá i Llevant** ("the plain and the east"), which in 2001 accuired the status of protected region of origin (D.O.). Here, too, red wine predominates. The palette of grape varieties is broader than at Binissalem, those grown here are Callet, Tempranillo, Cabernet Sauvignon, Manto Negro, Merlot, Monastrell, Syrah and Fogoneu. The white grape varieties grown here include Chardonnay, Macabeo, and Parellada.

There is wine in the west of Majorca, too: a single wine-producer near Andratx. Florianopolis (Santa Cate rina) is the name of the bodega belonging to the Swede Stellan Lundqvist; he makes a wide range of wines, using Cabernet Sauvignon, Merlot, Ull de Llebre (Tempranillo), and Chardonnay. These wines include red Gran Reservas and fruity whites.

SANGRIA
(Photograph above)

1 unwaxed orange, 1 unwaxed lemon
2 peaches
1-2 tbsp sugar
1 large bottle/1 liter red wine, chilled
3 tbsp/50 ml brandy
1 cup/250 ml mineral water, chilled

Rinse the citrus fruits in hot, running water, and dry them. Cut away the rind in a spiral, using a knife. Remove the pith from both fruits, and slice the flesh. Peel the peaches, halve them, and remove the pits. Cut the peach flesh into pieces. Place the fruit in a large, glass pitcher. Sprinkle with sugar. Pour in the wine and brandy, then the water. Stir. Sangría should always be served ice cold. A few ice cubes may be added.

Aragón

Harald Irnberger

Aragon

Aragon is a land of hearty meat dishes. The most delicious are made with lamb and mutton. Sucking lamb is the *pièce de résistance* of Aragonese butchers.

Because of its geographic location at the heart of several important traffic routes between the Mediterranean and the Atlantic, France and central Spain, Aragon has always been somewhere that people passed through on their way to somewhere else. Its culture is the result of centuries of foreign influence, and nature has not made life easy for its inhabitants. She demands submission – whether on the snow-topped peaks of the Ordesa National Park or in the desert-like south ("Africa's enclave in Europe"). Only on the central plains, intersected by the Ebro, is the climate milder. Countless Roman church buildings are a testimony to the type of ascetic religiousness that develops only under extreme environmental conditions. Despite, or perhaps because of these conditions, the native Aragonese, although surely somewhat taciturn by nature, are open-minded and have a strong sense of individuality. They have always had to contend with a climate that is just as harsh as the region's geographic conditions. Long, hard winters alternate with dry summers of African heat. Conditions such as these require a generous measure of sound resourcefulness, especially in the kitchen. The Aragonese kitchen is reputedly the plainest in Spain. It is based on meat, which was originally hunted and was later replaced by sheep breeding. Still, there were frequent periods of famine, which the Aragonese attempted to overcome with plain but highly nutritious meals. The olive oil of Lower Aragon provides lots of calories to help improve the chances of survival in a harsh environment with extremes of climate, and is often drizzled or poured on just about everything from bread to borage to enhance the nutritional value and improve flavors. Like all Spaniards, the Aragonese love sweet things, and no meal is complete without "something to nibble" at the end of it. Because of the extreme climatic conditions in the country, this used to be usually just a piece of fruit. However, the need to make fruit last longer, combined with people's own imagination, led to the creation of candied fruit, which is often coated with chocolate. And last, but not least, heavy Aragonese wines have for centuries provided both pleasing relaxation and comfort for the inhabitants of an area that has had to wrest its rather plain yet nourishing fare from the harsh unceasingly hostile environment.

Santiago de Compostela
Vitoria-Gasteiz
León
Pamplona
Aragón
Barcelona
Valladolid
Zaragoza
Madrid
Toledo
Palma de Mallorca
Valencia
Mérida
Ciudad Real
Murcia
Sevilla
Granada

Opposite: Powerful and imposing, the mountain world of Aragon. The topmost peaks are those of the Pyrenees; those shown here are in the province of Huesca.

TAPAS CULTURE

A trawl through the tapas bars in a Spanish town will satisfy the desire for adventure as well as hunger. It also poses something of a dilemma for the connoisseur: a few almonds, or some olives? Cheese, meat or air-dried ham? Perhaps some deep-fried seafood?

Tapas are those irresistible delicacies that are usually displayed behind glass at the bar, and which in Spain are either an introduction to the main meal or often a substitute for it. They are eaten hot or cold, served plain or as an artistic flight of fancy, and freshly made every day. Some inns, the *tascas* and *mesones*, offer a choice of three or four dozen different tapas, and the hot specialties of the day are usually written in chalk on a slate. Lots of tapas bars and restaurants now specialize in seafood or fish;

ham or certain types of sausage; vegetables or braised dishes. Tapas are served on small porcelain dishes or *cazuelitas*, the typical brown glazed dishes. Tapas are also called *pinchos* (skewers or kebabs) in the north, even if nothing is actually skewered. In Valencia, they are often served as *montaditos* ("the mounted"), either tiny bread croutons or slices of bread covered with a variety of delicious morsels. The actual ritual surrounding a typical tapas meal (*tapeo* or *chiquiteo*) is very much like the Spanish people themselves – after all, what could be nicer than eating, drinking, and chatting in a convivial atmosphere? Before the midday or evening meal, partakers stroll from bar to bar, sharing the day's woes and delights, rarely staying in one place for more than one drink. A morsel here, a morsel there to go with a glass of sherry or cider, beer or wine, and then on to the next bar.

The true origin of the tapas culture is still the subject of much debate. Was Castilian King Alfonso X the originator of these delights? After all, this monarch, who ruled over Seville, Cordoba, and Jaén in the 13th century, was advised by his doctors to cut back on his calories, so his personal cooks served him tiny morsels that supposedly tasted so good that they could well have been the precursors of the tapas culture. The Andalusians, however, laugh at this theory. There is no doubt at all in their minds that tapas actually originated from the sunny south. After all, southerners have always loved outdoor meals, invariably accompanied by a glass of sherry (or two). However, as the delicate aroma of this sweet beverage attracted hosts of irritating insects, a small cover (*tapa*) or dish was placed over the glass with a few olives, as well as a small amount of fish, ham, sausage, or other appetizing morsels.

It is also possible, though, that the Moors, of whom there are plenty of traces in Andalusia (and especially of a culinary nature), were really the inventors of the tapas culture. In their North African home, and especially among the Arab Bedouin, it is still both customary and a sign of refined hospitality for lots of tiny dishes to be served.

Seville is still considered to be the capital of the tapas, but Madrid and other cities have caught up, and many bars in Granada, Cadiz, and Cordoba have their own personal specialties that they swear by. In recent decades, the tapas culture has spread throughout the whole of Spain, and the basic rule of thumb is always the same, whether in Barcelona, Saragossa, or Toledo: if the locals congregate around long bars before a main meal, you can be pretty sure the reason is the quality of the tapas. Other signs of a good tapas bar are the variety on offer and the quality of its hams and sausages. If hams from the Iberian pig (*cerdo ibérico*) and homemade sausages hang from the ceiling, this usually means that the tapas are of above-average quality. In many Andalusian bars, it is still customary for the guest to be given, at no extra charge, a small tapa with every glass of sherry, wine, or beer. In a genuine "inns of little sins," you can be sure that the waiters will keep tally of the guests' consumption, and no matter how many beers are downed, guests will not be served the same tapa twice. After all, the choice is – almost – unlimited.

A small proportion of the varied fare available in tapas bars and restaurants is illustrated overleaf. Some of them are borrowed from the cuisines of other countries, some are indigenous Spanish recipes, but found all over the country, while others are local specialties. Each may seem small in itself, but after consuming several you will feel like you have eaten a hearty meal.

The times, they are a-changing: in former times, hearty tapas were accompanied by a wine from the region or a glass of sherry. Today, though, many Spaniards prefer a cool draft beer (*caña*) with their *tapeo*.

The mouth-watering delicacies displayed behind glass are often only a small sample of a tapas bar's repertoire. There is usually a whole range of hot tapas as well, which are freshly prepared in the kitchen.

FAVORITE SPANISH TAPAS

Flat *(boletos)* and other types of mushroom are fried in oil and flavored with a hint of garlic and parsley.

"Pain and destruction" *(duelos y quebrantos)* used to be made from eggs and brains, but now consists of eggs and bacon.

In the north, the delicate belly of the Atlantic tuna *(mendreska de bonito)* is served with a tomato and onion sauce.

The giant snail *(busano)* is a prickly variety that is steamed gently and served with lemon.

Pimientos de Padrón are tiny green capsicums (pimentos) from Galicia: though small, they are very flavorsome.

Centuries ago, almonds *(almendras)* were served with a good sherry, and today they are served in even the simplest bars.

Fried anchovies *(boquerones fritos)* are one of the absolute classics. Tiny ones are eaten whole.

Pickled anchovies *(boquerones en vinagre)* are particularly refreshing on a hot summer's day.

These fresh capsicums, which can be mild or surprisingly hot, are fried in hot oil to make a delicious dish.

Russian salad *(ensaladilla rusa)* is made from potatoes, various boiled vegetables, and a delicate mayonnaise.

Olives *(aceitunas)* are usually marinated in salt and vinegar. They can also be stuffed; anchovies and peppers are popular.

Artichokes in vinegar *(alcachofas en vinagre)*: the bitter aroma of the former and acidity of the latter combine well.

Fried *pimientos de Padrón* are eaten by themselves, sprinkled with a little coarsely milled sea salt.

Salted anchovies *(anchoas de l'Escala)* are a specialty of Catalonia. They go particularly well with tomato bread.

Button mushrooms *(champiñones)* are fried in olive oil with garlic and parsley, and served in an earthenware dish.

Braised loin *(lomo en adobo)*, usually of pork, is marinated in olive oil, wine, and vinegar before braising.

Wrinkled potatoes served with a spicy dip *(papas arrugadas con mojo)* are a specialty of the Canary Islands.

Escalivada, a vegetable salad, consists of fried eggplant, red capsicum, and onions, which are then marinated.

Tender young beans *(habas tiernas)* go especially well with air-dried mountain ham *(jamón serrano)* or sausage.

Goat cheese in olive oil *(queso de cabra en aceite)* continues to ripen in the oil, which gives the cheese a special piquancy.

Olive oil is drizzled over *pa amb tomàquet*, the popular tomato bread from Catalonia, which is made with fresh tomatoes.

Crispy fried spinach croquettes *(croquetas de espinacas)* are best eaten as soon as they are taken from the deep-frier.

Although tapas are ideal as a snack, since they take the edge off a hearty appetite, a good selection of them – *tapeo* – can stretch into a very cozy dinner for two.

Hard-shell clams are cooked in a wine-and-onion stock *(almejas a la marinera)*, or with tomatoes and spicy paprika.

Even canned tuna *(atún, bonito)* makes a delicious snack, and is good with fried capsicum or in a salad.

Small deep-fried calamari *(chipirones fritos)* served with lemon are one of the stalwarts of Andalusian tapas bars.

Mangold in a Béchamel sauce *(acelgas con bechamel)* is often found in the vegetable-growing regions of the north.

Favorite Spanish tapas

Pimientos del piquillo are barbecued red capsicums from Navarra, shown here with lots of garlic.

Tiny *chanquetes* are a type of anchovy. They are coated with flour and then deep-fried.

Baby elver *(angulas)* are one of the most expensive tapas. They are fried with fresh chilies and garlic in olive oil.

Catalan connoisseurs are particularly appreciative of this delicate mushroom salad, which is made from the saffron milk-cap, or lactarius, *(amanida de rovellons).*

Asparagus *(espárragos)* is usually eaten cold with mayonnaise; fat stalks from a can are very popular.

There are numerous different kinds of croquette *(croquetas)*, made, for example, with spinach, ham, or seafood.

Tortillas are a basic of any tapas bar, whether made with potato *(española)* or a wide range of other ingredients.

Each region has its own way of preparing tripe *(callos)*, but it is usually braised with vegetables, chickpeas, or sausage.

Snails *(caracoles)* are especially popular in the north. They are either broiled or braised, perhaps with blood pudding.

Tender lettuce hearts *(cogollos)* come mainly from Tudela in Navarra, and are served in a light vinaigrette dressing.

Meatballs in tomato sauce *(albóndigas con salsa de tomate)* are a classic – and a must in any tapas bar.

The common mussel *(mejillones)* is served warm or cold, either with an onion-and-wine marinade or steamed.

Deep-fried squid *(calamares a la romana)* are coated in flour before being cooked in hot oil.

Breaded large shrimps *(gambas rebozadas)* can be coated in breadcrumbs or dipped in flour and beaten egg.

Beef or pork tongue in a hearty tomato sauce *(lengua con salsa de tomate)* is a popular braised dish.

Chicory with preserved anchovies *(endibias con anchoas)* is a delicious blend of the bitter and salty components.

Langoustines *(cigalas)* are usually fried with olive oil and salt on a hotplate *(a la plancha)*.

Hard-shell clams with fava beans *(almejas con habas)* are a delicate blend of the aromas of land and sea.

Moorish kebabs *(pinchos morunos)* are usually pork, marinated in a piquant sauce and then broiled.

Razor shell clams *(navajos)* are steamed and served *au natur* with just a little fresh lemon.

The highly seasoned *chorizo* sausage is found in even the simplest bar. It is served either in chunks or slices.

These tasty little turnovers *(buñuelos)* are deep-fried from a dough of salt-fish, vegetables, or ham.

Rabbit *(conejo)* is often braised in an earthenware dish with garlic, seasoning, white wine, and potatoes.

Spicy blue-veined *Cabrales* cheese from Asturia goes especially well with hearty bread and an ordinary red table wine.

Shrimps with garlic *(gambas al ajillo)* are brought to the table in a small earthenware dish while still bubbling.

Air-dried mountain ham *(jamón serrano)* is good, and ham from the Iberian pig *(pata negra)* unsurpassable.

Jumbo shrimp and razor shell clams from the hotplate *(gambas* and *navajas a la plancha)* are popular throughout Spain. Another good way of enjoying shrimp is just to sprinkle them with coarse sea salt.

On a hot summer's day, a spicy seafood salad *(salpicón de mariscos)* is wonderfully refreshing.

Sea dates *(dátiles de mar)* are a relative of the common mussel, and are simply steamed in their own juices or in a broth.

Migas

"To encounter the culinary art of the stone age, it is only necessary to visit the Spanish mountain shepherds," noted Count von Keyserling, the traveling philosopher, at the beginning of the 20th century. Simple dishes made from grain, and sometimes enriched with a little fat and meat, have been around for thousands of years, and even the first Iberian inhabitants of Spain are known to have prepared a cooked dish made from stale bread. *Migas* in the exact sense of the word are actually only breadcrumbs. Shepherds and muleteers first ate *migas* on their travels throughout the land. Old bread was broken into small pieces, fried in sheep drippings or lard, and perhaps a little garlic, ground paprika, or a few herbs added. On good days, there would also be a piece of spicy sausage, ham, or bacon. At sunrise, the men sat around the fire with a plate of *migas*, and it was undoubtedly the shepherds who gave the morning star its colloquial name of *lucero miguero* (breadcrumb star) after their first meal of the day. A large number of *migas* variations on this basic shepherd's meal evolved throughout Spain, and they are still devoured today by hunters in the early morning mist or on rainy fall days. Traditionalists insist that the bread used for *migas* should be at least four days old and as dry as a bone. Because of the hardness of the crust and the amount of strength required to cut it up into small pieces, this job is usually left to the men.

In Aragon the traditional shepherds' *migas* (*migas de pastor*) are usually served with chorizo and grapes. As well as bacon, the *migas extremeñas* of southwest Spain are always served with hot red paprika, either as a vegetable or a ground powder. For *migas canas* the breadcrumbs are first softened in milk and then fried, either with garlic or sugar. *Migas de matanza* (butcher's *migas*) are fried in pork fat, and pork belly and spicy sausage added. A tomato sauce is also a popular accompaniment to these fried breadcrumbs (*migas con salsa de tomate*), and those with a really sweet tooth choose *migas negras* (also known as *migas de mulata*), which are made with milk, sugar, and melted chocolate.

Traditionally, *migas* are eaten from a *hortera*, a deep, coarse wooden plate whose name has also come to mean a narrow-minded, uncultivated person. Nonetheless, this "poor man's food" is also frequently found on middle-class tables, and in fact *migas* are often served on special occasions, such as a name-day or on religious fiestas.

Olive oil from Lower Aragon

The olive groves of Bajo Aragón are a direct legacy of Roman civilization. The land stewards tended to award premiums on the cultivation of this oil-producing fruit, so the hills and plains around Teruel were soon covered with luscious olive plantations. However, the Aragonese have to thank Arab technology for the skill of pressing the oil. The Moors developed oil mills which were operated by draft animals, and hand-operated presses. At the end of the 19th century the French introduced new technologies such as the hydraulic press. Clarification in centrifuges produced a clear, mild oil, which gastronome Dionisio Pérez mentioned at the beginning of the 20th century in his *Guía del Buen Comer Español*, where he describes olive oil from Alcañiz, and from anywhere in Lower Aragon, as "exquisite." Today, 90 percent of all olive trees are of the Empeltre variety, and 9 pounds (4 kilograms) of olives are required for 1 liter (4 generous cups) of oil. Colors range from golden-yellow to burnished gold. A fruity flavor of young olives dominates early in the harvest period, and becomes slightly sweet with a soft, pleasant aroma over time.

Migas de pastor
Shepherd`s *migas*
(Photograph left)

Generous 1 lb/500 g stale Spanish white bread
Salt
6 tbsp lard or olive oil
1¼ cups/150 g diced bacon
4 cloves of garlic, sliced

Dice the bread the day before you want to use it. Place it in a bowl and sprinkle over some slightly salted water; do not let it get too wet. Mix well and leave overnight.
Heat the lard or oil in a cast-iron skillet and fry the bacon. Add the garlic and fry until golden. Add the soaked bread to the skillet and, turning with a wooden spoon, fry until golden.
Shepherd's *migas* are often served with white grapes, chorizo or other spicy sausage, and/or fried eggs.

Migas a la extremeña
Migas Extremadura style

Generous 1 lb/500 g stale Spanish white bread
5–10 tbsp milk
6 tbsp lard or olive oil
1¼ cups/150 g diced bacon
7 oz/200 g chorizo, chistorra or other spicy
sausage, cut into thin slices
1 red bell pepper, seeded and cut into slices
2 cloves of garlic, finely diced
Salt
½ tsp mild paprika
Pinch of spicy paprika

Dice the bread the day before you want to use it. Place in a bowl and sprinkle over the milk. Leave overnight to absorb.
Heat the lard or oil in a cast-iron skillet and fry the bacon. Add the sausage and sliced bell pepper and fry. Add the garlic and bread, and, stirring frequently, cook until golden.
Season with salt and paprika, and serve while still very hot.

Migas canas
Sweet *migas*

Generous 1 lb/500 g stale Spanish white bread
¾ cup warm milk
4 tbsp oil
Sugar and ground cinnamon for dusting

Cut the bread into small dice. Place in a bowl, and sprinkle over the milk. Leave to absorb.
Heat the oil in a cast-iron skillet. Fry the bread until golden brown, stirring frequently. Dust with sugar and cinnamon before serving.

Ajoarriero

Although the technique of drying and preserving cod *(bacalao)* was already known to the Phoenicians, and later perfected by the Arabs, it was not until the Middle Ages that dried cod as we know it today became popular throughout the Iberian peninsula as a "poor man's fish."
Wandering shepherds and much-maligned muleteers *(arrieros)* stocked up with dried cod when in the large towns. They then ate the fish on their travels with a sauce made of bread, garlic *(ajo)*, and wild vegetables that they picked from the wayside.
Later, people began to cook dried fish of all varieties, and even vegetables *al ajoarriero*, "with garlic, muleteer-style." The cooking method remained the same for centuries, and can still be enjoyed today in *mesones* and *posadas*, simple inns and guesthouses encountered along country roads.
Bacalao al ajoarriero remains one of the most popular dishes in inland Spain, especially during Easter week. One ancient recipe calls for a whole head of garlic to each pound of dehydrated, boned dried cod, and two beaten eggs for binding. In most *ajoarriero* recipes, however, paprika is almost as important as garlic. Star chef José Mari Arzak confirms that there are as many recipes for *ajoarriero* as there were chefs in the ancient kingdom of Aragon. It is cooked with cauliflower or potatoes, spiny lobster or dogfish, snails or even river crayfish, a dish that Ernest Hemingway devoured with such relish while in Pamplona.

Bacalao al ajoarriero
Dried cod muleteer-style

Generous 1 lb/500 g dried cod, skin and bones
removed
2 dried red bell peppers
½ cup/125 ml olive oil
1 onion, finely diced
4 cloves of garlic, diced
1 tsp mild paprika
Salt and pepper

Soak the dried cod in water for 24 hours, changing the water at least twice. Soften the dried bell peppers in water. Remove the fish from the water, dry, and shred into pieces. Heat the oil in a deep pot and braise the garlic until translucent. Add the fish and the rehydrated bell pepper. Season with paprika and pour on some water if necessary. Cover and simmer on a low heat for 30 minutes. Season with salt and pepper to taste before serving.

HUNTING IN THE PYRENEES

According to Antonio, the Pyrenees are a paradise for huntsmen: some hunt stag for their spectacular antlers, some are devotees of the nocturnal hunt for wild boar, others prefer deer. But Antonio, who will shortly be celebrating his 60th birthday, yearns for his chamois. It's been ten years now since he shot his last one. First his luck was out, then age caught up with him. "But I have my memories of the days I spent stalking chamois on the rough cliffs – no one can take those from me, or the tiny, precious trophies hanging on the wall at home."

Chamois *(gamuza, rebeco)* is one of the most sought hunting trophies in the Pyrenees. During the famine that followed the Civil War, says Antonio, who has always been a passionate hunter and enjoys cooking in his spare time, it almost became extinct. In those days, people went into the mountains, some armed with muzzle-loaders that looked as if they could have come out of the Ark, to hunt just about anything that came into sight. Unlike Antonio, who was a conscientious huntsman and only went after corpulent "machos" or old and sterile females, these "hunters" went for young animals – kids. The situation improved, however, when the national preserves were established *(Reservas Nacionales de Caza)*, an area which encompasses most of the Pyrenees. The best huntsmen from the villages were employed as gamekeepers, and chamois stocks soon recovered.

Basically, there are two different ways of hunting game in the Pyrenees: stalking and driving. The latter is most widely employed for wild boar, and sometimes for red deer. Driving is advisable when dealing with a large number of animals. Antonio, however, believes stalking is more sporting. He prefers to select a particular animal, stalk it without the animal realizing, and to catch it unawares with a chest hit. Stalking is now the only permitted method of hunting chamois, ibex, deer, and stag. The huntsman is always accompanied by a gamekeeper who is responsible for selecting the animal. This method is therefore most suitable for choosing old and/or ill animals for culling.

There are five national preserves *(Reservas Nacionales de Caza)* in the Pyrenee of Aragon. With one exception, chamois is the main catch; in La Garcipollera it is stag. Next is wild boar, and in Los Valles deer as well. Still, chamois is far less frequently found in the region's restaurants than venison and wild boar. This is due in part to the low legal hunt quota, and in part to its comparatively poor flavor. It may on occa-sion be prepared for special guests, but in this case it would be more for entertaining friends than as the basis for a major gastronomic event. In Spain, it is common practice for the catch to remain with the hunt owner, whereas the huntsman is presented with the trophy and the skin. Antonio once reversed this custom, and this enabled him to experience the culinary quality of his favorite trophy. "The gamekeeper who was accompanying me made a mistake, and I accidentally shot a very young chamois. I was pretty angry when I realized it was practically still a kid. But then, when I had calmed down, I saw the positive side. The things I would be able to do with it in the kitchen! So we cleaned the animal out, there and then, and skinned it in the gamekeeper's hut. I then insisted that it be jointed and took the meat home, leaving behind the head, neck, and innards. Although it was still a young animal, there were still about eight to ten kilograms [18 to 22 pounds] of meat on it," he reports with satisfaction.

"We oven-roasted the fillet on the ribs. Delicious! This was definitely better than the tough, strong-smelling meat from older animals! Tender and aromatic, a sucking kid with the wonderful flavor of juicy mountain meadows. We made the leftover meat into a traditional ragout, and it cooked in less than an hour – delicious and tender. And that's how I came to eat the animal with a pleasure that matched the passion with which I hunted it." Antonio's delight at being able to sample this tender meat is clear. Over the centuries, hunting game in the harsh environment of Aragon became a way of life, and a necessity for survival. However, the huntsmen were well aware of which animals would provide the tastiest meal when they arrived home.

GAME SAUSAGE

In order to preserve game and make sure that just about every last morsel is used, hunters' wives made some of the catch into sausages. Very finely diced meat and innards are marinated, or just seasoned, stuffed into skins, dried in the kitchens and then gently smoked over a wood fire.

Today, venison and wild boar sausages often also contain pork meat and bacon, which helps to make the mass a little smoother. These sausages are usually seasoned with hot pepper, and can be hard or soft. Hunters in the Pyrenees wrap game sausages in brown paper to bake over glowing embers – but not for too long, as otherwise they would become tough. Game sausages are held in the hand, sliced with a long hunting knife, and accompanied by bread and olives or with vegetables for a hearty meal.

Jabali en salsa
Boar pot roast

1½ lbs/750 g loin of wild boar
2 carrots, sliced
2 large onions, diced
2 sprigs of thyme
2 bay leaves
½ tsp black peppercorns
3 cloves
3 cups/750 ml red wine
½ cup/125 ml olive oil
2 ripe beef tomatoes, skinned and diced
2 cloves of garlic, finely diced
Salt
2 medium-size potatoes, diced
7 oz/200 g mixed mushrooms, washed and diced

Wash the meat and pat it dry. Place in a bowl with the carrots and onions, and add the thyme, bay leaves, peppercorns, and cloves. Pour over the red wine. Leave in the marinade for 1 to 2 days, turning the meat several times.

Remove the meat from the marinade and pat it dry. Heat a generous (⅖ cup/100 ml of olive oil in a large pot and quickly brown the meat on all sides. Then pour in the marinade, including the carrots, onions, and herbs. Add the tomatoes and garlic, and season with salt. Cover with a lid and leave to braise for 25 minutes. Add the diced potato and cook slowly for a further 20 minutes.

Fry the mushrooms in the remaining oil until all the liquid has been absorbed. Then add to the meat in the cooking pot and heat everything together for a few minutes. Serve immediately.

SUCKING LAMB

Sucking lamb from Aragon is one of the best kinds of lamb available in Spain. The leg and loin of *Ternasco de Aragón* are especially prized. The flesh is a delicate pink and very juicy. Very young sucking lamb is not normally cut up, but cooked whole.

FROM HEAD TO TOE

The sheep is one of the oldest domestic animals in the world; it was tamed long before the cow and the pig. This was due not only to the legendary docility of the sheep, but also to the almost endless ways in which it could be used. The tasty flesh served as nourishment, the milk was used to make cheese, and the wool was made into clothing. Constantly under threat of famine, there was no end to the imagination that Spanish cooks have developed over the centuries. The head is split in half, seasoned or stuffed, and then baked in the oven. The trotters are served with a tomato or lemon sauce, made into dumplings, or stuffed with sausage. *Asadura de cordero* is a pot-cooked dish that is made from

innards (lung, liver, or heart), tomatoes, and onions. *Gallinejas y entresijos* are lamb's innards that are wrapped around wooden skewers and baked in oil. To make *madejas*, the innards are cut into strips and fried in oil; for *chiretas* they are stuffed with ham or sausage. The lung and other organs are finely diced, mixed with vinegar, oil, almonds, garlic, and seasoning, and made into *chanfaina*. Lamb kidneys became famous as *riñones al Jerez*, and doughnuts made from lamb's brains are known, ironically, as *buñuelos de talentos*: talent turnovers.
Lamb is fundamental to Aragonese cooking, which is based largely around meat of various types. It is not surprising that the animal has been exploited in almost every way possible in the kitchen.

THE MAIN SPANISH CUTS OF LAMB

1 *cabeza* – head
2 *cuello* – neck
3 *costillar* – rib, cutlet
4 *lomo* – loin
5 *falda* – breast
6 *paletilla/espaldilla* – shoulder
7 *pierna* – leg
8 *manos/patas* – trotters

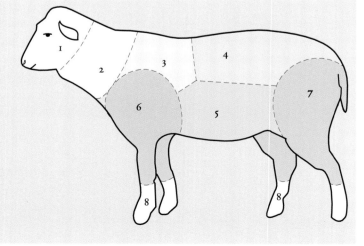

Since biblical times, man has happily sacrificed lambs to the gods. Legends handed down from ancient cultures that lived in Roman-occupied Palestine provide plenty of evidence of just how important lamb was: at Passover the number of lambs sacrificed was multiplied by ten to give an idea of the number of people present (one lamb will provide a feast for ten people).

Even in those times, the lambs were "barbecued" in the open air. The fat, which was considered to be impure, burnt away during the cooking process and prevented the flesh from drying out. A ceremony was performed, after which the believers consumed the lean meat.

The mountain meadows of Aragon provide excellent grazing for sheep and goats, and with stocks of around 2.5 million, lamb is considered to be the region's culinary "flagship." *Ternasco de Aragón* (sucking lamb from Aragon) is the meat from young indigenous breeds *Rasa Aragonesa*, *Roya Bilbilitana*, and *Ojinegra*. The mother of a *Ternasco de Aragón* feeds solely on the aromatic herbs in the mountain regions, and suckles her young with particularly fragrant milk. Shortly before the animals are slaughtered, the shepherds are allowed to add a natural concentrated feeding stuff.

A *Ternasco de Aragón* is no more than 90 days old when it is slaughtered, and weighs between 40 and 52 pounds (18 and 24 kilograms). It provides between 19 and 25 pounds (8.5 and 11.5 kilograms) of tender, juicy, pale pink meat with a firm, white layer of fat.

In the Pyrenees, sucking lamb is still prepared using the same methods as in prehistoric times. Around 1900, Dionisio Pérez, a much renowned gastronome, noted that "skewered sucking lamb *(ternasco asado al espeto)*, prepared in the open air and rubbed with salt and garlic and cooked over an open flame, is an extremely popular dish."

Oven-roast lamb *(cordero asado)*, another classic, is usually only rubbed with salt, garlic, and a little pork drippings before being placed in the oven, and is frequently basted with its own juices during cooking (recipe on p. 95). A sucking lamb roast such as this would undoubtedly have convinced those Spaniards who unthinkingly adopted the attitude of their ancestors that lamb was a "poor man's dish" and not fit for "decent" people's tables, since it stank. If the aroma and flavor alone are not sufficient to counteract this attitude, then the juicy price of *Ternasco de Aragón* surely is.

Opposite: On the juicy mountain meadows of Aragon, lambs feed solely on tasty herbs, and this has an obvious and beneficial effect on the quality of the meat.

Garlic and pork drippings, herbs, and a dash of vinegar; nothing else is needed for *cordero asado*.

A whole lamb is too big for a standard domestic oven. It is cut up then placed in a roasting pan.

Large amounts of diced garlic and fresh parsley are sprinkled all over the meat.

Pork drippings give the meat a hearty aroma, and help stop it from drying out during cooking.

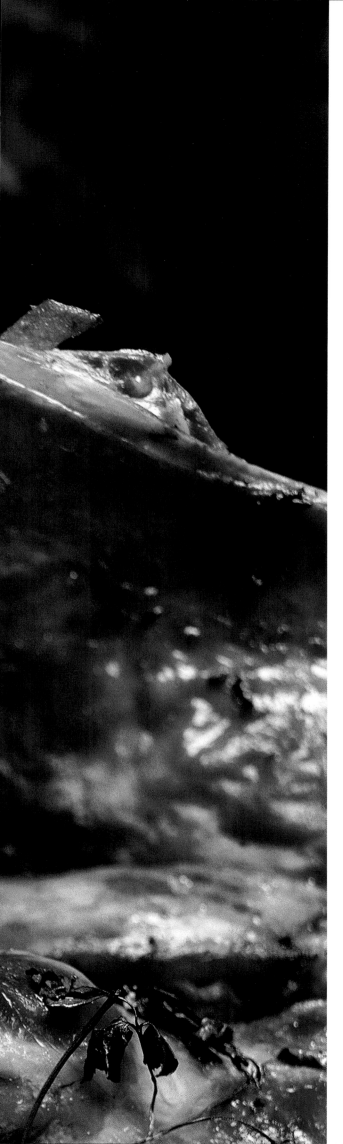

Delicious lamb

Ternasco al horno
Roast sucking lamb
Serves 6
(See opposite)

Leg and rib of 1 sucking lamb
Salt
Pepper
2 bunches of parsley, chopped
8 cloves of garlic, coarsely diced
2 sprigs of thyme
Generous ½cup/100 g pork drippings
1 cup/250 ml white wine

Wash the leg and rib, then pat dry. Sprinkle generously with salt and pepper and place in a large roasting pan.
Mix the parsley and garlic together, and sprinkle over the lamb. Add the thyme and dot the drippings over the top. Place in a preheated oven at 430 °F/220 °C for about 30 minutes. Turn the meat over and pour over the wine. Reduce the oven temperature to 350 °F/175 °C and roast the lamb for another hour (test for doneness). Baste frequently during the cooking process with water and the juices from the meat.

Piernas de cordero
con alcachofas
Lamb knuckles with artichokes

4 lamb knuckles, each weighing about 12 oz/350 g
Salt
Pepper
½ cup/125 ml olive oil
1 onion, finely diced
4½ oz/125 g Serrano ham, cut into strips
2 large cloves of garlic, diced
4 young artichokes, washed and halved
2 ripe beef tomatoes, skinned and diced
1 bay leaf
2 cups/500 ml meat stock

Wash the lamb knuckles and pat them dry. Rub generously with salt and pepper. Heat the olive oil in a large cast-iron pot and brown the knuckles on all sides. Remove the meat from the cooking pot and place on one side.
Cook the onion and ham in the oil until translucent. Add the garlic and artichokes, and fry. Stir in the tomatoes and the bay leaf, and pour over the stock. Then return the knuckles to the sauce and cover with a lid. Cook on a medium heat for about 1 hour. Season the sauce to taste with salt and pepper, and serve the knuckles in the sauce.

Cordero al chilindron
Lamb hotpot with paprika

2 large dried red bell peppers
2.2 lb/1 kg lamb haunch
½ cup/125 ml olive oil
2 onions, diced
4 cloves of garlic, diced
Salt and pepper
1 tsp mild paprika
4 ripe tomatoes, skinned and diced
2 green bell peppers, diced
1 cup/250 ml white wine
2 tbsp chopped parsley

Soak the dried bell peppers in 2 cups/500 ml of warm water for 1 hour. Remove from the water and dice.
Cut the lamb into bite-size pieces and brown on all sides in hot oil. Add the onions and garlic, and cook until slightly browned. Season with salt, pepper, and paprika, and pour over the water used to soak the peppers. Simmer for 20 minutes. Add the tomatoes, the red and green peppers, and wine. Cook for another 40 minutes, stirring from time to time. Add some more water if necessary to prevent the meat from drying out. Season with salt and pepper and garnish with the diced parsley before serving.

Paprika land

Together with its neighbors Navarra and La Rioja, Aragon is also known as *tierra de chilindrónes*, after the popular method of preparing a dish *al chilindrón*, that is, with fresh and dried bell peppers, tomatoes, and onions. Lamb, chicken, and even pork are cooked this way. It is said that this particular recipe dates back to the Moors, when manual artisans who wanted to join a particular workshop would serve their prospective colleagues chicken in a *chilindrón* sauce (see p. 122) to put them in a good mood. Later, these dishes were also served in the northern regions of Spain to seal a deal.

Poor man's fish

To the Aztec emperors of Mexico, frogs in a hot pimento sauce were just as much of a treat as other amphibians and insects were. The ancient Chinese also regarded them as a great delicacy, and in Europe in the Middle Ages dried frog was considered to be an aphrodisiac. In recent centuries, though, it has come to be thought of as a "poor man's fish," since in Spain the habit of eating frogs was considered to be something the gipsies did, as they were known to sell amphibians to make money.

However, in time frog became more acceptable, first as an emergency ration and subsequently as a delicacy. The Spaniards in the north consumed most of the creature, and the fried skin was very highly regarded. In Castile, though, only the legs and part of the upper body were eaten. Legend has it that frogs' tongues are poisonous, and so the head was removed in some regions, and in others only the front part of the head. As in France, the legs of the frog are the most popular, and eaten in many parts of Spain as part of traditional fare in restaurants.

Traditionally, frogs' legs *(ancas de rana)* are fried with garlic or (especially in the regions where large vegetable gardens are tended) with young vegetables and a hint of hot red paprika. *Ranas en salsa verde,* frogs in a green sauce made from white wine, onion, garlic, and parsley, are popular in northern Spain. Central Spain boasts three traditional recipes for frogs' legs: with garlic and oil *(al ajillo),* breaded and fried *(rebozadas),* and with tomato *(con tomate).* Rice with frogs was a quite a popular dish in Castile in olden times. However, increased contamination of rivers and lakes and the careless consumption of a creature that takes five years to reach maturity have had a dramatic effect on stocks in recent years. Frog hunting is banned today, but poaching is still a problem. Conservation organizations and the powers-that-be have adopted more rigorous methods, and this has meant that this traditional specialty is no longer on offer in the tapas bars. The frogs' legs that are available in smart restaurants have usually come from Thailand.

Snails

In spring, fall, and winter they take to vegetable fields and meadows: snail gatherers on the lookout for little shells with the delicious treats hidden inside. The vegetable growers are always pleased to see them, since they help to eliminate the problem that can decimate their crops. On the low plains of northern Spain, from Catalonia to the Basque country, snails have always been regarded as a delicacy, and most grandmothers' notebooks are full of recipes for *caracoles*. Higher up, in the valleys of the Pyrenees, the consumption of snails has always been looked down on, and poorer people were known derogatorily as "snail eaters."

Although almost 40,000 types of snail are known to man, only a tiny proportion ends up in the pot. On the whole, the Spanish do not differentiate between the different types, and the ones offered for sale on the market are usually a mixture of different varieties. The most common ones are *navarricas* or *boberos*. They are smaller than most of the varieties known in Europe, have a brown shell, and are more often found in fields than in the kitchen garden. Their fondness for herbs such as thyme and tarragon makes them especially tasty. Also popular are the tiny *caracol de huerta* (vegetable snail), the reddish, juicy *plana*, and the lighter-colored *caracolina*.

True connoisseurs are particularly appreciative of snails gathered in December and January, when they enjoy a kind of hibernation behind the sealed membrane of their tiny "house." As their digestive system has slowed down for the winter, there is no need for the laborious cleaning process that involves sawdust and salt water. Summer snails are hard to digest because of their well-filled digestive tract.

The snail is a modest creature; it will put up with just about any culinary treatment, and is frequently served in or with a sauce. Many Spanish recipes for snails are quite spicy, such as snails cooked the Madrid way, with saffron and hot paprika, or *caracoles a la riojina*, with paprika and onions. In Catalonia, snails are eaten in spicy-sweet dishes, and with *sobrasada* sausage on the Balearics. It is also not unusual to find them in hotpots made with lamb or rabbit. On the Levante, rice dishes are prepared with snails, peas, and saffron, but residents of the north prefer to barbecue or broil them, seasoned with just a drop of oil, a coarse grain of salt, and a seed from a hot chili pepper.

Left: In northern Spain, snails are barbecued or broiled, cooked in meat dishes with rabbit or lamb, or just seasoned with garlic and served in earthenware dishes.

Conejo con caracoles
Rabbit with snails
(Photograph above)

2.2 lb/1 kg rabbit, divided into portions
Salt
Pepper
Scant ½ cup/100 ml olive oil
1 large onion, diced
4 cloves of garlic, diced
1 tbsp flour
3 cups/750 ml meat stock
½ cup/125 ml red wine
2 tomatoes, skinned and diced
1 bouquet garni (parsley, oregano, thyme, rosemary)
2 bay leaves
1 cinnamon stick
½ tsp hot paprika
48 small snails
1 tbsp chopped parsley

Season the rabbit portions generously with salt and pepper. Heat the oil in a large cooking pot and brown the rabbit on all sides. Add the onions and garlic, and cook briefly. Sprinkle over the flour and brown slightly. Pour over the meat stock and red wine. Add the tomatoes, bouquet garni, 1 bay leaf and the cinnamon, and season with the paprika. Then cover with a lid and simmer for about 30 minutes.

Put 8½ cups/2 liters of water, the snails, and the remaining bay leaf in another pot and heat. Once the water is boiling, cover the pot with a lid and leave to simmer on a low heat for about 10 minutes.

Drain the snails and discard the bay leaf. Now put the snails in with the rabbit and leave everthing to bubble gently for another 10 minutes. Then remove the bouquet garni, the bay leaf, and the cinnamon stick.

Season to taste with salt and pepper, and garnish with the chopped parsley before serving.

Spanish Christmas

"And were a whole family to have to die together, but to go without celebrating Christmas Eve regardless of the dish placed before them? Never! Even a family with little inclination toward saving would start to put away a penny here, a penny there, in November so they would later be able to buy a turkey," is how Benito Pérez Galdós, a novelist of the late 19th century, described the Spaniards' feelings and emotions toward the Christmas feast.

Chestnut-roasters are the first to herald the approaching Christmas period, when they arrive in the towns to set up their stalls, and soon the country's consumption of sweetmeats rockets by 30 percent. The smell of baking cookies wafts from countless ovens. Woodcarving tools and vocal chords are honed in anticipation of the competition for the most beautiful cribs and the loveliest Christmas carols. Amateur thespians perform live nativity scenes (belenes vivientes), representing stories from the Bible, and of course scenes from the life of Jesus.

The highlight of the culinary year is the Christmas meal that is served in the evening of December 24, when the whole family congregates around the beautifully laid table. There is usually a capon or a turkey, steaming away gently on a silver platter. This will have been simply roasted in the oven, and perhaps stuffed using one of several regional recipes. In Galicia, a chestnut stuffing is made; in Asturia, local tastes are for apples; in Catalonia, a mixture of plums, raisins, and pine nuts is the preferred choice. However, roast lamb, kid or suckling pig, and baked fish dishes are popular alternatives at this festive meal.

As far as vegetables are concerned, artichokes have pride of place on the Christmas table, usually served in a béchamel or almond sauce. Red cabbage is another favorite.

However, many Spaniards are moving away from these old customs, choosing instead more modern specialties, such as smoked salmon, fine seafood, terrines, or possibly foreign cheeses. Increasingly, the stylish glasses will contain Spanish sparkling wine (Cava), although the sweet Moscatel wines, Amontillado and Oloroso sherries are not forgotten.

Young and old alike enjoy generous quantities of sweetmeats: marzipan and delicate almond cookies; sugar cracknel and deep-fried pastries; dried fruit boiled in wine or syrup, and sweet soups made from almonds, nuts, or chestnuts. But the Christmas sweet above all others is turrón, traditional almond nougat (see p. 382).

However, as far as the children are concerned, the event of the holiday happens early in the New Year – the arrival of the three Magi (Reyes Magos). In coastal towns, these wise old men from the East arrive on magnificent barques; when they arrive in the Canary Islands, they even have live camels with them to pull the highly decorated coaches that carry the Magi, accompanied by a large entourage and sometimes whole herds of animals. On January 5 in their homes, the children find the gifts that the Magi have brought them, and, full of anticipation and excitement, they pounce on the Roscón de Reyes, a dried-fruit ring cake that contains a surprise of a coin, a bean, or a small toy. The person who finds the gift is allowed to wear the king's crown for that day.

In Valencia, according to an old custom, children prepare a tray with turrón, sugared almonds, and three glasses of sweet wine, and leave it outside the door (with a bundle of hay) for the three Magi and their camels as fortification before they set off on their return journey to the East.

January 5 sees the arrival of the three Magi. The children are always particularly delighted to see them – possibly because they bring the children's gifts!

Capon de Navidad
Christmas capon
Serves 6

9 oz/250 g prunes, pits removed
Scant ½ cup/100 ml sherry
1 capon or turkey, weighing about 5½ lb/2.5 kg, ready to use
Salt and pepper
3½ lb/1.5 kg slightly sour apples, peeled and cored
Generous ½ cup/100 g lard
3 cloves of garlic
2 cups/500 ml Cava or dry sparkling wine
4 tbsp butter
Juice of 1 lemon
½ cup/125 ml light cream
9 oz/250 g mushrooms, washed and sliced

Soak the prunes in the sherry. Then drain in a sieve, reserving the sherry. Wash and dry the capon; then rub inside and out with salt and pepper. Stuff with the prunes and 2 of the apples, and secure the opening. Place the capon in a roasting pan.

Melt the lard in a small pot and cook the garlic until light brown in color. Remove the garlic and pour the lard over the capon. Roast in a preheated oven at 430 °F/220 °C for about 20 minutes. Reduce the heat to 350 °F/175 °C. Pour over the Cava and roast the capon for another 2 hours, basting frequently with the juices. Turn the capon around halfway through the cooking time so it browns evenly on all sides. Meanwhile, cut the remaining apples into quarters and fry in 2 tbsp butter. Add the sherry and cook until the apples are soft. Then pass through a sieve or purée with a hand-blender, and season with the lemon juice. Remove the capon from the oven and leave to stand a while before carving. Meanwhile, add some water to the juices in the roasting pan to loosen them, and pour in the cream; then season with salt and pepper. Sauté the onions in the remaining butter.

Arrange the capon on a large serving dish with the onions, apple purée, and mushrooms. Carve at the table, and serve the sauce separately.

SOPA DE ALMENDRAS
Sweet almond soup

1 cup/150 g skinned almonds
4¼ cups/1 liter milk
½ cup/125 g sugar
1½ tsp vanilla sugar
1 cinnamon stick
2 tbsp cornstarch
3½ tbsp light cream
Toasted bread slices or croutons

Dry-fry the almonds and then grind in a mortar and pestle.

Slowly bring the milk, sugar, vanilla sugar, and cinnamon to a boil. Mix together the cornstarch and the cream, and stir into the boiling milk with the almonds. Bring the liquid back to a boil again briefly; then remove the cinnamon stick and serve the soup with the toasted bread or croutons.

Christmas is also a time of sweet blessings, and these include almond nougat with various fillings, candied fruit, and pastries.

99

CANDIED FRUITS

In 1603, the French traveler Bartolomé Joly wrote in his book *Viaje por España* that it was common practice in Calatayud to make a gift of bread, wine, and candied fruit to friends from out of town. Even in those times, the rivers Jalón, Jiloca, Gallego, and Cinca were famous for the superb quality of the fruit that grew on their banks. Also, the inhabitants practiced the traditional method of fruit preservation by boiling it in syrup so the fruit was preserved by the sugar. Aragon has a long tradition of candying fruit.

Around 60 years ago, some enterprising Aragonese confectioners hit on the idea of covering candied fruit with chocolate. This proved to be so successful that these sweets soon

Frutas de Aragón are sugar-candied fruits. They are sometimes covered in chocolate.

became known as *Frutas de Aragón*. The idea was quickly copied elsewhere, and Aragonese manufacturers have now established their own regulations to protect their products. *Frutas de Aragón*, marked with a "C" for *calidad* (quality) may only be made from apples, pears, peaches, apricots, cherries, figs, plums, and oranges, and only sugar may be used for candying. Artificial preservatives and colorings are strictly forbidden. The chocolate must consist of at least 34 percent cocoa butter, and no other fat is permitted. Another feature of *Frutas de*

Aragón is the way the chocolate coating remains on the fruit. The fruit is extremely juicy and retains its aroma. The candies are sold in small wooden boxes, and are given to friends as a souvenir from Aragon – just as they were in Bartolomé Joly's time. A good tradition is worth preserving, and it seems likely that this one will continue for the next few hundred years.

Below: *Guirlache* was originally created by the Arabs, and is made from the best almonds and lots of caramelized sugar. Opposite: Peaches are often sold as dried fruit.

Frutas de Aragón, candied pieces of tender fruit, are wrapped in foil and packed in boxes.

The Spanish love *almendrados*, a light and airy almond pastry.

Tortas de alma have a "soul" of pumpkin, honey, and sugar.

These dainty little chestnuts *(Castañas de Huesca)* are made of marzipan.

Tray-baked *Coca de Fraga* is covered with apple or quince and dried fruit, and glazed with jelly.

SOMONTANO

Aragonese wine used to be considered heavy and coarse. At best, it was praised for its robust naturalness, since it was added to domestic and foreign wines to improve those with a weaker character. However, wine-producers in Somontano have put an end to this cliché in recent decades. First was the Lalanne vineyard, which, as long ago as the late 19th century, started to grow the French Cabernet Sauvignon variety as well as the traditional Moristel grape used for the typical reds and rosés of the region. Somontano is a strip of land on a high plateau at the foot of the Pyrenees; its southern boundary is formed by the Ebro. Barbastro is the main town and center of trade and commerce. The vineyards extend across hills and slightly elevated plains that slope down to the river valleys. The soils are sandy with plenty of chalk but little clay and hardly any organic material, all of which makes them particularly porous. The continental climate is tempered by the Pyrenees. The cold winters and mild summers with little rain provide a microclimate that is ideal for wine production. Some 2700 hours of sun every year guarantee that the grapes will ripen, and the small amount of moisture that there is protects the vines from pests and plagues. The potential of this region to produce quality wines has only recently been realized.

Today, the wine-producers of Somontano aim for lightness, elegance, and variety in their wines, to which end they acclimatize vines of international acclaim. Although local regulations cover only four white (Macabeo, Garnacha blanca, Alcañón, and Chardonnay) and five red varieties (natives Parreleta and Moristel, Tempranillo, Garnacha tinta, and Cabernet Sauvignon), in recent years growers have experimented with other (central European) grape varieties. Although new regulations prohibit the further planting of Riesling, Chenin blanc, and Sauvignon blanc, the Alsatian Gewürztraminer variety is still allowed to be grown.

Traditionally, Somontano red wines would also be offered for sale while still young. However, modern wines are generally stored for longer and have a fairly strong flavor of young wood. This emphasizes their strength of character, and is noteworthy in a country where red wines are traditionally stored in old wood for long periods of time.

Today, Somontano wines are known and appreciated for their clear fruitiness, their freshness and pleasantness. The red wines have a highly pronounced tannin note, and could have been made specifically for the paprika heat of the national dish, *cordero al chilindrón* (see recipe p. 95). The white wines are light, fresh and fruity. A few examples of rosé are also available in Somontano.

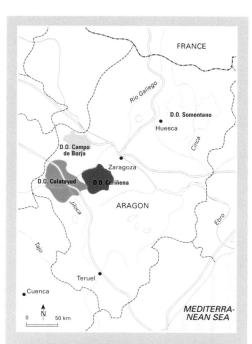

WINE-PRODUCING REGIONS IN ARAGON

D.O. Somontano
The most striking feature of this wine-producing area is the sheer variety it produces. In addition to the traditional heavy reds, a wide range of modern wines of great fruitiness and breeding are produced today. On the whole, the white wines are light, fruity, and expressive. There is a strong note of tannin in the red Cabernet Sauvignons, but the flavor is smoky with a pleasant fruit acidity.

D.O. Calatayud
The vineyards in this D.O. are up to 3280 feet (1000 meters) above sea level, and so are well protected against the extreme summer heat. The microclimate, two thousand years' of viticultural experience, and a keen interest in new technologies have all combined to produce a quality product: young, fresh, light wines – whites, reds, and rosés – with a strong, confident personality.

D.O. Campo de Borja
The character of these wines is determined by the extremely dry continental climate. In the 20th century, most of the wine production was shifted from numerous private cellars to large cooperatives. Garnacha and Viura, from which red, white, and rosé wines are pressed, dominate on the slopes of the Moncayo. The red are aromatic when young, acquiring a rounder bouquet as they mature. The rosés are fresh and mild, the whites fresh and light.

D.O. Cariñena
The vineyards of Cariñena are between 1640 and 2625 feet (500–800 meters) above sea level, and belong to 14 villages in the Ebro valley at the foot of the Pyrenees. Oddly enough, the Cariñena grape, which is grown all over the world, is not widely grown in Cariñena. Garnacha is the main variety, and Cariñena's reputation is actually based on its old red wines, some of which are mentioned in José Zorrilla's *Don Juan Tenorio*, written in 1844.

For a long time, heavy red wines that were used solely for blending were the only product of note created by the winegrowers of Somontano (photograph opposite: Alquézar). However, times have changed, and today Somontano is one of Spain's most promising wine regions – and that's not all: another four regions are "on the up" in Aragon, producing reds, whites, and rosés.

BUBBLY PIONEERS

Almost one hundred years after the first sparkling wine – known then as *Champán* – was delivered to Catalonia, an Aragonese vintner accepted a challenge to produce his own Cava. Miguel Angel Bordeje Cruz followed the traditional champagne method to the letter: the best grapes are picked by hand and pressed just until the so-called "tear must" is acquired, which is full of the finest aromas.

The wine is left to mature in bottles in the peace and quiet of the *cava* (cave) – in short, the sparkling wine is made by hand with absolutely no chemical intervention whatsoever.

In 1966 Miguel Angel Bordeje Cruz produced *Brut Nature*, and since then the Cavas Bordeje have become by far the region's most popular sparkling wines. The grapes all come from the vintner's own vineyards. While other producers always add a few Xarello and Parellada grapes, Fernando Bordeje, the son of the first Cava producer, swears by his own pressed *Brut Nature*, which is made solely from Macabeo grapes. He is also the only vintner in Aragon to grow Chardonnay, a variety that purists regard, derogatorily, as a "fashionable" grape, and produces a slim, elegant *Brut Nature 100% Chardonnay*. The name *Brut Nature* refers to the fruit sugar contained in the Cava, which is never, under any circumstances, added at a later stage. The top limit is 3 grams (one-tenth of an ounce) per liter of wine.

Today, the Aragonese Cavas are all produced by the champagne method, and each vintner decides himself how long to leave the bottles to mature; the minimum period is nine months. There are now five cellars in Aragon that are dedicated to this rite: Langa in Calatayud, the Cooperativa San Valero in Cariñena, the Bodegas Bordeje in Ainzón, Caytusa, and the Cooperativa San Cristo.

As far as production methods and grape varieties are concerned, the Aragonese Cava is virtually identical to the Catalan, but the peculiarities of the soil and the microclimate play a large part in determining the personality of the wine. While the Chardonnay Cavas develop an unmistakably French touch of mildness and elegance, the traditional Macabeo Cava is noted for its stronger personality and more pronounced local character and is well loved by purists who prefer a truly home-grown product.

Navarra

David Schwarzwälder

Navarra

Many different kinds of wild herb and fruit grow in the
mountains of Navarra. Their use to prepare excellent
liqueurs and elixirs in the monasteries dates back to the
Middle Ages.

Not so very long ago, cooks in the service of French aristocrats across the border were judged against the skills of their counterparts in Navarra. Centuries before, cooks in Navarra were already wielding their ladles with confidence, since the soil in their homeland in northern Spain has been producing the best quality ingredients for fine cuisine from time immemorial. The pride and self-assurance of the natives of Navarra have always been apparent, and they have always been keen to make their voices heard, whether in the realms of politics, culture, or cookery. Back in 850, the first king of Navarra, Iñigo Arista, gave his subjects comprehensive rights of free speech. These have been constantly reinforced over the centuries, thus strengthening the self-confidence of this small nation. Even when the kingdom of Navarra fell to the crown of Castile in 1512, following a protracted tug of war between Castile, Aragon, and the Frankish empire, the stubborn populace retained its special status and rights. It was not until 1841 that Navarra adopted a standard Spanish constitution, and to this day it continues to enjoy considerable independence as an autonomous region within the kingdom of Spain. The route taken by the pilgrims to Santiago de Compostela resulted in a cultural blossoming in the Navarra countryside during the Middle Ages, with innumerable monasteries and churches bearing witness to the rich heritage left by Christian pilgrims from all over Europe. Geographically, the region provides a cross-section in miniature of most of the climates and landscapes found in Spain; from the sheer mountain peaks of the Pyrenees in the north, the countryside falls away southward over deep forests of pine, oak, and beech. Pamplona, the famous capital with its notorious fiesta, forms the northern bridgehead of the gently rolling countryside of central Navarra as it merges with the fertile Ebro valley. Farther south, as a counterpoint to the luxuriant green of the north, lies the half-deserted wilderness of Bárdenas Reales. The cookery of Navarra benefits from the province's proximity to Aragon, Castile, the Basque provinces, and also France. In recent decades cultural exchanges with France have undoubtedly contributed to the emergence in Navarra of one of the first gourmet cuisines in Spain. However, it should not be forgotten that these new cooking methods also constitute a natural extension of the popular culinary tradition of Navarra: thanks to the availability of vegetables, it has always been light in character, with a certain natural elegance. Wines from Navarra vineyards, especially the rosé wines are considered some of the best wines in the whole of Spain.

Right: Navarra is Spain in miniature, with green hills and barren wastes. Fertile plains are bounded by rocky mountains, as shown here near Tudela.

Trucha a la Navarra
Trout Navarra style

4 fresh trout, gutted
Salt and pepper
4 slices of Serrano ham
Flour for coating
4½ oz/125 g smoked bacon, diced
2 tbsp olive oil
2 cloves of garlic, cut into slices

Wash and dry the trout; season with salt and pepper. Place a slice of ham inside each trout and secure with wooden picks. Coat the trout in flour, shaking off any excess. Cook the bacon in the olive oil in a large pan until the fat runs. Add the garlic and cook slowly until soft and transparent. Remove the bacon and garlic from the fat. Fry the trout on both sides in the fat until golden brown.
The diced bacon and garlic can be scattered over the trout before serving.

Variations: Wrap another slice of ham around the trout before coating in the flour, or fry the ham and trout separately and serve the fish on the slices of fried ham.

TROUT

In glowing terms, the American novelist Ernest Hemingway expressed his appreciation of the trout found in abundance in Navarra. The writer claimed to have caught the finest specimens of his entire life near Burguete. Even Alexandre Dumas, a French literary figure who was an implacable critic of Spanish cookery, had nothing but praise for the trout found in Spain, though he showed a particular preference for the succulent fish from Castile.

When it comes to fly-fishing in Spain, it is an undisputed fact that the angler has most luck in Navarra and Castile. Many rivers offering the conditions that trout love – very cold, clean water, rich in oxygen – have their sources in the Pyrenees and the Cantabrian mountains.

The most common catch in the north is the common brown trout (fario), a small species of trout with firm flesh and little fat. It is easily recognized by its silvery skin, which has a sprinkling of red and black spots. The salmon trout (trucha alsalmonada) is also found splashing around in Spanish streams; it has a very light skin and pale pink flesh, but is not a separate species. Its striking color and delicate flavor are acquired from the huge quantities of crayfish it devours. The multi-colored iridescent rainbow trout (trucha arco iris) now comes mainly from fish farms.

Trout is adaptable in the kitchen, and can be prepared either for a fast or for a feast. The famous trucha a la navarra (trout Navarra-style), like so many traditional popular dishes, was born of necessity. Hundreds of years ago, cooking oil was a luxury in the mountainous country of the Pyrenees; lard or bacon fat was mostly used for cooking. Trout were also cooked using pork fat; in times of plenty a little lean ham was added, for there is no doubt that the flavor of an air-dried jamón serrano and the tender flesh of mountain trout are a perfect combination. Nevertheless, the arguments still rage as to whether the ham should go underneath or inside the trout.

Variations on marinated trout (trucha en escabeche) are found throughout Spain. In earlier times, soaking in wine or vinegar was one of the few options available to preserve fish for any length of time. Different versions of stuffed trout are especially common in the southern half of Spain; ground meat or seafood are suitable fillings, as are vegetables or mushrooms. Trout soup is a Castilian specialty, and modern cooks like the combination of delicate fresh-water fish and roast red bell peppers.

1 Fresh trout are best bought already gutted and ready to cook. Then they just need washing.
2 Season the fish with salt and pepper, then stuff each trout with a slice of Serrano ham.
3 Secure the trout with wooden picks to prevent the ham escaping when it is fried.

4 Next, coat the trout in flour, so they turn beautifully crisp when they are fried.
5 Shake off any excess flour. Too much flour would form lumps and burn in the hot fat.
6 Cook the diced bacon in a skillet with olive oil until the fat runs. Then add the garlic.

7 When the garlic is golden brown, lift the diced bacon and garlic out of the oil and set aside.
8 Next, fry the trout in the remaining oil. Return the bacon and garlic to the skillet if a robust flavor is required.
9 Fry the trout, turning carefully, until they are brown and crisp. Then serve immediately.

FISHERMAN'S LUCK

I did not feel the first trout strike. When I started to pull up I felt that I had one and brought him, fighting and bending the rod almost double, out of the boiling water at the foot of the falls, and swung him up and onto the dam… .

While I had him on, several trout had jumped at the falls. As soon as I baited up and dropped in again I hooked another and brought him in the same way. In a little while I had six. [They were all about the same size.] I laid them out, side by side, all their heads pointing the same way, and looked at them. They were beautifully colored and firm and hard from the cold water. It was a hot day, so I slit them all and shucked out the insides, gills and all, and tossed them over across the river. I took the trout ashore, washed them in the cold, smoothly heavy water above the dam, and then picked some ferns and packed them

all in the bag, three trout on a layer of ferns, then another layer of ferns, then three more trout, and then covered them with ferns. They looked nice in the ferns, and now the bag was bulky, and I put it in the shade of the tree.

It was very hot on the dam, so I put my worm-can in the shade with the bag, and got a book out of the pack and settled down under the tree to read until Bill should come up for lunch.

(From: Ernest Hemingway, The Sun Also Rises, 1926)

VEGETABLES

Initial scepticism, when faced with the assertion that the best vegetables in the whole of Spain flourish here, would seem an entirely reasonable response. In the shadow of the dry slabs of the mountainsides, the Ribera de Navarra valley does not exactly give the impression of being particularly fertile. However, closer inspection reveals vegetable fields stretching out along the valley floor. *Ribera* quite simply means "a bank" or "irrigated plain." The term is used in Navarra, as well as in the neighboring regions of Aragon and La Rioja, to describe the fertile lowlands on the banks of the river Ebro, which produce vegetables of excellent quality.

The Arabs who occupied Spain stayed long enough in these riverside meadows to establish their sophisticated irrigation techniques, from which the population still benefits today. The vegetable fields of the Ribera, only occasionally interspersed with bushes or trees, have nothing in common with the cultivation practiced on a massive scale in the huge agricultural operations of southern Spain. A field of just under 5 acres (2 hectares) is considered large in Navarra, and most producers are family businesses.

Horticultural delicacies from Navarra include the cardoon *(cardo)*, a plant practically forgotten by large tracts of Europe and increasingly rare in Spain too. Botanically the plant is a relative of the artichoke, but the parts of the plant that are used bear a greater resemblance to celery. Cultivation of the cardoon is extremely expensive, and can be compared with that of asparagus; the growing shoots are painstakingly covered or earthed up by hand to prevent the stalks becoming bitter or stringy. After the stems have been cleaned and any threads removed, they are cut into pieces and boiled. Cardoon is often cooked in béchamel sauce in northern Spain, but it is also frequently served with fine herbs or vinaigrette. In Aragon, cardoon with almond sauce is a popular first course on the Christmas menu.

Of more than 30 varieties of lettuce grown in Navarra, the variety *cogollos de Tudela* is quite exceptionally tender. The young and extremely delicate lettuce hearts grow to a length of about 4 inches (10 centimeters), and are mostly served

as a first course with mayonnaise or a light marinade of olive oil and lemon, or vinegar, with salt. The delicate flavor is perfectly complemented by the addition of just a hint of garlic.

In early summer, young beans *(pochas)* are an indispensable ingredient in Spanish vegetable cookery. They are freshly cooked when they are still pale green, thus preserving their delicate, slightly sweet flavor. White asparagus *(espárrago)* and hot red peppers *(pimientos del piquillo)* have played the largest part in establishing the reputation of the vegetable-growing industry in Navarra.

Farmers in Navarra take pride in both new and old vegetable varieties. They grow (from left to right) lettuce, the cardoon (second from left), artichokes, green beans, young garlic shoots, and asparagus.

ASPARAGUS – VEGETABLE OF KINGS

The ancient Egyptians regarded asparagus as the food of the gods, as can be seen in the hieroglyphs inscribed on tablets from the kingdom of the Pharaohs. Later, the Roman censor and writer Cato described this fine vegetable as a *blandimentum gulae* (flattery for the palate), and the Roman master chef Apicius recommended asparagus as a first course to stimulate the appetite. When combined with egg and pepper, it was also supposed to heighten amorous pleasure. Asparagus shoots were also extolled by Pliny as the "vegetable of Venus," and its absence from any epicurean feast was unthinkable. In the Middle Ages asparagus stalks disappeared from the kitchen. They continued to be grown for a long time, but only behind monastery walls as a remedy for rheumatism, heart disorders, and skin diseases. It was not until the 17th century that the reputation of asparagus was restored in European cookery. The French Sun King, Louis XIV, is said to have been particularly fond of it, and when the Bourbon King Philip V ascended the Spanish throne in 1700, he is said to have re-established the vegetable on the Iberian peninsula as well.

Today the most famous white asparagus comes from Navarra. This delicate vegetable flourishes on the light-textured alluvial soils of the riverside meadows along the river Ebro, where the sun can warm the ground thoroughly and drainage is good. To ensure a harvest of dazzling white asparagus, the earth is piled up around the young shoots to prevent their exposure to sunlight, which would cause the tips to turn violet at first, and then green. However, color is no indication of the quality of the asparagus. In France and some regions of Spain green asparagus is particularly popular, since it has a stronger flavor than its white counterpart. In some areas it is still possible to find wild asparagus, which has a spicy flavor.

The "white gold," as it is known, is picked in Navarra between April and June. Harvesting asparagus remains a purely manual task, and even today many growers still peel the tender stalks by hand.

To earn its seal of quality, the asparagus *(espárrago de Navarra)* must be completely white, extremely tender, and not in the least fibrous. Most of it is taken straight to the regional canning factories after harvesting, since canned asparagus from Navarra is regarded as a delicacy throughout Spain. Very thick stalks measuring over an inch (3 centimeters) in diameter are much sought and very expensive. Fresh asparagus stalks, however, have also achieved something of a triumph in the kitchen in recent years. The following points should be noted when buying asparagus: freshly picked asparagus has tips that are tightly closed, and the cut surface of the stem is moist and pale in color. The stalks squeak when they are rubbed together, and they are easily broken. The asparagus should be perfectly white; any yellowing indicates that it has been picked for some time, and possibly that it is woody inside. Fresh asparagus can safely be kept for between three and four days in a refrigerator, wrapped in a damp cloth. Before cooking, asparagus must be washed, but under no circumstances soaked. White asparagus has to be peeled with a sharp knife or an asparagus peeler. Start just under an inch (2 centimeters) below the tip and peel from top to bottom. Cut off the woody end. Tender green asparagus, on the other hand, does not usually require peeling. Asparagus is best cooked in bundles for between 10 and 15 minutes in lightly salted boiling water. The flavor is enhanced by the addition of a pinch of sugar. The gentlest way to cook tender stalks is to place them upright in a narrow, tall pan, with the tips above the water so they do not become too soft during cooking.

Asparagus consists of nearly 95 percent water, and a 3½-ounce serving (100 grams) contains only 15 calories. It is rich in vitamins A, B, and C, as well as calcium, potassium, phosphorus, and folic acid. Asparagus tips are especially rich in vital nutrients. Because of its high levels of aspartic acid and potassium salts, asparagus has diuretic properties, cleanses the blood, and aids digestion.

There are very few different recipes for preparing asparagus in traditional Spanish cookery. It is usually eaten with vinaigrette or as *espárragos con dos salsas* (asparagus with two sauces), a dish in which the cooked stalks are accompanied by two kinds of mayonnaise, one pale and one colored with tomato. Modern chefs are beginning to experiment with more creative ways of using fresh asparagus, however, usually along French lines.

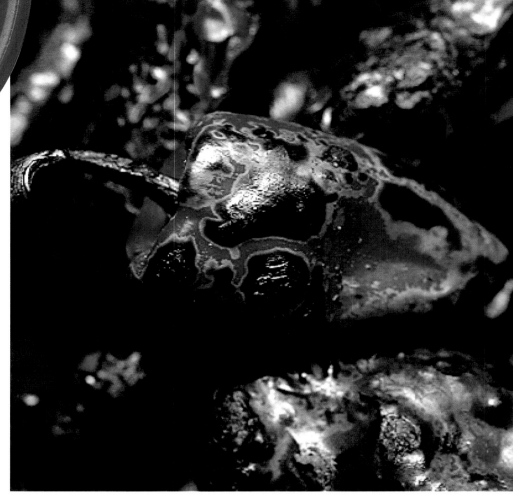

PIMIENTOS DEL PIQUILLO

For many Spaniards the very name *pimientos del piquillo* is enough to make the mouth water. These small, hot peppers are only about 3 inches (8 centimeters) long and are dark red in color. In their raw state they are not particularly appetizing because of their rather bitter taste. For this reason they are grilled over an open fire, and then skinned, seeded, and marketed as a preserve. Because of the expensive manual work involved in processing, *piquillos* are not cheap. The smoky tang from the wood fire and the hot, spicy nature of this variety of pepper combine well with seafood, fish, and mushrooms. Stuffed *pimientos del piquillo* thus have a universal appeal that is not confined to Navarra.

In a mysterious transformation, almost magical, the heat of the wood fire transforms the red peppers, which are extremely bitter in the raw state, into sweet delicacies to seduce the palate. The *pimientos del piquillo* must endure the heat of the fire and turn black as coal before their true character becomes apparent beneath the charred skins.

The red peppers, measuring only about 3 inches (8 centimeters), flourish on the alluvial sand of the *Ribera*.

The newly harvested peppers are sorted at the canning factory and are thoroughly washed before further processing.

The oven in which the peppers are to be roasted is wood-fired, just as it was two generations ago.

Next the peppers are put into the fire. In the oven the outer skin is charred, but the flesh of the fruit acquires exquisite flavor.

The women in the factory remove the charred skin, together with the stalks and seeds, of the *pimientos* by hand.

Traces of carbon are left on the peppers, but the delicate fruit must not come into contact with water.

Using soft cloths, and with great patience, the women remove the very last blemishes from every single pepper.

Finally the *pimientos del piquillo* are canned. They are available either whole, for stuffing, or in pieces.

Excellent vegetable dishes

Pimientos del piquillo rellenos
Stuffed peppers from Navarra
(Photograph below, left)

For the peppers:
12 small squid
2 tbsp olive oil
1 onion, finely chopped
2 cloves of garlic, finely chopped
1 tbsp chopped parsley
2½ oz/75 g air-dried ham, finely diced
2 tomatoes, skinned and diced
1 tsp flour
Salt and pepper
12 whole pimientos del piquillo, canned

Sauce:
1 onion, chopped
2 cloves of garlic, chopped
Scant ½ cup/100 ml olive oil
4 tomatoes, quartered
2 pimientos del piquillo, canned
1 bay leaf
1 slice of toasted white bread, cut into cubes
Salt and pepper

Clean the squid; remove the ink bags and set aside. Boil the squid for 10 minutes in 4 cups/ 1 liter water; then drain, reserving the liquid. Cut the squid into small pieces, setting aside a few heads for garnishing.
Heat the olive oil and cook the onion and garlic in it gently until soft and transparent. Add the parsley, diced ham, and tomatoes. Sprinkle with flour, add some of the squid stock, and leave to thicken. Season to taste with salt and pepper and add the chopped squids. Carefully fill the *pimientos* with this mixture and arrange them side by side in an earthenware casserole. Pour in 1 cup/250 ml squid stock and heat the *pimientos* through gently. Then add the squid and also heat gently.
Meanwhile prepare the sauce by cooking the chopped onion and garlic gently in the olive oil until soft and transparent. Add the tomatoes and the *pimientos* and fry briefly, stirring constantly.
Strain the ink from the ink bags through a fine sieve and stir into the remaining squid stock. Add to the sauce with the bay leaf and toasted bread cubes and simmer for about 20 minutes. Next remove the bay leaf and purée the sauce with a hand blender. Season with salt and pepper. Pour the sauce onto a warmed plate, arrange the stuffed *pimientos* on top and garnish with the squid heads.

Menestra de Tudela
Tudela vegetable stew
(Photograph below, center)

Generous 1 lb/500 g fresh peas
Generous 1 lb/500 g habas tiernas (young fava beans)
Generous 1 lb/500 g asparagus
Salt
10 young artichokes
Juice of 1 lemon
1 tbsp olive oil or lard
4½ oz/125 g air-dried ham, finely cubed
2 garlic cloves, chopped
1 tbsp flour
1-2 cups/250-500 ml vegetable stock
Pepper

Shell the peas and beans; peel the asparagus. Cook the vegetables in lightly salted boiling water for about 20 minutes, until just tender. Remove the outer, leathery leaves from the artichokes and cook them in salted water with the lemon juice until they too are just tender. Heat the olive oil in a shallow earthenware casserole and cook the ham in it until the fat runs. Add the garlic and cook gently. Sprinkle with flour and add between 1 and 2 cups/250 and 500 ml vegetable stock, according to taste, stirring constantly. Bring to a boil and cook for a minute or two; then add the vegetables and leave to stand for a few minutes. Season to taste with salt and pepper.

Fillings for Peppers

- Ground meat with béchamel sauce *(carne picada)*
- Oyster mushrooms *(setas de cardo)* with hard-cooked eggs and almonds
- Salt cod *(bacalao)* with cream and onions
- Hake *(merluza)* with ham and eggs
- Snow crab *(centollo)* with white sauce
- Crab meat *(carne de cangrejo)*
- Lobster *(langosta)*
- Snails and mushrooms *(caracoles y setas)*
- Lamb brains *(sesos de cordero)*
- Kidneys *(riñones)*
- Spinach and Béchamel *(espinacas y bechamel)*
- Scrambled egg with button mushrooms *(revoltillo con champiñones)*

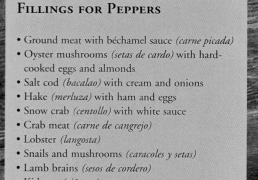
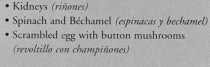

Alcachofas con almejas
Artichokes with clams
(Photograph below, right)

8 young artichokes
Salt
Juice of 1 lemon
1 tbsp flour
1 clove of garlic, finely chopped
2 tbsp olive oil
2 tbsp white wine
12 clams, cleaned

Remove the outer leaves from the artichokes. Boil the artichokes in lightly salted water with the lemon juice and a teaspoon of flour for about 20 minutes. Then remove from the water, drain and cut in half.

In an earthenware casserole fry the garlic in the olive oil until golden brown. Sprinkle over the remaining flour and add the white wine and 1 cup/250 ml artichoke stock. Cook the shellfish in this liquid until they have opened. Then add the artichokes and a little more stock if required. This makes an ideal first course. For a main course, double the quantities of ingredients.

Tortilla de esparragos y bacalao
Tortilla with asparagus and salt cod

14 oz/400 g salt cod
8 cooked asparagus stalks (bottled)
8 eggs
Salt and pepper
4 tbsp olive oil

Soak the salt cod in cold water the day before, changing the water at least twice. Next day lift the fish out of the water, pressing out any excess. Bring the fish to a boil with 2 cups/ 500 ml water; then remove from the heat and leave to stand for about 10 minutes. Drain off the water. Skin the salt cod, remove the bones, and shred the fish into small pieces.

Cut the asparagus into chunks. Whisk the eggs, carefully mix in the salt cod and asparagus, and season with salt and pepper.

Heat 1 tablespoon of olive oil in a metal pan and add a quarter of the egg mixture. Cook over a low heat until golden yellow, then turn over with the help of a plate or lid and cook the other side in the same way. Keep warm until all 4 tortillas have been cooked.

Borage

Early summer sees the arrival on the market of borage (borraja), a crop that in Spain is grown only in the provinces of Navarra and Aragon. Actually a wild flower, the blue-flowered plant was well known in earlier times for its healing properties. Borage contains many minerals, as well as a high level of vitamin C, and it is thought to be a tonic and metabolic stimulant. The robust stalks and young leaves, which have a slightly bitter taste, are the parts of the plant that are usually eaten. There are very few recipes for borage. Normally it appears on the table as a vegetable, boiled in salted water, or as a garnish for soups. Pancakes with chopped borage leaves have also become popular.

Spanish vegetable varieties

The artichoke (alcahofa) contains the bitter substance cynarine, which stimulates the liver and soothes the stomach.

Chard (acelga) contains high levels of vitamins B and C, as well as minerals.

Button mushrooms (champiñones) are mostly grown on specialist mushroom farms and are practically free of harmful substances present in the air or soil.

Spinach (espinaca) is full of flavor and rich in minerals, but it does not contain as much iron as was previously assumed.

The leek (puerro) is a member of the onion family and contains high levels of magnesium and potassium.

The cucumber (pepino) has only 15 calories per 3½-ounce (100-gram) portion and is rich in minerals.

Garlic (ajo), which is rich in minerals, also contains valuable essential oils and is thought to be effective as a remedy for disorders of the circulatory system and blood vessels.

Cauliflower (coliflor) is rich in vitamin C which is heat-sensitive; it should therefore be cooked as lightly as possible

There are several varieties of pumpkin (calabaza), which are especially popular in the Canary Islands. They contain many vitamins and minerals.

The onion (cebolla) is rich in vitamin C and has disinfectant properties.

Chicory (endibias) has a slightly bitter taste and stimulates the liver and digestive functions.

Stringless varieties of green beans (judías verdes) are the most common today. Green beans are rich in minerals.

Peas (guisantes) contain a great deal of starch and sugar, and are therefore high in calories.

White cabbage (col, repollo) contains a great deal of vitamin C and should therefore be eaten raw whenever possible.

Celery (apio en rama) has a high vitamin C content and also tastes very good raw.

There are many varieties of potato (patatas) in Spanish markets. The tubers have a high vitamin C content and are very easy to digest.

Asparagus (espárrago) consists of over 90 percent water, and contains only 15 calories per 3½-ounce (100-gram) portion. It stimulates kidney function.

Carrots (zanahorias) are low in calories and rich in carotene.

It is impossible to imagine Spanish cooking without eggplants *(berenjenas)*, zucchini *(calabacines)*, tomatoes *(tomates)*, and bell peppers *(pimientos)*. Indeed, they are the principal ingredients in the stew known as *pisto*, or the Catalan dish *samfaina*.

Fiesta time in Pamplona

"When I woke it was the sound of the rocket exploding that announced the release of the bulls from the corrals at the edge of town. They would race through the streets and out to the bull-ring."

This was how Ernest Hemingway in *The Sun Also Rises* described the famous San Fermín festival in Pamplona. Every July, in honor of the patron saint of the city, the city is plunged into total frenzy with bull-running and bullfights. The American novelist had a passion for Spain, and was fascinated by the symbolism of death that surrounds the bullfight.

The festival, which lasts for nine and a half days, commemorates Firminus, a devout Pamplona citizen, who died a martyr's death during the conversion of France to Christianity. During the festival his effigy is carried in solemn procession through the old part of the city. The climax of the San Fermín fiesta, however, is the legendary bull-run through the streets of Pamplona to the arena each morning. This race, a matter of life and death, is barely three minutes, but is enough to captivate thousands of people with its sense both of adventure and of death. In the afternoon, spectators fill the arena for the bullfight – and next morning, on the stroke of eight, the spectacle starts all over again with the next bull-run.

However, the festival in Pamplona is not devoted exclusively to San Fermín and the bulls; it is also regarded as a culinary experience of the first order. Hemingway, for instance, who was well known for his appetite for food and even greater appetite for drink, would habitually drink astonishing quantities of light Navarra rosé wine with the often very substantial meals at fiesta time.

It was once customary for the people of Pamplona to meet with friends during the fiesta for a festive banquet in one of the traditional restaurants, with seafood and lobster as the high points of such meals. Today the locals do not eat out as frequently as they used to, but wonderful cooking is still to be found in the *tabernas* and

mesones. The demand for fresh meat from bulls bred for fighting is so great that the 37,400 pounds (17,000 kilograms) of *carne de toro* available in Pamplona are not enough; steer meat from neighboring regions is therefore brought in before the festival actually begins. Braised steer *(estofado de carne de toro)* and the enormous cutlets *(chuletas)* seen sizzling on the grills in restaurants can be found all over Pamplona.

Young people are inclined to turn night into day before the bull-run. In the morning, according to old-established custom, they meet for a traditional late breakfast *(almuerzo)*. This meal includes a specialty which often takes foreigners some time to get used to: *cabeza y corada* is lamb's head with organ meat, seasoned with garlic and parsley – a relic from long ago, as is braised lamb organ meat *(patorrillo)*. However, there are of course other dishes on the table that require less of an adjustment, such as young beans, lamb ragout, or the popular drover's stew *ajoarriero*, which is made with salt cod, or even lobster, with peppers (see 89).

The *chistorra*, a thin air-dried sausage made mostly in central Navarra, is substantial fare, an eminently suitable basis for a long night of drinking. It is served fried as a tapa or snack, accompanied by fried potatoes and green bell peppers or scrambled egg. In Pamplona the specialty *chorizo cular*, the thickest version of the spicy pepper sausage *chorizo*, is kept from slaughtering time until the fiesta; because of its size it requires a long drying time. Traditionally it is sliced after the bull-run.

Chorizo cular (above), the thick pepper sausage, is not sliced until after the bull-run (left).

Meat from bulls bred for the bullfight appears during this famous festival in the guise of *estofado de carne de toro.*

Estofado de carne de toro
Braised steer

2.2 lbs/1 kg steer meat, or alternatively neck of beef
¾ cup/200 ml olive oil
3 onions, chopped
5 cloves of garlic, chopped
Salt
Pepper
2 tbsp flour
3 carrots, diced
1 cup/250 ml red wine
3 tbsp wine vinegar
2 bay leaves
2 cloves
2 hot red peppers, seeded and chopped
4 cups/1 liter meat stock
⅛ tsp cinnamon
2 tbsp chopped parsley

Wash the meat and pat dry. Cut into bite-size chunks. Heat the olive oil in a large pan and fry the meat briskly on all sides.

Add the onions and garlic and fry with the meat for a minute or so. Season with salt and pepper and sprinkle with flour.

Stir in the carrots and add the red wine and vinegar. Add the bay leaves, cloves, and peppers, then pour in the meat stock.

Bring to a boil, cover and simmer over a low heat for about 2 hours, stirring occasionally. Before serving, season to taste with cinnamon, salt, and pepper, and stir in the chopped parsley. Serve immediately.

Duck farming

Although Spaniards insist that their gastronomic culture is independent and try to disregard the French influence in their cuisine, there has always been a lively exchange of cultural and gastronomic traditions in the Pyrenean region near the French border. In Navarra it was recognized that the ducks, pigeons, and songbirds that often landed in Spanish cooking pots long ago had flown over the Pyrenees from France. Pigeons and collared doves, thrushes and swallows were popular as long ago as the 15th century, and were eaten quite unceremoniously with the fingers in Navarra, even at court.

Today the capture of songbirds is strictly prohibited. However, the pigeon catchers of Echalar continue to put out their nets every year to catch the birds when they land exhausted by the flight across the Pyrenees. Wild ducks have also traditionally enjoyed a good reputation in Navarra; the domestic duck, on the other hand, was something of a rarity, with the result that Spanish popular cookery had a limited repertoire of ways to prepare it. This also explains why the French tradition of duck farming has also taken a long time to gain a foothold in neighboring Spain.

The Landes region, France's most important center for rearing and processing ducks, lies directly over the border from Navarra, and the wave of gourmet cookery in 1970 caused many culinary influences to spill over into Spain. The first duck farm was established in Navarra in 1985 by the Martiko company, an enterprise that farms ducks belonging exclusively to the Mulard breed, and builds on the favorable results obtained by the French. Mulard ducks

Smoked duck ham (*jamón de pato ahumado*) is one of the finest delicacies from the duck farm.

are very meaty and can reach weights of up to 13 pounds (6 kilograms). As well as the fattened duck liver (*foie gras*), connoisseurs set great store by the ham made from this breed as it is more succulent and tender than that from other ducks. This is also the most important factor in producing high quality so-called *confit de pato*, or duck meat cooked in its own fat, for which the Spaniards, incidentally, have not yet coined a Spanish name. Other products on the market are fresh duck livers (*hígado de pato*), duck breast (*pechuga de pato*), duck hearts (*corazones de pato*), smoked duck ham (*jamón de pato ahumado*), and duck fillet (*solomillo de pato*), and of course whole duck.

In the meantime the pioneer of duck farming has been joined by other producers. In San Martí Sapresa in Catalonia, for instance, a subsidiary of the Mas Parés company offers both fresh and processed duck products. In addition, an increasing number of farms are being established in northern Spain on which free-range chickens are reared (*pollo de granja* or *pollo de corral*). This is because more and more cooks and chefs are viewing with a critical eye the birds that end up in their kitchens.

Ducks of the French breed Mulard feel just as much at home in Navarra as they do on the other side of the Pyrenees. The chicks are imported from France and are then reared on Spanish farms. This particular breed provides delicate livers and especially succulent ham, usually marketed as smoked duck ham.

The range of duck and goose products in Spain is becoming more varied.

Chicken *(pollo)*: the most important poultry species. A young chicken is called *pularda*, an older one *gallina*.

Capon *(capón)*: a chicken that has been castrated and then fattened up on grain. A very popular choice at Christmas.

Turkey, *(pavo, pava)*: very similar to a chicken, but larger. The meat is particularly rich in protein and low in fat.

Duck *(pato)*: strong, pale-colored meat, popular in the fall. Processed duck products are increasingly fashionable.

Goose *(ganso, oca)*: meat with a very high fat content, especially popular in Catalonia and a favorite for Christmas.

Partridge *(perdiz)*: succulent, yet very lean meat. It is often marinaded or served with a robust chocolate sauce.

Quail *(codorniz)*: exquisite meat that should be cooked with as little delay as possible. Quail eggs are also used.

Pigeon *(pichón, paloma)*: delicate meat with a faint, slightly sweet game flavor (except for domestically reared pigeons).

Pheasant *(faisán)*: firm meat with a distinct game flavor. It is usually marinaded before cooking.

Woodcock *(becada)*: delicate, slightly spicy meat. Woodcock shot in the fall are thought to be particularly tender.

Poultry in Spanish cooking

Pichones rellenos
Stuffed pigeon
(Photograph below)

2 young pigeons, with giblets
4½ oz/125 g smoked fat bacon, diced
2 cups/200 g mixed ground meat
2 shallots, finely chopped
1 clove of garlic, finely chopped
Salt and pepper
⅛ tsp cinnamon
2 tbsp pine nuts
1 tbsp breadcrumbs
2 tbsp chopped parsley
1 egg
1 tbsp lard
1 leek, washed and cut into rings
1 large carrot, sliced
½ cup/125 ml white wine
1 cup/250 ml chicken stock

Draw the pigeons, wash and dry thoroughly. Clean the giblets and chop. Heat the bacon in a dry pan until the fat runs. Add the ground meat, giblets, shallots, and garlic, and fry for 10 minutes. Remove from the heat and season with salt, pepper, and cinnamon. For the filling combine the ground meat mixture with the pine nuts, breadcrumbs, parsley, and egg. Use this to stuff the pigeons, and then secure with string.
Heat the lard in a roasting pan and brown the pigeons on all sides. Add the leek and carrot, and continue to fry for a minute or two. Add the white wine and pour in the chicken stock. Cook in a preheated oven at 350 ºF/175 ºC for about 30 minutes, basting repeatedly with the cooking liquor.
Lift the cooked pigeons out of the roasting pan. Strain the sauce through a sieve and season with salt and pepper to taste. Serve the pigeon and sauce separately.
Fresh apple compote often accompanies this dish.

Pollo al chilindron
Chicken with peppers

4 large dried red peppers
1 large oven-ready chicken, weighing about
3½ lbs/1.5 kg
Salt and pepper
Scant ½ cup/100 ml olive oil
1 large onion, finely chopped
4 cloves of garlic, finely chopped
4½ oz/125 g air-dried ham, diced
2 green bell peppers, seeded and cut into strips
3 ripe beef tomatoes, skinned and diced
1 tsp mild paprika
⅛ tsp hot paprika
2½ tbsp/40 ml brandy
1 cup/250 ml chicken stock
2 tbsp chopped parsley

Soak the dried peppers in water. Then pour off the water, drain and cut into small pieces.
Wash and dry the chicken. Divide into 8 portions and rub with salt and pepper. Heat the olive oil in a braising pan and fry the chicken pieces briskly. Remove them from the pan and place in a baking dish.
Cook the onions, garlic, and ham in the fat until they begin to brown. Add the soaked and fresh peppers and fry for a minute or two. Then stir in the tomatoes; season with paprika and add the brandy. Pour in the chicken stock and add the parsley. Simmer the vegetables for a few minutes and season to taste with salt and pepper. Spoon the mixture over the chicken portions and cover the dish with aluminum foil. Cook in a preheated oven at 350 ºF/175 ºC for about 1 hour. Serve straight from the dish.

Croquetas de pollo
Chicken croquettes

2 chicken breast fillets, each weighing about
5 oz/150 g
2 tbsp olive oil
3 eggs
2 tbsp butter
3 tbsp flour
Generous 1½ cups/375 ml milk
Salt and pepper
⅛ tsp ground nutmeg
1¾ cups/100 g breadcrumbs
Oil for frying

Fry the chicken breasts in the olive oil on both sides for about 5 minutes. Remove from the pan. Leave to cool a little, then chop quite finely in a blender with 1 egg and 1 egg yolk.
Melt the butter in a pan. Stir in the flour and cook gently until it turns pale yellow. Pour on the milk, stirring constantly, and bring briefly to a boil; then reduce the heat and leave to thicken for 10 minutes over a low heat. Remove from the stove top and stir in the chicken paste. Season with salt, pepper, and nutmeg.
Whisk the remaining egg with the egg white. Using a wet tablespoon, scoop out pieces of the mixture and form into croquettes. First roll them in egg, then in breadcrumbs, and fry in the oil in batches. Drain on paper towels and serve very hot.

Perdiz con chocolate
Partridge in chocolate sauce

2 oven-ready partridges
Salt and pepper
4 thin slices of green bacon
2 tbsp pork lard
6 shallots, finely chopped
2 cloves of garlic, finely chopped
2 carrots, diced
1 cup/250 ml white wine
2 tbsp sherry vinegar
1 cup/250 ml game or chicken stock
1 bay leaf
2 cloves
½ bunch of parsley
2 squares/50 g semisweet chocolate
A pinch of sugar

Wash the partridges thoroughly; then dry and rub with salt and pepper, inside and outside. Wrap the slices of bacon around the partridge breasts, then tie the birds securely in position using kitchen string.
Heat the lard in a braising pan and brown the partridges on all sides. Add the shallots, garlic, and carrots, and cook in the fat until they begin

Stuffed pigeon

to brown. Add the white wine, vinegar, and game stock, and season with the bay leaf, cloves, and parsley. Cover the pan with a lid and braise the partridge for about 20 minutes. Then remove from the pan and keep warm. Strain the sauce through a sieve and bring back to a boil. Crumble the chocolate and melt it in the sauce. Leave to thicken slightly and season with salt, pepper, and sugar.

Remove the slices of bacon from the partridges and put them back in the sauce. Leave to stand for 5 minutes. Serve in the sauce.

White bread or French toast is handed round as an accompaniment to this dish.

Duck with peaches

PATO CON MELOCOTONES
Duck with peaches
(see main photograph)

8 medium-size peaches
2 cups/500 ml white wine
2 tbsp sugar
1 oven-ready duck, weighing about 4½ lbs/2 kg
Scant ⅕ cup/100 ml olive oil
Salt and pepper
⅛ tsp ground cloves
⅛ tsp ground cinnamon
1 slice of toasted white bread

Peel the peaches and place in a pan. Pour in the white wine and stir in the sugar. Poach the peaches in the wine for 10 minutes; then remove from the heat and leave to stand in the wine syrup.

Wash and dry the duck. Combine the olive oil with the salt, pepper, ground cloves, and ground cinnamon. Brush this mixture over the duck, inside and outside. Then tie the duck securely in position with kitchen string.

Grease a roasting pan with olive oil and lay the duck in it. Brush with the spiced olive oil and roast in a preheated oven at 390 ºF/200 ºC for about 30 minutes, basting several times with oil. Turn the duck, pour over a few ladles of the wine syrup, and roast for another 30 minutes. At the end of the cooking time, lift the duck out of the roasting pan and keep warm.

Remove the peaches from the wine syrup. Strain the meat juices through a fine sieve into a casserole and skim off the fat. Add the wine syrup and boil rapidly to reduce. Pound the white bread with a little sauce in a mortar and pestle, stir into the sauce and cook until the sauce has thickened. Season with salt and pepper, place the peaches in the sauce and heat through. Divide the duck into portions and serve with the peaches and the sauce.

THE ZUGARRAMURDI WITCHES' COVEN

On June 23, the date of the summer equinox, bonfires burn all over Spain in honor of St. John, or *San Juan*. Each region has its own customs for celebrating this holy day, and superstition is by no means ruled out. The numerous natural caves in the Baztán valley, one of the most beautiful spots in the Pyrenees, have always had extraordinary power to unleash people's imaginations. So it comes as no surprise to learn that witches dance there every year on St. John's day.

The witches' coven of Zugarramurdi can be traced back to a historical event. In the 16th and 17th centuries, village women are said to have held black masses in the *Cueva de las Brujas*, or witches' cave, to worship the Devil, who appeared to them in the shape of a male goat. Every Friday, so it is said, they swooped down into this holy place, assisted by magic flying potions, to perform their rituals. At that time, however, the Spanish Inquisition was raging throughout Spain, including Navarra. In 1610, 40 women from the Zugarramurdi area were accused of witchcraft by the inquisitorial tribunal in Logroño, and 12 of them were burned at the stake. Despite this, many natives of Navarra remain devotees of the black arts to this day – if only for one day a year. They meet eagerly on St. John's day at the Zugarramurdi witches' coven to re-enact the ancient rituals of exorcism, known in northern Spain as *akelarre*. The villagers, dressed in witches' costume, dance around a huge fire until all the lights in the cave are extinguished as darkness falls. Men cloaked in sheepskins then make their entrance. The silence is broken only by the bells attached to their clothing and when they beat the ground with sticks. This pagan custom aims to drive out evil spirits.

Roncal

For centuries the people living in remote Pyrenean valleys were obliged to eke out a thoroughly wretched existence. The flocks of sheep they kept provided the sole reliable source of income for mountain people, and there were sometimes as many as 150,000 sheep roaming the countryside on the nomadic shepherds' tracks. In order to prevent disputes and over-grazing, local authorities began to regulate sheep husbandry at a very early stage. The seven main districts in the Roncal valley amalgamated during the Middle Ages, forming a cooperative known as the "union of the seven villages of the Roncal valley" *(Universidad de los siete pueblos de la val de Roncal)*. This regulated the times when the flocks were permitted to descend to the pastures in southern Navarra, and the times when they were driven back up to their native villages. Summer grazing land was allocated on an equitable basis, and was able to recover quickly as a result of the restrictions imposed. As well as permitting efficient husbandry of the pastureland, this perfect arrangement also solved significant social and ecological problems in the region as a whole.

Farmers in all the Pyrenean valleys in Navarra today still produce cheese traditionally from raw unpasteurized milk. The most famous cheese from the mountains of Navarra, *Roncal*, is manufactured between December and July. The lambing season falls in the winter and early part of the year and the sheep therefore produce sufficient milk during this period. Genuine *Roncal* cheese is made exclusively from raw ewe's milk from sheep belonging to the Lacha and Rasa breeds. Animal rennet is used and the cheese must be matured for at least four months. Young *Roncal* cheese has a slightly sharp flavor and is unusually buttery for a ewe's milk cheese; in the advanced stages of ripening it then develops its rounded, piquant character. Its outstanding quality led the Spanish government to bestow on *Roncal* in 1981 the first legally protected designation of origin, Denominación de Origen (D.O.), ever accorded to a cheese.

Every August the regional producers gather at the Roncal cheese fair to display their wares, which include thick ewe's milk curds known as *cuajada* or *gaztanbera*. This product is still made by hand on many farms, and in homes and restaurants, sometimes even using the traditional kaiku birchwood churn. As this cannot be placed over direct heat, stones are heated in a fire and plunged into the ewe's milk with a pair of tongs. As soon as the temperature of the milk is 100 °F (38 °C), fermentation is induced by the addition of animal rennet. This is a digestive enzyme obtained from the stomachs of newborn lambs (though artificially produced curdling agents have now largely replaced animal rennet). The thickened liquid is poured into small earthenware pots to cool.

The comparison that is frequently drawn between *cuajada* and yogurt is misleading; although their consistencies are similar, *cuajada* does not taste in the slightest degree acidic. It is characterized by a faint aroma of sheep, and if prepared in the traditional way using heated stones, it has a slightly smoky flavor.

The milk for *Roncal* is obtained from sheep of the Lacha and Rasa breeds in the Pyrenean valleys of Navarra.

Of the many varieties of sharp cheese made in the Pyrenees, *Roncal* is one of the best known. Many producers make it from unpasteurized raw milk.

Matured *Roncal* cheese is distinguished by its pronounced sharp flavor. It is usually served thinly sliced as a tapa.

Cuajada is fermented ewe's milk with a mild flavor. When it is made in the traditional way, using hot stones, it has a pleasantly smoky taste.

THE PILGRIM'S ROAD TO SANTIAGO DE COMPOSTELA

"Ultreia!" sang the pilgrims of St. James in the Middle Ages, as they traveled from Roncesvalles in the Pyrenees to distant Galicia, urging themselves "Onward! Onward!" through dark forests and over passes, in biting cold and scorching heat. This song accompanied millions of pilgrims on their journey to Santiago de Compostela, where they hoped to find redemption and spiritual peace.

The road taken by the pilgrims to Santiago *(Camino de Santiago)* is one of the most important pilgrimages in all European Christendom. Back in the early Middle Ages, pilgrims from practically every known country journeyed to the cathedral of Santiago de Compostela to pay homage to the apostle James the Elder (see page 248). Their long and arduous journey led them over the Pyrenees, then westward through the whole of northern Spain to their destination in Galicia. The typical pilgrim could be recognized by his dress – a voluminous cape, a broad-brimmed hat, a stave, a drinking vessel fashioned from a gourd, and a leather bag carried over the shoulder.

Over 460 miles (740 kilometers) of the pilgrim's route was on Spanish soil, and nearly a quarter of it passed through Navarra. The descent from the Pyrenees, from Roncesvalles to Pamplona, was considered particularly difficult in medieval times. Inns, hospitals, churches, and monasteries sprang up all along the arduous route. Pilgrims were cared for free of charge and were able to recover from their exertions. With the passage of time the pilgrim's route became a highly important trade route, along which new grape varieties from the Rhine and Moselle regions of Germany gradually spread, eventually reaching Galicia. Other commercial goods, as well as architectural styles, customs, and ways of thinking, also reached medieval Spain in the same way – and there was a reciprocal movement back over the Pyrenees to central Europe.

The way through unknown territory was found in the 12th century *Codex Calixtinus*, which can be regarded as the first medieval travel guide: it describes in minute detail the route to Santiago de Compostela and its places of religious worship. In those days the journey was measured according to the time it would take a horserider; the distance from the border between Navarra and France to Santiago de Compostela was reckoned to take 13 days. In addition to descriptions of the various stages of the journey and extremely amusing descriptions of the Spanish peasantry (see example below), the pilgrim's guide also gives an enormous amount of culinary advice, especially with regard to the delicate game and poultry dishes for which Navarra was famous even in those days.

Nevertheless, the traveler's simple fare appeared rather meager; rations for the journey included dry bread and hard cheese, with a little dried meat for the more affluent. The exhausted pilgrims were then fed and their strength restored in the monasteries and hospitals. In Roncesvalles alone, 25,000 emergency rations, consisting of a piece of bread and a cup of wine, were distributed to needy pilgrims each year. On feast days rations were supplemented by a little boiled mutton, and during Holy Week there might even be salt cod, pickled sardines, and vegetable broth on the table.

Today there are still many monasteries and inns lining the Spanish section of the route, some of which still offer lodging to pilgrims.

The two branches of the pilgrim's route from France meet in Puente la Reina. Since medieval times every pilgrim who makes the arduous journey to Santiago de Compostela has had to cross this bridge.

DIFFERENT TIMES, DIFFERENT CUSTOMS

The people of Navarra wear black tunics so short they only reach the knee, Scottish-fashion. Their shoes, which they call *lavarcas*, are made from untanned leather, still covered with hairs, and are bound to the feet with straps so that only the soles of the feet are protected, leaving the back of the heel exposed. They wear dark woolen coats that reach to the elbow, in the manner of a traveling coat, and they call these *saias*. They are poorly dressed, and they do not eat and drink well. The food is all mixed together in one pot, and it is the custom for all dwelling in a Navarra household – stableboy and master, maidservant and mistress – to devour it not with spoons, but with the hands, and they all drink from the same cup. To watch them eat is to imagine oneself confronted by dogs or pigs.

(From: *Codex Calixtinus*, c 1140)

The pilgrims in the Middle Ages were less fortunate than their modern counterparts; here, at the Bodega Irache, the pilgrim's fountain dispenses wine or water – welcome refreshment for pilgrims and tourists, and a clever marketing ploy.

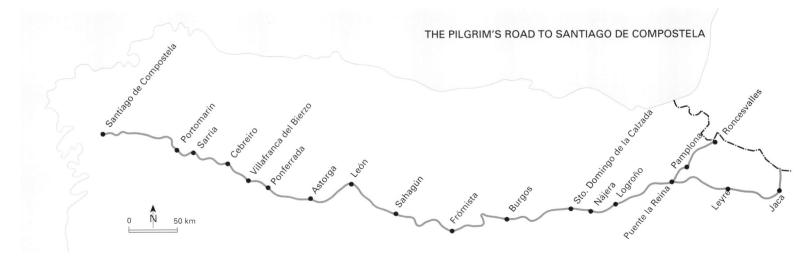

THE PILGRIM'S ROAD TO SANTIAGO DE COMPOSTELA

Santiago de Compostela · Portomarín · Sarria · Cebreiro · Villafranca del Bierzo · Ponferrada · Astorga · León · Sahagún · Frómista · Burgos · Sto. Domingo de la Calzada · Nájera · Logroño · Pamplona · Roncesvalles · Leyre · Jaca · Puente la Reina

0   50 km   N

NAVARRA WINE COUNTRY

Navarra is known to have been wine-making country even in Roman times – an ancient wine cellar has been excavated near the tiny village of Funes that had a capacity of nearly 20,000 US gallons (75,000 liters) about 2000 years ago. In the early Middle Ages, the monasteries that were gradually springing up along the pilgrim's route to Santiago de Compostela provided the focus for winemaking, and the reputation of the wine was spread from there throughout the world by the pilgrims who came from all over Europe.

ROSÉ WINES

For centuries Navarra has produced rosé wines in preference to any other kind, but the vintners for the most part pressed the grapes too heavily, and without a controlled cold fermentation the resulting *rosados* often had an oxidized flavor and were pale in color. Contaminated cask wines with a distinctly vinegary tang were not uncommon.

The continued domination of rosé wines in the region today is due to the fact that Navarra vintners, following the vine weevil disaster at the beginning of the 20th century, began planting the less susceptible Garnacha grape variety on a massive scale. Because of its tendency to oxidize rapidly, this grape variety is hardly suitable for producing durable red wines, so for decades *rosados* of rather dismal quality, marketed as cask wines, were the norm.

The breakthrough did not come until the 1950s, when the cooperative Vinícola de Navarra began draining the crushed grape mass (consisting of must, skins, stems, and seeds) after a fermentation lasting only a few hours. Without the aid of mechanical pressing, the must thus obtained, known as *lágrima*, or "tears," is released only by pressure from the weight of grapes above. It is then fermented.

After fermentation the wine has a distinctive luminous candy-pink color and an intense flavor of raspberries and strawberries. The procedure has been enshrined in the statutes governing wine production in Navarra, and brought the extremely fresh-tasting Rosados de Navarra global acclaim. By contrast, rosé wines in other regions and countries mostly continue to be produced from grape must that has undergone at the very least a light pressing.

NEW TRENDS

From 1970 onward, persuaded that they could produce great white and red wines as well, pioneers such as Juan Magaña began larger-scale planting of French grape varieties such as Cabernet Sauvignon and Merlot, as well as the aristocratic Spanish variety Tempranillo. At about the same time the wine research institute E.V.E.N.A. (Estación de Viticultura y Enología de Navarra) was founded, whose trial vineyards contained over 30 varieties of grape. The result is a magnificent panoramic landscape of wines in Navarra, due to the wide range of varieties and the very different types of wine on offer. Some of the blends of Tempranillo with Merlot or Cabernet Sauvignon now rank alongside the

The luminous candy-pink color alone would earn modern vinified rosé wines from Navarra their status as a jewel in the Spanish winemaking crown.

best wines produced in the country. With its modern methods Navarra has become a model for many Spanish wine-making regions.

The diversity of the wines produced in the **D.O. Navarra** demarcated wine-making area is mainly due to the differing climatic conditions of the five zones into which the area is divided.

In **Tierra Estella**, the northwestern sector, the Atlantic weather results in wines that are almost central European in character, including some good Chardonnays. Similar conditions are found in **Valdizarbe** in the north, where elegant, exquisitely fruity wines are produced in hilly countryside. **Baja Montaña** is the farthest east of all the zones and is undoubtedly influenced by the mountain climate; rosé wines from the Garnacha grape predominate here. **Ribera Alta** is the wine-producing center of Navarra and makes juicy wines, rich in extract, the character of which owes a great deal to the Mediterranean climate. **Ribera Baja** is the southernmost zone and accounts for 30 percent of the total area devoted to grape cultivation in Navarra. The area also produces Chardonnays.

ROSADO OR CLARETE?

This question is surrounded by confusion. *Clarete* is a term traditionally signifying a light red wine, *rosado* a rosé. In Castile and some other regions, however, the term *clarete* is also used to describe rosé wines. Indeed, it was once common for blends of red and white wines to be sold under this description – a method of production which has since been strictly prohibited by the E.U. in Brussels. Yet surprises are still possible. Nobody who dares order a *clarete* will ever know what exactly is in the glass – a genuine rosé; a wine with a high proportion of white grapes in the must that has turned red following fermentation; or even the despised mixture of red and white wine.

The reason for the confusion is that it was once normal to have mixed vineyards; red and white grapes were harvested and pressed together. The resulting light red wines were commonly known as *claretes*. Nowadays, however, the white grapes are usually pressed separately. The freshly pressed white wine must is then added to the red must, and they are fermented together as if making red wine. A genuine *clarete*, which can still be found in Valdepeñas today under the label Tinto de Valdepeñas or Aloque, contains at least 25 percent red grape must in the ferment. A genuine *rosado*, on the other hand, is pressed from red grapes that are fermented for a few hours before pressing. This fermentation is essential, since almost all red grape varieties in the world have white pulp that produces white must, like that from white grapes. The color is acquired only from the skin of the grape. To enjoy a genuine rosé wine, then, it is important to be armed with the right word when ordering – *rosado*.

The five zones into which D.O. Navarra is divided, each with a distinctly different climate and soil, make it one of the most diverse wine-making regions in Spain. The largest of the five, Ribera Baja (above) produces robust wines.

The pioneers of the Navarra wine revolution include the Magaña winecellars. For a quarter of a century this bodega has shown that Navarra can produce not only red wines that are rich in extract, but also magnificent rosé wines.

Pacharan

How very fortunate for those of a sensual inclination, when the pleasures of the flesh can be scientifically justified. *Pacharán*, for example, the traditional sloe liqueur from Navarra, is thought to be beneficial for the stomach and nervous system. Some resourceful medical practitioners even go so far as to claim that *pacharán* – consumed in moderation, of course – is effective in preventing heart attacks and arteriosclerosis.

Originally the national liqueur of Navarra was confined to farms, where it was usually made by the grandmother of the family.

The blue-black sloes *(pacharanes* or *endrinas)*, which are the fruit of the blackthorn tree, were picked in late summer and simply immersed in spirits. Later on, sloe-gatherers, or *pacharaneros*, began selling the fruit in the towns as well; the hoteliers rolled up their sleeves and very soon the liqueur was also being dispensed in city taverns.

Pacharán is very simple to make at home; sweet or semisweet spirits, with a slight flavor of aniseed, are poured into a bottle one-third full of very ripe sloes. A cinnamon stick or a few coffee beans can also be added, according to taste. The liqueur must then be left to stand for two to four months, shaking occasionally to enable the flavor of the sloes to permeate the spirits evenly. Villagers often stand the bottles on south-facing window sills to accelerate the process of making pacharán.

Since this Navarra specialty gained popularity throughout Spain, various brands of industrially produced pacharán have appeared on the market. Their alcohol content is between

Sloes, the fruits of the blackthorn tree, give flavor and color to the *pacharán*. To make the liqueur, sloes are steeped in sweet or semi-sweet aniseed-flavored brandy.

20 and 30 degrees, and no artificial flavorings or colorings are permitted.

The level of production has increased to such an extent that the sloe crop growing wild in Navarra is no longer adequate, and some of the fruit required has to be imported. Since 1992 blackthorn plantations have been established specially for the purpose of *pacharán* production.

Pacharán is best enjoyed as a *digestif* after a meal, at a temperature of between 37 and 45 °F (2 to 7 °C). The bottle should be well chilled; passionate devotees of pacharán advise strongly against ice cubes in the glass, as these dilute the liqueur too much. In the era of mixer drinks, a number of long drinks based on *pacharán* have become established – sloe liqueur is excellent mixed with orange or pineapple juice, and especially good with a shot of sherry.

Healing Elixirs

Since time immemorial, farmers and vintners have distilled spirits wherever they could find fruit and grapes. Strong drink is said to have enjoyed such great popularity in Navarra during the 18th century that the morals and work ethic of the general populace left much to be desired. It was for this reason that in 1757 the parliament of Pamplona prohibited the sale of drinks containing a high percentage of alcohol, with the exception of those serving a medicinal purpose; for a time spirits were available only on prescription. The people of Navarra were resourceful, however; the wide availability of both cultivated and wild fruit and herbs enabled all kinds of liqueurs to be produced. These had a lower alcohol content than hard liquor, explaining their therapeutic use in cases of gout. Alcoholic fruit and herb extracts have in fact always been considered infallible remedies for every complaint imaginable. The monasteries played an important role in the production of these sweet elixirs, as they always had a herb garden, and very often an apothecary's store *(botica)* containing all kinds of dried herbs, seeds, and spices. As a result the monks and nuns became truly expert at making liqueurs. They prepared elixirs using fennel, camomile, mint and angelica, roseships, blackberries, sloes, and bitter cherries. In the monastery at Leyre, on the route through Navarra followed by the pilgrims to Santiago de Compostela, the monks are still producing a liqueur from 30 different plants. A popular herb liqueur is also made in the monastery at Montserrat in Catalonia.

In many private households people continue to make liqueurs based on aniseed brandy as their grandmothers did, either with camomile, crab apples, or quinces. However, there are alternatives to herbs or fruit soaked in alcohol; one simple, but rather odd, variation is a cucumber liqueur flavored with aniseed *(anís de pepino)*. In the garden a clear glass bottle is placed over a cucumber plant bearing a young fruit. When the cucumber has grown to the required size, the stem is cut and the bottle, with the cucumber still in it, is topped up with aniseed-flavored spirits. After 40 days the liqueur is ready for drinking; it is said to be an effective remedy for colic pains.

Another recipe that has been handed down through the centuries uses green walnuts *(licor de nueces verdes)*. Green walnuts are placed in a vessel with 40 percent wine alcohol and water, with the addition of a little nutmeg, cinchona bark, lemon juice, and sugar. This mixture must then be left to stand for six weeks. In some regions of northern Spain this drink is also known as *ratafia de nueces*. Although it is not strictly speaking a liqueur, another popular festive drink in the wine regions of Navarra, La Rioja, and the Basque provinces is *zurracapote*, a kind of northern Spanish variant of Sangría. It is made from red or rosé wine with water, sugar, cinnamon, cloves, and lemon juice or peel. The drink is served cold in an earthenware jug.

In the monastery at Leyre (above), monks make liqueurs for both medicinal purposes and pleasure, just as in the Middle Ages (see main picture).

The essential extract for the liqueur is prepared from over 30 different herbs. In earlier times these came from the apothecary's store inside the monastery.

La Rioja

David Schwarzwälder

La Rioja

Grapes are La Rioja's gold, because the region depends almost entirely on wine. Here, grape juice is the elixir of life, providing jobs, income, and lots of pleasure.

"Do not encumber yourselves with a baggage train and travel light, because in this land you will find everything you need: linen shoes from Cervera, wool blankets from Ezcaray, baskets for provender in San Andrés, and moreover, everywhere hearty food, and glorious wine." To self-indulgent souls like the author Camilo José Cela, the smallest region in the Spanish mainland looms large in terms of the good things in life. La Rioja, the land on the banks of the Rio Oja, is regarded throughout the world as the premier home of quality Spanish wine. The picturesque scattering of vineyards is protected from all but the most extreme weather by the mountain ranges to the north and south. The east is flat, dry, and has an almost Mediterranean climate, while the west is damp and mountainous.

The Ebro meanders from east to west across 125 miles (200 kilometers) of gently undulating countryside. Fruit and vegetables flourish here – and, of course, the world-famous wine. As early as the first half of the 13th century, this wine is supposed to have inspired the monk Gonzalo de Berceo to intellectual flights of fancy. He devised the first verses ever written in Castilian Spanish by a famous author – inspired by the juice of the noble grape – in his study in the monastery of San Millán de Suso. "Henceforth I desire to create simple prose – exactly the same as people use with their neighbors, because people are not so well-educated as to have mastery of another language. I believe a glass brimming with good wine is best suited to this purpose." The region's culture flourished when King Sancho III of Navarra drove the Arabs from

the area and took up residence at Nájera. From 1076, La Rioja mostly belonged to old Castile; today it is an autonomous region in the kingdom of Spain. Its income is not just from wine – an abundance of fruit and vegetables grows here, while the mountains provide sheep and game, together with snails and mushrooms, which fill the larders of a people whose traditions are closely interwoven with those of the neighboring regions of Navarra, Aragon, Castile, and the Basque country. As a result, the cuisine is extremely varied, but clear distinctions from the neighboring regions are hard to spot. The culinary identity of La Rioja lies in the detail. In addition to the wine, which is flourishing strongly thanks to modernization, this includes chili sausage, goat's milk cottage cheese, and glowing red bell peppers which dry outside in the fall.

Santiago de Compostela
Vitoria-Gasteiz
Pamplona
León
Logroño
La Rioja
Barcelona
Valladolid
Zaragoza
Madrid
Toledo
Palma de Mallorca
Valencia
Mérida
Ciudad Real
Murcia
Sevilla
Granada

Opposite: the grapes at San Vicente de la Sonsierra grow on historic ground – the border between the kingdoms of Navarra and Castile once ran through here.

In La Rioja, grape harvesting is done by hand almost everywhere. Most vines are bush-trained, so modern machines cannot be used to aid the process.

Even in the vineyard, the wine-producers ensure that as few leaves or unripe grapes as possible are mixed in with the harvest. They can impair the wine.

Each year, at harvest time, migrant harvest labor converges on La Rioja. With the winemakers they must bring in the whole harvest in just a short time.

Many wine-producers still transport grapes to the bodega loose, on trucks. Modern businesses usually have stacking crates to protect the delicate fruit.

VITICULTURE

Today Haro is a tranquil little town in La Rioja. There is nothing to show that the community was once one of the richest in Spain. One hundred years ago three casinos, a lively nightlife, and a branch of the Spanish issuing bank lent Haro a very cosmopolitan atmosphere. The town achieved prosperity when phylloxera hit the vineyards in neighboring Bordeaux in the 1880s. In order to respond to the shortages there, massive wine shipments left Haro's rail station, heading for France, and returned with considerable wealth for the area.

There is very little trace now of the chic atmosphere, but Haro is still one of the most important wine towns on the Iberian peninsula. La Rioja's climate is mainly exposed to Atlantic influences due to the proximity of the Bay of Biscay. The Ebro valley is also affected by Mediterranean weather systems and continental influences. This sensitive meteorological balance of moderate temperatures, adequate rainfall, and occasional damaging frosts creates the right conditions for elegant wines. In general, due to the changing climatic conditions, quality is heavily dependent on the vintage. As is true for many other celebrated wine regions in Europe, genuine outstanding years in La Rioja are few and far between.

The current **D.O.C. La Rioja** wine-producing region is divided into three sub-regions, which extend into the neighboring areas, and produce different types of wine. La Rioja Alta, in the west, is famous for fine, elegant wines with only a moderate alcohol content. La Rioja Alavesa, which lies in the Basque country, produces especially fruity wines. Deep red grapes with high potential alcohol grow on the alluvial plains of the Ebro, in La Rioja Baja, which extends from east of Logroño to Navarra.

The most important grape in La Rioja is the fruity Tempranillo, which is regarded as altogether the premier Spanish grape variety. This is supplemented by the Garnacha, which lends color and body, the acidic Graciano, and the powerful and tannin-rich Mazuelo. White grapes account for only about ten percent of the area under cultivation, with the Viura taking center stage. Malvasía and Garnacha blanca are used only in small quantities for blending.

Although La Rioja is now one of the most modern wine-producing regions in Spain, viticulture has remained largely traditional. Hundreds of small family firms produce the grapes, which are later turned into wine by large cooperative cellars and bodegas. Vines are bush-trained across most of the area under cultivation, with low bushes, which means a lot of work, because only limited use of machines is possible.

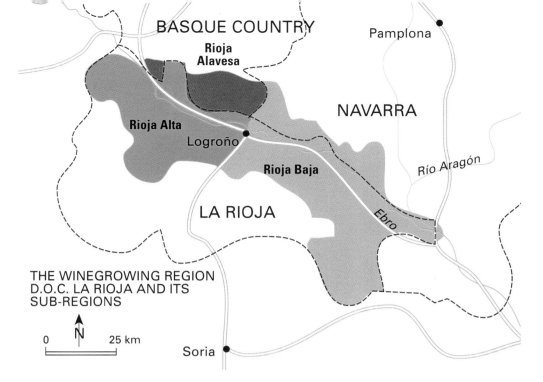

THE WINEGROWING REGION
D.O.C. LA RIOJA AND ITS
SUB-REGIONS

0   25 km
N

THE MAJOR GRAPE VARIETIES IN LA RIOJA

1 **Tempranillo:** the most important grape variety in La Rioja. It provides character and powerful, evenly structured wines.
2 **Garnacha:** the main variety from La Rioja Baja, mostly used for blending, harmonizes superbly with Tempranillo.
3 **Graciano:** mostly used for blending, it has very low yields. It lends acidity, freshness, and bouquet to the wine.

4 **Mazuelo:** also used for blending; small berries. It introduces acidity and aging potential.
5 **Viura** or **Macabeo:** the most important white variety in La Rioja, often used for young, lively, single variety white wines.
6 **Malvasía:** used in the same way as **Garnacha blanca** (not illustrated) to round out white wines.

In winter, the winemaker cuts back the shoots on the vine with shears to a specific number of buds, in order to focus the vine's strength. In very fruitful years, winemakers who are particularly quality-conscious go into the vineyard in July and cut out some of the bunches of green grapes, which are scarcely pea-size at this stage.

This "green harvest" gives the remaining grapes greater strength and also improves the wine's quality. The grape harvest begins in September in La Rioja and is, for the most part, purely manual labor. As few unripe grapes and leaves as possible should get mixed with the harvested grapes, because they might impair the quality of the wine.

A quality revolution means that some *bodegas* have introduced sorting tables. The grapes run along a conveyor belt, with leaves and damaged fruit being removed by hard-working helpers. The good grapes can then be made into the famous La Rioja wine, well-known throughout the world. The care taken at this time ensures that La Rioja's reputation is sustained.

At odds over wood

The quality of the wood used in the barrels plays a decisive role in aging a red wine. New wood releases tannin into the wine and slows the breakdown of the red pigments. This is why wines matured in wooden casks change color only very slowly. With time, however, minute quantities of oxygen penetrate the cask through the pores in the wood and react with the contents. This so-called micro-oxidation allows the wine to age slowly, and to mature too. The advantages of long-term storage in wood also include natural fining of the wine, since the residue is automatically eliminated by constant racking from barrel to barrel. (Racking is the process of "clearing" wine by siphoning it off from the dregs.) All these factors contribute to the clear, ruby-red color which glows in a classic, wood-matured La Rioja wine.

Wine enthusiasts always argue about whether French or American oak imparts the correct flavor to the wine – without ever reaching a definite conclusion. The classic *barrica*, as used in La Rioja, is produced from American wood. In 1996, some 650,000 such *barriques* were in use in the wine region, of which only 8 percent were made from French oak. The fundamental difference lies in the wood's structure; American white oak is more compact and has smaller pores than Limousin oak. Thus less oxygen can penetrate the barrel, and the wine develops more slowly. French oak imparts a sweeter taste, releases more tannin and flavor in the early years, but does not last as long as American oak. Furthermore, French barrels are almost twice as expensive as the American competitors. The decision to use either of the woods does not usually depend on price, however, but on the winemaker's taste and the type of wine he is trying to achieve. A wine matured in new French oak has stronger vanilla flavors, and is more familiar to many central European palates. New American oak has a less toasty flavor, but an unsuppressed, natural woody taste. Whether there really is a difference in quality will remain a matter of debate for all eternity. The ultimate judgment is one worthy of Solomon – it's all a matter of taste. Many people no doubt prefer the New World oakiness of American wood, but some may object that it does not belong in Europe.

AT THE COOPERAGE

The cooperage Tonelería Mecánica Riojana has been making barrels since 1898. Early on, the wooden casks served purely as containers for beer and pickled gherkins. But as the demand for wine barrels in La Rioja rose considerably, around the turn of the century, there was a speedy conversion to the French cask measure of 60 gallons (225 liters), and production began of the barrels known by the French term *barriques*, or *barricas* in Spanish. Suitable stands of oak were scarce in Spain, and very soon the coopers of La Rioja were importing their wood from the United States. The best white oak comes from Kentucky, Ohio, and the Appalachian Mountains in the state of Pennsylvania. There the wood is sawn along the grain, seasoned for a few months, and then shipped to Spain. At the cooperage, the boards are sawn to a thickness of 1⅜ inches (34 millimeters) and then stored.

In the meantime, Tonelería Mecánica produces around 11,000 *barriques* a year. Although a few modern machines are used in the process, coopering is still a genuine craft. The cooper selects suitable wood, and cuts it into 38 inch (95 centimeter) lengths with a band saw. In order to achieve the smoothest possible surface, he planes the planks on both sides by machine. Next the sides of the planks are gently rounded off with the saw – the staves are now ready for the barrel.

The cooper alternately places wide and narrow staves vertically on the rim of the barrel base, which are then squeezed together with temporary steel bands. In order to make the wood more pliable, the half-finished cask is next treated inside with hot water or steam, and then charred. To do this the cooper turns the barrel upside down over a small fire. The greater the "charring," the more the toasted flavor will be dominant in the wine later. Finally the cooper puts on the cask lid, and once more carefully planes the exterior of the barrel. The working bands can now be replaced by the proper barrel bands. To check the finished barrel's watertightness, and to clean it at the same time, it is filled with hot water. The cask is disinfected through the judicious use of sulfur, and then it is ready for use.

In the cooperages of La Rioja, repairing barrels is now just a small part of the work, because most of the large wineries employ their own coopers, who devote all their time to repairing used casks. The big cooperages are kept very busy with making barrels, because ultimately a good *barrique* makes a decisive contribution to the characteristics of a mature La Rioja wine. The wine's taste depends on both the barrels and the grapes.

1 The majority of the wood for *barriques* comes from America. It is imported to La Rioja in a rough-milled state.
2 The planks for barrels are sawn to 38 inches (95 centimeters) and then machine-planed.
3 Now the cooper positions staves of varying widths on the base of the barrel and secures them with temporary bands.

4 The barrel is shaped with the help of steam. Humidity and warmth make the wood pliable.
5 The soft staves are now pulled tight with the steel bands, until they take on the shape of a barrel.
6 The cooper turns the barrel upside down over a small fire. Charring the barrel gives the wine its toasted flavor later.

7 All that's missing now is the lid. For this, shorter pieces of wood are held together with thin metal pins.
8 After it is rounded off and planed, the lid must be individually adapted to every single barrel.
9 The lid is inserted into the rim of the barrel and knocked into place. Then the barrel gets the final bands.

As a finishing touch, each barrel receives the stamp of the cooperage, a trademark which will last for decades.

VINIFICATION

Toward the end of the 19th century, the first wine estates to mature their wines in *barriques* were established in La Rioja. Until that time, the only technique known here was oxidative wine-making in large wooden vats. As these were often quite poor quality wines, the French specialist Jean Pineau was brought to the area to teach a selected group of La Riojan estate owners the French method of making wine.

As the end of the century approached, more French wine merchants and winemakers came to La Rioja from Bordeaux, looking for replacements for their ravaged vineyards. It was at this time that the first great wineries, or *bodegas*, with massive warehouses and thousands of *barriques*, came into being. Thus started the story of a wine which today enjoys a world–wide reputation.

The La Rioja Alta estate is still regarded today as a bastion of traditional winemaking in La Rioja. As early as 1890, 3500 Bordeaux casks had been procured. The *bodega* has since concentrated on maturing wines in *barriques*, the small oak barrels which hold 60 gallons (225 liters).

To make a classic La Rioja wine, the grapes are stripped from the stalks after harvesting and

The wines are still racked by hand in the La Rioja Alta *bodega*. The winemaker first has to remove the bung from the cask before fitting the spigot.

The pulp is fermented in large fermentation tanks. Skins and fruit pulp impart color, tannins, and flavor to the juice, which is then run off.

The fresh, young wine streams from the barrel into an open tub. It is then transferred from this to another cask. A typical La Rioja red wine will be racked time and again over the period it matures in the barrel. With every racking the deposits remain on the bottom of the barrel and so, in time, the wine becomes clearer and clearer.

pressed. The resulting pulp is fermented in tanks. Skins and fruit pulp impart tannin, color, and flavor to the juice. The winemaker decides how long the juice remains in contact with the skins, depending on the type of wine required. The longer the maceration period, the more tannin and color is imparted to the juice. Excess maceration may, however, introduce undesirable astringents to the wine.

At La Rioja Alta, the winemaker often restricts the maceration period to a maximum of 15 days, even for premium-quality wines. Afterwards the juice is "drawn off." The free-run juice is run off, the pulp is gently pressed, and then the resulting press juice is put into fermentation tanks, where malo-lactic fermentation takes place. For the second, or malo-lactic fermentation, the juice is usually put into stainless steel tanks, or sometimes into massive wooden vats. During this stage, the malic acid contained in the grapes will be converted into lactic acid. For the time being, there is no question of the wines being described as having a fine bouquet; quite frankly, they stink.

After malo-lactic fermentation is complete, the winemaker separates the wines according to quality, and transfers them to oak barrels, after several rackings. The young wines, which still contain many deposits in suspension, must be racked again after just a few months, in order to draw the deposits from the barrels. In the cellars of La Rioja Alta, all qualities of wine are still racked by hand, without a pump, from top to bottom in rows of barrels stacked on top of each other. The liquid residue is later filtered, and offered to the employees, because according to an old law, a winery worker in this *bodega* is entitled to 2 pints (1 liter) of wine a day, and a further 64 pints (32 liters) a month, which he can take home.

Depending on whether the wine is to be matured as a Crianza, Reserva, or Gran Reserva, the red wines spend a certain amount of time in an oak barrel, whereby the prescribed maturation periods (see 143) are usually exceeded. In the sealed barrel, the wine is safe from damaging influences such as direct contact with the air and light, so that the components of the taste can develop and combine well. Furthermore, the wood imparts tannin to the wine and simultaneously increases its aging potential.

After aging in the cask the wines are filtered and bottled. In order for maturation to be completed, all qualities of wine now spend a certain period aging in the bottle, so that the wines become balanced and develop structure before they are sold. Bottle aging can smooth the rough edges off the wine's still rather coarse tannins, and balances the multi-faceted flavors. Such complexity of flavor is enjoyed by Rioja drinkers all over the world.

Preparations being made for racking, transferring the wine from one barrel to another: the cellar master first removes the bung that closes the barrel's outlet.

Next the spigot is fitted, but as yet the wine cannot flow. It is held back by the valve and the atmospheric pressure in the airtight cask.

When racking, only so much wine is run off from a barrel, until the precipitate – in other words, the part which contains the deposits – is left on the bottom of the barrel. The cellar master checks the condition of the wine again and again, with a clear glass and a candle. The color and clarity show how the wine is maturing.

In order to clean the barrels, a long iron chain is immersed inside. This is shaken thoroughly, thus removing impurities from the wood.

After the barrels have been cleaned mechanically, they are purified with sulfur, to eliminate bacteria. To do this, a sulfur candle is lit and then placed in the barrel.

Important bodegas in La Rioja

R. Lopez de Heredia

This winery, founded in 1877, is a legend in the Riojan wine world. Here, red and white wines are still always vinified according to strictly traditional methods. Wines from every great vintage of the 20th century are stored in the branching underground cellars. The Viña Tondonia red wines are finely crafted jewels, while some of the cask-matured white *Gran Reservas* are among the area's most extraordinary wines.

Bodegas Marqués de Murrieta

This fantastic estate close to Logroño, founded in 1872, is the second oldest *bodega* in the region, after Marqués de Riscal. Wines from this winery are characterized by powerful acidity when young, and are very slow to develop. Even in advanced age, they retain a liveliness that gives them a special place in the wines of the region.

Bodegas Muga

This winery has its headquarters in the railroad district of Haro, and adheres to a method of vinification not changed, in many respects, since the winery was founded in 1932. Fermentation is still carried out in wooden tubs made in the winery's own cooperage, and the wines are fined with egg white. The Prado Enea Gran Reserva is particularly highly regarded all over Spain.

Bodegas Breton

The *bodega* was first founded in 1983. Limiting production to 2.2 million pounds (1 million kilograms) of grapes makes it possible to maintain a constantly high level of quality. The wines are matured in American oak only. The best known are the Loriñon white wines, and red Dominio de Conte.

C.V.N.E.

The winery equipment at Compañia Vinícola del Norte de España (C.V.N.E.), founded in 1879, is always the most up-to-date; the fermentation room with rotary fermenters is famous. The *bodega* makes very good, cask-matured red wines, and a modern white wine. In 1974, C.V.N.E. founded the Viñedos del Contino estate in La Rioja Alavesa, where one of the most innovative La Rioja wines is produced.

Bodegas Juan Alcorta

This is one of the region's wine estates that controls the market due to its size alone. Over 70,000 *barriques* are stored in the underground cellars. The range of products stretches from simple white wines to the demanding Marqués de Villamagna Gran Reserva, which is only sold in exceptional years.

Bodegas Riojanas

The traditional house, from Cenicero in the La Rioja Alta, is still a family business, and owns over 200 hectares (494 acres) of the best vineyards in the region. The winery produces classic blended wines with attractive ripeness. Fermentation is still partly carried out in large oak vats.

Bodegas Roda

The new *bodega* in the railroad district of Haro produces a first growth wine (Roda I) and a second growth (Roda II), following the French trend. The grapes for both wines may come only from vineyards which are at least 30 years old. The first growth wine is only produced in very good years. It is characterized by a deep, dark color and unusual richness, and is the prototype of a modern La Rioja wine.

Marqués de Riscal

The oldest *bodega* in La Rioja was founded in 1860 by the Marqués of Riscal. The first wines in the region matured in *barriques* were developed here. The estate is very quality conscious and produces only *Reserva* and *Gran Reserva* quality wines. The grapes come only from vineyards which are at least 20 years old, and are still sorted in the bodega by hand.

Bodegas Martinez Bujanda

This *bodega* is one of the most reliable wineries in the whole of Spain. The *bodega's* cellars in Oyón contain in excess of 2.5 million bottles. The wines, which are known under the Conde de Valdemar brand, are characterized by their fruit and fullness. The winery plans to expand considerably over the next few years, with the construction of a new *bodega*.

Cosecheros Alaveses

The simple Cosechero red wines, vinified using the carbonic maceration method, have been made socially acceptable by this estate, which is known to many people by the brand name Artadai (se 177). Meanwhile, however, the *bodega* is far better-known for its wood-matured top wines such as Viñas de Gain, Viña El Pisón, Pagos Viejos, and the most expensive wines in La Rioja, the Reserva Especial Grandes Añadas.

Bodegas Campillo

This spectacular young estate was founded in 1990. Only premium-quality wines are produced from grapes grown on the estate's own 50 hectares (124 acres) of vines. The architectural pearl below Laguardia belongs to the owners of the Faustino Martinez winery.

Granja Nuestra Señora de Remelluri

This estate lies close to Labastida, and is one of the most attractive in the whole of La Rioja. It is managed by the son of the family, who trained in Bordeaux. Red Riojas are produced by following the château method – in other words, purely with grapes from one's own vineyards. The house produces only *Reservas* and *Gran Reservas*, which are usually characterized by concentrated fruit.

La Rioja Alta: The *bodega*, founded in 1890, still vinifies its wines according to traditional methods. In accordance with an old custom, practically the only casks used in this winery are American oak.

Top wines from La Rioja

904
Gran Reserva 1987
(La Rioja Alta): delicate
smoky aromas; ripe fruit;
long and timeless.

Viña Tondonia
Gran Reserva Blanco 1976
(Bod. López de Heredia):
delicate acidity; classic oak;
elegant hints of age.

Dominio de Conte
Reserva 1994
(Bodegas Bretón):
fruity; richly flavored,
with lively acidity.

Viña Albina
Gran Reserva 1987
(Bodegas Riojanas): ripe
raspberry and strawberry
flavors; soft tannins.

Castillo Igay
Gran Reserva 1964
(Marqués de Murrieta):
marked acidity; delicate
mix of oak and fruit.

Imperial
Gran Reserva 1989
(C.U.N.E.):
finely balanced with deep
fruit flavors; long.

Marqués de Vargas
Reserva 1994
(Marqués de Vargas):
chocolatey; fruity;
powerful.

Prado Enea
Gran Reserva 1987
(Bodegas Muga): elegant;
fine ripe fruit; classic
mature oak flavors.

Faustino I
Gran Reserva 1987
(Faustino Martínez):
ripe; good length with
lots of potential.

Campillo
Gran Reserva 1987
(Bodegas Campillo):
smooth tannins; neat
fruit.

Marqués de Arienzo
Gran Reserva 1987
(Bodegas Domecq):
round; soft, red
fruit flavors.

Barón de Chirel
Reserva 1994
(Marqués de Riscal):
highly concentrated late
developer.

Contino
Reserva 1991
(Viñedos del Contino):
closed; bouquet of charred
wood and tobacco.

Viña El Pisón
Reserva 1994
(Cosecheros Alaveses):
concentrated; minerally;
soft tannins.

Viña Pomal
Gran Reserva 1982
(Bodegas Bilbainas):
venerable; soft, ripe
tannins; fine fruit.

San Vicente
Reserva 1994
(Señorío de San Vicente):
cinnamony, with glowing
cherry fruit.

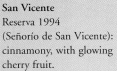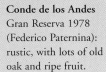

Conde de los Andes
Gran Reserva 1978
(Federico Paternina):
rustic, with lots of old
oak and ripe fruit.

Remelluri
Gran Reserva 1989
(Granja Nuestra Señora
de Remelluri): extremely
compact, lots of tannin.

Quality standards for La Rioja wines

The officially stipulated quality standards in the
Denominación de Origen Calificada (D.O.Ca.)
Vinos de La Rioja relate to the length of time the
wines have matured in *barriques*, and in bottles.
The label on the back of the bottle provides
information on the quality of the wine. Quality
standards, however, represent only a statutory
minimum maturation period. Many traditional
businesses in La Rioja allow their wines to age for
far longer than prescribed by the controlling
body, which leads to a very complex range of
great wines. It specifies the following categories:

Vino sin crianza / vino joven
A young La Rioja whose rear label shows only the
designation *Garantía de origen* (guaranteed region
of origin). This wine – whether white, rosé, or red
– is sold when just a few months old. It may well,
have been matured in oak, too, for a time before
bottling.

Crianza
A wine in this category must be at least two years
old, one year of this being spent in the cask for red
wines, and six months for white and rosé wines,
before bottling.

Reserva
Red wines in this category may leave the winery
only after they have matured for three years, 12
months of which period have to be spent in
barriques. White *Reservas* require a total of 24
months, six months of which in the barrel.
Almost no rosé *Reservas* are produced any more.

Gran Reserva
These wines require a
maturation period of at
least 24 months in oak
barrels and further 36
months in bottles. A
few traditional *bodegas*
still produce white

Gran Reservas, which are among the great white
wines of the world. The prescribed maturation
period is a total of 48 months, six months of
which must be spent in oak barrels.

143

Vintage wines

Generally, in La Rioja, as in other wine-producing areas of Europe, only wines from very good vintages really age. Not only are there requirements specific to the area, such as a climate which is not too mild, and poor, chalky soil (so that the grapevine really has to battle to survive and develops long roots), but the vinification of La Rioja wine is also decisive for its aging potential. Long maturation in *barriques*, first in new wood, and later in used casks, strengthens the structure of the tannin and protects the wine's fruit.

Cellars with an even temperature of 50–55 °F (10–12 °C), and stable humidity of between 70 and 80 percent, are important for maturing the wine. Although the wines change due to long maturation in wood, even very well-aged Riojas, whose fruit and tannin have already been consumed by age, retain a certain acidity which lends them life. This makes these wines so unique that most *Gran Reservas* from the region can age for 20 to 25 years without a problem. When the best storage conditions are present, La Rioja wines from exceptional years can reach 60 years of age, or even older. If you are lucky enough to open an old La Rioja (1964 or older), the wine should not be decanted, just allowed to breathe briefly before pouring. Most old Riojas shake off the dusty storage smell of vintage wines very quickly, and you should take the opportunity to enjoy the secondary and tertiary aromas, before they evaporate.

Wine is best stored in a dark and well-ventilated cellar, at a temperature between 55 and 60 °F (12 and 16 °C), and 60 to 70 percent humidity. Basically, the bottles should be stored in a horizontal position, so that the cork always remains in contact with the wine. Apartments, and even cellars in modern houses, are usually too warm and dry for this sensitive drink. If you don't have a wine cellar, it would be a good idea to purchase a special wine storage cabinet (also known as a temperature-controlled wine store) to store fine vintages, so that you will be able to enjoy the precious drops for as long as possible. Vintage wine can be very expensive, and it would be a shame nor to be able to enjoy the delicate flavors of La Rioja at their best, the wine having been stored in the right environment for many years.

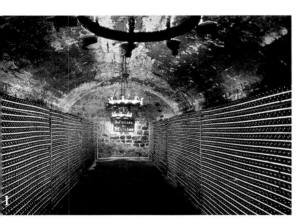

1 Wine is best stored in damp, cool cellars. Low temperatures and high humidity provide the correct climate for fine wines, as shown here in the old, vaulted cellars of Bodegas Paternina.

2 Good La Rioja wine generally matures for several years in oak casks before being bottled – and even then it is not ready for sale. It is bottled and matures in bottles for a very specific period.

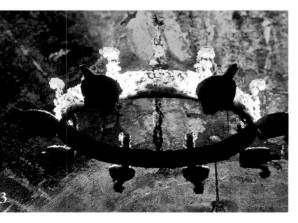

3 Cobwebs and rust in a *bodega* are not first-hand evidence of traditionalism – and have nothing to do with sloppiness. They are simply unavoidable when a damp climate suitable for storing wine prevails in such deep, vaulted cellars.

4 The casks are marked with chalk, so it is possible to see how often the wine has been racked. The six marks on cask number 3014 indicate six rackings, with the last having taken place on July 1, 1997.

Rioja Vintages

La Rioja vintages are officially classified by the controlling body according to how good they are:
E = excellent, VG = very good, G = good, A = average, P = poor

2003 G	1986 G
2002 G	1985 G
2001 A	1984 A
2000 G	1983 G
1999 G	1982 E
1998 VG	1981 VG
1997 G	1980 G
1996 VG	1979 A
1995 E	1978 VG
1994 E	1977 A
1993 G	1976 G
1992 G	1975 VG
1991 VG	1970 VG
1990 G	1968 VG
1989 G	1964 E
1988 G	1958 E
1987 VG	1955 E

Wine-tasting

Whether with friends in your own living room, buying wine at a *bodega*, or with professionals in the trade – the most important way of assessing wine is to taste it *(cata)*. Ultimately, you can confidently rely on the human senses being more sensitive than any refined chemical-physical analysis. Above all, the nose is by far superior to any technology for the purpose of perceiving the aromas and flavors.

Usually groups of wines with similar characteristics, such as white wines aged in

The eye enjoys a drink too: first the glass, filled one-third full, is held up to the light, in order to assess the consistency, color, and clarity of the wine.

When you smell the wine, its "nose" gives the first indication of the range of flavors, and the bouquet. The first impression the aroma makes is decisive.

It is only when you taste it that the wine reveals its true self in terms of richness, body, and tannins. The flavor which lingers is important too.

barriques, or red *crianzas* from one vintage, are tasted "blind," with the label concealed. At the same time the wines are evaluated according to appearance, nose, taste, and "body," the feeling which develops in the mouth as the wine is tasted, and which it leaves behind. The number of points that a wine achieves is calculated according to a system that is primarily based on these criteria.

A ten-point system prevails in Spain. Of course, wine-tasting is a very personal matter. Basically, any kind of description which helps wine enthusiasts explain complex nuances of smell and taste is permissible. Many years of experience, however, have led to the development of a jargon that is not always comprehensible to everyone. Terms such as "lemon," "raspberry," "smoky," or "vanilla" are understandable and unambiguous. Attributes such as "elegant," "slender," or even "wet saddle," which creep into wine-tasting notes time and again seem, on the other hand, extremely subjective and dubious. Even professionals do not interpret all of these terms in the same way.

So how does one go about tasting wine? The glass, which should be filled one-third full, is first held up to the light, or against a white surface, and inspected closely. It is possible to determine in this way whether the wine is clear. The color of the wine provides information about its age and condition. The general rule is, the more purplish and deeper the color, the younger the wine. As a wine ages, it first has red-brick or russet colors, which later shade to brown. The change can always be detected on the rim of the liquid first: therefore another term which is used is "age rim."

The "tears," which run down from the rim of the glass when the wine is swirled, may be a sign of a wine rich in qualities. But beware: the tears may also indicate an excessive alcohol content, which will immediately be confirmed on the nose.

After the visual assessment, the foot of the glass is moved in small circles on a firm surface, so that the liquid swirls, and the aromas have a chance to develop. After the wine's "nose" has been assessed, take a sip, and let it roll over your tongue. Never take too big a gulp of wine! There should still be enough room in the mouth for a little air, because this allows the delicate flavors to rise up between the mouth and nose. After tasting the wine, a professional taster notes down his discoveries, stage by stage, and the results are discussed when the tasting is completed.

Wine-tasting is an acquired skill, which takes patience to develop. Once you are able to distinguish the many aspects of the flavor of wines, the experience is very enjoyable.

Quality wines from Spain

Since Spain joined the European Union in 1986, Spanish wine regulations have been amended to comply with European guidelines. As a result there is now differentiation between table wines and quality wines, and the Spanish system of quality wine control is one of the strictest in the world. Each Spanish quality wine region with the designation D.O. *(Denominación de Origen)* has its own supervisory body, the *Consejo Regulador*. This controlling body includes the president, appointed by the Ministry of Agriculture, as well as representatives of Spain's winemakers, wineries, and merchants. The controlling body regulates, amongst other things:
• the areas under vine
• viticulture (grape varieties, density of planting, pruning, harvesting, etc.)
• vinification (volume of juice, vinification, and maturation)
• chemical and sensory analysis of the finished wines
• control of sales.

The *Consejo Regulador* only issues the back labels with the inspection numbers to wines which comply with all the respective D.O. quality standards. These labels make it possible to trace every bottle to its point of origin. The only Spanish wine region to hold the protected *appellation* D.O.Ca. *(Denominación de Origen Calificada)* is La Rioja. In this, the highest category, specifications are even stricter and the quality standards higher than for a normal D.O. Above all, the quality of the grapes, vinification, and sale are most strictly regulated here. You will find descriptions of all the Spanish quality wine regions in the wine sections for the respective regions described in this book.

Even when simply pouring wine, connoisseurs observe closely how the wine flows into the glass. This gives them an indication of the consistency, and the age.

FRANCE

GALICIA   ASTURIAS

CANTABRIA

BASQUE
COUNTRY

NAVARRA

CASTILE-
LEÓN

LA RIOJA

CATALONIA

ARAGON

PORTUGAL

MADRID

VALENCIA

BALEARIC ISLANDS

EXTREMADURA

CASTILE-
LA MANCHA

MURCIA

ANDALUSIA

CANARY ISLANDS

LANZAROTE

LA PALMA

LA GOMERA

TENERIFE

FUERTEVENTURA

EL HIERRO

GRAN CANARIA

0   100 km

N

Winegrowing regions
with protected appelation (D.O.)

D. O. Cava

WINEMAKERS' CUISINE

A stone hut points the way to the place of worship – the smoke stack rising up from the ground is the first sign of a cave *bodega*, then the door cut into the mountain is revealed. These underground wine cellars can be traced back to the prehistoric Iberian race of La Rioja. Because nature had eroded hardly any hollows in the plains of the Ebro, the Iberians dug out their places of worship themselves. They met here for religious ceremonies, paid homage to higher powers, and also sacrificed animals as part of a ritual sun worship. They consecrated the best

Below: the winemakers of La Rioja like their food. After all, their hard work makes them hungry. They enjoy meeting in their cave *bodegas*, in the evening, for a chat.

cuts of meat to the gods and the rest was grilled on the fire, then consumed. The Iberians probably also drank ready-fermented juice during their festivals.

The Riojanos have been storing their wine in these caves since the early Middle Ages, until the first great wineries were established in the villages around 1900. But even after that, the underground *bodegas*, which are located on the slopes of mountains near many communities, remained social and culinary meeting places. On weekends, people meet here at sunset, to savor a communally prepared meal and good wine. Guests are also welcome and so, then as now, cave *bodegas* are regarded as the epitome of Riojan hospitality.

On warm fall evenings, the scent of vine wood fires rises into the air, lamb chops *(chuletas de cordero al Sarmiento)* sizzle on the barbecue over glowing coals, with juicy red bell peppers from the garden. The popular lamb stew *calderete*, on which there are countless variations with

vegetables, potatoes, or pulses, also belongs with a winemaker's hearty meal. Dried salt cod, potatoes, or snails are also often served *a la riojana*, with tomatoes and the spicy red peppers, which can be seen hanging out to dry on many balconies all over La Rioja in the autumn.

PATATAS A LA RIOJANA
Potato stew La Rioja style

½ cup/125 ml olive oil
2 onions, peeled and sliced
2 green bell peppers, seeded and diced
Generous 2 lbs/1 kg potatoes, peeled and diced
5 cloves of garlic, peeled and minced
4 dried red bell peppers
1 bay leaf
1 cup/250 ml dry white wine
Salt and pepper to taste
⅛ tsp cayenne pepper

Right: the time to serve *pochas con codornices* – tender young fava beans with quails – is in spring, when the young vegetables are ripening in gardens along the Ebro.

Heat the olive oil in a saucepan. Sauté the onions and the green bell peppers in the hot oil, until they start to brown. Add the diced potatoes, garlic, dried red peppers, and bay leaf. Then add the white wine and top up with enough water to cover the vegetables completely. Season to taste with salt, pepper, and cayenne.

Bring to a boil, then put the lid on the saucepan, and simmer over a medium heat for about 25 minutes, or until the vegetables are tender. Remove the red bell peppers and the bay leaf, reserving the red peppers. Chop the red peppers. Adjust the seasoning with salt and cayenne. Sprinkle the chopped red bell peppers over the stew and serve immediately.

CALDERETE
Lamb stew

½ cup/125 ml olive oil
8 oz/250 g lamb's liver
1 tsp sweet paprika
1 cup/250 ml dry white wine
1½ lbs/750 g shoulder of lamb, boned and cut into ½ inch/1.25 cm cubes
2 onions, peeled and chopped
3 cloves of garlic, peeled and minced
Salt and pepper to taste
2 carrots, peeled and sliced
1½ lbs/750 g potatoes, peeled and diced
1 bay leaf
1 fresh red chili, seeded and finely chopped
1 red bell pepper, seeded and diced
4 artichoke hearts

Heat 2 tbsps of the olive oil in a skillet. Sauté the lamb's liver until sealed. Remove from the skillet, put in a food processor with the paprika and white wine, and blend to a smooth purée.

Heat the remaining olive oil in a large saucepan. Add the cubed lamb and sauté quickly until browned. Add the onions and garlic, reduce heat, and sauté until the onions start to soften. Add enough boiling water to cover the lamb. Season to taste with salt and pepper. Cover the skillet and simmer over a medium heat for approximately 40 minutes.

Add the carrots, potatoes, bay leaf, chili, bell pepper, and artichoke hearts, then stir in the puréed liver. Bring the stew to a boil again, cover, and simmer over a low heat for about 30 minutes, or until the meat is tender, adding more hot water if necessary. Season to taste with salt and pepper before serving.

POCHAS CON CODORNICES
Baby fava beans with quails
(Photograph above)

4 oven-ready quails
Salt and pepper to taste
1½ lbs/750 g fresh fava beans
3 tbsp olive oil
1 onion, peeled and sliced
2 cloves of garlic, peeled and minced
1 bay leaf
5 slices/150 g prosciutto, chopped
2 red bell peppers, seeded and diced
1 tomato, halved

Rub the quails with salt and pepper, then tie them up with kitchen thread. Shell the beans. Heat the olive oil in a large saucepan, or flameproof casserole. Sauté the onion and garlic until translucent. Add the beans, bay leaf, and chopped prosciutto, together with 4 cups/1 liter of hot water. Bring to a boil, add the quails, and simmer for 10 minutes. Then add the red bell peppers and tomato halves, and simmer for another 20 minutes. Serve with crusty white bread, and preserved green chiles.

Variation: If you want a heartier dish, sear the quails first in hot oil, and add them to the beans halfway through cooking.

TRUCHAS CON SETAS AL VINO TINTO DE LA RIOJA
Trout with mushrooms in red Rioja wine

4 trout, cleaned and gutted
Salt
Pepper
½ cup/125 g butter
Generous 1 lb/500 g wild mushrooms (e.g. porcini, chanterelles), cleaned and sliced
1 cup/250 ml red La Rioja
1 cup/250 ml hot meat stock

Preheat the oven to 355 °F/180 °C. Rinse the trout, pat them dry, and rub them with salt and pepper.

Butter a roasting pan, and lay the trout side by side in it. Add the mushrooms and dot the trout with the remaining butter. Bake in the oven for 10 minutes.

Add the red wine and meat stock, and cook the trout for another 10 minutes.

Remove the trout from the oven and arrange on a warmed serving dish, together with the mushrooms. Carefully strain the juices through a sieve, into a clean saucepan. Bring to a boil and simmer until the sauce is slightly reduced and thickened.

Season to taste with salt and pepper. Pour the sauce over the trout, and serve immediately.

GOLMAJERIAS

The La Riojanos are not just lovers of sweet treats, they even have their own word for them. Here, all sweets are known by the old Arabic word *golmajerías* and, in the Arabian fashion, two of the best-known desserts are made from almonds. No one knows why the marzipan balls, *mazapanes de Soto*, developed in the Cameros mountains, of all places: not a single almond tree grows in the harsh climate of the Sierra. Be that as it may, the paste is prepared from almonds, boiled potatoes, sugar, and lemon zest, and shaped into balls. These are then placed on top of wafers, and dried in the oven. Finally they are dipped in a sugar syrup. *Fardalejos*, small puff pastry pockets which are filled with an almond mixture, and deep fried, come from Arnedo. Available throughout Spain puff pastry *milhojas* are filled with cream, flavored crème patissière, or liqueurs, and also enjoy great popularity with sweet-toothed La Riojans. Visitors to the area are also no doubt seduced by the wonderful variety of La Riojan desserts.

The Spanish adore the lightness of puff pastry. It is absolutely irresistible with warm vanilla and/or chocolate sauce *(milhojas calientes)*.

Mazapanes de Soto, marzipan balls made of a boiled potato and almond paste, come from the village of Soto en Cameros.

Boozy Desserts

Melocotones con vino
Peaches in wine (photograph left)

4 large, firm peaches
3 cups/750 ml red wine
3 tbsp sugar
2½ tbsp brandy
1 cinnamon stick

Peel the peaches. Put them into a saucepan where they just fit snugly. Blend together the red wine and sugar, and pour it over the peaches. Add enough water to cover the peaches completely. Add the brandy and cinnamon, then bring to a boil. Reduce the heat and simmer the peaches very gently, until tender. Serve hot or cold, as liked, with a little of the syrup.

Sorbete de La Rioja
La Rioja wine sorbet

¾ cup/150 g sugar
1 cinnamon stick
1 cup/250 ml red La Rioja
Grated zest of 1 orange
2 egg whites
Mint leaves to decorate

Put the sugar in a saucepan with the cinnamon stick and a scant cup/200 ml of water. Bring to a boil and simmer until the sugar has dissolved completely and the syrup is clear. Remove the cinnamon stick and let the syrup cool.
Mix together the sugar syrup, red wine, and orange zest. Beat the egg white until it forms soft peaks, then fold into the red wine mixture. Transfer the mixture to a metal bowl and place in the freezer for 3 hours. Break up the ice crystals occasionally by whisking with a balloon whisk. Before serving, the sorbet should be whisked again, then divided between chilled glasses. Decorate the sorbet with mint leaves.

Variation: The sorbet can also be served in tall glasses, which are then topped up with chilled Spanish sparkling wine (Cava).

Camerano Cheese

"Our *Camerano* is the only cottage cheese in Spain with character. Why should La Rioja need more types of cheese?" a fan from La Rioja once crowed. The good man may indeed have rated the cheese of his homeland above all others, or perhaps he just wanted to excuse the lack of a wider choice. Indeed, it is amazing that a region which produces such a wide range of high quality wines has never developed a cheese industry worth the name. The only cheese that can be considered a genuine Riojan product is the *Queso Camerano* in question. It comes from the Sierra de los Cameros, the mountains to the south of the Ebro which, geographically and culturally, cut off the fruitful river valley, with its world-famous wine–producing region. This is why this cheese is completely unknown, even to many inhabitants of La Rioja. It is rarely available in restaurants; it is most likely to be found in good delicatessens in the area, or at local outdoor markets. The production area for *Camerano* cheese lies in the high valleys of the Sierra, and includes a small part of the Castilian province of Soria. Formerly, the farmers produced the moist cottage cheese in their mountain huts almost exclusively for their own use. Because it keeps for only ten days at most, it never became as popular as its delicate flavor merited. For some years now, though, a cheese-maker has been producing the gastronomic relic using a modern process and, despite manual production methods, is able to produce about 300 cheeses per day.
Camerano cheese is made from the unpasteurized milk of mountain goats, which are milked only once a day. In the fall and winter, when the animals are fed in stalls, 12½ cups (3 liters) of milk make about

2 pounds (1 kilogram) of *Camerano*, whereas in summer, when the goats graze on the mountainside, and the milk is less rich, it takes 21 cups (5 liters) of milk to make about 2 pounds (1 kilogram) of cheese.
The milk is coagulated for about three hours, using animal rennet. Previously the curds were then packed into the typical wicker baskets of the area, a practice which is now banned, for reasons of hygiene, for cheese which is to be sold commercially. The baskets have therefore, unfortunately had to be replaced by plastic tubs.
A *Camerano* cheese weighs between 1 and 2 pounds (500 grams and 1 kilogram), and differs from many other types of curd cheese due to its spicy taste. Gourmets in the know particularly enjoy the Riojan goat milk cottage cheese with anchovies from Santander. Otherwise it is usually served as a dessert, either with *carne de membrillo*, the Spanish quince bread, or with herby mountain honey from La Rioja.

Below: the mountain farmers of La Rioja have been making their goat milk cottage cheese for centuries. It was formerly packed in wicker baskets, but now it is sold in plastic tubs (above).

País Vasco

Harald Klöcker

BASQUE COUNTRY

A good *Idiazábal* cheese, and perhaps a glass of wine to go
with it; like these farmers, many Basques maintain their
national culture and stand up for their independence.

"The Basques are generous, and hospitable, and sometimes astound with their greediness and love of drinking. A Basque eats as much as three Andalusians together – and exceptionally well." The German Walter Haubrich, an authority on Spain, used these words to describe his culinary experiences in the Basque country. And yet the region on the Bay of Biscay was not always blessed with plenty. A Bohemian pilgrim noted in 1416, "Horses are no use in this country. There is no hay, no straw, and no stabling; moreover, the inns are poor. Wine comes in goatskin sacks. There is neither bread nor meat nor fish, people mainly eat fruit." In the Middle Ages many Basques were seamen, because there was so much poverty, and they helped to conquer the New World. The Basque country only caught up with the times in the middle of the 19th century, when one of the most important centers of Spanish industry grew up around Bilbao, with its shipbuilding and heavy industry. Poets and philosophers such as Pío Baroja and Miguel de Unamuno come from this region, and today many citizens of the Basque country can be found in top positions in politics, finance, and the Church. The Basques have always looked to maintain their independence, though. They defend their individuality patriotically, and regard themselves as Basques first – and as Spanish only second. They have withstood conquest and oppression, such as the prohibition of the Basque language during Franco's rule, with passionate nationalism and a strong sense of unity. The Basques love their homeland, have never completely abandoned their farming traditions, and enjoy a markedly communal way of life. This also includes communal cooking in gastronomic societies. The Basques like to spend money on food and drink, and lots of it. Fish and seafood, vegetables and meat, game, mushrooms, and wine all come from their region. Furthermore, many raw materials from other areas are here transformed into refined delicacies for the first time. Following the lead of a few top chefs, Basque cuisine has been going through a phase of creative renewal over the last 30 years. Inspired by French *nouvelle cuisine*, the Basque country is nowadays regarded as Spain's uncontested gourmet stronghold. Do not expect to find artificial creations here, though; the only thing which matters to Basque cooks is the absolute freshness and pure flavors of the very best basic ingredients. Traditional dishes are given a new dimension by using unusual ingredients with very carefully matched, complementary flavors. Moreover, the Basques are unique in Spain, being true masters of the use of refined sauces.

País Vasco

Santiago de Compostela
Bilbao
Vitoria-Gasteiz
León
Pamplona
Barcelona
Valladolid
Zaragoza
Madrid
Toledo
Palma de Mallorca
Valencia
Mérida
Ciudad Real
Murcia
Sevilla
Granada

Right: from the island of Santa Clara, looking toward San Sebastián, which the Basques call Donostia – the most elegant coastal resort on the Bay of Biscay.

BACALAO

In 1871, a Spanish fish merchant called Gurtubay, from Bilbao, ordered *30 o 40 hatillos de bacalao* from Norway. There, however, the "*o*" was misread and he was supplied – would you believe it? – not with "30 or 40 bundles of dried cod," but with 30,040. The poor man was facing financial ruin. But just a short while later, the third Carlist War broke out. Bilbao was besieged, provisions were running out, and finally, only Gurtubay was still able to supply the population – with almost endless quantities of dried cod. The fish merchant made a fortune from the pauper's fish.

The Vikings valued dried fish as a foodstuff on their long sea crossings. After the discovery of the Americas, Portuguese seamen sailed to the coast of Newfoundland to catch cod. On the ships the fish were gutted and heavily salted, being dried on the rocky seashore under the home sun, only after weeks at sea. "Stockfish" is also dried on large wooden frames, but without salting. However, the name has been adopted for salted, dried fish too.

In the 16th century, Spanish fishermen also discovered *bacalao*, and the Basques introduced it to the whole of Spain. The dried fish could be transported to every part of the country, without the need for special cooling equipment and so, especially in the interior, it became an important source of protein, particularly for Fridays and the Lenten fast.

Because stocks of cod in the oceans of the world have been drastically reduced by overfishing, *bacalao* has become expensive. Much of it is now caught off the Scandinavian, African, and American coasts.

Allow 4–6 ounces (100–150 grams) stockfish per person for a main meal. Before preparation, the fish has to be "reconstituted" by soaking. Usually *bacalao* is soaked in cold water for 24 hours, the water being changed two to four times during this period. Very thick pieces should be soaked for 36 hours; 12 hours is long enough for pieces which are very thin. For the last two hours, it is best to soak the *bacalao* in warm water, to be sure of drawing out all the salt. The fish can then be drained, patted dry, and prepared.

Over the last few years, creative Basque cooks have rediscovered the delicate flavor of fresh cod. *Bacalao fresco* is popular when carefully poached with mussels or seafood; in wafer-thin slices like carpaccio; or delicately smoked. Cod roe is also regarded as a delicacy – a fish at one time eaten only by the poor has now made it big.

PURRUSALDA
Stockfish with leeks and potatoes
(Photograph bottom left)

10 oz/300 g stockfish
½ cup/125 ml oil
1 onion, peeled and finely diced
2 cloves of garlic, peeled and finely diced
4 medium potatoes, peeled and diced
2 leeks, washed, trimmed, and cut into 1–1½ inch /3–4 cm chunks
1 bay leaf
Salt and freshly milled pepper, to taste
A few saffron threads

Soak the stockfish for 24 hours, changing the water twice at least. Place the fish in a large skillet, or fish kettle, and add 2 cups/500 ml water. Bring to a boil, and simmer on a low heat for about 8 minutes. Lift the fish out of the pan with a fish slice, drain, and leave it to cool a little. Reserve the fish stock. Skin and bone the fish, and cut into small chunks. Heat the oil in a saucepan, add the onion and garlic, and sauté until translucent. Add the diced potatoes, leeks, and hot fish stock, and season with the bay leaf, salt, and pepper. Bruise the saffron, with a splash of fish stock, in a mortar, then stir it into the stew. Add the chunks of fish. Cover the pan, and simmer for about 25 minutes, or until the vegetables are tender.

CARPACCIO DE BACALAO FRESCO
Carpaccio of cod (Photograph bottom left)

Generous 1 lb/500 g piece of cod fillet
Juice of 1 lemon plus 2 unwaxed lemons
Salt to taste
1 tsp pink and 1 tsp black peppercorns
4 tbsp olive oil

Rinse the cod, pat it dry, and wrap in aluminum foil. Put it in the freezer for 2 hours. Take it out and slice it very thinly, using a sharp knife. Divide the cod slices between 4 plates, and arrange them in overlapping layers. Drizzle the lemon juice over the cod, and season to taste with salt. Lightly crush the peppercorns in a mortar and scatter them decoratively over the cod. Then drizzle the olive oil over the fish. Garnish each plate of *carpaccio* with half a lemon, and serve immediately.

BACALAO A LA VIZCAINA
Stockfish Biscay style

1¼ lbs/600 g stockfish, in pieces
8 large, dried red bell peppers
Salt to taste
½ cup/125 ml olive oil
4 slices bacon, diced
4 slices prosciutto, diced
3 Spanish onions, peeled and diced
4 cloves of garlic, peeled and minced
1 tbsp fresh, white breadcrumbs
2 tbsp chopped fresh parsley
½ tsp cayenne pepper
1 cup/250 ml hot fish stock
Freshly milled pepper to taste

Soak the stockfish for 24 hours, changing the water twice at least. Soak the bell peppers in water for 1 hour, take them out of the water, and scrape out the flesh. Drain the fish, pat it dry, and remove any bones. Preheat the oven to 350 °F/175 °C. Season the fish sparingly with salt. Heat the oil in a large skillet, and sauté the fish for about 5 minutes on each side. Do not let it brown. Remove the pieces of fish from the oil, and reserve them.

Sauté the bacon, prosciutto, onions, and garlic in the oil until translucent. Stir in the pepper flesh, breadcrumbs, and parsley. Season to taste with cayenne and a little salt, and add the hot fish stock. Simmer the sauce for about 40 minutes, adding a splash of water if it is reducing too much. Season the sauce with pepper to taste, and pour about one third of the sauce into a flameproof dish. Place the pieces of stockfish on top, skin uppermost, and pour over the remaining sauce. Bake in the oven for about 15 minutes. Serve immediately.

The fish stew *purrusalda* (top right) is made from stockfish, the fine *carpaccio* from fresh caught cod.

The bacalao trade

In many towns there are fishmongers who specialize in the sale of *bacalao*, and sell the dried, salt cod in various forms.

- *Bacalada* is the name for whole *bacalao* (up to 2 feet/60 centimeters long). Larger specimens are cut into portions that are then sold individually.
- *Morro* and *lomo* are thick and squarish or rectangular, bone-free pieces. They are thus the most valuable parts of the stockfish; *filete* is the name for the strip either side of the backbone.
- *Vientre* or *loncha* is the name for the belly portion of *bacalao*, flat, long-grained pieces, usually without bones (frequently cut into triangular shapes and therefore also known as *oreja* – ear).
- *Cola* – the rear part of the fish with the big bones, has strong-flavored, often rather tough flesh.
- *Rosario* is the name given to the main bones and the flesh on them. This cut is primarily suited to making fish stocks and sauces.

Above: Fresh cod is dried on wooden frames and thus cured to make "stockfish." If, on the other hand, it was dried on rocks at the edge of the sea, it would in the past have been known as "klippfish." Nowadays, after the obligatory salting, the fish is usually dried in specially ventilated rooms, due to the great demand and vast quantities produced.

Below: *Bacalao*, dried cod, is sold in highly specialized stores. Prices for the individual cuts of fish vary greatly.

In the *bacalao* store, whose strong aroma pervades the street outside, the dried fish can be cut into conveniently sized portions.

In order to be able to use stockfish in cooking, it must first be soaked in water thoroughly, to remove the salt. This takes between 24 and 36 hours.

HAKE

The hake lives in a shoal, and during winter it becomes extremely sluggish. The reason is that at this time, the predatory fish encounters huge shoals of sardine along the coastline, and then becomes extraordinarily gluttonous. During the day it rests in deep water, but at night it rises very close to the surface, to hunt. The hake then consumes enormous quantities of the tiny fish. It stuffs itself so full that it loses a lot of its maneuverability. Slow and clumsy, as though in a daze, it then becomes easy prey for fishermen. It is no wonder then, that Spanish metaphors based on the hake (*merluza*) are not exactly flattering: *cojer una merluza* doesn't mean "to catch a hake," but "to drink oneself stupid." And if someone calls you a *merluzo*, you will have to come to terms with being regarded as a "simpleton" or "stupid fool."

Nowadays, hake for the Spanish market is fished in almost all the seas of the world, and sold internationally. The differences in quality are enormous – the best is freshly caught *merluza* from the Bay of Biscay, especially the angled hake *(merluza de anzuelo)* caught just off the Basque coast. The taste is incomparable, because a fish that has been caught on a hook

These fishermen hunt the hake with massive nets. The specimens from the Bay of Biscay, caught with a rod and line, are considered particularly delicious.

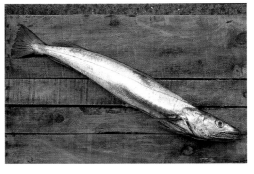

Hake is a must on any Spanish menu. The exquisite fillets are very popular and the cheeks (*kokotxas*) are considered a delicacy.

has not had a long battle with the trawl net, and it goes into the pot almost immediately it is caught. In the past, the fish heads were boiled up on board the boats, with lots of garlic, to make a warming soup. Nowadays though, the fishermen sell freshly angled hake to the best restaurants at scandalous prices. Stores and fish markets, on the other hand, usually sell hake which is caught in trawl nets and then deep frozen – the best of these also coming from the Bay of Biscay. The cheapest, less flavorsome hake comes from Africa, California, and South America, and has to travel a great distance before it reaches the consumer's table.

Basque cuisine primarily uses fillet or medallion of hake. At the start of the 20th century, the cheeks and gills (*kokotxas de merluza*) still made their way straight into the garbage. Since then,

however, this delicacy has found its way onto the market, at sky-high prices. Usually the two extremely delicate, gelatinous pieces of flesh from the hake's gills are cooked very slowly in olive oil with garlic (*al pil-pil*) and sometimes also with chopped parsley (*en salsa verde*), until the fish protein combines with the oil to form a thick, creamy sauce. *Pil-pil* onomatopoetically reproduces the sound that the fish makes when it makes contact with the hot oil.

Hake roe (*huevas de merluza*) should not be overlooked either. This expensive product is gathered by hand, from the bellies of female fish, by experienced craftsmen. The delicate product is then either consumed fresh – surely the most elegant form – or preserved in cans; in its own liquor, in vegetable oil, or in a delicate vinaigrette. Hake roe is seen as a reasonably priced substitute for caviar, and is popularly used in canapés and tapas, as well as for egg dishes, and for garnishing fish and other dishes.

MERLUZA A LA KOSKERA
Hake with asparagus and peas
(Photograph above, right)

4 hake fillets, weighing 7 oz/200 g each
Salt to taste
Flour for coating
5 tbsp olive oil
4 cloves of garlic, peeled and minced
1 shallot, peeled and minced
½ cup/125 ml dry white wine
8 oz/250 g hard-shell clams, scrubbed and rinsed
7 oz/200 g cooked peas, fresh or frozen
7 oz/200 g asparagus tips, steamed
Freshly milled pepper to taste

Rinse the hake fillets and pat them dry. Season them with salt, and leave them to cure for a few minutes. Toss the fillets in the flour, shaking off the excess.

Heat the olive oil in a large skillet or flame-proof casserole. Add the garlic and shallots, and sauté until transparent. Put the hake fillets in the pan, and seal them quickly on each side. Pour on the white wine, and add the clams. Turn the heat down low, cover, and simmer for 10 minutes, shaking the skillet occasionally. Carefully fold in the peas and asparagus tips, and heat them through. Season to taste with salt and pepper.

The Basques combine the versatile hake with very different ingredients. There is the perfect marriage of the fruits of both earth and sea in *merluza a la koskera*: hake with peas, tender asparagus tips, and hard-shell clams (above). Creative cooks don't shy away from preparing the fish with mushrooms or fruit either. Hake cheeks (*kokotxas de merluza* below) are very delicious and combine well with the fish when poached.

Slice the cloves of garlic thinly and sweat them in the olive oil until golden.

Then add the hake cheeks. The skillet should be shaken well all the time during cooking.

When the fish juices have combined with the oil to make a thickish sauce, the parsley can be added.

Kokotxas should be served piping hot. In restaurants, this classic dish commands a high price.

KOKOTXAS DE MERLUZA AL PIL-PIL
Hake cheeks with garlic sauce
(Photograph below left)

1¾ lbs/800 g hake cheeks
Salt to taste
Scant 1 cup/200 ml olive oil
3 cloves of garlic, thinly sliced
1 tbsp chopped fresh parsley

Take the hake cheeks off the bone and season them with salt. Heat the olive oil in a deep skillet or flameproof casserole dish, and sauté the garlic until pale golden brown. Add the hake cheeks and reduce the heat. Sauté the hake and garlic for 10 minutes, shaking the skillet all the time, so that the oil combines with the fish protein from the hake cheeks, and forms a thick sauce. Just before serving, sprinkle the chopped parsley over, and serve straight from the skillet.

Variation: Cook 2 tablespoons of chopped fresh parsley in the sauce with the hake, in order to create *kokotxas en salsa verde* (hake cheeks in green sauce).

Lobster

Considered the king of the crustacean world, the lobster (*bogavante* or *lubigante*), the darling of gourmets, prefers to live in waters with a rocky bed. It impresses lesser creatures with two large claws, which are never the same size. The stronger claw (usually on the right) is used to grasp and crush prey, the smaller one for probing and breaking. It is easy to distinguish between a lobster and a spiny lobster, because the latter does not have claws.

During the day, the lobster lives in caves and beneath rocks, hunting only at night to track down favorite foods – squid, small crabs, and fishes. As it grows, the lobster keeps shedding its carapace. The growing body cracks open the outer shell, and the naked lobster retreats to a sheltering cave for a few weeks, until its thick, leathery skin hardens into a new shell.

In Spain, lobsters are caught from June to August, with lobster pots or dragnets that are pulled over the sea bed. Since the noble crustaceans are usually sold alive, they have to be handled very carefully after catching, because stress is detrimental to quality.

Due to massive overfishing in most waters, the Northern lobster (*Homarus gammarus*) has become a highly priced rarity. This is why American lobster (*Homarus americanus*) is often also found on Basque markets. It is caught off the coast of Newfoundland, where stocks are still more plentiful. Overall, the American lobster is somewhat stockier and has larger claws with a greater proportion of meat. While its carapace is reddish black, the carapace of the Northern lobster is darker, sometimes almost bluish. It takes on its striking red color only after boiling.

Lobster is best bought live, from a tank. In order to tell whether a specimen has lots of meat inside, which is hard to gauge from external appearances, you should lift it up high and watch its reflexes. If its claws show a strong, lively reaction, it is almost certainly meaty. If it moves sluggishly, this indicates less meat. If covered with a damp cloth, a fresh lobster can be kept in the refrigerator for up to two days. Lobster needs to be cooked for only 15 to 20 minutes, so that the meat is still tender, and the delicate flavor is retained.

SALPICON DE LUBIGANTE
Lobster vinaigrette

2 bay leaves
Salt to taste
1 lobster, weighing about 5½ lbs/2.5 kgs
1 fresh red chili, seeded and finely diced
7 oz/200 g green olives
2 tbsp white wine vinegar
Freshly milled pepper to taste
5 tbsp olive oil
1 tsp chopped fresh parsley

Fill a large saucepan with water, add the bay leaves and a pinch of salt, and bring to a boil. Plunge the live lobster into the water head first, and cook at a fast boil for about 20 minutes. Remove the lobster from the pan, drain, and leave it to cool. Take the meat out of the claws, legs, and tail, then slice it. Arrange the lobster meat attractively on a serving dish, garnished with the diced chili and olives.

To make the vinaigrette, whisk together the white wine vinegar, salt, pepper, and olive oil. Drizzle the dressing over the lobster, and sprinkle with chopped parsley.

EATING LOBSTER SKILFULLY AND WITH PLEASURE

To eat a lobster, twist off the claws, and cut the lobster in two, using a knife. Now there is nothing to stand in the way of your enjoyment of this delicate meat.

Next crack open the large claw. As this part of the lobster has the hardest shell, using a lobster knife is recommended.

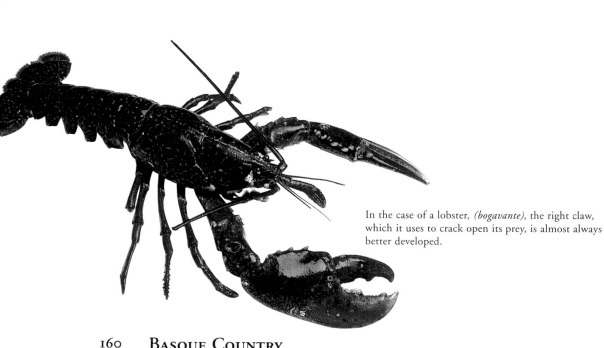

In the case of a lobster, *(bogavante)*, the right claw, which it uses to crack open its prey, is almost always better developed.

The lobster meat can be lifted out of the shell using a knife and fork. The greenish part is especially choice – the extremely tasty liver.

After you have cracked open the shell on the lower section of the claw in several places, with the lobster knife, use a lobster pick to remove the flesh.

Now the shell can be opened with a lobster knife and pick and the tasty meat lifted out. Opening the shell by hand is also considered acceptable.

It is easy to loosen the meat in the lower section of the claw with a pick. Separate the upper and lower claw at the joint, and the meat is easily accessible.

The reward for all your hard work may not be that plentiful, but a very fresh lobster pays back your efforts a thousandfold with tender meat and a delicate flavor.

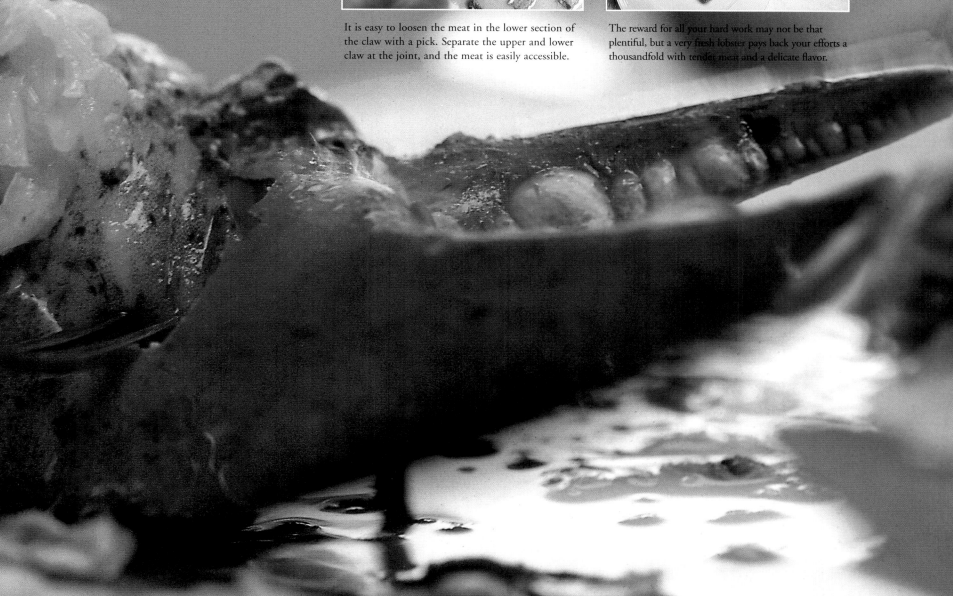

SPANISH SEAFOOD

Shrimp *(gambas* and *langostinos)*: various different species commercially available; particularly good varieties come from Catalonia, Valencia, and Andalusia. Smaller varieties are called *quisquillas* and *camarones.*

Lobster *(bogavante)*: the star of the crustacean world, up to 1½ feet (45 centimeters) long. Should always be bought live. Extremely tender meat.

Langoustine *(cigala)*: Deep sea crustacean with very tasty flesh. Langoustines from colder waters are especially good.

Spiny lobster *(langosta)*: seabed crustacean without claws; very tasty meat; bought live.

Blue crab *(nécora)*: difficult to crack open; little meat; but very tasty nonetheless.

Snow crab *(centollo, txangurro)*: popular in northern Spain in particular; extremely tasty meat.

Edible crab *(buey de mar)*: tender meat, especially in the claws; fine liver.

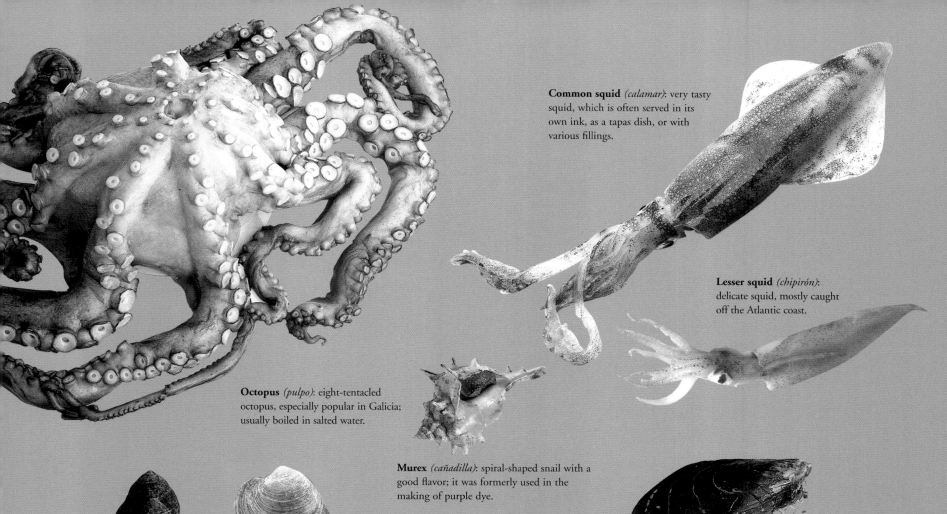

Common squid *(calamar)*: very tasty squid, which is often served in its own ink, as a tapas dish, or with various fillings.

Lesser squid *(chipirón)*: delicate squid, mostly caught off the Atlantic coast.

Octopus *(pulpo)*: eight-tentacled octopus, especially popular in Galicia; usually boiled in salted water.

Murex *(cañadilla)*: spiral-shaped snail with a good flavor; it was formerly used in the making of purple dye.

Whelk *(bígaro)*: from the Atlantic; mostly cooked briefly in boiling water.

Hard-shell clam *(escupina)*: uses its rippled shell to bury itself in the sea bed.

Common mussel *(mejillón)*: popular throughout Spain; best in winter; can be prepared in several different ways.

Goose barnacle *(percebes)*: extremely tasty little crustacean, usually simply cooked in boiling water.

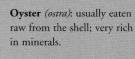

Cockle *(escupiña)*: very thick-shelled; less delicate flavor.

Razorshell clam *(navaja)*: tasty; usually eaten broiled or steamed.

Oyster *(ostra)*: usually eaten raw from the shell; very rich in minerals.

Clam *(almeja)*: one of the most popular shellfish in Spanish cuisine.

Heart clam *(berberecho)*: roomy shell; little meat, but delicate flavor.

Calico scallop *(zamburiña,* above) and **common scallop** *(vieira)*: among the most delicate shellfish of all.

Sea urchin *(erizos)*: only the tasty corals from both male and female urchins are eaten.

163

Basque
SEAFOOD CUISINE

MARMITAKO
Tuna stew
(Photograph below)

1¾ lbs/800 g fresh tuna
Salt and freshly milled pepper to taste
½ cup/125 ml olive oil
2 onions, peeled and finely diced
2 cloves of garlic, peeled and minced
2 large green bell peppers, seeded and diced
2 ripe beef tomatoes, skinned and diced
4 large potatoes, peeled and diced
2 cups/500 ml hot fish stock
1 tbsp chopped fresh parsley

Wash the tuna and pat it dry. Cut it into bite-size pieces, and season with salt and pepper. Heat the olive oil in a cast-iron pan, or a flameproof casserole. Sweat the onions and garlic in the oil until translucent. Add the bell peppers and sauté briefly. Add the tomatoes and potatoes, and pour in the fish stock. Simmer for 20 minutes, or until the vegetables are just tender.

Add the tuna pieces, and fold them into the vegetables. Take the pan off the heat, and let the tuna cook through for about 10 minutes. Season to taste with salt and pepper. Sprinkle the chopped parsley on top and serve the stew immediately, straight from the pan. Serve with slices of toasted white bread or croutons.

Tuna fish, potatoes, and garlic (above) are the main ingredients in *marmitako*, which is flavored with onions and bell peppers. Eating the stew is a sociable event (right).

Filetes de lenguado al txakolí
Fillets of sole in Txakolí wine

8 fillets of sole
Salt and freshly milled pepper to taste
All-purpose flour for coating
4 tbsp olive oil
8 large, ready-to-cook langoustines
1 onion, peeled and finely diced
2 cloves of garlic, peeled and minced
1 large, ripe beef tomato, skinned and diced
1 cup/250 g mussels, scrubbed and rinsed
1 cup/250 ml Txakolí or other dry white wine

Rinse the sole fillets and pat them dry. Season them with salt and pepper. Toss them in the flour, and shake off any excess. Heat the oil in a deep skillet, and sauté the sole fillets on both sides, until golden brown. Remove the fillets and keep them warm. Sauté the langoustines in the oil for a few minutes, remove, and keep them warm too. Sweat the onion and garlic until translucent. Add the diced tomato and sweat it until softened. Add the mussels to the skillet, cover, and steam for 5 minutes over a high heat, shaking the skillet occasionally. Pour in the wine and bring the mussels to a boil. Discard any mussels that have not opened. Place the sole fillets and langoustines in the sauce, and heat them through carefully for 2 to 3 minutes.

Setas con almejas
Mushrooms with clams

½ cup/125 ml olive oil
1 large Spanish onion, peeled and finely chopped
3 cloves of garlic, peeled and minced
2.2 lbs/1 kg mixed wild mushrooms, e.g. porcini, chanterelles, field mushrooms, wiped and cut into bite-size pieces
2 tbsp chopped fresh parsley
A few saffron threads
½ tsp cayenne pepper
1 cup/250 ml dry white wine
Salt and freshly milled pepper to taste
2.2 lbs/1 kg ready-to-cook, hard-shell clams

Heat the olive oil in a deep, cast-iron skillet. Sweat the onion and garlic until translucent. Add the mushrooms, and sauté them until almost all the juices have evaporated. Fold in the parsley. Crush the saffron in a mortar with the cayenne, and a splash of water. Stir into the mushroom mixture, then add the white wine. Season to taste with salt and pepper. Add the clams to the skillet, cover, and steam on a high heat for 5 minutes, shaking the skillet occasionally. Before serving, discard any clams which have not opened.

Txangurro relleno
Stuffed snow crab
(Photograph below)

3 carrots, peeled and sliced
1 leek, rinsed and sliced
1 rib of celery, scrubbed and diced
Handful of fresh parsley, roughly chopped
1 onion, peeled and halved
Freshly milled salt to taste
4 medium-size snow crabs
2 shallots, peeled and finely diced
2 cloves of garlic, peeled and minced
4 tbsp olive oil
2 carrots, peeled and diced
1 leek, washed and thinly sliced
2 tomatoes, skinned and diced
3 tbsp/50 ml dry sherry
Freshly milled pepper to taste
2 tbsp fresh white breadcrumbs
1 tbsp chopped fresh parsley
2 tbsp butter

Bring a saucepan of salted water to a boil. Add the sliced carrots, leek, chopped celery, parsley, and halved onion, and bring to a boil again. Slide the crabs into the boiling water and boil for 8 minutes. Remove the crabs from the pan and drain them. Reserve the cooking liquid. Open the shell with a sharp knife, cut off the legs and claws. Scrape the meat out of the shell and legs, and chop it finely. Reserve the crab shell.

Preheat the oven to 390 °F/200 °C. Heat the olive oil in a skillet; sweat the shallots and garlic until translucent. Add the carrots, leek, and tomatoes, and sweat them for 5 minutes. Fold in a few tablespoonsful of the cooking liquid, together with the crab meat. Simmer for another 10 minutes, then add the sherry, and season to taste with salt and pepper. Pile the mixture into the crab shell. Combine the breadcrumbs and parsley and scatter over the filling. Dot the butter over the breadcrumbs, and bake in the oven until crisp and golden brown. Serve immediately.

Snow crab

The snow crab, also known as a spider crab, is a crustacean enjoyed by people in the Basque country more than in any other region of Spain. The rounded prickly protuberances on the shell, measuring between 4 and 8 inches (10 and 20 centimeters) across, and two delicate claws, are typical of the snow crab. It has four thin legs on each side to help it get around, so it really does look like a spider (photograph on page 162). It lives in depressions, and between stones on the sea bed, and feeds on water plants and mollusks. The females are regarded as somewhat more flavorsome than the males – but both end up in the cooking pot.

There are a number of dishes which can incorporate the snow crab. The one described above is typical of the region. The Basques may have a special liking for this sea creature, but it is also found in the cuisines of other areas of northern coastal Spain.

Eel

Catching eels has always been a popular sport for men in northern Spain. In days gone by, when the farmers didn't have much work, they tried their luck at setting fish traps or nets in the nearby streams or lakes, and made eel baskets. Up to 50 years ago, they still were lucky most of the time, and were able to provide their wives with plump eels for the cooking pot. But stocks of the European common eel (Lat. *Anguilla anguilla*, Span. *anguila*) have been considerably reduced by water pollution, the building of dams, and the proliferation of the air bladder worm. The eel has become an expensive rarity. Eel larvae are spawned in the Sargasso Sea, to the south of the Bermudas, in the western Atlantic. They are then driven toward Europe by the Gulf Stream, feeding on plankton on the way. The long journey may take up to three years. They reach the Old World in the form of elvers *(angulas)* – young and tender, transparent, and just about the size of a matchstick. For many of the young, the journey ends at this early stage, because in the Basque country elvers are regarded as a delicacy. While the male elvers, if they escape the fishermen, remain in the brackish water at the river mouth, the females swim up the river until they find a suitable habitat. They remain there for ten to twenty years, feeding on worms, snails, crustaceans, and small fish. Then, if they have not fallen prey to Basque anglers, they swim back to the sea in the Bay of Biscay, and start the long journey home back to the Sargasso Sea in the western

Young elvers are only a couple of inches (5 centimeters) long. They have hardly reached the Spanish coast after their long journey when they land up in the cooking pot.

Elvers turn white when cooked (above). They are usually served in ceramic bowls with garlic, olive oil, and hot chilies (below).

Atlantic, where they mate, reproduce – and then die. Eels caught in fresh water may be almost 5 feet (1.5 meters) long and weigh over 13 pounds (6 kilograms). Smaller specimens, weighing between 1 and 2 pounds (500 to 1000 grams) are more tender and tastier, though. Eel meat contains almost 25 percent fat and is therefore very hard to digest (in comparison, trout has just 2.7 percent fat). In contrast to central and northern Europe, eel is rarely smoked in Spain, but is usually stewed, braised, or sautéed. Eel pasty is also a popular specialty in the north of the country.

Angulas
Elvers

1⅔ cups/400 ml olive oil
6 cloves of garlic, peeled and thinly sliced
2 dried red chilies, seeded and cut into strips
Generous 1 lb/500 g fresh elvers

Heat the olive oil gently in a saucepan or flameproof casserole dish. Sauté the garlic until golden brown. Add the sliced chili, and reduce the heat. Then add the elvers, and cook for 1 minute, stirring with a wooden spoon. Do not sauté them. Divide the elvers and flavored oil between 4 warmed ceramic bowls, and serve very hot. In the Basque country elvers are served with wooden forks to prevent you from burning your mouth. So be careful if you want to enjoy this delicacy at its best.

Most species of eel live in the sea, and even the so-called river eel is born in the western Atlantic, before it begins its long journey to Europe. The conger eel *(congrio)*, small, expensive elvers *(angulas)*, and fully grown river eels *(anguilas)* are usually found in Spanish markets.

ALLIPEBRE
Garlic and chili eels (from Valencia)

1 eel, weighing about 2.2 lbs/1 kg
Salt to taste
½ cup/125 ml olive oil
1 onion, peeled and finely diced
½ tsp paprika
1 tbsp all-purpose flour
2 hot red chilies, seeded and cut into strips
3 cloves of garlic, peeled and minced
A few saffron threads
1 slice of white bread, toasted
Freshly milled pepper to taste
1 tbsp chopped fresh parsley

Gut the eel, cut off the fins, and make a diagonal cut through the skin behind the head. Peel the skin away from the meat and pull it off. Cut off the head and tail. Rinse the eel and pat it dry. Cut into chunks and season them with salt.
Heat the olive oil in a deep skillet or flameproof casserole. Then sauté the onion until translucent, and stir in the paprika and flour until fully blended. Add 1 cup/250 ml warm water, stirring all the time, and bring to a boil.

Add the eel chunks and the chilies. Add more water, if necessary, so that the eel is always completely covered. Simmer on a low heat for 10 minutes. Break the slice of toast into pieces. Crush the garlic in a mortar with the saffron, the toast, and a little of the liquor from the eel. Stir this mixture into the cooking liquor, and cook for another 10 minutes. Season to taste with salt and pepper, and sprinkle over the chopped parsley. Serve immediately.

ANGUILAS CON HABICHUELAS
Eel with lima beans

2½ cups/400 g dried lima beans
1¼ lbs/600 g eel, gutted and skinned
Salt to taste
5 tbsp olive oil
1 onion, peeled and diced
1 green bell pepper, seeded and finely diced
2 large, ripe beef tomatoes, skinned and diced
Freshly milled pepper to taste
1 tbsp chopped fresh parsley

Soak the beans overnight in cold water. Next day, bring them to a boil, with the soaking water, and add more hot water, so the beans are completely covered. Simmer on a medium heat for 30 minutes.
Wash the eel, and cut it into chunks. Add them to the beans, and season with salt. Simmer on a low heat for 20 minutes, or until the eel is tender.
Meanwhile heat the olive oil in a skillet, and sweat the onion until translucent. Add the bell pepper and sauté quickly. Fold in the diced tomatoes and season with salt and pepper. Cook for 15 minutes. Add the tomato mixture to the bean stew, and simmer for a few minutes longer, on a low heat, for the flavors to combine. Before serving, sprinkle over the chopped parsley.

Vegetables and mushrooms

Babarrunak and *zizak* are the cornerstones of Basque vegetable cuisine: beans and mushrooms. *Alubias negras de Tolosa* are among the most expensive Spanish legumes. These black beans are soft, with a powerful flavor and pleasant creaminess. They play an important role in stews, and as an accompaniment to hearty meat dishes.

It is difficult to beat the Basques when it comes to mushroom consumption. Only the Catalans eat greater quantities. The most popular, and most expensive, culinary mushroom in the Basque country is the *perretxiku* (Lat. *Tricholoma georgii*, Span. *perrechico*) or St. George mushroom. The Basques prefer to eat this mushroom as simply as possible, to let the characteristic aroma of cornmeal develop fully. It is usually sautéed, baked in the oven, or served with scrambled eggs. The perretxiku also holds its own in combination with snails, meat, or even fish. Porcini, field mushrooms, chanterelle, and oyster mushrooms are all popular in the region too.

Potatoes from the Alava province are sold under the protected appellation *arabako patata*. Spinach is especially popular in the area around Bilbao. Basque cuisine also treasures small, green peppers from the area around Guernica (*gernikako piperra*), as well as celery, turnips, leeks, fresh peas, beans, teasel, and artichokes.

The *perretxiku* (also known as *seta de Orduña*, *seta de abril*, or *seta de San Jorge*) grows in spring in meadows and in undergrowth, especially under whitehorn and scrub.

Alubias negras de Tolosa
Tolosa black beans

2½ cups/500 g dried black beans or navy beans
5 oz/150 g bacon
3 tbsp olive oil
Salt to taste
4 chorizo sausages or other chili sausage
1 small onion, peeled and finely chopped
4 cloves of garlic, peeled and minced
1 leek, washed and thinly sliced
Freshly milled pepper to taste

Soak the beans overnight in water. Drain the beans, and put them into a saucepan. Add the piece of bacon, 1 tablespoon of the olive oil, and a pinch of salt. Add enough cold water to cover all the ingredients completely. Bring to a boil and simmer over a low heat for 45 minutes, topping up the water if necessary. Prick the sausages with a fork, and add them to the beans. Simmer for another 15 minutes. Heat the remaining olive oil in a skillet and sauté the onion and garlic until translucent. Add the leek and sauté until lightly browned. Stir the onion and leek mixture into the stew. Season to taste and serve very hot.

The fine, creamy *alubias negras de Tolosa* are among the best beans in the land. They have a delicate flavor and need little preparation.

Piperrada
Bell pepper omelet
(Photograph left)

5 tbsp olive oil
1 onion, peeled and finely diced
2 cloves of garlic, peeled and minced
4 oz/100 g prosciutto, cut into thin strips
1 red and 1 green bell pepper, seeded and cut into thin strips
4 ripe tomatoes, seeded and diced
Salt and freshly milled pepper to taste
4 eggs

Heat the olive oil in a deep skillet. Sauté the onion, garlic, and prosciutto until translucent; then add the bell peppers and sweat them in the oil. Fold in the tomatoes and continue cooking until the vegetables are almost cooked. Season to taste with salt and pepper.

Beat the eggs and pour over the vegetables. Do not stir the eggs. Cook the omelet over a low heat until it is set.

Transfer to a warmed plate to serve.

PERRECHICOS FRITOS
Sautéed St. George mushrooms

4 tbsp olive oil
2–3 cloves of garlic, peeled and minced
Generous 1 lb/500 g St. George mushrooms or other
wild mushrooms, wiped and cut into bite-size pieces
Salt and freshly milled pepper to taste

Heat the olive oil slowly in a saucepan, and sweat the garlic gently until translucent. It should not take on any color. Add the mushrooms and sweat them, until all the juices have evaporated. Season to taste with salt and pepper. Serve hot.

HOJALDRE DE ESPINACAS Y GAMBAS
Puff pastry with spinach and shrimp

16 oz/450 g shop-bought frozen puff pastry
Generous 1 lb/500 g fresh spinach
1 onion, peeled and finely chopped
1 clove of garlic, peeled and minced
1 tbsp olive oil
4 oz/100 g prosciutto, cut into thin strips
1 tbsp butter
1 tbsp all-purpose flour
1 cup/250 ml milk
Salt and freshly milled pepper to taste
⅛ tsp ground nutmeg plus ⅛ tsp ground cinnamon
Pinch of sugar
2 eggs, separated plus 1 egg yolk, beaten
7 oz/200 g cooked, shelled shrimp

Defrost the puff pastry. Roll out and cut into 12 equal squares. Pick over the spinach and wash it thoroughly. Heat the olive oil in a large saucepan, and sauté the onion and garlic until translucent. Add the prosciutto and spinach, cover the pan, and steam for a few minutes. Then remove the lid and continue cooking on a low heat.

Melt the butter in another saucepan. When it is foaming, add the flour, stirring all the time, and cook until fully incorporated, and a roux forms. Still stirring all the time, add milk and simmer until a thick, white sauce forms. Fold the sauce into the spinach, season with salt, pepper, nutmeg, cinnamon, and sugar (mixture should be sweetish). Remove from the heat and whisk the egg whites together with a pinch of salt, until very stiff. Fold the egg yolks into the spinach mixture, then carefully fold in the egg whites, then fold in the shrimp.

Preheat oven to 430 °F/220 °C. Rinse a baking sheet with cold water and place 4 squares of puff pastry on it. Divide half of the spinach mixture between the pastry squares, spread it, and cover with a square of pastry. Spread remaining spinach mixture on top and cover with the remaining pastry squares. Brush the pastry with the beaten egg yolk and bake for about 15 minutes, or until golden brown. Serve immediately.

Fresh ingredients for Basque vegetable dishes are best bought at the market. San Sebastián has several undercover markets to choose from, and vegetables are delivered fresh daily to other towns in the region.

Porcini *(boleto)* are among the most popular ingredients in Spanish mushroom cookery. They are traditionally sautéed with just a little garlic, but in modern recipes they are commonly combined with meat and fish too.

MEN'S WORK

In times gone by, a black bean was enough to deny a man entry to culinary paradise. In the past, some gastronomic societies *(txokos)* used the legumes to vote on who could become a member of their circle, and who could not. The aspirant longed for white beans only, because the vote had to be unanimous.

Txokos are a kind of gastronomic brotherhood, whose members meet regularly to cook together and devote themselves to the pleasure of eating and drinking. Since time immemorial, these institutions have been regarded in the Basque country as a cultural asset, and are still enormously popular. The *txokos* uphold the traditions of regional cuisine, but also like to experiment with new creations.

The first *txoko* was founded in 1843 in San Sebastián, and further gastronomic societies sprang up around 1870. Around the turn of the century the epicurean clubs spread like wildfire, as increasing prosperity brought about by industrialization made grandiose celebratory meals a possibility. *Txoko* means "corner" or "harbor" and the industrial and shipyard workers came in numbers, with their colleagues, at the end of the working day, to relax over a good meal and plenty of wine.

Today there are some 300 *txokos* in the Basque province of Guipúzcoa alone. San Sebastían has more restaurants, taverns, and bars per square mile than any other Spanish city. It is not surprising that it is still regarded as the stronghold of the *txokos*, with several gastronomic societies for every district in the *Parte Vieja*, the old town. People from all walks of life are represented there. It doesn't matter whether one is a banker or bus driver, stevedore or schoolteacher – anyone can be a *tripazai*, a cook in a gastronomic society. The only thing that matters is one's love of culinary pleasures, real commitment at the stove, and punctual payment of the monthly membership subscription.

A *txoko* usually has its own clubhouse with a fully equipped kitchen, bar, dining room, and storage space for food and drink. Whereas some *txokos* might have just a dozen members, other societies welcome up to 200 pleasure-seeking men. Duties are loosely allocated, and everyone pitches in – whether with shopping or chopping; setting the table or washing the dishes; arranging the dining room; or managing the money. After hours of grafting and pottering in the kitchen, the cooks then present their tastebud ticklers to the massed members, who enjoy deliberating on whether or not the dishes are a success. The menu is heavily seasoned with the latest gossip, and an exchange

Every member of the *txoko* has to knuckle down. If cooking isn't your thing, you can shop, chop ingredients, or set the table for the main meal.

BASQUE IS IN THE BLOOD

The Basques call their homeland *Euskadi* and call themselves *Euskaldunak* – "those who speak the Basque language." Their language, which was forbidden during the Franco dictatorship, has been preserved up until today. Basque *(Euskera)* is a non-Romance, pre-Indo-European language, whose origins and relationships cannot be conclusively explained by academics. Even on a menu, you will often come across terms which have very little in common with the Spanish language: *txangurro* is what they call snow crab here, *zurrukutuna* and *purrusalda* are stews made with stockfish, while *perretxiku* is the name for the most popular edible mushroom in the Basque country. In this region, the popular little delicacies *(pintxos)* are not enjoyed as *tapeo*, but rather as *txikiteo*. If you don't stumble over *gazia* (cheese) or *kafe huts* (black coffee) at your *hamaiketako* (mid-morning snack), you will surely get tongue-tied when saying thank you *(eskerrik asko)*. In a bare schoolroom, *Euskera* is truly a closed book. The secrets of this strange language are most readily revealed in a *jatetxea* (restaurant) after two or three glasses of *txakolí*, the light, dry, fruity, domestic white wine, which loosens tongues.

The *txoko*, the male gastronomic society, is a haven of the pleasures of the flesh for many Basques. Even today, women are not allowed to enter the charmed circles.

of views on the motor sport, or soccer team, of the moment. In many *txokos*, political discussions are traditionally taboo, in order to avoid the possibility of any social friction.

Women and other honored guests are welcome in the *txokos* clubhouses only at certain times of the year. In San Sebastían, the doors are open to visitors on the patron saint's day (January 20) and the Assumption of the Blessed Virgin Mary (August 15). Usually, though, the men cling firmly to the tradition of meeting in a men-only environment. Some *txokos* have retained another custom: if a young man wants to join, he has to wait until an older member dies.

Harrijasotzaile is one of the most popular Basque trials of strength. Colossal men compete to carry massive quarry stones.

HOW BASQUE MEN WORK UP AN APPETITE

A bell rings – and they let fly; two *aizkolariak*, famous throughout the region, are in their element. Each "lumberjack" has an imposing length of beech trunk in front of him. The men swing their axes at a dizzying speed. "Thud, thud, thud!" – the splinters fly, people yell encouragement. The beech trunk in front of one of the giants splits in two: "I've won!"

Herri kirolak (country sports) is the name the Basques give to their own sports that are based on strength, and that have their historic roots in the day-to-day activities of fishermen and farmers, charcoal burners, and woodsmen. In the past these hardworking men would meet at the weekend, to try their strength. Who could carry the heaviest sandbag? Who could mow a field fastest with a scythe? Who could reach his destination fastest by rowing? Even then, the spectacle took place in public, before the eyes of a baying crowd. Today, these strongmen, with their bizarre sports, are still heralded as folk heroes throughout the Basque country. Many have won the title of Basque champion, and there are even professional country sportsmen, who earn their living with the help of their muscle power.

The competitions usually take place in the open, in a village square or stadium, where the program of events may completely bewilder lazy office workers:

aizkolari: chopping thick tree trunks with an ax
txingas: a race where the competitors carry two 110 pound (50 kilogram) weights
zakua: the so-called "smugglers' sprint" with a 175 pound (80 kilogram) sandbag on your back
segalari: a mowing competition using a scythe
harrijasotzaile: carrying quarry stones weighing up to 660 pounds (300 kilograms)
idi-probak: carrying weights on an ox yoke
soka-tira: tug-o'-war
traineras: rowing regatta

BARBECUE

The *parrillada* is really not a new invention: only the almost endless variety of meat, fish, and vegetables that often sputter over the coals separates the modern barbecue from the traditional meals of charcoal burners, herders, and fishermen. Centuries ago, shepherds cooked a whole lamb on a metal spit (Basque *burruntzi*) over glowing wood embers, while the fishermen grilled sardines on a rack over an open fire.

Today a barbecue is as much a part of a Spanish summer weekend as sun and wine. The Basque farms produce everything that is needed for a *parrillada* or *barbacoa*, a proper barbecue – the finest beef and lamb, fresh fish, and crisp vegetables. The stars of a Basque *parrillada* are hearty steaks, preferably from the native Basque Raza Vasca cow. A standard-size steak is known as a *chuleta*, an outsize steak is respectfully called a *chuletón*. In the opinion of the natives, the *chuletones* from Tolosa and Berriz win hands down when it comes to size and taste. These massive steaks are coated in a well-seasoned marinade of olive oil, parsley, and garlic, and then prepared as *chuletones a la brasa*, on a charcoal grill. In many country inns and cider houses *(sidrerías)* they also prepare the stomach for a night of heavy drinking.

Lamb and pork chops also sizzle on the barbecue, as well as spareribs, lamb shanks and kidneys, various sausages, sliced duck livers, sardines, or jumbo shrimp, trout, and heavily seasoned snails. Small pieces of meat and fish are imaginatively combined with vegetables to form kebabs. A whole, spit-roasted lamb is still, however, the highpoint of a Basque *parrillada*. As an accompaniment bell peppers, tomatoes, and onions are baked on the racks. Whole bulbs of garlic, including the skin, are roasted round the edge of the barbecue. The contents of the soft cloves are mashed with a fork, and spread over grilled meat, or onto a slice of toasted bread. Potatoes, wrapped in aluminum foil, bake in the hot coals. Fish is stuffed with butter and herbs, wrapped in aluminum foil *(en papillote)*, then placed directly on top of the hot charcoal. More delicate fish is cooked on the barbecue itself.

The Basques love drinking their dry Txakolí white wine with their barbecues, but a glass of cold beer is increasingly common too. The atmosphere is just perfect when someone takes out their *txistu*. This traditional Basque flute has only three holes and is played with one hand. The other is free to beat time – or turn a juicy steak on the barbecue.

Lamb is very good for barbecues. The chops *(chuletas de cordero)* are brushed with oil, sprinkled with some herbs, if liked, then slapped straight onto the barbecue.

To make a delicately flavored rabbit terrine, chop the meat very small with a sharp knife.

Purée the rabbit liver in a mixer, and then put it in a large bowl.

Line a terrine with the slices of bacon. As much of the bottom and sides as possible should be covered.

Poultry and Game

Terrina de conejo
Rabbit Terrine
(Photographs left and right)

2¼ lbs/1 kg boneless rabbit meat
1 rabbit liver
8–10 slices bacon
2 tbsp olive oil
1 onion, peeled and finely chopped
1 clove of garlic, peeled and minced
1 sprig fresh thyme, finely chopped
1/8 tsp ground nutmeg
½ tsp paprika
1/8 tsp cayenne pepper
1 tbsp all-purpose flour
2 tbsp brandy or 3 tbsp sherry
2 eggs
Salt and freshly milled pepper to taste
4 slices bacon, cut into strips

Sauté the onion and garlic in the olive oil until soft, then add them to the puréed liver.

Add the spices – thyme, nutmeg, paprika, and cayenne give the terrine a spicy kick.

Add the chopped rabbit meat to the liver mixture, together with a splash of brandy, or perhaps sherry.

First dice the rabbit meat, then chop it very fine or grind it. Purée the liver in an electric mixer, or grind it, and put it in a large bowl. Line a terrine with the slices of bacon.

Heat the olive oil in a skillet and sweat the onion and garlic until translucent. Add the onion and garlic to the puréed liver, with the thyme, nutmeg, paprika, and cayenne. Fold in the ground rabbit, flour, and brandy or sherry. Beat the eggs with a fork, and add them to the rabbit mixture. Season to taste with salt and pepper, and stir well until all the ingredients are thoroughly combined.

Preheat the oven to 430 °F/220 °C. Pile the rabbit mixture into the terrine lined with bacon, pressing it down well. Trim off any ends of bacon which overlap the dish. Then lay the strips of bacon across the top of the dish in a lattice pattern. Cover the terrine with a lid, or a saucer. Fill a roasting pan with boiling water, so it comes about halfway up the sides of the terrine. Bake on the bottom shelf of the oven for 1½ hours. Check the water level in the roasting pan after an hour, and top up as necessary. The terrine may be eaten hot or cold. It will keep in the refrigerator for up to 1 week.

Beat the eggs with a fork. Add to the rabbit meat mixture, and mix thoroughly.

Pile the rabbit meat mixture into the bacon-lined terrine. Press the meat mixture down firmly.

Trim any pieces of bacon which overlap the sides of the dish, using a sharp knife or scissors.

Cover the terrine with the strips of bacon in a lattice pattern.

Cover the terrine, and cook it in a *bain marie* for about 1½ hours.

When the terrine is cooked, the bacon on top is translucent. The terrine can be eaten immediately or kept in the refrigerator.

Liebre a la bilbaina
Hare Bilbao style

1 large hare, skinned and gutted
½ cup/125 ml olive oil
1 onion, peeled and diced
2 cloves of garlic, peeled and minced
1 tbsp all-purpose flour
1 cup/250 ml red wine
1 cup/250 ml hot meat stock
⅓ cup/50 g dark chocolate, grated
2 tbsp ground hazelnuts
1 apple, peeled, cored, and finely chopped
7 oz/200 g wild mushrooms, e.g. porcini,
chanterelles etc., wiped and chopped small
Salt
Pepper
1 tbsp chopped fresh parsley

Rinse the hare and pat it dry. Cut it into portions. Heat the olive oil in a deep skillet or large saucepan, and seal the hare quickly. Add the onion and garlic, and sweat them until soft. Sprinkle the flour over the hare mixture and add the red wine and stock. Simmer for 20 minutes. Then stir in the chocolate and hazelnuts. Fold in the chopped apple and mushrooms; then simmer for another 20 minutes. Season to taste with salt and pepper. Sprinkle the chopped parsley over just before serving.

Pichones rellenos con foie gras
Pigeons stuffed with foie gras

4 large dried figs
4 oz/100 g foie gras
4 young oven-ready pigeons
Salt and freshly milled pepper to taste
3 tbsp olive oil
2 shallots, peeled and finely diced
1 cup/250 ml hot game stock
1 tbsp raspberry vinegar
Scant ⅓ cup/100 ml medium dry sherry

Wash the figs, soak in cold water for 4 hours and drain them; then stuff them with the foie gras. Rinse and pat dry the pigeons. Rub the skin with salt and pepper. Place a stuffed fig in the belly cavity of each pigeon, close it with a wooden pick. Preheat the oven to 430 °F/220 °C. Heat the oil in a roasting pan and seal the pigeons all over. Remove them from the pan and keep warm. Sauté the shallots in the pigeon juices until translucent. Add the hot stock, vinegar, and one third of the sherry. Put the pigeons back in the pan and transfer it to the oven. Braise for about 20 minutes, basting occasionally with the remaining sherry. Arrange the cooked pigeons on a warmed serving dish. Strain the gravy through a fine sieve, season to taste with salt and pepper, and serve separately.

Ensalada de espinacas con codornices
Spinach Salad with quails

8 oz/250 g fresh spinach
½ head Belgian endive
4 oven-ready quails
Salt and freshly milled pepper to taste
2 tbsp sherry vinegar
6 tbsp olive oil
4 slices bacon
8 quail eggs, hard-cooked

Pick over the spinach and trim the Belgian endive. Wash and drain the spinach and endive, and tear into bite-size pieces. Divide between 4 plates. Rinse the quails and pat them dry. Cut each one into four portions. Season with salt and pepper. Whisk together the sherry vinegar, salt, pepper, and four tablespoons of the olive oil, to make a dressing. Drizzle it over the salad leaves. Heat the remaining olive oil in a skillet and sauté the bacon in it until crisp. Remove the bacon from the skillet and keep it warm. Sauté the quail portions in the juices until golden brown. Arrange the quail portions, bacon, and quail eggs on top of the salad leaves, and serve immediately.

Below: Rabbit terrine

Great quantities of *Idiazábal* cheese of varying degrees of maturity are sold in markets. It can either be bought as a whole cheese, or as a section. Individual slices are not sold in Spain – in any case it would be a shame to put the smoked cheese in a sandwich.

IDIAZÁBAL

The sheep in the Basque mountains are the hippies of their race. Most are members of the hardy and extremely long-haired *Lacha* (Basque *Latxa*) breed. Almost 150,000 of these shaggy animals typical of the region wander around the Basque meadows. In flocks they are very peaceable, are ideally suited to the cool, damp mountain climate, and produce high quality milk, with a very high fat content. Many farmers still produce *Idiazábal* cheese by traditional methods, but a proportion of the fresh sheep's milk is also sent to the large dairies. 100 registered cheesemakers produce 1.9 million US gallons (7.5 million liters) of sheep's milk each year, and manufacture around 1320 tons (1200 tonnes) of *Idiazábal*.

This rinded cheese ripens for two to five months. The Basque shepherds discovered by pure chance that it can also be smoked. In the past they stored the ripened cheeses, before they went to market, in the shepherds' huts. When a fire was lit in the fireplace, the smoke drifted throughout the hut. In time, it became clear that the smoke did the stored cheese no harm at all, and gave its aroma and flavor an interesting twist. Later, cheeses were hung directly in the smoke room. Traditionally, the shepherds and smaller family businesses fire these with whitebeam or cherry wood. However; the large cheese manufacturers increasingly use oak or beechwood. This gives the cheese a noticeably darker color. *Idiazábal* cheese has a soft, almost buttery consistency, as well as a slightly acidic and piquant, but in no way sharp taste which is pleasingly accentuated by the smoked flavor. The fat content of *Idiazábal* is at least 45 percent. The Basques are rightly proud of their sheep's milk cheese, one of the many excellent varieties to be found in Spain.

For the most part, Basque cheese is made from sheep's milk, because thousands of the shaggy creatures inhabit the meadows in the hinterland (main photograph). While *Idiazábal* is smoked, other varieties are matured without smoking.

Idiazábal cheese is produced by 37 cheesemakers in the Basque country. The only milk permitted by law is that from Lacha sheep. Smoking gives each cheese its own inimitable taste.

Txakolí is a slightly sparkling, uncomplicated wine. Once you have discovered the dry, acidic nature, plus the freshness and sweetness of this white wine, you will greatly enjoy Txakolí with fish and seafood.

Txakolí

"Txakolí is an acquired taste," Basque wine buffs will say with a smile. The strange name conceals a slightly sparkling, sweet, and lively white wine with fresh acidity and rather restrained fruit. The name Txakolí (Span. *Chacolí*) is derived from the Arabic *chacalet*, which means something weak, light, or thin. The fresh, light wines are an integral part of any Basque folk festival, as well as barbecues and summery lunches.

Txakolí is produced in three officially designated quality regions: **D.O. Getariako Txakolina** *(spanish Txakoli de Guetaria)* with 432 acres (175 hectares) of grapes in the province of Guipúzcoa; **D.O. Bizkaiko Txakolina** *(spanish Txakoli de Vizcaya)* with 395 acres (160 hectares) in the province of Vizcaya; **D.O. Arrabaco Texakolina** *(spanish Chacoli de Álava)* with 148 acres (60 hectares) in the north of Álva province. The white grape variety Hondarribi zuri (from 85 to 90 percent of vines under cultivation) is permitted, as well as the black Hondarribi beltza, from which the rare red Txakolí wines are vinified. The wines have a relatively low natural sugar content, due to the Basque country climate, which is not exactly overendowed with sunlight. As a result the wine has a lot of acidity and dry freshness.

A classic Txakolí is light, medium dry, and uncomplicated. It has 10–11 degrees of alcohol and is drunk young, and chilled, preferably at about 46 °F/8 °C. Txakolí goes extremely well with fish and shellfish. It also proves to be an unassuming accompaniment to heartier dishes with a marked salty flavor. It is popular as a apéritif, due to its appetite-stimulating acidity. Two Basque *bodegas* also turn the residual grape pressings from Txakolí into fine brandies, called *Orujo de Txakolí.*

Txakolí wine comes from three officially designated areas of origin in the Basque Country. The grapes grow in the hilly hinterland (above) but in Guetaria they also grow in very close proximity to the sea (right).

White Txakolí is produced from the typical regional Hondarribi zuri grape variety. The rarer red Txakolí comes from Hondarribi beltza grapes.

RIOJA ALAVESA

One of the three sub-regions of the La Rioja wine–producing area actually lies in the territory of the Basque province of Alava: Rioja Alavesa. The red wines from this area are generally paler than those in the other sub-regions of Rioja Alta and Rioja Baja, predominantly due to the high proportion of chalk in the soil. Rioja Alavesa wines have a very individual character and, when young, contain an astounding amount of freshness and fruit. The Tempranillo grape variety dominates; but Garnacha, Graciano, and Mazuela are also cultivated. In addition to the cooperatives and renowned major bodegas, which mainly produce good *Reservas* and *Gran Reservas*, a few smaller producers have recently concentrated on red wines that are full of character and which, although they are marketed as young wines, display a highly individual, complex mix of flavors. A typical characteristic of these young winemakers' red wines *(cosechero)* is that they are produced by the carbonic maceration method *(maceración carbónica)*. For Rioja the black grapes are normally stripped and pressed immediately after the harvest, before the juice is pumped into the fermentation tanks. However,

carbonic maceration uses whole grapes, including the stalks. Firstly a fermentation tank, open at the top, is filled about half full with whole bunches of grapes. The berries that split release some juice, which sinks to the bottom of the tank and starts to ferment. The carbon dioxide released by the fermentation settles in a blanket over the grapes and prevents the incursion of oxygen. The berries start to ferment from inside. In order to assist this process, the tank is regularly pumped over, or stirred. After ten to twelve days, the first wine (the *lágrima*, the so-called "tear wine") is drawn off. Then the grapes are pumped over again, and continue fermenting. After a few days, the grapes are pressed, and the so-called heart, or middle wine is drawn off. Then the grapes may be given a final pressing to release the press wine, which is too coarse and tannic for use in winemaking, and is often distilled into brandy. The tear wine and middle wine are combined, and mature for just a few weeks in large wooden vats or steel tanks, and are then bottled. The result is generally a fruity, light, and relatively good value red wine, which is totally different in nature from the expensive, tannic *Reservas* or *Gran Reservas* of Rioja. In fact, it seems strange, perhaps, that this highly individual wine should be given the name Rioja at all.

SWEET TEMPTATION AT THE CAKE SHOP

The Spanish don't need a special reason to consume quantities of pastries, confectionery, and all kinds of other sweet stuff. After all, there are plenty of opportunities for temptation. A cookie is even part of breakfast, and the age-old tradition of *merienda* means that on summer afternoons, after the siesta, a cup of coffee and a nice piece of cake, or a pastry is *de rigueur*.

If a family is celebrating a birthday, or other family occasion, then the sweet dishes are more lavish, the gateaux bigger and richer. This is customary for celebrations which fall into the top B.B.C. category: *bodas* (weddings), *bautizos* (baptisms), and *comuniones* (first communions). At these special celebrations, a beautifully decorated cake generally graces the table, in addition to the usual dessert. The cake is usually enjoyed with a cup of coffee, or cappuccino. Depending on the occasion, and the family's tastes, it might be a walnut tart *(tarta de nueces)*, a lemon tart *(tarta de limón)*, a custard tart *(tarta de crema)*, an apple tart *(tarta de manzana)*, a cheesecake *(tarta de queso)*, a chocolate gateau *(tarta de chocolate)*, or an almond cake *(tarta de almendras)*. In recent years, many convents relied for survival on their traditional manufacture of cakes and pastries. They offer a wide range of products for sale, which the locals know to be delicious. And so in many towns it has become the custom for the celebration cake for a very special day to be ordered from a convent bakery (see also page 446 f). Whether from the convent or cake shop, it is worth trying some of the delicious varieties shown right.

Whether a gateau or a cookie – the appeal of a Basque cake shop is difficult to resist.

SWEET TREATS FROM ALL OVER SPAIN

Goyescas: soft toffees

Vasquitos: fine caramel candy ("little Basques")

Pastel vasco: covered "Basque tart" with delicious ice-cream filling

Tartaleta de frambuesa: small tart with raspberries and fruity raspberry jam

Trufa montada: tartlet filled with chocolate truffle, topped with coarsely grated chocolate

Suspiro de Bilbao ("Sigh of Bilbao"): airy almond meringue

Orejones: puff pastry "ears" with whipped cream or custard filling

CANUTILLOS DE BILBAO
Bilbao puff pastry rolls
(Photograph above)

Pastry:
2½ cups/300 g all-purpose flour
1¼ cups/300 g butter
½ tsp salt

Custard filling:
6 egg yolks
8 tbsp/100 g superfine sugar
2 tsp vanilla sugar
2 cups/500 ml milk
Grated rind of 1 lemon
⅛ tsp ground cinnamon

Flour for the work surface
Confectioners' sugar for dusting

Make a puff pastry dough using the flour, butter, salt, and 1 cup/250 ml water (alternatively, you could use purchased frozen puff pastry).

To make the custard, whisk together the egg yolks, sugar, and vanilla sugar until creamy. Gradually stir in the milk. Fold in the lemon rind and cinnamon. Put the mixture in a bowl over a saucepan of simmering water, and whisk continuously until thickened and creamy. Remove the bowl from the pan and leave it to cool.

Preheat the oven to 430 °F/220 °C. Roll out the pastry thinly on a floured work surface, until it forms a rectangle. Cut the pastry into 4 inch/10 cm squares. Rinse *canutillos* molds (small metal tubes about 2 inches/5 cm in diameter, or use cornet molds) in cold water, and wrap a piece of pastry around each mold. Bake for 15 minutes, until golden brown. Take them out of the oven and remove them from the mold immediately. Leave them to cool on a wire rack.

Pile the custard into a piping bag fitted with a tip, and pipe it into the pastry cases. Dust each pastry with confectioners' sugar and serve immediately.

Variation: The finished *canutillos* can also be glazed with sugar syrup.

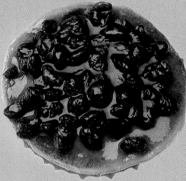

Pastel de yema con pasas al ron: tartlet with egg custard and raisins soaked in rum

Turrón: almond nougat with various flavorings from cream, via chocolate truffle, to liqueur

Brazo de gitano: Jelly roll sponge with different fillings (custard, fresh cream, or jam)

Bizcocho: sponge cake layered with buttercream filling, but other creams, custards, fresh cream, or jam may be used

Carbayones: small puff pastry envelopes filled with marzipan and a fine egg custard

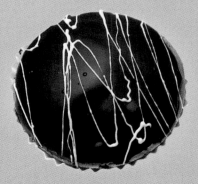

Pastel franchipán: tartlet filled with almonds and topped with various glazes, such as chocolate or lemon

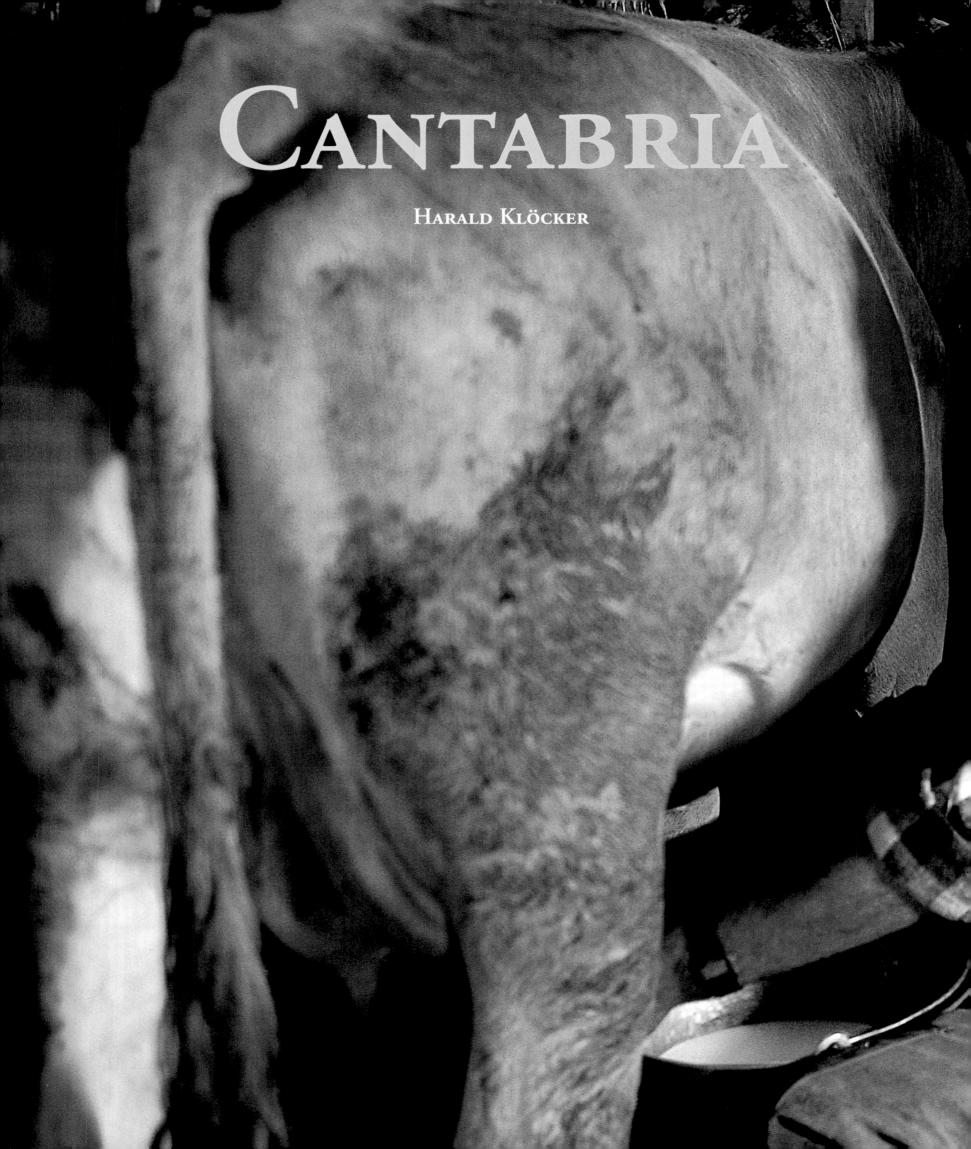

CANTABRIA

Harald Klöcker

CANTABRIA

SARDINES AND ANCHOVIES
CANNED FISH AND SEAFOOD
FISHERMAN'S MEALS
MOUNTAIN CUISINE
DAIRY INDUSTRY
SPANISH MILK AND
 CUSTARD DISHES

A cow in the shed has always been money in the bank
for Cantabrian farmers. They won't get rich, but the
family will always have a supply of fresh dairy products.

"*Cantabrum indoctum iuga ferre nostra,*" noted the Roman writer Horace in the first century BC – "The Cantabrians will not bow to our mastery." The people who live in this mountainous region are alleged to have once been as wild and restless as the Cantabrian sea. Certainly, they stubbornly resisted the advance of the Roman army, and it was only around the time of the birth of Christ that the conquerors succeeded in subjugating this people, who had retreated into the dark ravines and forests of their homeland. Many discoveries testify to Cantabria being inhabited even during prehistoric times. In the cave at Altamira, aptly known as the "prehistoric Sistine Chapel," Stone Age artists created powerfully expressive rock paintings, giving an insight into the everyday life of the early Cantabrians some 15,000 years ago.

To some extent, ancient traditions and ways of life have persisted to the present in the mountains of Cantabria. The inhabitants come across as closely linked to nature. In this smallholding economy, farmers still chop their own firewood, as in days gone by, and mow the grass with a scythe, so it can be carried to the village by horse-drawn cart. Many farms still bake their own bread and make their own cheese, while the old custom of nomadic herdsmen still survives up here in the mountains. For some time, the neighboring regions of Asturia and the Basque country have successfully drawn attention to their many culinary treasures and unique dishes. Cantabria, though, like its people, is rather reserved in this regard – almost as if the epicurean wonders that the tiny region has to offer should under no circumstances be made public. The mountain scenery, with its green upland meadows, bubbling streams, and fruitful valleys, produces the best dairy produce, usually manufactured by small family businesses. Meanwhile, the Cantabrian coast is dominated by dishes based on fresh fish and fine seafood. The fresh and processed anchovy specialties from Laredo, Santoña, and Colindres, have a first-class reputation throughout the whole of Spain.

One Cantabrian beauty, however, has always known how to show herself off to the best advantage – Santander. Once the grain import/export harbor of Castile, and the royal summer residence, it still exudes a worldly charm. It has come to be regarded by gourmets as the new shrine of the North for pilgrim gourmets.

Opposite: The nature of Cantabria is determined by the elements of earth and water. In some places, sea inlets reach far inland towards the green mountain meadows.

Above: sardines (right) and anchovies are found by the ton on Cantabrian markets. Both are used fresh, or the canned varieties are found in store cupboards.
Background: anchovies are salted before canning. Traditionally, they are cured in brine in a wooden barrel. Sardines, on the other hand, are canned fresh, in oil.

SARDINES AND ANCHOVIES

Whole shoals of shimmering, silvery fish swam into the nets of the seamen of antiquity as they fished off the coast of the island of Sardinia, in the Mediterranean. The fish soon acquired the name of sardines from the Latin word for this Italian island. At that time, however, opinions differed as to their culinary value. The Romans are supposed to have thought very highly of sardines. The Greeks, on the other hand, connected them with the realm of the goddess of the dead, Hecate. This is why, at best, they found a place only on the tables of the lower classes. The culinary attraction of the sardine was also disputed in subsequent ages, when they were generally regarded as food for the poor. There have always been gourmets, however, who were convinced that the sardine deserved a place in *haute cuisine*.

The sardine is a type of herring that lives in the Atlantic, between Ireland and the Canary Islands, and also occurs in the Mediterranean. The fishing season is between June and November. The Spanish prefer to eat sardines fresh – either gutted, with the head removed, and broiled, or filleted and marinated. Before broiling, the fish are often brushed with a mixture of olive oil, chopped herbs, garlic, and freshly milled salt and pepper. When only canned sardines, often contemptuously referred to as "sardines in oil," are available, gourmets insist that the fish should be left in the can or jar to mature for as long as possible before consumption, thus markedly increasing the flavor, as with some red wines. Experts store top-quality canned sardines for many months, even well beyond the specified "best by" date. Only then do they savor the delicacy, preferably with a splash of lemon juice drizzled over them. It is easy for the practiced eye to distinguish the sardine (Lat. *sardina pilchardus*) from the anchovy (Lat. *engraulis encrasicholus*). The slightly protruding lower jaw and silvery flanks with dark, round spots, which diminish in size toward the tail, are typical of the sardine. The anchovy, however, is smaller and slimmer. It can be recognized by its very protuberant snout, the striking large eyes, the mouth packed with teeth, and a slightly greenish back. Anchovies pass through the Bay of Biscay in early fall on their way to Norway, and return in the spring well-nourished and with a resultant cushion of fat. This is when the Cantabrian fishermen start to fish for anchovies, which are sold either fresh or preserved. The meat is darker and has a much stronger flavor than that of sardines.

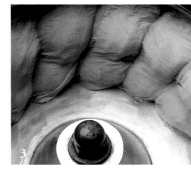

1 Anchovies for canning are first cured for a few months, minus the head and intestines, in a brine solution.
2 The anchovies are rinsed, and then dried. To do this, they are hand-rolled in cloths.
3 The anchovies wrapped in the cloths are placed in a centrifuge, which removes the very last drop of water from them.

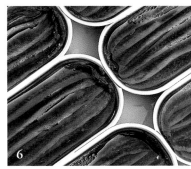

4 The dried anchovies can now be processed further. Each fish is divided into two fillets by hand.
5 Skilled hands now layer the anchovy fillets, piece by piece, in the cans. All the fillets should remain in one piece.
6 To preserve them, the fish are covered with sunflower oil. The cans are then sealed.

The centers of the Cantabrian fish-canning industry are the coastal towns of Santoña, Laredo, and Colindres, which have specialized in producing first–class canned anchovies. Those anchovies which have been processed using the traditional *anchoada* method to give tender anchovy fillets are viewed as a particular delicacy. The heads and intestines are first removed from the anchovies, and they are layered in wooden barrels that are then filled with a brine solution. The barrel is topped off with a heavy weight, that carefully presses down the layered anchovy fillets over time. The anchovies remain in the barrel for three to six months. They are then rinsed, dried and divided into two fillets by hand. Finally, they are packed in cans with the addition of olive or sunflower oil. Anchovies and anchovy fillets are perfect for garnishing and are usually served as a tapa – they are popular combined with olives, cheese, bell peppers, or melon.

Fresh anchovies, that have not been cured in brine, are known as *boquerón*. They are eaten fresh or baked with cheese. Usually though, *boquerones* are marinated in fillet form, in a mixture of olive oil, vinegar, and herbs, and then served as tapas. In the north of Spain tapas, the popular Spanish snack, are also known as *pincho* (from *pinchar*: "spear" or "skewer"). Refreshing, acidic *boquerones en vinagre* are just as popular as anchovy fillets with bell peppers, chicory, olives, or melon. Shrimp in batter, marinated mussels or clams, broiled sardines, or a hearty salad of sautéed or marinated squid are also found in the windows of northern Spanish tapas bars. See pp. 84–87 for a selection of delicious tapas, which act as appetizers or can form a main meal.

Deep-fried anchovies *(boquerones fritos)* are a popular tapa throughout Spain.

Canned fish and seafood

There's no doubt that the Spanish love fresh fish, which arrive on tables every day fresh from the sea, as natural and unprocessed as possible. Yet in a country whose shores are washed by the Atlantic and the Mediterranean, canned fish and seafood also enjoy a kind of cult status. It doesn't matter whether they come in cans or jars – canned products are not regarded as an expression of culinary barbarism. Indeed, on Spanish tables they have won the right to a place of their own.

Galicia, the region with the greatest volume of production, takes first place for canned fish and seafood. However, Cantabria, the Basque country, and the Atlantic province of Andalusia are renowned for the outstanding quality of their products. Although canned fish have been sold for decades almost exclusively as a cheaper food, many producers are now increasingly offering at inflated prices unusual delicacies such as classic preparations of tuna or anchovy, as well as seafood in various dressings and marinades. These specialties are also exported, but in the case of mass-produced canned fish, products from Asia continue to be more competitive on the international market even if they are sometimes not as tasty.

Like these anchovies (above) and sardines (facing page), most seafood is processed and packed by hand in Cantabrian canning factories.

Clams (almejas) come in widely varying sizes, and are prepared for the can in many different ways.

Salted, preserved anchovies (anchoas) from Cantabria are regarded as particularly tender and delicate, and are not too salty.

Canning tuna (atún) is not considered a sin in Spain. Canned tuna is mainly very popular for use in salads.

Heart clams or cockles (berberechos) are not very meaty, and are therefore not very cheap when canned.

Mackerel (caballa) is also very popular in canned form in central Europe, where it is exported in very great quantities.

Larger squid (sepia) are divided into pieces and preserved. It is enjoyed cold as a tapa, or hot too.

Often only the pouch-shaped body of baby squid (calmar) is canned. They are suitable for stuffing, or for tapas.

Mussels (mejillones) come canned in a wide variety of often very tasty dressings and marinades.

Razor shell clams (navajas) are usually prepared very simply, so the delicate flavor is not overpowered.

Octopus (pulpo) must be handled very carefully during processing so that the meat does not become dry and tough.

Sardines (sardinas) are filleted and canned in large pieces. "Sardines in oil," like these, are coveted throughout Europe.

Calico scallops (zamburiñas), with their refined flavor, are one of the most popular varieties of canned seafood.

FISHERMAN'S MEALS

SARDINAS AL HORNO
Baked sardines
(Main photograph)

2.2 lbs/1 kg small sardines, heads removed and gutted
Salt and freshly milled pepper to taste
Scant ½ cup/100 ml olive oil
3 cloves of garlic, peeled and minced
2 tbsp chopped fresh parsley
Juice of 1 lemon
½ cup/125 ml white wine
3 tbsp fresh, white breadcrumbs

Preheat the oven to 355 °F/180 °C. Rinse the sardines and pat them dry; then rub them inside and out with salt and pepper. Brush a shallow baking dish with olive oil, and lay the sardines in it side by side. Sprinkle the garlic and parsley over them, then pour over the lemon juice, white wine, and remaining olive oil. Scatter the breadcrumbs over the sardines. Bake in the oven for about 20 minutes. Serve straight from the oven.

Variation: Large sardines can be stuffed with prosciutto, wrapped in vine leaves, and then baked in the oven.

BOQUERONES EN VINAGRE
Preserved anchovies

Generous 1 lb/500 g fresh anchovies
½ cup/125 ml sherry vinegar
6 large cloves of garlic, peeled and thinly sliced
2 tbsp chopped fresh parsley
Salt and freshly milled pepper to taste
1 cup/250 ml olive oil

Cut open the bellies of the anchovies and remove the backbones and heads. Rinse the fish thoroughly and pat them dry. Cut them in half lengthwise. Place them side by side in a dish and pour over the vinegar. Add enough water to cover the anchovies completely. Cover the dish with plastic wrap, and leave to marinate overnight in the refrigerator.
Remove the anchovies from the vinegar mixture and drain them well. Place them in a serving dish, scatter the garlic and parsley on top, and season with salt and pepper. Pour the olive oil over the anchovies and marinate for 1 to 2 hours. Serve with fresh, crusty white bread.

For sardines baked in the oven *(sardinas al horno)*, it is not necessary to gut the fish. They are baked in a ceramic dish with garlic, oil, and herbs.

Lubina a la montañesa
Sea bass with mushrooms

4 sea bass fillets, or bream, each weighing about
6 oz/150 g
Salt
Pepper
1 onion, peeled and finely diced
1 leek, rinsed and thinly sliced
Scant ½ cup/100 ml olive oil
2 ripe tomatoes, skinned and diced
1 carrot, peeled and sliced
7 oz/200 g mixed wild mushrooms
(e.g. porcini, chanterelles),
wiped and chopped
½ cup/125 ml dry sparkling wine

Preheat the oven to 355 °F/180 °C. Season the fish fillets with salt and pepper, and leave them to marinate a little. Sauté the onion and leek in 3½ tbsp/50 ml of olive oil, until translucent. Add the tomatoes and carrots, and sweat them for 10 minutes. Stir in the mushrooms and sweat for another 5 minutes. Pour the remaining oil into a baking dish. Dip the fish fillets in the oil to coat them, then lay them in the dish. Scatter the vegetable mixture on top and pour on the sparkling wine. Bake in the oven for about 10 minutes, until the fish is tender and flakes easily.

Mejillones al modo de Laredo
Mussels with olives

4½ lbs/2 kg mussels
Salt to taste
1 onion, peeled and spiked with 1 bay leaf
2 shallots, peeled and diced
2 cloves of garlic, peeled and minced
3 tbsp olive oil
4 ripe tomatoes, skinned and diced
7 oz/200 g pitted black olives, diced
3 anchovy fillets, diced
1 cup/250 ml dry white wine

Scrub the mussels thoroughly under running water and remove the beards. Place 4 cups/1 liter water, 1 teaspoon salt, and the spiked onion in a large saucepan, and boil. Add the mussels, cover the pan, and simmer on a low heat for 5 minutes. Remove the mussels from the liquor with a skimmer, drain, and leave to cool a little. Discard any unopened mussels. Remove the mussels from the shells, reserve, and keep them warm.
Sauté the shallots and garlic in the olive oil, until translucent. Add the tomatoes, olives, and anchovy fillets. Pour on the white wine and boil to reduce the sauce a little. Return the mussels to the pan and heat them through in the sauce, but do not let it boil.

Arroz santanderino
Santander style rice

4 salmon steaks, each weighing 8 oz/250 g
Salt and freshly milled pepper to taste
Juice of 1 lemon
1 cup/250 ml milk
1 cup/250 ml hot fish stock
1 cup/200 g arborio rice
2 tbsp butter

Rinse the salmon steaks and pat them dry; then rub them with salt and pepper. Drizzle over the lemon juice, and let them marinate for at least 10 minutes.
Preheat the oven to 355 °F/180 °C. Put the milk and fish stock in a flameproof casserole and bring to a boil. Add the rice, bring to a boil again, and simmer for 10 minutes.
Melt the butter in a skillet and sauté the salmon steaks, until sealed and golden on both sides. Remove the salmon steaks from the pan and lay them on top of the rice. Pour the melted butter from the skillet over the salmon. Bake in the oven for 10 minutes. Serve straight from the oven.

Below: Sardines have been grilled for as long as the Cantabrian fishermen have had traditions. The fish are brushed with oil, and seasoned with herbs.

Plump stone age prey

Bison and brown bear, deer, wild boar, and mountain goats were among the favorite foods of Stone Age man. The Altamira cave, discovered close to Santillana del Mar in 1879, looked like a kind of outsize menu when revealed for the first time. Some 15,000 years ago, hunters armed with slings and spears painted their menu on the walls of the cave with pigments made from charcoal, soil, animal fat, and blood. The cave paintings are now seen as one of the most important European testimonies to Stone Age art. As late as the 19th century, Cantabrians hunted for bear in the mountains. Bear meat was considered very nutritious, because it was fatty, and was mainly served as a ragout or as dried meat. The

warm pelt was also highly prized. The mountain people also hunted bear to keep them away from the villages and their herds of sheep and cows. As a result of excessive hunting, as well as the enormous threat to their habitat from roads and farming, there are now fewer than 100 brown bears left in the Cantabrian mountains. They have since become strictly protected and can no longer be hunted. Farmers or herdsmen, who can prove that a sheep or cow has been mauled by a brown bear, receive compensation from the nature conservation authorities. In this way, most of the inhabitants now assist in protecting these rare animals. Other rare species indigerious to the mountains along the border between Spain and France have been accorded similar protection.

Mountain cuisine

"I had never before seen such a vast tract of the world at my feet, never before had I felt so close to my Maker, never before had seeing His works filled me with such deep and homely feelings." The mountains of his homeland inspired a huge measure of enthusiasm in Cantabrian author José Maria de Pereda in the late 19th century – not just because of the breathtaking panoramas, but also because of what he saw in the cooking pots of Cantabrian farmers' wives. Today, some hundred years later, Pereda's successors prize the Liébana valley *(Valle de Liébana)* almost as a mountain Garden of Eden – and the smallest imaginable culinary paradise. The mountainous world of the Picos de Europa, with its sheer rock walls, has created unique conditions in the sheltered Liébana valley. A mild sunny climate, from spring to fall, enables grape vines, and fruit and almond trees to flourish. In addition to *garbanzos de Liébana*, especially tender chickpeas, it is predominantly *orujo de Liébana*, a spicy, fruity *marc*, or brandy made from wine pressings, that attracts foodies from all over Spain. It is distilled in traditional copper stills, *(alquitaras)* according to methods which have been handed down through the ages. Simple farmer's fare also includes hearty stews: the *cocido montañés* made from lima beans, cabbage, and pork, and *cocido lebaniega* (see illustration) based on chickpeas with blood sausage, beef, boiled ham, bacon, bell peppers, and lots of cabbage.

This land of milk and honey also presents visitors with wild salmon, and milk-fed lamb. Finally, Cantabrian veal, fattened on the high mountain pastures *(carne de alta montaña)* is regarded as a delicacy. The Tudanca breed of cow, of which there are very few left, is typical of the region, and is perfectly adapted to the Atlantic mountain climate. It provides especially good and flavorsome meat. The beef is popular when prepared in combination with cheese from the region, or with fresh herbs.

It is almost obligatory to end a day out in the Valle de Liébana in one of the ancient country inns, such as the "Bearkeeper," the *Mesón del Oso*, built of massive natural stone blocks, in the village of Cosgaya. At weekends, hundreds of tourists enjoy the rustic atmosphere and consume hearty stews and homemade cheesecake – and, of course, the landlord pours a glass of brandy from the Liébana valley to accompany it.

Opposite: The Altamira cave and its drawings are regarded as one of the most impressive examples of Stone Age art in Europe. The paintings mainly depict animals.

Hearty stews with legumes, meat, and vegetables warm body and soul. Chickpeas from Liébana are especially fine. They form the basis of *cocido lebaniego* (above), which also contains lots of meat.

Cocido montañes
Cantabrian style stew

1 cup/250 g dried lima beans
2 tbsp pork drippings or butter
Generous 1 lb/500 g pork shoulder, diced
½ pig's trotter
4 oz/100 g bacon, diced
1 onion, peeled and diced
Salt and freshly milled pepper to taste
2 potatoes, peeled and diced
2 carrots, peeled and sliced
½ small head of white cabbage or savoy cabbage,
cut into ribbons
3 cloves of garlic, peeled and minced
2 tbsp olive oil
1 tsp paprika
1 Spanish blood sausage
1 chorizo sausage or other chili sausage

Soak the beans overnight in cold water. Melt the drippings, or butter, in a large saucepan, and seal the pork shoulder, pig's trotter, and bacon. Add the onion and sauté until golden. Add the beans and soaking liquid, and top up with a splash of water if necessary, so that all the ingredients are covered. Season with salt and pepper, cover, and simmer on a low heat for 1 hour. Remove the pig's trotter. Add the potatoes, carrots, and cabbage, and simmer for 10 minutes.
Heat the olive oil in a skillet and sauté the garlic until golden brown. Put the oil, garlic, and paprika in a mortar and pound it until a paste forms. Stir the paste into the stew. Add the blood sausage and chorizo, and cook for 10 minutes. Then remove the sausages and slice them thickly. Return the sliced sausages to the pan and season the stew to taste with salt and pepper.

Ciervo a la montañesa
Roast venison with mushrooms

2.2 lbs/1 kg shoulder of venison
1 bay leaf
1 carrot, peeled and sliced
2 sprigs each of fresh rosemary, thyme and parsley
2 cloves of garlic, peeled and minced
2 cups/500 ml red wine
½ cup/125 ml wine vinegar
Salt and freshly milled pepper to taste
Scant ½ cup/100 ml olive oil
4 oz/100 g bacon, diced
4 oz/100 g prosciutto, cut into strips
12 shallots, peeled
1 tbsp all-purpose flour
1 cup/250 ml hot meat stock
8 oz/250 g wild mushrooms, wiped and diced small
2 ripe tomatoes, skinned and diced

Rinse the meat and pat it dry. Put it in a bowl and add the bay leaf, carrot, rosemary, thyme, parsley, and garlic. Pour over the wine and vinegar. Cover, place in refrigerator, and leave for 1 to 2 days.
Remove meat from the marinade, and pat it dry; then rub it with salt and pepper. Reserve the marinade. Heat the oil in a large casserole and sear the meat quickly on all sides. Add the bacon, prosciutto, and shallots, and sauté them briefly with the meat. Sprinkle the flour over the meat and cook it, stirring all the time, until the flour bubbles and turns golden. Deglaze the dish with the meat stock and add 4 cups/1 liter of the marinade. Cover and braise for 1 hour. After 45 minutes, add mushrooms and tomatoes. After 1 hour, remove the meat from the casserole, place on a warmed serving dish, and keep warm. Reduce the gravy. Season. Serve the gravy separately from the meat.

Dairy industry

Green meadows and black and white cows; here and there, a little farmstead; and up in the mountains the typical *cabañas*, the shelters for sheep – for centuries Cantabrian farmers have made their living from the dairy industry. According to statistics from the Cantabrian Chamber of Agriculture, in 2002 there were precisely 3988 milk-producing businesses in the region. According to E.U. guidelines, the whole of Spain may produce 6.6 million US tons (6 million tonnes) of milk per year. Of this, the small province of Cantabria produces almost one tenth.

The Cantabrian farmers predominantly keep Friesian cows, but they also have a few animals from the old Cantabrian Tudanca breed. A cow

which is well fed and cared for gives between 21 and 63 US pints (10 and 30 liters) of milk a day. As the average Cantabrian farmer only has 22 cows, this is too few to be able to make a living. The cost of energy, food, vet's bills, and insurance have risen constantly in recent years, while milk prices on the Spanish and other European markets have fallen further and further. Large corporations and multinational groups set the purchase price for milk, and earn massive profits from trade in dairy produce, while the situation for farmers in Cantabria and elsewhere is visibly worsening.

Many small dairy farmers who can no longer cope with the increasing price pressure have already given up farming and found jobs in the city. Some offer a couple of bed and breakfast rooms on their farm, in order to get a toe in the door of tourism. But many still cling firmly to

their traditions, as one farmer wistfully confirmed: "It really can't have anything to do with the product. Our milk is first class, especially in April and May, when the cows have eaten the fresh, lush spring grass with the many wild flowers, herbs, and clover. Then the milk tastes of fresh grass and sweet flowers." The farmers make their own cheese and other dairy products from a small proportion of the milk they produce. The rest goes to the dairy *(lechería)*, and has a long way to go before the consumer can pour a glass of milk.

Immediately after the herd is milked, the fresh milk is cooled to 38–46 °F (4–8 °C). The dairy's drivers collect the milk from the producers in refrigerated tankers. At the dairy's laboratory the milk is tested for fat content and bacteriological safety, and then processed in various stages.

Centrifuging: The cream is separated from the milk in a large centrifuge. When the centrifuge is rotated at very high speed, the globules of milk fat remain at the center of the centrifuge. The heavier skim milk, which contains more water, is pushed to the rim of the centrifuge by the centrifugal force. The cream is later turned into butter or cream, and the skim milk is processed to make drinking milk, sour cream, or cottage cheese-type products. To make drinking milk, cream is added after centrifuging, to obtain the desired fat content.

Homogenization: drinking milk is homogenized ("made uniform") by pushing it through narrow nozzles under high pressure. This reduces the size of the fat globules and distributes them evenly through the milk. It is no longer possible for the fat and water to separate and the milk will not form a layer of cream on top.

Pasteurization: standard drinking milk, which should keep for several days, is usually pasteurized. In other words, it is heated to around 170 °F (75 °C) for a maximum of 30 seconds, and then cooled down again. In this way, bacteria in the milk are made harmless. The milk will keep for up to a week, and for the most part the vitamins are retained.

Ultra Heat Treatment: milk which is supposed to keep for several months, and which is sold in light–fast and airtight cartons (**tetrabriks**), is heated for 3 to 10 seconds to 265–300 °F (130–150 °C), to kill any bacteria. During this process, however, up to 20 percent of the valuable vitamins are lost. UHT milk also tastes different to pasteurized milk, and its flavour can sometimes be off putting.

Freshly expressed cow's milk is the basis for many products, from drinking milk, via yogurt, to countless varieties of cheese. Spanish farmers are permitted to produce more than 5.6 US tons (5 million tonnes) of milk each year. Almost one tenth comes from Cantabria, and the milk from the mountain pastures is reputed to be the best in Spain.

There are almost as many cheeses in Cantabria as there are small dairy farmers and there are some produced industrially in large cheese factories. It is mainly the *quesucos* whose fame has crossed the regional boundaries – small, fine truckles, which weigh a maximum of 1 kilogram (2.2 pounds). *Quesucos de Liébana* in particular are well known to gourmets.

Opposite: healthy dairy cows graze on lush meadows. They give good milk that in spring tastes – according to the farmers – of flowers and herbs.

Milk products

Cream *(nata)*: the cream which is separated from the skim milk by centrifuging. Usually 10 percent fat, but at least 30 percent fat for heavy cream. Sour cream is produced by the addition of lactic acid bacteria and contains 10–15 percent fat.

Butter *(mantequilla)*: butter is made from sweet or sour cream which has been pasteurized and stirred at various different temperatures for several hours until the desired consistency is achieved. Contains at least 80 percent milk fat, 16–18 percent water, and about 2 percent solids. It is usually slightly salted.

Sour milk products: milk products which are soured by the addition of lactic acid bacteria. These convert part of the lactose into lactic acid, which causes the milk to thicken, by coagulation, and gives the product its characteristic flavor.

Yogurt *(yogur):* To make this, pasteurized or ultra heat treated milk is cultured with lactic acid bacteria at temperatures between 104 and 117 °F (40 and 47 °C). Then the souring process is arrested by cooling to 43 to 46 °F (6 to 8 °C). The fat content is up to 10 percent. More than 80 percent of yogurt is sold as fruit yogurt (with the addition of sugar and fruit preparations).

Quark *(requesón)*: pasteurized milk is coagulated through the addition of lactic acid bacteria and rennin. It is then centrifuged again, until the whey is removed, and a loose, homogeneous mass forms. Usually sold in Spain with a full fat content of 40 percent. Low–fat quark contains less than 10 percent fat.

Fermented milk *(cuajada)*: fermented by the addition of rennin, or sometimes lactic bacteria; usually sheep's milk in Spain. The consistency is such that it would hold the outline of a spoon (see page 125).

Cottage cheese *(queso fresco)*: unmatured cheese with a slightly acidic flavor (e.g., *Mató, Camerano*). Pasteurized milk is coagulated by the addition of lactic bacteria, fermented herbs, or rennin. It is sold immediately. The fat content is between 10 and 40 percent. The high water content (over 70 percent) qualifies the fat content, which relates to the dry weight of a cheese. Low-fat cottage cheese is also available.

Fine slices of custard are deep-fried in hot oil (background).
They are then sprinkled with sugar and cinnamon (above),
after which there is nothing else to do but enjoy them.

Spanish milk and custard dishes

Flan

Flan is not exactly baked custard. But the Spanish national dessert is still a custard made with eggs, sugar, and milk, then baked in a *bain-marie*. Practised tongues with expert tastebuds can distinguish between the many industrially produced custards which keep well, but have no finesse, and the homemade variety, the *flan casero*, for which almost every housewife has her own recipe.

The milk used is instrumental in the success of a custard. A top quality, unpasteurized whole milk is best. Also required are egg yolks, and a little vanilla, lemon peel, or brandy for flavor. A fresh, homemade custard has a light, creamy texture, and it should be possible to taste the egg yolks and milk.

To elevate the custard's taste to gastronomic heights, place one or two green fig leaves overnight in the milk. It will take on a sweetish flavor – an old trick from Mexico. Variations on custards are apple custard (*flan de manzana*), which is popular in northern Spain, orange-flavored custard (*flan de naranja*), and custard with rum (*flan al ron)*, with chestnuts (*flan de castañas*), or with strawberries (*flan de fresas*).

Flan al caramelo
Caramel custard
(Photograph opposite, below)

1¼ cups/250 g sugar
4 eggs, plus 2 egg yolks
2 cups/500 ml whole milk

Put half the sugar and ½ cup/125 ml of water in a saucepan and bring to a boil; then simmer until the syrup thickens and turns golden brown. Pour the caramel into 4 ramekins, tilting the ramekins so that the bottoms are evenly covered.
Preheat the oven to 300 °F/150 °C. Beat together the eggs, egg yolks, and remaining sugar. Bring the milk to a boil in a saucepan, then take it off the heat to cool a little. Stir the milk into the egg mixture and pour into the ramekins. Place them in a roasting pan, and fill the pan with hot water so it comes halfway up the sides of the ramekins. Bake the custards for about 45 minutes. Check that the water does not evaporate; top up as necessary. Remove the custards from the roasting pan and leave them to cool completely; put into the refrigerator.
Before serving, dip the base of each ramekin in hot water, and carefully loosen the sides of the custard with a sharp knife. Turn out onto dessert plates and serve.

1 To make fine custard slices you need milk, butter, flour, and egg yolks, as well as sugar, vanilla, and lemon.
2 Bring milk to a boil with the sugar, lemon peel, and vanilla. Then remove the flavorings.
3 After the taste of flour has been cooked out in the butter, add the milk, and stir until a smooth sauce results.

4 Add the egg yolks, then leave the mixture to set in the refrigerator. Cut the custard into even-size pieces.
5 Now beat together two eggs and dip the custard slices in it, followed by a coating of breadcrumbs if liked.
6 Heat the oil in a skillet, and add the custard slices. Fry until nicely golden brown.

Leche frita
Deep-fried custard slices
(Photographs above and opposite, above)

2 cups/500 ml milk
Grated rind of 1 lemon
4 tbsp sugar
1 vanilla bean, split
5 tbsp/75 g butter, plus butter for the dish
1⅓ cups/150 g flour
4 egg yolks, plus 2 eggs
4 tbsp dry white breadcrumbs
Oil for deep-frying
Cinnamon and sugar for dredging

Put the milk, lemon rind, sugar, and vanilla bean in a saucepan, and bring to a boil slowly. Take the pan off the heat, remove the lemon zest and vanilla bean; let the milk cool.
Melt the butter in another saucepan until foaming and add the flour; cook until the flour foams and turns pale golden, stirring all the time. Slowly add the warm milk, still stirring. Cook the sauce for 5 minutes on a low heat until it thickens. Remove from the heat and beat the egg yolks into the sauce. Butter a shallow dish. Pour the custard into the dish and leave it to set in the refrigerator for at least 4 hours. Cut the cold custard into squares or triangles. Beat the eggs lightly and dip the pieces of custard first in the beaten egg, then in the breadcrumbs. Heat the oil in a deep-fat frier or deep saucepan, and fry the custard slices in batches until golden brown. Take the custard slices out of the oil and drain them briefly on paper towels. Combine the sugar and cinnamon, and dredge the warm slices in the sugar mixture. Serve lukewarm, or cold.

Arroz con leche
Rice pudding

2 cups/500 ml milk
1 vanilla bean, split
1 cinnamon stick
Rind of ½ lemon
½ cup/100 g pudding rice
5 tbsp/75 g sugar
¼ cup/60 g butter
3 egg yolks
1 tsp ground cinnamon

Put the milk, vanilla bean, cinnamon stick, and lemon rind in a saucepan and bring to a boil slowly. Remove the vanilla, cinnamon, lemon peel, and add the rice. Simmer the mixture for about 20 minutes, until the rice is soft. Fold in the sugar and butter, and take the pan off the heat. Beat in the egg yolks. Pour the rice pudding into a warmed serving dish. Sprinkle the cinnamon on top and serve immediately.

ASTURIAS

Harald Klöcker

ASTURIAS

Asturias is the apple paradise of Spain and farmers
demonstrate their skill with three dozen varieties which
are either eaten fresh or made into *sidra*.

It is with chests swelling with pride that Asturians recall what was probably their greatest contribution to the fortunes of Spain. In 722, under the leadership of the prince Pelayo, they repelled the Moorish assault in mountains not far from Covadonga, thereby securing their independence and laying the groundwork for the Christians' reconquest of their country. However, following this great historical achievement, Asturias fell into a slumber centuries long. For many years the region was regarded as the poorhouse of Spain, a place where simple folk lived off millet, corn, chestnuts, and wild fruits.

It was only the end of the 19th century that marked the beginning of more prosperous times and inspired the writer Jesús Fernández Santos during his journey from the barren plateau of Castile towards the Atlantic. He declared "Up there on the mountain ridge is where Asturias begins. If you continue farther, it is truly as if you have crossed an invisible line, the threshold to the promised land." Today, the principality of Asturias (*Principado de Asturias*) is part of "Green Spain," along with the Basque country, Cantabria, and Galicia. The high mountains of the Picos de Europa, with their alpine pastures, deep ravines, and fast-flowing rivers, descend gently, opening out across countryside that is kept constantly green by its proximity to the Atlantic and that leads down to a rocky coastline with sandy beaches. The industrial and economic center is in the triangle of the towns of Oviedo, Gijón, and Avilés. The east and west are dominated by flowery meadows, market gardens, woods and apple orchards, and villages, churches, and chapels that date back to the Middle Ages.

Historically, the Asturians are a people of farmers, shepherds, and fishermen. The culture of allowing sheep to roam still prevails here and there are over 30 recorded varieties of cheese – in particular, the three-milk cheese made from cow, sheep, and goat milk. Gourmets will find their paradise in the mountainous region of the Picos de Europa in eastern Asturias. On a cheese trail they can sample the different varieties and come across quite unexpected gems that are only produced in small quantities and never found in the stores.

No official seal is needed to demonstrate the obvious quality of specialty hams and sausages, wild boar and venison, trout and wild salmon, as well as a large variety of fish and seafood from the Atlantic, which is served up as simply as possible. Each year, the Asturians pay tribute to their extraordinary culinary delicacies with special festivals and competitions which are keenly fought.

Opposite: The mountains feed streams with crystal-clear water. Trout can be seen jumping and even wild salmon are still to be found in rivers such as the Río Sella.

Every farming family in Asturias has a few apple trees on its land. The apples are harvested by hand in the fall and made into *sidra*.

The different varieties of apple are packed in nylon sacks and transported to the press. Here the fruit has to be processed as quickly as possible.

First, the apple varieties are mixed according to the particular taste required, then they are thoroughly washed and chopped up small.

In many places the farmers still press their apples in old wooden presses. The apples, which have previously been softened, are shoveled in.

The must is then fermented in chestnut barrels. The carbonic acid which is released makes the liquid start to foam.

At a first tasting (*espicha*) a glass of *sidra* is tested. To eliminate any cloudiness, the fresh cider is poured from the barrel through a fine filter.

Sidra

"The Asturians have a drink they call *zythos* which is made from fermented apple juice," commented the Greek geographer Strabo in the first century B.C. Even the Celts had cultivated apples in northwest Spain to make this intoxicating cider. By the mid-18th century there were around 250 apple presses in the region. These produced some 1.2 million gallons (4.5 million liters) of juice a year, a large proportion of which was fermented into cider. Nowadays, the legendary *zythos* is referred to as *sidra* and is the Asturians' regional drink.

On the Atlantic coast of northern Spain, over 30 different varieties of apple thrive in market gardens and large-scale plantations. Some of these are marketed as eating apples, since only certain varieties are suitable for the production of *sidra*. Small, sour varieties of crab apple give the cider its freshness, while sweet and bitter varieties produce its slight variations in taste. The cellarman's skill therefore depends on his choice of a well-balanced mixture of apples.

In the farmer's press, the fruit is first washed and chopped up, then softened in water and finally pressed. The solid residue is fed to the cattle. The apple must is fermented in chestnut barrels until its alcohol content is about five percent. Throughout the winter before the *sidra* is bottled, friends and neighbors get together for the notorious first tastings (*espichas*), where everyone tries the cider straight from the barrel. It is accompanied by spicy Cabrales cheese, ham, sausage, and bread. The process of decanting the cider into dark green bottles of thick glass does not begin until February or March, (most of the bottles are left unlabelled).

In the *sidrería*, where the cider is traditionally sold, even the most sceptical Asturians are happy to display their religious side with an old saying: "We may have lost paradise because of the apple, but we'll get it back with cider." The fundamental principle of the *sidra* communion is that the mildly foaming elixir is always drunk in company, as it raises the spirits, loosens the tongue, and animates the conversation.

The Asturians consume their regional drink from large, rustic glasses, observing a traditional ritual in its serving. The bartender grabs the bottle with a flourish, raises it with a twist of the arm above his head, and lets the *sidra* cascade from the bottle golden and foaming into the glass which he holds below. It is said that the cider develops its potential flavor only at the moment that it falls onto the bottom of the glass. The *escanciador* usually pours only about one or two inches into the glass, after which the *sidra* is drunk immediately. Only a drop is left to rinse out the glass. The *escanciador* then refills the same glass and passes it on to the next member of the group. Dry cider is traditionally drunk with tapas and *fabada*, the Asturian bean stew, or with fish dishes, such as baked sardines (*sardinas al horno*) or salt cod omelet (*tortilla de bacalao*). Even when eating, the rule that the *sidra* must not be left standing in the glass still applies – a rule people are only too happy to observe!

The cider produced in Asturias compares well with that made in other parts of Europe where apples are cultivated extensively, such as in Normandy in France. Asturians also use their apples to make other drinks, such as brandy, and cider vinegar.

Cider

A distinction is made between two types of *sidra*:

Sidra natural: This cider, which is usually produced by small-scale operations, is fermented using a natural process without any additives. It has a pleasantly tart, sharpish flavor and is naturally cloudy with a strong bouquet. *Sidra natural* should always be drunk young. Even bottles of cider which are securely corked should not be kept for longer than a year following purchase.

Sidra gasificada (also *sidra dulce* or *champanada*): This is the popular name given to industrially manufactured *sidra*, which has carbonic acid and varying amounts of sugar added and is then stabilized in high-grade steel tanks. This cider is usually significantly sweeter and has fewer subtle variations of flavor than *sidra natural*. It keeps longer than the natural version and is drunk less in Asturias itself than in other parts of the country. Among industrial cider cellars which market their branded products under their own label, a distinction is made between:

Sidra Extra (semi-dry)

Sidra Selecta (dry)

Sidra Refrescante (high carbonic acid content).

Now and then you may be lucky enough to be offered a small glass of **apple brandy** (*aguardiente de manzana*). Quite unashamedly, the Asturians name it after its famous French cousin calvados – although this, of course, cannot be officially printed on any labels. In most cases, however, the distillates from the small cider cellars never reach the stores, but are sold exclusively to friends and acquaintances or savored within the family. For centuries Asturian farmers have also been using their *sidra* to produce **cider vinegar** (*vinagre de sidra*) for their own use. Nowadays, it is also mass-produced. Making it involves fermenting *sidra natural* for a second time and maturing it in oak barrels for up to two years. (Simple apple vinegar, on the other hand, is fermented straight from the must – without turning it into wine first.) The new wave of health-consciousness has won it many devotees.

This ritual of pouring *sidra* is said to improve its flavor.

Cooking with Sidra

Merluza a la sidra
Hake in cider
(Main photograph, right)

1½ lbs/750 g hake fillet
Salt and pepper
Flour for coating
Scant ½ cup/100 ml olive oil
14 oz/400 g potatoes, peeled and diced
1 small onion, finely chopped
2 cloves of garlic, finely chopped
2 apples, peeled and diced
9 oz/250 g clams, cleaned
2 cups/500 ml sidra or apple cider
1 tbsp chopped parsley

Wash the hake and pat it dry before seasoning with salt and pepper. Coat with flour, shaking off any excess.
Heat the olive oil in a flameproof dish and fry the fish on both sides. Remove the fish and keep it warm. Fry the diced potato in the oil until golden brown. Add the onion, garlic, diced apple, and clams. Cover and sweat for a few minutes, shaking the dish several times. Remove the lid, return the fish to the dish, and pour over the *sidra*.
Bake, uncovered, in a preheated oven at 345 °F/ 175 °C for about 10 minutes.
Place the fish on a warm serving plate, pour over the remaining ingredients, and sprinkle with the parsley.

Chorizo en sidra
Chorizo in cider
(Main photograph, front)

Generous 1 lb/500 g chorizo or smoked garlic sausage
3 cups/750 ml sidra or apple cider

Cut the sausage into chunks. Place it in a terra cotta dish and cover with *sidra*. Bring it to a boil and leave on a low heat to reduce the liquid by half. Serve in the dish.

Manzanas a la sidra
Apples in cider
(Main photograph, back)

4 apples
4-6 cups/1-1.5 liters sidra or apple cider
⅔ cup/125 g sugar
1 cinnamon stick
A piece of lemon rind

Peel the apples leaving the stalk intact. Place the apples in a pan and pour in enough *sidra* to cover them. Add the sugar, cinnamon stick, and lemon rind and simmer for 15-20 minutes. Remove the lemon rind and cinnamon stick.
Store the apples in the syrup or serve warm with the syrup in small dishes.

Sidra natural is still made in the traditional manner in Asturias and the neighboring Basque Country. Many producers label their products, but most bars serve from unlabeled bottles.

CUNNING FROM THE COOKPOT

Even 170 years ago the rulers of Asturias had recognized the disarming effect of good food. During the first Carlist war, which began in 1833, the government handed out weapons to the liberal civil militia. At the end of the war the men were reluctant to return their weapons. The authorities shrewdly laid on a banquet for the fighters in Oviedo. There was chickpea soup with spinach for everyone, as well as steamed salt cod and tripe, red wine, and plenty of *sidra*. The brave warriors surrendered to the hearty fare and heavy wine – and handed over their weapons. Today the festival of *El Desarme* (The Disarmament) is a gastronomic occasion commemorating this historical event at which similar amounts of food and wine are consumed.

HOME BUTCHERING

"A cada puerco le llega su San Martín," say the Spaniards almost affectionately – "Every pig has its St Martin's day." In rural areas the butchering season traditionally starts on November 11. No other domestic animal is more venerated and exalted in its use as a food source than the pig. Folk songs, fairy tales, and popular sayings all pay tribute to the pig as a walking larder, a nutriment and delicacy rolled in one. In Asturias and Galicia the pig is regarded in some churches as a *gaitero*, a mystical creature that plays the northern Spanish version of the bagpipes *(gaita)*. It is little wonder, therefore, that in many areas the pig is blessed by the village priest before it meets its maker.

Once the crops have been harvested in the autumn, each farmer sets aside a weekend for the home butchering ceremony *(matanza)*. This is a ceremony which is thought by many to have a long tradition. According to popular belief, the men must be sexually abstinent on the day before the butchering, otherwise the ground pork will go off. In rural areas it is customary for the whole family to help with the butchering. The neighbors are often there as well and the family will drag them in to lend a hand. The fattened pig will have reached a weight of 220 to 440 pounds (100 to 200 kilograms) by the time it is butchered. First, the pig has its throat cut. This is traditionally a man's job. The blood is collected and used while it is still completely fresh. Next, the bristles are burnt off, after which the dead pig is carefully cleaned with hot water on a wooden table. The butcher cuts the animal in half and the organs are removed. This is where the veterinary surgeon takes over. Only when the expert has inspected the pig's tongue and liver and confirmed that they show no sign of disease can the animal be released for processing.

Step by step, the cuts of meat are used. *"Todo es bueno en el cochino, desde el hocico al estantino"* is something that has held true for thousands of years – "Everything is good on the pig, from the snout to the spleen." It is true that every part of the pig is used: the brain and ears, the fore and hind trotters, the skin, blood, organs, and even the tail. While the men remove the ham and individual joints of meat, the women are already busy making sausages (see 206).

Of course, those at the butchering celebration are there not only to work hard, but to play hard too. The table is adorned with fresh pork products, starting with the blood sausage and fresh cooked sausages. In Asturias, these also include a pig liver soup *(sopa de fégadu)*, as well as potatoes in their skins with pig head.

There is no doubt that a well-fattened pig is a valuable source of food. Many tasty dishes are made from the various cuts of pig meat available in Asturias, and elsewhere in Spain. Sausages are popular throughout the country, and Asturias produces some fine examples.

FROM THE FAT POT

Apart from ham, bacon, and smoked sausage, another indispensable element of the Asturian larder is a ceramic pot of pig fat *(manteca)*. The melted, rendered fat is used primarily for enriching pot roasts and other meat dishes. Pig fat is also frequently used in a wide variety of sweet and savory baking, such as *ensaïmadas* or *tortas de manteca*. In rural households, *manteca* is also used to conserve meat and sausages, so that they can be enjoyed fresh, tender, and moist. The leftover rind *(chicharrones)* is used to enrich the flavor of vegetables or meat dishes, as well as in baking: a specialty is the wholesome dessert *torta de chicharrones* or *coca de llardons*.

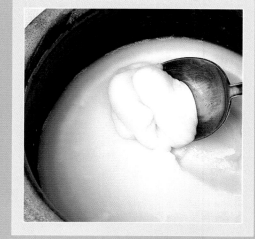

When a pig is butchered the fresh blood must be collected first. It must be used immediately.

Once the bristles have been burnt off, the pig's skin is cleaned with hot water and brushes.

To cut up the pig, the butcher lays it on a wooden table. The trotters are cut off first.

Before the pig is cut in half, the head is removed. Like everything else, this can be used.

The pig is then divided down the middle, to remove the organs and inner cuts of meat.

Almost every part of the pig is used. The trotters and innards are collected in a wooden trough.

Piece by piece, the men have cut up the pig. The meat is taken into the house in baskets and it is here that the women get to work – they are in charge of sausage-making.

The pig trotters (above) are cooked on the day of butchering, along with the skin and ears (below). A rich broth is welcome after the day's toil.

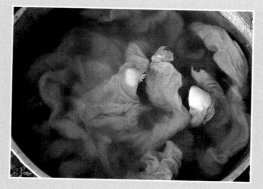

Once the pig's intestines have been carefully cleaned, they are well boiled to make them sterile so that they can be used as sausage skins.

The meat set aside for sausage-making is removed from the bone and diced up small. The fat is also used to prevent the sausage from becoming dry.

The meat is passed through the grinder, and garlic, spices, and herbs are then added, depending on the variety of sausage. The ground meat is mixed thoroughly.

The ground meat is then introduced into the skins by the sausage machine. For sausages, the pig's small intestine, appendix, and large intestine are used.

A whole host of different types of sausage are produced from various parts of the pig, with inspired combinations of spices and different intestines. These can then be boiled, smoked, or simply air-dried.

SAUSAGE-MAKING

The women's job at the butchering ceremony is to make the fresh meat into sausages. Little by little, vast quantities of meat are fed through the grinder and mixed with spices and other ingredients. They are then squeezed into the skins, which have been carefully cleaned beforehand. Sausages which are made from raw meat must be eaten within a few days and are usually boiled or fried.

Something which proves particularly popular at every Spanish butchering event is blood sausage (see inset right), which in Asturias is either fried and served immediately or smoked over oak. The *chorizo*, a sausage seasoned with garlic and paprika, and lomo embuchado, marinated pork loin, are also popular throughout Spain (see 344 f). As in other areas of Spain, two varieties of hard sausage, *longaniza* and salchichón, are commonly found (photographs 346).

A region's climate determines what happens to the sausage after it has been made. While sausages and hams can be air-dried in the arid south and west of Spain, it is usually too damp for this in the Atlantic north. As a result, in Asturias and neighboring regions most types of sausage and ham are dried for a short time and then smoked as well.

Professional butchers have special smoking rooms that they use for this. However, farmers still hang their hams and sausages in the smoke over the fireplace, as was commonplace in their grandmothers' day. Farmers prefer to use spicy oak for this. Depending on how thick and firm the sausages are, the smoking process over smoldering chips can take ten days or more. Experts ensure that the fire is kept as low as possible for smoking, because the slower and more even the process, the better the smoky flavors are able to penetrate the meat, right into the very middle. These flavors are accompanied by antiseptic substances which also penetrate the sausage, so that it keeps particularly well. If the smoking is too quick, too aggressive, or too hot, the quality and life of the product diminishes, because the meat has not been evenly smoked through.

As with *chorizo* and blood sausage, superior sausages made from venison or wild boar are also usually smoked. Asturian hams are generally air-dried for a further six months after smoking. Exquisite hams with a spicy, smoky flavor are produced in the west of Asturias, particularly in the areas around Tineo and Ibias. The smokiness of the pig meat produced in Asturias is one of the main attractions for many, a virtue born out of necessity. When it comes to sausage-making, this Atlantic region, once considered the poor house of Spain, holds its own.

Blood sausage

Even in pre-Christian times, pig and sheep blood was reputed to bestow exceptionally beneficial properties on those who ate it. Blood sausage began its triumphant advance in the Middle Ages and it is now an established feature of Iberian cuisine. Historically, *morcilla* has simply been referred to as "sausage," but nowadays it is almost always taken to mean blood sausage. In Catalonia and Andalusia, however, there are several types of *morcilla blanca* which, as the name suggests, are white because they contain no blood.

As a genuine blood sausage, *morcilla*, along with *chorizo*, is the main ingredient of many stews, such as the Asturian *fabada* or the Castilian *cocido*. Boiled or fried, dried or smoked, cold or hot, eaten alone or with other food, it goes best with a wide variety of vegetables, making it also suitable for stuffing bell peppers or cabbage leaves.

When a pig is butchered the blood must be used immediately, to prevent it from thinning. To do this, the warm blood is first stirred continuously. If the sausage is to contain pieces of meat, these are coated in a mixture of spices. Apart from meat, blood, and bacon, the filling may contain a wide variety of different ingredients: potatoes or squash, almonds or nuts, cinnamon or garlic, salt and/or sugar. The western Asturian *fiyuela* blood sausage contains white beans, rice, and sugar. However, all blood sausages have one thing in common – they are boiled before being hung up to dry. In the north they are frequently also smoked to make them keep longer, because the sausages have to last a whole year, until the next butchering ceremony. On St. Martin's Day, the cycle will begin again, and more sausages will be made.

In Asturias and neighboring regions, the fresh sausages are usually smoked. Oak is a popular wood for this, because it imparts a delicate flavor. Once they have been dried and smoked, the sausages will keep until the following year.

207

STEWS

The Christian reconquest of Spain began with heavy artillery. In the Battle of Covadonga, the Asturian Pelayo and his men gained the first victory over the Moors in 722. Legend has it that the soldiers were fed a hearty bean stew (fabada) for extra energy before going into battle, and many villagers later surmised that the rumbling and aroma had driven the Moors into retreat.

Today, the fabada asturiana is the flagship of Asturian cooking, although it has never aspired to be haute cuisine. The film director, Luis Buñuel is alleged to have once said, "This is a dish that was discovered by a nation of hungry people." Only in recent decades has this dish become more widely acceptable. Today, the recipe can even be found among the scribblings of gourmet chefs and fabada is canned and exported as far afield as South America.

As with other Asturian stews and soups, the faba plays a central part in a genuine fabada. This is a large, flat, white bean grown especially around Villaviciosa, Pravia, Cangas de Narcea, and Luarca. It comes from the New World and was brought back by Asturian sailors in days gone by.

CORN FROM THE FARM GARDEN

In around 1600 a sailor from the small Asturian town of Castropol is said to have brought back from America a cedar chest full to the brim with corn kernels. These were successfully sown in the area around Tapia and the grain spread from northern Spain to the south. Corn was easy to grow and produced higher yields than other varieties of grain in the wet climate of northern Spain. Moreover, Asturians liked the bread made from cornmeal because it was heavy and nutritious and kept far longer than other breads commonly eaten until then. By the 18th century corn had become the most important foodstuff among the rural population, alongside millet and turnips. Nowadays in Spain, corn is grown almost exclusively for cattle fodder. Cornmeal is still used for recipes which have been passed down, such as the traditional farmhouse/country/peasant breads from Asturias and Galicia or for fariñón, a coarse blood sausage from the Candàs-Luanco area. Corn porridge with water, milk, and sugar, known as (fariñes, farrapes or pulientas), is still eaten for breakfast here and there.

Fabes, of which around 1100 tons (1000 tonnes) are produced each year in Asturias, number among the most expensive types of bean in Spain, but they can boast a unique flavor – delicately buttery, they are fine-skinned with creamy, firm flesh. They should be bought snow-white, without any blemishes or marks.

Fabes are ideal for dishes which require long, slow cooking, particularly soups and stews. They are not only perfect in a real fabada (recipe below), but also have an astonishing ability to complement game, fish, or seafood and absorb their flavors. So Asturians also regularly eat beans with clams or eel, hake or salmon, chicken or goat, rabbit or mushrooms. These delicate beans are also popular as a side dish.

FABADA ASTURIANA
Asturian bean stew
(Main photograph)

Generous 1 lb/500 g lacón (cured, air-dried pork shank), boned, or cured belly pork or spareribs
14 oz/400 g large, dried, white beans (fabes)
¾ cup/150 g smoked streaky bacon, finely diced
1 onion, chopped
1 clove of garlic, chopped
2 tbsp olive oil
1 bay leaf
A few saffron threads
½ tsp sweet paprika
Pepper
2 Spanish blood sausages
2 chorizos
Salt

Soak the shank overnight, changing the water once. Soften the beans overnight in cold water. Sweat the bacon, onion, and garlic in a pan containing the olive oil until transparent. Add the meat and beans and just enough water to cover the ingredients. Season with the bay leaf, saffron, paprika, and pepper. Bring to a boil and simmer on a medium heat for around 1½ hours. Stir several times during cooking and add more water if necessary.

When the beans are almost soft, add the sausages. Adjust the seasoning and leave to simmer until the beans are completely soft. Before serving, remove the meat and sausage from the pan, cut it into pieces, and combine with the beans.

FABES CON ALMEJAS
Beans with clams

Generous 1 lb/500 g dried white beans (fabes)
2 tbsp olive oil
1 small onion, chopped
1 clove of garlic, chopped
1 bay leaf
Salt and pepper
Generous 1 lb/500 g clams
1 cup/250 ml white wine
1 tbsp chopped parsley

Soak the beans overnight in cold water. Heat the oil in a pan, add the onion and garlic, and sweat until transparent. Add the beans and just enough water to cover them. Season with the bay leaf and salt and pepper, then leave to simmer over a medium heat for 1 hour. Stir several times during cooking and add more water if necessary.

Clean the clams and remove any which are open. Add them to the beans and pour over the wine. Once the clams have opened, sprinkle on the parsley.

POTAJE DE GARBANZOS Y ESPINACAS
Chickpea and spinach soup

1¼ cups/250 g chickpeas
Salt
1 onion, spiked with 1 bay leaf and 2 cloves
2 carrots, peeled
Generous 1 lb/500 g leaf spinach
1 onion, finely chopped
3 cloves of garlic, finely chopped
2 tbsp olive oil
1 tsp mild paprika
2 slices white bread
Pepper
4 eggs

Soak the chickpeas overnight in plenty of water. Next day add some salt, the spiked onion, and carrots to the soaking water, and pour on enough water to cover all the ingredients. Bring to a boil and leave to simmer for about 40 minutes.

In the meantime, wash the leaf spinach and sweat the onion and garlic in the olive oil. Sprinkle on the paprika, add the spinach, and cook for a short time. Remove the onion and carrots from the chickpeas and take out the cloves and bay leaf. Mash the carrots and onion in a mortar with the white bread. Combine with the chickpeas and add the spinach mixture. Continue to cook for 10-15 minutes and season to taste with salt and pepper. Divide the soup between 4 ovensafe dishes, break an egg into each one and leave to set in a preheated oven at 390 °F/200 °C.

Fabada asturiana, a bean stew, is Asturias' regional dish. The *fabada* is traditionally served in shallow, earthenware bowls and eaten with wooden spoons.

Scissors are carefully used to open the sea urchin's mouth on the flat side.

Beneath the spiny shell is a sort of connective tissue which is severed.

Tweezers are now used to open up a hole large enough to remove the delicate catch.

The orange-colored, edible coral can now easily be removed with a teaspoon.

The sea urchin's reproductive organs, often referred to as coral, taste delicious.

Sea urchins are exceptionally delicate creatures. Beneath their spiny shell is concealed a soft, delicate center, which goes off quickly if the animal is robbed of its element. Once sea urchins have been removed from the water, they should be stored in ice or eaten there and then, raw with a little lemon.

Sea urchins

Even in ancient times, Greek and Roman gourmets celebrated the fine flavor of sea urchins, which were served up at feasts and banquets alongside oysters. They were the high point of a meal and were also said to give a boost to declining virility! Because sea urchins prefer to feed on plankton, algae, and other plant life, they offer a fairly concentrated taste of the sea. Due to their high iodine and mineral salt content, sea urchins are also regarded as an effective remedy for neck ache.

Sea urchins *(erizos de mar,* or in the Asturian dialect, *oricios de mar)* live in all seas in temperate to cool climatic zones and are therefore found in both the Atlantic and Mediterranean. In Spain they are mainly collected in winter along the rocky and sandy coastline of Asturias, as well as in Cantabria and Galicia and along the Costa Brava in Catalonia and the coast of the Andalusian province of Cadiz.

Only on still days with a calm sea can sea urchins be found in the shallow coastal waters. They are carefully lifted out of the water using an implement resembling a pair of tongs. Once

Opposite: In Asturia and other regions, sea-urchins are often caught by professional divers. The men collect the animals with nets from the sea-bed.

robbed of their element, sea urchins go off very quickly, which is why connoisseurs eat their delicate catch raw, straight from the sea.

To eat the flesh of a fresh sea urchin, first open the animal's mouth using a pair of scissors or a sharp knife. Then slit open the flat side around the mouth and drain off the sea water. The small piece of orange to purple-red flesh (or coral) can now be lifted out from the inside of the spiny shell and eaten raw. (Incidentally, the coral is nothing more than the reproductive glands of the male and female sea urchins.) Occasionally, the flesh is also boiled briefly; it can also be served with scrambled egg or *au gratin* with cider or sparkling wine.

Some Asturian producers are now marketing canned sea urchin delicacies. To obtain the delicate sea urchin roe *(caviar de oricios)*, the shell is first removed from the female sea urchin and the tender roe is then carefully detached. This product, which is both quite exquisite and rather expensive, is canned by hand and sold in 70, 120, or 280 gram (about 2½, 4¼, or 9¾ ounces) weights.

Sea urchin pâté *(paté de oricios)* is made from sea urchin flesh, hake, and Asturian butter. This delicate pâté can also be made at home. Sea urchin pâté or roe can be used to enrich sauces, soups, or scrambled egg. The flavor of the sea urchin comes across just as well served on a piece of toast.

For those not wishing to eat the fresh sea urchins immediately, they are best served *au gratin* (photograph) – or with scrambled eggs.

In Spain sea urchins *(erizos)* come in various colors.

Wild salmon are caught with flies. Anglers use bait made from feathers or plastic, which look like real flies and float on the water.

Fat wild salmon are not a rarity in Asturias. They frolic in rivers like the Río Sello (main photo) and may only be caught when they are over 22 inches (55 centimeters) long.

WILD SALMON

Wild salmon was not always a delicacy. But today it is one of the most sought-after freshwater fish and should be prepared in such a way that it retains its flavor.

During the Middle Ages the monasteries were constantly complaining about the farmers. This was because only the monks had official fishing rights over many Asturian rivers – a fact which the farmers frequently ignored. Without seeking the clergy's consent, they would fish for salmon, taking cartloads of fish to sell at market. Historical documents even suggest that farmers would occasionally mix secret tinctures made from green walnuts or a plant related to the bay *(Daphne laureola)* and tip them into rivers to drug the salmon and make them easier to catch.

However, salmon was not a particular delicacy in those days. It was regarded as quite an ordinary food. Reports even chronicle an "anti-salmon campaign" launched by the building workers who constructed the church of Santa María in the Basque town of Tolosa in the 17ᵗʰ century. With violent protest, they succeeded in ensuring that the clergy, who had undertaken to feed the builders, could not give them wild salmon to eat more than twice a week – they were so tired of it.

Even at the start of the 18ᵗʰ century, 12,000 salmon a year were being caught in the Río Sella alone. The national fishing encyclopedia even claims that between 1791 and 1795 up to 2000 salmon a day were caught at the height of the season. Although the number of wild salmon in northern Spanish rivers has declined greatly since 1900, they have not yet died out completely. Even in nonadays, there are years when anglers pull over a thousand wild salmon out of Asturian waters. The Sella, Cares, Eo, Esva, Narcea, and Deva rivers are regarded as particularly good fishing waters. The conservation regulations are strictly enforced, to prevent salmon and trout from being overfished. Each angler may catch a maximum of three salmon a day and these must be at least 22 inches (55 centimeters) long.

Anglers are seen standing next to the rivers mainly in spring and early summer, when the predatory wild salmon returns from the expanse of the open sea and battles its way upriver, to spawn in the upper reaches. The anglers generally use homemade flies as bait, which they model themselves to resemble an insect and which have a hook attached to the middle. Catching a fully grown wild salmon, which may be over 5 feet (1.5 meters) long and weigh over 110 pounds (50 kilograms), is naturally an outstanding event. Farm-bred salmon simply pale with envy at the firmness of its flesh and intensity of its flavor.

The best way of doing justice to the noble wild salmon is to eat it as naturally as possible, as steaks or fillets. Sophisticated methods of preparing wild salmon are virtually unheard of in traditional cooking. Dishes commonly found in Asturias are *salmón a la ribereña* (salmon with *sidra*) and *marmita de salmón*, a salmon and potato casserole. Another popular way of cooking salmon is very simple. First lay it in milk and season it with lemon juice and herbs. Then simply broil it.

SALMON A LA RIBEREÑA
Salmon Asturian style

4 salmon fillets, each weighing 7 oz/200 g
Salt and pepper
Flour for coating
2 tbsp olive oil
2 tbsp butter
2½ oz/75 g air-dried Serrano ham
½ cup/125 ml fish stock
½ cup/125 ml sidra *or apple cider*

Rinse the salmon fillets, pat them dry, and season with salt and pepper. Turn them in the flour and shake off any excess. Heat the olive oil and butter in a skillet and fry the salmon for about 5 minutes on each side on a medium heat. Lift from the skillet and keep warm. Cut the ham into fine strips and fry it in the oil. Deglaze the skillet with the fish stock and *sidra* and leave it to reduce for a while. Place the salmon fillets on a preheated serving dish and pour over the sauce.

Serve with potatoes in their skins and broiled tomatoes, accompanied by *sidra* or a light wine.

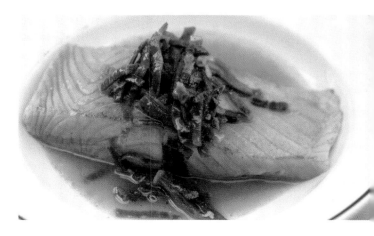

CABRALES

Asturias is *the* cheese center of Spain. Over 40 officially registered varieties of cheese are produced by several hundred usually small-scale, family businesses situated in this mountainous region. Particularly in the high mountain known as Picos de Europa, which still inhabited by bears and rare birds of prey, herders continue to roam through the mountains with their cows, goats, and sheep, and produce their own varieties of cheese. Although most businesses have adapted their standards to comply with modern hygienic requirements, many varieties of cheese are still made to traditional recipes from fresh, unpasteurized milk and are sold only in small quantities locally.

Queso de Cabrales, a cheese which the author Benito Pérez Galdós described as having a "pestilent aroma," is the only one to have made a name for itself far beyond the boundaries of Asturias. *Cabrales* comes from the area around Cabrales and Peñamellera Alta and is a three-milk cheese. Unpasteurized cow milk is mixed with varying quantities of goat and sheep milk. It is then warmed and curdled by adding small amounts of rennet. Once the whey has been drained off, the cheese is broken up into pieces the size of a hazelnut and pressed into cylindrical molds. The cheese is then left for one to two weeks to dry.

Cabrales obtains its characteristic blue veining in the limestone caves typical of the region. These natural maturing chambers, which were created thousands of years ago, are evenly ventilated throughout the year by cool winds which blow through the porous stone. These are accompanied by a high atmospheric humidity of around 90

Cabrales, the traditional three-milk cheese, is produced in several small villages in the Picos de Europa mountain range. The cool winds help it to mature.

Farmers' wives, who still produce *Cabrales* in the traditional way, use a mixture of sheep, cow, and goat milk, which is thickened with rennet.

A mature *Cabrales* cheese has a blue vein running through it. It used to be packed in moist maple leaves, but now is mainly sold in printed foil.

percent and low temperatures of between 46 and 54 °F (8 and 12 °C). Under these conditions, bacteria, yeast, and the fungus in the caves (*penicillium claverum*, similar to the *Roquefort* fungus) act on the cheese's metabolic process. The cheese must be turned several times during the maturing process and the rinds must be cleaned, so that they have sufficient air to enable the mold to continue to develop. Three to six months later, a firm, blue-veined cheese will emerge. *Cabrales* was traditionally sold wrapped in moist maple leaves. However, modern European Union hygiene regulations increasingly require this packaging to be replaced by foil with a leaf motif stamped on it.

Although the famous *Cabrales* has been protected by a quality classification (D.O.) since 1985, there are still significant differences in quality. The best comparison is offered by the cheese market in Arenas de Cabrales, held each year on the last Sunday in August, where the area's cheese producers exhibit their products.

Although overshadowed by the famous *Cabrales*, its relative *Queso de Gamonedo* is still an insider's tip. It is also a three-milk cheese, made from cow, sheep, and goat milk. The cheese is compressed, making *Gamonedo* more compact than *Cabrales*. It is also lightly smoked and then matured in limestone caves, where it develops a fine blue veining only around the edge, due to its density. This cheese used to be wrapped in ferns after it had matured. *Gamonedo* will often outstrip *Cabrales* in terms of flavor and aroma. However, it is usually only sold locally.

TERNERA AL CABRALES
Veal fillet with *Cabrales* cheese

4 slices of veal fillet, each weighing 5 oz/150 g
2 tbsp oil
5 tbsp/75 g butter
½ cup/125 ml brown stock
½ cup/125 ml cream
3½ oz/100 g Cabrales or another blue cheese, finely diced
Scant 1 cup/200 ml brandy
Salt and pepper

Fry the veal steaks in hot oil for a minute on each side. Remove them from the skillet and keep warm. Melt the butter in the skillet and fry the mushrooms in it. Deglaze with the brown stock and pour in the cream. Melt the cheese in the sauce, add the brandy, and season with salt and pepper. Return the veal steaks to the sauce for a few minutes, depending on how they are to be cooked, and serve them in the sauce.

Fresh *Cabrales* cheese is snow-white (above). Its characteristic blue veining develops only during lengthy maturing in cool, damp, limestone caves (background), where the *Penicillium* bacteria can act effectively.

WHAT IS RENNET?

Many cheese-making processes involve the milk being curdled by adding animal rennet *(cuajo)*. This liquid is extracted from the mucous membrane of the stomachs of suckling calves, sheep, and goats. It contains the proteolytic enzyme chymosin, which enables the young to digest their mothers' milk. Even in ancient times, the process of adding animal rennet to milk to curdle it was well known, probably as the result of a fortuitous discovery. In those days, calves' stomachs were used to store and transport milk, which then miraculously thickened.

This property was put to good use and even the Romans used rennet to process milk into cheese. The amount of rennet used and the curdling temperature are the two factors crucial to the consistency of the cheese. The more rennet used and the warmer the milk (up to 113 °F/45 °C), the firmer the end product.

Because cheese consumption is constantly on the increase, there is now no longer sufficient animal rennet available to meet demand. Tests involving pig and chicken rennet have proved unsuccessful. As a result, cheese makers are using rennet substitutes more and more frequently. This is usually microbial rennet obtained from fungus. In many countries, rennet which has been genetically manufactured with the aid of microorganisms is used. This method is not yet permitted in Spain.

Spanish Cheese

Cow Cheese

Tetilla ("little tit"): a very mild, creamy cow cheese, briefly matured, from the Galician provinces of A Coruña and Lugo.

San Simón: a tangy, semi-cured cut cheese from Galicia, matured for three weeks and then smoked over birch wood.

Arzúa-Ulloa: a semi-cured cut cheese, similar to Tetilla, but with a slightly stronger flavor due to longer ripening.

Mahón-Menorca: a fairly sharp, semi-cured cut cheese from the island of Minorca. The milk is thickened with herbs, rather than animal rennet.

Sheep Cheese

Burgos: a snow-white, moist, lightly salted fresh cheese made from Castilian sheep milk.

Zamorano: a tangy hard cheese from Castile, which used to be molded in baskets made from esparto grass.

Manchego: made from the milk of Manchego sheep, at varying stages of ripeness. The definitive Spanish cheese.

Torta el Casar: a sheep cheese from Extremadura made from the milk of the Churra sheep, with a soft to runny center and a very strong flavor.

Idiazábal: a Basque hard cheese made from the milk of the long-haired Lacha sheep.

Roncal: a hard cheese from Navarra, with a flavor ranging from delicate to very piquant.

Tronchón: a hard cheese from Aragon and the hinterland of Valencia. Sometimes goat milk is also added.

Tupí: a soft cheese from the Catalan Pyrenees, sometimes also produced with goat milk and a small amount of liqueur.

Mixed Cheese

Picón: a Cantabrian three-milk blue cheese from the mountains of the Picos de Europa. Particularly creamy and tangy, it used to be wrapped in leaves.

Cabrales: a blue cheese from the Picos de Europa in Asturias, matured in limestone caves. With a distinctive, tangy flavor, it used to be wrapped in maple leaves.

Quesucos: a small cheese from northern Spain (about 2¼ pounds/1 kilogram) made from a mixture of milk or individual types of milk, or smoked and plain varieties.

Goat Cheese

Queso curado al vino de Murcia: a Murcian goat cheese made from the fragrant milk of the *cabra murciana* breed, cured for a while in red wine.

Ibores: a hard cheese from Extremadura, frequently rubbed with oil and paprika, which gives it its reddish hue and spicy flavor.

Queso de cabra: a pure, hard goat cheese from the mountains of Andalusia, as well as other regions.

Montsec: a hard goat cheese from Catalonia, snow-white and creamy inside, the outside is rubbed with wood ash during the maturing phase.

Majorero: a cut cheese from the Canary Island of Fuerteventura, made from the milk of goats which graze in meadows, living mainly off marjoram.

Camerano: a fresh goat cheese from the mountains of La Rioja, made traditionally in wicker baskets.

Mató: a fresh goat cheese from Catalonia, previously made with vegetable rennet, although now animal rennet tends to be used.

Goats live almost all over Spain. They thrive in the mountainous regions of the north, where their milk goes to produce three-milk cheese. They can also be found on the plateau and in Mediterranean areas, where although vegetation is frequently sparse, they are able to survive and produce particularly aromatic milk for tangy varieties of cheese.

CAKES AND COOKIES FROM NORTHERN SPAIN

SOBAOS PASIEGOS
Cantabrian butter sponge cake

1¼ cups/300 g softened butter
1½ cups/300 g sugar
1 envelope vanilla sugar
Pinch of salt
Grated rind of 1 lemon
5 eggs, separated
2½ cups/300 g flour
Butter and breadcrumbs for the cake pan

Beat together the butter, half the sugar, the vanilla sugar, salt, and lemon rind until light and creamy. Gradually add the egg yolks. Beat the egg whites until stiff, while slowly adding the remaining sugar. Mix half the egg white into the butter mixture, then carefully fold in the sifted flour and the remaining egg white.
Butter a loose-based cake pan and sprinkle with breadcrumbs. Add the sponge mixture and bake in a preheated oven at 355 °F/180 °C for about 45 minutes. Leave the cake to cool slightly in the pan for 15 minutes, then turn it onto a wire rack to cool completely.

CASADIELLES
Walnut popovers

Pastry:
4⅓ cups/500 g flour
1 tsp salt
1 cup/250 g butter

Filling:
7½ cups/600 g ground walnuts
2 cups/400 g sugar
5 tbsp honey
2½ tbsp aniseed

Oil for frying
Confectioners' sugar for decorating

Make the pastry dough using the flour, salt, butter, and a cup of water and leave it to stand for 30 minutes. In the meantime, mix the ground walnuts, sugar, honey, and aniseed together well for the filling.
Roll out the dough thinly and cut it into rectangular pieces. Place some filling on each piece and wrap the dough around it. Press the long sides of the dough together using a fork.
Fry the pastry pockets individually in hot oil. Lift them out of the oil and drain on paper towels. Sprinkle with confectioners' sugar before serving.

Variation: The filled pastry pockets can also be coated with beaten egg, placed on a buttered baking sheet, and baked in a preheated oven at 395 °F/200 °C until golden (see photograph).

FRIXUELOS
(photograph left)
Sweet pancakes

3 eggs
2 cups/500 ml milk
Pinch of salt
Scant 1¼ cups/125 g flour
8 tsp olive oil
Jam for filling

Beat the eggs in a bowl with the milk and salt. Sift in the flour and whisk until the batter is smooth. Leave it to stand for 1 hour.
Heat a teaspoon of olive oil in an iron skillet and pour in one-eighth of the batter. When the underside is lightly browned, flip the pancake over and cook the other side. Remove it from the skillet and keep warm until all 8 pancakes are ready. Spread the pancakes thinly with jam, roll them up, and serve immediately.

Variation: *Frixuelos* can also be filled with cream or simply sprinkled with sugar.

CARBAYONES
Almond boats

Pastry:
1 cup/250 g butter
Generous 2 cups/250 g flour
1 tsp salt

Filling:
2 eggs, separated
Grated rind of ½ lemon
⅔ cup/125 g sugar
2½ tbsp brandy
2½ cups/250 g ground almonds

Butter for greasing

Egg custard:
6 egg yolks
1 cup/200 g sugar
Grated rind of 1 lemon
1 tbsp arrowroot

Chocolate frosting or plain white icing for decorating

Prepare the pastry dough using the butter, flour, salt, and ½ cup/125 ml of water and leave it to stand in the refrigerator for 30 minutes.
In the meantime, cream the egg yolks with the lemon rind and sugar for the filling. Mix in the brandy and ground almonds. Beat the egg whites until stiff, then fold them in carefully.
Roll the dough out thinly. Butter some small, rectangular baking molds and line them with the dough. Divide the filling between the boats and cover with aluminum foil, to prevent them from burning in the oven. Bake the boats in a preheated oven at 395 °F/200 °C until golden brown. Remove from the oven and leave to cool slightly. For the egg custard, beat the egg yolks with the sugar until light and creamy. Add the lemon rind. Dissolve the arrowroot in a little water and add to the egg and sugar mixture. Beat constantly over warm water until a thick custard forms, then spread over the Carbayones. Leave the boats to cool completely and finally spread them with a thin layer of chocolate frosting or plain white icing.

Opposite: Apple tart *(tarta de manzana)* is particularly popular in the north, but today it is common all over Spain and is often served as a dessert.

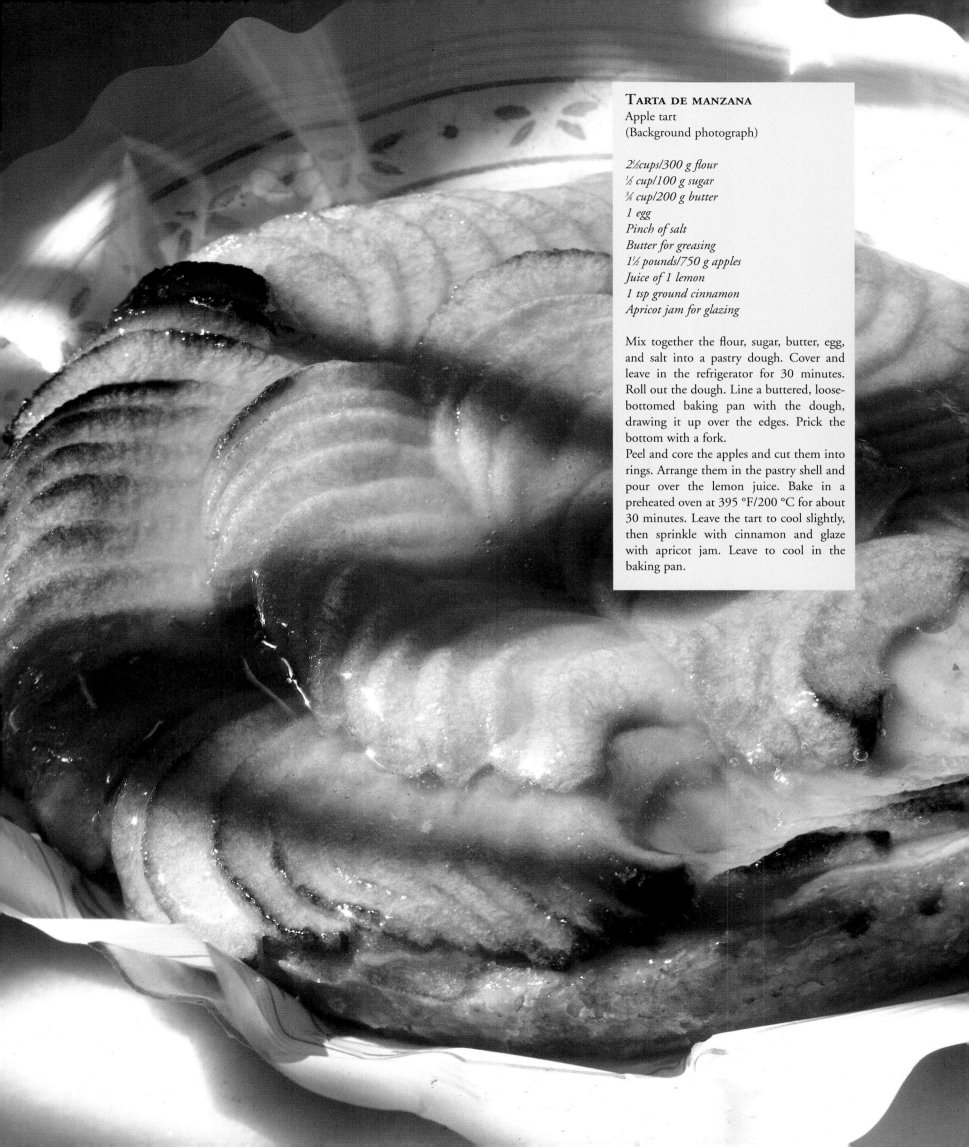

TARTA DE MANZANA
Apple tart
(Background photograph)

2½cups/300 g flour
½ cup/100 g sugar
¾ cup/200 g butter
1 egg
Pinch of salt
Butter for greasing
1½ pounds/750 g apples
Juice of 1 lemon
1 tsp ground cinnamon
Apricot jam for glazing

Mix together the flour, sugar, butter, egg, and salt into a pastry dough. Cover and leave in the refrigerator for 30 minutes. Roll out the dough. Line a buttered, loose-bottomed baking pan with the dough, drawing it up over the edges. Prick the bottom with a fork.

Peel and core the apples and cut them into rings. Arrange them in the pastry shell and pour over the lemon juice. Bake in a preheated oven at 395 °F/200 °C for about 30 minutes. Leave the tart to cool slightly, then sprinkle with cinnamon and glaze with apricot jam. Leave to cool in the baking pan.

GALICIA

Harald Klöcker

Galicia

The Galicians enjoy hearty food and the butcher provides the raw ingredients: pork, beef, and lamb with fresh vegetables from the fields.

No Galician is ever seen without his rubber boots, woolen scarf, and umbrella – the Spaniards in the sunny south enjoy making the odd jibe at this region which lies in the extreme northwest of their country. And such mockery is not entirely unfounded – mist and strong wind, drizzle and an often depressingly overcast sky characterize both the weather and the mood of Galicia. The people themselves are seen as reserved, taciturn, and very superstitious – alternating, like the weather, between one obstinacy and the next. They speak their own language, the ancient *gallego*, and unlike most other regions of Spain, the northwest holds virtually no trace of an earlier Moorish presence. Instead, Celtic settlements and Roman bridges shape the character of the hinterland of a dramatically rugged coastline running for 745 miles (1200 kilometers). The landscape is defined by small to minute cultivated fields lying between barren hills, wild, overgrown bush land, eucalyptus woods, meadows, and vineyards. Most people living in this economically underdeveloped region were left with only two employment options: eking out an existence as a small farmer or fisherman. Many Galicians were forced to emigrate abroad, as there was no lucrative employment to be found at home. Those who remained proudly and obstinately respect Galician customs, Celtic traditions, and folklore rituals. The Galicians attribute super-natural powers to the elements of fire, water, and wind, and many believe even today in the transmigration of souls, as well as the existence of witches and spirits. Galician soil is sacred to its inhabitants; people do not trade with their own piece of land and would never sell it. So in this region the hard-earned products of soil and sea enjoy the respect of a possession that cannot be taken away from anyone, whether rich or poor, and that must be augmented and cherished. Eating and drinking are the veritable elixir of life for the locals, removing the toil and drudgery of everyday existence and raising the spirits. The Galicians catch over 80 different types of saltwater fish, both along their coast and farther afield, as well as an almost equal variety of mussels and other shellfish. In the hinterland, farmers cultivate fruit and vegetables; raise poultry, pigs, and beef cattle; catch freshwater fish; and use milk to produce cheese. And, not least, the excellent wines and brandies produced in their region fill the Galicians with an almost patriotic pride, providing warmth which is usually lacking in the region's somewhat inhospitable weather.

Opposite: Fisterre, the most westerly tip of the Spanish mainland, was considered to be the end of the world in the Middle Ages.

VEGETABLES

Large estates with vast expanses of land, such as those found in Castile or Andalusia, are unheard of in Galicia. In the northwest of Spain, subsistence or small-field farming still has a firm hold. The land is divided into thousands of parcels, often less than a couple of acres in size. The reason for this is that until now the traditional division of inheritance has been observed. If the head of a family dies, all his children inherit a piece of land, and they all keep their patch of earth, whether they farm it or not. Because a small parcel does not yield much, teams of oxen are still used for plowing in many areas.

The Galician vegetable garden supplies the kitchen with different types of cabbage, beet, beans, peppers, tomatoes, squash, garlic, onions, potatoes, and turnips *(nabos)*. The flowering stalks of this plant *(grelos*, see main photograph) are particularly sought. They are succulent with a slightly bitter taste and form the basic ingredient of many hearty winter dishes. *Grelos* are traditionally served with pork or sausages, but nowadays they also accompany fish or seafood.

While elsewhere in Spain people may sometimes turn their noses up at the unusual flavor of turnip leaves, *pimientos de Padrón*, small capsicumsonly 2–3 inches (5–7.5 centimeters) long, are universally regarded as a delicacy. The cultivation of these green peppers guarantees a living for around two hundred families living in the towns of Padrón and Herbón to the south of Santiago. The aromatic pods go well with meat dishes or *chorizo* and are also served by themselves in bars as tapas. For this the *pimientos* are fried in olive oil and sprinkled with coarse sea salt (photograph on 84). But beware, for amidst the mildly mouth-watering baby peppers there is always one that proves fiendishly hot. It looks like all the others but brings tears to the eyes of the eater, leaving him at the mercy of his table companions and their cutting jibes.

In contrast, the large, fleshy green bell peppers from La Limia are completely harmless and ideal for stuffing. The region of La Limia, situated to the southwest of Orense on the Río Miño, is also known for its excellent potatoes. International and Spanish varieties are grown. The Kennebeck variety is sold under the seal of quality as *Patacas de Galicia*. However, most households only distinguish between two varieties. *La roja* (a reddish potato) is hardy and remains exceptionally firm when boiled. It is a particularly good accompaniment to fish dishes. *La blanca* (white potato) is considerably lighter, softer, and more mealy, making it ideal for the *cocido gallego* and other stews. Most of all, though, the Galicians love their *cachelos*: new potatoes eaten in their skins.

Galician cuisine is clearly very healthy. It is well supplemented with vegetables of all types, and they provide the basis of as many dishes as the meat, fish and cheese produced in the region.

Following an old tradition, Galician farmers store corn and occasionally other vegetables like onions, garlic, squash, and other field crops in *hórreos* or typical granite storehouses. The *hórreos* were inherited from the Celts. They stand on wooden or stone stilts, designed to protect the stored food from damp rising from the soil, as well as rats and other rodents. The roof may be made of wooden laths, stone slabs, tiles, or – less commonly today – a thick layer of straw. A particularly large number of *hórreos* have survived to date in the coastal town of Combarro.

Above: Potatoes and cabbage from the farm garden provide the basis of many Galician dishes.

Right: Tender, young turnip leaves are the main ingredient of many hearty casseroles.

FERTILIZER FROM THE SEA

Long before the manufacture of artificial fertilizers, Mother Nature had prepared everything the soil needs to be productive. In the coastal regions of Galicia, farmers can still be seen today gathering seaweed, sea grass, and algae at low tide to nourish their land. In years gone by, this harvest washed ashore by the tide would have been laboriously loaded onto oxcarts and transported to the pasture. Nowadays, tractors help to move the sea's nutritious resources to the fields. This free fertilizer is rich in iodine and minerals. It is often plowed into the soil where corn is later to be grown, as this is a crop which leaches the soil of many nutrients. In addition to this, farmers who work land close to the coast are still happy to use the calcareous shells of mussels and crabs to fertilize their fields. By contrast, farther inland where woods and heathland flourish, chestnut shells or a variety of broom referred to in Galician as *toxo* are used as organic fertilizers for fields and gardens. These natural fertilizers are often thought to be superior to any produced artificially.

At low tide, farmers gather valuable fertilizers for their fields along the Atlantic beaches: algae, seaweed, and sea grass are a source of minerals.

225

Hearty food for colder days

Caldo gallego
Galician soup

1½ cups/250 g dried white beans
1 ham knuckle
Salt, pepper, and sweet paprika powder
Generous 1 lb/500 g potatoes, peeled and diced
Generous 1 lb/500 g turnip tops, alternatively
spring or savoy cabbage, rinsed and coarsely
chopped
2 chorizos, cut into pieces

Soak the beans overnight in plenty of cold water.
Next day, bring the beans and the ham knuckle
to a boil in 8½ cups/2 liters of water. Season with
the salt, pepper, and paprika, and simmer for
about 1 hour. Remove the ham bone and add the
potatoes, vegetables, and *chorizo*. Continue
cooking for another 30 minutes.
Serve the soup in earthenware bowls.

Lacon con grelos
Cured pork shoulder with turnip tops

2¼ lbs/1 kg cured pork shoulder (lacón), *cured
belly pork or cured pork spareribs*
8 small potatoes, peeled
2¼ lbs/1 kg turnip tops, alternatively spring
cabbage, washed and chopped
4 chorizos
Salt
Pepper

Turnip tops and potatoes are an essential ingredient of
every *caldo gallego*. Spicy *chorizo* is added to them.

Cover the pork shoulder with cold water and
soak for 24 hours, changing the water several
times. Put the pork shoulder in a pan with
plenty of water. Bring it to a boil and simmer
for around 2 hours until tender. Remove the
meat and keep it warm. Cook the potatoes,
turnip tops, and *chorizos* in the stock for 25
minutes, then season with salt and pepper. Lift
the *chorizos* out of the stock and drain the
vegetables. Save the stock for soup. Cut the
meat into pieces and transfer it to a large
serving plate with the *chorizos* and vegetables.
Serve piping hot.

First of all, white beans are boiled until they are almost cooked; a ham knuckle produces the heavenly flavor.

The potatoes, vegetables, and sausage are only added 30 minutes before the end of the cooking time.

The slightly bitter turnip tops and spicy *chorizo* are an ideal combination.

Cocido gallego
Galician stew

1½ cups/250 g dried chickpeas
4 slices of belly pork
9 oz/250 g beef
½ pig's head, cut into four
1 slice fat streaky bacon
1 ham knuckle
Salt
Generous 1 lb/500 g turnip tops, alternatively savoy or spring cabbage, washed and coarsely chopped
8 small potatoes, peeled
4 chorizos or other paprika sausages

First soak the chickpeas overnight in plenty of cold water.
Bring the meat, pig's head, bacon, and ham knuckle to a boil in 12 cups/3 liters of salted water. Cover and simmer for about 1 hour.
Cook the chickpeas in a pan with some of the meat stock for 1 hour. In a second pan, boil the turnip tops in some meat stock for about 30 minutes.
After 1 hour remove the ham knuckle and add the potatoes to the meat; lay on the *chorizos* and cook for another 25 minutes. Then lift the meat, potatoes, and sausages from the stock. Drain the chickpeas and turnip tops. Arrange all the ingredients separately in a preheated serving dish and serve immediately.

Right: For centuries the kitchen was the focal point of every house. Warming stews bubbled in the pot over an open fire – in days gone by, this too was the scene in the home of Galician writer Rosalía de Castro in Padrón. Today her house is a museum.

THE KITCHEN MEETING PLACE

During that cold season, the kitchen became the main focal point of the house, as a place where mainly women would come to chatter and relax. Barefoot, a few would shyly venture in, scarves fastened in triangles around their heads; others would sigh contentedly as they approached the luxuriously warm kitchen fire; yet others would grasp their spindles and, their skirts full of flax from their belts, begin to spin, but only after they had warmed their hands, or produced chestnuts from their pockets and laid them to roast in the glowing embers. And gradually the soft whispers grew to a chattering crescendo. Sabel was the queen of this tiny royal household. Warmed by the fire, with sleeves rolled up and eyes moist from the smoke, she would receive the incense of adulation, dip the iron ladle into the pot, and fill bowls with the soup, whereupon one of the women would immediately leave the circle, withdrawing to a corner or a bench where she could be heard eagerly chewing, blowing the boiling hot broth, and slurping it by the spoonful. There were evenings when the girl did nothing other than tirelessly fill the mugs or bowls, while a constant stream of women came in, were served, and withdrew to make space for another.

(Extract from: Emilia Pardo Bazón, *The Estate of Ulloa*, 1886)

FAIRGROUND OCTOPUS

The ancient Greeks firmly believed that octopus *(pulpo)* increased male virility and potency, and even today the question of whether the meat of *Octopus vulgaris* really holds any aphrodisiac properties is enthusiastically debated at Galician festivals – perhaps in anticipation of what is to come after the festivities.

However, all mythical and mystical speculation aside, there is also a quite profane reason why octopus is traditionally served at Galician festivals – the delicious mollusk has always been an inexpensive delicacy requiring little preparation. The flesh must be nice and tender, but still firm with enough bite. The Galicians are particularly keen on octopus caught in their own waters, due to its freshness. However, octopus caught off Africa is often served as well. It is darker and less tender.

Pulpo a feira (fairground octopus) is unimaginably easy to prepare. To tenderize the octopus, once it has been thoroughly cleaned, its tentacles are banged against a hard surface about ten times. Modern chefs simply leave the octopus in the freezer for three days to tenderize the flesh. The octopus is then briefly dipped in boiling water three times and finally left to simmer gently in water with a whole onion and a bay leaf for around 2 hours. Once the octopus has been drained, its tentacles are cut into small pieces using a pair of scissors, arranged on a wooden board, and seasoned with coarse sea salt, medium-hot paprika, and a good, cold-pressed olive oil. If liked, a hint of crushed garlic may also be added. In Galicia it is customary to drink red Ribeiro wine with *pulpo a feira* – preferably from a typical white, porcelain bowl.

Large pots are to be found everywhere: *Pulpo a feira* is prepared out in the open at Galician festivals. The octopus is quite simply boiled in water.

Shearing the manes and tails of wild ponies, once a hard job, has now been turned into a festival in La Estrada-Sabucedo.

GALICIAN FESTIVALS

There is scarcely a week in the annual calendar that does not provide the occasion for a festival. The Galicians celebrate the festivals in the Christian calendar, the feast day of the village's patron saint, and the famous *curros*, which are held each summer in over 20 locations. In a colorful spectacle, semi-wild mountain ponies are driven into pens *(curros)*. Here they are branded, their manes and tails cropped, and then the festivities begin.

The Galicians have been taming wild ponies since the Bronze Age. However, clipping their manes and tails was not always a labor of love. It used to be hard work and afterward the men would get together with food and drink to relax and celebrate. The tradition lives on and today it is a festival for everyone, where there is singing and dancing, and people have a few drinks and polish off vast quantities of turnovers *(empanadas)* and octopus *(pulpo a feira)*.

If you are a fan of a particular specialty, there is every chance you will find it has its own fiesta, because Galicia boasts no fewer than 300 culinary festivals. These usually last a whole weekend and are devoted to individual products or dishes – oysters or clams, glass eel or lamprey, potatoes or chestnuts, Albariño wine or marc brandy *(orujo)*. Music and dance is naturally always an integral part of these celebrations, yet there is no sign of flamenco. Instead, the sounds of the bagpipe, flute, and drums are more reminiscent of Ireland or Britanny, and the *morriña*, the proverbial Galician melancholy, which is also expressed in the music, can make you forget for a few hours that you are actually in Spain. The roots of Galician culture are to be found way back in the region's Celtic past (see also 254), a history very different from elsewhere in Spain.

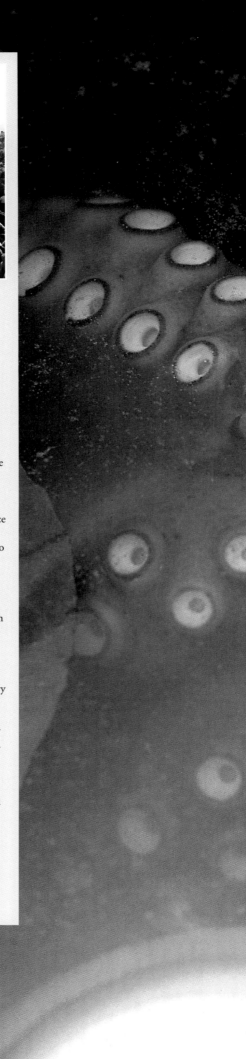

The octopus is boiled in plenty of boiling water with an onion and bay leaf.

The octopus is cooked until it is nice and tender, then removed from the water and briefly drained.

The tentacles are cut into bite-size pieces using a pair of scissors and then heavily seasoned.

In Galicia, the favorite way of serving *pulpa a feira* is on rustic wooden plates.

GALICIA THE FISHING NATION

Each year 16,200 boats with a total gross register tonnage of half a million transport almost 1.43 million tons (1.4 million tonnes) of fish. The Spanish fishing fleet, the largest in Europe, glows with superlatives. New fishing grounds are constantly being opened up and new techniques developed, because of the insatiable appetite for fish. Unlike the Mediterranean, large parts of which have already been overfished, the cold waters of the Atlantic, rich in oxygen and plankton, are still home to an astonishing quantity and variety of edible fish. Due to its exposed position on the northwest tip of Spain, Galicia has for centuries been associated with shipping and fishing. Since the discovery of abundant fish stocks off the coast of Newfoundland in the 16th century and the large-scale fishing associated with this, the Galicians have ventured far out into the Atlantic.

The high demand on domestic and foreign markets decimated fish stocks in almost all the world's seas and relentless international competition have meant that nowadays the Galician fleet operates almost world-wide. State-of-the-art trawlers sail as far as the coasts of Canada, South America, and Africa, equipped with navigational computers for locating shoals of fish and exploring the ocean bed. The catch is usually sorted and graded on board, so that the fish can be processed in the Galician canning factories as soon as the boat returns. Certain top-quality products, which are particularly sought on international markets, are exported direct to other European countries, Australia, or Asia, completely by-passing the Spanish fish auctions. This is how Galician fishermen sell large quantities of black halibut (*fletán negro*), caught at depths of 3280 – 4920 feet (1000 to 1500 meters) off the coast of Newfoundland, straight on to Japan, where it commands the best possible prices.

Vigo, with a total of 500,000 inhabitants the largest city in Galicia and often lauded as the "Barcelona of the Atlantic," is Spain's most important fishing port and the third largest in Europe. Every day the local newspapers publish the latest fish and seafood prices, because the town lives from its trade in the sea's resources, the associated canning industry, and production of fish meal and oil. Fresh produce leaves Vigo and A Coruña on modern transport systems to reach the major cities, above all Madrid and Barcelona. Galicians are very proud of their fishing traditions, although clearly today this is big business, which benefits from the new technologies at its disposal.

GALICIAN TURBOT

The Spaniards' love of fish has led to a substantial increase in the number of fish farms in Galicia over the last 20 years. Breeders have experienced particular success with the farming of turbot (*rodaballo*). The world's largest breeding installation is located in the Galician Lira-Carnota, where 1200 tons (1100 tonnes) of turbot are reared each year. The work is costly, which is why the fish command such a high price. They are fattened for four years until they have reached a weight of 7½ pounds (3.5 kilograms) and can be sold. Wild turbot are smaller, but far outstrip their farm-reared cousins. Their flesh is firmer and has a better flavor. However, the small quantities of wild turbot caught go almost exclusively to Madrid's top restaurants and can seldom be found in Galicia. The richer people in the capital are willing to pay a high price for this fish.

Fish auction

Early morning in the port of A Coruña. The previous day, several trawlers have returned with vast quantities of fish and seafood. During the night, the catch was unloaded, graded according to type, size, and quality, and moved to the auction hall *(lonja)*. It is not quite seven o'clock, yet the atmosphere is indescribably hectic. Dozens of wholesalers or *asentadores* dash through the halls, casting an expert eye over the different qualities of produce lying side-by-side in crates, soon to be auctioned: swordfish, sardines, cod, hake, lobster, crayfish, and different types of tuna. A few dealers shout into their mobiles, gesticulating wildly, trying to agree a final price with their customers, while others jot down the results of their checks.

Although the eight new, automatically cooled auction halls have only been opened in February 2004, no computers are used for the auctions. "They are simply too slow," says one of the persons responsible. According to the old tradition, the fresh goods are sold to buyers calling out. *Se canta* is how it is described, "Singing time." Somebody working for the *lonja* calls out the starting price, reducing it to

find a buying price, until an *asentador* finally shouts out clearly *"Mío!"* or "Mine!"

The *asentadores* must be officially registered with the *lonja* and have a license, as well as a great deal of experience. They often only have seconds to assess the quality of the merchandise being auctioned. Split-second agreements then have to be reached with customers – and a certain amount of cash has to change hands if you want to buy the largest lots possible at the best price.

Things get under way. The *asentadores* take their places. A batch of sardines is called on – 18 crates in all, going for 55 Euro a crate. "50 Euro, 45 Euro," the salesman calls. But many dealers continue to hesitate. Being professionals, they also have in their heads the prices at Spain's other trading centers and those who are really well informed know that several trawlers with larger catches of sardines are expected in the next few days, which means that the price is going to fall. The tension rises: "40 Euro, 35 Euro, 30 Euro." Bingo! An *asentador* has finally called out "Mío." The sardines have their buyer.

Just recently landed, a crate of langoustines stands on the quay, ready for auction early that morning.

Only first-class produce will attract purchasers with money to spend, so these swordfish are being cleaned.

Hundreds of wholesalers attend the auction of freshly caught fish from the Atlantic.

Crushed ice cools the fish before the auction. They are moved on as quickly as possible afterward.

GOOSENECK BARNACLES

Gooseneck barnacles force the Galicians into a waiting game. The only time they have any opportunity of getting hold of this small, thumb-length crustacean is during the winter months, and even then only when there is a spring tide at new or full moon, followed by an extremely low tide when the rocks to which the *percebes* attach themselves lie dry. For weeks on end the gooseneck barnacle collectors *(percebeiros)* must wait, sometimes for this one month. If the weather is clear at low tide and the Atlantic breakers are not crashing against the rocks with their usual ferocity, the perilous work can begin. The bravest and most experienced men climb down with a rope secured around their waist, held by a fellow mate, onto the slippery rocks below where the gooseneck barnacles grow in clusters. A notoriously risky undertaking. Another quick look at the waves and off he goes. One of the men is already grabbing his first cluster of barnacles. With his right hand he stabs a sharp knife into the limestone layer between the rock and the barnacles, so that the catch slides into a net which he has attached in front of his stomach. Quick as a flash he gathers one cluster of barnacles after another. From higher up rings out the timely command *"Moita mar!"* – which roughly translated means "Look out, high waves!" On hearing this, the *percebeiro* quickly climbs up the rocks to safety.

Lovers of the delicate gooseneck barnacle can often barely conceive of the danger involved in this work. Yet it is not without reason that diners in the gourmet restaurants of major cities are willing to pay up to about US$ 50 for them as an appetizer. However, on the northwest coast of Galicia, where the *percebeiros* take their catch straight to the locals, they are significantly cheaper. The best way to buy *percebes* is at the local fish markets.

Gooseneck barnacles are about the size of your finger but shaped like elephant's legs. They have triangular, shingle-shaped shells, which could be mistaken for the neck of a freshly hatched gosling – probably the origin of the English name. From a strictly scientific point of view, however, *percebes* are not barnacles, but crabs, which cling to the rocks.

Gooseneck barnacles are simply boiled in water with a bay leaf and then served warm or cold. To eat them, break open the shell press out the thick, fleshy skin to reveal the pink-colored flesh, and bite it off the shell.

Right: Safely secured, the men climb down into the surf to search the rocks for barnacles – a rather daring venture.

1 To harvest gooseneck barnacles, the fishermen sail their boats to rocky fishing grounds along the coast.
2 In actual fact, gooseneck barnacles are small crabs which cling to the rocks. They are about thumb-size.

3 Those who have gathered the food from the sea also have the pleasure of sorting and cleaning their delicate catch.
4 Gooseneck barnacles are easy to prepare: they are boiled in water, either with or without a bay leaf.

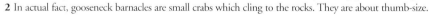

The edible part of the gooseneck barnacle is attached to the triangular, shingle-shaped shell. The pink-colored flesh is compact and juicy. You simply bite it off the shell and the salty flavor and taste of the Atlantic immediately tickle your palate.

Mussel farming

They look like giant rafts - platforms made from eucalyptus wood bobbing about on the water in the Bay of Arousa. Yet they are certainly not intended to take wood away from Galicia. These *bateas*, as they are called, are firmly anchored to the sea bed and are used for mussel breeding. Spain's northwest coast offers ideal conditions for this.

Galicia's rugged coastline is over 745 miles (1200 kilometers) long. Here, the Atlantic has produced granite cliffs and reefs, countless islets, and occasionally bizarre rock formations. Particularly typical are the numerous shallow river estuaries or *rías*. The water in these fjord-like bays is usually only about 6½ feet (2 meters) deep, so it warms up easily. In addition, the tides bring in a constant flow of water rich in minerals and oxygen, which provides a perfect breeding ground for numerous micro-organisms and algae. This creates perfect living conditions for many types of mollusk, such as

Below: A crane lifts the catch from the sea in a big basket and transports it onto the boats.

Razor shell clams

During the fall and winter months, dozens of people are commonly seen on Galicia's sandy beaches, wearing rubber boots and rain clothes and poking about in the sand at low tide. They are patiently searching for razor shell clams. The *navaja*, which can be up to 6 inches (15 centimeters) long, with its distinctive, elongated shell, is concealed in the mud and can bore down with lightning speed up to 20 inches (half a meter) into the wet sand, if it senses danger. Locating and removing them unharmed from the mud takes skill and experience and for many people on the Galician coast it is a welcome way of supplementing their income. On a good day over 330 pounds (150 kilograms) can be gathered, bringing easily 20 Euro at auction. Razor shell

Searching for razor shell clams in the sand is a thankless task, which is why they command such a high price.

clams are either boiled in stock or barbecued on an open charcoal fire. Either way, they are very tasty.

oysters, scallops, common mussels, clams, razor shell clams, and heart clams (cockles). Most mussel farms are situated in the Ría de Arousa. One platform can hold up to 600 33–39 feet (10–12 meter) nylon ropes and 265–440 pounds (120–200 kilograms) of mussels can grow on each of these. A single platform can hold up to 88 tons (80 tonnes) of shellfish.

Roughly 95 percent of the 297,000 tons (270,000 tonnes) or so of mussels produced by Spain each year come from Galicia. Nearly a 33,000 tons (30,000 tonnes) are exported abroad fresh. Before they are sold, the mussels are cleaned in the cleaning plant *(depuradoras)* and checked for quality, so that the reputation of Galicia for good seafood is maintained.

On the boat the ropes on which the mussels have grown must be removed.

The mussels are tipped by the hundredweight onto the boat taking the fresh produce ashore.

Factory workers wash and sort the mussels by hand on long sorting tables.

The mussels are cleaned in a sort of washing installation until they are a shiny blue-black. Then the *mejillones* can be packed and transported by the fastest routes to all four corners of the country.

COMMON MUSSELS

Common mussels *(mejillones)* are harvested throughout the year, but in particularly large quantities in September and October. The blue-black shellfish arrive on the market precleaned and ready to captivate the eater with their juicy, orange-colored flesh.

Before mussels can be cooked they must be thoroughly cleaned and scrubbed if necessary. After this, the byssus threads (beard) are either pulled off or removed using a knife and the mussels cleaned again under running water. They are now ready to be cooked. Individual mussels that do not open during cooking are inedible and must be discarded.

In Galicia, common mussels are normally served up as simply as possible. They are popular steamed in a little water with salt and a bay leaf *(mejillones al vapor)* or cooked in a stock made from white wine, onions, and garlic *(mejillones a la marinera)*.

Fresh mussels also taste wonderful in tortillas or as a filling for turnovers.

PILGRIM SCALLOPS

The beautifully shaped pilgrim scallop *(vieira)* is a symbol of the pilgrims who, after completing their pilgrimage, walked from Santiago de Compostela to Fisterra on the Atlantic to find a pilgrim scallop as a symbol of their journey and take it home with them.

The main season for pilgrim scallops is between October and March and although nowadays they can be bought deep-frozen and in cans, they naturally taste best fresh. The flesh of the scallop, a tender piece of muscle located between the two shells, and the delicate roe (coral) call for careful preparation and should not be overpowered by strong seasoning (photograph, page 238).

The Galicians like to eat *vieiras* broiled with a little garlic, parsley, and onion, or enriched with a dash of sherry or white Albariño wine. More experimental modern cuisine also combines scallops with a potato gratin or wild mushrooms, such as porcini, served with a refreshing Galician white wine.

The mussels are still covered in patina from the sea when they are removed from the ropes by the farmers.

The delicate pilgrim scallop is farmed in Galician bays, with each rope carrying up to 440 pounds (200 kilos).

Oysters taste best straight from the sea. Mussels are supplied by farmers each day straight to Vigo's oyster alley – they don't get much fresher than this.

OYSTERS

Oysters are fascinating creatures. They can change sex as circumstances require - male one minute, female the next. What has become the object of laborious research by modern-day scientists, must have been suspected by the ancient Romans. It was not purely by chance that they glorified oysters as an effective aphrodisiac – an opinion that is still widely held today. The angular mollusk with its surprisingly tender center is particularly rich in protein, with a considerable proportion of vitamins and minerals, and is often prescribed for anemia, due to its high iron content. At the same time, oysters are virtually fat-free, thereby guaranteeing a minimum level of harmful substances, since these can only accumulate in the fatty tissue of marine life.

OYSTER FARMING

Even centuries ago, Galician oysters enjoyed a good reputation among Spain's upper classes. As early as the 16th century, they were being marinated and sent in the form of *ostras en escabeche* from Vigo to the royal court in Madrid. Today, however, native oysters are virtually unheard of along the Galician coast. Nevertheless, breeders in special oyster farms have been experimenting with different varieties of the mollusk for around 25 years. The main type of oyster bred in Galicia is the European oyster *(Ostrea edulis)*, which is imported from France and has produced outstanding results. The Portuguese oyster *(Crassostrea angulata)* and Japanese oyster *(Crassostrea gigas)* are also farmed on a smaller scale.

The bays found along the Galician coast provide ideal conditions for oyster breeding, with their constant supply of fresh Atlantic water. While the varieties originating in France need roughly four years in their native waters to reach harvesting size, the ideal water temperature and high concentration of food found in Galician bays mean they can be harvested after only two to two-and-a-half years.

The breeding process involves mature animals being sent to the oyster farms' laboratories in vessels filled with sea water. Heating the water stimulates fertilization. The eggs soon develop into free-swimming larvae, which cling to rocks or empty mussel shells in their natural habitat. In the breeding plants, the ropes on which the oysters are to grow are prepared with cement, so that the larvae can cling to them. They feed on phytoplankton from the brackish water and gradually grow a slate-like shell. Depending on their size, the water temperature and amount of food available, oysters can process up to 5.2 gallons (20 liters) of water an hour, to filter out

Oysters find ideal living conditions in Galicia. They feed off plankton which they filter from the water.

the necessary nutrients and ultimately add to the size and flavour of the oysters for the consumers' benefit.

OYSTERS FRESH ON THE TABLE

Unlike France, where different varieties of oyster have a real cult following, Galician consumers usually tend to choose by size alone. The largest, fleshiest oysters are the most sought. However, real oyster connoisseurs value the smaller specimens for their delicate flavor of the Atlantic.

Galicia's most important center for the oyster trade is the port of Vigo, where mussels are sorted by size and sold in markets and at auction. In the old town and around the harbor area there are special *ostrerías* – stores specializing in fresh oysters. On weekdays in the Ría da Pescadería, the oyster alley above the ferry port, the *ostreras* (oyster women) sell fresh oysters to eat there and then or take out. Business is brisk, particularly around lunch time, when locals and visitors slurp their *ostras* down with relish – usually with no accompaniment whatsoever, just a small glass of white Albariño wine.

However, in high-class restaurants diners will also find oysters baked with breadcrumbs and seasoning; a particularly popular dish in Vigo is oysters with mushrooms *(ostras a la viguesa)*. Occasionally, creative cooks will enrich their oysters with some leek and truffles. Oyster soup is even occasionally found on Galician menus and, as in the time of the Hapsburgs, *ostras en escabeche* (marinated oysters) are still a great delicacy.

Purists will, however, argue that the only way to eat oysters is straight, washed down with sea water.

EUCALYPTUS FROM GALICIA

It is true that the eucalyptus is native to Australia. Yet in 1884 Father Rosendo Salvador, a Spanish bishop in Australia, brought a few trees with him back to Galicia from the other side of the world and planted them. To begin with they were used purely for ornamental purposes in the parks of the wealthy, but soon the economic benefits of the eucalyptus became evident too. The tree grows very quickly in Galicia's mild climate and after only ten years reaches a substantial size. After 1950 General Franco had whole eucalyptus woods planted in Galicia and today there are nearly 444,600 acres (180,00 hectares). Galician cellulose factories are the main customers for the wood, which helps many a farmer earn his crust. Eucalyptus is also suitable for wooden floors, and because the light wood floats very well, it is the preferred choice for the construction of platforms in mussel farms. The fragrant, essential oil of the eucalyptus is used in medicine, for cosmetics and candy. However, the disadvantages of eucalyptus cultivation are becoming increasingly evident. The monoculture system draws excessive amounts of water from the soil and leaches it, leaving other trees with insufficient ground water and nutrients. Their cultivation has therefore now become a controversial issue in the region.

DELICIOUS RECIPES FOR FISH AND SHELLFISH

MEJILLONES EN ESCABECHE
Marinated mussels

4½ lbs/2 kg mussels
½ cup/125 ml olive oil
½ cup/125 ml white wine vinegar
1 tsp mild paprika
½ tsp hot paprika
Salt
2 bay leaves
8 peppercorns

Wash the mussels thoroughly, then steam them in a pan over a low heat with a little water until they open. Discard any mussels that have not opened. Remove them from their shells and leave to cool.
Heat the oil in a deep skillet and fry the mussels in it. Remove the mussels and set them to one side. Return the skillet with the cool oil to the heat and add the wine vinegar, ½ cup/125 ml of water, paprika, salt, bay leaves, and peppercorns. Simmer for 10–15 minutes. Leave to cool, then marinate the mussels in the liquid overnight. Serve the mussels in their shells with the marinade poured over.

VIEIRAS A LA GALLEGA
Pilgrim scallops Galician style

16 fresh pilgrim scallops
2 tbsp lemon juice
1 onion, finely chopped
1 clove of garlic, finely chopped
4 tbsp olive oil
1 tbsp chopped parsley
1 tsp sweet paprika
Pinch of ground cinnamon
Salt and pepper
½ cup/125 ml white wine
2½ tbsp orujo, alternatively grappa
Oil for the shells
4 tbsp breadcrumbs

Open the scallops with a knife. Clean them well and remove any inedible parts. Separate the corals (orange-colored roe) from the white scallop meat and drizzle the scallops with lemon juice.
Sweat the onion and garlic in 3 tbsp olive oil until transparent. Finely chop the corals and mix them with the parsley. Season with paprika, cinnamon, and salt and pepper. Pour over the white wine and orujo and bring to a boil. Clean 8 scallop shells and brush them with oil. Place 2 scallops in each shell and pour over the sauce. Sprinkle with breadcrumbs and drizzle over the remaining oil. Place the scallops in a preheated oven at 355 ºF/180 ºC for about 12 minutes until golden brown.

BERBERECHOS A LA MARINERA
Heart clams (cockles) in onion and garlic sauce

2¼ lbs/1 kg fresh heart clams (cockles)
Salt
5 tbsp olive oil
1 onion, finely chopped
2 cloves of garlic, finely chopped
½ cup/125 ml dry white wine
1 tbsp breadcrumbs
Juice of ½ a lemon
1 bay leaf
Pepper
2 tbsp chopped parsley

Clean the heart clams (cockles) thoroughly, discarding any open shells. Bring the clams to a boil in a wide-bottomed pan with 1 cup/250 ml of water and a pinch of salt. Cover and cook until all the shells have opened, shaking the pan several times. Discard any clams that have not opened. Remove the cockles from the cooking liquid using a skimmer, then pour the liquid through cheesecloth and set aside.
Heat the olive oil in a deep pan and sweat the onion and garlic until transparent. Pour over the white wine and stir in the breadcrumbs. Pour in the cooking liquid with the lemon juice and bay leaf, and season with salt and pepper. Add the clams to the sauce, sprinkle with the parsley, and return to a boil. Transfer to a warmed dish and serve immediately.
Mussels, small scallops, and razor shell clams can also be prepared in this way.

The pilgrim scallop provides the connoisseur with two treats in one – the orange roe (coral) and the tender, white scallop meat.

Turbot with seafood

RODABALLO CON MARISCOS
Turbot with seafood
(Photograph above)

2 onions, finely chopped
2 cloves of garlic, finely chopped
1 tomato, skinned and finely diced
2 tbsp olive oil
Salt
Pinch of hot paprika
2¼ lbs/1 kg turbot, skinned and boned
8 pilgrim scallops
12 bay scallops
20 peeled shrimp
½ cup/125 ml white Albariño wine

Sweat the onions, garlic, and tomato in the olive oil for 10 minutes. Season with salt and paprika. Lay the turbot in an earthenware baking dish. Place the scallops and shrimp on top, spoon on the onion mixture and pour over the wine. Bake for about 20 minutes in a preheated oven at 355 °F/180 °C.

XOUBAS CON CACHELOS
Sardines with potatoes in their skins

2¼ lbs /1 kg small sardines
Sea salt
Generous 1 lb/500 g small new potatoes
1 bay leaf
½ cup/125 ml olive oil
1½ lbs/750 g small green chili peppers

Wash the sardines, pat them dry, and rub with sea salt. Leave them to stand for 1 hour, then grill until crisp on a charcoal barbecue (or under the broiler).
Put the potatoes in their skins in salt water with the bay leaf. Bring to a boil and cook for about 20 minutes. Drain off the water and return the potatoes to the pan; cover with a damp cloth and leave to continue cooking off the heat.
Heat the olive oil in a deep skillet and fry the chili peppers in it. Remove the peppers from the oil, drain and sprinkle with sea salt.
Arrange the sardines, potatoes, and fried peppers on four plates. Remember that the potato skins should be eaten.

CALDEIRADA
Galician fish stew

2¼ lbs /1 kg potatoes, peeled and thickly sliced
1 onion, coarsely chopped
1 bay leaf
Salt
2¼ lbs/1 kg fish fillet (hake, monkfish, turbot, sea bass, skate, or another white fish)
Pepper

For the garlic sauce (ajada):
6 tbsp olive oil
8 cloves of garlic
½ tsp sweet paprika
Pinch of hot paprika

Boil the potatoes with the onion and bay leaf for 20 minutes in 6 cups/1.5 liters of salt water. Wash the fish and cut it into bite-size pieces. Place them on the potatoes and season with salt and pepper. Cover and cook for 10 minutes. Drain off the liquid, reserving 1 cup/250 ml, and discard the bay leaf.
For the *ajada*, pour the olive oil into a skillet and brown the garlic cloves. Lift them out and remove the skillet from the heat. Then add a ladle of the reserved liquid and the paprika and stir well. Leave the sauce to simmer for about 10 minutes; then add to the fish stew and serve immediately.

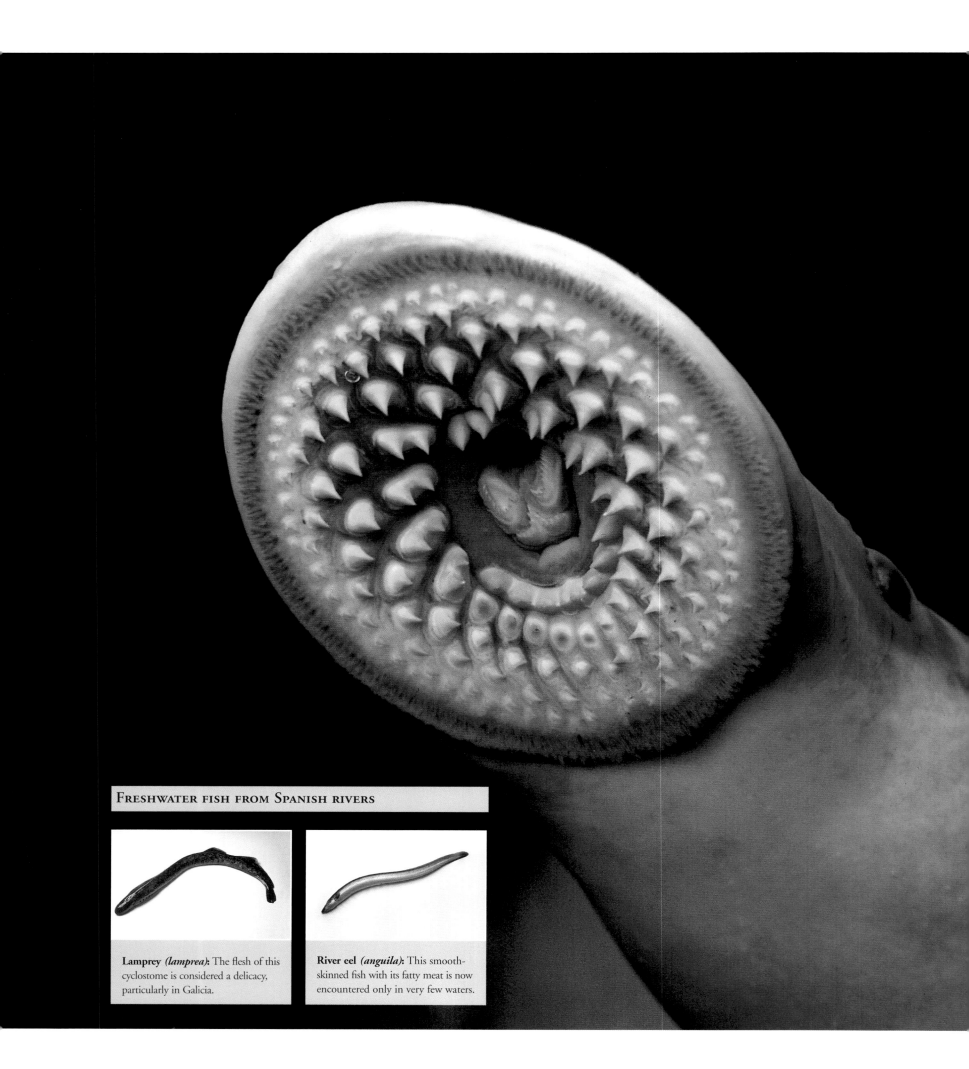

FRESHWATER FISH FROM SPANISH RIVERS

Lamprey *(lamprea)*: The flesh of this cyclostome is considered a delicacy, particularly in Galicia.

River eel *(anguila)*: This smooth-skinned fish with its fatty meat is now encountered only in very few waters.

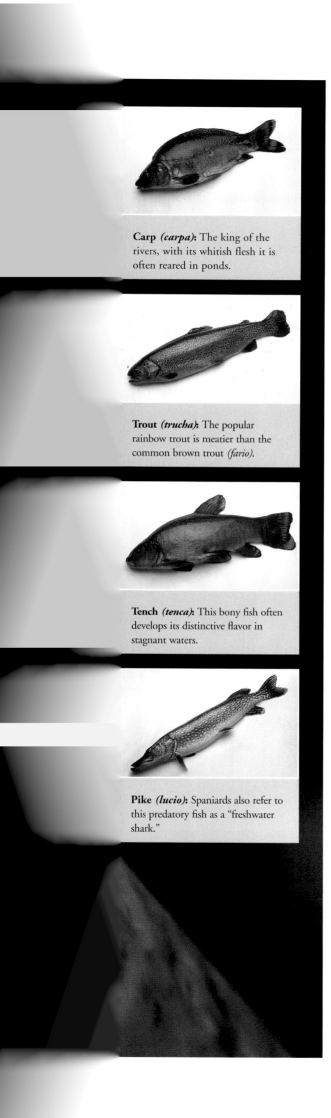

Carp *(carpa)*: The king of the rivers, with its whitish flesh it is often reared in ponds.

Trout *(trucha)*: The popular rainbow trout is meatier than the common brown trout *(fario)*.

Tench *(tenca)*: This bony fish often develops its distinctive flavor in stagnant waters.

Pike *(lucio)*: Spaniards also refer to this predatory fish as a "freshwater shark."

LAMPREY

In Roman times, the lamprey was regarded as a mysterious river creature. In those days, not only did people eat the fish, but fish ate the people. The Roman governors in Galicia would punish rebellious slaves by throwing them into the rivers and seas, which were teeming with the eel-like monsters.

However, all evil associations aside, the lamprey has always been regarded as a delicacy, particularly in France. It is said that in the Middle Ages the *lamproies* of Nantes were so sought that Parisian fishmongers would travel right out of the city to their suppliers, for fear of going away empty-handed.

The lamprey *(lamprea)* belongs to the vertebrate group of cyclostomes, which means, strictly speaking, that it is not actually a fish. It fixes itself to fish and other aquatic animals by the suckers and horny teeth of its round mouth, and then sucks their blood and other bodily fluids. Behind its nostril and single eye, the lamprey has seven gill slits on each side of the neck. It can grow up to 5 feet (1.5 meters) in length, and has a smooth, slimy skin. Its upper body is dark-brown or gray-blue with dark flecks, while its underside is lighter in color.

In winter, the lamprey swims from the open sea to spawn in the rivers. However, the species has become very rare throughout Europe, due to the pollution and congestion of the rivers. In Spain, the *lamprea* can now be found only in the lower course of the Río Guadiana in Extremadura and in Galicia, particularly in the Río Miño.

Lamprey are caught between January and April using *biturones*, a sort of spiral-shaped trap. At this time of year, gourmets from all over Galicia gather up their kith and kin and flock to the Arbo area to enjoy a well-prepared lamprey. The season culminates in the festival of Saint Joseph *(San José)* on March 19. On this day, restaurants on the Río Miño renowned for their *lamprea* dishes are all packed.

Experts make sure of buying their lamprey alive, so that they are absolutely fresh. This ensures that the dark, fatty, slightly sweet flesh, which many connoisseurs even prefer to eel, is of the best quality.

A popular way of preparing lamprey is to boil or braise it in its own blood, if possible with red Ribeiro wine. However, it also goes well with garlic, onions, and a wine vinegar sauce; with mushrooms in an onion and wine sauce, or as

a filling for *empanadas* (see page 242). In Galicia, *lamprea* dishes are served with rice and toasted breadcrumbs *(picatostes)*. A less common way of preparing lamprey is to smoke or air-dry it. *Lamprea* preserved in this way must be soaked overnight before being eaten. A hearty lamprey dish should be accompanied by a tannic rosé or red wine, preferably a drop of decent wine from the banks of the Río Sil or the Ribeiro and Condado de Tea regions.

LAMPREA GUISADA
Lamprey in its own juices

1 lamprey, about 3¼ lbs/1.5 kg
¾ cup/200 ml olive oil
¾ cup/200 ml wine vinegar
½ cup/125 ml dry red wine
2 cloves of garlic, finely chopped
Salt and pepper
Pinch of ground cinnamon

Wash the lamprey well under hot water and pat it dry. Remove the gall bladder from beneath the mouth. Slit the fish lengthwise along its belly and collect the blood. Then gut and clean the fish and rinse out the belly cavity.

Combine the blood, olive oil, wine vinegar, and wine, and bring to a boil in a large pan. Add the garlic and season the liquor with salt, pepper, and cinnamon. Lay the fish in the cooking liquor, and bring it back to a boil. Cover and leave on a low heat for around 25 minutes without letting it boil. Then cut the fish into portions and return it to the cooking liquor. Serve immediately, with fresh white bread or rice. Galicians also like serving it with toasted breadcrumbs.

Left: The lamprey with its horn-teeth and suckers looks like a fabulous creature. But don't be put off, the fish does not bite and it tastes delicious.

EMPANADAS

According to an old Galician saying, "Making love and kneading dough are two things that shouldn't be rushed." And who better qualified to judge than a people who discovered the *empanada*. This turnover was even immortalized in the cathedral of Santiago de Compostela. If a hungry pilgrim eats an *empanada* there, it is said that the pleasure he feels will last for all eternity. The figure has indeed been carved in stone – a religious monument for the aficionado.

For centuries now the Galicians have valued the *empanada* as a tasty snack. Like a filled pizza, it is a popular and practical meal for fishermen, farmers, and forestry workers, as well as a provision to sustain pilgrims on their travels. There were also countless Galician emigrants who chose to take some sort of *empanada* with them on their long journeys overseas, in addition to dried fish. Today, this specialty, which undoubtedly originated in Galicia, is known in every part of Spain and throughout South America. The *empanada* has grown from being a food simple folk would take with them on journeys, to being a delicacy fit for the most demanding gourmet.

The outer case of the *empanada* is made quite simply from either bread dough or puff pastry. It is essential for the latter to contain fresh pig fat. After baking, the dough must be soft and the crust crisp and golden-yellow. The *empanada* can be round and as big as a tart, but it is often also served on a baking sheet in a rectangular shape. Cut into small pieces, it is mainly served as a tapa. *Empanadillas* are a pocket-size version of the *empanada* – small, filled pastry cases, each the size of an individual portion. The filling ingredients vary from province to province and season to season. In rural areas, the *empanada* can be eaten hot or cold and popular fillings include chicken with onions and chili peppers or pork with chorizo and vegetables. Fresh mushrooms also make a wonderfully tasty filling. In the province of Orense, the turnovers are often prepared using freshwater fish, such as eel or lamprey; along the coast, fillings of mussels, salt cod, and sardines or anchovies are the most popular. *Empanadas* are often also a way of using up the previous day's leftovers. Every housewife and every restaurant in Galicia swears by their own particular recipe. It could be said that every empanada is different, as little variations are constantly being used in the recipes for this most basic food.

EMPANADA GALLEGA
Galician turnover

For the dough:
4½ cups/500 g flour
1 tbsp white wine
1 tsp olive oil
1 tbsp clarified butter
Salt
Pinch of sugar
Flour for rolling out
Butter for greasing
Egg yolk for glazing

Sift the flour into a wide bowl and make a well in the middle. Add the white wine, olive oil, clarified butter, salt, sugar, and a few tablespoons of lukewarm water. Knead all the ingredients into a flexible dough. Leave the dough to rest in the refrigerator, then divide it into two. Roll out one half on a floured work surface and use it to line a buttered pan, making sure that the dough overlaps at the upper edge. Add the filling. Roll out the remaining dough and lay it on top of the filling. Press together the edges of the dough. Brush with egg yolk and bake in a preheated oven at 355 °F/180 °C for about 30 minutes until golden brown.

1 Ingredients for a bread dough, vegetables, fish, or meat for the filling (according to taste) and egg for glazing - all you need to make a Galician *empanada*.
2 The dough is made from wheat or corn flour. Pour the flour into a wide bowl and gradually add the olive oil, white wine, and all the other ingredients.
3 Roll out half the dough with a rolling pin. Lay it in the pan and press it down until the base and edges are completely lined.

4 Spoon the finished filling into the dough case. Make sure that the mixture has cooled down and is not too runny, otherwise the dough may become soggy during baking.
5 Now comes the top of the *empanada*. Press out the remaining dough by hand to form a lid. It should be as close as possible to the correct size.
6 Lay the top carefully on the filling and make sure that the pastry edges are well sealed. Brush the *empanada* with egg yolk then off it goes to the oven.

Meat filling
for *Empanada de carne*

4 tbsp olive oil
Generous 1 lb/500 g pork loin, cut into thin
strips
2 large onions, finely chopped
2 cloves of garlic, finely chopped
2 green bell peppers, finely chopped
4½ oz/125 g air-dried ham, diced
2 tbsp tomato paste
Salt and pepper
1 tsp sweet paprika

Heat the olive oil in a large skillet. Fry the strips of pork, then remove them from the skillet. Sweat the onions and garlic in the oil until transparent. Mix in the peppers and diced ham, and fry briefly. Return the meat to the skillet with the tomato paste and season with salt, pepper, and paprika. Spoon the filling onto the dough.

heart clam (cockle) filling
for *Empanada de berberechos*

4½ lbs/2 kg heart clams (cockles)
2 bay leaves
Salt
3 tbsp olive oil
4 small onions, finely chopped
2 cloves of garlic, finely chopped
2 green bell peppers, finely chopped
Pinch of hot paprika

Clean and rinse the heart clams (cockles) thoroughly, rejecting any that have opened. Bring the clams to a boil in a wide-bottomed pan with the bay leaves and plenty of salt water. Cover and leave to simmer until all the shells have opened, shaking the pan several times. Discard any clams that have not opened. Drain the clams and leave them to cool, then remove the clams from their shells. Heat the olive oil in a large skillet and sweat the onions, garlic, and peppers. Season with salt and paprika, and finally stir in the clams. Spoon the filling onto the dough.

Sardine filling
for *Empanada de sardinas*

6 large onions, finely chopped
5 tbsp olive oil
2 green bell peppers, finely chopped
4 beef tomatoes, skinned and finely diced
Salt and pepper
2¼ lbs/1 kg small sardines, cleaned and gutted

Pour the olive oil into a large skillet and sweat the onions until transparent. Add the peppers and diced tomato. Season with salt and pepper and leave to simmer for 10 minutes.
Arrange the sardines evenly over the dough and pour over the vegetable sauce.

Galician beef

Galicia is Spain's Wild West – and not only geographically speaking. Cowboy country starts in the hinterland of the province of Lugo. A winding road, unfinished for the last few miles, leads from the coast up to the pastures where Galician cattle graze. This place is home to the *vaqueiros*, the cowboys from San Isidoro. No one up here bats an eyelid at the sight of ruggedly dressed men riding through the village on their horses, tethering them in front of their houses at lunch time, and then galloping away again after their siesta over the hills and meadows to see to their cattle grazing in the pastures beyond.

Dairy and beef cattle are still regarded as being of considerable value in Galicia. As a result, these animals are always jealously guarded and meticulously cared for. The cattle spend most of the year in pasture, grazing on grass and herbs. Only in winter is their diet supplemented by hay or wheat.

The daily work of the *vaqueiros* involves keeping the herds together; driving them to the feeding points; separating the young animals from the older ones at the prescribed time; and maintaining fences and shelters. Every year on August 24, the feast day of Saint Bartholomew (San Bartolo), the beef cattle are driven amid great spectacle down from the pasture to the village, where they are blessed. Of course, the residents of San Isidoro also take this opportunity to hold a colorful fiesta in honor of their patron saint, with music, lots of superb food, and copious quantities of wine.

Galician veal

Increasing numbers of Galician cattle breeders favor the region's typical breed, *Rubia Gallega*. It is extremely resilient, has adapted perfectly to the Atlantic climate, and produces superb meat. The *Rubia Gallega* is of average size with short horns and a light-brown hide, which occasionally has a reddish hue. Apart from this predominant breed of cattle, there are still a few other native breeds to be found in Galicia, which are generally referred to as *Morenas del Noroeste* (northwest brunets). They have a dark-brown hide, but are otherwise almost identical to the *Rubia Gallega*, and there has been a good deal of crossbreeding between the two types.

The top-quality veal produced by the *Rubia Gallega, Morena del Noroeste* or a crossbreed of the two is protected by the *Ternera Gallega* (Galician veal) seal of quality. Calves awarded this seal must have been born, raised, and butchered in Galicia. Only free-range production is allowed. This means the cattle graze exclusively on grass, clover, and herbs, which makes the meat moist and gives it a particularly aromatic flavor. Around 11,020 tons (10,000 tonnes) of veal bearing the *Ternera Gallega* seal of quality are currently served up each year, representing roughly 1.5 percent of the total veal eaten throughout Spain.

For beef to be marketed as veal *(ternera)*, the animal must be no more than ten months old when it is butchered; *añojos* may be between 10 and 18 months old; *cebones* are butchered at 18 to 36 months of age. Although they have a rather short life, free-range production ensures that it is pleasant and many argue that it improves the meat's flavor.

Right: Cattle reared in the Galician hinterland lead a pleasant life. They usually graze in luscious meadows, which produces delicious meat later on.

Vilalba capon

In rural areas of Galicia a typical Christmas menu will include a crisp, roasted capon. This culinary tradition is particularly strong in Terra Chá, a fertile plateau surrounded by mountains in the province of Lugo. Here, the locals cultivate fruit, grain, and vegetables, while the farmers rear more capons than anywhere else in Galicia, with the birds commanding a high price on the market. The center of capon rearing is the small town of Vilalba. The capon is a castrated cock which has been fattened up and has particularly tender, juicy, flavorsome meat. The chicks are born at Vilalba's breeding stations in March and April. They are fed up on grain and chestnuts until they have reached a live weight of at least 4½ pounds (2 kilograms) in December. Many farmers even add a little wine or marc *(orujo)* to the feed, to improve the flavor of the meat still farther. A popular way of preparing a typical *capón de Vilalba* in Galicia is to lard it with onions, garlic, and ham, then roast it in the oven for 1½–2 hours, basting it during the cooking time with chicken stock that has had the fattiest parts of the capon added to it. A real delicacy for local holidays and festivals is *capón con ostras*, a capon filled with oysters. As with all other Galician meats, capón de Vilalba is very popular, and farmers take pride in rearing high quality birds. The proof is in the eating, when the meat is served in one of the many traditional ways.

Rubia Gallega: a light-colored breed of cattle from Galicia, which produces good milk and high-quality veal.

Asturiana de los Valles: a breed from the north, renowned for its good milk and excellent veal.

Retinta: from Extremadura. Free-range rearing on dry meadowland produces a particularly aromatic meat.

Morucha de Salamanca: a breed of cattle indigenous to Castile, whose meat has a highly aromatic flavor.

Avileña Negra Ibérica: from Castile, one of the oldest breeds in Europe, with delicate, light-colored meat.

Almost all types of Galician cheese are made from cow's milk. Many are sold as fresh cheese (photograph above). *San Simón* and *Arzúa* are matured for two or more weeks (main photograph). Galician cow's milk is also used to produce good-quality butter, which is decoratively rolled in cabbage leaves before being sold.

To produce *Tetilla* cheese, the curds obtained by curdling the cow's milk with rennet are transferred to plastic molds.

Once all the whey has drained from the curds, the cheese becomes firmer. When it has set, the mold can be removed.

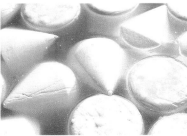

The cheese is immersed in a salt solution. This is followed by several weeks of maturing until the *tetilla* or "little tit" is ready.

Tetilla, *Arzúa*, and many other Galician cheeses are semi-cured with a light-colored rind and a mild, creamy texture.

246   GALICIA

Cheese

Despite their thin hides, cattle seem to feel far more at home in Galicia's damp Atlantic climate than sheep or goats. This is perhaps why the region in the extreme northwest of Spain produces the widest variety of pure cow's milk cheese. The milk usually comes from the *Rubia Gallega* breed or from Friesian cows.

Until now, Galician cow's milk cheese *(queso de leche de vaca)* has frequently been produced by small farms not yet affected by official European Union regulations. Just as in their forefathers' day, the farmers take the fresh, unpasteurized milk and add natural rennet, then leave it to curdle at temperatures of between 82 and 90 °F/28 and 32 °C. The resulting curds are carefully pressed to drain out the whey. The cheese is then salted and stored for at least seven days in a cool but not excessively damp environment. Many varieties of cheese are also smoked.

In recent decades, Galicia has inevitably seen the emergence of an increasing number of cooperatives and large-scale operations producing cow's milk cheese on a commercial basis, while observing rigid legal requirements. These companies can only use pasteurized milk for their products.

Queso de Tetilla usually comes from the province of A Coruña and a few areas in the neighboring province of Lugo. This cheese – Galicia's favorite – is molded in the shape of a soft, well-formed breast. In fact, *tetilla* actually means "little tit." *Tetilla* cheese needs to ripen for 15 to 20 days, after which it is sold as a very mild, creamy, delicately tasty cheese. The rind is pale yellow, and the cheese itself white to yellowish in color and strikingly soft and stringy. *Tetilla* is a popular tapa or dessert, cut into small chunks and consumed with a little quince jelly *(carne de membrillo)*.

The aromatic hard cheese *San Simón* comes mainly from the area of Vilalba in the province of Lugo. It looks like a slightly misshapen pear and matures for about three weeks before it is smoked to varying strengths over birchwood. This gives the cheese its typically light-brown rind and a unique flavor that is dominated by a tangy smokiness.

Apart from these two main types of cheese, which are available as unpasteurized cheese and industrially manufactured variants, *Queso de Cebreiro* is another cheese from the mountain regions of Piedrafita and Becerreá which can be found on Galician markets. This cheese is usually still made by hand and produced in correspondingly small amounts. It is shaped rather like a flattened chef's hat. *Cebreiro* cheese has a fresh, mildly acidic taste, similar to Quark, although it has a firmer, drier consistency.

A cheese virtually unknown outside Galicia is *Queso de Arzóa-Ulloa*, which used to be left to mature in grain stores *(hórreos)*. This cow's milk cheese is produced by 13 communities in the province of A Coruña, following a procedure similar to that used for *Tetilla* cheese. However, *Arzúa-Ulloa* is left to ripen slightly longer. This makes it develop a stronger flavor, producing a smooth, bright yellow rind. The cheese itself is dense, soft, and ivory-colored. Galicia's cheeses may not be famous, but they are still extremely flavorsome.

Chestnuts

They are not only delicious and nutritious, but absolutely free. Perhaps this is why chestnuts have been a much sought winter food in wooded areas of the provinces of Lugo and Orense since time immemorial. Farmers would keep up their strength as they worked in the fields by eating freshly roasted chestnuts.

Even today, Galicians can be found wandering through the woods in October and November, gathering *castañas* to roast in their ovens at home. Chestnut festivals are the "in-thing," taking place on or around November 11 in the provincial capital Orense or on an October weekend in the monastery of San Esteban del Río Sil, when hundreds of visitors flock to the historical courtyard to savor the delicious flavors of roasted chestnuts. To boil chestnuts, begin by making a cross in the brown outer skin and then place the chestnut in boiling water for a while. This makes it easy to peel off the shell and skin. In Galicia chestnuts are traditionally eaten for breakfast boiled in hot milk (occasionally flavored with aniseed) or in the form of chestnut cakes and flans. Chestnut soup made with milk and lard is a traditional recipe now used by only a few cooks. Plain chestnuts are often used to make a tasty stuffing for goose, capon, or turkey dishes, or are boiled until soft in a brown stock enriched with chunks of celery. To roast chestnuts, first make a cross in them with a knife, to make the shell easier to remove. Once they have been roasted in the oven or on the stove top, the sweet kernel is best eaten immediately while hot or still warm. A young, fruity red wine will complement them well. In recent decades, chestnuts have also been elevated to the status of high-quality candy in Galicia. This involves grading the chestnuts, then peeling and sterilizing them. Next, they are boiled until tender in a syrup made from sugar water and vanilla. Finally, they are coated with syrupy sugar and dried in special ovens. Glazed chestnuts can be found in shops packaged in pretty glass jars or small wooden boxes and sold under the French label *marron glacé*. The modern range of chestnut products includes chestnuts in syrup or brandy and delicate chestnut purée, which is used mainly for tarts, cakes, and a whole host of delicious desserts to round off a hearty meal.

TARTA DE SANTIAGO

No one knows exactly why the almond tart *tarta de Santiago* was named after the apostle St. James. It may be that a pilgrim once brought the recipe to Galicia with him or that another devout individual, in a sublime moment, dedicated the simple cake to the well-known saint and patron of the whole of Spain. Whatever the answer, for centuries now the top of the tart has been adorned with the cross of the knights of St. James, made in confectioners' sugar. Many visitors to Santiago de Compostela buy one of the tarts, which are popular throughout Spain, as a souvenir of their visit to the pilgrim's city.

TARTA DE SANTIAGO
Galician almond tart

For the pastry:
1½ cups/200g flour
⅛ cup/75g sugar
1cup/100g butter
1 egg

For the filling:
4 eggs
1¼ cups/250 g sugar
Peel of 1 unwaxed lemon
2 cups/250 g ground almonds
Pinch of ground cinnamon

Flour for rolling out
Butter for greasing
Confectioners' sugar for dredging

Knead a short pastry with the flour, sugar butter and egg, adding a little milk if needed. Form a ball, wrap in foil and leave to stand in the fridge for 30 minutes.
For the filling, beat together the eggs and sugar until creamy. Fold in the lemon rind, ground almonds, and cinnamon.
Roll out the pastry on a floured work surface. Line a greased, loose-bottomed pan with the pastry. Prick it all over with a fork and spoon the filling on top. Bake in a preheated oven at 355 ºF/180 ºC for about 30 minutes, until golden brown.
Leave the almond tart to cool in the pan. Once cool, transfer it to a serving plate and dredge with confectioners' sugar before serving.

Almonds, flour, good-quality butter, sugar, and eggs, as well as freshly grated lemon rind and a hint of cinnamon, are the only ingredients needed to make a delicate *tarta de Santiago.*

The cathedral of Santiago de Compostela is the goal of many thousands of pilgrims from all over the world.

The pilgrim scallop is the symbol of the St. James pilgrims. Carved in stone, it adorns the cathedral of Santiago.

SANTIAGO DE COMPOSTELA: EVERY PILGRIM'S DREAM AND GOAL

"The envious on the other side of the mountains should blush with shame at their claim to having relics or parts of the body. Because the apostle's body lies here in *toto*. It is magnificently illuminated by precious, heavenly gems and continuously venerated by divine aromas; it is adorned by heavenly candlelight and angels celebrate it with their declarations of goodwill." The French pilgrim, Aimeric Picaud, was in no doubt: the "real St. James" had found his final resting place in Galicia. In around 1140 Picaud described in the pilgrim's guide *Codex Calixtinus* the history of the St. James pilgrimage and the veneration of the saint in the cathedral of Santiago de Compostela.
It is said that early in the 9th century a hermit, guided by a special star sign, discovered the legs of the apostle St. James in Galicia. Due to the heavenly apparition, the site was first named Campus Stellae (constellation), but later took the name Santiago de Compostela (*Sant'Jago* means Saint James). In the 11th and 12th centuries a mighty cathedral was built over the grave. Throughout the Middle Ages Santiago was regarded as the "Jerusalem of the West" – one of the most important places of pilgrimage for Christians. Even today, the Galician city of Santiago de Compostela remains the dream and goal of pilgrims throughout the world, who exhibit their reverence in the cathedral of St. James, asking for help or expressing thanks for the granting of their innermost desires. Many pilgrims still cover the entire historical route on foot, or at least a good portion of it (see p. 126). Nevertheless, anyone arriving on horseback or by bicycle is still accepted as a genuine pilgrim, receiving their certificate from the pilgrims' office at the cathedral. However, anyone pulling up in a car or arriving by bus may well be equal in the eyes of God and St. James, but they must forego the much sought document.
On high church holidays, the *botafumeiro* – a heavy, silver censer – is used in the cathedral to honor the saint. In full view of the worshippers, eight monks in red robes swing the vessel through the cathedral nave on long ropes – a magnificent spectacle and an unforgettable experience.
Standing on the cathedral square is the *Hostal de los Reyes Católicos*, the former pilgrims' hospice. It was founded at the end of the 15th century by the Catholic King Fernando and his Queen Isabella. This shelter was used to care for sick, ailing, and weak pilgrims during the Middle Ages. Today, the expensively restored building with its picturesque inner courtyards and magnificently decorated façade houses a luxury hotel. And even today, the first ten pilgrims to reach the city each day are given three days' accommodations free of charge – in memory of days gone by. Today's beneficiaries of charity do not have to be sick or weak.

To make the tart base, line a well-greased, loose-bottomed pan with pastry.

Ground almonds and sugar create the basis of the moist filling.

Four whole eggs add consistency to the filling and make it a golden yellow color.

Beat the filling vigorously until all the ingredients are well mixed together.

Galician confectioners use a metal template to decorate the *tarta de Santiago*. This represents the shape of St. James' cross. The templates used to be forged by hand. Nowadays they are regarded as valuable antiques.

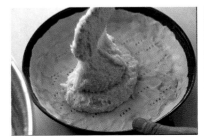

Then carefully spoon the almond mixture onto the pastry base in the pan.

Smooth the filling from the middle outward using a spatula.

Once baked, dredge the tart with confectioners' sugar.

A true *tarta de Santiago* should bear the cross of the knights of St. James.

Albariño

The origin of the Albariño grape is still disputed. The Germans are keen to assert that this grape variety was taken to Galicia by Cistercians from vine-growing regions on the Mosel and Rhine. Documentary evidence suggests that German monks planted the first grapes of this variety in the monastery of Armenteira in the Val do Salnés in the year 1185. This would provide a logical explanation of the name *Albariño*, meaning "the Rhine white." Galician white wines – headed by those produced from the Albariño grape – are among the most striking that Spain has to offer. The usual home of the Albariño is the Rías Baixas region, extending along the southwest coast of Galicia and the lower course of the Río Miño, which forms the border with Portugal at this point. Albariño production is centered around the town of Cambados.

The Albariño grape is best suited to Galicia's damp, rainy climate. The method of cultivation usually involves the grapes growing up granite posts. Later they ripen along wires running between the posts, almost 6 feet (2 meters) above the ground. This protects the grapes from the excessive moisture at ground level and also reduces the risk of a fungal attack.

The Albariño grape has enormous flavor potential, but the fruit are strikingly small and not particularly juicy. Albariño wines are therefore expensive, something which is compounded by growing demand, particularly on the Spanish market. There is no disputing the pleasant freshness and varying depths of fruitiness characterizing the charm of these white wines. Most of their class and elegance is developed while the wines are still young, during the first and second years following production, after which they tend to lose their vitality. In terms of taste, Albariño wines tend to resemble a mixture of Riesling and white Burgundy, and they go particularly well with seafood and light fish dishes. In Cambados homage is paid to them each year when a fiesta is held on the first weekend of August.

Several wine routes *(rutas del vino)* now follow the wine's tracks along the Rías Baixas. A free brochure and special description indicate the paths to historical, vine-growing monuments and important cellars *(bodegas)*, and also provide information on tasting opportunities in the region. Many tourists and connoisseurs are now taking advantage of this new feature of the region's hospitality.

A characteristic feature of the Rías Baixas vine-growing region and the Albariño grape is the high-growing vines. Trellises protect against moisture.

VINE-GROWING REGIONS OF GALICIA

For centuries there were no blanket controls on vine-growing in Galicia. It was only after 1980 that the innovative technique of reallocating arable land, coupled with the refinement of local regional grape varieties, led to significant quality improvements in almost all areas of cultivation in Galicia. Today there are five cultivation areas covered by the legally protected mark of origin *Denominación de Origen (D.O.)*.

The region's best known cultivation area is the **D.O. Rías Baixas** with its sub-zones Val do Salnés, O Rosal, Condado de Tea, Soutomaior and Ribeira do Ulla. Albariño, the predominant grape variety, produces fresh, aromatic white wines (see left).

D.O. Valdeorras has also earned a good reputation for quality wine. It is around 90 miles (150 kilometers) from the coast on the banks of the Río Sil, surrounding the town of El Barco de Valdeorras. Although red wines are also produced here – usually from the Alicante and Garnacha grapes – modern production of white wines made from the native Godello grape is of far greater interest. The vintages produced from this grape by a few small growers are characterized by their solid acidity, soft fruit, and strikingly spicy bouquet.

D.O. Ribeiro lies on both banks of the Río Miño, mainly in the province of Orense. The most important wine center is Ribadavia, where both red and white wines are produced. In the past, the reds could only ever be described as pleasant, table wines. However, in recent times a few growers have shown that by vigorously selecting their grapes, which are usually of the Mencia or Garnacha varieties, they can produce extremely elegant reds with delicate bouquets. Nevertheless, whites remain the region's leading product, and these are produced using up-to-date cellar technology from the Treixadura, Loureiro, Torrontés, and/or Godello varieties.

The two growing areas **D.O. Ribeira Sacra** (province of Lugo) and **D.O. Monterrei** (province of Ourense) were awarded the status of a protected mark of origin in 1996. By and by, the potential of the high slopes with their slatey soil is being assessed. Some of these red wines have a district mineral note. **D.O.** In the Ribeira Sacra, ambitious growers concentrate on red wines made from the Mencía grape. Monterrei specializes on white wines with a harmonious blend of Doña Blanca, Treixadura, and Godello. The red wines are light and pleasant, but lacking in depth.

ORUJO

The *poteiro* is an genial combination of craftsman and faith healer. Like an alchemist, he watches over the brew gurgling and bubbling in his copper kettle. Sticking meticulously to the distilling formulae passed down through the generations, he never ever reveals his own personal distilling secret.

In Galicia there is a long tradition of high-proof distillates made from grape residue *(aguaradientes de orujo* or *orujos* for short). Even today, many private individuals distil their own *orujo* in the vine-growing regions. The basic ingredient is the residue from wine production - in other words, the grape skins from the presses, along with the seeds and stalks. The residue should not be over-pressed, to ensure that the distillate takes on the flavor of the grapes. The pressed grapes are first fermented in open fermenting vats and wine residue or must is often added. Then the distillation process follows.

The most important piece of apparatus used by the *poteiro* or *orujo* distiller is the *pota* or *alquitara*, a copper kettle that can hold up to 53 US gallons (200 liters). The fermented grape residue is slowly poured into this and distilled over an open fire which gives off an even heat. The alcohol evaporates and is collected in cooled coiled tubing. A distilling cycle or *potada* should last at least six hours, until the crystal-clear *orujo* with its aromatic

A hydrometer measures the specific weight of the liquids. This instrument enables the *poteiro* to find the precise alcohol content of the *orujo*.

bouquet finally emerges. The grape residue is distilled once or twice, depending on taste. Only the "middle run" of the distillate is ever bottled, because the liquid released at the beginning and end of the distilling process contains harmful alcohol and fusel oils. An *orujo* distilled by an expert *poteiro* is still regarded in Galicia as something extra special. Nevertheless, it is fair to say that many marcs produced in modern, fully automated distillation plants are on a par with the traditionally distilled *orujos*, in both flavor and bouquet. Moreover, they are often more cleanly distilled, which is an important consideration.

Galician *orujo* can be distilled from various types of grape. Each *poteiro* uses the grape varieties which are grown in his particular area and are therefore readily available. Top-quality *orujos* are usually made from the Albariño, Godello, Treixadura, and Loureiro grapes.

55 *orujo* producers of 65,000 US Gallons (250,000 liters) of marc a year have been awarded the quality seal of the *Denominación Específica* (D.E.) *de Orujo de Galicia*. The control board distinguishes between the crystal-clear marc simply called *orujo* and the aged variety *(orujo envejecido)*, which is matured in oak for at least two years and is characterized by its amber color. The alcohol content of an *orujo* can be anything between 37 and 50 percent volume. However, where the alcohol content exceeds 45 percent volume, the strength of the alcohol frequently overwhelms the typical fruit flavor.

Surprisingly enough, there is no great tradition of marc in most other vine-growing regions of Spain. Although there has always been some small-scale distilling in the villages of La Rioja, most of the grape residue has been sold to alcohol factories. In recent years, however, a few *orujos* with a delicate, woody flavor and some nice fruit, similar to the French marcs, have appeared on the market. A few Catalan cava cellars are also producing outstanding marcs under the label *Marc de Cava*. These are based on the Macabeo, Xarel.lo, and Parellada grape varieties and in most cases the distillate is matured in oak casks adding to its characteristic flavor.

For some time now, the residue from wine-making has been more than mere waste. By distilling the pressed grapes, fine marc *(aguardiente de orujo)* can be produced.

QUEIMADA

"Owls, toads, and witches,
malevolent demons and devils,
spirits of the snow-covered pasture.
Ravens, lizards, and sorceresses..."

When winter arrives in Galicia and the cold oppresses both body and soul, it is as if an entire universe of mysterious beings is waiting to burst forth. In this region, with its countless rainy days, mysterious mists, and howling winds, the pagan belief in supernatural forces, spirits, and witches has remained fairly strong until today. Many myths and customs date back to Celtic times. These also include the belief in the purifying and fortifying power of fire. *Queimada*, the Galician draft made from schnapps seasoned with herbs, is a fiery potion thought to fortify the heart and mind for whatever tribulations fate may have in store. "*Queimada* gives us confidence in our own strength," say the Galicians. "It makes us courageous and determined and drives out the dark forces that have a habit of making our lives difficult."

A genuine *queimada* is celebrated by the *bruxo* or Galician sorcerer, who dresses in a costume of skins and straw and wears the horns of a he-goat on his head. This is often the host of the party. Uttering mysterious sounds and oaths, the sorcerer ignites a fragrant liquid in a large kettle. Then he grabs the *gaita* or old Galician bagpipes and starts playing. Again and again, he interrupts the tune to stir the flaming *queimada* with his ladle, while casting an impressive spell on the hot, potent drink:

"I ladle the flames from this fire, the fire of hell. Witches will take to their broomsticks in flight and bathe in the waves breaking on the shore."

Time and again the *bruxo* calls upon the spirits to impart strength and invigorating substances to the magic potion. It is supposed to quicken the mind, avert illness and disease, and purify the body, restoring its energy and vitality:

"Hark! Hark the groans of all those who cannot warm themselves on the fire water that purifies them. As this drink flows down our gullets, it will free us from the sufferings of the soul and from any bewitchment."

Once again, the master of ceremonies stirs the flaming elixir, then ladles the magical potion ceremoniously into porcelain bowls. In this moment the whole world is enveloped in a universal ritual:

"Powers of heaven and earth, spirits of sea and fire, I call to you all. If it is true that you have greater powers than we mere mortals, then let the souls of all those friends who cannot be here today share this queimada with us here and now."

Now the master observes how a red glow slowly rises in the faces of his guests. Gone are the trials and torments of everyday life, forgotten is the wind whistling at the door. Many appeal to the spirits of the fire in its afterglow, imploring that this night of magic may never end and simultaneously hoping for another glass of this wonderful brew!

The ritual is just as alive now as in Celtic times – the sorcerer prepares a *queimada* in a stunning, fiery ceremony that is held, if possible, on the beach at dusk.

THE LAND OF WITCHES AND DRUIDS

When the Galicians celebrate, they go back to their roots. The bagpipes and drums create a melancholy mood and it is precisely this melancholy that characterizes the mood of life in this mysterious region. In around the 6th century B.C., Galicia fell under the influence of the Celts. They set up fortified settlements *(castros)* and influenced the region's culture more than in any other part of Spain. Celtic villages, monumental stone circles, and other remains of settlements from the Celtic age have survived in many parts of Galicia. The remains of the Celtic culture are also expressed in the regional language *gallego*, which is today one of Spain's four official languages, and in the mythology and pagan customs. The main instrument of Galician folk music is the bagpipes or *gaita* as the Galicians call them, which are common throughout the entire area of Celtic culture. Ceramics also reflect the influence of Celtic designs. Something that is characteristic of Galician folklore is the fusion of pagan and Christian rites

and rituals. Many Galicians believe the sea and rocks possess supernatural powers. Worshipping the dead and ancestors is just as much a part of everyday life as believing in the transmigration of souls and the existence of witches *(meigas)*, who are believed to have great healing powers. Even quality daily newspapers frequently carry reports of cases in which people have come back from the dead, long-lost ancestors have emerged from the mist, or a terminally ill child has been miraculously healed by a witch's spell. Particularly in the hinterland of the provinces of Lugo and Orense, where the mist often hangs in the valleys for weeks on end during winter, sightings of witches are said to be a daily occurrence. Many religious processions and sacrificial rituals summon up the miraculous force of supernatural beings or are intended to placate dead ancestors. Until now, the Galicians have also credited many wild animals with mythical powers and the ability to determine fates. Many similar benefits and rituals are still found in other parts of Europe, particulary in Brittany and parts of the British Isles.

Queimada
Galician fire drink

4 cups/1 liter orujo, alternatively Italian
grappa
6 tbsp sugar
Rind of ½ unwaxed lemon, cut into thin strips

Pour all but 3 tablespoons of the marc into a flameproof bowl. Add 4 tablespoons of sugar and the lemon rind, and stir well.

Put the remaining sugar in a ladle, add the rest of the marc, and light it.

Slowly pour the flaming liquid into the bowl, stirring constantly. To put out the flames, place a lid on the bowl.

Serve the hot *queimada* in small clay bowls. Pieces of fruit or coffee beans can also be added, depending on taste, as can coffee, orange liqueur, and/or port wine.

CASTILLA Y LEÓN

David Schwarzwälder

CASTILE-LEÓN

Baking bread

Pork dishes

Dried legumes

Great Spanish stews

Jewish cookery

Sheep farming

Substantial meat dishes

Castilian beef

Wine-production on the banks of the Duero: Vega Sicilia

Top Duero wines

Sweet self-indulgence

Not a great deal grows on the high plain of Castile, but there is no need for Castilians to go hungry; sheep, pigs, and cattle provide meat in abundance.

"Instead of countryside, we are discovering space," observed author Gustav Faber, a keen traveler in Spain, writing about Castile-León. In the stillness and isolation of this sparsely populated region, it is easy to imagine the sharp sounds of battle: swords clashing and steeds snorting; the surroundings harbor lingering memories of the ruthless Middle Ages and the romantic age of chivalry. Indeed, it is a fortress that assumes pride of place on the Castilian coat of arms.

The two kingdoms of Castile and León, amalgamated in 1230, were constituted as a result of the various campaigns waged by the Christians to reconquer Spain, during their initially timid advances southward from the mountains of the north. Two hundred years later Isabella of Castile, one of the most famous women in Spanish history, joined her husband, Ferdinand of Aragon, in laying the political foundation stones on which Spain was to build to become a world power. This marked the birth of the Spanish nation. Although it is not quite central to the country geographically speaking, Castile-León lies at the very heart of Spain, and is now the largest administrative unit in modern Europe.

Castile-León, more than any other region, exemplifies the three traits which have defined the essence of the Spanish character over many centuries – pride, melancholy, and mystical religious fervor. The vast expanses of the landscape and the light are awe-inspiring; winters here are bitterly cold, and summers blazing hot. Although often described as aloof, Castilians are only outwardly reserved; their gruff exterior conceals a cheerful and hospitable nature. The sharp contrasts of Castile, together with its huge capacity for integration, are clearly reflected in its varied gastronomy, in which Jewish, Arab, and Christian elements mingle in a cuisine that has only regained the recognition it richly deserves in recent decades. Stews are a traditional feature in the cooking of all three of these cultures, the only basic difference being the type of meat used. For Christians, pork was central to physical well-being, whereas Arabs and Jews ate lamb for religious reasons. The famous stews *olla podrida* and *cocido* originate from the high plateau of central Spain. Meat remains a universally used ingredient in Castilian dishes today, and when served in classic style is accompanied only by a little green salad. Since sheep still dominate and characterize the Castilian landscape, lamb is ranked alongside pork as the preferred choice of meat at table. Sauces and sophisticated methods of preparation are even now practically unknown in Castilian cookery, which always focuses on essential methods and ingredients.

Santiago de Compostela
Vitoria-Gasteiz
Pamplona
León
Castilla y León
Valladolid
Barcelona
Zaragoza
Salamanca
Madrid
Toledo
Valencia
Palma de Mallorca
Mérida
Ciudad Real
Murcia
Sevilla
Granada

Opposite: Castile owes its name to its numerous forts and castles (*castillos*). The castle of Peñafiel was built in the 13th century, high above the Duero river.

Baking bread

The history of baking bread stretches back over thousands of years. On the Iberian peninsula the Celts were already preparing products resembling bread. They used wheat flour and acorn meal, which they cooked as unleavened dough cakes on hot stones. The Iberians are said to have used the froth from beer to induce fermentation, thereby producing leavened bread. And the Romans imported the skill of building ovens, which they had acquired from the ancient Greeks. Soon the vast plains of the Iberian peninsula were transformed into a rich granary.

As was the case all over Europe, the baker's art was regulated in the Middle Ages; the first Spanish baker's guild to be documented dates from the year 1395. However, not all villages had a baker in medieval times. Housewives baked at home or kneaded the dough in their own kitchens and then took the loaf, wrapped in cloth, to a communal oven, in which all members of the community were allowed to bake their bread for a small sum. Rural bakers' shops are largely a phenomenon of the 19th and 20th centuries. Over the years, however, their number has been considerably reduced by regional bread factories.

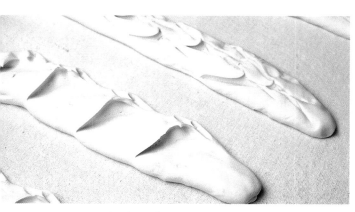

Traditional patterns are etched into the loaves using a sharp blade. When the dough rises, the decorations unfold in all their glory in the time-honored fashion.

Many bakers in Castile-León still heat their ovens in the traditional way, feeding them with wood while the dough rises, then putting the bread in the oven.

Bread sticks need less than half an hour before they are baked to a golden brown color. The wood-burning oven gives them a crisp crust and imparts the characteristic slightly smoky flavor. In rural areas the oven is often stoked afresh after the bread has been baked, as many people have a suckling pig roasted by the baker on weekends.

Nevertheless, it is still possible today to find the odd baker in Castile who makes bread quite traditionally in a wood-burning oven.

On Saturdays the *panadero* is often in his bakery as early as three in the morning to knead the dough for the three basic types of bread – *barra* and *colín* (bread sticks), and *pan candeal*, the typical Castilian round loaf. All of these are made from wheat flour, water, yeast, and salt. The loaves stand for about an hour on long wooden shelves while the dough rises.

Meanwhile the baker lights the enormous brick oven. This has internal walls running right through it, so that it heats up evenly. Sometimes over 220 pounds (100 kilograms) of oak are stacked up in the bakery, since a few suckling pigs frequently follow the bread into the oven to be roasted on weekends.

The round loaf, weighing about 2 pounds (900 grams), takes longest to bake and must therefore go into the oven first. Using a razor blade inserted into a handle, the baker cuts diamond shapes into the surface of the rounds of dough. After being decorated in this way they are baked for 35 minutes, until the crust is light brown and between ½ inch and 1 inch thick (1 to 2 centimeters). Then the bread sticks are put into the oven; these weigh 14 ounces (400 grams) and take just under half an hour to bake. The popular *colínes* are similarly decorated with a pattern before baking and have a thicker crust than the *barras*. In the livestock slaughtering season the baker also prepares huge round loaves with a thinner crust. The crumbs are added to the fillings used to make sausages – *morcilla* (blood sausage), for instance, and the Salamancan specialty, *farinato*.

PAN CANDEAL
Castilian round loaf

4⅓ cups/500 g bread flour
2 tsp/10 g salt
1 cake/15 g compressed yeast
Olive oil for greasing baking sheet and glazing

Sift the flour onto the work surface and make a hollow in the center. Add the salt, crumbled yeast, and ¾ cup/200 ml lukewarm water. Knead all the ingredients into a smooth dough. Cover and leave in a warm place to rise until doubled in volume. Make the dough into a round loaf, about 12 inches/30 cm in diameter. Carve a diamond pattern on the surface with a sharp knife. Place on a greased baking sheet and brush with olive oil. Bake in a preheated oven at 390 °F/200 °C for about 25 minutes until golden brown.

CHASTITY BREAD

Lent must once have been extremely hard for the men of Salamanca, for abstinence was required, and not just in culinary matters. The pious 16th-century King Philip II issued an edict that all women of easy virtue were to leave the cities for the duration of the fasting period. So in Salamanca the prostitutes were sent from the city in Holy Week and were not allowed to return until the Monday after Easter. On this day the loose women were strictly forbidden to enter the city via the bridge – it was deemed unthinkable that the devout souls inhabiting the town should encounter these women, who were regarded as sinfulness personified. It was the students and the official responsible for prostitution – laconically referred to by the people as *padre putas* (the whores' priest) – who rowed across the river in boats decked with flowers to fetch the women back. This event was celebrated on the banks of the river with free-flowing wine and *hornazos*, pies filled with meat and eggs.

The custom has survived in similar form until the present day; even devout Spaniards are not averse to celebrating the *lunes de aguas*, or festival of the waters, on Easter Monday. Many families take a picnic lunch out into the countryside, and eat the traditional *hornazos*. To make these, pastry is filled with lean pork, ham, paprika sausage, and hard-cooked eggs. It is then baked (see photograph on page 263).

Bread from a wood-burning oven, produced by the traditional method, has an almost mystical aura – it is an important cultural phenomenon.

Crisp bread sticks feature among the most important foodstuffs for Spaniards. Some people even go so far as to claim they would rather eat nothing at all than sit down to a meal without bread. Ultimately, bread – a food we know to be thousands of years old – does more than satisfy mere physical hunger. Bread is part of our culture, part of the rituals associated with meals and communication. And on a more mundane level, Spaniards love using bread to mop up a good sauce.

Pork dishes

Roast sucking pig (*cochinillo asado* or *tostón*), which epitomizes Castilian cuisine, enjoys cult status in the villages. It has aroused such passion among its devotees that many recipes are reminiscent of romantic poems addressed to the dearly beloved, extolling the virtues for instance of "fat, tender, healthy piglets, 25 days old, and barely 9 pounds (4 kilograms) in weight." The bakers stoke up their ovens even on weekends, to roast sucking pigs. These are put in the oven at the local bakery whenever there is a cause for a celebratory feast.

A Castilian *cochinillo* is fed exclusively on its mother's milk and is no more than a few weeks old when it is slaughtered. In central Castile it is traditionally roasted whole in the oven, while in Burgos and Palencia it is sometimes also spit-roasted over an open fire. However, the pig's legendary status comes from the famous rotisseries (*asadores*) of Segovia. To dine on suckling pig in such restaurants is an experience, for most of them have their own walled ovens (*horno de leña*). The arguments about the perfect method of heating these ovens occasionally reach philosophical heights; some experts insist that holm oak is the best wood, because it gives a hotter fire, while others favor pine wood, because it burns more slowly and evenly. Whatever the method, the young pigs must be roasted very slowly. The sucking pig is served whole on a large earthenware platter and, in a conclusive demonstration of the tenderness of the meat, is divided into portions using the edge of a plate.

Pork, of course, is also a feature of Castile's various specialties. The famous hams from Guijuelo and Candelario in the south of the province of Salamanca are made from black Iberian pigs (*jamón ibérico*, see also 338 ff). Salamanca also produces an excellent *longaniza*, a thin sausage that has dark red meat and a sprinkling of mold on the outer skin. It is air-dried for between one and two months and can then be eaten raw, fried, or boiled. The quick-dried *chorizo di Cantimpalos* is dried for a short time and may contain up to 15 percent beef. This and the *chorizo* from Villarcayo, which is reputed to be particularly hot and spicy, are Castilian variations on the pepper sausage. Blood sausage from Burgos, which contains rice (*morcilla de Burgos*), is a good partner for stews made with legumes, while the small sausages (*salchichas*) from Zaratán in the province of Valladolid are best fried.

In the rotisseries (*asadores*) of Segovia, the pigs are cooked whole in wood-burning ovens. The meat is so tender as a result, that it melts in the mouth.

Tender pink sucking pigs are so popular in Castile that they have been written about in the most ardent terms – and not just in cookbooks. Owing to its symbolic significance, the pig is revered, and is "sacrificed," especially on feast days.

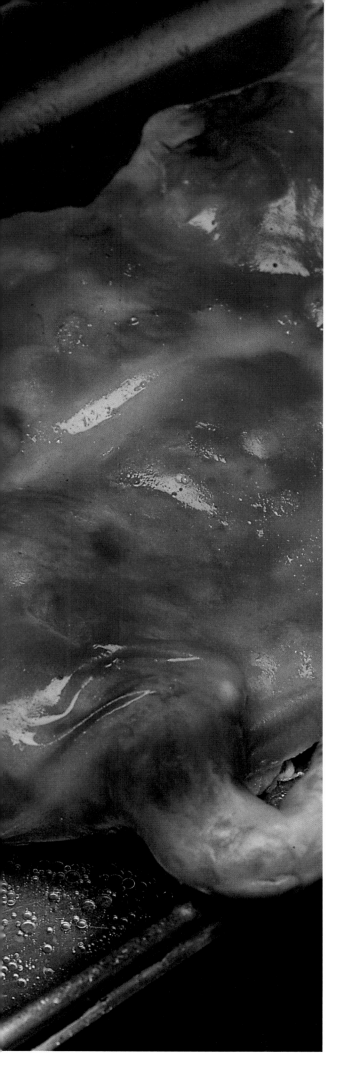

Traditional Castilian pies (*hornazos*) are filled with pork, ham, pepper sausage, and eggs, but there are many variations.

Fat bacon (*tocino*) or pork belly (*panceta*) is often air-dried and then used in stews; it is much sought after, especially that from Iberian pigs.

The traditional pork butcher's is full of wonderful things. Every part of the pig is used in cooking – the ears, organ meat, the trotters, and even the tail.

Pig trotters can be a real delicacy, when they are salted, for instance (*manos de cerdo saladas*). They are excellent for stews and in pot-roasts (see recipe on page 272).

Farinato, a soft sausage made from bread crumbs, lard, flour, onions, and aniseed, is an unusual specialty, which is usually eaten fried. El Bierzo, the mountainous region in the north, is famous for the *botillo*, made by stuffing pigs' stomachs with head, rib, and tail meat, which is then marinated in paprika, garlic, and oregano. The resulting sausages are smoked. The *botillo* is often the main ingredient in potato and vegetable stews. It is also good served with *berza*, a type of cabbage.

COSTILLAR DE CERDO LACADO
"Lacquered" pork ribs

4½ lbs/2 kg pork ribs (spareribs)
Salt and pepper
6½ tbsp/200 g runny acacia or woodland honey
2 tbsp wine vinegar

Wash and dry the spareribs and rub with salt and pepper. Stir the honey and wine vinegar together and then brush the mixture evenly over the ribs. Leave to stand for a minimum of three hours in the refrigerator. Lift the ribs out of the marinade and drain. Cook on a hot charcoal grill or under a preheated broiler in the oven for approximately 30 minutes, turning and basting with the honey marinade several times.
Divide the cooked ribs into portions along the bones and serve very hot.

THE PIG AS A SYMBOL

There is a popular Castilian saying that ham is more likely to produce Christian converts than the Spanish Inquisition. The common destiny shared by pigs and the human population of Spain has left its mark on huge tracts of the landscape, and for centuries it split the population into three political and religious camps. Consumption of pork was proof of a good Christian; Jews and Muslims, on the other hand, were forbidden to eat pig meat.
Pigs were being fattened up and eaten in Spain long ago, in Roman times. When the Muslim Moors conquered large parts of the Iberian peninsula at the beginning of the 8th century, they banished pigs from the menu, since they were branded unclean by the Koran. As the Moors were driven back during the reconquest of Spain and the Christian rulers regained control, the pig once again became a symbol of the division between religions; people who refused pork were open to the suspicion that they were not true believers in Christ. When the Christian forces were victorious, many Muslims and Jews converted to Christianity in order to avoid expulsion from the country. Naturally the moral arbiters of the Spanish Inquisition were aware that many of these conversions were merely for the sake of appearance, so anyone who was accused of refusing to eat pork, was persecuted as a false convert. Today, Jewish converts and their descendants are still called *xueta* – from the old word for pork fat.

Dried legumes

Legumes (*legumbres*) are among some of the world's oldest cultivated plants. Stone Age peoples collected ripe seeds from plants belonging to the *papilionaceae* family (legumes), such as lupins and lucerne, and ate them with the game that they hunted in the vast forests of Europe. For centuries, beans and chickpeas rivaled bread in Spain as the most common foodstuff, and they form the basis of many substantial dishes. The plants are content with extremely poor soil, and adapt perfectly to the weather conditions of the country, which are sometimes extreme. Furthermore, they act as a valuable organic fertilizer for the fields (see inset on opposite page).

Because poultry, beef, and game were enjoyed only by the nobility and holders of high office in medieval Spain, the diet of the ordinary people relied largely upon pork and also legumes, which were known as "poor man's meat." This non-meat protein source played an extremely important role, not least during periods of fasting, as legumes contain up to 25 percent valuable plant protein.

Spain is the only country in Europe where the chickpea (*garbanzo*), which many people disdain, was able to gain a foothold. Originally a native of ancient Persia, it was brought to the eastern Mediterranean by the Greeks and the Romans; eventually the seeds are thought to have reached Spain via the Carthaginians. Today, tender Castilian chickpeas from Fuentesaúco and Pedrosillanos and *garbanzos* from Extremadura and Andalusia both appear on the market as a delicacy.

Most varieties of bean (*alubias, judías*) were brought back from the Caribbean and Latin America by the Spanish conquerors, and replaced those varieties that the Arabs had already established on the Iberian peninsula. Although Castilians still continue to claim that their region has around 200 indigenous varieties of bean, most of these are regional variants of the twenty or so main varieties that are natives of Spain. The best Castilian beans include the white varieties of *judías de el Barco de Avila, alubias de La Bañeza,* and *judiones de La Granja,* as well as the red variety of *alubias rojas de Ibeas.*

In ancient times, lentil dishes were very popular in Mesopotamia, or what is now Iraq, which led the Romans to incorporate them in their own cuisine. Today the best Spanish lentils are grown in the Armuña, a belt of land in the province of Salamanca.

Legumes are the basic ingredient in the traditional Spanish stew *cocido* (see 266) and in many *platos de cuchara* (dishes eaten with a spoon), food which was once eaten exclusively by hard-working rural people for the sustenance of both body and soul. Now, however, even the best chefs are singing the praises of legumes and conjuring up all manner of culinary masterpieces with them.

The best Spanish legumes include *lentejas de La Armuña,* (left), *alubias rojas de Ibeas* (above center), *fabes Asturianas* (above right), *Garbanzos de La Bañeza* (below right), and *judiones de La Granja* (below center).

NITROGEN-FIXING NODULES

Legumes are more than just a cornerstone of human nutrition; the soil also benefits greatly from their presence. Beans, lentils, peas, and chickpeas, in addition to clover and lucerne, break up the soil with their deep roots and work tirelessly to absorb nitrogen. In the swellings, or nodules, on the roots of legumes live so-called nitrogen-fixing bacteria; these absorb the nitrogen that is so essential to all living plants and convert it into a chemical compound that the plant can utilize. In return the bacteria receive valuable nutrients from the plant. Because of this important function, legumes are often planted in rotation on land whose nutrients have been exhausted, where they enrich the soil by restoring its precious nitrogen content. They are therefore an ideal organic fertilizer.

Background: chickpeas (*garbanzos*) flourish happily on the poorest ground, and even restore nutrients to the soil. Legumes also provide valuable minerals in the human diet.

GREAT SPANISH STEWS

"The huge dish steaming there at the front looks to me as though it might be *olla podrida*, and such a great diversity of comestibles is contained in such dishes that I cannot fail to discover in it something both palatable and wholesome."

Don Quixote's simple observation sums up everything there is to be said about *olla podrida*, the quintessential Castilian stew, in which there is room for anything – legumes and vegetables, meat and sausage, ham and bacon, sometimes even potatoes or noodles. Chickpeas were the principal ingredient in this substantial dish back in Cervantes' time, except in Burgos, where they prefer red beans.

Olla simply means a pot or kettle. The adjective *podrida* should not be translated as meaning "spoilt" (from the Spanish *podrir*), but as meaning "powerful" or "potent" (from the Spanish *poder*, "to be able"). This indicates that in earlier times only wealthy Spaniards could afford such an opulent stew with its extravagant meat ingredients, and also that the dish was considered substantial and satisfying.

The Castilian *olla podrida* ranks alongside the Jewish *adafina* (see 268) as a kind of archetypal Spanish stew. It spread throughout the country under the name of *cocido* or *puchero*, and each region developed its own variant using locally grown ingredients. In Madrid housewives add cabbage and beet, in Galicia turnip tops, in the Levante green beans and pumpkin, and in the Basque provinces spinach and hard-cooked eggs, with the regional meat or sausage specialty providing the finishing touch wherever it is made. The Catalan variation *escudella i carn d'olla* (see photograph top right), which unlike the central Spanish stews contains poultry and fine-textured meatballs, is a particularly lavish variant. It should nevertheless be possible to taste every single ingredient, and herein lies the challenge for the cook.

Almost every type of *cocido* is served in three parts (*tres vuelcos*), called *sota, caballo y rey* (knave, horse, and king) – a reference to the hierarchy of chess pieces. The broth is served first, the legumes and vegetables follow, with the meat as the climax. The exception to this rule is found only among the inhabitants of a small Castilian village in Astorga, Castrillo de los Polvazares. For centuries they have eaten the meat first, followed by the legumes and vegetables, with the soup served last, accompanied by the ultimate extravagance of a delicious sweet vanilla cream.

Opinion is divided about the reasons for this. Some say that after a rich meal the stomach needs a soothing broth. Others are of the opinion that if anything is to be left uneaten, it should be the soup. A third version involves the senior officers who occupied Astorga with their troops during the Christian reconquest of Spain; they did not take much time off from their fighting to eat, and so started directly with the meat course. Whether this is true or not, today *cocido maragato* usually has to be ordered in advance in Castrillo de los Polvazares: since this most aristocratic of stews contains between eight and ten different kinds of meat and sausage, the preparation is correspondingly time-consuming and costly.

In addition to the various *cocidos* made from chickpeas or beans with vegetables and meat, there are, of course, other dishes featuring legumes in Spanish cookery. Fine braised dishes with lentils and the sausage specialty of the particular region predominate in central Spain. In the coastal regions plump white beans are combined with mussels, crabmeat, or other seafood, eel or snails, and are also served as an accompaniment to various kinds of meat and game.

OLLA PODRIDA
Castilian stew
Serves 6

1¼ cups/300 g dried chickpeas
9 oz/250 g beef
Generous 1 lb/500 g pork ribs (spareribs)
1 pig trotter
1 pig ear
3½ oz/100 g piece smoked bacon
3½ oz/100 g piece air-dried ham
1 onion, stuck with 1 bay leaf and 2 cloves
2 carrots, chopped
2 white beets, chopped
2 chorizo sausages, or other pepper sausage
2 Spanish blood sausages
2 cloves of garlic, chopped
Salt and pepper
1 tbsp lard

Leave the chickpeas to soak overnight in plenty of water. Next day place the chickpeas, together with the water in which they have been soaked, the beef, pork ribs, pig trotter, pig ear, bacon, and ham in a large pan, and add enough water to cover all of the ingredients. Add the onion, stuck with the bay leaf and cloves, and boil for approximately 1 hour.

Stir the carrots and beets into the stew and add the sausages. Crush the garlic with a little salt and add to the stew. Mix well, then season with pepper and stir in the lard. Cook for an additional 15 minutes.

Lift the meat, bacon, ham, and sausages out of the stew, and cut into small pieces. Strip all the meat from the ribs and pig trotter, and cut into cubes. Return the meat to the pan and reheat in the stew. Season to taste with salt and pepper before serving.

Note: Many Spanish housewives are of the opinion that *olla podrida* has to be simmered for several hours before all the ingredients can develop their full flavor.

ESCUDELLA I CARN D'OLLA
Catalan meat and vegetable stew
Serves 6 (Photograph above)

1 cup/200 g chickpeas
Salt
1 calf foot
1 pig trotter
2 soup bones
1 pig ear
7 oz/200 g smoked bacon
2¼ cups/250 g mixed ground meat
1 egg
2 tbsp breadcrumbs
⅛ tsp ground cinnamon
1 tbsp parsley
Pepper
1 tbsp flour
½ chicken, divided into portions
2 medium/250 g potatoes, quartered or halved
½ head of white cabbage, cut into strips
2 carrots, cut into strips
1 bunch of green onions, chopped
1 clove of garlic, finely minced
2 Spanish blood sausages (butifarras negras)
9 oz/250 g vermicelli

Leave the chickpeas to soak the night before in lightly salted water.

Wash the calf foot, pig trotter, soup bones, and pig ear well and bring to a boil in a large pan with a generous 6 US pints/3 liters water and 1 tsp salt. Add the chickpeas, cover and boil over medium heat for 1 hour. Mix the ground meat, egg, breadcrumbs, cinnamon, and parsley together well. Season with salt and pepper. Form into a long loaf shape and sprinkle with the flour. Leave to stand.

Add the chicken pieces, potatoes, white cabbage, carrots, green onions, garlic, and ground meat loaf to the pan, and cook for another 25 minutes. Add the blood sausages 10 minutes before the end of cooking time.

Arrange the meat, chicken, bacon, and sausages on a warmed platter. Put the vegetables on another platter, keeping the different kinds separate, and keep everything warm. Boil the vermicelli in the stock until just tender.

Serve the noodle soup first, followed by the meat and vegetables.

JEWISH COOKERY

On March 31, 1492 a royal edict brought to an end the era marked by a Jewish presence on Spanish soil – an era that had lasted for a thousand years. This decree was a warrant for the expulsion of Jews from Castile and Aragon, and to a large extent it also set the seal on the very gradual decline of the Spanish economy. For centuries the Jews had been making their mark on the social and political life of the country. Religious tolerance was the norm in Castile, especially during the reign of King Alfonso X (1221-1284), known, not without good reason, as Alfonso the Wise. Jews were able to live unmolested among Christians and Arabs, for the most part abiding strictly by the tenets of their faith.

The Jewish way of life featured strict rules concerning food, in Spain as everywhere else. These are called *Cashrut* in Hebrew, and are still of fundamental importance in all Jewish communities throughout the world. These rules not only prescribe how individual foodstuffs must be prepared, but also determine the sequence in which food is eaten and the amount of time that must elapse between courses. Thus milk, for example, may not be consumed at the same time as blood in the form of meat or fish – an interval of several hours is required. The logistical burden imposed on an orthodox Jewish family as a result of this is by no means to be underestimated, since two completely separate sets of crockery and cutlery are required for dishes containing blood and those containing milk.

A practicing Jew eats the meat only of poultry and cloven-hoofed ruminants – sheep, goats, and cattle. It is also essential for the animal to have been weaned. The animals authorized for consumption by the Thorah, the book of traditional Jewish commandments, must be kosher, meaning impeccable, and the stricture forbidding the ingestion of blood under any circumstances is paramount. During the ritual slaughter procedure, the gullet and windpipe of the animal are severed in addition to the carotid artery, so that the animal is bled dry. After this the carcass must be irrigated for half an hour. The meat is then heavily salted and hung for over an hour on a grid. Finally, it is thoroughly rinsed with water on three consecutive occasions – only after this is it deemed kosher and ready for cooking.

As far as fish are concerned, Jewish cuisine is restricted to species with fins, gills, and scales. It is forbidden to eat shellfish. In Spanish fish cookery the influence of the Sephardim, the Spanish or Portuguese Jews who were forced to leave Spain in 1492 and fled to north Africa, Italy, and the Ottoman Empire, is still much in evidence. Recipes are still found in these areas for stuffed fish in which the Spanish-Levantine influence can be seen.

Saturday is the Sabbath, the seventh day of the week in the Jewish religion; all work, including household tasks and cooking, must cease on this day of rest and religious observance. To avoid this dilemma and still have a hot meal on the table to enjoy on the Sabbath, the pious Jewish housewife begins preparing a stew the day before, on the Friday. *Adafina* is the Jewish equivalent of the Christian *puchero* or *cocido*. For an ordinary Jewish family this dish would traditionally consist of kosher goat meat or mutton, oil, chopped onion, and garlic, cooked with saffron and various herbs. Wealthier Jewish families may opt for a much richer meal which would include beef, poultry, legumes, or noodles. The stew prepared on Friday is kept warm until the Sabbath by wrapping it in thick cloths or even tucking it under the bed covers to retain as much heat as possible. In earlier times the custom was for the housewife to put the pot in glowing coals, where it cooked overnight.

Above: The Jews have made their mark on Spanish life. The legacy of their rich culture can be seen in the Jewish quarter (*Barrio Judío*) in Toledo.

Right: The Jews were protected by the Castilian crown until the 14th century. In Toledo they built a synagog, which was later used by the Christians as a church.

Tender sucking lamb sizzles in the wood-burning oven – an image reminiscent of a holy shrine. *Lechazo asado*, roast sucking lamb, is as sacred to Castilians as sucking pig, and the method of preparation has something of the ritual about it. The quartered lambs are placed on earthenware plates with the cut side upward (see inset) and roasted. They are turned later on (main photograph).

SHEEP FARMING

On the Iberian peninsula, long ago, the Romans discovered tracks in the pastureland along which herdsmen had driven their livestock since time immemorial. The Goths called the common grazing land *mesta*, and held regular meetings at which they discussed all kinds of problems relating to sheep rearing. When Alfonso the Wise created the *Honrado Consejo de la Mesta* in 1273, sheep farming had long since become a cornerstone of the Castilian economy. In creating the "honorable councilor for grazing land," the king acknowledged the amalgamation of sheep breeders from Castile and León, which was to develop into one of the most powerful guilds in Europe. The shepherds were granted extensive privileges for their grazing lands, as well as rights to water and rights of way. The network of drovers' tracks (*cañadas reales*) sanctioned by the crown was consolidated, and it continued to expand with the reconquest of Spain by the Christians. Soon the roads were to stretch from the mountains of Asturias in the north down as far as Valencia and Seville. The monarchy was very keen to encourage rotation of grazing land. Ultimately the livestock tax imposed on flocks was to provide a considerable source of income for the rulers. Wool

Castile produces some fine ewe's milk cheeses, such as this *Queso Zamorano*, in varying stages of ripeness.

production was vital to the Castilian economy; the wool was shipped to Flanders, England, and France via the ports on the Bay of Biscay. During the reign of the Catholic monarchs Ferdinand and Isabella in the 15th century, there were more than three million sheep in Castilian flocks. However, the economic decline of the wool industry began as early as the 17th century. Replacement of grazing land by cultivated fields became the watchword, for more and more grain was required to feed the rapidly growing population. The influence of the "councilor for grazing land" declined steadily as a result, until his office was abolished in 1836.

ROAST SUCKLING LAMB

Sheep from the high plain of Castile still provide milk for varieties of cheese such as *zamorano* or *manchego*, as well as meat of excellent quality. Castile and La Mancha are something of a Promised Land for connoisseurs of the famous suckling lamb (*cordero lechal* or *lechazo*). The best quality lamb is of the Churra or Castellana breed: it must be no more than thirty days old, and must have been fed exclusively on its mother's milk.

The suckling lambs are roasted in ancient vaulted ovens (see photograph on facing page). These should have walls of clay (*adobe*) or brick, as they absorb the heat better and retain it for longer than fireclay; as a result the meat cooks very slowly. For roasting, on the bone, a suckling lamb aged between 25 and 30 days is quartered. The pieces are laid, cut side upward, on large earthenware plates, and a glass of water containing a soupspoon of pork lard is poured over each piece. The quarters are put into the oven at a temperature of 445 °F/230 °C, and the heat is then reduced to approximately 355 °F/180 °C. After an hour and a half the meat is turned, salted, and then cooked for another 15 minutes. The use of herbs or lard is a matter of personal taste – the most important factor is the quality of the meat.

This picture could easily be thousands of years old. Back in Roman times herdsmen were crossing the high Castilian plain with their sheep, and for a while their rights were even protected by the crown. Although today some of the ancient drovers' roads (*cañadas*) have been blocked and intersected by roads, they are still officially in existence. There is even one ancient *cañada* that leads through the center of Madrid – right through the chic Castellana shopping area.

SUBSTANTIAL MEAT DISHES

PICHONES RELLENOS
Stuffed pigeons
(Photograph opposite)

4 oven-ready pigeons, with giblets
Salt and pepper
2 tbsp olive oil
1 clove of garlic, chopped
3½ oz/100 g Serrano ham, finely diced
2 hard-cooked eggs, chopped
2 slices of stale white bread, softened in milk
⅛ tsp mild ground paprika
8 thin slices fat green bacon
Oil for the baking pan

Wash and dry the pigeons and rub with salt and pepper. Clean the giblets and cut into small pieces. Heat the olive oil and fry the giblets briskly. Stir in the garlic and continue frying for a minute or two. Remove from the heat and mix with the diced ham, the eggs, and the bread (after squeezing out excess milk). Season with salt, pepper, and paprika. Use this mixture to stuff the pigeons, and sew up with kitchen string. Wrap each pigeon in 2 slices of bacon. Brush a baking pan with oil. Stand the pigeons in it and then roast in a preheated oven at 430 ºF/220 ºC for about 25 minutes.

MANOS DE CERDO A LA CASTELLANA
Pig trotters Castilian style (Photograph below)

4 pig trotters, from the front of the animal, split lengthwise
1 onion, stuck with 1 bayleaf and 2 cloves
1 clove of garlic
2 carrots, chopped
Salt and pepper
1 tbsp lard
1 onion, finely chopped
2 cloves of garlic, finely chopped
1 tbsp almonds, coarsely chopped
1 tbsp flour
½ cup/125 ml white wine
⅛ tsp hot ground paprika
2 bay leaves

Wash the pig trotters thoroughly. Place in cold water with the spiked onion, garlic, and carrots, and bring to a boil. Season with salt and pepper, cover, and simmer for about 2 hours. Then lift out the pig trotters and divide into portions. Strain the cooking liquor and reserve. Heat the lard in a braising pan and cook the onion and garlic gently until soft and transparent. Stir in the almonds, sprinkle with flour, and brown slightly. Pour in 2 cups/500 ml of cooking liquor and the wine, stirring constantly. Season with salt, pepper, and paprika, and add the bay leaves. Boil for 10 minutes; then add the trotters and leave to simmer for another 10 minutes.

SOPA BURGALESA
Soup with crayfish and lamb
(See also inset on opposite page)

2 tbsp lard
14 oz/400 g lamb, cut into thin strips
1 onion, finely chopped
1 tbsp flour
Generous 4 cups/1 liter meat stock
16 crayfish tails, cooked and shelled
Salt and pepper
1 tbsp chopped parsley

Heat the lard in a pan and fry the strips of meat briskly. Add the onion and cook gently until soft and transparent. Sprinkle with the flour and let it brown slightly. Pour over the stock, stirring constantly. Bring to a boil and simmer for 15 minutes. Add the crayfish tails to the soup and heat through without letting it come to a boil. Season with salt and pepper to taste and sprinkle with the chopped parsley before serving.

GALLINA EN PEPITORIA
Chicken in almond and wine sauce

1 large chicken, weighing about 3¼ lbs/1.5 kg
Salt and pepper
5 tbsp olive oil
2 onions, finely chopped
½ cup/125 ml white wine
1½ cups/375 ml stock
1 bay leaf
2 sprigs of thyme
2 cloves of garlic, chopped
2 tbsp ground almonds
A few saffron filaments
⅛ tsp ground cinnamon
2 hard-cooked egg yolks
1 raw egg yolk

Wash the chicken under running water and dry thoroughly; then cut into 8 portions. Rub well with salt and pepper. Heat the oil in a casserole and fry the chicken pieces briskly on each side. Add the onions and cook gently until they are soft and transparent. Add the white wine and pour in the stock. Add the bay leaf and thyme, cover, and cook the chicken over a medium heat for approximately 25 minutes.
Meanwhile, crush the garlic in a mortar and pestle along with the ground almonds, saffron, cinnamon, hard-cooked egg yolks, and 2 tbsp of stock. Stir this paste into the braising liquor and simmer for a few more minutes. Then remove from the heat, discard the bay leaf and thyme, and stir in the raw egg yolk. Season with salt and pepper to taste and serve immediately.

CATCHING CRAYFISH ON ST VITUS' DAY

Now, whether or not the water of the Moradillo is good for skin diseases remains an open question. One thing is certain, though; the stream has an abundance of crayfish, and back in those early days of the 20th century, on an afternoon with a north wind blowing, and armed with a drag net and four helpers to beat the surface of the water, it was possible to fill three or four bags without too much trouble. Things were not as strictly regulated in those days as they are now, and you could catch crayfish properly with a crab catcher, or with a fixed net, or with a dragnet, or just by hand, provided you did not mind getting a wet backside, which is the inevitable lot of those

bent on catching fish. Anyway, on St. Vitus' Day, the families of the village traditionally lined the banks of the stream to catch crayfish, gathering in the afternoon at the *Encapuchados* monastery for tea. Each of us had his allotted position on the bank, and Mama, Papa, the twins, Aunt Marcelina, and I used to sit beneath the seven poplars that stand at the edge of the wood and are known in the village, although I do not know why, as the Seven Sacraments. There, very carefully, Papa would set up the crab catchers in the deepest and stillest spots, after he had pushed aside the rushes with a forked branch. Papa always used dried meat for bait, but if things were not going too well, he would hand me the axe and have me look for worms in the damp earth. It was very rare for crayfish to spurn such bait. Ponciano, on the other hand, baited his crab catchers with roast potatoes, and Valentin,

the secretary, used horse spleen, and there were a few people in the village, like Don Justo del Espíritu Santo, the priest, who even used crusts of rye bread.

(From: Miguel Delibes, *Four Old Stories from Old Castile*, 1964)

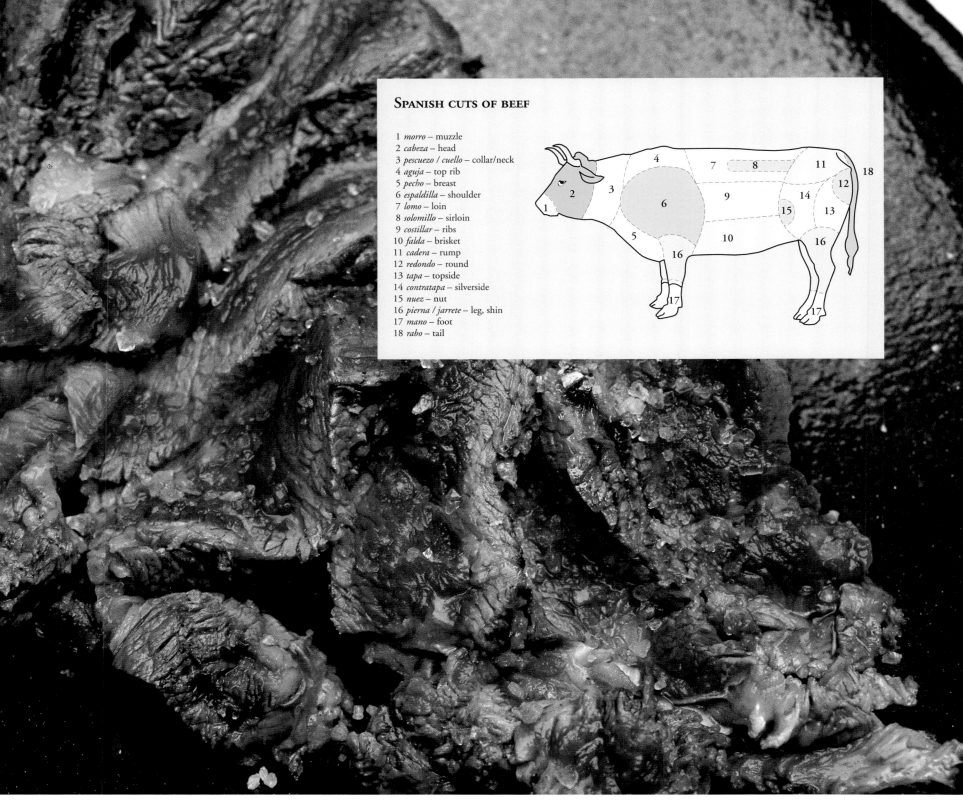

SPANISH CUTS OF BEEF

1 *morro* – muzzle
2 *cabeza* – head
3 *pescuezo / cuello* – collar/neck
4 *aguja* – top rib
5 *pecho* – breast
6 *espaldilla* – shoulder
7 *lomo* – loin
8 *solomillo* – sirloin
9 *costillar* – ribs
10 *falda* – brisket
11 *cadera* – rump
12 *redondo* – round
13 *tapa* – topside
14 *contratapa* – silverside
15 *nuez* – nut
16 *pierna / jarrete* – leg, shin
17 *mano* – foot
18 *rabo* – tail

Beef from the Morucha de Salamanca and Avileña Negra breeds is far too good to be overcooked. It is best eaten seared, so that the meat is still red on the inside. In many restaurants the thick rib steak or *chuletón* is cut into pieces (main picture) before it continues to cook on its hot earthenware platter. It is most important to avoid cooking the meat for too long if it is to retain its tenderness and delicate flavor.

A proper Castilian *chuletón* weighs at least 14 oz (400 grams) and is at least a couple of inches (several centimeters) thick.

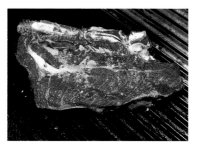

The thick pieces of rib are seared over a very fierce heat on a grill, hotplate, or in a skillet.

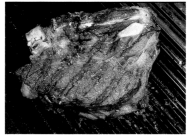

After a short time the *chuletón* is turned. It should be browned on the outside, but never cooked right through.

Next a flat earthenware platter is heated until it is very hot. The meat is served on this, so that it can continue to cook slowly.

CASTILIAN BEEF

"The shepherd's meal for tomorrow, consisting of a generous ration of *cecina* and ham, is already packed," wrote Enrique Gil y Carrasco in his book *El Pastor trashumante*, published in 1843. Dark red dried beef, or *cecina*, has been produced in the area around León for centuries. Because it can be kept for long periods of time, *cecina* was once an ideal provision for wandering herdsmen and journeymen.

As in other mountainous regions of Europe, the raw beef is salted and smoked, and is then air-dried for several months. The long periods of frost and strong winds in northern Castile encourage even ripening, while the smoking over oak wood fires imparts a strong flavor. Villarramiel in the province of Palencia produces a variant of *cecina* using horseflesh, and in earlier times *cecina* was made from donkey meat. In Vegacervera in the province of León goat's meat is also used; *cecino de chivo* is made from adult female goats, *cecina de castrón* from castrated male goats.

Wafer thin slices of *cecina* are served with a drizzling of the finest cold-pressed olive oil, accompanied by robust farmhouse bread. This excellent dried meat also graces any plate of cold cuts on which the finest products of Castilian ham and sausage producers are displayed. If served warm, it goes particularly well with wild vegetables and mushrooms.

Fresh beef is also very popular in Castilian cookery. There are several indigenous breeds in the region that are able to turn the barren countryside to their advantage, for it is precisely from feeding on the infertile pastures of the stony mountain valleys and Mediterranean forests that the meat derives its characteristic flavor and a wonderfully succulent, firm texture. The black Avila cattle (*Avileña Negra Ibérica*), which are reared in the mountains all around León and graze on large tracts of pasture, belong to one of the oldest breeds of cattle in Europe.

The animals are sold as calves, yearlings, or young steers. Its meat has a refined, subtle flavor and is very pale in color with a pronounced grain (see photograph on page 245).

The gray Morucha cattle are directly descended from the ancient Iberian breed known as Bos Taurus Ibericus and are kept only in the province of Salamanca. The animals live out in the fields all year round in all conditions, and as a result their muscle fiber tissue is very fine-grained with hardly any fat running through it. The lean meat has a strong, very spicy flavor (see photograph on page 245).

Every self-respecting Castilian inn now offers top quality beef on its menu, which is preferably cooked on a charcoal fire (*a la brasa*), or grilled (*a la plancha*). In Salamanca, the home of Morucha cattle, a Castilian specialty is often served – thick rib steaks (*chuletones*) are briefly seared and then brought to the table almost raw on glowing hot earthenware platters, on which they sizzle and continue cooking (see opposite page).

By special request the meat, which can weigh 14 ounces (400 grams) or more, can be served in a whole piece on the bone if the customer wishes, but in many restaurants the *chuletón* is cut into slices that are much easier to turn on the earthenware platter for the convenience of the customer.

REARING BULLS FOR THE FIGHT

The bull has been a powerful symbol throughout the history of the entire Mediterranean region, as shown by the world of Greek mythology and the enduring impression made by the Minotaur, even up to the present day. The bull was the embodiment of supernatural strength and a symbol of virility, synonymous with unbounded potency and fertility. The first specimens are thought to have been brought by the Carthaginians to the Iberian peninsula, where the bullfight as a ritual proof of masculinity continues to delight the crowds. Fighting bulls (*toros de lidia*) are mainly bred in central and southwest Spain, and most breeders are found in the province of Salamanca in southern Castile. A medium-size farm breeding bulls for fighting has between 300 and 400 animals, with about 50 cows serviced by one bull. By means of stringent selection procedures over the centuries, Spanish breeders of fighting bulls have developed five breeds from the extinct European bison that are distinguished by particularly "brave" behavior. Today nearly 95 percent of all fighting bulls are of the Vistahermosa breed – a uniformity that many bullfighting enthusiasts find regrettable.

In order to produce steers with the best possible temperament for fighting, the breeders employ a complicated selection process. This involves observing the behavior of the bulls and cows used for breeding when they are branded, while they are grazing, and during a simulated bullfight. The purpose of this is to

Above: Fighting bulls are reared in the far-flung regions of west and southwest Spain.

determine which of the breeding stock can produce the most belligerent offspring. Before they enter the arena, the prospective stars must not have experienced any threatening situation; otherwise these intelligent animals would remember, and attack immediately. A group of hooligans organizing an improvised bullfight under cover of darkness could ruin the prospects for those bulls in the arena.

A "brave bull" (*toro bravo*) is not ready for the arena until its fourth year of life, and in most cases breathes its last after its grand entrance. Bulls aged six or seven years are not used for a classic *corrida*, as by this age they have become too clever and thus too dangerous. A fighting bull of "pensionable age" that has never seen the inside of an arena is only suitable for the bull-running held in many towns.

To make authentic *cecina*, fresh beef must be smoked and air-dried before it can be sliced and eaten.

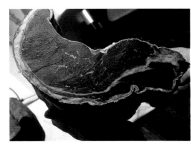

Inside, the *cecina* is deep red with little fat. Its flavor is strong and ideally should be so tender it melts in the mouth.

Delicious *cecina de León*, dried beef, is served in thin slices.

WINE-PRODUCTION ON THE DUERO: VEGA SICILIA

"Barren and desolate, inhabited only by bears, wild boar, and other diverse beasts of prey" – such was the description by the 11th-century king, Alfonso VI, of the menace of the countryside that stretched from the southern bank of the river Duero to the mountain ranges of central Spain. At first sight it is difficult to imagine the Duero, Castile's largest river, having any economic importance, even now, as it is not navigable. It is, however, of significant importance for the plateau, because in the close environs of the river its waters temper the extremes of the continental climate – its blazing hot summers and bitterly cold winters. This is particularly beneficial for wine-production.

Wine was being made in this area as long ago as the Roman era, and the Visigoths carried on the tradition. As a result of the continual military clashes between Moors and Christians during the reconquest of Spain, however, most of the population moved away and the region declined to become a no-man's land. Only with the resettlement of the area, largely pioneered by monastic orders, did the real, ongoing story of the wines of the Duero begin.

Although the winemaking districts of Rueda and Toro benefit from the advantages bestowed by the river, Duero wines are today mainly understood to mean wines from the Ribero del Duero region. For half a century the ultimate in Spanish wine – Vega Sicilia – has been pressed in the western part of this area. Wine connoisseurs the world over have been arguing for decades as to what makes this wine so exceptional. Three main factors play a fundamental role: ancient, well-tended vineyards; a unique philosophy in the wine cellar, where very slow fermentation and maturation are of paramount importance; and the outstanding skill of the winemaker.

Meticulous selection of grapes from the harvest and extravagant technological fermentation methods do not appear significant; it is the aging process alone that makes the flagship wine of the *bodega*, Vega Sicilia Unico (meaning "the only one"), such a special wine. This is made only in the very best years; a must obtained from healthy grapes, with a rich color, powerful tannin content, highly concentrated fruit, and high levels of extract is required. Only such a must will be equal to the long passage through the wooden vats of varying size and age, which characterizes the making of this famous wine, and the equally long, if not longer, period of aging in the bottle.

The first important decision, therefore, has to be made immediately after alcoholic fermentation – whether to make a Unico this year, and if so, which of the many separately fermented batches of wine, which come from different vineyards, to use. The wine chosen is placed in large wooden barrels with a capacity of nearly 8000 US gallons (30,000 liters) for the second fermentation, where it matures for at least six months, and sometimes for as long as 18 months. After this phase the wine is transferred to *barriques*, or casks, made from new wood, where it is kept for between four and eight months. The wood imparts stabilizing tannins (tannic acid) and strong toast notes to the wine. The clarity of the wine improves constantly as a result of the regular transfer, since on each occasion the sediment is left at the bottom of the barrel. The winemaker tastes the wine intensively during this phase, in order to gauge the right moment for another transfer – this time to old barrels, where the wine settles

Above: the monastery of Valbuena is situated quite close to the Duero. It has become a kind of emblem for the Vega Sicilia *bodega*, where many of the vines are over a hundred years old (main photograph).

These Vega Sicilia wines have made history on the banks of the Duero: (left to right) the flagship wine Unico Reserva Especial, the Unico 1970, the Unico 1985, and the Tinto Valbuena.

The Duero and its waters are a blessing for the wine-making area Ribero del Duero. The river tempers the climate, thus ensuring that great wines can be made here.

Tempranillo and Tinto Fino grapes, nowadays mostly identical, are the most important for Ribera wines and also for Vega Sicilia and Pesquera wines.

and becomes smooth. This is followed by a further period of maturing in old oak, which imparts no further oak notes and serves merely to age the wine.

An Unico spends a total of at least five years in wooden barrels. It is then bottled and kept for at least another five years in the bottle before it is marketed. Vintages such as the 1970 (matured on the estate for 24 years), the 1974 as well as the exeptionally dense 1989, and the 1981 (available since spring 1998) are absolutely supreme Vega Sicilia wines and naturally contribute greatly to its legendary reputation.

It is remarkable that after being aged in the wood for such a long time, the wood flavor does not dominate a Vega Sicilia Unico. The reverse is true; some Unicos develop extremely subtle nuances of flavor on many different levels, which are revealed only gradually. By contrast, the estate's second wine, the Vega Sicilia Valbuena, is less complex, and somewhat more loosely structured; it is aged in oak for between 18 and 26 months, depending on the vintage, and is marketed in its fifth year. The producers' crowning glory is the Vega Sicilia Unico Reserva Especial, the most expensive wine from the *bodega*, which is only made every two to four years from a blend of various excellent vintages.

THE CHALLENGER

Although Vega Sicilia is legendary, the Ribero del Duero has long been a blank page for wine connoisseurs. For instance, the first wines pressed by Alejandro Fernández from Pesquera in the 1970s were bottled straight away in carbonated drink bottles with a snap lock, for domestic consumption. He achieved fame as a result of his 1982 Tinto Pesquera, which one of the world's authorities on wine at the time compared with Château Petrus; the Tinto Pesquera caused a stir with its incredibly dense fruit and soft, sweet tannins.

After this, Fernández was to prove that Ribera wines can aspire to true greatness even without being matured for long periods in the barrel. The Pesquera wines, which have since attained legendary status, spend only the minimum time required by the regulatory authorities in small oak barrels, and yet they are as complex as few other wines in the whole world. The highly complex premium wine of the estate, Janus, is made only in certain years, using single variety grapes.

Alejandro Fernández Pesquera – a new wine god

TOP DUERO WINES

Vega Sicilia Unico Gran Reserva 1970: very ripe fruit, raisins, spicy notes, complex, profound, long on the palate.

Janus Gran Reserva 1991 (Pesquera): profound, concentrated, full-bodied, nuances, enormous potential.

Torremilanos Gran Reserva 1990 (Peñalba López): elegant fruit, finely structured, strong integrated oak notes.

Dehesa de los Canónigos Reserva 1994: very clear, intense fruit, medium-bodied, with subtle resonance.

Alión Reserva 1994: Exudes an intense aroma of berried fruit, spicy, close-textured, with sweet woody note.

Viña Pedrosa Gran Reserva 1992 (Pérez Pascuas): pronounced acidity with fine fruit and clear oak notes.

Valsotillo Gran Reserva 1994 (Ismael Arroyo): a traditional Ribero. Dense fruit, pronounced sweet tannin, great depth.

Matarromera Reserva 1994 (Viñedos y Bodegas): intense fruit, a memorable wine, juicy and harmonious.

Señorío de Nava Reserva 1990: balanced, with pleasant fruit, and dry but delicate wood tannin.

Emilio Moro Reserva 1994: berried fruits and wood notes in bouquet, soft on the palate, eucalyptus in finish.

Valduero Reserva 1989: fine oak, rich in extract, elegant fruit, finely textured, firm-bodied, with potential.

Viña Sastre Reserva Oscar 1995 (Hermanos Sastre): berried fruit notes, powerful tannin, soft on palate, rounded.

Pago de Carraovejas Reserva 1993: opulent black and red berried fruits, dense, with very juicy tannin.

Briego Reserva 1992: fruit and oak in bouquet, firm in mouth, powerful acidity, a great deal of tannin on the palate.

López Cristóbal Reserva 1995: fruit in the nose, firm-bodied, soft tannin, echoes of eucalyptus in the finish.

Teófilo Reyes Reserva 1995: intense, many layers of fruit, fine wood, very deep and lingering.

Arzuaga Navarro Reserva 1994: fine wood and vanilla notes, blazing fruit, juicy tannin, good length.

Valtravieso Reserva 1994: very expansive fruit bouquet, perfectly integrated woody notes, sumptuous and rounded.

Wine-producing areas in Castile-León

D.O. Ribera del Duero

In the D.O. (*Denominación de Origen*) created in 1982 just for red wine on the Duero river, nearly 30,000 acres (about 12,000 hectares) of chalk, clay, and alluvial silt are devoted to grape cultivation. The main grape variety is Tinto Fino (also called Tinta del País), a local version of the top Spanish grape, the Tempranillo, which produces extraordinarily concentrated fruit and very pronounced tannin under the weather conditions prevailing on the plateau. Cabernet Sauvignon, Merlot, Malbec, Garnacha, and white Albillo grapes are also permitted. These are sometimes added to red wines in very small quantities in order to raise their acidity. Infertile soils and the extremes of the continental climate, somewhat tempered by the river, yield high quality grapes from small quantities. The wines are very fruity, deep, almost black in color, and very rich in extracts. They are exceptionally well suited to aging in the cask. However, many estates market younger wines and Semi-Crianzas (an official term for wines spending less time aging in the wood than is legally prescribed for Crianzas), since the opulent fruit and sweet tannins emerge very well from short periods of maturation in the cask. For Crianzas and Reservas, the regulations prescribe 12 months in the barrel and one or two years in the bottle. For Gran Reservas a total of five years' aging is required, two of which must be in the barrel.

Vega Sicilia and Pesquera have long since ceased to be the only wines worthy of note in Ribero del Duero. Several dozen bodegas press high-class wines – a number that is increasing each year. Of course, every ideal picture has its dark side, and this is all too frequently in evidence in Ribero; the harsh climate occasionally brings late frosts and hail, which in some years destroy parts amount of the harvestor impair its quality. Although there is no wine shortage because extensive new vineyards have been planted the prices remain on a sensitively high level.

D.O. Toro

The smallest D.O. in the region is known as the new red wine wonder of Spain. Elite winegrowers from La Rioja and the neighboring regions of Castile have invested into the Toro region and are producing top red wines. Unlike the extremely alcoholic wines produced in the past (around 16 percent alcohol by volume), red wines from Toro are now lighter and fruitier, but, thanks to modern vinification methods, are concentrated and multifaceted. The main grape variety is the indigenous Tinta de Toro, a relative of the famous Tinta del País (Tempranillo). Other varieties permitted are the red Garnacha and the white Verdejo and Malvasía grapes. Red Toro wines are eminently suited to aging in the wood. However, the wonderful fruit of the Tinta de Toro has induced some vintners to press Semi-Crianzas and even wines to be drunk young.

D.O. Cigales

This D.O. stretches out over open-textured, chalky soil in the immediate vicinity of Valladolid. Cigales-Rosé, once one of Spain's most famous wines, which used to be made using a blend of red and white (*clarete*, see page 129), is now struggling for survival. The greater part of today´s *bodegas,* many of them equipped with highly modern technology, is now concentrating on red wines natured in the cask. Modern techniques are also appired for rosé wines, called Cigales Nuevo, and numerous high-quality reds which are mainly pressed from the Tinta del País grape. In the case of the rosé, the fruit is combined with a lively acidity, and the red has body and warmth. Other permitted grape varieties are the red Garnacha and the white Verdejo, Albillo, and Viura varieties, which have until now been used only in rosé and red wine blends.

D.O. Rueda

This area restricts itself exclusively to white grapes, of which the indisputable champion is the Verdejo. This indigenous variety produces light, well-structured white wines, with a restrained fruit supplemented by subtle mineral tones and hints of aniseed. The transformation that has occurred during recent decades from white wines oxidized during aging to the fruity, sensitive wines of today is quite spectacular. A typical Rueda is a young white wine that has not touched a cask, though nowadays more and more producers do let the white drops ferment in oak barrels. The possibilities offered by the leading Verdejo variety are far from exhausted.

The other varieties permitted are Sauvignon Blanc and Viura; Palominois nearing extinction. Since the year 2000 red wines carry the seal of quality of the D.O., with the main varity, Tempranillo, flanked by Cabernet Sauvignon, Garnacha, and Merlot. A sparkling wine fermented in the bottle, called Espumoso Rueda, is produced in the region, and a legacy from the past exists in the form of the fizzy, oxidized Dorado Rueda and Pálido Rueda wines.

D.O. El Bierzo

The Castilian wine-producing areas in the extreme western part of the region differ somewhat from the norm in terms of climate and type of wine produced. Instead of raw, highland weather conditions, the climate reflects the geographical transition from damp Galicia to dry Castile. From the center of a wide valley emerge fruity and tannin-rich red wines resulting from the potential of the numerous old vineyards that provide exellent grapes for concentrated wines of exceeding warmth. The main red grape variety, Mencía, held to be a descendant of the French Cabernet Franc variety, is partly grown on sloping terraces of infertile soil containing slate. Its character is shown to best advantage in a young wine or a Crianza matured for a limited time in the wood (six months). In addition, white wines produced from the Godello grape and are worthy of note.

Background: An ancient aqueduct still runs through the Vega Sicilia vineyards. In earlier times it provided water for the fields of wheat and vegetables in the area.

SWEET SELF-INDULGENCE

The dedication shown by Castilians in their consumption of sugary sweet confections sometimes resembles that of a religious cult. Pastries and all kinds of other sweetmeats are ranged in confectioners' windows like devotional objects, and in such abundant variety as would delight the heavenly host. Each village, district, and town has its own unique tradition of making confectionery; some of the recipes have long since been forgotten, while some specialties are made only for certain occasions.

The nuns in the convents of Castile have been especially active in preserving an impressive number of recipes. Ultimately, religious customs always affect everyday life and a country's consumption of sweet food. In all the regions of Spain there is a close connection between pastries, cookies, and other sweetmeats, and the feast days honoring the patron saint of a town or village.

The main ingredients of Castilian confectionery are almonds, flour, lard, sugar, eggs, and uncooked almond paste. Chocolate also plays an important role. Almonds are the basis of almond cookies (*almendrados*), but they are also found almost everywhere in candied form as *almendras garrapiñadas*. The sweetmeat *roscones* is a common specialty, and few festivities are complete without various pastry rings called *rosquillas*. Some are flavored with aniseed or pine nuts, and some are filled with honey. The Castilian lard and butter tartlets (*mantecadas*) are among the best in Spain, especially those from Astorga, and the crumbly cookie *bollo maimón* is a specialty of Salamanca.

A major role, however, is played by *yemas*, a sugary sweet egg yolk confection – above all, the famous *Yemas de Santa Teresa*, which have very little at all to do with the Saint. They were brought to Avila, probably in the 17th century, by a confectioner who was born in Castile, but owned a confectionery business in Madrid. He later opened a branch in Avila, and it was one of his sons who later gave the house's trademark confection its most illustrious name – a stroke of true marketing genius, if one considers that the term *Yemas de Santa Teresa* is now used to refer to all Spanish *yemas*.

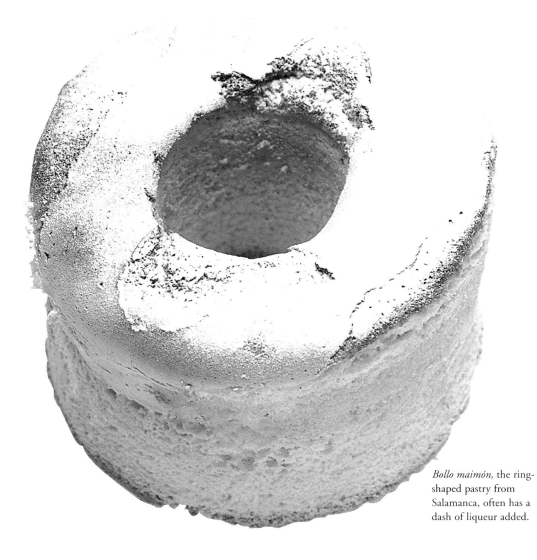

Bollo maimón, the ring-shaped pastry from Salamanca, often has a dash of liqueur added.

YEMAS DE SANTA TERESA
Saint Teresa's egg yolk confection

1 cup/200 g sugar
1 cinnamon stick
Rind of 1 unwaxed lemon, peeled
in a spiral
10 egg yolks
Confectioners' sugar for coating
Paper cases

Boil the sugar with 6-8 tbsp of water to make a clear, heavy syrup. Remove from the heat and add the cinnamon and lemon rind. Leave the syrup to cool for a while, while continuing to stir. Then remove the cinnamon stick and lemon rind from the syrup.

Beat the egg yolk in a bowl until it is foaming. Slowly add the syrup, stirring constantly. Stand the bowl in a *bain-marie* and beat until thick and creamy. Remove from the *bain-marie* and leave until cold. Make a long roll with the mixture, cut into small pieces and roll them quickly into small walnut-sized balls. Coat with confectioners' sugar and then place in paper cases.

All over Spain there are pastries made with lard or butter to tempt people with a sweet tooth. One particularly old tradition is that of the *mantecadas de Astorga*, made with a lot of good quality butter and up to ten eggs for every 2⅔ cups (300 grams) of flour. If these sugary sweet temptations are made with lard, they are frequently called *mantecados*. Usually, people do not distinguish between the two – the most important thing is the taste.

Castile has a wide variety of ring-shaped pastries (*roquillas*), made with or without yeast, cooked in the oven or deep-fried.

Chochos de Salamanca are sugary sweet bonbons; in places the term is also used to refer to sugared almonds.

Perrunillas are cookies containing cinnamon and lard; they are mostly found in southern Castile and the Extremadura.

Wafers *(obleas)* from the village of Cipérez near Salamanca have become a souvenir typical of the entire province.

MADRID

WALTER TAUBER

Madrid

A coffee and a brandy: A day in the pulsating metropolis can begin like this, and end in precisely the same way 20 hours later as the sun comes up.

The Puerta del Sol is the center of Spain. The distances on the kilometer stones on the national highways are measured from this square in the center of the capital, the focal point of the routes which bind the whole country together. At the same time, a walk around the Puerta del Sol provides a whistle-stop tour of the whole nation. For the immigrants have left their mark on Madrid, and in the bars and taverns of the old city there are Galicians, Basques, and Andalusians offering for sale the typical fare of their native regions. Madrid was a village when King Philip II chose it as his capital in 1561. And for a long time this city remained provincial. For industrialization came late to Spain and began on the periphery – in Catalonia and in the Basque region. Madrid remained nothing

more than an administrative capital inhabited by bureaucrats right up until the end of the Civil War. It is only the meteoric development of the last 50 years which has turned it into a metropolis with millions of citizens. But however small Madrid may have been, it very soon became the capital of an empire which spanned the world, and the seat of the royal house of the Hapsburgs, which had one foot in Austria, and then later of the Bourbons, a dynasty which thought (and ate) in the French style. Madrid was both *corte* and *villa*, a court and a small town at the same time.

The culinary culture of Madrid was thus also always somewhat contradictory; it was simple and robust, but simultaneously refined and aristocratic as well. The *castizo* cuisine, the tradition handed down by the ordinary people, was soon

merging in the cooking pots of the capital with the upper-class cuisine of the Hapsburg court and its master chefs. The common people, whose roots were firmly anchored, above all, in La Mancha, grew more and more knowledgeable due to the influence of the many citizens who came to Madrid from all over the country and from the colonies. Never mind whether it was fish from Cantabria, fine seafood from Galicia, or chocolate from Mexico – all of these received an enthusiastic welcome from the chefs of Madrid. And they were all put to the best use as well. And so a cuisine soon arose which outgrew its origins and achieved world-class status. As Franco's dictatorship came to an end, the whole city threw off its shackles in what was nothing less than a cultural renaissance. Now Madrid has become a European metropolis.

Opposite: Madrid is always an experience, and the gourmet's temples are often located in dreamlike houses from the Belle Epoque – as here on the Gran Vía.

Breakfast

Desayunar means to break one's fast, corresponding to the French *petit déjeuner* and the English "breakfast." In Spain, of course, it is only rarely that anyone does this at home. Having breakfast is a social act, and it can take different forms, depending on locality and social class – starting with just coffee, black or with a mere dash of milk, gulped down on the way to work. Anyone needing a real shock to wake up puts away a glass of aniseed schnapps in the bar on the corner. Nor does this suggest an alcoholic. There are people with this habit who are teetotal the rest of the time. For those who want to still the first little hunger pangs of the day, this is usually done with something sweet. Pastries of every kind entice the customers in the morning from beneath the glass bells on the counter in the *cafetería*. It is a long time since the only things on offer were *churros* and *porras*, which can also be ordered from the *churro* baker. The *croissant* is now at home in Spain. Another very popular snack is the *tostada*, a slice from a white sandwich-type loaf, toasted on the *plancha* (the grill), with butter and marmalade. Swiss visitors need not worry if they find *suizo a la plancha* on the menu, as this merely refers to a type of roll from Andalusia. *Ensaïmadas*, a Majorca specialty made with yeast dough, have already become a feature of breakfast all over the country, and *magdalenas*, little cakes baked in paper cases, are especially popular for dunking in white coffee. Like these, the elongated *sobaos*, spongecakes, in wax paper now come from the large commercial bakery.

But breakfast is quite a different matter for workers who have already been hard at it for hours. For them, *bocadillos*, rolls, are the norm, filled with *tortilla*, ham, or cheese, and frequently accompanied by a glass of beer or wine.

However, after only two or three hours of work, the *madrileños* feel the urge to visit a café. The cafés are crowded from ten o'clock onward, with people discussing last night's football match or television program at the tops of their voices. Some may still order *chocolate*, the thick, viscous drinking chocolate made according to the old tradition. But nowadays the majority tend to drink white coffee (*café con leche*) from the typical large cups. Many cafés offer low-price breakfast menus from nine to eleven or twelve o'clock – a fixed price for a cup of white coffee, sweet bread, and often freshly squeezed orange juice as well.

In Spain, sweet bread can tempt even habitual late risers to get up. It forms part of breakfast, together with a cup of strong coffee.

A type of cookie press is traditionally used to force the thick *churro* dough into the deep fryer. Machines now do this in the modern *churrerías*.

Freshly baked *churros* are wrapped in paper and sold "straight into your hands." In a traditional *churrería*, hot chocolate is available to drink.

CHURROS AND CHOCOLATE

Deep-fried pastry and hot chocolate are still a breakfast cult in Madrid. They have helped many night owls to face the cold gray light of day. In many families, they form part of the Sunday ritual. The well-loved, slender pastry fingers (*churros* and *porras* the thicker version) are made in special machines in the *churro* store, but at home people just use a type of cookie press. *Churros* were probably invented simply and solely for dipping into hot chocolate, without which breakfast time in Spain is difficult to imagine.

Linguistic researchers trace the word *chocolate* back to the Aztecs. It is supposed to have evolved from the words *pócholt* (holly) and *cacacaúlt* (cocoa). The Spaniards brought chocolate back from their colony in Mexico in the middle of the 16th century. Going from palace to palace, the drink won over the royal houses and the nobility of Europe. In Spain, it had so many admirers that it even became a problem for theologians. They had to ask the Pope to exclude the drink from the regulations governing fasting, since the inhabitants of Madrid would otherwise have fallen into sinful ways. "*Liquidum non rumpit jenjunium,*" to quote the ecclesiastical Latin of the Bull granting the dispensation: "Liquid does not break the fast."

Nowadays, the Spaniards prepare their beloved thick chocolate, *chocolate espeso*, with milk and special chocolate bars that can be bought in any supermarket. According to the old custom, of course, the ingredients are water, chocolate, and also cornstarch, since traditionally the drink must be thick enough for the wooden spoon to be able to stand up in it.

There is hardly any breakfast experience more sensual than to indulge in dunking freshly baked *churros* in a cup of thick, sweet chocolate – food fit for the gods.

BULLFIGHTING

The *corrida* is a didactic drama, an intimate tragedy, which tells of female power, seduction, passion, and death. This is the ritualized story of a man and woman kept apart by fate, a story told from the perspective of the man, who pays for his unquenchable desire with his life.

This view of bullfighting as something deep-rooted, mythical even, is taken from the book *Toros, Toreros,* by the anthropologist Lorenz Rollhäuser. But the *aficionados*, the bullfight fans, who flock to the arenas in ever-increasing numbers, rarely take their analysis that far. In the end, the bullfight is primarily a fiesta, or even *the* Spanish *Fiesta Nacional*, blending artistry and traditional entertainment.

Strict rules govern the procedure, like a religious ceremony in honor of a powerful heathen god. Those who do not understand the ritual usually fail to notice the little signal given by the master of ceremonies with a handkerchief. Then the trumpets ring out, and the actors in the drama strut around the ring to the march rhythm of the *paso doble*. Two *alguaciles* – officials representing the master of ceremonies – lead the procession, followed by the bullfighters, each of whom will kill two bulls ("if God sends good fortune," as

the set phrase has it). They are followed by nine *banderilleros*, who have to irritate the bull with decorated colored goads. The *picadores* ride past on horseback. They have to weaken the bull with their lances, and they will have to endure the scorn of the crowd if they go in too hard. Last come the mules that drag out the corpses of the conquered when it is all over.

Way back in the first century BC, the Greek historian Diodoros was already noting that bulls were sacred for the Iberians. Julius Caesar fought bulls on horseback and introduced the spectacle to the Roman arena. In the early Middle Ages, the nobles of Castile are said to have taken part in similar activities. Initially, the skillful riding of the noble lords held center stage, and the *matador*, who had to kill the bull right at the end, was only a minor figure. This altered in the 17th century, and today the fine gentlemen on horseback are themselves only really of minor importance. The *matador* is in the foreground – alone and on foot.

During the San Isidro *feria* in Madrid, which lasts 30 days, the spectators are particularly critical. The *aficionados* go there with their *peña*, or group of fellow enthusiasts. People tremble, cheer, and complain together, then meet up afterward for a glass of wine to discuss the events of the day (see box on opposite page).

Crowds literally flock to every bullfight that takes place in Madrid's "second cathedral." To the fans, the Las Ventas arena is no less than holy ground.

The bullfighting season runs from March to October, but the high point is the San Isidro *feria*, from May 15 through the middle of June. Every seat is taken during this period.

The encounter between the bullfighter and the *toro bravo*, the brave bull, in the arena is like a mythical dance. The *torero* needs nothing but his cape, the *capa*.

The *banderillero* has the most thankless task. He has to weaken the bull with his slender lances. If he is too cruel, the crowd show their disapproval by whistling.

The *aficionados*, the bullfight fans, follow a *corrida* with an extremely critical eye. A pair of binoculars can be a great help for those in the highest seats of the giant arena.

A LITTLE GLASS OF SOMETHING AFTERWARD

When the last bull has been dragged out of the arena, the second part of the great day begins for the *aficionado*, the passionate bullfighting fan. For what good would a *corrida* be if no one could talk about it afterward? This is known as the *tertulia*, the discussion within the circle of connoisseurs. The fans are traditionally attracted to certain bars and restaurants that are usually decorated with posters and photographs of famous matadors. The hotels where the famous matadors stay also stage discussions with experts. Among the most popular meeting places in Madrid are the Gran Hotel Reina Victoria in the Plaza Santa Ana, the Hotel Miguel Angel in the street of the same name, the Hotel Wellington in the Calle Velázquez, and the Restaurante Los Timbales in the Calle Alcalá, right next to the arena. Ernest Hemingway visited the Casa Botín, Juan Belmonte liked to frequent the Casa Ciriaco, and everybody goes to the Casa Lucio. One particularly celebrated meeting place is the unique Malcatín, while the Casa Paco is full of pictures of *toreros* and La Hoja can be recommended to those who prefer the Salamanca quarter located in the old city.

COOKING THE BRAVE BULL'S MEAT

Once the *toro bravo*, the brave bull, is dead, the *aficionado* is interested only in its meat. *Rabo de toro* (the bull's tail) is considered the greatest delicacy, and indeed the demand is such that top chefs complain that the tail of a genuine fighting bull is hard to obtain.

In contrast to the ox, which also has to donate its rear appendage to the culinary arts, the fighting bull from the arena has a distinctive taste. Adrenalin in the blood tinges the bull's meat with bitterness, for which reason it is usually cooked *estofado* (braised) or in stews, and served with white beans in both cases. The gelatin content means it requires very long and careful preparation.

The once popular bull's testicles (*criadillas de toro*) now appear only rarely on the table. In La Mancha, bull's testicles are still served, together with the brain, in scrambled eggs (*huevos a la porreta*), while in Andalusia they are served coated in breadcrumbs and fried.

After appearing in the arena, a fighting bull is slaughtered. The meat is somewhat bitter and so is usually best eaten stewed.

Bull's testicles (*criadillas de toro*) can be found only rarely, and are mainly eaten in restaurants in Andalusia.

Bull's tail (*rabo de toro*, above) is still very popular all over the country. It is usually served in a stew (right).

VARIETY MEATS

When Phillip II made Madrid his capital in 1561, a creative tension arose between the refined upper-class cuisine and the innovative spirit of the people. What are nowadays famous as specialties are often traditional favorites of the *castizos*, the poor people of Madrid. The ingredients not thought good enough for the tables of the rich were made into exquisite dishes by the poor: variety meats such as the heart and the brain, the kidneys and the liver, the tongue and the sweetbread.

The most popular of such dishes in Madrid is tripe (a cow's stomach cut into strips). The Spanish word *callos*, from the Latin *callum*, points to the ancient origin of the dish. And yet the skill of the *madrileños* lay in the fact that they made this dish socially acceptable in high society as well: it was referred to in print as long ago as 1599. In the innumerable *mesones*, the inns for visiting merchants and local people, stews made from entrails were already a specialty hundreds of years ago. Around 1900, the taverns of Madrid would vie with one another to see who could serve the best tripe, and there are still some restaurants which specialize in it. In contrast, other traditional dishes using variety meats, such as *gallinejas*, made from chicken livers and stomachs, or *asadura de cordero*, crispy fried lamb's intestines, appear only rarely on Spanish menus nowadays.

CALLOS A LA MADRILEÑA
Madrid style tripe

Generous 1 lb/500 g cooked calf's tripe
Generous 1 lb/500 g cooked ox cheek
4 tbsp olive oil
1 onion, finely chopped
2 cloves of garlic, finely chopped
3½ oz/100 g smoked bacon, diced
1 chorizo sausage, sliced
2 cups/500 ml meat stock
½ cup/125 ml white wine
1 bay leaf
1 tsp mild paprika powder
Salt and pepper
1 tbsp chopped parsley

Cut the tripe and the ox cheek into strips. Heat the olive oil in a deep pan. Cook the onion, garlic and bacon in the oil until transparent. Add the sausage, tripe, and ox cheek. Then pour on the meat stock and white wine. Season with the bay leaf, paprika, salt, and pepper. Leave to cook for around 30 minutes on a medium heat. Sprinkle with chopped parsley before serving.

GALLINEJAS
Fried giblets

Generous 1 lb/500 g mixed chicken liver, stomach, and heart
1 cup/250 ml olive oil
4 cloves of garlic
Salt

Wash the liver, stomach, and heart well, then pat them dry. Cut them into strips about 2 inch/12 mm wide. Heat the olive oil in a deep pan. Peel the garlic cloves and leave them to brown in the olive oil. Remove the garlic cloves from the oil and fry the liver, stomach, and heart until crispy brown in the oil. Remove from the oil with a slotted spoon and leave to drain briefly on paper towels, season with salt, and serve very hot.

HIGADO ENCEBOLLADO
Liver and onions
(Photograph top right)

Generous 1 lb/500 g calf's or lamb's liver, sliced
1–2 tbsp flour
Scant 1 cup/200 ml olive oil
Generous 1 lb/500 g onions, cut into fine rings
1–2 cloves of garlic, finely chopped
2 tbsp chopped parsley
½ cup/125 ml white wine
Salt and pepper

Wash the liver, then pat it dry. Toss it in the flour, shaking off the excess. Heat ⅔ cup/150 ml of the olive oil and cook the onion rings in it until pale yellow. Then mix in the garlic and parsley, and pour on the white wine. Season with salt and pepper, and leave to simmer a little. Meanwhile fry the slices of liver in the remaining oil. Arrange the liver on warmed plates, pour the onion sauce all over it, and then serve immediately.

LENGUA DE VACA ESTOFADA
Stewed cow's tongue

1 cow's tongue, about 2¼ lbs/1 kg
Salt
2 tbsp pork fat
2 onions, chopped
4 carrots, cut into thick slices
½ cup/125 ml white wine
1 bay leaf
A few sprigs of thyme
1 toasted slice of white bread
2 cloves of garlic, chopped
Pepper

Liver and onions
(*hígado encebollado*).

Wash the tongue, then cook it in lightly salted water for about 12 hours. Remove from the pan and let it cool; then remove the skin. Heat the pork fat in a deep pan and fry the onions in it until transparent. Place the tongue on top and arrange slices of carrot around the tongue. Pour on the white wine and 2 cups/500 ml of the tongue stock. Add the bay leaf and thyme, and bring it all to a boil. Crush the toasted bread in a mortar with the garlic and 2 tbsp of the stock. Season with salt and pepper. Spread the bread paste on the tongue, cover and let it simmer for 1–1½ hours. Remove the tongue from the pan. Blend the sauce to a purée. Cut the tongue into slices and arrange on a warmed dish. Pour the sauce over it and serve.

MOLLEJAS EMPANADAS
Fried calf's sweetbreads

1 lb 10 oz/750 g calf's sweetbreads
Salt
1 bay leaf
4 tbsp flour
2 eggs, beaten
4 tbsp breadcrumbs
Oil for frying

Leave the calf's sweetbreads in cold water for 3–4 hours, then remove the external membrane and veins. Place the sweetbreads in a saucepan of cold water. Add some salt and the bay leaf, and bring to a boil. Simmer for 5 minutes; then remove the sweetbreads from the pan and rinse with cold water. Place the sweetbreads on a flat dish, cover with a plate and press down a little so that the sweetbreads are lightly compressed. After 1 hour, cut the sweetbreads into thick slices. Place the flour, egg, and breadcrumbs in 3 separate soup plates. Coat the sliced sweetbreads, first in the flour, then in the egg, and finally in the breadcrumbs. Fry the sweetbreads until golden brown on both sides in the hot oil and serve with tomato sauce.

BREAD

"Better bread with love than chicken with grief," runs the old Spanish proverb. For bread is the most important basic foodstuff of the Spaniard. In 1937, the poet José Martinez Ruiz, known as Azorín, went into romantic raptures in his Parisian exile over the hunger he had suffered in the poverty-stricken years of his youth. At that time, one roll – carefully divided and cut up into slices – was all he had to eat for a whole day.

Until not so long ago, every Spaniard ate on average a kilogram (2¼ pounds) of bread a day. In addition to the religious significance which it has had in almost all civilizations since ancient times, bread is also used as a symbol of social intercourse. It is almost impossible to think of sitting around the table together without a loaf of bread there to share. Many Spaniards would rather do without a meal altogether than have to eat the food without any bread. No one considers it bad manners to mop up the juice of a meat dish with bread at a Spanish table – quite the contrary in fact. Those unwilling to do this miss out on the best part of the dish. On the other hand, something that surprises many northern Europeans is that in Spain bread is not provided with soup. In contrast, good bread plays an important part in accompanying tasty *tapas*. Last but not least, it acts as the basis for *bocadillas* and *montaditos*, the popular sandwiches and delicious filled rolls (see opposite page).

Good white bread is still the norm in Spain. Wholewheat varieties have become much more significant only in recent years, since Spain entered the European Union. However, the white bread is made in different ways from place to place. The *pan blanco* (or *pan candeal*) of Castile is a large, flat round made from the finest flour, into the top of which patterns have been carved with a blade. It becomes hard relatively quickly, but can then be used again to wonderful effect in some of the substantial stews typical of central Spain. In Catalonia and the Balearic Islands, the round loaf called *pa de pagès* predominates, a traditional tasty farmhouse bread with a thick crust, which keeps well and is suitable for rubbing with tomato (see page 16). In Catalonia, the traditional rolls are known as *llonguet*, and anyone lucky enough to be given some straight from the charcoal oven will not forget the strong taste in a hurry. The Andalusian bread, *piquito*, is decorated with strange lacy patterns. In Asturias, *borona*, a cornbread, is baked. The bread in San Sebastian, *sopako*, is very dark. Its composition is somewhat spongy, but it is tasty and particularly suitable for bread soups. Almost every village is proud of its own specialty, and so a visit to the baker can always lead to a wonderful new discovery.

White bread occupies the number one position in Spanish bakeries, but the choice has grown. They have French sticks, bread rings, barley bread, oat bread, and wholewheat bread, as well as breads containing nuts or raisins.

The prospects are good for rustic bread like grandma used to make. These types of bread are usually baked in charcoal ovens, which gives them a pleasantly smoky taste. They go well with smoked products or strong cheeses.

The *bocadillo* is a cult. It can be eaten at any time of day – and, of course, can provide the basic stamina for long nights. Imagination is the only limit on what filling is put in the middle, and many *bocadillo* stores turn this into a real art. A ham *bocadillo* is certainly one of the more simple variations, but it is still a classic.

BOCADILLO AND MONTADITO

A *bocadillo* is everything and nothing. It is in no way a meal. At most, it is a substitute for one: a fresh, white roll, which can be filled with any delicacy imaginable. Historically, it could be considered as a continuation of the *almuerzos* of the poor. As a snack between meals in the fields, they had bread together with some sort of "taste enhancer" such as sausage, dried meat, or bacon. The word *companaje* ("what accompanies the bread") comes from central Spain, and gives an idea of the relative proportions which used to prevail in those days.

Nowadays, and particularly in the big cities, *bocadillos* are a quick snack to keep you going. They can be found in every bar, with rich fillings such as cooked or uncooked ham and cheese, and often *chorizo*, the spicy sausage. However, this is only the bare minimum, and a tavern with any self-respect will boast a long chalk-written list.

There are *bocadillos* with hot meat or fish fillings, while a cold *bocadillo* can have any filling, from mayonnaise salad to tuna fish in oil with tomato. There are really splendid fillings, like the exquisite Iberian ham, or *cercina* (dried beef). Every possible kind of *tortilla* can be crammed into a *bocadillo*. As an intriguing alternative, a selection of the high-quality delicacies may be more likely to please the palate: just arranged on the plate, with bread to go with them. Or as a tasty morsel for more refined occasions, there are the mini-versions of *bocadillos*, the *montaditos*.

POPULAR MONTADITOS

1 *salmón* – salmon
2 *huevas* – caviar
3 *anchoas ahumadas* – smoked anchovies
4 *rollito de salmón* – rolled salmon
5 *anchoas en salazón* – salted anchovies

6 *queso Brie* – Brie cheese
7 *merluza frita* – fried cod
8 *chorizo* – spicy sausage
9 *morcilla* – blood sausage
10 *solomillo* – loin of pork
11 *tortilla* – omelet

12 *queso manchego* – La Mancha cheese
13 *lomo ibérico* – air-dried Iberian loin of pork
14 *salchichón* – salami sausage
15 *queso Roquefort* – Roquefort cheese
16 *chorizo ibérico* – paprika sausage made from Iberian pork
17 *jamón ibérico* – Iberian ham

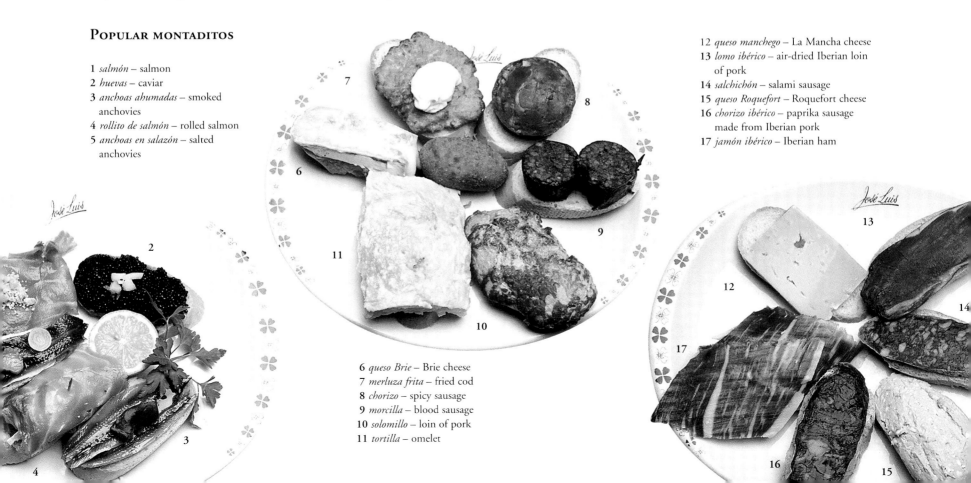

Fresh fish

Madrid is a seaport. In the middle of the high Castilian plateau, some hundreds of miles away from the coasts, the metropolis ranks as the biggest "inland harbor" of Europe for fish – way ahead of Paris or Milan. Almost 80 percent of the fish landed at Spanish ports is consumed within the country. If the average consumption of fish for every Spaniard is around 40 pounds (15 kilograms) a year, then the figure for the citizens of Madrid is undoubtedly much higher. Even centuries ago, the people here liked a juicy sea bream for Christmas. That was what Enrique de Aragón wrote in 1423 in his *Arte Cisoria*, the Bible of Spanish medieval cuisine. Nowadays, even women gathering mussels on the Galician beaches are working mainly for *madrileños*, since the *navajas* (sword mussels) which they laboriously dig out of the sand are quickly transported to the capital overnight. Fish from Cantabria or shrimp from the Mediterranean are available in the capital's covered markets almost as quickly as at the fishermen's auction sales on the coast. No celebration is considered complete without *gambas*, *centolla*, or *chipirones* (shrimp, snow crabs, or cuttlefish) For special occasions the expensive *percebes* (goose barnacles) or *angulas* (elvers) are a necessity as well. And even today, Christmas in the capital would be almost unthinkable without *besugo*, a delicious oven-cooked sea bream.

Besugo al horno
Oven-cooked sea bream
(Photograph on right)

1 sea bream, about 2¼ lbs/ 1 Kg, prepared for cooking
Salt and pepper
2 slices of lemon
3 cloves of garlic thinly sliced
4 tbsp breadcrumbs
½ tbsp chopped parsley
2 cup/125 ml white wine
4 potatoes, cut into slices
Scant ½ cup/100 ml olive oil

Wash the fish, and pat it dry. Rub in salt and pepper inside and out. Place the fish in a baking dish and make four incisions on top with a knife. Halve the lemon slices and place them in the cuts. Arrange the garlic around them. Mix the breadcrumbs and parsley and sprinkle over the fish. Pour on the white wine and arrange slices of potato around the fish. Pour the olive oil over the fish and the potatoes. Cook for about 25 minutes at 355 °F/180 °C in a preheated oven (check to see if cooked).

The Zarzuela

The Teatro de la Zarzuela lies behind the Cortes, the Spanish Parliament in Madrid. The traditional entertainment here is a type of musical comedy, which is a mixture of dialogue, songs, music, and dance, following each other in an intoxicating sequence. The *zarzuela* goes back to the 17th century, when traditional theatrical presentations were often a dazzling mixture of music and dramatic scenes. A good century later, the poets Lope de Vega and Calderón de la Barca elevated this gloriously colorful entertainment into an art form and wrote the first scripts for the *zarzuela*, which was later replaced by the operas brought in from Italy. In the 19th century, however, the *zarzuela* enjoyed a renaissance. Satirical and amusing, with its roots among the ordinary people, this mixture of music and drama still lives on today. With its colorful mixture of anything and everything, the *zarzuela* is probably also the origin of the name of Spain's popular fish stew.

Merluza a la madrileña
Madrid style stuffed hake

1 cod, about 2¼ lbs/1 kg, prepared for cooking
Salt and pepper
Juice of 1 lemon

Filling:
10 shelled shrimp tails
1 shallot, finely chopped
1 tbsp chopped parsley

Sauce:
½ cup/125 ml olive oil
1 onion, finely chopped
3 cloves of garlic, finely chopped
9 oz/250 g tomatoes, peeled
and diced
2 tbsp chopped parsley
2 tbsp breadcrumbs
½ cup/125 ml dry sherry

Wash the cod and pat it dry. Rub in salt and pepper and sprinkle with lemon juice. Leave to steep for 10 minutes. For the filling, cut the shrimp into small pieces and mix them with the shallot and parsley. Put everything into the stomach cavity of the fish and secure the opening with wooden picks.

Heat a scant ½ cup/100 ml of olive oil and cook the onion and garlic in it until they are transparent. Add the diced tomato and leave to cook for a few minutes. Remove from the stove and mix in the parsley. Place half of the onion mixture in a baking dish, lay the stuffed cod on top, and cover with the remaining onion mixture. Scatter the breadcrumbs on top. Sprinkle with the remaining olive oil and pour on the sherry. Cover the baking dish with aluminum foil. Cook in a preheated oven at 440 °F/225 °C for 30 minutes, removing the foil for the last 5 minutes of cooking time. Serve very hot in the baking dish.

Congrio con salsa vinagreta
Conger eel with vinaigrette sauce

2¼ lbs/1 kg conger eel, prepared for cooking
Salt
1 bay leaf
1 bouquet garni (e.g., thyme, rosemary,
parsley)
3 tbsp wine vinegar
Pepper
2 cup/125 ml olive oil
1 onion, finely chopped
1 pickled gherkin, finely chopped
2 hard-cooked eggs, finely chopped
1 tbsp chopped parsley

Divide the eel into portions. Rub in some salt and leave for 10 minutes. Then bring 4 cups/ 1 liter of water to a boil with the bay leaf and the bouquet garni. Add the eel, cover and leave to steep for 20 minutes on a low heat.

Meanwhile, stir the vinegar, salt, pepper and olive oil together to make a vinaigrette. Then stir in the onion, pickled gherkin, eggs, as well as parsley. Remove the cooked eel from the cooking liquid and then leave to drain thoroughly. Then place the eel on a warmed serving dish. Serve the sauce separately along with boiled potatoes as a side-dish.

Soldaditos de Pavia
Stockfish "Pavía soldiers"

1 lb 5 oz/600 g skinless stockfish
1 tsp mild paprika powder
Salt and pepper
Juice of 1 lemon
2 tbsp olive oil
3 tbsp flour
3 eggs, beaten
Cooking oil

Cut the stockfish into pieces and soak for 24 hours, changing the water at least twice. Let the fish drain thoroughly and cut the fish into uniform strips. Blend the paprika, salt, pepper, lemon juice, and olive oil into a marinade in a bowl. Place the strips of stockfish in this and leave them to marinate for 2 hours. Remove the strips of stockfish from the marinade and pat them dry. Coat them first in flour and then in egg. Fry in plenty of hot oil until golden brown.

Serve the hot stockfish strips sprinkled with paprika in *bocadillo* rolls or on plates in the usual way accompanied with a spicy tomato sauce.

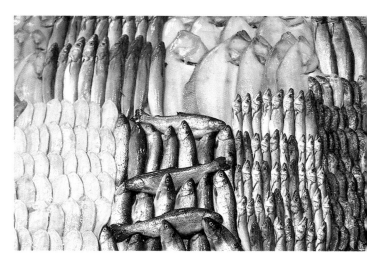

The fish on sale in the markets in Madrid is almost as fresh as the fish sold on the coast. The range of choice in the city is indescribable, and fish is excellently prepared.

295

1 *Café solo:* A little cup of black coffee is just as popular as a substitute for breakfast as it is after a good meal.
2 *Cortado:* Those who like their coffee not quite so strong add a little dash of milk to a black coffee.
3 *Leche manchada:* The main ingredient in the "stained milk" is hot milk, with a very small amount of coffee.

4 *Café con hielo:* A little cup of black coffee is served with a glass filled with ice, into which the sweetened coffee is tipped.
5 *Café del tiempo:* As a remedy for a thick head in the morning, coffee is served with ice, plus a slice of lemon.
6 *Café canario:* This specialty from the Canary Islands mixes a regular *café solo* with sweet condensed milk.

Café con leche: A little cup of black coffee, with hot milk poured in by the waiter at the table, is the typical drink with a breakfast sweet bread. But it tastes just as good when friends meet in the coffee house in the afternoon.

IN THE COFFEE HOUSE

"The coffee house is the Council of State for every man who is never asked for his opinion." Such was the verdict of a chronicler of the Spanish capital. The men who met in coffee houses in the first decades of the twentieth century talked politics. True, scarcely anyone listened, but they did leave their mark on the intellectual life of the country.

Today, there are a few surviving relics of that coffee house era. At best, they furnish material for the more mediocre writers of the capital. And yet there is still something fascinating about places like the Gijón or the Comercial. Imagine: over there sits an old anarchist, a survivor from the Civil War. The tribulations he has suffered and his strict moral standards keep his back very straight. At the next table, a young woman, an 18-year old student. Her father's nylon shirt, knotted at the navel, gives everyone a good view, and around her neck she wears the black scarf of anarchy. The old man notices and realizes that he no longer understands this world.

For at some point progress arrived. Many coffee houses were replaced by boutiques. Interior designers invented the glittering Art Nouveau style, which arrived with a flourish and did nothing for the spirit. But then came a glimmer of light – the Barbieri was restored to what it had been 50 years ago and the *tertulia*, the discussion group in the coffee house, was back – in spite of the consumer society and television. Perhaps many such places still serve the voyeuristic purpose of sitting and watching attractive people. But a few corners of Madrid have witnessed the return of civilization, of people taking an active part in the intellectual life of the nation.

COFFEE FROM THE COLONIES

Coffee's roots lie buried in innumerable myths and legends. Most probably, the drink which is now popular all over the world came from the Arab countries. The Venetians brought coffee to Europe in the 17th century, and it probably first arrived in the Iberian peninsula in the baggage of the first Bourbon king, Philip V, whose reign began in 1700. At all events, the drink spread throughout the country in the 18th century. This uncertainty about the actual origins of coffee contrasts with the precise details historians give of how it was taken to America in the 18th century. First, the French brought the valuable seed to Guyana and Martinique, and from there it also reached Brazil. The plant reached Colombia as well, along somewhat winding paths. The former colony is still Spain's main source of coffee today.

The *carajillo* ranks as one of the stars among the Spanish specialty coffees. Aniseed schnapps or brandy is stirred in, with the desired amount of sugar added.

Depending on the time of day, personal desire and mood, a coffee bean or a piece of raw lemon rind can also be added to the typical small glass.

Strong black coffee is not poured into the glass until right at the end. Many people treat themselves to this magic potion even as early as at breakfast time.

Court cuisine of the Hapsburgs

The Hapsburg Emperor Charles V (Carlos I of Spain) ruled over an empire on which the sun never set. In the 16th century, his ships brought gold and silver from America to Seville, and made Spain the superpower of Europe. The conquerors also brought culinary riches such as tomatoes or chocolate back to the mother country, and the Hapsburg kings of Spain knew how to appreciate these as well. From the mighty Emperor Charles and the much-feared Philip II to the weakly Carlos II, whose death in 1700 marked the end of the Hapsburg line in Spain, the *Austrias* maintained an expensive lifestyle in their palaces. Eating and drinking was of central importance, no matter how many of their subjects were starving outside the palace gates.

Oficio de boca (literally, "the department of the mouth") was the collective name for the personnel who were responsible for the physical well-being of the entire royal house. The head chef (*cocinero mayor*) lorded it over his subordinates like a minister. His staff included many different types of specialist. Thus the *guardamangier* was responsible for the stores, the *comprador* for purchasing, and the *summellier* for the wine. There were cooks at the court who specialized purely in sauces, desserts, cakes, and even tripe. There was someone else whose field was spices, and even the fruit on the royal table had been approved by the fruit specialists.

Mealtimes were a wearisome ritual for the king and particularly for the court. After the priest had blessed the table and the food, the *panetier*, who was responsible for the bread, and the *trinchante* ("he who carves the food"), brought in the meal. They were accompanied by half a dozen other servants, who endeavoured not to get under one another's feet.

In those opulent times, drinking was just as complicated as eating. The *copero* (from *copa*, "glass"), poured the wine into a beaker with a lid. Next, the doctor examined the drink thoroughly. Not until then, when the drink had been approved, was the cup-bearer allowed to bring the beaker closer (accompanied by two more court officials, presumably to convey greater dignity) and to present it, on his knees, to the king. While the king was drinking, the *copero* had to hold a tray in position so that no drops of wine could fall onto the royal clothing. Finally, he handed over a napkin to dry the royal lips. Then the entire procession withdrew again, taking the beaker. Despite the wearisome ritual, the Hapsburgs enjoyed eating and always took pains to ensure that they employed only the very best chefs available in the country.

A Christmas court menu which has come down to us includes twelve first courses, twelve second courses, and twelve main courses – a list which, even today, would make the mouth of the most discriminating gourmet water. The list naturally included *olla podrida*, that most Spanish of all stews, and also Savoy veal in puff pastry. Tender pigeons, turkeys, or quail always formed part of a fine meal, as did fillets of pork, calf's livers, or hare pâté. A popular dish was pigeons in a chocolate-based "black sauce." Rabbit captivated when served with capers, and there was no lack of larded kid, or of sea bream and trout. It remains only to mention that not every guest managed all the courses: ceremonial meals of this kind offered plenty of variety so that every guest could make an ample selection, as in a modern buffet.

Of course, it was not only when the Hapsburgs were celebrating Christmas that such great abundance was available. Even a simple royal "snack meal" (*merienda*) meant the monarch was faced with more than 30 dishes on the table, including trout pie, tongue, choice sausages and dried meats, roasted pigeons, and rolled veal in pastry, in addition to chicken and loin of pork. As regards the "sweet sins," cocoa from the colonies was so popular that Carlos II was said to be "enchanted" by it, and reputedly drank 20 to 30 cups of hot chocolate a day.

Cocido madrileño

As it grew dark in Madrid, a figure swathed in a black shawl slipped out of the palace, quickly crossing Calle Bailén and disappearing into the alleys of *Madrid de los Austrias*, the old city built under the Hapsburg kings. Everyone knew who this young woman was, and even 130 years later, all the regulars seated at the bar in the taverns of Madrid know her story.

They still refer to this princess, who had grown weary of life in the palace, by the affectionate nickname of *chata* ("snub nose"). The Infanta Isabel, sister of Alfonso XII, habitually went out into the Madrid night to satisfy her voracious hunger for working-class *cocido* and working-class men. *Cocido madrileño*, the Madrid stew made from *garbanzos* (chickpeas), vegetables, and meat, is the staple diet of the city, whether it is the enriched variety with meat, paprika, and blood sausage or the basic version with a little bacon and chicken. In each case, the basic element is always chickpeas, which were brought to Spain from central Asia by the Phoenicians. The *cocido* is usually eaten, like most Spanish stews, in three distinct stages: first the soup was served, then the vegetables, and lastly the meat.

The *cocido madrileño* is certainly cooked like a typical stew, but it then suffices for a complete meal with three courses: the soup is usually served as the first course.

Chickpeas and other vegetables come next, and then there should still be some room in the stomach for the high point – any amount of sausage and other meat.

Wine from Madrid

A good *cocido* should be accompanied by a good red wine. "It must be almost black," say the local experts. Garnacha, a wine from Navalcarnero, is particularly suitable. For a long time, the *vino de Madrid* produced on the southern boundary of the region was sold only on draft. But for a few years the winemakers producing it have also been putting well-matured wines on sale in bottles, under the registered description of origin of **D.O. Vinos de Madrid**. The vinegrowing area is divided into the subregions of Navalcarnero, San Martin de Valdeiglesias, and Arganda. The soils are rich in lime – hence the whitish color which is characteristic of large parts of the countryside around the capital. The lime gives the wines structure, which is most apparent in Tempranillo wines. They have a deep color, with powerful tannins and juicy fruit. Recently, experiments have also been carried out with Cabernet, Merlot, and even Syrah. However this grape, from the Rhône Valley in France, is not yet officially permitted. The white grapes are dominated by Malvar, a grape which grows only in Madrid and has an original nutty character.

White varieties made from Albillo and from the Airén grape, which can be found everywhere in central Spain, are also bottled – and let's not forget the neighboring area of La Mancha.

Thus the hearty reds of Navalcarnero and the whites from Arganda are gradually replacing the wine from Valdepeñas, which has been popular in the capital since time immemorial. Nowhere else in the country are there so many wine merchants, and nowhere else do the restaurants offer such a rich variety of top-quality wines from all over Spain.

Background: *Cocido madrileño*, the stew native to Madrid, is traditionally cooked in a clay pot, and nowadays, to please the eye, in small individual pots as well.

Beer has become socially acceptable, and many of the more traditional beer taverns (*cervecerías*) also appeal to those seeking a certain informality which sometimes seems to be lacking in typical Spanish gastronomy. In a genuine *cervecería* (above), draft beer can naturally be obtained (background) and the choice of beers available is steadily growing.

BEER

When the sun is high in Spain, the *caña*, a glass of draft beer, is more and more replacing the *chato*, the little glass of red wine from the barrel. Spain is certainly not a traditional beer-drinking country like for instance Germany or Denmark, and yet nowadays the local breweries offer a multiplicity of beers which are perfectly capable of facing up to the competition from the north. Of course, beer did not originate in Europe. The Sumerians are thought to have brewed a type of beer in the Orient as far back as 6000 years ago. According to the mythology of ancient Egypt, Osiris, the god of agriculture, taught human beings the art of brewing beer from barley, which was spiced with dates, honey, or cinnamon. Hops have been used since the 7th century BC. In the year 133 BC, the first storage jars full of beer reached the Mediterranean harbors of the province of the Roman Empire that was then called Hispania. In the time of the Emperor Vespasian (AD first century), the Romans also noted that the *Hiberi*, the ancient inhabitants of the Iberian peninsula, had a drink fermented with yeast, called *ceria*, in honor of the fertility goddess Ceres. The conquerors who overran the country in the succeeding centuries then decided the fate of beer in Spain for long years to come. The Germanic tribes were great drinkers, but the Arabs, who crossed the Straits of Gibraltar in 711, and conquered almost the entire peninsula, disapproved of alcohol, following the prohibition imposed by Mohammed.

In the 16th century, King Carlos I (Emperor Charles V of the Holy Roman Empire) boosted a renewal in the brewing of beer. Having been born in Flanders, he did not want to be deprived of his favorite drink. When he retreated to the monastery of Yuste toward the end of his life, he had a brewery built there. Thanks to royal concessions, several brewers established themselves in Madrid and Santander in the same century, and a hundred years later the Madrid breweries were already producing 66,000 US gallons (250,000 liters) of foaming ale annually. The end of the royal monopoly in the 19th century gave a boost to production and consumption, which had reached around 22 million US gallons (83 million liters) a year by the Civil War (1936–39). But in the hungry years after the war there was a considerable drop in consumption. Beer was too expensive in comparison to wine. It was only from 1970 onward that Spain became established as a significant beer producer, and in 2002 it produced 728 million US gallons (2.8 thousand million liters). On average, a Spaniard drinks 19 US gallons (73 liters) of beer a year. The European average is a little more: 20 US gallons

Cervecerías are a tradition in Madrid. The typical beer taverns are found in the old city, where people go to enjoy a beer fresh from the barrel *(caña)* and some tapas before a meal.

Nibbles provided in bars such as almonds (*almendras*), peanuts (*cacahuetes*), and olives (*aceitunas*) make sure that the beer does not go straight to one's head.

(77 liters), and the Germans drink 31 US gallons (120 liters) a year.

By definition, beer is an alcoholic beverage obtained from grain or other cereals containing starch by means of yeast fermentation. Beer is usually made from barley and flavored with hops before boiling. Beers made from other cereals must be described as grain beer (*cerveza de cereal*). Since the starch contained in the cereal cannot be fermented, it is converted into sugar through the malting process. The barley is allowed to begin to germinate and is then roasted, in order to interrupt the germination and form flavorings. The grains, malted in this way and then crushed, are mixed with water and hops and boiled down. Yeast is added to the cooled "wort," which ferments a large part of the sugar to alcohol and carbon dioxide. Beers in which the yeast floats on the fermenting wort are known as top fermenting; if the yeasts act at the base they are referred to as bottom fermenting. Bottom fermenting lagers and pils beers form the main part of Spanish production. Well-known European brands are made under licence. But recent developments such as dark beers, special light beers, non-alcoholic beers, "wheat beer" (made from wheat, malt, and top-fermentation yeast), Irish-type stout, and a pils brewed to conform with the German purity law testify to the efforts of Spanish breweries to serve an increasingly choosy market.

Estrella Damm   Aguila estilo Amstel   Mahou clásica   San Miguel 1516

Alhambra Pilsner   Aguila Reserva   Damm Edel   Cruzcampo

Tortilla

The *tortilla de patatas*, the popular Spanish potato omelet, appears in written form as early as the notebooks of Francisco Martinez Montiño. He was the head chef for the Hapsburg kings Philip III and Philip IV and was also the author of one of the most important works of Spanish gastronomy: *Arte de cocina, pastelería, bizochería y conservería*. This simple egg dish was initially known as *tortilla de cartuja*. It was created by the Carthusian monks and the eggs were mixed with cream. Another recipe in Montiño's collection describes the preparation of *tortillas de agua*, which involves putting a few drops of water in the pan after the oil has been poured out and before the eggs are added. This is the most original form of the *tortilla* now described in Spain as "French," a very simple omelet *(tortilla francesa)*. Over the following centuries, the potato omelet then became so typical that it eventually attained the rank of a national dish, the *tortilla española*.

Nowadays, almost anything can be used to make an omelet in Spain: spinach or beans, elvers or ham, tomatoes or mushrooms. For the *tortilla al modo de Palencia*, several *tortillas* are stacked and tomato sauce is poured over them all. Many people like to consume the three-story *tortilla de tres pisos* with quite outrageous amounts of mayonnaise. In Valencia, *tortilla* is made with rice and ham, or even with the leftovers from a paella; the *tortilla del Sacromonte*, with brains and bull's testicles, is typical of Granada. Those who like to eat in style will need eight eggs and 7 ounces (200 grams) of potatoes to serve four. Others use three eggs to 2¼ pounds (1 kilogram) of potatoes. For the simplest Madrid-style variation, the potatoes are fried, together with finely sliced onions or cloves of garlic. This *tortilla* is so popular that it is often confused with the original recipe for *tortilla de patatas* (note, without onions!). For the *tortilla de escabeche a la madrileña* (with marinated tuna fish), potatoes and onions must be sliced particularly fine, and for the *tortilla de esparagos* (asparagus omelet) asparagus from Aranjuez is especially popular in Madrid.

Tortilla de patatas
Potato omelet

⅔ cup/150 ml olive oil
2¼ pounds/1 kg large potatoes, peeled and thinly sliced
2 tsp salt
6 eggs

Heat a scant ½ cup/100 ml of olive oil in a heavy iron pan. Put the sliced potatoes into the pan, season with 1 tsp of salt and toss once in the oil. Then reduce the heat and fry the potatoes for 15–20 minutes, turning them occasionally. Drain off the surplus oil. Beat the eggs with 1 tsp of salt until they are frothy, using a whisk. Carefully fold in the sliced potatoes and then leave the entire mixture to rest for a time. Heat the remaining oil in an iron pan and put the potato and egg mixture into it. Smooth it out and let it thicken for a few minutes on a low heat. Turn the potato omelet over with the help of a plate or a lid and brown it in the same way on the other side. Serve hot or cold.

First the potatoes are peeled and cut into pieces, then they are fried in large amounts of olive oil.

In the meantime, the eggs and salt are beaten with a fork or with a whisk until they are frothy.

The fried potatoes are mixed with the frothy eggs and the mixture is then put into the hot skillet.

When the *tortilla* is cooked on one side, it is turned over with the help of a plate and fried on the other side.

Huevos fritos
Fried eggs, usually cooked in very generous amounts of oil. They are popular *a la cubana*, with rice and tomato sauce.

Huevos fritos con migas
Fried eggs on diced fried bread with diced ham and/or *chorizo*.

Huevos cocidos a la madrileña
Sliced hard-cooked eggs *(huevos duros)* covered in a tomato and paprika sauce, served with diced raw ham.

Huevos revueltos (revuelto, revoltillo)
Scrambled eggs. Almost as widespread and with almost as many variations as the *tortilla*. Particularly popular with young garlic as *revuelto de ajos tiernos*, or with mushrooms *(setas)* or asparagus *(espárragos)*.

Matahambre madrileño/manchego
The "hunger killer," prepared in the style of Madrid or La Mancha, is a type of omelet in which the egg is whisked together with stale bread softened in milk, garlic, and parsley.

Duelos y quebrantos
The classic Cervantes recipe for "aches and afflictions" combines scrambled eggs with bacon and lamb's brain. Nowadays usually made with bacon and *chorizo*.

Huevos mollets
Soft-cooked eggs. As *huevos mollets a la Alicantina*, they are served on split potatoes with shrimp and Béchamel sauce.

Huevos escalfados
Poached eggs (cooked in vinegar water without shells), often served in a *sofrito* made from tomatoes, crushed paprika pods, and olive oil.

Huevos empanados (huevos rebozados)
Fried or boiled eggs, tossed in a thick Béchamel sauce, coated with breadcrumbs and fried, frequently with tomato sauce.

Huevos al plato al modo de Avila
Baked eggs on a bed of seasoned and fried sliced tomatoes with blood sausage.

Piperrada
Scrambled eggs with tomatoes and bell peppers.

Huevos al estilo de Sóller
Fried eggs with *sobrasada* sausage and vegetable purée made from peas, carrots, and leeks (from Majorca).

Huevos a la flamenca
Baked eggs served on a bed of tomatoes, bell peppers, peas, green beans, asparagus, paprika sausage, and Serrano ham.

Huevos rellenos
Stuffed eggs, containing, for example, tuna fish, olives, and mayonnaise, with mushrooms or sardines.

Tortilla de mariscos: with seafood such as mussels, shrimp and cuttlefish.

Tortilla de sardinas: with pieces of sardine, which are carefully laid over the omelet.

Tortilla de hierbas aromáticas: with fine herbs such as thyme, oregano, tarragon.

Tortilla de atún: with tuna fish, fresh or canned, depending on availability.

Tortilla de hígado de pollo: with fresh chicken liver, coarsely chopped.

Tortilla murciana: with fresh vegetables, depending on what is available.

Tortilla de caracoles: with snails, which must be cleaned and cooked in advance.

Tortilla de angulas: with young elvers. An aristocratic variation on the basic dish.

Tortilla de espinacas: with spinach, lightly braised beforehand. Garlic is also suitable.

Tortilla de espárragos trigueros: with green wild asparagus, – has a subtle bitter taste.

Tortilla a la cazadora: the "huntsman's *tortilla*" with mixed fresh wild mushrooms.

Tortilla catalana: with spicy *Butifarra* sausage and plump, precooked beans.

Anis

What botanists know as *Pimpinella anisum* is an umbelliferous plant from the Near East. It can grow to a height of well over 20 inches (50 centimeters), and has white flowers and small, strongly aromatic fruit. In Spain, the aniseed spirit *(anís)* made from it is an indispensable part of the Spanish way of drinking. This schnapps is made all over the country, usually in small distilleries. The *anís* distillates from Ojén or Cazalla in Andalusia are both famous, but far outstripping them all are the varieties from the small town of Chinchón, only 32 miles (52 kilometers) south of Madrid. *"Chinchón – anís, plaza y mesón"* ("Chinchón – aniseed, square, and inns") as a familiar saying goes: the town is a favorite destination for excursions from the capital, which may include the purchasing of a bottle of *anís* as a souvenir, a visit to the *Plaza Mayor*, the famous main square, and a meal in a good restaurant.

In Chinchón, the old art of *anís* distillation goes back to the days of the Moors. A contract dating from 1777 provides for the local vineyards to supply the royal house with about 26,000 US gallons (100,000 liters) of schnapps every year. The vineyards in the district made it possible to produce the alcohol, which was then subjected to a second distillation with aniseed.

Growing real aniseed is not easy, since the plants need to be tended carefully. In other places, substitute plants are often used (fennel in France), but Chinchón is proud of the fact that it preserves the true tradition. Even today, the *Sociedad Alcoholera de Chinchón*, the distillery, guarantees not to use either substitute plants or extracts and to distil only genuine *anís*.

Dry aniseed usually has an alcohol content of 45–50 degrees (though the *Alcoholera de Chinchón* can also supply a "special dry" variety registering a mighty 74 degrees). The sweet variety, in contrast, usually registers around 38 degrees of alcohol. Various manufacturers spice up the pure aniseed spirit by adding herbs of every kind – which accounts for the multitude of local aniseed schnapps varieties in the country.

And there are just as many different ways of drinking it. Some drink *anís* or a *carajillo* (a dash of *anís* in black coffee) to wake themselves up at breakfast time. Dry varieties in particular are suitable digestifs after an ample meal, and even those who like a sweet *copa* are beginning to desert the imported fruit-based spirits and liqueurs and find their way back to the home-produced *anís*. When mixed with golden brandy, the transparent *anís* becomes *sol y sombra* (sunshine and shadow). *Anís* is also more and more frequently drunk with ice, which makes the sweet varieties in particular easier to digest.

The best-known aniseed schnapps in the entire country (background) comes from Chinchón. The *plaza* of the little town (above) is traditionally used to stage religious dramas.

CHINCHON IN THE GOLDEN AGE

The irregular, slightly sloping square – with the fountain on one side and surrounded by mainly three-story buildings with wooden balconies – is one of the most beautiful in Castile. Every year since 1502, the *Plaza Mayor* has been transformed into a bullfighting arena for the Chinchón *fiesta*. And almost 150 years ago, the tradition of the *beneficiencia*, the charity bullfight, was also introduced here, as practiced, for instance, during the *Feria de San Isidro* in Madrid.

A very different kind of spectacle was provided by the heavy wooden wagons of the theatrical groups, which in the 16th century during the festival of Corpus Christi were pushed together on the square to form a stage. The dramas performed were *autos sacramentales*, one-act plays with religious themes. Originally simple dramatizations of the Last Supper, the presentations became increasingly more complex, but they were always allegories from the Old or New Testament. Well-known authors like Lope de Vega or Tirso de Molina wrote plays of this kind, but the high point of this art form is represented by Pedro Calderón de la Barca. From 1649, Calderón was the only author permitted to write *autos sacramentales* for Madrid and, in a letter written shortly before his death, he stated that he had written 70 of these pieces. But the *autos* gradually degenerated into simple farces, and in 1765 they were banned. The town of Chinchón again commemorated the original tradition in 1963, when it once more staged a Passion Play at Easter. Since then, the inhabitants of the town have all come together in their square on Easter Saturday each year to perform such a religious drama.

Anís de Chinchón

Anís Castellana

Anís Marie Brizard

Anís Machaquito

Anís Tunel

Anís del Mono

Aniseed originates from the eastern Mediterranean and was first used as a spice in breadmaking in Europe.

Aniseed seeds give the Spanish aniseed schnapps its delicate flavor. The drink is based on grape distillates.

307

Mojito, the national drink of Cuba, made from rum, limes, sugar, and mint, conquered the Spanish bars long ago.

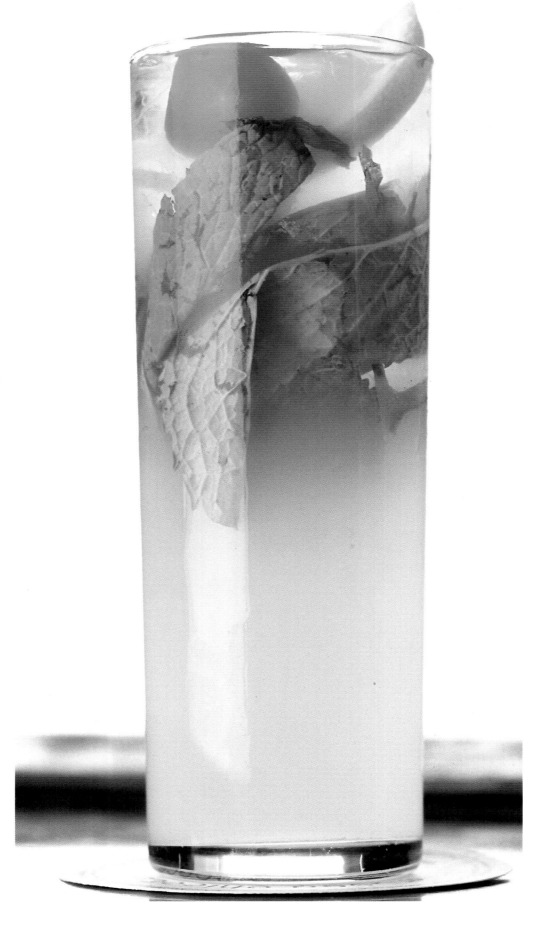

Cubata or **Cubalibre** is mixed from rum and cola with a little lemon.

Ginebra tónica or **Gin and tonic**, contains gin and tonic water.

Caipirinha consists of limes, cane spirit, and some sugar.

Quemadillo is a grog made from rum and water, often with milk.

Agua de Valencia is orange juice with champagne, or a liqueur.

Lumumba a warm winter drink containing rum and chocolate milk.

THE CASTELLANA

The Paseo de la Castellana (photograph right), which is now the most popular place to go for a stroll in Madrid was once a *cañada*, a sheep drovers' track. Even 30 years ago, shepherds regularly drove their flocks along Spain's noblest avenue, and the Calle Alcalá, which crosses the Castellana at right angles, is legally still a part of the *Cañada Galiana*. Alfonso the Wise introduced the *cañadas reales*, the royal shepherds' tracks, in 1273, since his income was based on wool. From the mountains of Asturia all the way to Valencia and Seville, the paths stretch out for the flocks in search of pastures. There are 62,000 miles (100,000 kilometers) of *cañadas* today, roamed over by around 400,000 sheep (see also page 271). They now come only for protests or for traditional *fiestas*.

Night without end

Madrid leads a double life. During the day, Spain's capital is noisy and dusty. But when night falls, the oppressive atmosphere disappears. True, the pace remains hectic until far into the night, but the mood becomes magical and the air is clean, as the wind from the *sierra* blows the grime of the day from the atmosphere and from people's heads. *Marcha* (march) or *movida* (movement) – these are the watchwords for the night life of Madrid. In earlier times, when the capital had still not awoken from the lethargy of Franco's dictatorship, this description referred to its stimulating cultural life. Nowadays, it means movement in its purest form, since many people appear to believe that standing still is the same as dying. So they go off to the bars, which are full to bursting, since the only fun places are those that are already full of people.

To a citizen of Madrid, it would be unthinkable to spend the whole evening at the same table in the same bar. Once work is over, the evening begins with an *aperitivo* in a tapas bar – at around eight o'clock or later. No one wants to eat until ten o'clock in the evening, and as soon as the meal is over, the struggle for a *copa* begins, as people drift amiably from one drink to the next. The point is to see and be seen in the right places – which keep changing with the moods of fashion:

Drinking habits

Whether the drink is an *aperitivo*, a *vino*, or a *copa*, drinking in Madrid is still governed by strict, traditional rules. It would be uncivilized to go straight from the office or from home to a restaurant to eat. The *aperitivo* can extend over several bars. A few tapas are accompanied by a beer, a sherry, or even a glass of *cava*, which is often served from the barrel. Other wines are also frequently drunk with tapas (served in a small bar glass known as a *chato*). In the south, people also drink red wine on such occasions, with lemonade or soda and a slice of lemon, a drink known as *tinto verano* (summer red wine). Wine is still king during the meal, even if the rules which prescribe white wine for fish and red for meat have long since ceased to be applied strictly. In a simple restaurant (*tasca*), the set menu for the day will be accompanied by a modest wine from the barrel, and at lunchtime it is often mixed with *gaseosa* (sweet lemonade soda). This seemingly barbaric habit is understandable, in view of the summer heat and the heaviness of the red wines from the Priorato or Aragon. But legend recounts that the wine waiter in an upmarket bar in Madrid fainted when a *nouveau riche* customer ordered a lemonade with a noble Rioja. You just need to know

where the limits are. The fact that the consumption of wine is steadily falling in Spain, as elsewhere, means that here, as in other places, the market is becoming more interested in quality than quantity. If the bottle is empty once everyone has had a second glass, Spaniards will not order another, since after the meal they will go on for a *copa*. As regards the digestif, there is first and foremost one simple drinking rule: the more refined, the better. But nothing has been discovered as yet which goes down better than golden brandy, white *orujo* (grape spirit), or *anís* (see page 306 ff.).

After leaving the restaurant in the evening, people go on to the nearest bar for a *copa*. The word means a glass or a beaker, but it usually refers to a strong drink such as brandy or whisky – either neat or mixed. Standard mixtures known the world over – such as gin and tonic or rum and cola – can be obtained everywhere in Spain as well. People also like to indulge in exotic mixed drinks, from Cuba Libres through Caipirinhas to the really off-the-wall mixtures with coffee or chocolate milk. For the totally unsophisticated palate there is *calimocho*, a mixture of cola and cheap red wine. In contrast, a glass of Spanish champagne *(cava)* is always an elegant choice, and it can also be enjoyed with freshly pressed orange juice as the drink called *agua de Valencia*.

in summer, naturally, these are the *terrazas*, the open-air café terraces on the chic streets such as the Castellana or Paseo Pintor Rosales. The streets of Madrid are still full of chaotic traffic jams at three o'clock in the morning. After midnight, the body needs movement (otherwise, it falls asleep). So there is nothing for it but to go off to a disco. From

salsa or samba to the hardest techno, all kinds of music clamour for attention in every kind of hot venue. Those who want to can start on Friday evening and go on till Monday morning – and many discos are open all day as well. What a fascinating experience to tell all your friends about – if you can survive!

The *Museo Chicote* bar (above) was a meeting-place in the Franco era. But the times have changed. Nowadays anyone who wants to be considered important goes to the bars on the Castellana.

Castilla-La Mancha

Walter Tauber

Castile – La Mancha

Each year, the farmers of La Mancha wallow in a tidal wave of crocus flowers, which bloom in the barren landscape and supply the much sought saffron.

La Mancha may be a harsh region, but the high plateau can also offer some special surprises. Magic touches this region very early in the day, when there is scarcely enough sunlight to make out the soft hues of the gray-green olive groves, and late in the evening, when the setting sun turns the gold of the wheat fields into red fire. At other times, let your imagination soar: be like Don Quixote who put on his armor to tilt at windmills; be brave and scorn physical hardships. This is the basic rule – not just for brave knights, but for anyone entering the heart of Spain. For only a spirit in contemplative mood is ready to comprehend the particular greatness of Don Quixote and his land.

Lying in the heart of Spain, the plain is sometimes scorched by drought and burning sunshine, and sometimes tormented by icy winds. It is surrounded by dark ranges of hills, where the sessile oaks and sparse grass provide a home for many kinds of animal. For a long time, this flat region was a world apart, the border between Christendom and Islam. Here the religious knights of Calatrava once rode out against the pagan foe. Here the Berber soldiers of the Caliph's army rustled the Christian king's sheep. A long time has passed since thousands of flocks of sheep roamed endlessly across La Mancha. But this sparsely inhabited area, which has a population density of scarcely 20 people to a third of a square mile (a square kilometer), still produces excellent roast lamb.

Nowadays, the shepherds share the land with the farmers. The farmers supply their splendid white bread to accompany cheese and meat, with light, beguiling wines, and vegetables which are transformed into a fragrant miracle in the clay pot. A journey through the scorching, barren waste is often suddenly interrupted by glimpses of Paradise – a carpet of saffron crocuses catches the eye amid the dusty acres, or a rugged cliff suddenly opens out into a green valley, with a babbling river and leaping trout. It is a modest life in La Mancha, but those travelers, usually French, who have condemned the allegedly crude Castilian cuisine so frequently and so loudly, have simply failed to recognize the miracles before them. The ingredients mixed together by the shepherd in his iron skillet were undoubtedly simple: bread, oil, and garlic, the most essential foundations of Castilian cuisine, were always to hand. To this he added whatever the land provided, day by day: a hare, a red-legged partridge, or even a wild boar. And, of course, his imagination.

Saffron

The Greeks of antiquity used saffron as a cosmetic for their beautiful women. The Emperor Nero had the streets of Rome covered with the golden threads before he rode into the city. Wealthy Romans drank a saffron broth at their orgies, so that they could devote themselves more energetically to the service of Venus, the goddess of love. And saffron also gives fabrics a color which ranges from yellow to a deep gold. It was a prized material for the veils of Phoenician brides, and after the death of the Buddha his priests approved the noble spice as the dye for coloring their robes. Saffron has always been one of the world's most valuable products, with a price which could sometimes be higher than that of gold.

Crocus sativus is the name botanists give to this treasure. This type of crocus originally came from Asia Minor, where it has been cultivated since ancient times. The Arabs brought the spice *az-zafaran* (literally, "yellow") to Spain during their tempestuous drive west over a thousand years ago, and today over 70 percent of the world's production is grown on the high Castilian plateau. The miracle happens each year in October. The crocus flowers open up in the dark, and the red light of dawn shines on a purple carpet, the *manto*. From Toledo to Albacete, pure chaos reigns. Safran *(azafrán)* must be gathered within a day. Otherwise, the valuable threads lose their flavor. The harvest period lasts scarcely ten days. The farmers pluck the flowers between their index fingers and thumbs. The women sit at long tables and separate out the reddish stigma with practiced skill, their fingers moving as fast as lightning. Finally, the stigma is roasted on a sieve. In earlier times, this was done over charcoal. Nowadays, gas burners tend to be used. About 200 crocus flowers

are needed to obtain a single gram of saffron, and the average harvest obtained by a family enterprise is around 8 Castilian pounds (a Castilian pound equals 460 grams, approximately 1 pound, avoirdupois weight). Since time immemorial, the "red gold of La Mancha," dried and preserved in the closet between layered sheets, has acted as a savings bank for the farming families. Saffron was once accepted as a currency, and even today the Spanish expression for bartering is "to pay in *especie*" ("spice").

The saffron harvest has always brought life to the sleepy, dazzlingly white villages of La Mancha. In the old days, helping out with the harvest was a good opportunity for a young man to visit the home of a farmer's daughter he loved. Perhaps he could steal a kiss unnoticed during the bustle of the harvest. (After all, from olden times love has been connected with the valuable plant: in a Roman fable, a lovesick youth called Crocus is turned into a flower.) The "Saffron Rose Festival" *(Fiesta de la Rosa del Azafrán)* is the highpoint of the year in Consuegra. On the last Sunday in October, at the foot of the white windmills against which Don Quixote once battled, the farmers celebrate with music and dancing, and choose the most captivating local beauty to be crowned as *Dulcinea de La Mancha* in honor of the beloved Don Quixote.

The laborious work in the crocus field (background) pays off. The money rolls in from the saffron crop. And saffron adds the spice to the *tojunto* made from beef or rabbit and potatoes (top).

The fresh stigma of the saffron crocus flower (bottom) perishes quickly. If the saffron is to be used as a spice (top), it must be first dried over a fire.

Crocus sativus grows wild on poor soils. The saffron extracted from its stigma has been much sought for thousands of years as a dye, a medicine, and also a spice.

The saffron crocuses are harvested in October. The farmers go out into the fields and use their thumbs and index fingers to pick thousands of flowers.

Women pull the reddish threads from the stigma of each individual flower. Around 200 crocus flowers are needed to obtain a single gram of saffron (0.035 oz).

The fresh saffron threads are roasted in a sieve. In earlier times, there was usually a wood or charcoal fire burning underneath. Nowadays, it might also be a gas burner.

Sancho's heart's desire

The governor (Don Quixote's companion, Sancho Panza - Ed.) waited with intense yearning for nightfall and suppertime; and although it seemed to him that time stood still and the hands of the clock never moved, nevertheless the longed-for hour finally arrived. He was given chopped beef with onions, and a pair of steamed calf's trotters, which had put in a good few years' service. He took greater delight in all this than if he had had Milanese grouse, Roman pheasants, Sorrento veal, partridges from Morón, or geese from Lavajos put before him. And during the meal, he turned to the doctor and said to him: "Mark you, Sir Doctor, take no trouble in future to have them bring me special dishes and choice things to eat, for in that way you would lead my stomach off its track, since it is used to goat meat or beef, bacon and dried meat, turnips and onions. And perhaps, if it is offered the food the gentry eat, it will be reluctant to accept it, or now and then might vomit it up. What the steward can do is to set an *olla podrida* before me more often, full of things like cabbage and turnips all mixed up together, and the more they are mixed up the better it tastes, and he can put in and mix in anything he likes, as long as it's something to eat, and I'll just thank him and reward him."

(From: Miguel de Cervantes Saavedra, *Don Quixote,* Vol. 2, 1615)

Windmills and fortresses are the famous symbols of La Mancha. But only the windmills are kept in good repair in this harsh region. However, people can still always tilt at windmills if they feel so inclined, as Don Quixote did.

DON QUIXOTE

Alonso Quijano, a member of the minor nobility, from a little village in La Mancha, has read too many books on chivalry. He imagines that he is a knight too, and he sets out on a crazy quest. The powerful novel *El ingenioso Hidalgo Don Quijote de la Mancha* by Miguel de Cervantes Saavedra (1547–1616) is a satire on the romances of chivalry popular at the time. But it is also the story of a decidedly human hero, and the monumental work encompasses many aspects of the life of that age: love, politics, and religion – and also food.

Food, drink, and physical well-being, and particularly the lack of all three, form a recurring theme in *Don Quixote*: around it the thoughts of the anti-hero constantly circle. And it is no accident that Quixote's rotund companion is named *Sancho Panza*: *Panza* is the Spanish word for belly or paunch.

Quixote can be seen as a living panorama of a world power in decline: Cervantes gives an ironic picture of the customs of the aristocracy and extols the simple life of shepherds and journeymen. And so the novel is peppered with popular sayings concerning gastronomy: one good example is "Wine brings a gleam to the eye, gives you good teeth, and cleans out your bowels."

Cervantes and his hero know the right and proper way to cook: an important piece of advice is "If you don't want to eat a stew right away, leave it to keep cooking". Finally, by virtue of patience alone, a good meal can be had from chickpeas and meat – something like *olla podrida* (see also page 266). In addition to this famous stew and *pisto manchego*, made from fresh vegetables (page 319), other dishes we know of through Don Quixote are *duelos y quebrantos* (scrambled eggs which, in the days of the brave knight, were mixed with lamb's brain, and are nowadays made with ham and paprika sausage); *tiznao* (dried cod with vegetables); *gachas de matanza* (a shepherd's dish made from flour, water, and salt, together with the leftovers when an animal is slaughtered); and the popular *migas de pastor* made from stale bread and bacon (see pages 88 ff.).

Faced with one crisis after another, Don Quixote learns to value his daily bread much more highly, as a source both of physical well-being and of deep philosophical insight. "Yesterday's bread, today's meat, and mature wine safeguard health the whole year round," – insists the clever knight. He also observes: "While I am eating, I know nothing. But when I have finished eating, I begin to understand."

Main photograph: The life of the noble knight of La Mancha inspired Anton von Werner (1843–1915) to paint "Don Quixote among the Goatherds."

THE LOGIC OF PERFECT FORM

Pottery was known in Spain as long ago as the Stone Age, and in the second century BC, when the Greeks developed potter's wheels which were operated with the foot, these were soon to be found on the Iberian peninsula. But it was the Arabs who turned pottery into a fine art. In the areas where they ruled for the longest periods – in Andalusia, in parts of eastern Spain, and in Toledo – true masterpieces of Spanish ceramics were created. There were still some fifty potters in Consuegra only a few decades ago.

The basic materials for the potter's art are aluminous silicates known as loams. These loams are mixed with various substances, depending on the application – for example, silica sand is used to increase the moldability. The rich white clays and the lean reddish varieties are obtained from open-cast mining or from quarries. Some shafts at Mota del Cuervo in Cuenca province are up to 165 feet deep (50 meters). The deep *olla* and *puchero* and the shallow *cazuela* are the traditional forms for Spanish clay cooking pots, which are always glazed inside, and often outside too. These clay vessels are indispensable for many dishes forming part of the traditional cuisine. Above all, it is the storage and transportation containers that reflect the logic of perfect form. Their ancestors are the amphorae of antiquity, but it was the Arabs who made their use widespread in their Spanish caliphates. The *cántaro* is used to store water for domestic use. The smaller, flat-bottomed variation stands on the table; larger pitchers with pointed bases are storage jars and three or four of these can be mounted in a special wooden holder, the *cantarera*. The *tinaja* is used to store large quantities of wine or olive oil. Such vessels normally have pointed bases, so that they can be pushed down into the ground itself. Vessels of this kind are unglazed, and the smaller types are sometimes decorated with fine lines or crazed patterns. The *tinajas* of Valdepeñas are famous, the largest being more than 15 feet high (5 meters). They formed part of the basic cellarage equipment until they were made obsolete by oak casks and steel tanks. But the king of the pots is the *botijo*, a water container which can be carried by a handle, with a wide opening for filling and a narrow one for drinking. In the summer, the water slowly forces its way through the pores of the unglazed vessels and evaporates – so the contents stay cool even in the hot sun. The *botijo de carretera* (highway *botijo*) is hung over the shoulder on a strap and taken out by those working in the fields. The countless variations of the *botijo* have become decorative objects or collector's items, and they are still made to high standards of quality today.

To begin with, every clay pot is a thick, unformed mass of clay.

With the help of the potter's wheel, the object takes on its crude form.

Then the potter shapes the details; a casserole or perhaps a wine jar.

Vegetables or meat can be braised in the *cacerola* (casserole), which has a lid.

The *puchero* is used mainly to cook substantial stews.

The *cazuela*, the most versatile cooking pot, has a smaller version: a *cazuelita*.

The *cántaro* (a pitcher with a handle) is used to store water.

VEGETABLES

The sun-scorched soil of La Mancha conceals a never-ending abundance. In the pots which dexterous master craftsmen form from the clay, gloriously colorful vegetables of all kinds can be prepared: tomatoes, garlic, and onions of course, but also turnips, hefty potatoes, zucchini, eggplants, and peppers. In many places, the cabbage fields stretch as far as the eye can see, and the capital Madrid obtains its salads, beans, and spinach from this wide plain.

In the area around Almagro, southeast of Ciudad Real, the eggplant is king. The town is best known nowadays for its festival of classical theater; but in the 16th century it was the headquarters of the Fugger banking family. Every year, it produces more than 3300 tons (3000 tonnes) of the *Solanum melongena var. depressum*

– the botanical name for a small, oval variety of eggplant which is found only in this region. It now flourishes on the plain where once the holy warriors of Calatrava rode out to do battle with the Moors. In contrast to the big eggplant, the greenish center is surrounded by thick leaves. It is picked when it is still small – 3 to 4 inches (7-10 centimeters) long and slightly more than 1½ inches (4 centimeters) thick. The crop-pickers work in the fields from July until the first frost at the end of November, and there are four factories in Almagro which process the produce from around a hundred farming families.

The fresh eggplants are cooked within 48 hours, and then preserved in water, vinegar, salt, garlic, caraway, and peppers. A piece of red pepper, pushed into the heart of the eggplant and secured by a fennel stalk, serves as decoration. *Berenjenas de Almagro* are sold locally by the *orza*, a small clay jar. Almost all the cans filled with this

exquisite vegetable go to Madrid, where this specialty is very popular. Gourmets can sometimes find eggplants from Almagro in Spanish stores in other countries.

There is a second town in La Mancha which depends essentially on one single product. Villanueva de la Jara in Cuenca province produces 5500 tons (5000 tonnes) of mushrooms in giant sheds. All in all, the province of Cuenca produces 55,000 tons (50,000 tonnes) of mushrooms - almost half of the entire Spanish production. In earlier times, this crop was grown in natural caves in the bare cliff, and even today these are still used as additional production sites in summer. Fresh Villanueva mushrooms have a texture almost as delicate as fish. Part of the crop is processed and preserved, and half of this is exported. Around a thousand families in Villanueva earn their living from mushrooms, and on May 8 they hold a tremendous festival that honors the little fungus.

PISTO MANCHEGO
Braised mixed vegetables

Scant ½ cup/100 ml olive oil
2 onions, chopped
2 cloves of garlic, finely chopped
4 small zucchini, cubed
1 red and 1 green bell pepper, cubed
2 ripe beef tomatoes, skinned and cubed
Salt and pepper
2 tbsp chopped fresh herbs, e.g. parsley

Heat the olive oil in a clay pot or a deep pan, and fry the onion and garlic in it until they are translucent. Add the vegetables and season with salt and pepper. Leave to braise for around 15 minutes on a medium heat until the cooking liquid has completely evaporated. Sprinkle with fresh herbs before serving.

Variation: Anyone wanting a more substantial dish can brown some cubed ham or bacon in the olive oil before the vegetables are added.

BERENJENAS RELLENAS
Stuffed eggplants

4 small eggplants
12 oz/350 g lamb, chopped
1 egg
1 onion, finely chopped
3 cloves of garlic, finely chopped
3 tsp ground cinnamon
Salt and pepper
1 tbsp chopped parsley
½ cup/125 ml olive oil
½ cup/125 g grated Manchego cheese

Wash the eggplants and cut them in half lengthwise. Hollow them out with a spoon.
Combine the lamb together thoroughly with the egg, onion, garlic, cinnamon, salt, pepper, and parsley, and fill the eggplants with the mixture. Heat the olive oil in a flameproof baking dish and put the eggplants in it. Sprinkle the filling with cheese. Cover the dish with aluminum foil and cook in a preheated oven at 390 °F/200 °C for about 40 minutes. Remove the foil 10 minutes before the end of the cooking period.

CHAMPIÑONES AL AJILLO
Mushrooms with garlic

Scant ½ cup/100 ml olive oil
6 cloves of garlic, sliced
Generous 1 lb/500 g mushrooms,
thickly sliced
A pinch of hot paprika powder
Salt
3½ tbsp/50 ml sherry
2 tbsp chopped parsley

Heat the olive oil in a deep pan, but do not let it become too hot. Brown the garlic slightly in it, then add the mushrooms. Cook, stirring constantly, until all the oil has been absorbed. Season with the paprika powder and a little salt. Add the sherry and sprinkle with parsley just before serving.

The garlic is sorted in long wooden troughs. Depending on the quality, the bulbs are put on the market immediately, kept in storage, or processed into various products.

The finest and juiciest bulbs are woven into strings. Created by hard work in La Mancha, they are sold everywhere as typical Spanish souvenirs.

The finished strings are washed (main photograph). Then they are put into large sheds to dry before being shipped off to destinations all over the world.

Many tons of garlic are processed in Las Pedroñeras each year. The employees of one firm proudly display the bulbs which are responsible for their village's prosperity, and for a characteristic scent in the air.

GARLIC FROM LA MANCHA

"Eat neither garlic nor onions, for thy smell will betray the peasant in thee," Don Quixote admonishes his squire, Sancho Panza. Like Cervantes, innumerable Spanish and foreign authors have long despised garlic as a poor people's spice. In the 14th century, King Alfonso of Castile forbade any knight smelling of garlic to enter his palace for an entire month. Around 1920, the novelist Julio Camba expressed his rather sceptical views on society in a comment on Spanish cooking, which he claimed was "full of garlic and religious prejudice."

But the days in which kings banished the pungent bulbs from their courts are long past. Garlic, together with bread and olive oil, is part of the trio that forms the foundation of Spanish cuisine. "There are many cuisines in Spain," says the culinary elder statesman Xavier Domingo, "but they all have one thing in common: garlic." The cultivation of the once despised peasant food has long outgrown the private vegetable garden, and in La Mancha it is an important sector of the modern economy. The area in which garlic is cultivated has quadrupled over half a century. On average, every Spaniard eats over 3 pounds (1.5 kilograms) of the bulb known to scientists as *Allium sativum* each year.

Spain produces almost 193,000 tons (175,000 tonnes) of garlic a year, one-third of which is exported all over the world. Just over 16,530 tons (15,000 tonnes) goes to Brazil alone. The capital of the beloved *ajo morado* (purple garlic) is Las Pedroñeras, a place in La Mancha where garlic is honored in a great festival at the end of September. Practically all the 6,800 inhabitants live off the "white gold" of the farmers, either directly or indirectly. The average family-run farm has almost 10 acres (4 hectares) of land, and yields approximately 53,000 pounds (24,000 kilograms) of garlic. In most rural areas everywhere, the general complaint is that there is a flight from the land – but not here. The young people want to stay and take over their fathers' fields. And they have been proved right to do so. Are we not all familiar with the picturesque garlic strings or the wreaths woven from the white bulbs which appeal to every visitor to Spain? It is certainly true that the low prices charged by their rivals in China threaten the supremacy of the village in La Mancha. But in Las Pedroñeras, where there is an unmistakable aroma in the air (and not only during harvest time), the people are well-prepared for the fight. Quality is their hallmark, even if China can threaten them with quantity. Nowadays, cold stores guarantee satisfactory produce the whole year round, and the modern industry is continuously looking to develop new packaging and exciting new products, such as garlic cloves pickled in oil with herbs and spices, or a whole range of exquisite ideas for sauces and marinades.

SOPA DE AJOS
Garlic soup

8–9 slices/250 g stale white bread
6 tbsp olive oil
6-8 cloves of garlic, chopped
1 tbsp mild paprika powder
1 tbsp hot paprika powder
Salt
Generous 4 cups/1 liter meat stock
4 eggs

Cut the white bread into cubes. Heat the olive oil in a saucepan and fry the bread cubes in it until it is golden brown. Add the garlic and let it color a little. Season with the paprika powders and pour on the meat stock. Cover and leave to simmer for about 15 minutes.

Fill 4 earthenware bowls with soup. Carefully slip 1 egg into each bowl and leave to cook in a preheated oven at about 390 °F/200 °C for around 10 minutes. Serve the soup very hot.

Hunting is a very serious affair. There is a lot to do, and the various tasks are allocated to the hunters present before they are able to go out into the field.

Young and old take their shotguns into the woods in Spain. Centuries ago, hunting red-legged partridges was a way of putting meat into the cooking pot.

Many a hunter treasures a finely crafted weapon which he has inherited from his father or grandfather, and which he will pass on to his own children later.

Apart from red-legged partridges, hares and rabbits are most frequently shot. That pleases any cook, since they figure in many traditional dishes.

Hunting in Spain

Sometimes it seems as though the whole of Spain were just one big shoot. On potholed country roads or remote tracks, on trees and posts – everywhere there are the black and white disks bearing the text *coto privado de caza* (private hunting reserve). In fact, the marked areas cover three-quarters of the country. And even that still does not seem to be enough for the hunters, for every fall they swarm all over 98 percent of the territory of Spain. There is scarcely any nook or cranny where hunting does not take place.

In Spain, hunting is a national sport, more popular than bullfighting or football. A million and a half men roam over fields and through the undergrowth and bag a total of 70 million animals a year. The business based on hunting has a turnover of about three billion US $. It employs about 20,000 people full-time and gives casual work to two million. The Spaniards call their country the "hunting grounds of Europe." And the heart of these hunting grounds is located in the *Montes de Toledo*, the range of hills in La Mancha, colored dark by its stone oaks.

But today there is more than one kind of hunting in Spain. Some take part in what the writer Xavier Domingo has described as "social hunting." This extravaganza was long symbolized by the image of the small dictator Franco in front of a pile of slaughtered stags, and nowadays members of high society pay up to US $ 4,000 for the right to shoot a stag in fenced-off areas. Even specially reared red-legged partridges are driven in front of their guns. This kind of hunting long ago produced a standardized international cuisine. Venison or wild boar has been prepared the same way at the courts of Europe since the Middle Ages. So, although the French master chef Escoffier was certainly pleased with the recipes *à la mode d'Alcantara* that were captured by Napoleon's troops in Extremadura, game has long been prepared in exactly the same way in Germany or France as in Spain.

Hunting as a mass sport is a new phenomenon. In earlier times, workers on the land earned a meager wage, but were able to survive by adding game to their menus. Shepherds and farmers have also made a considerable contribution to Spanish cuisine with their shotguns, traps, and creative ideas. Red-legged partridges and quail are the most popular game birds, but pigeons, guinea fowl, and pheasants are also hunted. Rabbits and hares are used for *gazpachos manchegos* (pages 322 ff.). But the red-legged partridge heads the list, especially those that live near vineyards and like grapes. For *Perdiz en escabeche* the bird is marinated in wine vinegar – a dish which can serve as a proud testimony to the culinary skills of a hunting nation (recipe, page 327).

To shoot a wild boar *(jabalí)* is every hunter's dream. The meat has a decidedly dry taste, and must be expertly prepared.

Hunters go after the stag *(ciervo)* mainly as a trophy. But the exquisitely gamey taste can inspire chefs as well.

The deer *(corzo)* is rare in Spanish cuisine, in spite of having tender meat, with a discreetly gamey taste.

The Iberian ibex *(cabra montés)* is mainly hunted as a trophy, but it can be hunted only in specified areas.

Spanish cuisine has innumerable ways of preparing rabbit *(conejo)* which enhance the gamey taste of the extremely tender meat.

When eaten at eight or ten months old, the hare *(liebre)* has tender meat, with a slightly gamey taste.

Poachers and the Guardia Civil

Tragic or absurd, a serious drama played out by people with a twinkle in their eye – many stories are told of the games of hide-and-seek played by poor farmers hunting on the gentlemen's estates to feed their families and dodging the members of the green-uniformed rural police force, defending the gentlemen's rights. Indeed, such stories epitomize the history of Spain in the twentieth century. For a long time, the land belonged to only a few in Spain: it was once claimed that a squirrel could jump from tree to tree all the way from the Basque Country to Cadiz without leaving the lands owned by the Dukes of Alba. For far too long, the nobility and the church held far too much in their hands. As a result the country exploded, torn apart by the Civil War (1936–1939). But under Franco's dictatorship, the main task of the rural police, the *Guardia Civil*, was to defend the rights of the powerful. They were brutal in their pursuit of those who dared to shoot a stag which belonged to a nobleman. Even in the 1960s, when Spain was becoming increasingly orientated toward modern ways and was attracting Europe's vacationers to its *costas*, the Guardia was still making sure that, in the villages at least, the feudal era lived on.

Red-legged partridges *(perdices)* are usually hunted with decoys. The hunters rear these at home until the time comes for them to play a star role in the hunting season. Their job is to lure other partridges by their mating calls.

Wash the meat and pat it dry; then rub salt and pepper into it. Heat the drippings in a deep skillet and sear the meat on both sides. Add the onion, herbs and spices and pour on the red wine. Cover and leave to cook on medium heat for about 1½ hours.

Then remove the venison from the skillet and keep it warm. Pour the cooking liquid into a pan through a sieve and boil down until it has reduced to taste. Add the brandy and season with salt and pepper.

Cut the venison into equal slices and finally serve with the sauce.

Espaldilla de gamo rellena
Stuffed shoulder of fallow deer

1 shoulder of fallow deer, drawn by butcher, in one piece
2½ cups/300 g of mixed chopped meat
1 cup/150 g of finely diced smoked bacon
1 cup/150 g of finely diced cooked ham
1 egg
2 tbsp breadcrumbs
Salt and pepper
⅛ tsp ground nutmeg
4 carrots, cut into pieces
2 large onions, stuffed with 2 cloves and 1 bay leaf
1 bouquet garni (e.g. thyme, oregano, parsley, rosemary)
2 cloves of garlic
2 cups/500 ml dry white wine

Spread out the drawn shoulder of fallow deer on a clean dish towel.

Mix the chopped meat, diced bacon and ham, egg, and breadcrumbs together for the stuffing. Season with salt, pepper, and nutmeg. Spread this mixture over the meat and roll it up with the help of the dish towel. Tie the roll tightly with kitchen twine.

Put 2 cups/500 ml water into a large saucepan with the carrots, onions, bouquet garni, garlic, wine, and salt. Place the stuffed shoulder in the pan and bring to a boil; then cover and simmer for 2 hours on a low heat. When the cooking time is over, remove the meat from the stock. Strain off the stock and let it boil down to one-third of the quantity. Cut the meat into equal slices and place in a preheated dish. Pour the stock over it and serve immediately.

These game dishes are popular in all areas of central Spain: braised beans with red-legged partridge (*judias estofadas con perdiz*, top), rabbit with garlic (*conejo al ajillo*, left), and roast venison (*carne de ciervo asada*, right).

A GLANCE INTO THE HUNTER'S POT

JUDIAS ESTOFADAS CON PERDIZ
Braised beans with red-legged partridge
(Photograph above, top)

1¾ cups/250 g white beans
Salt and pepper
4 red-legged or common partridges, ready for cooking
Flour for coating
Scant ½ cup/100 ml olive oil
1 onion, chopped
3 cloves of garlic, chopped
2 cloves
1 bay leaf
1 cup/250 ml white wine
Vinegar for seasoning

Soak the beans overnight in cold water. The following day, drain the beans and place in a pan of fresh water. Bring to a boil, then simmer for 30 minutes.

Meanwhile, rub salt and pepper into the partridges and coat with flour.

Heat the olive oil in a flameproof casserole and brown the partridges on all sides. Then brown the onion, garlic, cloves, and the bay leaf. Add the white wine, beans, and cooking liquid. Cover and leave to braise for approximately 40 minutes.

Finally, before serving, season with salt, pepper, and vinegar.

CONEJO AL AJILLO
Rabbit with garlic
(Photograph above, on left)

1 rabbit, ready for cooking, cut into small pieces
Salt and pepper
1 cup/250 ml olive oil
6 cloves of garlic, thinly sliced
Scant ½ cup/100 ml white wine

Rub plenty of salt and pepper into the rabbit portions. Heat two-thirds of the oil in a pan and brown the rabbit pieces in batches until they are golden brown. Then place the rabbit portions in a clay pot. Sweat the sliced garlic lightly in the remaining oil. Pour the garlic and oil over the rabbit and add the wine. Cook for about 15 minutes in a preheated oven at 390 °F/200 °C. Fresh homemade mayonnaise can be added (see recipe, page 68).

CARNE DE CIERVO ASADA
Roast venison
(Photograph above, on right)

Generous 2 lbs/1 Kg venison, drawn
Salt and pepper
2 tbsp drippings
1 onion, stuffed with 2 cloves and 1 bay leaf
3 sprigs of thyme
3 sprigs of marjoram
⅛ tsp ground nutmeg
2 cups/500 ml red wine
2½ tbsp/40 ml brandy

PERDIZ EN ESCABECHE
Marinated red-legged partridge
(Photographs on right)

4 red-legged or common partridges,
ready for cooking
Salt and pepper
½ cup/125 ml olive oil
1 onion, finely chopped
5 cloves of garlic, halved
2 large carrots, thinly sliced
½ cup/125 ml white wine
½ cup/125 ml white wine vinegar
½ tbsp black peppercorns
2 bay leaves
2 cloves
2 sprigs of thyme
2 sprigs of oregano
A pinch of sugar
½ tbsp hot paprika powder
Lemon slices and a few stalks of parsley

Wash the partridges and pat them dry; then rub salt and pepper into them, inside and out. Tie into shape with kitchen twine.

Heat half the oil in a deep pan and brown the partridges until they are golden on all sides. Then remove from the pan and put to one side. Brown the onion, garlic, and carrots in the pan juices. Pour in the wine and vinegar, then add the spices. Cover and simmer for 10 minutes. Then put the partridges back in the pan, cover and simmer for about 45 minutes on a low heat. Remove from the stove top and leave the partridges to cool in the stock.

Then take the partridges out of the stock and remove the kitchen twine. Place the partridges in a clay casserole. Strain off the stock and pour it over the partridges. If necessary, add a little more white wine, until the partridges are completely covered. Pour the remaining oil on top. Leave to marinate in a cool place for at least one day. Before serving, cut the partridges in half and pour a little sauce over them. Garnish with lemon slices and parsley.

Variation: The partridges can also be heated slowly in the stock and served hot.

A BIRD WHICH BINDS A NATION

The red-legged partridge *(perdiz)* is honored almost as a sacred animal in Spain. In the Middle Ages, it was set before kings, princes, and church dignitaries on very special occasions. Painters and poets have put everything into works inspired by this relative of the common partridge, and a popular proverb points out that a meal which includes red-legged partridges is the epitome of happiness: "*Fueron felices y comieron perdices*" – "They were happy and they had red-legged partridges to eat."

For *perdiz en escabeche*, red-legged or common partridges are used with the ingredients for a spicy marinade.

Bind the birds into shape with twine. Then roast them in hot oil until they are golden brown on all sides.

Remove the partridges from the oil; then brown the onion, carrots, and garlic in the pan.

When the vegetables have been well browned, pour in the white wine and a good wine vinegar.

Next add the bay leaves, herbs, and other seasonings. Leave the stock to simmer for a while.

Add the partridges and cook them thoroughly. The birds can be kept in the stock for several days.

SHEPHERDS' FARE

If the farmer's wife created a "take it slowly cuisine" in her home by braising vegetables and legumes, the shepherds' tradition can be thought of as "fast food." On long journeys with their flocks, they took only a few provisions in their baggage. But living off the land in this way did not mean they had to do without delicious dishes. The *gazpachos manchegos* is a kind of game stew on a dough base, and it marked the first decisive step away from the subsistence peasant fare of bread, garlic, and olive oil toward a cuisine that is much more refined.

The name *gazpachos* comes from the word *caspa*, which dates from pre-Roman times. It means a fragment or leftover, and that is precisely what is involved in this higgledy-piggledy stew. Strictly speaking, the dish mentioned in *Don Quixote* under the name *galianos* is a soup made from *pan ázimo*, a thin, flat round made of unleavened bread, which is also referred to simply as *torta*. Incidentally, the high priest of the culinary arts, Nestor Luján, insists on the plural, in order to distinguish the *gazpachos manchegos* from the Andalusian *gazpacho*.

Gazpachos manchegos is a winter dish from the Albacetes mountains, which form the boundary between La Mancha, eastern Spain, and Extremadura. So imagine the scene: the tepid sunshine is dissolving the mist above the slope, which is overgrown with stone oaks. The shepherd's dog retrieves the hare or the red-legged partridge the man has shot. The warming fire heats up the ground, while the shepherd sits on a tanned sheepskin and prepares the round flat bread made from wheat flour, salt, and a little water (but without any yeast!). It must be five hands wide and very thin – the old rule was "no thicker than a coin." Then the shepherd rakes back the embers and lays the bread on the hot earth before covering it with embers again. At least, that's the way it used to be. Nowadays, anyone in a hurry buys a *torta* in the supermarket. The basic ingredients of the stew are paprika and tomatoes, oil and garlic, mixed together in the *gazpachera*, the shallow pan which is a standard feature in every shepherd's pack. What else goes into the mixture depends on the luck of the hunter. It might be a hare or quail, a pigeon or hen. A few recipes also include mushrooms. Finally, a finely sliced *torta* is added. A second piece of bread serves as a plate onto which the *gazpachos* is placed. Alternatively, it can be used instead of a knife and fork to scoop the food straight from the pan.

Gazpachos manchegos is known all over Spain, as is *migas de pastor*, which is made from breadcrumbs and bacon (see pages 88 ff.). But La Mancha also has quite a number of other satisfying shepherds'

When the shepherds roam the land with their flocks, food has to be simple. All the shepherd has in his bag is garlic, flour, and oil. But these ingredients can be combined with game to produce satisfying dishes.

dishes, which in earlier times could easily be prepared out in the open:

• **Morteruelo**

This inspired combination of the hunt and the slaughterhouse is mentioned in documents as far back as the 11th century. As the name implies, the ingredients are crushed in the mortar *(mortero)* and a kind of *pâté* is created, based on pig's liver. To this are added hare, partridge, ham, and bacon. It can be eaten hot or cold.

• **Gachas manchegas**

In La Mancha, the thick porridge which people in other rural areas of Spain prepare using wheat flour traditionally consists of water and *harina de almortas*, blue vetch flour. To this are added bacon, pig's cheek, or some other pork, and possibly also sausages and spices. If strained pig's liver is added, the dish is called *gachas de matanza*. For *gachamigas manchegas*, pieces of bread are used as the base, and cooked in water with salt.

• **Guisado de trigo (guiso de trigo)**

This stew, which is also popular in Andalusia and Murcia, represents the ultimate in simplification. The name simply means wheat stew. The whole wheat germs, cooked with chickpeas, vegetables, and knuckle of pork, replace the bread. In earlier times, the shepherds would add wild vegetables and meadow herbs.

Gazpachos manchegos
La Mancha shepherd's stew

For the bread:
2¼ cups/250 g flour
A pinch of salt
Flour for work surface
Oil for baking sheet

For the stew:
½ rabbit or hare
1 partridge
Salt and pepper
2 cups/500 ml olive oil
6 cloves of garlic
1 onion, chopped
1 green bell pepper, cubed
2 sprigs of thyme
1 bay leaf
2 large, ripe beef tomatoes, peeled and cubed
1 tbsp mild paprika powder
A few threads of saffron

Sift the flour into a large bowl. Add the salt and ½ cup/125 ml of water. Knead everything into a smooth dough, adding a little more water if necessary to make the dough more flexible.

Divide the dough into 3 pieces, and form each piece into a ball; then roll out on the floured work surface into rounds about ⅛ inch/ 2 mm thick. Place the pieces of bread on an oiled baking sheet and bake them in a preheated oven at 355 °F/180 °C for about 25 minutes; then leave to cool on a wire rack. Break 2 pieces up small before they become hard.

Wash the rabbit and the partridge, then pat them thoroughly dry. Divide them into portions and then season with salt and pepper. Heat the oil either in an iron pan or an earthenware casserole and brown the meat well on all sides with the garlic. Take out the garlic cloves and cut them in half. Add the onion and bell pepper to the meat, then the thyme and the bay leaf, and briefly brown them all. Mix in the cubed tomatoes, the paprika powder, and the saffron and cook them together for 5 minutes. Then pour on just enough water to cover the meat. Add the halved garlic cloves and simmer for about 30 minutes on medium heat. Finally add the broken-up pieces of bread and then let the stew simmer for about another 5–10 minutes, until the bread has softened and the stew has thickened well. Leave the stew to stand for 10 minutes before taking to the table. It is traditionally served on round, flat pieces of bread.

The stew for *gazpachos manchegos* usually consists of rabbit and partridge. The meat is cut into relatively small pieces and seared in a pan.

Onions, garlic, and a bay leaf (above) provide the right seasoning for the *gazpachos manchegos*. The finished stew is served on a round of unleavened bread (right).

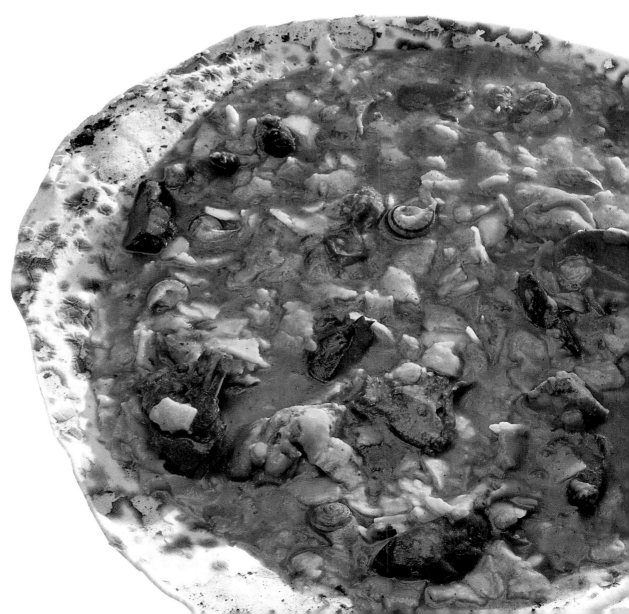

For hundreds of years, the shepherds of La Mancha have been making tasty *manchego* cheeses from the fresh, unpasteurized milk of the local sheep.

When the milk has been thickened with rennet and the mass has been broken up into curd, the whey is squeezed out – traditionally with linen cloths.

MANCHEGO CHEESE

Archeological finds such as sheep bones and pressing molds indicate that sheep-rearing and cheesemaking were going on in La Mancha during the Iron Age. In later times, the tasty Spanish sheep cheeses were prized by the Greeks and Romans. Despite this, they were for a long time merely the by-product from sheep-rearing. The animals were important for their wool, for this was a significant source of finance for the crown. When the Arabs conquered Spain, they brought with them from North Africa a breed of sheep which was adapted to desert climates. In the harsh landscape of La Mancha, that for a long time was the frontier country between the Christian kingdoms and the Muslim caliphate, the flocks of both sides flourished and interbred.

Cheese was originally only something for the shepherds to eat on their travels. Like the *pan candeal*, the typical wheat bread, sheep cheese was tasty and it kept for a long time. It was not until the nomadic way of life came to an end that La Mancha cheese also became economically important. In 1836, following the dissolution of the "Honorable Councils of Breeders" (*Mesta*, see page 271), modern animal husbandry replaced the nomadic economy. From that time onward, the economic importance of dairy products also increased at a rapid rate. Countless types of cheese were developed in many small enterprises.

Culinary high priest Xavier Domingo complains of the restrictive policies of modern authorities, which have long disregarded the interests of small local producers. Indeed, 20 varieties of Spanish cheese are threatened by the unchecked importation of cheap mass-produced goods. But the *Queso Manchego* has pulled through, and since 1984 it has carried the seal of the protected denomination of origin, the *Denominación de Origen (D.O.)*. Of the 20 varieties of Spanish cheese with a D.O., it is the best known. It was the consumption of fine *manchegos* which first created a new cheese culture in Spain. It educated people's palates, leading to the high level of demand existing today, which has promoted the survival of countless other types of cheese made with milk from sheep, goats, or cows. The basis for genuine *Manchego* cheese is the pure milk of the sheep of La Mancha, a robust breed that can exist on harsh pastures and in very dry conditions. 670,000 animals yield about 11.7 million US gallons (45 million liters) of milk a year, which is high in fat and aromatic. 80 % of this milk goes into making *Manchego* cheese which amounts to about 7700 tons (7000 tonnes) of cheese.

The fresh cheese mass is compressed in molds, which nowadays are made of plastic, until the cheese has reached the desired density.

The finished and formed cheese "loaves" are immersed in brine for two days. They are then dried off and taken to the cellar to mature.

The milk is heated and then coagulated using rennet. In earlier times animal rennet was used for this, but now it is usually obtained from vegetables. After being drained, the mass is formed and squeezed until the whey has separated out. The resulting curd is shaped into a cylinder and immersed in brine for 48 hours. It then matures for at least 60 days at a temperature of between 46 and 53 °F (8 and 12 °C) and an atmospheric humidity of between 80 and 85 percent. Around 15 percent of *Manchego* production comes from manually operated dairies. Cheeses with the *artesanal* label must be made from unpasteurized milk. Nowadays, of course, the majority of *Manchego* products is manufactured from pasteurized milk in industrial dairies, in steel and plastic containers. One thing common to all *Manchegos* is the logo depicting a flower, together with the herringbone markings on the sides – a pattern which in earlier times was left behind by the esparto grass used for pressing the cheese, and which is now left behind by the molds. A *Manchego* cheese weighs up to 7¾ pounds (3.5 kilograms), and has a fat content of about 50 percent. The *Manchego* has a hard rind, which can vary from pale yellow to greenish-black. The cheese is marketed at three stages of maturation:

• *Fresco*: This is how very young cheese is described, which is put for sale as soon as the

minimum maturation period of 60 days has been completed. The interior of the cheese is a pale ivory color, and still very pliant and soft.

• *Semicurado*: Cheese which has been maturing for up to six months if from artisan production, and between two and four months if from an industrial dairy. It is already decidedly compact.

• *Curado*: The mature cheese described in this way must have matured for more than six months. It is now a hard cutting cheese.

Naturally, the only obligatory limit for the dairies is that the cheeses must have been matured for at least the minimum period. Thus manufacturers offer a large number of different grades of *Manchego* for sale, and it can be a gastronomic adventure to discover them. *Añejo* (ancient) is the name given to a cheese which has been matured for a very long time: seven, twelve, or even twenty-four months.

The ivory-yellowish sheep cheese tastes slightly sharp and full-flavored, and more or less piquant depending on the length of maturation. The Spaniards like to eat it best on its own as a tapa, since *Manchego* disdains any accompaniment except a full-bodied red wine or a dry sherry. As a dessert, of course, it is also popular with figs, grapes, apples, or *carne de membrillo* (preserved quince pulp).

In earlier times, the pattern on the *Manchego* came from esparto grass baskets. Nowadays it's from plastic molds.

A good *Manchego* needs no accompaniment. When mature, it should be eaten on its own.

Honey sweet

Gorse and umbrella pines cling to wild, jagged slopes. The sun has burned the coarse grass brown. But suddenly a delightful valley opens up with a tinkling stream – such are the stark opposites of a romantic landscape. In Alcarria, at the northern edge of La Mancha, beekeeping is often the only productive way to make use of the land. Hundreds of bee colonies make Spain's most famous honey, *Miel de la Alcarria*, from the flowers of rosemary, thyme, and lavender. There is scarcely a village in this area which does not offer its own honey for sale. No visitor goes home without a jar of it, and every restaurant has its own specialty: cheese with honey, perhaps, or honey with nuts.

So it should come as no surprise that fine confectionery made with honey has also developed in La Mancha. This is due to a combination of nature and history, for it was the Arabs who left behind their skill in combining honey and almonds. Marzipan used to be made here with honey as well (see box), as did the *alajú* from Cuenca, a kind of nougat served between two wafers, and made from almonds, honey, and figs.

This goes well with a taste of the local liqueur: *Resolí*. It was traditionally made by tavern-keepers and pastry cooks, and there was fierce competition between them at Easter time when the liqueur was in great demand. But modern industrial companies also produce versions of the drink that include coffee, brandy or aniseed schnapps, cinnamon, caramelized sugar or honey, and orange rind extracts.

Torrijas
Sweet fritters

6½ tbsp/100 g sugar
1 cup/250 ml lukewarm milk
8 slices of stale white bread
3 eggs
1 cup/250 ml oil
1 tsp ground cinnamon

Stir half the sugar into the lukewarm milk. Leave the slices of bread to soak in the mixture for 10 minutes, turning them over once. Beat the eggs and dip the slices of bread in them. Fry them in batches in hot oil until golden brown on both sides. Then remove the slices and drain on paper towels; keep them warm until all the slices have been browned. Mix the remaining sugar with the cinnamon. Sprinkle this mixture over the bread slices before serving. *Torrijas* can also be served with honey.

Marzipan from Toledo

Toledo, Venice, and the Orient all have rival claims to have invented marzipan. The Arabs brought to the Iberian peninsula a sweet mixture of almonds and honey, which they are thought to have called *mautha-ban* or *mahsaban*. On the other hand, the Venetians like to say that *marzipane*, the "bread of Saint Marcus" was named in honor of the patron saint of the city in the lagoon. However, there are also different stories: During the reconquest, at the battle of Navas de Tolosa in the year 1212, it is said that the nuns of the San Clemente convent took care of the Christian soldiers. They are supposed to have ground up their stores of almonds in mortars and then kneaded them together with sugar to create emergency rations. This type of bread *(pan)* produced with a pestle *(maza)* is supposed to have given rise to the name *maza-pan*. At all events, the sweet almond food was very popular in central Spain in the Middle Ages, and even healers appreciated its effects. Marzipan could make bitter medicines taste a little more palatable, and it was also popular as a tonic to counter weakness and illness. In 1613, a Toledo confectioner, Gaspar de Atienza, laid down the rules for creating genuine marzipan. The main ingredients at that time were almonds, sugar, and honey. Even today, the finest varieties of Toledo marzipan consist only of sugar and almonds. Cheaper kinds may also contain rice flour and potato starch. Anyone making marzipan at home may also add some egg white in order to make the mixture more flexible and malleable.

Toledo

Bizcochos borrachos
Tipsy sponge cakes

Syrup:
½ cup/125 g sugar
2 tbsp honey
⅛ tsp ground cinnamon
Rind of 1 orange, grated
2½ tbsp/40 ml brandy
Scant ½ cup/100 ml sherry

Sponge:
¾ cup/100 g flour
4 eggs, separated
6½ tbsp/100 g sugar
Ground cinnamon for sprinkling over sponge cakes

Boil the sugar together with the honey, cinnamon, and orange rind, stirring the mixture constantly. Remove from the stove top and stir in the brandy and sherry; leave to cool. Sift the flour. Beat the egg yolks with the sugar syrup to a thick cream in a bain-marie. Beat the egg whites until very stiff and pour over the egg yolk cream. Add the flour and carefully blend the mixture with a whisk. Spread the mixture over a baking sheet lined with wax paper and bake in a preheated oven at 430 °F/220 °C for about 10 minutes, until it is golden brown. Turn out the finished sponge onto a moist dish towel. Peel off the wax paper and spread the sponge with the sugar syrup. Sprinkle with cinnamon and cut into squares measuring about 2 x 2 inches/5 x 5 centimeters, then serve.

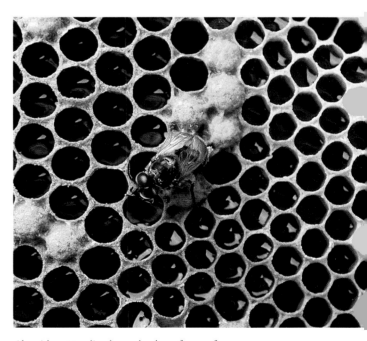

Alcarria's outstanding honey has been famous for centuries. But sweet gold flows into honeypots in other regions as well. Orange blossom honey comes from Valencia, eucalyptus, chestnut, and heather honey from Galicia; licorice honey from the Catalan Pyrenees; and gorse and tree heather honey from Tenerife.

Alajú from Cuenca is "a dessert fit for a king." It is made from almonds, figs, and honey.

Before the conquest of the Americas, buttercake was made with honey. Today sugar is used.

Nicanores are puff pastry cakes usually sprinkled with large amounts of confectioners' sugar.

La Mancha wine

The following question regularly comes up on the paper for the most difficult wine examination in the world: "What is the most commonly grown white grape variety in the world?" Anyone who wishes to be accepted into the illustrious group of the Masters of Wine will fail if he or she chooses Chardonnay or Riesling. The answer is: Airén.

This grape is grown mainly in the La Mancha region. The area, which even the Arabs once considered as desolate, now contains the largest continuous wine-producing area in the world – approximately 1540 square miles (400,000 hectares). The legally protected area of origin covered by **D.O. La Mancha** accounts for almost half of all the vines grown in Spain. It also produces half of all Spanish wines, which until a few years ago were considered, at best, as only reasonable table wines.

In order to accommodate the extreme variations in temperature on the high Castilian plateau, the gnarled plants stay close to the sandy, chalky soil. The Airén grape yields light white wine which can be fruity or dry. In addition, Cencibel, which is related to the famous Tempranillo variety from the Rioja region, and Garnacha supply soft red wines of great power. The sun is nearly always shining here, and ensures that the wines have an alcohol content of up to 15 percent.

But this does not please everybody. The bureaucrats of the European Union have determined that there is too much table wine being produced and are asking the Spaniards to root out thousands of hectares of vines. Apart from the hardships this might bring for the growers, this would also be an ecological catastrophe, for it would leave the dry soil at the mercy of erosion.

In northern Europe, over half a million tons of sugar are mixed with grape must every year just to produce wine. This process is called chaptalization. It is absolutely legal, and its use is one argument deployed by critics as evidence of the power of the sugar lobby. But the winemakers of La Mancha see absolutely no reason why the consumer should have to drink a wine which can be fermented only artificially. Where they live, the sun does that all on its own. Moreover, the people here have been trying for years to replace table wine, which is becoming less popular, with carefully structured wines of certified origin and quality, stored in oak casks. A lot of effort has been put into modernization in the last few years, both in the vineyards and in the wine cellars. And even if most of the country's gourmets still remain loyal to their favorite vintages from La Rioja, Penedès, or Duero, a Señorío de Guadianeja from Manzanares can be seen as quite capable of measuring up to them.

La Mancha's wine history developed in the shadow of old fortresses (above), and many *bodegas* still have cellars dating from Roman times (background).

La Mancha's soils are poor. Those vines which flourish are those that can withstand extremes of weather. The most common grape is the Airén.

In earlier times, La Mancha produced mainly low-price table wine. But recently producers have begun to develop vintages which mature in the cask.

The Marquis from Toledo

Carlos Falcó, Marquis of Griñon, is a cosmopolitan. This aristocrat, who was born in Seville, plants almost nothing but French vines on his property at Valdepusa near Toledo. He was already experimenting with Cabernet Sauvignon when this was still considered a heresy in Spain. He continually takes his experiments further, and nowadays his products, Marqués de Griñon and Dominio Valdepusa, are among the best Spanish wines – even without a regional appellation. Falcó plants types of vine with a potential that can reach full development in the extreme climatic conditions of La Mancha. One big surprise was his full-bodied red wine made from the Syrah grape, which is native to the Rhône Valley.

Wine-producing in La Mancha

D.O. La Mancha

For a long time, this area – the largest winemaking area in the world with a denomination of origin – produced simple white table wine. Important varieties of grape are the white Airén and the red Garnacha and Cencibel.In recent years, cooperatives have made big investments in modern equipment, and nowadays they also markete, well-balanced, red wines with a powerful aroma, some of them natured in the cask. Despite intensive efforts, most of the output is still sold from the wood, and some is also exported as a low-cost table wine.

D.O. Valdepeñas

Valdepeñas, which nestles within the southern part of the La Mancha wine-producing area like a kind of enclave (see map), is creating first-class vintages that mature in the cask. The low productivity of the dry soil, and the frequent sunshine create good grapes. In Valdepeñas too, the winemakers are turning away from cask wine to produce powerful but very soft red bottled wines from the Cencibel grape. Apart from the popular white wines, the traditional Tinto de Valdepeñasis is made, a red wines mixed with white grapes (which may no longer be described as *clarete*).

D.O. Almansa

Located on the border with Valencia, this D.O. mainly uses grapes from eastern Spain: the red Monastrell and Garnacha and the white Merseguera. Although close to the Mediterranean, the climate here is still continental and harsh, and the vineyards' height of around 2300 feet (700 meters) makes for correct, light red wines.

D.O. Méntrida

This is still a little-known wine area, the red wines of which are very powerful, and consist of Garnacha and Tempranillo. The quality of these reds hase risen, due to new investments. Recently, some soft and juicy Cabernet Sauvignons have also begun to make a name for themselves.

D.O. Mondéjar

This small region east of Alcalá de Henares produces mainly thick and decidedly rugged red wines made from Cencibel and Cabernet Sauvignon, which are marketed young by the comparatively few bottling firms. The white grapes Malvar, Macabeo, and Torrontés are also cultivated here.

D.O. Ribera del Júcar

This D.O. region is named after the river and lies on a plateau in southern Cuenca province. Only red wines are produced here, they are light and fruity. The grape varietres grown here are Tempranillo, Garnacha, Cabernet Sauvignon, Syrah, and also Bobal.

D.O. Manchuela

This D.O. area in the south-west covers parts of Albacete and Cuenca province. Its proximity to the Mediterranean brings fresh winds to the region, which helps to moderate the extreme climate of the southern Meseta. Dry soil and low productivity make for powerful red wines pressed from the Bobal, Tempranillo, Garnacha, Cabernet Sauvignon, and Merlot varieties as well as the lesser-known Moravia Dulce.

D.O. Dominio de Valdepusa

In 2002, this *Finca* near the Montes de Toledo covering 104 acres (42 hectares) was graded the status of denomination of origin. Since the 1980´s, Carlos Falcó has been producing high-quality wines known as Marqués de Griñón, pressed according to modern standards of viticulture and wine production.

D.O. Finca Elez

This *finca* with its own denomination of origin lies in the mountains of Albacete and is owned by Manuel Manzaneque. The wines pressed from his 94 acres (38 hectares) of vineyards carry his name, they are modern, fruity white and red wines predominantly made from international grape varieties.

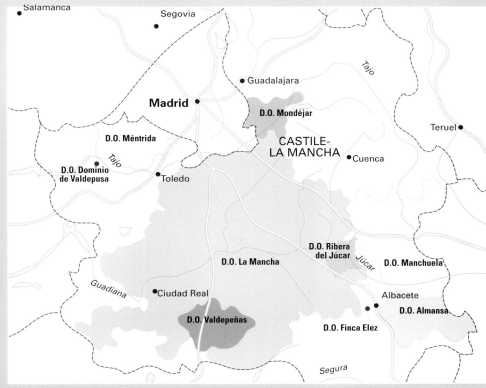

EXTREMADURA

David Schwarzwälder

EXTREMADURA

Small red chili peppers, grown by the farmers of La Vera, bring color and spice into the daily lives of the people – and into the cooking pots of Spain.

Extremadura – extremely hard? This seems the obvious translation for anyone traveling through the arid southeast of Extremadura, which is very sparsely populated. But it is not at all correct. The name derives from *extremo del Duero* – the no-man's-land on the south bank of the Duero river. During the reconquest of Spain, this formed the boundary between the Christians and the Muslims, which moved farther south as the Moors retreated. The conquerors of the New World – Hernán Cortés, Núñez de Balboa, and the Pizarro brothers – inaugurated an age of military glory for the region from which they came. The soldiers brought back more than gold and silver. Potatoes, corn, tomatoes, and paprika also found their way into Extremadura, thus enriching a cuisine which had evolved from Christian, Jewish, and Moorish eating habits. The landscape of Extremadura, characterized by extensive cork and stone oak forests, has scarcely altered for hundreds of years. Only a million people live here, in an area larger than Switzerland. However, the region holds many surprises – not confined to the unspoilt riches of nature. The towns and villages between the central mountains and the Sierra Morena have something to offer to connoisseurs of both cuisine and culture. The palatial architecture of Cáceres and the festivals at the Guadalupe monastery would be major features of the cultural landscape of Europe if only they were not so far off the beaten track. Extremadura is making only slow progress toward relative prosperity. Some gentle tourism, together with an agriculture which is more strongly orientated toward quality, are slowly changing the sterotype that this region is the poorhouse of the Spanish nation.

Against this background, it quickly becomes apparent that this is not an area for fanciful cooking. Over the centuries, the gastronomy of Extremadura has been dominated by the Iberian pig, lamb, and goat. Historically speaking, the local cuisine can be described as austere, or ascetic. But it can also be seen in a positive light: the clear simplicity of most of the recipes is as free and open as the boundless expanses of the landscape. The centerpieces of this cuisine are stews based on lamb, goat's meat, pork, and shepherds' recipes based on bread and vegetables. It is not so well known that the people of Extremadura have a passion for trout and other freshwater fish. And even if the gastronomic traditions of the region do not impress by their elegance or ease of preparation, they can still offer a selection of recipes which are richly varied and sometimes very original.

Opposite: Every spring, when the rain makes the barren pastures bloom, the no-man's-land of Extremadura can be seen in a completely new light.

The Iberian pigs feed mainly on acorns from the cork tree and the stone oak.

THE DEHESA

More than any other landscape, the Dehesa epitomizes the character and the culture of Extremadura. The light forests of stone oak and cork trees, with less than 15 trees per acre (35 trees per hectare), cover a large part of the provinces of Cáceres and Badajoz, as well as some adjacent areas in western Andalusia, southern Castile, and La Mancha. The Iberian pig is at home here, and the Mediterranean woods also provide shelter and nourishment for many migratory birds including flamingos, storks, and eagles, as well as for 55 other animal species threatened with extinction. Since ham from Iberian pigs has now acquired the status of a luxury product, it has once again become profitable for the inhabitants of this region to rear these animals, and they are again making their contribution to the preservation of the Dehesa. Iberian pigs are very mobile and provide an ecologically acceptable way of keeping the enormous wooded areas uniformly tidy. The animals do this by grubbing for roots, which keeps the undergrowth down, and their manure also ensures the continued growth of plants and trees. For its part, the forest regulates the numbers of animals which can be reared through its restricted food supplies. In recent years, Spanish nature conservation organizations have been making ever greater efforts to protect this area of the original Spanish landscape from destructive intensive cultivation.

Background: The Iberian pig's preferred habitat is the light Mediterranean forests of the Dehesa.

Ham which is intended to become genuine *jamón ibérico* spends at least two weeks under a layer of salt.

Because most (not all!) Iberian pigs have black trotters, the ham is also known as *pata negra*.

Jamón ibérico spends many months maturing in cool cellars, to develop its full-bodied taste.

THE IBERIAN PIG

It is undemanding, stolid, and placid, and it copes equally well with both extreme heat and harsh winters. *Cerdo ibérico*, the Iberian pig, is a semi-domesticated breed which, over thousands of years, has adjusted best to the climate of the Spanish south and southwest. The ham from this species is legendary, and as far back as the sixteenth century there was a market each year in Plasencia on San Andrés day (November 30), when 40,000 Iberian pigs changed hands. Even then the *pata negra*, the black trotter, was considered as a mark of the breed, and to this day the high-quality aromatic ham from the Iberian pig, *jamón ibérico*, is also known simply as *pata negra*.

The black pig lives in the *dehesa*, a lightly forested area dotted with evergreen stone oaks and cork trees. Most of this region lies in Extremadura, but it also extends to parts of western Castile and northern Andalusia (see box opposite). The animal can get by for long periods with little to eat. In spite of this, it will rapidly develop fatty tissue which permeates its entire body and leads to finely marbled meat. The Iberian pig roams far and wide over its grazing areas feeding on grasses, herbs, and roots. It frequently also eats olives, which gives an additional aroma to the meat. In the summer, when the Dehesa can become very arid, the pigs are also fed grain. The final fattening period (*montanera*) starts in the fall when the acorns (*bellotas*), the staple diet of the Iberian pig, are dropping from the trees. The animal now develops an astonishing appetite, and puts on about 130 to 176 pounds (60 to 80 kilograms) within a few months. The acorns give the meat a particularly aromatic taste.

PREPARING THE HAM

The pigs are slaughtered in winter, at the age of 14 to 18 months, at a maximum weight of 397 pounds (180 kilograms). It takes a lot of time, patience, and skill to create a genuine *jamón ibérico*. For the quality of the *pata negra* ham is determined by more than the animal's breeding, what it eats, and the climate. The maturation process also plays a role, perhaps the main role. The most important centers for the maturation of Iberian pig products are all in western Spain. In Extremadura, the villages of Jerez de los Caballeros, Fregenal de la Sierra, Oliva de la Frontera, and Higuera la Real in Badajoz province have all made a name for themselves. The ham-producing villages of Guijuelo and Candelario are in the southern part of the Castilian province of Salamanca. In Andalusia a ham with an almost legendary status is produced in Jabugo, in the Sierra de Aracena. A little farther to the east, in the province of Córdoba, a number of small and medium producers are concentrated around the Pedroches Valley. All these places are in the mountains where there is plenty of fresh air, and are therefore very suitable for drying fine hams in the open air.

After slaughter, the rear legs of the pigs are drawn back into a V-shape, and the animals are completely drained of blood. The meat is then salted, spending up to 14 days sealed off under a layer of salt (depending on the animal's weight and the external temperature). The meat is rearranged regularly during this period. The higher (and therefore cooler) the location, the less salt is needed. Finally, the precious hams are washed, and then kept in cool storerooms for four to six weeks, at a temperature of 43–46°F (6–8° C). Here the meat dries out and sets.

It is only now that the real maturation process begins. The hams are suspended from ropes or hooks in special drying halls (*secaderos*). The amount of fresh air supplied is regulated as required through flaps. As the temperature rises in spring, the hams begin to "sweat." They lose about a third of their weight, and slowly develop their aromas. The maturation process is rounded off in cool storage cellars (*bodegas*), where the hams are suspended for a further period of up to 14 months. It is during this time that the hams can be marked by the "noble rot" *Penicillium roquefortis*, which gives the meat other very distinctive flavors.

Toward the end of the maturation period, the *calador* (tester) checks the quality of the ham with the (*cala*) or a probe made of horn or bone. He jabs this into various places on the ham. He removes a little meat. He then decides, on the basis of the aroma, whether the meat has attained the desired quality. A good Iberian ham can be matured for 24 months (or even 30 months, in exceptional cases) before it is put on the market. The weight is usually between about 13 and 18 pounds (6–8 kilograms).

Other excellent products obtained from the Iberian pig are *chorizo* and *lomo* (see p. 344 ff.). There are also rare but outstanding specialties, such as a sausage made from the meat of the head. Sometimes fresh loin of Iberian pig can also be found in high-class butcher's stores, and the fresh meat is often prepared in impressively imaginative ways.

QUALITY GRADES FOR IBERIAN HAM

- **bellota:** Ham from pigs which are at least 75 percent Iberian by breed, and which have put on at least 40 percent of their live weight under free-range conditions, feeding exclusively on acorns and vegetation from the Dehesa.
- **recebo:** Ham from Iberian pigs which have also been fed on grain during the final fattening process (a maximum of 30 percent).
- **pienso** (also known as **cebo** or **campo**: Ham from Iberian pigs which have been fattened exclusively on grain.

Jamón ibérico from black pigs is finely marbled with fat and tiny white crystal inclusions. These can be traced back to the fact that a large part of the mast is made up of acorns. The finest of all hams is best eaten on its own as a tapa.

IBERIAN HAM

Iberian ham is one of the most famous Spanish delicacies, and it is as rare as it is expensive, due to the lengthy and costly production process. The meat is deep red in color and develops an intensely nutty flavor at room temperature. It should be shot through with a fine marbling of fat, which must be soft and also yield when pressed in with the fingers. Because the pigs have been fed on acorns, little white points also often occur in the meat on a ham. These are due to crystals of the amino acid tyrosine and are not harmful in any way. They can even be taken as a guarantee of a genuine *bellota* ham. In Spain, Iberian ham is usually sold just as it is when it comes out of the maturation cellar, namely with its fine coating of "noble rot," which is considered to be a particular mark of quality. However, since the fungus is not acceptable to some consumers, washed Iberian hams are also sold.

THE GREAT ART OF CUTTING IBERIAN HAM

Cutting Iberian ham is something of a ritual act in Spain. The guests at a tapas bar may sometimes have to wait for the chef to do it, since he will not let anyone else cut the precious meat. In Extremadura and Castile, there are even competitions to find the best ham cutter.

A whole ham should be stored after purchase, for a period not exceeding three months – suspended in a cool place, but never stored in the refrigerator. To cut it up, a *jamonera* is used, a special piece of equipment made of metal or wood. If the ham is intended for immediate consumption, it is clamped into the *jamonera* in the classic way, with the trotter facing upward. If the leg is not going to be eaten immediately, the ham should be clamped in the *jamonera* with the trotter facing downward and "opened up" along the narrowest side of the ham. This part dries out most rapidly, and so should be carved first.

First the rind and the excess fat are removed with a hefty knife. A layer of fat as thick as a finger is left on the sides to preserve the meat. With a long, narrow, and flexible knife, wafer-thin slices are now cut off, following both the grain of the fibers and the shape of the bone. A dew-like film of sweat forms on fresh-cut ham, on the surface of the slices, which provides an indication of the creamy consistency of the meat. Each cut should start at a point covered by the ham's own fat.

When ham is bought in smaller quantities, it is recommended that the butcher should be asked to cut the meat into very thin slices. This should then be kept in the refrigerator in plastic wrap.

About half an hour before the ham is to be consumed, the packaging should be removed and the ham should be allowed to "breathe" at room temperature, so that it can be allowed to develop its full flavor. The noble Iberian ham is best served as a tapa, accompanied only by a little white bread – and should never be served too cold.

An Iberian ham is one of the finest delicacies that Spain has to offer.

To cut the noble meat, the ham is clamped into a *jamonera*.

First the rind is removed on one side with the help of a hefty knife.

Excess fat is also cut off – it is very useful for cooking purposes.

Iberian ham is always cut into wafer-thin slices because this is the best way to bring out its fine flavor. It is served with a little bread and requires nothing else.

A knife with a flexible blade is used to cut the ham into slices.

Beginning on the narrowest side, the expert always cuts parallel to the bone.

Then the ham is turned in the frame. Once again, the rind is removed first.

Part of the fat is cut off so that the meat is revealed.

Only a limited amount of fat is cut off, to ensure that the ham cannot dry out quickly.

As far as possible, large slices are always cut from the haunch.

The rind remains as long as possible on the sides which have not yet been cut.

The nearer to the bone, the more precisely parallel to it the cutting must be.

No more beautiful big slices of ham can be cut. Now the detailed work begins.

The rind and the fat are particularly thick on this part of the haunch.

It certainly requires some strength to remove the surplus fat here.

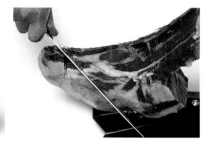

The interior of the meat is shot through with a great deal of fat near the joint.

Even when cut parallel to the bone, the pieces are smaller here.

Care is required now – the knife must not contact the bone.

The meat around the hip is removed with very great care.

The fat is kept for substantial stews, or else for roasting meat.

The parts of the meat which lie to the side of the hip are now cut up further.

Gourmets also appreciate the small pieces, since fat makes the meat juicy.

The meat in the deeper layers shows whether the ham is thoroughly mature.

The meat on the haunch has been neatly removed, but the process is not over yet.

The meat along the bone is now cut off, all the way down to the trotter.

A little meat is concealed here under a thick layer of rind and fat.

The meat from these thin areas of the ham is always the most thoroughly matured.

When all the meat has been removed, the bone can still be used to make tasty stock.

Various types of pepper are cultivated to make powdered spices in La Vera. The round peppers (above, right) produce light orange, mild paprika powder *(pimentón dulce)*, while the elongated dark-red peppers (above, left) yield medium hot powder *(pimentón agridulce)*. Hot paprika powder *(pimentón picante)* is obtained from various elongated types of pepper.

Pimenton

The sovereigns were struck dumb with surprise. Christopher Columbus brought paprika back to Spain with him from his second voyage to America, and introduced it to their Catholic Majesties Ferdinand and Isabella in the monastery of Guadalupe. The biting sharpness of some peppers almost took the noble pair's breath away. But that did not prevent the monks of the monastery from passing on the new vegetable to the brothers of their order, so that the peppers spread initially throughout Extremadura and then over the entire country.

However, it was not until the 17th century that *pimentón*, the crushed powder from the small red spicy pepper, began its triumphal progress through Spanish cuisine. A hundred years later, the traveller Baron von Bourgoing wrote: "The Spaniards like strong spices: pepper, tomato sauce, and hot paprika powder, which adds color and fire to many dishes." Even now, paprika spice is wrongly referred to in many languages as "Spanish pepper."

Today, the finest paprika powder in Spain is made in northern Extremadura, not far from the place where the first plants bloomed in the monastery garden 500 years ago. The home of the famous *pimentón de La Vera* is the delightful area around La Vera in northern Extremadura, the most fertile part of central Spain. The spicy peppers find ideal conditions on the low-lying alluvial soils around the Tiétar River. The climate is mild and there is adequate precipitation. Here the farmers cultivate different varieties of the paprika genus *Capsicum annum*, each with varying degrees of pungency. This factor is determined by a substance known as capsaicin, which is absent in the delicate, mild peppers, just as it is in the bell peppers grown as vegetables.

The farmers sow the pepper seeds in March. The harvest begins in September and lasts until November. Entire families go out into the fields, sometimes assisted by seasonal workers, to harvest the little red peppers. It is a wearisome manual task. Buildings equipped with little skylights are scattered around the edges of the fields: the drying houses.

It is not until the fresh peppers are smoke-dried that any real skill comes in. The amount of oakwood required must be five times as great as the amount of paprika powder to be obtained. No other wood can be used if the genuine *pimentón de La Vera* is to have its typical taste. The peppers are placed whole on a wooden grid at a height of just under 8 feet (2.5 meters). Then the fire is lit. The farmer has to go into the smoking house (*secadero*) once a day, to turn over the layer of peppers by hand.

The paprika varieties for mild, medium hot, and hot powder are supplied ready-dried to the mill.

Only if the mill turns very slowly does the paprika powder retain its attractive color and its consistency.

When the stalks and parts of the seed core have been removed, the peppers are mechanically milled.

Paprika powder from La Vera is packed in cans and sold in mild, medium hot, and hot varieties.

Like fiery volcanoes, tons of paprika powder are heaped into mounds in the mills of La Vera – representing a whole year's work for the region's farmers. Smoke-drying over oakwood accounts for the variations in the taste.

It is just over 30 inches thick (80 centimeters). The drying phase lasts 13 to 15 days. Then the peppers are sent to one of the little paprika mills of the region. There the stalks are removed, together with part of the core – not all of it, of course, since the cores contain fatty acids which decisively affect the consistency of the powder. Finally, the peppers are milled by electrically operated stone wheels. This must be done very slowly, since friction heat could impair the pure flavor and color. *Pimentón de La Vera* is marketed in several varieties – mild (*dulce*), medium hot (*agridulce*), and hot (*picante*). It normally keeps for two years. The precious powder is indispensable for many types of Spanish sausage such as *chorizo* or *lomo* contain paprika. Although in La Vera the peppers are smoke-dried, the traditional method in the Murcia region is to lay them out in the sunshine. But nowadays the modern companies there have hot air drying chambers, and some producers sterilize the powder with steam so that it will keep longer. Moreover, a steam solution process makes it possible to obtain dye extracts from the peppers. This resin-type dye is used in the meat and pharmaceutical industries. Paprika powder is also produced in the Balearic Islands.

Chorizo & Co.

"In every respectable household in Spain, they make as many *chorizos* as there are days in the year: 365 sausages for their own consumption, and 50 more for days when they have guests." This custom impressed the French writer Alexandre Dumas, who toured Spain in 1846-7 and wrote at great length about Spanish cuisine. There is a lot of evidence that *chorizo*, the star turn among Spanish sausages, originated in Extremadura. Nestor Luján, the great authority on gastronomy, points to the letter written in 1576 by a priest from Badajoz who used the word *churico* to mean sausage. Another somewhat far-fetched explanation is the possible relationship with the word *churre*; in Castilian Spanish this means something like "dripping fat" and may refer to the fact that the sausages are hung up to dry. What is certainly undisputed is that the *chorizo*, which nowadays usually has a bright red color, was a decidedly pale fellow until the Spanish conquistadores introduced the pepper plant.

There are more than a thousand small and medium-size companies today, located all over Spain, producing some 55,100 tons (50,000 tonnes) of *chorizo*. The national sausage comes in many varieties: thick and thin, plain or smoked, as an exquisite tapa with a great deal of lean meat, or a fatty variety used for stews and fried dishes. Depending on the type of *chorizo*, lean and fat pork is chopped up in varying proportions and kept in a mixture of seasonings for two days – garlic, paprika powder, salt, and herbs. A dash of white wine is often added as well, to accelerate the natural fermentation process. This process gives the *chorizo* its typical, slightly acidic taste. The obligatory paprika powder also lends color and seasoning, and its etheric oils mean the sausage can be kept longer. Industrially manufactured *chorizo* are also allowed to contain limited amounts of chemical conservation agents such as nitrite salts. The seasoned meat is stuffed into skins by a sausage machine. The skins are then tied and the sausages are hung up to dry. In the wet northern area of the region, *chorizos* are often slightly pre-smoked.

Another product of the *chacinería*, the pork butcher's store, is *lomo embuchado*, air-dried loin of pork, which is a really exquisite delicacy. To make it, the loin of pork, which is between 19 and 27 inches long (50–70 centimeters), is cut tidily from the carcass. All the fat is removed and it is then marinated in a mixture of fine seasonings, just like the *chorizo*. The marinated loin is stuffed into a beef skin and is slightly smoked, or else it is air-dried for three to four months so that it will retain its tender suppleness. A *lomo embuchado* (also known as *lomo curado*, can weigh over 3 pounds /1.5 kilograms). The meat varies between pink and bright red. Together with Spanish ham, it is considered as the highest expression of the Spanish butcher's art. Naturally the quality of the meat plays an important role in the quality of all these specialties. Pride of place is always given to the products based on the Iberian pig: *lomo ibérico* and *chorizo ibérico*, both of which are distinguished by their typical nutty aroma.

Extremadura is well known for its excellent ham and sausage specialties. Gourmets from all over the world long to get their hands on products made from the meat of the Iberian pig – whether these are fine hams, air-dried loin of pork, or *chorizo* sausages. The meat products from white breeds of pig are not to be overlooked either.

In damp, cool regions in particular, sausages are not only air-dried, but also smoked (above and main photograph). This guarantees their fine flavor and ensures that they will keep.

The *chorizo* gets its bright red color and spicy taste from hot paprika powder. In Extremadura and Majorca, people still swear by the local varieties of paprika.

SPANISH SAUSAGE SPECIALTIES

Chorizo del Pirineo: smoked hard sausage from the Pyrenees.

Chorizo de Teruel: hard sausage from Teruel, the sausage and ham town in Aragon.

Salchichón del Pirineo: spicy salami-type hard sausage from the Pyrenees.

Chorizo de León: Castilian hard sausage with much garlic – can be eaten raw or cooked.

Chorizo de ciervo: peppery hard sausage made from Pyrenean venison.

Llonganissa de pagès: spicy farmhouse sausage from the Catalan mountains, eaten raw with bread.

Longaniza: hard sausage found all over Spain, containing seasoning which varies from region to region, and eaten raw or fried.

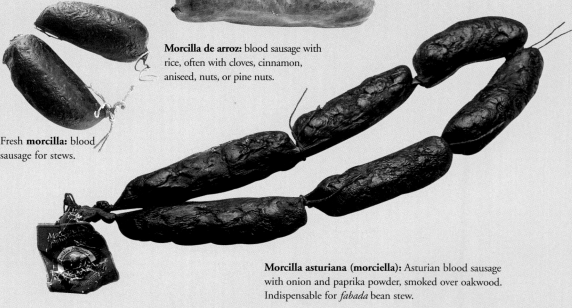

Morcilla de arroz: blood sausage with rice, often with cloves, cinnamon, aniseed, nuts, or pine nuts.

Fresh **morcilla:** blood sausage for stews.

Sobrasada from Majorca is simply spread on rustic farmhouse bread for a picnic in the country.

Morcilla asturiana (morciella): Asturian blood sausage with onion and paprika powder, smoked over oakwood. Indispensable for *fabada* bean stew.

Chorizo cular: a long and thick mature *chorizo* from Navarre. Sliced up, following an old tradition, at the Sanfermines festival after the bull-running.

Bisbe: Catalan specialty made from a pig's liver, stomach, and rind, finely seasoned with pepper and nutmeg and then stuffed into a thick skin.

Chistorra: the national sausage of Navarre, made from pork, frequently with a little beef added – usually served fried with peppers.

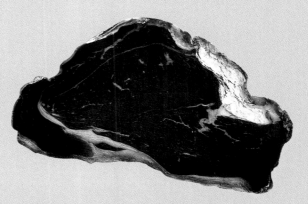

Butifarra negra: Catalan blood sausage made from blood, bacon, and pork rind, usually with pepper and nutmeg – for stews or eaten raw.

Butifarra blanca: national Catalan sausage with many variations – always contains pork, together with bacon, rind, variety meats, and various seasonings.

Cecina: Castilian dried beef, donkey meat, or horse meat – salted, seasoned, and then air-dried, frequently also smoked until tender.

Morcón: specialty from Extremadura, made from coarsely chopped lean pork, which is marinated with paprika powder and garlic.

Sobrasada: Majorcan spreading sausage with paprika powder.

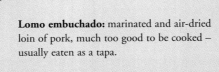

Lomo embuchado: marinated and air-dried loin of pork, much too good to be cooked – usually eaten as a tapa.

Salchichón: hard sausage, popular all over the country, made from chopped pork, pepper, and seasonings which vary from region to region.

347

Wild vegetables and stockfish, the typical food during fasts, are carried in a basket by this Lenten symbol (*figura de la cuaresma*) from Ripoll. The seven feet represent the seven weeks of Lent.

CULINARY ARTS BEHIND MONASTERY WALLS

They were not short of time or money, and apart from having to fast in Lent the monks of Extremadura liked to eat well. Living in seclusion, comfort, and relative safety, the servants of the Lord could dedicate themselves energetically to the art of cooking. As far back as the 13th century, the San Benito monastery in the village of Alcántara made a name for itself as the center of the mounted order of chivalry of the same name. The Church's warriors did great service to the crown in the struggle against the Moors and were rewarded with estates and wide-ranging privileges. High-ranking nobles, and even kings, broke their journeys in the monasteries.

Thus the Benedictines were able not only to strengthen their relations with the ruling class of Christian Spain, but also to develop the culinary arts to the very highest level. The collection of recipes from the Alcántara monks is legendary, and was taken back to France by Napoleon's troops. Alcántara-style poultry dishes can still be found in French cook books today. No less famous is the monastery of Guadalupe, a place of pilgrimage for devotees of the Black Virgin, the patron saint of Extremadura and the national saint of Mexico. Many Spanish conquistadores, including Christopher Columbus, made the pilgrimage to Guadalupe to thank the Virgin for the success of their enterprises. Richly endowed by illustrious visitors, the monastery developed into a cultural

center of the highest rank and raised cooking to an art form. The monks invented the omelet, under the name *tortilla cartujana* (little Carthusian cake), and they are the fathers of the *consumo* or *consumado*, a simple but tasty broth. French soldiers are supposed to have stolen the recipe from the monastery during the Napoleonic wars. The French authority on cooking, Escoffier is reputed to have said later, about the fine broth: "This was the best trophy and the only advantageous prize which France gained from this war." The dish from Extremadura later left France as *consommé* to make a triumphal progress all round the world.

Background: The omelet was invented centuries ago behind the walls of the monastery of Guadalupe.

Lenten fare

The practice of temporarily fasting is known to all the great religions. The Spanish word for Lent, *cuaresma*, can be traced back to the Latin term *quadragesimam diem* (the fortieth day), and recalls the forty days which Jesus spent in the wilderness, fasting and meditating. The fast period laid down by the Catholic Church begins the night before Ash Wednesday and ends on Easter Sunday.

In the Middle Ages in particular, Lent was a favorite theme for Spanish chroniclers and popular story-tellers, since the abstemiousness required by the church was often seen as bitterly ironic by the poor people. Recurrent famines and the chronic poverty of large segments of the population made any order from on high to abstain from eating somewhat meaningless. In the *Libro del Buen Amor*, the great religious work by a senior cleric from Hita, written in the 14th century, the narrator displays some biting irony: "He fasted for two days a week, and if he had nothing to eat, the poor sinner explained that he was on a starvation diet." On the other hand, anyone who had money could make Lent a little easier to bear through a *Bula de la Santa Cruzada*. If a small sum of money was paid, the Papal crusade bull permitted the eating of meat on certain specified days during Lent.

But in general the church's rules on fasting were almost always obeyed in Catholic Spain. From Ash Wednesday to Easter, it was usually watery stews and soups made from legumes, corn, and vegetables which simmered in the cauldrons. Dishes made from bread, milk, and eggs were also permitted, such as tortillas or sweet dishes. Since fresh fish from the coast was at that time a rarity inland, people also ate salted freshwater fish. Snails and frogs' legs were eaten occasionally for a change. They were considered to be "neutral" foods and were not covered by the fasting restrictions.

When the trade in stockfish (*bacalao*) began around 1700, this became a Lenten symbol. The *guiso de Viernes Santo*, a "Good Friday stew" which is almost forgotten today, consisted of stockfish, cauliflower, artichokes, and split hard-cooked eggs. These were all rolled in flour and deep-fried together, then served in a sauce. The famous *sopa de cuaresma* (Lenten soup) is still prepared today. Its ingredients are stockfish, spinach, and chickpeas. Anyone who took the injunction to abstinence particularly seriously consumed nothing more during a fast period except water to drink and *caldo de vigilia*, which was essentially a light broth containing fish and various different kinds of vegetables.

Bacalao monacal, "monks' stockfish", is allowed even during Lent, for the pious dish contains no meat. The monks' meal is so tasty that people are happy to eat it after Easter as well.

Bacalao monacal
Monastery style stockfish
(Photograph above)

2 firm pieces of stockfish, 10 oz/300 g each
Generous 1 lb/500 g spinach leaves
1 small onion, finely chopped
2 cloves of garlic, finely chopped
½ cup/125 ml olive oil
Salt and pepper
Generous 1 lb/500 g potatoes, thinly sliced
Flour for coating
1 cup/250 ml stock
8¾ oz/250 grams fresh sheep cheese

Soak the stockfish for 24 hours, changing the water twice. Remove from the water and leave to drain thoroughly. Sort the leaf spinach and wash thoroughly. Cook the onion and garlic in 1 tbsp of olive oil until translucent. Add the wet spinach and blanch briefly. Season with salt and pepper and remove from the stovetop. Heat the remaining olive oil in a deep pan and fry the potatoes. Remove the sliced potatoes and place in a heat-resistant mold. Add spinach on top. Coat the fish in flour and fry briefly in the oil on both sides. Place on top of the spinach and pour the stock over the mixture. Divide the fresh cheese and the fish into portions and cook everything together in a preheated oven for 15 minutes at 430 °F/220 °C.

Caldo de vigilia
Lenten soup

3 onions
3 cloves of garlic
2 bunches of herbs and vegetables for making soup
1 bay leaf
3 cloves
2 bunches of thyme
7 black peppercorns
Salt
Scant 1½ lbs/750 g of filleted fish, cut into bite-size morsels
Pepper
1–2 tbsp vinegar
2 tbsp chopped parsley

Cover the onions, garlic, soup herbs, and vegetables, and all seasonings with 8 cups/ 2 liters of water. Bring to a boil and leave to simmer for about 1 hour. Remove from the stovetop and leave to cool. Then strain the stock and bring to a boil again. Add the pieces of fish and simmer in the stock for 10 minutes. Season with salt, pepper, and vinegar, and garnish with chopped parsley before serving.

Wild vegetables and mushrooms

The green north of Extremadura is the complete opposite to the dry, wide Dehesa and the steppes of the south, concealing a remarkable wealth of wild vegetables and mushrooms in its little woods and along the banks of many streams and rivers. The absolute star among the "collector's items" is wild asparagus (*espárrago triguero*), which is already thrusting its head up out of the ground very early on in the year. Its preferred habitat is in olive groves and bushy landscapes. But it can also be found in the Dehesa, sheltered by the oak trees. Wild asparagus differs from white asparagus, which must always be covered by earth to prevent discoloration. It must be allowed to grow until its slim, matt-green stalks project over 8 inches (20 centimeters) out of the ground. Only then is it picked.

Triguero asparagus does not need to be peeled. All that is necessary is to cut off the hard, woody end. Wild asparagus, with its elegant, slightly bitter notes, is best appreciated fried, in scrambled eggs, with poached eggs, or boiled for use in salads. Genuine devotees also swear by heavily salted *triguero* asparagus cooked on a charcoal grill or, if necessary, in a pan or on a hotplate (*a la plancha*).

The golden thistle (*cardillo*) and the thistle (*cardo*, see also page 110) can be found in uncultivated fields or along the banks of streams. They are usually precooked and then served cold in salads, fried in oil, or covered in Béchamel sauce. In damp areas, watercress (*berro de agua*) can also be found. It needs only a light vinaigrette dressing to become a healthy and delicious side-dish. One refreshing traditional combination is made up of cress, orange segments, and freshly chopped garlic.

Mushrooms have a rather low profile in the traditional cuisine of Extremadura. This seems all the more surprising given that at the time of the Roman Empire this part of the province of Lusitania was the main source of supply for the legendary edible fungus *Amanita caesarea* (golden agaric), which was the favorite of the rulers in Rome. Today Extremadura exports huge quantities of wild mushrooms to France, the Basque Country, and Catalonia. Truffles (*criadilla de tierra* or *garamuelo*) are popular in local gastronomy, though these are actually poor relations of the white-fleshed truffle. These Spanish truffles have a delicate flavor, which should not be masked. So they are usually prepared in a light omelet. Other fungi popular in the west of Spain are the parasol mushroom (*parasol*), the ceps (*boleto negro* and *boleto de pino)*, the saffron milk cap (*níscalo*), and the meadow mushroom (*champiñon de campo*).

Revuelto de esparragos trigueros
Scrambled eggs with wild asparagus

Generous 1 lb/500 g wild asparagus, or
substitute green asparagus
Salt
3 tbsp olive oil
2 cloves of garlic, finely chopped
8 eggs
⅛ tsp hot paprika powder

Blanch the asparagus in salted water. Remove from the water and drain. Cut into pieces.
Heat the olive oil in an iron pan and cook the garlic in it until it is translucent. Add the asparagus and brown it. Then beat the eggs and pour them over the asparagus. Stir the mixture on a low heat until it thickens. Season with salt and paprika, and serve immediately.
Variations: A combination of 9 oz/250 g of wild asparagus and 9 oz/250 g of forest mushrooms can also be used for this dish, or 7 oz/200 g of wild asparagus with 5 oz/150 g of forest mushrooms and ⅔ cup/150 g of cooked shrimp.

Left: Tender wild asparagus (*espárrago triguero*) is best eaten in an omelet or with delicate scrambled eggs.

Right: Green asparagus is also grown in Spain, but there is nothing better than genuine wild asparagus, with its exquisite, slightly bitter flavor.

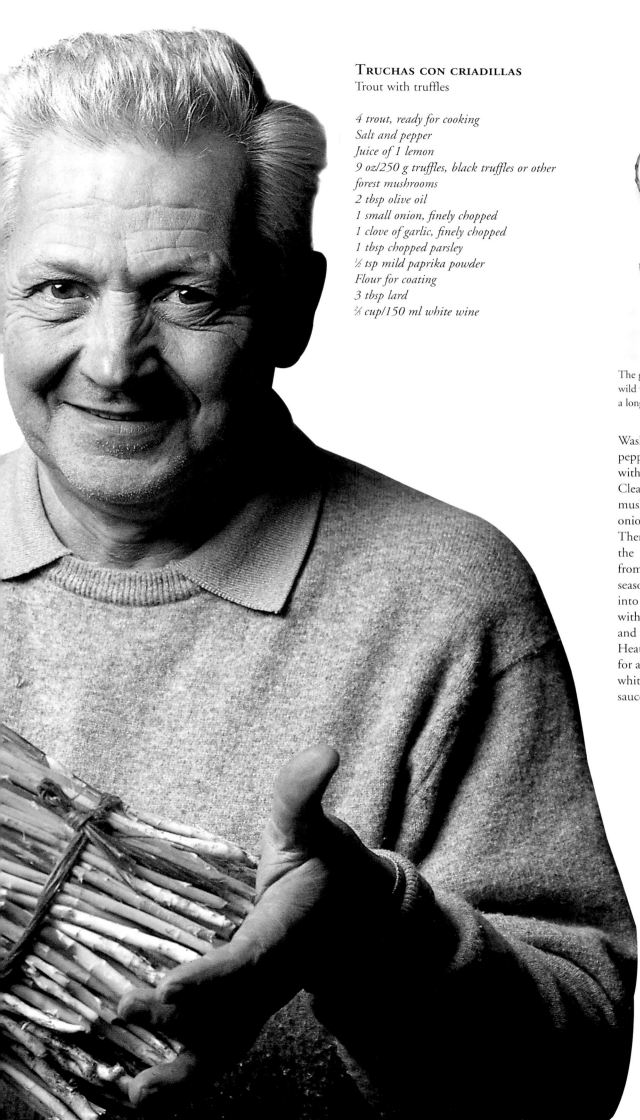

TRUCHAS CON CRIADILLAS
Trout with truffles

4 trout, ready for cooking
Salt and pepper
Juice of 1 lemon
9 oz/250 g truffles, black truffles or other
forest mushrooms
2 tbsp olive oil
1 small onion, finely chopped
1 clove of garlic, finely chopped
1 tbsp chopped parsley
½ tsp mild paprika powder
Flour for coating
3 tbsp lard
⅔ cup/150 ml white wine

The golden thistle (*tagarnina* or *cardillo*) is one of the wild vegetables gathered by farmers in Extremadura for a long time. It is still popular with many of them today.

Wash the trout and pat it dry. Rub salt and pepper into it inside and out, and sprinkle it with lemon juice. Leave it to marinate a little. Clean and coarsely chop the truffles or mushrooms. Heat the olive oil and cook the onion and garlic in it until they are translucent. Then add the mushrooms and simmer until the cooking liquid has evaporated. Remove from the stovetop, stir in the parsley, and season with paprika powder. Stuff the mixture into the trout and close the stomach cavities with wooden picks. Coat the trout in the flour and tap any excess flour off.

Heat the lard in a large pan and fry the trout for about 5 minutes on each side. Then add the white wine and let the trout simmer in the sauce for a few minutes. Serve with potatoes.

Golden thistles and truffles (right), the typical fungi of Extremadura, are easily pickled and stored.

The way to a man's heart

A recipe for true love: gather various magical herbs before the sun comes up, mix them with blood and dried lizard, strain the mixture through three pubic hairs. In the Middle Ages, men and women used elixirs of this kind to charm their beloved into bed.

Aphrodisiacs – substances which are supposed to be able to stimulate erotic desire and passion – owe their name to Aphrodite, the Greek goddess of love. People still have quite a few ideas on how to encourage fertility and conception, as well as increase the pure pleasure of "the mating game." Tales of love potions and titillating foods, perfumes and incense, stimulating powders and mysterious mixtures from the siren's kitchen abound all over the world. The ancient Indians and Egyptians laid special emphasis on the power of fragrances to arouse the senses. The Persian king Xerxes insisted that his wives were instructed for a year in the art of using scents and spices before they were allowed to approach him, perfectly perfumed, for the first time.

Soon love found another way, through the stomach. Every culture has developed its own recipes to increase the raptures of love. Seafood has held an honored place on the menu in Spain since time immemorial, with the slippery oysters in the lead, thanks to their high content of iodine, zinc, and other minerals. But octopus and fish roe were also supposed to keep lovers in the mood.

Those hungry for love have also sworn by the effects of artichokes and asparagus since the year dot, and modern medicine even has an explanation for this. Both vegetables have a dehydrating effect and activate the digestion, which relaxes the pelvic area and stimulates the flow of blood. Celery, parsley, and garlic have a similar effect. Truffles, morels, and ceps, as well as spices such as pepper, chili, ginger, and cinnamon, are supposed to have an infallible effect on both sexes. In the Middle Ages, experts on love particularly recommended poultry and eggs in spiced red wine.

Particularly exotic are those recipes in which powdered rhinoceros horn or even milled lion's penis is sprinkled over food. On the other hand, it seems only logical that in a country like Spain, where bull fighting is regarded as a ritual of proof of manhood to this day, fried bull's testicles (*criadillos de toro*) are considered to be an aphrodisiac.

Of course, if the eager lover has used too high a dose of the "little something," a small glass of wine containing extract of rue can come to the rescue. An anti-aphrodisiac that is considered to be just as effective is eating raw onions, or sucking pig brawn with poppyseed, lemon juice, or juniper, all said to have the power "to make the body damp and cold." And those who have had their passions stirred up against their will can best be helped by a medieval ritual against love enchantments. Put on new shoes or boots, and walk as fast and as long as you possibly can, until your feet are really sweaty. Then take off the right shoe, pour wine into it, and drink it all down – all erotic thoughts will have disappeared.

Above: The final seasoning for an aphrodisiac meal was often a "little something" from a herbal pharmacy.

Right: The way to a man's heart is through his stomach. Casanova could always be tempted with cocoa.

SPANISH FLY

No one really knows why the gleaming, metallic green beetle with the Latin name *Cantharis vesicatoria* ever came to be known as "Spanish fly." It is assumed that the term goes back to the legendary hot-bloodedness of Spanish Latin lovers. At all events, the powdered remains of the dried fly have the reputation of being able to drive sensual desire to the highest peaks. The Spaniards usually call the aphrodisiac insect *cantárida*, but the term *mosca de España* is also known. Spanish fly contains the poison cantharidin, and as far back as the Middle Ages the milled beetle powder had the reputation throughout Europe of also being an effective remedy against rheumatism. What is certain is that the substance stimulates the circulation of the blood, and it is this which led it to enjoy a real boom as an alleged aphrodisiac in the first half of the 20th century. However in the 1950s the sale of Spanish fly was prohibited, because more and more people were poisoning themselves by taking large doses, with serious consequences. Even a tiny amount (4 milligrams) of cantharidin is a fatal dose for human beings. Spanish fly can still be obtained in minimal amounts as an ingredient in some aphrodisiacs sold in sex shops. So scatter it hopefully into the beloved's soup – but remember, the actual effect remains in dispute.

PALETILLA DE CABRITO AL HORNO
Baked leg of kid

1 leg of kid on the bone, weighing about
3¼ lbs/1.5 kg
Salt and pepper
½ cup/125 ml olive oil
7 cloves of garlic, coarsely chopped
1 onion, coarsely chopped
2 ripe tomatoes, skinned and cubed
1 bay leaf
2 sprigs of thyme
1 cup/250 ml white wine
2½ tbsp brandy
2¼ lbs/1 kg potatoes, cut into quarters
2 tbsp pine nuts

Wash the leg and pat it dry; then rub salt and pepper well into it. Heat the olive oil in a large ovenproof braising pan and brown the leg well all around. Remove from the pan and put to one side. Cook the garlic and onion in the oil until they are translucent. Add the tomatoes and cook lightly. Add the bay leaf and thyme, then the brandy and white wine. Return the leg to the pan and place in a preheated oven at 347 °F/175 °C for 1½ hours. After 30 minutes, add the potatoes and pine nuts, and pour in some water. Baste the leg frequently. Serve the cooked leg on a preheated dish with the potatoes. Pass the cooking liquid through a sieve. Season with salt and pepper, and serve separately.

Meat and game dishes

Codornices al modo de Alcantara
Alcántara style quail
(Photograph below)

1 small onion, finely chopped
1 clove of garlic, finely chopped
1 tbsp olive oil
7 oz/200 g chicken liver, finely chopped
or minced
3½ oz/100 g black truffles, cleaned and sliced
Salt and pepper
4 quails, each weighing about 7 oz/200 g
Generous 4 cups/1 liter port
2 tbsp lard

Cook the onion and the garlic in the oil until they are translucent. Add the liver and brown it. Then mix in the sliced truffles and lightly braise the mixture. Remove from the stovetop. Season with salt and pepper and leave to cool. Wash and dry the quails; then rub salt and pepper into them. Fill with the cold truffle stuffing and tie the birds securely with kitchen twine. Place the quails in a china dish and cover with the port; then place in the refrigerator to marinate for 2 days.

Take the quails out of the port and wipe them dry. Melt the lard and fry the quails until golden brown on all sides. Add the port and leave to simmer for about 20 minutes on a low heat; then take the quails out of the sauce and keep warm. Boil the sauce down and season with salt and pepper. Halve the quails and serve with the sauce on preheated plates.

Variation: The dish can be prepared using red-legged or common partridges *(perdiz)*.

Caldereta extremeña
Extremadura style meat stew
(Photograph below, right)

Scant 1¾ lbs/750 g cubed kid or lamb
½ cup/125 ml olive oil
1 onion, chopped
7 oz/200 g kid's or lamb's liver
2 dried mild red peppers, softened in water and cut into strips
1 dried red chili, de-seeded and chopped
1 cup/250 ml white wine
1 slice of toasted white bread
2 sprigs of thyme
1 bay leaf
2 cups/500 ml stock
Salt and pepper
2 cloves of garlic
1 tsp mild paprika powder
1 tbsp vinegar

Sear the meat in the olive oil in a stewpot. Then mix in the onion, liver, peppers, and chili, and fry the mixture briefly. Add the white wine, white bread, thyme, and bay leaf, and lastly the stock. Season with salt and pepper and then cook for 30 minutes.

Crush the garlic to a creamy paste in a mortar with the paprika powder and the vinegar. Stir this mixture into the stew and leave to simmer for another 15 minutes. Remove the bay leaf and thyme before serving.

Extremadura's Cheeses

In view of the harsh landscape of Extremadura, the wide choice of hand-made cheeses is impressive. Two of the great names from the Spanish cheese tradition are at home here: *Queso de la Serena* and *Torta del Casar*. Both have been handed down from the days of the wandering shepherds. They are made entirely from sheep's milk and are among those rare types of cheese that are coagulated using vegetable rennet from the wild artichoke plant.

Queso de la Serena comes from the southeastern part of Badajoz province. It is made from the milk of the Merino sheep, which has a high dry extract due to the poor pastures. Between ¼ and 1½ US gallons (5 or 6 liters) are needed to produce approximately 2 pounds (1 kilogram) of cheese, but for this very reason it has a particularly full-bodied taste. It can never be predicted in advance just how a *Serena* cheese will develop. It depends on the milk and on the external conditions. If the cheese matures into a genuine *torta*, it is very creamy; it runs when it is cut into and has a sharp, spicy aroma. If it is harder in consistency, it can mature for up to a year and then has a very piquant taste. *Torta del Casar* is obtained from the milk of the Churra sheep and is named for its place of origin, Casar de Cáceres. The viscous interior of a *Casar* cheese has an intense taste, very rich, and with a stronger aroma than that of its relation from Badajoz. *Torta del Casar* is eaten by cutting a round hole in the surface and spooning out the creamy contents.

Alcántara style
quails.

Caldereta extremeña, the traditional
stew made with goat's meat or lamb.

CORK

Dom Pérignon, the French Benedictine monk who invented the champagne cork, is said to have taken the idea of closing bottles with corks from Spanish pilgrims, who plugged up their gourds or leather flasks with raw cork. Other sources maintain that the worthy brother had spent quite some time in a monastery in Extremadura, and that it was there he discovered the advantages of the flexible bark. Whatever the truth may be, it was not until about 1670 that the cork and the bottle paired up, although clay amphorae had been sealed with this material as long ago as 500 B.C. In Extremadura today, just over 58 square miles (15,000 hectares) are covered by cork oak woods. The cork obtained from them is famous all over the world, and is among the region's most important exports.

The types of oak tree native to Extremadura create their cork bark extremely slowly, and thus give it a particularly flexible and dense quality. A cork oak takes almost 30 years before it is ready to be stripped for the first time. Then another ten or twelve years must go by before

Below: The bark is peeled off the cork oaks in sheets. Then the tree must be allowed to regenerate.

The quality of a cork depends, above all, on the quality of the bark. Barks with very fine pores supply particularly compact and dense corks (top). Corks with many holes (bottom left) are of lesser quality.

the bark has regenerated. Given that it is not until the third time the bark is stripped that the quality is good enough for bottle corks, it rapidly becomes clear why high-quality corks are so valuable and expensive.

Although corks are now produced mechanically, the trees still have to be stripped by hand. Then the bark is stored for a year before being washed and steamed. Depending on the desired length of the cork, the bark mats are cut to various thicknesses. Then the corks are punched out along the line of the trunk. After a thorough quality inspection, the edges are rounded off and the corks are polished. To complete the manufacturing process, the corks are carefully sterilized. In contrast to the simple corks for wine bottles, champagne corks generally consist of three sections – two flat discs made from normally stamped cork enclose a cylinder made of cork granulate and resin. The individual constituents are then bonded together, with the help of a special adhesive.

The bark from gnarled cork oaks supplies the material from which corks are manufactured in Extremadura.

Only mature bark is suitable for best-quality corks. The bark is first stored for a year.

The cork is steamed to remove the tannic acid and make the cork malleable.

Next, the cork sheets are cut into handy pieces which then go on to be mechanically processed.

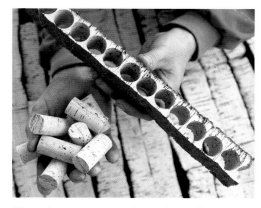

The corks are stamped out by machine. The residue is used to make granulates for composition corks.

Women sort and grade the corks by hand. In many companies, this work is now computer-assisted.

The name of the *bodega* which has placed the order is mechanically branded on each individual cork.

Not a scrap of the valuable cork is wasted. Granulates are also made into corks – or into floors.

Wine from Extremadura

In the 16th century, in the time of Carlos V, Extremadura was one of the most important winemaking areas on the Iberian Peninsula. Indeed, one of the Emperor's favorite sayings was: "For living, the wine of Jarandilla – and for dying, the monastery of Yuste." But today the vintages of Extremadura are unknown to most lovers of wine: there are no outstanding wine-producing areas. On the other hand, there are a handful of vineyards which have been able to move away from a table wine image and produce better wines from modern blends. The local varieties of white grape, Cayetana blanca and Pardina (or Pardillo), produce soft white wines marked by apple notes, with a pleasant acidity. The red varieties grown are Tempranillo, the French Cabernet Sauvignon, and Garnacha, which is found all over the country.

D.O. Ribera del Guadiana

In 1997, the winemakers of Extremadura came together to set up the protected demonination of origin D.O. Ribera del Guadiana. It is divided into the sub-areas Tierra de Barros, Ribera Alta, Ribera Baja, and Matanegra in Badajoz province, and Montánchez and Cañamero in Cáceres province. From a total winemaking area of 220,000 acres (89,000 hectares), only about 46,900 acres (19,000 hectares) belong to the D.O. and over two-thirds of this are in the Tierra de Barros sub-area. The Inviosa *bodega*, in the heart of this wine region, is one of the pioneers with regard to high-quality wines. Since the business was established in 1931, the firm has relied on the characteristic features of the deep soils. It produces wines which are developed in wooden casks, a character that combines the typical earthy flavors of the region with a fine, fruity delicacy. Inviosa's cellars also produce one of the few sparkling wines prepared outside Catalonia that is entitled to call itself *Cava*. But modern developments in Extremadura have changed everything. In Tierra de Barros, an area in Badajoz province, some outstanding *bodega* projects were developed, producing fruity red wines with a full body, natured in oak barrels. The percentage of reds aged in the *barrique* has risen steadily. Even the huge wine cooperations have modernised their equipment to perfection. Due to their excellent price / performance ratio, the wines from this region have found their way to the export market. Traditional white wines fermented without refrigeration are hardly found anymore.

Grapes flourish even on really arid soils, and the wines of the region are getting better and better.

VALENCIA

Heike Papenfuss

Valencia

Paella, an ambassador for Valencian cuisine, is
considered by many as the national dish of the whole of
Spain. Many cooks prove their ability with giant paellas.

"The bell has drowned out the sound of the muezzin's voice. I mourn your loss, oh Valencia, nard and blossom, song and young tongue," an Arabic poet lamented after being driven out of Valencia by the Christians. If you soak up the lavish sun, clear light, and mild air in this region today, it is all too easy to understand this yearning. The ancient Romans called the stretch of land which lies along the Mediterranean coast *Valentia* (the Strong) and gave plots of this land to deserving veterans as gifts. Over the centuries Goths, Arabs, Castilians, Aragonese, and Catalans have also contributed to the region's character. The Moors ruled the region in the 8th century, marking the start of an era whose influence can still be seen today: they brought new cultivated plants such as rice, sugarcane, oranges, and almonds with them from North Africa and the Near East; they created ingenious irrigation systems and built magnificent palaces; and their poets and scholars gave the culture a new impulse. In 1094 Rodrigo de Vivar, known as El Cid, liberated the Moor stronghold of Valencia for a while, but it was only in 1238 that King Jaime I of Aragon managed to recapture the town once and for all for the Christians. Since then the region has been characterized by a powerful dualism: the nobility, established there by Jaime, lived in feudal splendor in the mountainous hinterland, while the townspeople lived as cosmopolitan tradesmen along the coastal strip. Whereas Castilian Spanish *(Castellano)* has been spoken in the hinterland for centuries, the inhabitants along the coast keep up *Valenciano*, which is very similar to Catalan. There are even two sides to Valencia's cuisine: on the hot, fertile coastal plain the orchards and vegetable gardens are an inexhaustible source for simple and light delicacies. Meat plays a secondary role here, as fish and seafood dominate. These are caught fresh off the coast and are generally served naturally and unadulterated. Rice, which Valencians prepare imaginatively, is an indispensable part of the local cuisine. No dish has achieved as much fame as paella, which is well-known far beyond Spain's borders. In contrast to the coast the mountainous hinterland is more barren. Here game and kid are often used in a cuisine which is very earthy and not sparing with the calories.

Opposite: Valencia lives off the riches of the fertile fields and orchards. The *barracas*, former dwellings of small farmers, have become symbols of the region.

RICE-GROWING

When the Aragonese King Jaime I captured Valencia in 1238, rice fields extended as far as the city. In order to prevent malaria epidemics the king ordered the cultivation of rice to be restricted to the Albufera lagoon area. Since then the city of Valencia has expanded to the edge of the lake and once again huge rice fields almost reach the city limits. The flat marshland criss-crossed with channels is one of the most famous rice-growing areas in Europe. And it is regarded as the birthplace of paella.

The starchy plant *Oryza sativa* has been cultivated for about 6000 years. The Moors brought the tropical meadow grass, which comes originally from India and China, to the Iberian peninsula from North Africa – and along with it the necessary art of irrigation. The Spanish word for rice, *arroz*, originates from the Arabic word *ar-ruzz*.

Over time farmers have constantly reduced the size of the freshwater lake in order to gain new areas of cultivable land. They call the small, fenced areas that they wring out of the lake to use for farming *tancats*. As rice-growing is extremely labor-intensive for a very low return, it is a second occupation for many small farmers who also work in farmers' cooperatives or perhaps in industry.

After the rice is sown in the spring, the fields of the Albufera are flooded. The seeds begin to germinate at temperatures of about 54 °F (12 °C). When the plants are some 8 inches (20 centimeters) tall, they are pulled out in clumps and then planted separately 4 inches (10 centimeters) apart in another rice field, which is already flooded. The water can be drained off and the rice harvested from September. After it has been threshed, the rice is dried in the sun or in mechanical driers. The husks are then removed from the grains and the rice is then polished between millstones to give it its familiar white shine. The rice fields are again flooded in winter in order to regenerate them. To irrigate 2½ acres (1 hectare), 1,235,990 cubic feet (35,000 cubic meters) of water are required per year.

Most of the rice grown in Spain is the Japanese subspecies, in particular the Senia and Bahía varieties. These medium-grain types can absorb a lot of water and are particularly suitable for paella and other rice dishes, as well as for sweet dishes. Long-grain rice only accounts for 6 percent of that grown in Spain. It absorbs less liquid, has a shorter cooking time, and is usually served as an accompaniment rather than the main ingredient. Brown rice is not often found in Spanish cuisine.

Even alfalfa thrives marvelously in the damp region of the Albufera. The plant which is rich in vitamins is mainly used as animal fodder, though in recent years it has been introduced into salads.

ALBUFERA NATIONAL PARK

Albuhaira, the little sea, was the name given by the Moors to the bay south of Valencia. At the time of the Romans it was an impressive 116 square miles (30,000 hectares) in size, but over the centuries it has been increasingly reduced through silting up – a process that farmers have helped to accelerate over the last 200 years. They began to separate off and fill up parts of the lagoon in order to gain new land for cultivating rice. The lake was thus reduced to a tenth of its original size. Today a 3940 foot (1200 meter) wide sand bar, the Dehesa del Saler, separates the lake from the open sea. In 1986 the Albufera and adjoining Dehesa were declared a national park. It is an important habitat and breeding ground for numerous types of waterfowl. However the ecological balance of this sensitive area is still threatened by sewage from the towns and the use of chemicals in farming. The Valencians' traditional love for the Albufera cannot, though, be diminished. Every year on August 4 the lake is crowded with lavishly decorated boats. During the *Fiesta al Cristo de la Salud* the inhabitants of the village of El Palmar ask God for plentiful fishing, a good harvest, and the best of health. As far as food is concerned, the Albufera is particularly well-known not just for its rice but also for its eels. The *anguilas* caught in this region are often served in the typical Basque dish, which originates from Valencia, *all-i-pebre*: braised with garlic and bell peppers (see recipe details on page 167).

Above: The Albufera is one of Spain's most valuable humid regions. The farmers who sow rice at the edge of the lake must respect the ecological balance of this sensitive area (main photograph).

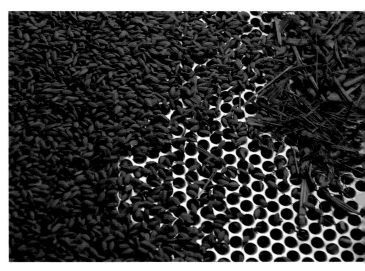

After the freshly harvested rice has been dried, impurities such as stalks and other parts of the plant are extracted. Then the husks can be removed from the rice.

The rice, with husks removed, is polished between special rollers. The grains become snow-white, but lose valuable nutrients along with the bran and silver membrane.

The end product is white rice, eaten all over the world. Medium-grain varieties are particularly popular. They absorb a lot of liquid and are suitable for paella.

FROM THE PAN OF PANS

Many call it *paellera*, but deep-rooted Valencians disagree: the large, black pan has given the Valencian national dish its name – it must, therefore, be called *paella* plain and simply. The term comes from the Latin *patella*, a flat plate on which offerings were made to the gods. By the 16ᵗʰ century the Castilian word *paila* was being used for a vessel similar to the paella pan, while the word *paela* already existed in Valenciano.

The large surface area of this pan is very important for the preparation of paella, since it is this that allows the liquid in which the rice is cooked to boil away, producing a lot of *socarrat*, the rice that sticks to the bottom and edge of the pan and is a bit brown and crunchy.

You cannot go far wrong when buying a paella pan. Many cooks prefer iron to stainless steel as it conducts heat better. A pan for four to five people should be about 16 inches (40 centimeters) in diameter, for six to eight people 19½ inches (50 centimeters). Before it is used for the first time some water with a dash of vinegar must be boiled in the pan. It is then left to dry and some olive oil rubbed over the inside of it. It is advisable to follow this procedure faithfully after each use so that the pan does not rust.

Paella

Andar de paella, or in English "to go for a paella," is very much a social occasion in Valencia. Saint's days and birthdays are celebrated, patron saints honored, and Sunday outings made complete by the famous rice pan. When the Valencians celebrate their festival of fire magic in March, the *Fallas*, and traditionally burn giant papier mâché figures in the streets, steam and delicious smells of a different kind come wafting throughout the night from huge, black pans over open fires.

The Valencians' national dish originated in the country outside the city, and it was the agricultural workers who were the first to make a fire in the fields at lunchtime and cook rice in a flat pan. They added what they could find to the pan. They cooked snails and vegetables with the rice; on special occasions rabbit, and later chicken, was added. Beside this traditional "original paella," Valencians are particularly fond of *paella marinera* with fish and seafood, and *paella mixta* with fish, seafood, and meat. Paella, however, can also include liver, blood sausage, artichokes, and other ingredients.

The success of a paella depends on many factors. Ideally it should be prepared on a wood fire, which must be very hot to start with, though the heat is continually reduced during cooking. The correct amount of oil is another decisive factor: the paella should never be too greasy. And finally, a true pro will measure out the water exactly. Valencians are convinced that paella can be made successfully only when Valencian water is used. It is, therefore, not unusual for them to go to the extraordinary lengths of taking local water with them when they want to prepare paella outside their region.

The prepared dish is placed in the middle of the dining table, as it is traditionally eaten straight from the pan with a wooden spoon.

Paella valenciana
Valencian style paella Serves 8
(Photograph opposite, top)

1¼ cups/250 g garofó *or dried white beans*
Salt and pepper
4 tbsp olive oil
1 chicken, weighing about 2¾ lbs/1.3 kg
1 ready-to-cook rabbit
24 snails, cleaned
2 cups/500 g tavella *or other young bean seeds*
2¼ lbs/1 kg ferraura *or other green beans*
2 medium-size/250 g tomatoes, peeled and diced
2 cloves of garlic, finely diced
½ tsp saffron powder
3 cups/750 g medium-grain rice

Soak the white beans overnight and drain the following day. Wash the chicken and the rabbit thoroughly and pat dry. Cut into small pieces. Season with salt and pepper.

Heat the olive oil in a paella pan and brown the chicken and rabbit on all sides on a medium heat; then add the snails and fry briefly. Remove the meat and snails from the pan and set them aside.

Add the bean seeds, green beans, tomatoes, and garlic to the oil and brown. Add the white beans and pour in 10½ cups/2.5 liters water. Simmer for 10 minutes. Then add the saffron and rice, and mix well. Boil for 10 minutes; then add the meat and snails and cook for another 10 minutes on a low heat, until the water has boiled away. Continue to simmer for a few more minutes so that the crust *(socarrat)* forms.

Paella marinera
Paella with fish and seafood
(Photograph opposite, bottom)

¾ cup/200 ml olive oil
4 jumbo shrimp
4 langoustines
9 oz/250 g small squid or squid rings
2 tomatoes, skinned and diced
2 cups/400 g medium-grain rice
4 cups/1 liter fish stock
Salt
A pinch of saffron powder
1 cup/250 ml meat stock
9 oz/250 g cooked mussels

Heat the oil in a paella pan. Brown the shrimp and langoustines, remove and set aside. Brown the squid in the oil and mix in the tomatoes. Add the rice, pour in the fish stock, and season. Stir the saffron powder into the meat stock and add to the pan. Boil for 10 minutes, then simmer on a low heat for another 10 minutes. Add the mussels, langoustines, and shrimp and reheat in the rice. Leave to stand briefly before serving.

Paella de verduras
Vegetable paella

¾ cup/200 ml olive oil
4 cloves of garlic, finely diced
1 large eggplant, cut into large cubes
1 large red and 1 large green bell pepper, diced
9 oz/250 g each of flageolet and white beans
9 oz/250 g mangel, roughly diced
4 artichoke hearts
2 tomatoes, skinned and diced
2 cups/400 g medium-grain rice
Salt
⅛ tsp hot paprika
A few saffron threads

Heat the olive oil and fry the garlic briefly. Add the vegetables and fry briefly. Pour in 4 cups/1 liter water and stir in the rice. Season with salt, paprika, and saffron. Boil for 10 minutes, then simmer for 10 minutes on a low heat, adding water if necessary. Leave to stand briefly before serving.

1 For *paella valenciana* you need rabbit and chicken, various beans, tomatoes, snails, and rice.
2 First brown the meat in oil in the paella pan, then add the cleaned snails.
3 Remove the meat and snails from the pan and fry the green beans, tomatoes, and garlic.

4 After adding the haricot beans pour on water. Then add the rice.
5 Saffron gives it a yellow color and delicate flavor. Add a few threads to the paella if liked.
6 Shortly before the end of the cooking time return the meat and snails to the paella to warm through.

Rice for every day

Arròs a banda
Rice with fish

4½ lbs/2 kg ready-prepared mixed fish,
e.g. red mullet, monkfish, or ray
Salt and pepper
Juice of 1 lemon
1 onion, spiked with a bay leaf and
2 cloves
3 tbsp olive oil
2 cloves of garlic, diced
2 cups/400 g round-grain rice
½ envelope of saffron
½ tsp mild paprika

Wash and pat the fish dry. Cut it up into reasonable size pieces, rub in salt and pepper, and squeeze over the lemon juice. Leave to marinate for 10 minutes.

Meanwhile bring 4 cups/1 liter water to a boil in a pan with the spiked onion. Put the fish in the pan, reduce the heat, and simmer for 15-20 minutes. Then remove the fish from the stock and keep warm.

Heat the olive oil in a deep pan and brown the garlic and rice. Pour in the fish stock and season with saffron, paprika, salt, and pepper. Simmer for about 20 minutes, until the rice has absorbed all the liquid. Traditionally, the rice is served first, and then the fish, accompanied with *alioli* (see recipe page 17).

Arrós negre
Black rice
(Photograph below)

2¼ lbs/1 kg small fresh squid
Salt
½ cup/125 ml olive oil
1 large red bell pepper, sliced
1 clove of garlic, diced
2 ripe tomatoes, skinned and diced
Juice of 1 lemon
2 tbsp chopped parsley
2 cups/400 g round-grain rice
½ cup/125 ml white wine
Pepper

Carefully remove the ink sac from the squid and set it aside. Clean the squid (follow detailed directions on page 375) and boil in salted water for 10 minutes.

Heat 2 tbsp oil in a pan and fry the bell pepper on a gentle heat. Dice the pepper together with the oil, garlic, tomatoes, lemon juice, and parsley in a food processor.

Heat the remaining oil in a pan. Stir in the pepper mixture and then stir the rice in. Pour on 3 cups/750 ml water and bring everything to a boil.

Meanwhile empty the ink sac and mix the ink with the white wine. Pour it through a strainer onto the rice. Then mix in the squid. Season with salt and pepper and cook for 15–20 minutes. Serve with *alioli* (recipe page 17).

Arròs amb costra

Below: *arròs negre*

Arròs amb fesols i naps

FIDEUA

It does not always have to be rice that is cooked in Valencia's paella pans. *Fideuà* is a type of paella with noodles, and the cooking-crazy Valencians like to disagree as to how the dish actually came about.

In the harbor area of Gandía they insist that fishermen from the village had the idea when they had no rice onboard their cutter. Wanting to eat the fish that they had caught, after the catch they found only noodles in the galley.

In the hinterland, on the other hand, it is said that hungry hikers resorted to noodles because they had left the rice for a proper paella at home. What is, however, certain is that, like paella, the preparation requires a certain skill to get the paella just right. The proportions of the ingredients and the amount of heat must be correct. There is now even a *Concurso de la Fideuà* which takes place annually in Gandía. Foreign cooks now come to Spain to take part in this competition – and are more than able to hold their own against the Valencians.

FIDEUA
Valencian noodle paella

Generous 2 lbs/1 kg fish scraps
1 onion, spiked with 1 bay leaf and 1 clove
Salt and pepper
5 black peppercorns
4 tbsp olive oil
2 onions, diced
2 cloves of garlic, diced
1 ripe tomato, skinned and diced
14 oz/400 g monkfish fillet
1 tsp mild paprika
1 tbsp chopped parsley
14 oz/400 g fideos (short noodles)
4 langoustines
8 shrimp

Make a rich fish stock out of the fish scraps, 6 cups/1.5 liters water, the spiked onion, salt, and peppercorns.

Heat 2 tbsp oil in a paella pan and sweat the onion and garlic until translucent. Then add the tomatoes and pour in 3⅓ cups/800 ml fish stock. Bring to a boil and add the fish. Season with paprika and parsley. Stir in the noodles and then season with salt and pepper. Simmer until the stock has almost all boiled away.

Meanwhile fry the Norway lobsters and shrimp in the remaining oil.

Arrange the seafood over the noodles and finally cook for another 5 minutes in a preheated oven at 345 °F/175 °C.

ARRÒS AMB CROSTA
Rice with a crust (photograph above)

Scant ½ cup/100 g chickpeas
2 cloves of garlic, diced
1 small onion, finely diced
1 bay leaf
1 chicken, cut into 8 portions
5¼ oz/150 g Valencian blood sausage
3 tbsp olive oil
3 ½ oz/100 g smoked ham cubes
2 cups/400 g rice
Salt and pepper
½ tsp mild paprika
½ envelope of saffron powder
2 eggs
2 tbsp breadcrumbs

Soak the chickpeas overnight. Next day bring them to a boil in a good 6 cups/1.5 liters water with the garlic, onion, and bay leaf. Add the chicken portions and blood sausage; simmer until tender. Take out the chicken portions and blood sausage; discard the bay leaf. Drain the chickpeas, keeping the water. Heat the olive oil in a flameproof casserole and sweat the rice and ham until translucent. Pour in 4 cups/1 liter stock from the chickpeas and season with salt, pepper, paprika, and saffron. Boil for 10 minutes. Slice the blood sausage. Mix the blood sausage and chicken portions into the rice and simmer for another 5 minutes. Beat the eggs and pour over the rice. Sprinkle with the breadcrumbs and then bake in a preheated oven at 435 °F/225 °C until golden brown.

ARRÒS AMB FESOLS I NAPS
Rice with navy beans and rutabaga (Photograph above)

¾ cup/200 g dried navy beans
2 onions, roughly diced
1 pig trotter
9 oz/250 g veal
7 oz/200 g smoked bacon in a piece
Salt and pepper
2 black Valencian blood sausages (negrets)
2 white Valencian blood sausages (blanquets)
4 small rutabagas, peeled and diced
1 cup/250 g round-grain rice
½ envelope of saffron

Soak the beans in cold water overnight. The following day bring the beans to a boil in a good 6 cups/1.5 liters salted water with the onions, pig trotter, veal, and bacon and simmer for 30 minutes. Then add the blood sausages and rutabaga, and simmer for another 30 minutes. Take the pig trotter, veal, bacon, and blood sausages out of the stock. Remove the pork from the bone. Keep everything warm.

Put the rice in the stock and season with saffron, salt, and pepper. Cook for approximately 15 minutes. Meanwhile cut the meat, bacon, and blood sausages into small pieces. Shortly before the end of the cooking time mix the meat into the rice.

Citrus fruit

The conveyor belts do not stop. They move through the huge sheds in endless loops, transporting oranges, satsumas, and clementines. It is November, and therefore high season for citrus fruit. Every day farmers deliver freshly harvested produce to the loading stations at the Valencian cooperatives. Here the fruit is washed and then packed in bags and crates according to variety and size. The trucks are already waiting outside to take the fruit to various European countries. Many producers also export to the U.S.A. and Canada.

According to tradition the first oranges are supposed to have arrived in the eastern Mediterranean region with Alexander the Great's caravan (356–323 BC). The Arabs cultivated the bitter orange as an ornamental plant, and as Islam spread, it reached Spain, where it became famous as the Seville orange.

The recent history of the orange in Europe began at the end of the 18th century when a catholic priest in Carcagente, near Valencia, laid out the first commercially exploitable orange groves. The results were so encouraging that other plantations quickly sprung up. Within a few years 7400 acres (3000 hectares) of uncultivated barren land had been irrigated and planted with orange trees. By the early 19th century the area had already increased tenfold.

Clementine *(clementina)*: this is a seedless fruit with dark, sweet flesh.

Grapefruit *(toronja)*: smaller than the pomelo and slightly bitter.

Pomelo *(pomelo)*: the largest citrus fruit, yellow or pink.

Limequat: cross between the lime and kumquat, contains a lot of juice.

Limette *(lima)*: has a discreetly sharp quality, suitable for cocktails.

Orange *(naranja)*: most important citrus fruit with sweet and bitter types.

Kumquat: slightly bitter miniature orange with a thin, edible skin.

Lime *(lemon)*: sharp fruit with a high vitamin C content.

Today citrus plantations stretch along the Mediterranean coast from Catalonia to Andalusia. The main areas of cultivation are the Valencia and Murcia regions. The large number of varieties means that harvesting can take place from October through July. More than 3.3 million tons (3 million tonnes) of oranges were harvested throughout the country in the 2002/2003 season. Spain grows the largest number of different varieties in the world. These varieties differ in ripening time, storage time, color, juice content, flavor, and taste. The most famous are the various navel oranges (Navel, Navelina, Newhall, and Navel Late). They owe their name to the visible "navel" at the end where the blossom was. As well as oranges, different varieties of satsuma, clementine, and mandarin are cultivated in Valencia. The latter have almost disappeared from the market because of their many seeds. The seedless satsumas with their flatter shape and the bright orange, sharp clementines sell better. Lemons, limes, and the fashionable limequats and kumquats also grow here.

1 Citrus plantations stretch across the Valencia region as far as the eye can see. The sophisticated irrigation system using channels *(acequias)* arrived in the country with the Arabs.

2 As well as oranges, Valencia's fruit farmers cultivate many other citrus fruits, including different varieties of flat mandarins, clementines, and satsumas.

3 The citrus fruit is picked by hand. To make the work easier, low-growing trees have been planted as a priority during the past few decades.

4 The pickers transport the fruit to the trucks in plastic baskets – heavy work as the trucks can drive up to the picking area only in some places.

5 The delicate fruit is loaded from the baskets into stackable crates so that it is not damaged. A truck can carry several tons of fruit.

6 The crates are carefully stacked and secured on the trucks. Then the quickest route is taken to the packing station as the market demands freshly picked produce.

7 While men and women often work together in the orange groves, sorting and packing the fruit in the factories is mainly women's work.

8 Packed in crates, the fresh citrus fruit goes immediately to the customers. The majority are in Europe, but some of Valencia's producers also export overseas.

Mysticism surrounding the orange

In spring, when the orange groves are in blossom, a bewitching fragrance fills the air. So it is not surprising that the coastal area south of Valencia bears the name Costa del Azahar, "Coast of Orange Blossom." Sailors are supposed to have been able to smell the fragrance of their native oranges up to ten nautical miles off Valencia. The Roman scholar Pliny the Elder lauded the healing power of oranges in his Natural History, while an old Chinese tradition maintains that the evergreen trees bring their owners luck. The tree, with its fragrant blossom, also played an important role for the Moors. It was one of the three basic components when creating a garden – in addition to colorful mosaics and gushing ornamental fountains. However, in those days orange blossom was not only used for decoration. It was also used during religious ceremonies and for preparing dishes. The Jews as well as the Arabs extolled the healing and invigorating effect of orange blossom honey. Juice from the blossom obtained by fermentation was used as a perfume and medicine. The harmonizing and very stimulating effect of orange blossom has been rediscovered in recent years in the new field of aromatherapy, which uses fragrances to aid healing.

Background: The orange, which in ancient times was regarded as a lucky charm and medicine, is today Valencia's most successful export.

COOKING WITH CITRUS FRUIT

PECHUGA DE POLLO A LA NARANJA
Chicken breasts with orange
(Main photograph, left)

4 chicken breast fillets, skinned and boned
Salt and pepper
4 tbsp olive oil
2 carrots, diced
1 onion, diced
1 tsp sugar
Juice of 3 oranges
Juice of 1 lime
½ cup/125 ml white wine
Orange slices to garnish

Season the chicken breast fillets with salt and pepper. Heat the olive oil in a deep pan and fry the chicken breasts on both sides until golden brown; then remove and keep warm. Brown the diced carrot and onion in the meat juices. Add the orange and lime juice and pour in the white wine. Let the sauce boil down a little to intensify the flavors. Purée in a blender, then season with salt and pepper. Place the chicken breasts in the sauce and simmer, covered, on a medium heat for 10 minutes. Serve garnished with orange slices.

RAPE AL LIMON
Monkfish medallions in lemon sauce
(Main photograph, bottom right)

1 clove of garlic
Grated rind of ½ lemon
Juice of 1 lemon
Salt and freshly milled pepper
1 cup/250 ml dry white wine
4 monkfish medallions, weighing about
5 oz/150 g each
2 tbsp olive oil
2 tbsp capers
Lemon slices to garnish

Peel the garlic and crush using a mortar and pestle with the lemon rind, lemon juice, salt, and pepper. Mix this paste with the white wine. Fry the monkfish medallions in the oil in a pan on a medium heat until golden brown on both sides. Pour the wine sauce over and leave to boil down a little on a low heat; finally heat the capers in the sauce. Serve on a warmed platter with lemon slices.

ENSALADA DE NARANJAS
Orange salad
(Main photograph, top right)

2 large oranges
3½ oz/100 g black olives
Juice of 1 pink grapefruit
Juice of 1 orange
4 tbsp cold-pressed, fruity olive oil
(for example of the Picual *variety)*
Mint leaves to garnish

Carefully peel the oranges, being careful to remove the pith completely. Cut the oranges into thin segments and arrange in a dish or on dessert plates. Place the olives on top. Mix the orange and grapefruit juice together and pour over the oranges. Leave to marinate. Before serving drizzle olive oil over and garnish with mint leaves.

Juicy oranges are not only delicious as fresh fruit, they are also excellent with fish and meat dishes, as well as for sweet dishes.

Diluted orange juice drinks from a bottle are rarely served in Valencia. Orange juice *(zumo de naranja)* is nearly always fresh here, squeezed by sophisticated machines. The orange halves, complete with rind, are put in a basket, then at the press of a button one orange after another is pulled in and squeezed. The fresh juice, rich in vitamins, is usually served with a small envelope of sugar as the Spanish like it sweet.

DRINKS WITH CITRUS FRUITS

During long nights Valencians like to switch to cocktails. Many are mixed with orange, lemon, or lime:

Agua de Valencia
2 tsp each of vodka, rum, and Cointreau with a scant ½ cup/100 ml orange juice; sometimes just Cava (sparkling wine) with orange juice

Caipirinha
3½ tbsp Cachaça (sugar-cane schnapps) or white rum, 1 lime, squeezed, brown cane sugar

Planter's Punch
2½ tbsp brown rum, a generous tbsp lemon juice, 3½ tbsp each of orange and pineapple juice, 2 tsp grenadine, with a dash of Angostura Bitters

Campari Orange
2½ tbsp Campari, ⅔ cup/150 ml orange juice

Screwdriver
2½ tbsp vodka, ⅔ cup/150 ml orange juice

Tequila Sunrise
2½ tbsp tequila, ⅔ cup/150 ml orange juice, a shot of grenadine

Gin Fizz
2½ tbsp gin, 4 tsp lemon juice, 2 tsp sugar syrup, 3½ tbsp soda

Whisky sour
2½ tbsp whisky, 4 tsp lemon juice, 2 tsp sugar syrup

COOL PLEASURES

Iced fruit in the fruit bowl is a particular specialty in Alicante. The fresh piece of fruit is hollowed out and then ice cream is mixed with the fruit flesh and put into the fruit shells. Beside citrus fruit, apple, melon, pineapple, and mango can be used. The skilled ice cream makers in Alicante only usually use natural base products as a rule. They do not use stabilizers or colorings, and the only preservative for their ice cream is the cold.

LECHE MERENGADA

4 ¼ cups/1 liter milk
1 stick of cinnamon
1 ¼ cups/250 g sugar
Grated rind of 1 lemon
3 egg whites
2 tbsp confectioners' sugar
1 tsp ground cinnamon

Bring the milk to a boil with the cinnamon stick and sugar. Remove from the heat and leave to cool. Remove the cinnamon stick and stir in the lemon rind. Transfer to a bowl and place in the freezer until frozen. Beat the egg white with the confectioners' sugar until very stiff. Fold into the frozen milk and freeze for at least 2 hours. Before serving sprinkle with ground cinnamon.

ORANGE SORBET

2 cups/500 ml freshly squeezed orange juice
⅔ cup/150 g sugar
2 ½ tbsp orange liqueur
2 egg whites

Mix the orange juice well with the sugar and orange liqueur. Transfer to a bowl and place in the freezer until frozen. Beat the egg white until partly stiff and carefully fold into the frozen orange juice. Freeze in the freezer compartment for a minimum of 2 hours. Whisk now and again during this time.

ORANGE ICE

1 cup/250 g sugar
Scant ½ cup/100 ml orange juice (blood oranges)
1¼ cups/300 ml light cream
Juice of ½ lemon

Bring the sugar to a boil in ½ cup/125 ml water and boil until a clear syrup is formed, then remove from the heat. Add the orange juice and mix with the cream and lemon juice. Freeze the mixture. Finally, serve in the halved, hollowed out orange shells.

PATO A LA NARANJA
Duck in orange sauce

1 duck, weighing about 4½ lbs/2 kg
Salt and pepper
3 tbsp olive oil
1 cup/250 ml freshly squeezed orange juice
½ cup/125 ml white wine
1 tsp honey
2½ tbsp brandy
orange slices to garnish

Wash and dry the duck; then rub with salt and pepper. Prick the breast and legs several times. Place on the rack of the roasting pan and cook in a preheated oven at 390 °F/200 °C for about 1 hour. Halfway through the cooking time turn the duck over, and then coat with olive oil every 10 minutes. Take the roasted duck out of the oven and keep warm on a serving plate. Pour the meat juices through a sieve, discard the fat, and bring to a boil with the orange juice and white wine. Stir in the honey and brandy, and let the sauce thicken. Season with salt and pepper. Pour the sauce over the duck, decorate with a garnish of orange slices, and serve immediately.

FLAN DE NARANJA
Orange crème caramel

1½ cups/300 g sugar
4 eggs
2 egg yolks
Grated rind of 1 orange
2½ cups/600 ml freshly squeezed orange juice

Boil half the sugar and ½ cup/125 ml water to form a golden brown caramel. Pour the caramel into 4 individual ramekins, tilting the ramekins so that the bottoms and sides are evenly covered.
Mix the eggs, egg yolk, and orange rind with the remaining sugar, but do not beat so much that it becomes frothy. Now bring the orange juice to a boil; then leave to cool a little and begin stirring into the egg mixture. Pour this mixture through a fine sieve and divide between the ramekins. Cook in a bain-marie in a preheated oven at 300 °F /150 °C for about 50 minutes. Check that the water does not evaporate; top up if necessary. Leave to cool and refrigerate overnight. Before serving briefly immerse the base of each ramekin in hot water and turn the dessert out onto a plate.

The Huerta, Valencia's fertile irrigated area, is well-known for its extremely good artichokes. The slightly bitter vegetable steams well and is usually served as a tapa.

Water tribunal in Valencia

From him that cheats the water is taken away, and so is his livelihood. This is according to the unwritten laws of the Huerta, the irrigated area around Valencia. The water tribunal has met in Valencia for over a thousand years, its function being to settle disputes about water rights in the irrigated region. It was set up by the caliph of Cordoba around 960. Throughout the centuries and up to the present day all Spanish heads of state have protected and upheld the privileges of this court. *El tribunal de las aguas* is made up of eight men who each represent one of the main canals which provide the Huerta with water. The judges still meet today each Thursday at noon, in the square in front of the cathedral. Their arbitration award is irrevocable, even though it is not based on any written laws. Even the judgment pronouncement is made only verbally; the punishment is usually lenient. However, if a neighbor suffers financial damage, this must be compensated and not just symbolically.

Background: For 650 years farmers have been coming to sell the fruits of their labor at the *Tira de Contar*. Today the farmers' market is part of the large market hall.

FARMERS' MARKET

The gardens awoke slowly, and their yawning grew louder and louder. The cock crowed in the farmers' houses. The roads filled up with small black dots, like ants marching toward the town. Outside the houses those going to the town and those staying to work in the fields greeted each other.

The Valencian writer Vicente Blasco Ibáñez often described the everyday life of farmers in the Huerta, the lush vegetable and fruit garden outside the gates of Valencia. In *La Barraca* from 1898, Blasco Ibáñez wrote about the trials and tribulations of the work which often provided only a poor living for the large families. This passage describes how the farmers set out early in the morning to sell their produce at the markets in the town, returning later to the fields.

A good hundred years has passed since then. Working conditions and distribution methods have changed drastically, but there are still farmers' markets in Valencia. The market with the longest tradition is the *Tira de contar*, which was mentioned in documents as long ago as 650 years ago. The name refers to the farmers' practice of setting up their stands in a row *(tira)*. Here they sold their fruit and vegetables by the piece and not according to weight, so they had to count *(contar)* the individual items. Even today some 300 farmers come each day from the huerta to the *Tira de contar*, which is now housed on the site of the large market Mercavalencia.

Valencia's Huerta is one of Spain's most important irrigated regions, with an incredible variety of fruit and vegetables (see also page 392). Many vegetables, including beans, artichokes, bell peppers, tomatoes, potatoes, eggplants, mangels, carrots, onions, cabbage, and citrus fruits flourish here. The three varieties of beans that are found in a real *paella valenciana* are typical: the white *garrofó*, the wide, green *ferraura*, and the *tavella*, the young seeds of which are used.

The high-quality vegetables form the basis of many Valencian stews. A *hervido valenciano* contains potatoes, onion, and green beans which are cooked and salted, then drizzled with oil and vinegar. The *olleta* or *olla churra*, a typical dish from the interior of Valencia, consists of white beans, chickpeas, pumpkin, and mangel stalks, as well as rice with pork and sausage. *Borra* is a fish stew with various different vegetables and potatoes, to which eggs and oil are added at the end.

Even in peaceful times many look for the opportunity to let off steam. Every year thousands of "fighters" and onlookers travel to Buñol for the pleasure of having very ripe tomatoes thrown at them. Fortunately this war is harmless, though not a single shirt or eye remains dry during the *Tomatina*.

BATTLE OF THE TOMATOES

Buñol on the last Wednesday in August: if you want to take a stroll through the usually sleepy little town this morning, you must be careful. There is an air of anticipation. Crowds of people pour into the town center, most of them wearing running shoes, old pants, and T-shirts. Those particularly keen for a fight even come equipped with helmets and enormous goggles. The *Tomatina*, Buñol's legendary tomato battle, is imminent. From all directions trucks bring the apples of paradise – bright red and overripe. The starting gun goes off on the dot of 11. Those who want to take part in the spectacle arm themselves with tomatoes. Battle commences. A young man enthusiastically squashes three juicy fruit on his neighbor's head, another skids on the slippery road and with great delight wallows in a sea of tomato juice. If you prefer to remain a spectator, you will have to keep your distance to escape the mushy projectiles. Even in the back row the sweet, red drops rain down from the sky. After a good hour it is all over and it is time to clear up. The streets are cleaned, house fronts scrubbed – and it will all start again next year.

The tomato battle dates back to 1945. At the festival honoring the patron saint, San Luis Bertrán, a scuffle broke out during the procession in front of a greengrocery store. Some of the townspeople were unhappy as they had wanted to carry the traditional papier mâché figures through the village during the procession and had been turned away. The situation escalated as some people, outraged, grabbed tomatoes and used them as missiles. A police officer stopped the tomato battle without further ado, imprisoning those involved, but they were soon released. The next year some visitors brought tomatoes with them to the procession as a precaution. The sweet, red spectacle was repeated. From then on, new anecdotes circulated every year about the *Tomatina*, as the fight came to be called. The town authorities tolerated the new festival, although it succeeded in temporarily banning the *Tomatina* in 1957. The protest by fans was, however, so great that the legendary tomato battle was officially authorized in 1959. Since then it has attracted thousands of visitors from all over the world. The "weapons," though, have to be imported from other regions of Spain, because no tomatoes actually grow in Buñol.

SQUID

It is hard to understand why scientists call the *calamar* "common" since *Loligo vulgaris* (the common squid) is the culinary king of the cephalopods. For a long time in Europe its exquisite taste was experienced only on the coasts of the Mediterranean, although it is found in all stretches of water from Norway to the Canary Islands. It is normally 12 to 20 inches (30 to 50 centimeters) in length, and has a long body with two side fins, eight arms, and two long feelers. In order to catch squid, fish traps are used.

The smallest variant is served in Spain with the Basque name *txipirón*, very often *en su tinta* (in its own ink). The best known are the breaded, fried rings *calamares a la romana*, which are not known under this name in Rome (although *calamaretti fritti* are very popular there too). In Spain they are available as a tapa in almost every bar. The *calamares* are usually frozen and prepared with a thick layer of breadcrumbs. This, though, does not always indicate poor-quality squid, despite its tendency to share the sharp tang of fast food.

With its pouch-like shape, the *calamar* is particularly suitable for stuffing. Spaniards from the north and south like to put the tentacles inside, cut up and mixed with air-dried ham. (The Greeks and Turks prefer to use rice.) In Menorca the stuffing is prepared with milk, while in Tossa on the Costa Brava an apple is used. A meat stuffing is very popular in the northeast.

A LA PLANCHA

Fish and seafood from the hot plate, as natural as possible: in the Levante in particular, but also in other parts of Spain, delicacies from the sea are eaten *a la plancha*. Everything can be prepared on the hot iron plate, whether it is fish, meat, or vegetables. Bread is toasted and fried eggs cooked on the *plancha*. You need only a little oil, so it is a healthy way of cooking and the produce will keep its own, unadulterated taste. Even the nutrients are largely preserved. In particular the delicate shrimp from the Valencian coast, the famous *langostinos* from Vinaròs, and the excellent *gambas* from Denia, are enjoyed at their best without anything added – simply *a la plancha*.

CALAMARES RELLENOS
Stuffed squid
(Photograph opposite, top)

4 medium-size fresh squid
3 cloves of garlic, finely diced
1 onion, finely chopped
2 tbsp finely chopped parsley
4 ½ oz/125 g smoked ham, finely diced
2 tbsp breadcrumbs
1 egg
Salt and pepper
1 tsp mild paprika
Flour for coating
4 tbsp olive oil
2 ripe tomatoes, skinned and diced
Juice of ½ lemon
½ cup/125 ml white wine

Clean the squid thoroughly, then cut the tentacles into small pieces. Mix the tentacles with 2 cloves of garlic, half the onion and parsley, the ham, breadcrumbs, and egg. Season the mixture with salt, pepper, and some paprika, and stuff into the squid bodies. Then close the openings by using wooden picks to pierce the flesh. Toss the stuffed squid in flour. Heat the oil in a deep pan and brown the squid on all sides. Remove from the pan; then sweat the remaining garlic and onion in the oil until translucent. Stir in the diced tomato and the remaining parsley. Season with the remaining paprika and the lemon juice. Return the squid to the pan, pour in the wine, and bring to a boil. Simmer, covered, on a low heat for about 1 hour. Season with salt and pepper before serving.

Variation: Squid can also be stuffed with various other foods such as ground meat, monkfish, seafood, or ham and mushrooms.

SEPIA CON CEBOLLA
Squid with onion
(Photograph opposite, bottom)

Generous 1 lb/500 g medium-size squid, ready to use
¾ cup/200 ml olive oil
Generous 1 ½ lbs/750 g onions, thinly sliced
2 bay leaves, crushed
Salt and pepper
2 cloves of garlic, finely diced
Juice of ½ lemon
1 tbsp finely chopped parsley
Wedges of lemon to garnish

Wash the squid, pat dry thoroughly, and cut into bite-size pieces.
Heat the olive oil in a flameproof casserole and brown the squid. Add the onions and fry briefly. Season with the bay leaves, salt, and pepper; then stir in the finely diced garlic. Cover and cook slowly on a low heat for a good hour, stirring occasionally.
Finally, season with salt, pepper, and lemon juice before serving. Put into a warmed dish, sprinkle with parsley, and then garnish with the wedges of lemon.

The "common" squid definitely knows how to behave in the kitchen. It goes best with garlic and oil but is also suitable with an enormous variety of stuffings.

Large squid are most suitable for stuffing. For instance, they are often served as *calamares rellenos* with a hearty ham stuffing. A more unusual variation is with a filling of ground meat or seafood.

There are several versions of squid with onion *(sepia con cebolla)*: sometimes it is made simply with olive oil, garlic, and parsley, sometimes more fiery with tomatoes and a pinch of sweet or hot paprika.

CALAMARES IN THE KITCHEN

First wash the squid. Then remove the skin, working upwards toward the head.

Now hold the body and tentacles in both hands and carefully pull them apart.

By pulling carefully, the head and innards can be removed from the body pouch.

It is imperative that great care is taken to avoid damaging the ink sac.

Then take a very sharp knife and cut the tentacles off the head.

Don't throw away the silver-gray ink sac. It is used in many dishes for the sauce.

Finally pull the pen (this is the name for the transparent backbone) out of the body.

If you want to use the squid in rings, then you need to cut the usable parts into small pieces.

CALAMARES A LA ROMANA
Squid in batter

4 medium-size fresh squid, ready to use
4 cloves of garlic, finely diced
Salt
4 tbsp flour
3 eggs, beaten
Oil for frying
Lemon slices for garnishing

Cut the body pouch of the squid into rings about ½ inch/1 cm thick. Mix with the garlic and some salt and marinate for one hour. Toss the squid rings in the flour, then in the beaten egg, and fry in the hot oil in batches. Drain and serve immediately garnished with lemon slices.

Fish in spanish cuisine

The grouper *(mero)* has firm, tasty flesh, which is particularly suitable for broiling and for baking in the oven, as well as for stews and rice dishes.

The moray *(morena)* with its snakelike body can grow up to 6 ½ feet (2 meters) long. It has very oily, compact flesh with a fine taste.

The *sama* is a small dentex and is regarded as a typical food of the Canary Islands. It has delicate flesh, and it is usually eaten broiled.

The cod *(bacalao)* was used only as salted, dried fish for centuries. Recently more and more fresh cod has been used in cooking.

The anchovy *(boquerón)* is popular throughout Spain as a tapa. Anchovies are eaten salted and in oil *(anchoas)* or in a vinegar marinade *(en vinagre)*.

The sardine *(sardina)* is found off all Spanish coasts. It is often grilled or cooked in the oven and is regarded as one of the successes of the canning industry.

The dogfish *(cazón)* is a small, harmless shark which is regarded particularly highly in Andalusia. There it is eaten in a saffron or tomato sauce.

The swordfish *(pez espada)* is found in the Mediterranean and Atlantic. Its flesh is similar to that of the tuna, and it is particularly good baked as steaks.

The monkfish *(rape)* has become fashionable in recent years. Each region has numerous ways of preparing its white, extremely delicate flesh.

The ray's bream *(palometa negra, zapatero, japuta)* is found particularly off Spain's north coast and is often used in place of tuna.

The hake *(merluza)* is one of the most popular fish used in Spanish cuisine. It can be prepared in many ways; the tender gill cheeks are considered to be particularly delicious.

Spanish fishermen haul in their nets in seas throughout the world and bring a large variety into the kitchen. The Spanish fishing fleet travels as far as the coasts of America and Africa. Which nations have the right to which fishing grounds has become a matter of politics and constantly causes arguments in international bodies.

The white seabream *(sargo)* does not have such delicate flesh as other types of bream, but, like its relatives, is cooked in a salt crust or in the oven.

Both the bluefin tuna *(atún,* above) and the long-fin tuna *(bonito)* are found in Spanish waters. The long-fin tuna has more delicate tasting flesh.

The red scorpionfish *(cabracho, escorpión)* with its spines is outwardly one of the most exotic fish. It has very tasty, white flesh.

The axillary seabream *(besugo)* with its delicate, white flesh is the typical Christmas meal in many Spanish households. It is baked in the oven.

The red bream *(palometa roja)* belongs to the bream family. It is very similar to the *alfonsiño* and, like its relatives, is extremely tasty.

The parrot-fish *(vieja)* is mainly caught in the waters around the Canary Islands. It is usually served there baked with a hot sauce *(mojo verde)*.

Every Spanish market has its own fish counter which sells a large variety of freshly caught fish and fresh seafood.

The fisherman's work is not over once the fresh fish is at the market. As has always been the case, the nets have to be kept in a good state of repair. However, this sort of romantic scene should not hide the fact that fishing is hard work, which today mainly takes place onboard ultra-modern, computer-controlled trawlers.

The mackerel *(caballa)* comes mainly from the Atlantic and has very oily flesh. It is particularly suitable for broiling, but can also be baked or braised.

The Atlantic john dory or St. Peter's fish *(pez de San Pedro)* has only a small amount of flesh because of its large head, but has a pleasant taste and a firm consistency.

The plaice *(solla)* is a flatfish which is found in the Atlantic Ocean and Mediterranean Sea. It is usually cooked whole on the hot plate.

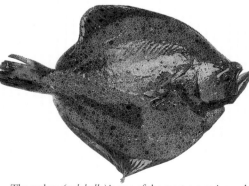

The turbot *(rodaballo)* is one of the most expensive and delicate fish. Those from the Atlantic are particularly sought after, though it is also often bred on fish farms.

The conger *(congrio)* can grow to 10 feet (3 meters) and weigh 155 pounds (70 kilograms). In the north it is often eaten with a garlic and parsley sauce *(salsa verde)*.

The brill *(rapante)* is found in both the Mediterranean and Atlantic. It is closely related to the turbot, and tastes just as good, but is very much cheaper.

The red *alfonsiño* is a specialty of the Canary Islands, where it is found in its waters. It has very firm, white flesh and is usually eaten baked.

The ballan wrasse *(maragota)* is rarely found on the market. It feeds on crabs and mollusks, which makes its flesh full of flavor.

The bib *(faneca)* is not found very often on menus in Spain. It is caught in the Atlantic and Mediterranean and has a very delicate flavor.

The sole *(lenguado)* with its tender, delicate flesh is usually simply baked so as not to adulterate the flavor. Wine sauces also go well with it.

The red gurnard *(rubio, perlón)* is a member of the gurnard family. It is full of flavor and is suitable for stews. Because of its big head there is a lot of waste.

The horse-mackerel *(jurrel or chicharro)* has very oily flesh and is mainly canned. It is also found marinated *(en escabeche)* or broiled.

The gilthead bream *(dorada)* with a golden stripe between its eyes has very tasty, white flesh and is often baked in a salt crust or in the oven.

The megrim *(gallo)* is a flatfish which can often be sold as sole. It has delicate flesh and is best baked with very few accompaniments.

The garfish *(aguja)* is mainly found in the Gulf of Biscay. Its firm, delicate flesh makes it suitable for braising.

The sea bass *(lubina)* has lean, white, firm, and very palatable flesh, which is prepared differently by every region – often in the oven.

The bogue *(boga)* belongs to the bream family and lives mainly in the Atlantic. It has many bones and is often prepared on the grill or in stews.

The gray mullet *(mújol, lisa)* has palatable, white flesh. In Murcia the salted and dried roe is considered to be a delicacy.

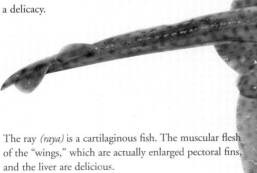

Several subspecies of the red mullet *(salmonete)* are found, especially in the Mediterranean. The delicate flesh goes particularly well with vegetables.

The ray *(raya)* is a cartilaginous fish. The muscular flesh of the "wings," which are actually enlarged pectoral fins, and the liver are delicious.

ALMONDS

In January the almond trees on the Sierra Espadán north of Valencia are in blossom, and the mountains are covered in a haze of white and pink. At this time of year there is a similar scene in many regions along the Spanish Mediterranean coast, since the majority of Spanish almonds *(almendras)* grow from Tarragona via Valencia to Málaga. They also grow in the Andalusian hinterland near Granada and Almería as well as on the Balearic Islands. On average, Spain harvests between 220,400 and 330,600 tons (200,000 and 300,000 tonnes) of almonds year after year. A large proportion of these are exported.

The almond tree is a robust, long-lived plant that blossoms every year. The Roman Agronom Columela said that all this tree requires is hard, dry ground. The almonds in Valencia are cultivated on such ground and are harvested in August and September. Unlike oranges which have to be watered regularly, the almond tree is extremely undemanding. It gets the moisture it requires through roots which extend deep into the ground. An almond tree is best grown from the bitter almond. Young trees have a smooth, light brown trunk which becomes increasingly darker and gnarled with the passage of time. In order to develop new varieties and achieve good quality, almond trees are as a rule grafted. Wild forms of the almond, as well as sometimes peach or apricot trees, are used as the rootstock. When the fruit is ripe its external, hairy fruit layer splits open and the almond kernel appears. Before the fruits fall, farmers spread large cloths under the trees to make it easier to collect them. After being harvested the almond kernels are broken out of their shells. This used to be done laboriously by hand, but today special machines are used.

1 The Mediterranean coastal regions are covered in a veil of white and pink when the almond trees are in blossom.
2 When the almonds are ripe, the outer fruit layer splits open and the kernels appear.
3 The fruits are collected in huge cloths that are spread out under the almond trees.

4 The almonds are collected in large baskets. Stalks and leaves naturally also get mixed in with them.
5 Leaves and twigs now have to be separated from the valuable almonds. Today this is done by a machine.
6 This just leaves the almonds, but they still have their fruit layer. This must also be removed.

7 The almonds are sorted by machine according to size. Then the kernels are broken out of the fruit shell.
8 Some of the almonds go straight on the market unshelled. The rest are shelled, fully automatically nowadays.
9 So that only the best produce is packed, the shelled almonds are sorted again at the end, by hand.

Above: Almond varieties *Marcona* (above) and *Largueta*, both with the fruit layer, the almond kernel, and shelled. Background: During the harvest, cloths catch the almonds.

Above: The last almonds are brought down from the trees using long poles. None are to be wasted.

There are numerous varieties of almond in Spain with such pleasant-sounding names as *Larguetas* and *Marconas* (see photograph), as well as *Planetas* and *Valencias*. Some are Spanish varieties that grow throughout the country, such as the long *Largueta* or the heart-shaped *Planeta*. Other varieties of almond are only of regional importance.

Whereas today almonds are usually served as appetizers or nibbles, for a long time they were an important source of protein for the rural population. Modern dietetics can now confirm their high nutritional value: almonds consist of 54 percent fat, and contain iron, calcium, phosphorus, and vitamin B. There is as much linoleic acid in just two almonds as there is in 2.6 U.S. pints (1.25 liters) of milk. So this polyunsaturated fatty acid is particularly beneficial to the heart and circulatory system.

Almonds are eaten roasted, salted, or even coated with a layer of sugar. In addition they are traditionally used in the making of *Turrón* (see page 382 f), marzipan, cookies, and cakes. They can also enhance fish dishes and sauces. Sweet almond oil is used in the cosmetics industry where it is utilized in the manufacture of soap and perfume. The actual fruit of the bitter almond tree is not eaten, as it contains the glycoside amygdalin from which the poisonous prussic acid separates during digestion. However, bitter almond oil is used in the cosmetics and drugs industries and even in tiny amounts in baking.

For soft *turrón (turrón blando)*, the *turrón duro* (hard *turrón*) mixture is processed further. It is first ground between rollers to form a homogenous paste.

Then the paste is reheated and slowly stirred into a smooth mixture. The addition of almond oil binds the mixture; egg white can also be added.

After the mixture has been left to cool in square metal containers, the *turrón blando* is cut into portions mechanically and then packed.

Traveling turron salesmen

Traveling salesmen made *turrón* famous in Spain. They must have been successful because in Madrid in the 16th century these early commercial travelers were only allowed to sell *turrón* that was not made in the city from special shops in the Plaza Mayor. If the traveling hawkers were caught selling outside the specified areas, their goods were seized and distributed to charitable institutions.

As late as the end of the 19th century the occupation of traveling *turrón* salesman was very common. Emigrants from eastern Spain started up business in North Africa and sold their wares in Algiers, Rabat, or Fez. Others set themselves up in the colonies. They traveled to Havana, Montevideo, Buenos Aires, and California, and established companies, some of which still exist today. Inevitably, an enormous number of tall stories have grown up around the traveling *turrón* hawkers. One anecdote tells of a man from Jijona who took it into his head in the 19th century to sell his luxurious sweet stuff in the Vatican. However, in Rome he came across Garibaldi's hungry troops and was forced to hand over his goods to the soldiers at giveaway prices. Another salesman allegedly went from Spain to Morocco, where as well as successfully selling excellent *turrón* he is supposed to have sold his wife.

TURRÓN

It is said in Catalonia that a master confectioner called Pablo Turrons invented the almond nougat *(turrón)* in Barcelona at the beginning of the 18th century, at the time of the War of the Spanish Succession. Using the only available foodstuffs, almonds and honey, he made a survival ration for the besieged town. It is more likely, however, that the sweet delicacy was brought to Spain by the Arab conquerors. In Jijona near Alicante, Arabs and Jews produced the candy long before the days of Pablo Turrons under the name of *halvo*. A similar candy, called halva, is still found today in Turkey and the Near East.

In Valencia *turrón* was early on sold as a delicacy. In the 16th century the councilors of Alicante would entertain important visitors with *turrón* and fig bread *(pan de higos)*. They must have been very generous with it, because in 1595 King Philip II wrote to the town dignitaries, urging them to exercise moderation when proffering the exquisite gift. Although

turrón is known throughout Spain today and is enjoyed everywhere, in particular at Christmas, the Valencian town of Jijona is still regarded as the main center of *turrón* production. The production process, requiring skill and watched over critically by a *turronero*, has been preserved down the centuries. Almonds and honey are still the basic ingredients of a true *turrón*, and as far as purists are concerned there are only two true varieties:

• soft Jijona turrón *(turrón blando)*, and
• hard Alicante turrón *(turrón duro)*.

To produce hard *turrón*, the almonds are firstly roasted and chopped up. They are then mixed with honey and simmered over a constant heat, during which time the mixture is stirred with large wooden spoons. Finally some egg white is added as a binding agent. Then the mixture is cooled, cut into pieces, and packed, usually by machine. To obtain soft Jijona *turrón*, the cooled block of *turrón* is ground with the separated almond oil to form a glutinous paste. It is then reheated, and beaten for hours into a soft, even mixture. Finally it is bound with egg white. Apart from the classic versions which are

Many producers still refer to old traditions in the style of packaging.

made only from almonds, honey, and egg white, there are now all sorts of modern variations of *turrón*. Ingredients range from egg yolk and sugar, through hazelnuts, pine nuts, shredded coconut, and candied fruit, to milk and dark chocolate. Often *guirlache*, a type of almond bread made from caramelized sugar and almonds that have not been roasted, is regarded as *turrón* (illustration page 100).

1 For real *turrón* from Jijona the shelled almonds are first roasted in a large drum. Then they are chopped up and mixed with honey.
2 The *turrón* mixture is simmered at a constant heat. The *turronero* constantly stirs it with large spoons. Egg white is added to bind the mixture.
3 The hard version *(turrón duro)* is now almost ready. When the mixture has cooled, the workers cut portion-size amounts from the sticky mixture by hand.
4 The *turrón* mixture is covered with wafers and then packed. The sweet delicacy can be bought in *turronerías* (below), but they are also available in supermarkets.

Horchata, tiger nut milk which is often sweetened, is available in Alboraya and other Valencian towns in special *horchaterías*. *Horchata* comes in liquid form (front), as well as mixed with crushed ice as *granizado* (back). Although the delicious drink made from fresh tiger nuts (*chufas*, photograph center) is perfectly satisfying on its own, it is also served with cakes such as *fartons*, yeast sticks with syrup (left), or with all sorts of excellent puff pastries.

The tiger nut *(chufa)* grows well in the sandy soil around Valencia. The young seedlings are planted in the spring.

Tiger nuts are tubers that grow below ground. Before they are harvested the foliage is burnt off or even mowed.

The work has become easier: today the *chufas* are lifted out of the ground using harvesters instead of bare hands.

There are usually impurities among the freshly harvested tiger nuts. Naturally, these must be sorted out.

If you want to make tiger nut milk *(horchata)*, first wash the *chufas* thoroughly with plenty of water.

Then grind the *chufas* finely and put them straight into a food processor where they are mixed with fresh water.

Sugar and lemon juice are added, and the tiger nut mixture is mixed together thoroughly in the machine.

Finally filter the whole thing, and the *horchata* is then ready. It can be drunk immediately or bottled.

Tiger nuts

The tiger nut *(chufa)* is an ancient tuber. It has even been found as a burial object in the urns of 6000-year-old Egyptian desert tombs. Later it was evidently placed in sarcophaguses as food for the dead. Although it has been known for a long time, the tiger nut was of only regional importance as a foodstuff. In Spain *chufas* are mainly grown in the Alboraya region, a few miles from Valencia. The town is, therefore, regarded as the birthplace of the drink *horchata*, tiger nut milk.

The tiger nut (lat. *Cyperus esculentus*) is the brown tuber of the nutsedge and is rich in starch, oil, and sugar. Its taste is very reminiscent of almonds or hazelnuts. The *chufas* are planted in April or May, generally in sandy soil. They can be harvested in the months of October through December. As the fruit ripens under the ground, the first job at harvest time is to mow the green parts of the plant growing above the ground. After this the tubers have to be dug up. This laborious task used to be carried out by hand, but nowadays machines are used.

Chufas are an extremely tasty and healthy foodstuff. They contain a high proportion of unsaturated fatty acids, in particular linoleic acid, as well as biotin (vitamin H), which improves skin and hair, and rutin (vitamin P), which protects blood vessels. In addition, tiger nuts contain more than 25 percent fat, about 30 percent starch, and a good 7 percent protein, as well as many minerals (calcium, magnesium, potassium, and sodium). Tiger nuts are now classified as a healthy whole food product, rich in fiber. They are considered to be good for the nerves as well as providing an energy boost. They can also be eaten raw as flakes, such as in muesli, with yogurt, or quark, or with raw fruit and vegetables. Medical experiments have confirmed the positive effect of the tiger nut in the treatment of certain intestinal illnesses.

To make the popular tiger nut milk *horchata*, the *chufas* are first harvested, then dried and sorted. Thoroughly cleaned, they are then ground, and water, sugar, and some lemon juice is added to this mixture. Then it is all filtered. A real *horchata* should always be prepared fresh. It can be drunk as a liquid or as *granizado* – that is, mixed with crushed ice. The drink can be stored cold or even frozen for quite a long time. Today *horchata* can also be bought in bottles, and in this case is usually diluted with milk.

Like every drink in the social culture that is Spain, *horchata* is best enjoyed with friends and conversation around a café table.

Fruit from Valencia

Grapes from the bag
In 1919 the mayor of Novelda in the sunny Vinalopó valley had an inspired idea. In the fight against the "grape plague," when a moth destroyed the fruit, he put paper bags over his grapes in order to protect them from the dreaded pest. The system worked, and the unusual cultivation method has changed little to this day. About 20 days after the plants have flowered, when the growing grapes are the size of a peppercorn, poor panicles are removed from the vine. The good panicles are wrapped in special white paper bags which open at the bottom. In this way the fruit is protected from unwelcome, external influences such as moisture, fungal diseases, and insects. Over and above this, there is a special microclimate inside the bag, which allows the grapes to ripen slowly and evenly and attain an optimum flavor by the time they are harvested. The grapes can be picked from August through December, depending on their variety and location.

In the Valencia region grapes are not only grown for wine but also for eating. The best ones come from Novelda in the Vinalopó valley.

The grapes from Novelda grow in special paper bags in which there is a favorable microclimate and which also protect them from pests.

Dates from Elche
The Carthaginians originally planted dates around Elche. Later the Arabs continued to cultivate the groves. In the 13th century there are supposed to have been almost one million palms in Elche's palm grove. Today there are estimated to be several hundred thousand. This makes Elche the only town in Europe in which large stocks of this tree have survived. Some of the date palms tended here are up to 200 years old and grow to between 98 and 130 feet (30 and 40 meters) tall. Around 2200 tons (2000 tonnes) of dates *(dátiles)* are picked each year in Elche. They are sold fresh, dried, or even as an excellent date liqueur.

Europe's largest palm grove is in Elche near Alicante. The dates hang in the tops of the palms in thick bunches.

Dates are picked in whole bunches. They contain a lot of sugar, iron, calcium, and B-group vitamins, and are considered to aid digestion.

Medlars
Many cultures call the medlar the "fruit of love" and consider it an aphrodisiac. The medlar tree has been grown in Japan and China as an ornamental plant for more than a thousand years. It reached Spain via Mauritius 200 years ago from where it spread to the whole of the Levante and the southeast of the country. Today the small delicate fruits grow in particular in Callosa d'en Sarrià in a sheltered valley in the area which surrounds Alicante. They are picked by hand between the end of March and the end of May. Medlars have a yellowy orange flesh, are extremely juicy, and have a distinct sweet, tangy flavor. Although the fruit has a fine skin it must always be peeled before eating. It can be eaten fresh on its own, in muesli and desserts, or as an exotic accompaniment to duck or chicken. Medlars are considered to be healthy and very digestible. They only contain 44 calories per 3½ ounces (100 grams), and also provide plenty of calcium and phosphorus, as well as the important vitamins A and C.

WINE-PRODUCING IN VALENCIA

D.O. Utiel-Requena

Almost 154 square miles (40,000 hectares) of land in the mountains around the small towns of Utiel and Requena are covered in vines. The principal grape variety, the red Bobal, enjoys a solid reputation as a rosé grape and certainly also has the potential for good red wines (see opposite). There are, however, also some interesting red wines made from Tempranillo/Garnacha or Cabernet Sauvignon blends, which are very good value. Some bodegas are also trying out Cabernet Franc and Graciano. The most important white variety in this region is the Macebeo, followed by the Merseguera. White wines, though, play a secondary role in the D.O. Utiel-Requena. Some villages in this wine-producing area are officially allowed to market their red wines under the D.O. Valencia label, since the latter has hardly any red wines.

D.O. Valencia

The white grape Merseguera, which produces very light and pleasantly fresh white wines, is predominant in this region which has 62 square miles (16,000 hectares) of vineyards and 16 permitted types of vine. The white wines produced from the Mersegura grape are often lemony and somewhat grassy to the nose. They reveal pleasant hints of apple and almond in the mouth. The classic Moscatel wines, which leave a strong impression of pure, sweet fruit in the mouth, come from the Turís-Cheste-Godelleta triangle, which is in the heart of the Moscatel de Valencia area. The farther inland you go, the more you find sweet wines with hints of raisins and a pleasant sharpness.

D.O. Alicante

The Moscatel wines from Alicante have a similar structure to those in the D.O. Valencia, but with more hints of honey. There are now also producers who create naturally sweet wines to which no wine alcohol is added. The D.O. Alicante vines grow as far as the Mediterranean and extend into the adjacent highland. Roughly equal amounts of red and white wines, characterized by a great variety of aromas, are produced on 56 square miles (14,600 hectares). The white varieties are Merseguera, Moscatel, Romano, Macabeo, Planta Fina, and Airén. Red grapes grown include Monastrell, Garnacha, Merlot, Tintorera, and Tempranillo. Recently wine-producers have also planted Chardonnay, Riesling, Cabernet Sauvignon, and Pinot Noir. Some bodegas now sell "big," intense, and very complex red wines, which are pressed predominately from Tempranillo and French varieties. The local Monastrell grape produces wonderfully fruity red wines, but they soon lose their color and oxidize in the barrel.

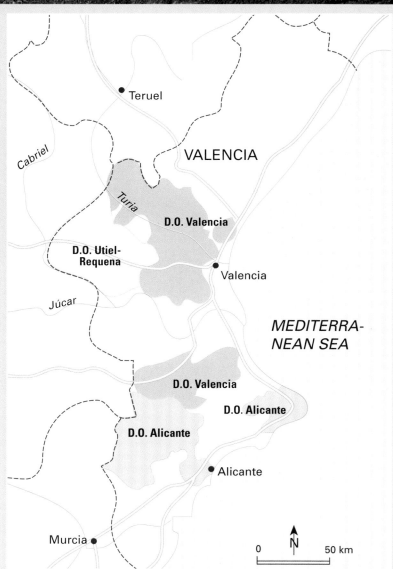

WINE FROM UTIEL-REQUENA

Wine has been grown in Valencia for two thousand years. The wine-producing region has not, though, enjoyed the best of reputations over the last few decades. For a long time mainly red cask wines have come out of the towns of Utiel and Requena. In spite of the enormous area covered by vineyards, almost 154 square miles (40,000 hectares), the wines from this area were supposedly poor quality and mass-produced, causing a headache for Brussels bureaucrats before Spain joined the E.U. The good rosé wine from this region was largely simply forgotten.

Ninety percent of Utiel-Requena's vineyards are occupied by the red Bobal, a resistant, firm grape which is very suited to the region's climatic conditions. The vineyards are situated at an average height of 2460 feet (750 meters), on brown, chalky soil in Valencia's mountainous hinterland. The summers are extremely hot and the winters often very cold. Until recently fear of early frosts meant the Bobal grapes were usually not left on the vines long enough to produce good red, barrel-aged wines. So for decades rosé wines and thick, almost black *doble pasta* wines in particular were pressed in Utiel-Requena. The latter were used mainly for blending.

A *doble pasta* is a by-product, as it were, of rosé production. Large quantities of fresh rosé wine are obtained from the Bobal grape, with the grapes being only lightly pressed after a short maceration time. Large quantities of must are left over which still contain a lot of juice. This must is added to an unpressed red wine must in fermentation tanks. The result is red wine which is fermented from a double quantity of red grape flesh and skin, the so-called *pasta*. You can imagine the intense color of *doble pasta* wines and what a stroke of luck this wine represents for numerous red table wines, many of which would appear as colorless wines without the addition of *vinos de doble pasta*.

In 1987 the region was awarded the protected designation of origin **D.O. Utiel-Requena**, and the wines' reputation began to improve. Today more and more wine-producers in the region are aware of the characteristic properties of their wine and sell it in bottles. The predominant grape variety is still the Bobal from which red wines and, above all, fresh, fruity rosés are pressed. These rosé wines are really best drunk young, and are today considered to be some of the best rosé wines in Spain.

Even if there are no Bobal red wines which have yet been successfully barrel-aged, the research station of the D.O. looks set to produce impressive results. And once the wine-producers begin to exploit the possibilities of the Bobal grape fully, there may be some surprises in store for wine connoisseurs. The success enjoyed by other Spanish wine regions, such as La Rioja and Navarra, may at last be shared by Valencia and its bad reputation for wine will be forgotten.

SUGAR-SWEET DROPS

The Valencian wine regions also produce excellent liqueur wines and dessert wines. Generally grapes of the Garnacha, Malvasía, Pedro Ximénez, or Moscatel varieties are used to produce liqueur wines. A base wine is first produced to which wine alcohol and unfermented must or Mistela sweet wine are added. As a rule, the liqueur wines are stored in a wooden keg for two years before they appear on the market. During this time the characteristic flavor of raisins and honey develops. Valencia's dessert wines include the famous Fondillón, which took its place on the world's grand tables a hundred years ago and is produced only in Alicante. The Fondillón is a late vintage wine made from the red Monastrell grape, with a very high sugar content and 16 to 18° alcohol. It is left to mature for eight years in oak casks. During the aging process the younger wines pass through several series of butts, in accordance with the *solera* system, and are successively mixed with older wines.

The Moscatel Romano grape is the base for the Moscatel wine of the same name, a luscious, sweet dessert wine. Mistelas are sweet wines produced from filtered unfermented must to which wine alcohol is added so that Mistelas achieve an alcohol content of around 15°.

Left: Traditionally mainly Bobal grapes are grown in Utiel-Requena's vineyards. Red wines and fresh, fruity rosés are pressed from them.

MURCIA

Harald Irnberger

Murcia

Murcia, the region on the Levante coast, is blessed
with sunshine. Farmers here harvest fresh vegetables
all year round for the whole of Europe.

Thanks to its very mild climate and calm coastal waters the region of Murcia is one of Europe's oldest settlements. Archeological finds and Greek travel accounts testify to four Iberian tribes who at one time inhabited this region. Later, Greek and Phoenician traders set up businesses on the coast and in the interior of the region. They exported natural products, such as the esparto grass which grows in abundance, and silver from Murcian mines. The Carthaginians founded the city of Cartagena, which at the time of the Punic Wars (before the start of the Christian calendar) was the busiest port on the Mediterranean coast. Under Roman rule the activities of fishing, hunting, and agriculture developed into the basic pillars of the Murcian economy, and this tradition continues today. Even then cooks benefited from the geographical and climatic division of the region into three. The waters of the Costa Cálida, the "warm coast," provided plenty of ingredients for the popular pungent sauce garum, which was exported throughout the Roman empire. Olive and fig groves were planted in the fertile meadows of the Río Segura, and in the very dry, mountainous hinterland heavy wines were produced which were even then exported in quite large numbers. In the middle of the 8th century the Arabs conquered the region and helped it to achieve a significant cultural and economic upturn. To the Mediterranean region they also brought with them many Middle Eastern foodstuffs and sophisticated cooking techniques. Above all, the irrigation system, which is still partly intact today, changed the hot, dry region into what it has remained until the present day: a flourishing irrigated area. The population explosion at the beginning of the 20th century led to a mass migration of agricultural workers, with no possessions, into the towns, as happened in so many regions of Europe. The attempt at land reform came to an end along with the Spanish Republic during the Civil War of the 1930s. What remained – poor farmers and a hard life – finds expression not least in culinary traditions: here what dominates is a poor man's Mediterranean cuisine, based on excellent and varied ingredients. It makes use of produce from the intensive horticulture in the interior, of fish and seafood from the Mediterranean and Mar Menor, and of game and wine from the province's hinterland. The fruit and cultivation techniques imported by the Arabs have successfully merged into the regional cuisine, just like the descendants of the former conquerors have merged into the Murcian population.

Santiago de Compostela
Vitoria-Gasteiz
León
Pamplona
Barcelona
Valladolid
Zaragoza
Madrid
Toledo
Valencia
Palma de Mallorca
Mérida
Ciudad Real
Murcia
Sevilla
Granada
Murcia

Opposite: The Mar Menor symbolizes life. The Murcians have lived off the treasures of this lagoon, which puts fish in the stomach and sunshine in the

Spain's market garden

The Murcians owe their market garden, the Huerta, to the Arabs. Tools have been found, though, that verify that people sought to make use of the ideal conditions on the Río Segura during the Neolithic Age: water close at hand, fertile ground, and a hot climate. For the inhabitants the river was always both a blessing and a curse. While, on the one hand, it guaranteed survival, frequent floods cost many lives, and destroyed harvests and houses, including whole towns.

The Romans safeguarded their estates, on which they grew figs, olives, and grain, by using irrigation systems. The Arabs, who arrived in the country from the 8th century, perfected the irrigation systems with ditches and scoop wheels. Diverting the water to higher dry land, they introduced as then unknown varieties of crops: citrus fruits, almonds, eggplants, and rice. After the Moors had been driven out, the plantations were divided up into plots of land and given to immigrants from northern Spain. With time the large cultivated areas were turned into a colorful patchwork of small orchards and vegetable gardens. These *minifundios*, plots of land up to 2 ½ acres (1 hectare) in size, still exist on the banks of the rivers Segura and Guadalentín, and people in the Huerta still enjoy fruit all year round. Cherries, apricots, plums, peaches, figs, pomegranates, quinces, pears, apples, and almonds sustain the inhabitants of the Huerta from April through November. Oranges are also available between December and March. The Huertanos grow vegetables and pulses, and in addition produce their own preserved vegetables.

As in the neighboring cultivated areas of Valencia, today almost 80 percent of the agricultural produce is exported to Central Europe. The area of irrigated farmland has doubled in the past 30 years thanks to new technologies. Farmers can till their land all year round and harvest it up to four times a year. Regular crop rotation is relatively rare. Fruit and vegetable cultivation is adapted to suit prevailing market requirements.

Since the setting up of the first canning factory by the Río Segura in 1886, this branch of industry has experienced an enormous boom. About 75 companies all around Murcia are currently involved in the canning of vegetables and fruit. Distribution channels recently set up by the agricultural industry have done so well that it has been possible to secure an income far above the Spanish national average even for small family businesses. Murcia, therefore, receives many envious glances from Valencia's

Farmers in the Huerta de Murcia can harvest fresh vegetables all year round. Beans are one of the most popular – even on regional menus.

Fieldworkers have the laborious task of picking the green beans by hand. A hat provides protection from the scorching sun – whether it be a straw hat or baseball cap.

Even Murcia is not spared by the modern age. Outdoor cultivation is certainly predominant, but there are also large greenhouses here and there.

The farmer plants what the city dweller wants. Produce from Murcia goes to the whole of Europe. Broccoli is very much in demand, so it is found in fields here.

Capers

Capers have long been used in the Mediterranean for scurvy and rheumatism, and as a dehydrating remedy. The Romans also used them as a condiment and aphrodisiac. The caper is the small, heart-shaped flower bud of a wonderful shrub called *Capparis spinosa*. This grows wild in rock crevices and cracks in walls in hot Mediterranean countries. Between the end of May and early October in the Murcia region, first the buds and stems of the caper shrub are harvested, then the fruits.

The pink and white flowers have an extremely short life. They open in the early morning and are dead by midday. They must be picked by hand while they are in bud. On the same day they are hurriedly pickled in brine where they remain for two months. However, the characteristic sharp taste develops only when the capers are put in wine vinegar afterward. The delicate buds are sorted by size before they are sold – then they are either pickled in jars and bottles, or dried, salted, and loose.

As is the case with all pickled vegetables, the smallest capers *(alcaparras)* are the most aromatic and therefore the most expensive. The top quality are the *nonpareilles*, which can be no larger than ⅓ inch (7 millimeters). At the opposite end of the quality scale is the *alcaparrón*, the giant Spanish caper, which is not the bud but the fruit of the caper shrub. *Alcaparrones* are also pickled, but are far coarser and less tasty. In Murcia capers are not usually used as a condiment in dishes, but eaten as a piquant counterbalance to them. So a bowl of gherkins, mild chili peppers, and capers are always placed on the table. This tasty little vegetable is used all over the world to bring piquancy and tartness to sauces, condiments and a variety of dishes.

cultivated areas with their endless mono-cultures: the huge production of citrus fruits in large parts of the neighboring region has led to overproduction and the collapse of prices. That is why plans are afoot in the Valencian Huerta to diversify again, to cultivate plums, apricots, and cherries, to grow flowers for cutting and ornamental plants, or even to return to the traditional cultivation of vegetables. They are tempted by the tried and tested example of the Huerta de Murcia which has achieved modernization without giving up traditional variety of produce.

The Arabs brought sophisticated irrigation systems to Murcia, as this waterwheel at Lorquí shows. In addition they introduced many new varieties of vegetable, including the artichoke (background).

Many irrigation channels *(acequias)* in southern Spain originate from the time of the Arabs. They are not just tourist sights though, they still provide the fields with valuable water.

Cooking with vegetables

Olla gitana
Gipsy stew
(Photograph right)

¾ cup/150 g chickpeas
¾ cup/150 g dried white beans
Salt and pepper
9 oz/250 g green beans, washed
9 oz/250 g pumpkin flesh, diced
2 carrots, sliced
2 cooking pears, peeled and sliced
2 medium-size potatoes, diced
1 onion, finely diced
Scant ½ cup/100 ml olive oil
2 ripe tomatoes, skinned and diced
1 clove of garlic, diced
1 tsp mild paprika
A few saffron threads
A handful of mint leaves (hierbabuena),
cut into thin strips

Soak the chickpeas and white beans overnight. The next day put into fresh water with some salt and bring to a boil; then simmer for about 30 minutes. Mix in the green beans, pumpkin flesh, carrots, cooking pears, and potatoes, and cook for another 15 minutes.

Meanwhile sweat the onion in the oil until translucent. Add the tomatoes and cook together with the onion. Crush the garlic using a mortar and pestle with the paprika, saffron, and some salt. Stir this mixture into the tomato sauce and then simmer on a low heat for 10 minutes.

Next add the sauce to the stew, stir well, and simmer for another 5 minutes; season with salt and pepper. Finally, sprinkle over the mint leaves before serving.

Zarangollo murciano
Murcian zucchini

2 large onions, diced
2 cloves of garlic, finely diced
½ cup/125 ml olive oil
2 ¼ lbs/1 kg zucchini, cut up into small pieces
Salt and pepper
1 tsp oregano

Sweat the onions and garlic in the oil until translucent. Add the zucchini and steam, covered, on a low heat for 15 minutes. Season with salt, pepper, and oregano, and cook for another 5 minutes until the zucchini are soft.

Rice from Calasparra

The rice grown around Calasparra, on the flood plain of the Río Segura. was the first Spanish rice with the protected designation of origin *Denominación de Origen (D.O.)*.

It owes its reputation to the particular ecological conditions in which it grows, as well as to a very special cultivation system. The purity of the drinking water and the coolness of the river water at a height of 1475 feet (450 meters) delay the ripening of the grain, which benefits the quality of the rice. Furthermore, farmers are concerned about preserving the wealth of minerals in the soil by crop rotation. In a two-year cycle rice is grown from May through October, wheat from November through June, legumes from July through April. The foliage of the legumes, which is plowed in after harvesting, serves as a natural fertilizer for the rice that follows. The rice varieties *Balilla x Sollana* and *Bomba* are grown in Calasparra. Because of its natural dryness the grain of the *Bomba* variety needs larger amounts of water and a longer cooking time than other rice. During cooking it increases to up to three times its original volume. The loose consistency, but simultaneous firmness of the grains, remains for a long time after cooking. The *Balilla x Sollana* variety has similar qualities and, unlike the husked, white *Bomba*, is also available as brown rice *(arroz integral)*

and organically grown brown rice *(integral de cultivo ecológico)*. The latter is cultivated without the use of any chemical fertilizers, herbicides, pesticides, and insecticides, and the rice is also processed without chemicals being added. Calasparra's rice producers had to fight for a long time for the right to the appellation of *Denominación de Origen* for their modest production (2800 tons/2500 tonnes a year), since some of the large associations, such as the rice producers of Valencia or in the Ebro Delta, felt that it threatened their prestige. The appellation, which is a guarantee for the consumer of the product's origin and quality, was, however, finally awarded in 1986. The controlling body, *Consejo Regulador*, issues numbered labels to the producers within the D.O. and subjects both the plantations and the treatment of the rice to rigid controls.

Arroz con verdura de la huerta
Rice with green vegetables

3 cloves of garlic, finely diced
4 tbsp olive oil
1 ripe beefsteak tomato, skinned and diced
7 oz/200 g green beans, washed
9 oz/250 g fava beans, shelled
½ cauliflower, cut up into florets
1 green bell pepper, seeded and diced
2 young artichokes, washed and quartered
1 cup/200g Calasparra rice, or
medium-grain rice
1 dried red paprika pod
Salt and pepper
A handful of green garlic, or green onions,
cut up small

Cook the garlic in the olive oil in a paella pan just until it has obtained some color. Add the vegetables and brown while stirring. Stir in the rice and cook briefly, and then pour in 2 cups/500 ml of boiling water.

Crush the red paprika pod using a mortar and pestle, and stir this into the vegetable rice. Season with salt and pepper and then simmer for approximately 20 minutes. Stir in the green garlic or green onions 5 minutes before the end of the cooking time.

Pimientos rellenos
Stuffed bell peppers

1 onion, diced
2 cloves of garlic, finely diced
Scant ½ cup/100 ml olive oil
2 cups/400 g ground lamb
Salt and pepper
1 tsp mild paprika
½ tsp ground cinnamon
1 egg
4 tbsp cooked rice
4 large green bell peppers
2 tbsp breadcrumbs

Sweat the onion and garlic in 2 tbsp olive oil until translucent. Add the ground lamb to the pan and cook until crumbly. Season with salt, pepper, paprika, and cinnamon.

Remove from the heat and leave to cool a little. Mix the meat mixture with the egg and rice.

Wash the bell peppers and remove the stalks and all the seeds. Fill the peppers with the meat mixture.

Pour the remaining olive oil into a baking pan. Place the bell peppers in it meat-side up and sprinkle the breadcrumbs over the peppers. Cook in a preheated oven at 430 °F/220 °C for approximately 30 minutes.

SALZILLO – MASTER OF THE "PASOS"

The Salzillo procession is the most important parade in the Murcian Holy Week. The procession begins at seven o'clock in the morning on Good Friday when the "kiss," the first ray of sunshine, falls on the standard of the brotherhood or in the face of the *Dolorosa*, the Lady of Sorrow. Then whole scenes *(pasos)* are carried through the streets of the town. The most popular is the representation of the Last Supper with real food on fine table linen. Francisco Salzillo Alcaraz, the son of a Neapolitan sculptor and a Spanish mother, was born in Murcia in 1707. In his youth he took up his father's profession, but increasingly specialized in wood. At the age of twenty he had to support his large family through commissions. When he died in 1783, famous and esteemed, Salzillo left almost 1800 life-size sculptures, some of which can be seen in the Salzillo Museum in the Iglesia de Jesús in Murcia. His famous crib is here, too. There is hardly a church in the province that does not own at least one Madonna or apostle from his workshop. Salzillo's figures are full of meaning and reveal much about social conditions in 18th century Murcia. Saints, sinners, foot mercenaries, shepherds, farmers, and priests are represented with stark realism with their brightly painted faces and carefully chosen attire.

SEMANA SANTA

In contrast to Holy Week in Central Europe with its strict reflection and fasting, the Spanish *Semana Santa* is a religious public festival. The pagan forerunners celebrating the reawakening of nature after the winter combine with the Christian story of the Resurrection to present an artistic spectacle. The piety with which this is staged is impressive – often without the assistance of priests. The *Semana Santa* with its large processions of penitents begins on Palm Sunday and culminates in a real celebration on Easter Sunday itself. Every region has its own individual traditions and customs.

The country's most ornate *Semana Santa* is without doubt celebrated in Murcia. It begins with laments in the first light of dawn, when the street is filled with tunics and pointed penitents' hats of all colors. The wearers of these form endless processions along with drummers, crucifixes, huge foghorns fixed to carts, and above all the *pasos*: life-size, carved holy figures which are carried through the streets on the shoulders of the faithful. Many brotherhoods parade past in old gardeners'

The Holy Week processions range from religious mystique to carnivalesque hustle and bustle, whether it be with groups of penitents (left) or people on horseback (below).

Many *Semana Santa* processions of penitents begin very early in the morning. It is still dark when the cloaked figures set off – an impressive sight.

costumes under their habits, showing lace borders on the finely worked long johns, and traditional straw shoes.

Along the procession routes some traveling confectionery salesmen with carts offer for sale a considerable assortment of brightly colored sticks of candy, glazed apples, burnt almonds, candy floss, and such like. They are a tolerated commercial addition that has gradually become part of the tradition. However, the tradition also stipulates that nothing is actually sold here, but is given away – according to the

old maxim: "He who does not give out candy during Holy Week will not be forgiven by God and cannot enter the Kingdom of Heaven." So during the processions members of the brotherhoods hand out large amounts of candy, cookies, hard-cooked eggs, and Easter chicks from their *barrigas*, fat "bellies" made of sacks tied together, to the spectators waiting at the side of the road.

After the carnival procession it is traditional to discuss the spectacle just witnessed with relatives and friends in convivial surroundings and, as a reward for the service rendered during it, to share some food. Consequently there are typical *Semana Santa* dishes which are always prepared throughout the country. In Murcia these include the vegetable stew *(menestra murciana)* and dried cod rissoles *(albóndigas de bacalao)*, two dishes that can easily be precooked or quickly prepared, because during Holy Week everyone wants to be on the streets following the spectacular events. Certainly nobody is expected to stay at home and cook for hours on end.

Dried cod dishes in particular are also served in other regions during *Semana Santa*, but vegetables such as roasted or stuffed bell peppers, and salads and egg dishes are also typical Holy Week fare. The sweet dishes, above all, are so delicious that they can send those celebrating into real raptures. If that is not heaven on earth…

Why the fish in the Mar Menor is different

The Mar Menor is a lagoon near Murcia which is separated from the Mediterranean Sea by a 12½ mile (20 kilometer) long sand bar. The fish and, above all, the jumbo shrimp from the Mar Menor have more tender flesh and a more distinct taste of the sea than those from the open sea. The reasons for this are the constantly warm climate, the calmness, and the shallowness of the water (13–16 feet/4–5 meters on average). Another factor is the significantly higher salt and iodine content of the lagoon (4 percent as opposed to 1–2 percent in the Mediterranean Sea), and the different flora and fauna on the seabed that are the result of this. Consequently very few species are found in the Mar Menor – but those that are have an incomparable flavor: the famous shrimp *(langostinos del Mar Menor)*, as well as the gilt head bream *(dorada)*, sea bass *(llobarro* or *lubina)*, striped sea bream *(mabre* or *herrera)*, and the now almost extinct gray mullet *(mújol)*. By catching fish with the *paranza* (see description opposite) most of the fish remain alive in the net. This ensures absolute freshness and maintains the first-class quality of the fish.

Fishermen bring real gems out of the Mar Menor. The finest shrimp (top photograph) and gray mullet (bottom photograph) are highly sought.

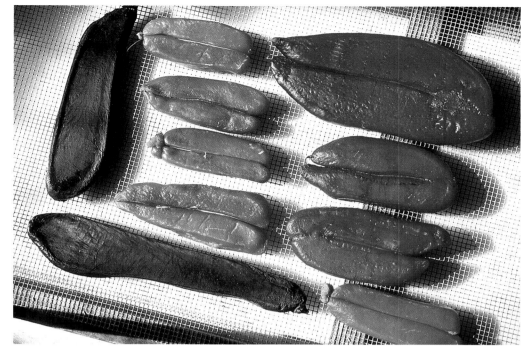

Highlights from the Mar Menor: gourmets pay a small fortune for salted tuna fillets (*mojama*), as well as for salted and dried roe (*hueva*) from the gray mullet and ling (from left to right).

FISHERMEN ON THE MAR MENOR

Originally Paco did not want to go out onto the Mar Menor at all that gray December morning. "Too cold," croaks the fisherman, and washes down his coffee with a brandy. And this is at 10 °C (50 °F) plus? I am amazed. "Besides, the season has been over for a long time," says Paco. "Yes, in October, November, then you could bring up 200 kilograms (440 pounds) of fish per net. But now…"

Finally Paco agrees to show me his boat, a motorboat. It bobs up and down peacefully in the fishing port of Lo Pagán, one of the small villages on the shores of the lagoon which have been completely swallowed up by the frenzied building boom. Paco jumps nimbly onboard and invites me to do the same. He wants to check on the *paranza*. Paco says he has always fished with the *paranza*. His son Manolo, on the other hand, works with *tres malles*. This is why certain local restaurants only buy their fish from him, Paco, personally.

"*Paranza? Tres malles?*" I ask. "You will soon see," Paco mumbles. He tugs at the starting cord of his outboard, and we chug out into the grayness, where water, air, and land seem to become one. After a few minutes the motor stops. "*La paranza!*" Paco announces. I can only see a couple of corks bobbing gently on the water's surface. "Hold this, we'll bring the *bolsa* up!" He presses a rope into my hand, and we both pull until we have heaved the *bolsa*, a sack-like net, onboard. Lots of silvery fish – sardines, gilthead bream – and amongst them the famous Mar Menor *langostinos* thrash about and wriggle in the net. However, Paco is disappointed: "Fifty kilograms (110 pounds) at the most. That is why I didn't want to go out fishing until tomorrow."

As we release the slippery, live fish from the net Paco explains the essence of the *paranza*. Whereas in the Mediterranean Sea the boats drag the nets along behind them, in the Mar Menor the nets are installed permanently. The fish remain alive in the *paranza*, a type of giant fish trap, until the net is brought up. *Tres malles*, on the other hand, are three taut nets side by side which break the neck of the fish which swims against it. *Tres malles*, therefore, always contain dead fish, which taste inferior. According to Paco, first-class fish from the Mar Menor always come from *paranzas*.

Paco throws the net back into the lagoon and is suddenly in a great hurry. He wants to get the meager catch to the fish market while it is still alive, he says. "In the past, when we used sailing boats, there was always time for breakfast. We would sail gently with the morning breeze to the nearest shore, make a fire out of old nets and trash, and calmly cook sardines over it. A bit of bread and garlic with it and a drop of wine to help warm us up. What more did you need… in the past?" The pressures on modern fishermen mean that such relaxing starts to the day are no more than distant memories for Paco and his contemporaries.

The gilt head bream (*dorada*) owes its name to the golden stripe between its eyes. It tastes delicious baked in a salt crust (background).

DELICACIES WITH FISH

DORADA A LA SAL
Gilt head bream in a salt crust

*1 gilthead bream, about 2¼–2½ lbs/1–1.2 kg,
ready to use
Pepper
Juice of ½ lemon
½ bunch of parsley
A few sprigs of thyme or rosemary
4 ½ lbs/2 kg coarse-grain sea salt
Oil for the baking pan*

Wash the fish and pat dry. Season with pepper and drizzle lemon juice into the abdominal cavity. Place the herbs in the fish. Put a third of the sea salt in an oiled baking pan. Lay the fish on top and cover with the remaining salt, smoothing this out. Bake in a preheated oven at 390 °F/200 °C for 30 minutes. Gently crack open the salt crust and remove lumps of salt. Remove the skin on the top side of the fish, and take the fish fillet off the bones. Remove the main bones and take the remaining flesh out of the skin. Serve with *alioli*.

SALT FROM THE LEVANTE COAST

"*Es Torrevieja un espejo, donde Cuba se mira,*" says a line of an old folk song: "Torrevieja is a mirror in which Cuba looks at itself." What applied to the small town in Valencia was also the case for many towns on the Levante coast a good hundred years ago: the people acquired wealth and fame through their salt works with their glasslike patches of water. The band of salt works stretches along the Mediterranean coast from the south of Catalonia through Valencia and Murcia to the Cabo de Gata in Andalusia. In the Murcia region the salt works at San Pedro del Pinatar on the Mar Menor (photograph top left) still produce 88,160 tons (80,000 tonnes) of sea salt a year.

A large part of the yield is sold as moist salt. After harvesting, the salt is simply washed and cleaned. In the kitchen, coarse-grain salt (*sal gorda* bottom photograph) is used to make *salazones*, salted meat and fish products. Shrimps are cooked on the hot plate with coarse-grain sea salt added, and many dishes such as octopus *(pulpo)* or roasted green bell peppers from Galicia *(pimientos de Padrón)* are sprinkled with sea salt before eating. And naturally *sal gorda* is needed in abundance to cook fish in a salt crust (main photograph).

Garum – The Roman's relish

Around 2000 years ago the Murcian coastal region was an important Roman production center for salted mackerel and for garum. To make this delicious spicy sauce, either mackerel, sardines, or anchovies were salted and then placed in the blazing sun for weeks to ferment. Some recipes also recommended the use of fish innards. Once the mixture was cooked through, the liquid was drained off, leaving a fish-flavored salty, oily, spicy sauce, similar to the fish sauces from Asia which are common today. It was used to garnish or improve a variety of dishes. Gourmets throughout the Roman empire enjoyed this spicy sauce so much that they literally licked their lips at the thought of this delicacy and were willing to pay horrendous prices for garum from Murcia. Ancient lime basins at La Unión verify that large amounts were stored here before they were bottled and shipped to Rome. Even sealed amphorae containing the fossilized remains of garum were found on the seabed off the coast. Escombreras, the name of a small island off Cartagena, reflects the tremendous amount of mackerel *(escombros)* fished there.

Caldero murciano
Murcian fish stew

2 ¼ lbs/1 kg fish scraps
½ cup/125 ml olive oil
Salt
5 black peppercorns
1 bay leaf
A bunch of herbs and vegetables for making soup
1 ¼ lbs/600 g fish fillets, e.g. scorpionfish, red mullet, gray mullet, gilt head bream, cut into bite-sized pieces
2 hot, dried paprika pods
4 cloves of garlic, diced
Generous 1 lb/500 g of tomatoes, skinned and diced
1 ¼ cups/250 g round-grain rice

Brown the fish scraps in half the olive oil. Pour in 6½ cups/1.5 liters water and season with salt, the peppercorns, and bay leaf. Add the soup herbs and vegetables. Simmer for 30 minutes, then strain the stock, and set aside.
Heat the remaining olive oil and brown the fish fillets. Grind the paprika pods using a mortar and pestle with the garlic and some salt, and cook with the fish briefly. Pour in the stock, then stir in the tomatoes. Simmer, covered, on a low heat for about 10 minutes until cooked. Remove the fish from the stock and keep warm. Pass the stock through a sieve; then return to the pan and add the rice. Cook for 20 minutes, adding some water if necessary. Serve the rice as the first course, then the fish with *alioli* (see page 17).

Full use is made of the fish for the *caldero*, from the head to the bones. First make a stock from the fish scraps.

In the meantime, brown the fish fillets on all sides in the olive oil. Then just add seasoning to taste.

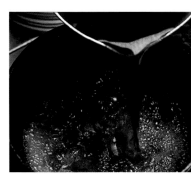
Fry the paprika and garlic briefly and then pour the fish stock over the fish fillets.

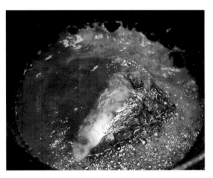
Add the skinned and diced tomatoes to the pan and cook the fish in the gently simmering stock.

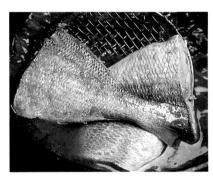
Lift the fish fillets carefully out of the stock with a skimmer and keep them warm. Then sieve the stock.

Right at the end, cook the rice in the spicy fish stock. Round-grain rice is the most suitable.

The fish/rice stew provides two courses of a sumptuous meal. With *caldero murciano* the rice, which has absorbed the flavors of the different fish, is served first. However, you should not eat too much of this course. The rice is followed by the fish which is traditionally served with a freshly prepared *alioli*.

Poisonous green tomatoes?

In spite of the once common belief, those who think that they can get rid of unpleasant peers with a salad of green tomatoes are much mistaken. Green tomatoes are not poisonous, and at least no less digestible than other unripe fruit or vegetables. However, it is advisable, as it is with ripe red tomatoes, to remove the white stalk, where the flower was, before eating as the tomato is a member of the nightshade family. The plants of this genus contain the poison solanine in the fruits, shoots, and leaves, which can lead to stomach or bowel upsets.

With the stalk removed, green tomatoes can be made into a delicious jam. Pickled green tomatoes are also a piquant delicacy. For this green tomatoes are pricked several times, and placed in gently boiling salted water until the skin splits. They are then carefully taken out, drained, and put in layers in a large jar. Next, a mixture of wine vinegar and water in a ratio of 1:1 is poured over. The vinegar/water is poured off into a pan the next day, and sugar (2¼ pounds to 4¼ cups/ 1 kilogram to 1 liter) cooked in it until a clear syrup forms, which is seasoned. The tomatoes are simmered in the syrup for 10 minutes before they are returned to the jar covered with the liquid.

Background: Sun ripened tomatoes are a sweet, firm pleasure. No wonder they are called "apples of paradise" in many languages.

Tomatoes

At the end of the 19th century the confused author of the Vienna food encyclopedia reported: "In Spain they even eat tomatoes raw by cutting them down the middle horizontally, and then sprinkling salt on both halves." This custom seemed very exotic to the author. It was thought at that time that tomatoes must be cooked for at least three hours before they could be eaten. As a member of the nightshade family the red fruit had a reputation for being poisonous.

The tomato (lat. *Lycopersicon esculentum*) came to Europe in the early 16th century from Peru and Mexico, and for a long time was treated exclusively as an ornamental plant. For the first time in 1544 the Italians described the new fruit from overseas as the "golden apple" *(pombo d'oro)* since the fruits common at that time were yellow – and small like cherry tomatoes. Special powers were attributed to the tomato as the "apple of love" or "apple of paradise" because of its bright red color. It is still called *Paradeiser* in Austria today. The Spaniards, however, adopted the Aztec name *tomatl*.

The tomato was used more widely as a food only in the 20th century. As it likes a lot of sun and well-watered soil, Spain is a favored region today for growing both bush tomatoes, which take on a salty flavor near the sea, and the milder cordon tomatoes. It produces about 4.4 million tons (4 million tonnes) a year. The first type are particularly suitable for sauces, pulp, paste, and juice; the slightly mealy beefsteak tomatoes are generally used primarily for salads. The globular tomato is particularly versatile. Its harmonious, mild flavor is suitable for both salads and vegetables and, because of its deep red color, it is also used as a garnish. The juicy, sweet and sour plum or egg tomatoes are recommended particularly for vegetables as well as soups, and the small, sweet cherry or sugar tomatoes mostly for decoration.

In August, the best month for tomatoes, country-women still bottle mountains of tomatoes as *sofrito*. This mixture of stewed tomatoes, onions, and garlic is put into large jars, and used as the base for numerous sauces, rice dishes, and stews. In Catalonia, making tomato bread *(pa amb tomàquet)* is tantamount to a patriotic ritual, and there are as many recipes as cooks for the world-famous Andalusian *gazpacho*, a cold tomato soup. What is always important is a lot of ripe tomatoes to give both color and flavor to the "Andalusian blood." Fully ripe tomatoes are easy to skin, others must first be blanched. Then they are seeded, and the flesh is diced for salad or lightly crushed to make a sauce. The skin and seeds which are left over are suitable for clearing stock as they usefully bind fat as well as scum.

Well-ripened tomatoes have an intense flavor and are highly nutritional. Beside plenty of vitamin C, they also contain a lot of beta-carotene, pro-vitamin A. The human body can, however, only use it in conjunction with fat, so it should be noted that oil should always be added to any tomato dish.

Ajotomate
Murcian tomato salad

1 large ripe beefsteak tomato, skinned and sliced
4 cloves of garlic, diced
2 tbsp wine vinegar
Salt and pepper
A pinch of cumin
A pinch of paprika
4 tbsp olive oil
Generous 1 lb/500 g firm tomatoes

Crush the beefsteak tomato slices using a mortar and pestle with the cloves of garlic. Then mix in the wine vinegar, salt, pepper, cumin, paprika, and olive oil.
Wash, dry, halve, and slice the tomatoes. Put them into a salad bowl and then pour over the tomato dressing. Mix together well, season with salt, and serve.

SALADS

The naturalness of Spanish cuisine is revealed by the pleasures that come straight from the garden to the table, in the form of salads. The mild temperatures and the many hours of sunshine per day encourage the early ripening and excellent quality of lettuce, tomatoes, bell peppers, cucumbers, and other fresh sources of vitamins. They are harvested when fully ripe for the regional market and this brings out their unique flavor.

The oldest known salad to have originated from the Mediterranean region is the *ajotomate* (recipe page 403). *La busca* (the search) has been well-known in Spain for centuries. This salad consists of wild herbs and vegetables (for example wild asparagus, thistles, fennel, and dandelion), which are picked and diced. They are then cooked, and served dressed with oil, salt, and lemon.

The best example of a modern salad is the popular *ensalada mixta* with freshly picked lettuce, large slices of sun-ripened tomatoes, strong, juicy onion rings, and olives. Red and green bell peppers, on the other hand, are served as "roasted salad" *(ensalada asada)*: roasted where possible on a wood fire with rosemary and thyme, they must sweat for at least an hour in a dish. The fragrant juice that they release is used later as the base for the exquisite marinade, which is completed with oil, vinegar, salt, and garlic.

Today Spain produces alone almost 1.1 million tons (1 million tonnes) of varieties of lettuce *(lechugas)* per year on 145 square miles (37,000 hectares), the majority of which are grown in Murcia. New varieties are constantly being developed, and growing, harvesting, and transportation methods are constantly perfected. Romaine lettuce *(lechuga romana* or *larga)*, as well as heart or crisphead lettuces *(lechugas acogolladas)*, are the most common. However, as the choice grows, so cooks can enjoy experimenting, combining the fresh green salad with various types of fish or meat. Creations with dried cod, red-legged partridge, or pies evolve, and are even given a touch of sophistication with the addition of fresh fruit, such as oranges or grapes.

In Spain salads have more than a minor role. They are served as a separate course, and sometimes even as the main course in summer. They are mostly dressed just with cold-pressed olive oil, some lemon juice or vinegar, and a pinch of salt. According to a Spanish proverb you need exactly four people to dress a good salad: a spendthrift to put on the oil, a skinflint the vinegar, a wise man to sprinkle on the salt, and a madman to mix it all together.

Ensalada catalana: slightly underripe tomatoes, strips of roasted bell pepper, with artichoke hearts, *Butifarra* sausage, anchovies, and hard-cooked eggs.

Ensalada asada: roasted bell pepper, tomatoes, eggplants, and onion, marinated in their own juice with olive oil, garlic, and vinegar or lemon.

Ensalada de habas tiernas, tomates y sardinas: young beans, pieces of tomato, green onions, and salted sardines, dressed with lemon.

Ensalada de mar: "sea salad" consisting of mussels, shrimp, squid, mushrooms, and capers, marinated with lemon juice and the finest olive oil.

Oakleaf lettuce
(hoja de roble)

Iceberg lettuce
(lechuga iceberg)

Batavia

Endive
(escarola)

Lollo Bianco

Lollo Rosso

Romaine lettuce
(lechuga romana)

Salpicón de patatas: boiled potatoes, with ripe tomatoes, small pickled gherkins, and hard-cooked eggs in a marinade of vinegar, oil, and salt.

Ensalada de apio y naranjas: celery, ripe oranges, and pieces of tomato, dressed with olive oil, red wine vinegar, salt, and sugar.

Endibias con Cabrales: Chicory with a cream made from Cabrales, the strong blue cheese from Asturia, and cream, lemon juice, salt, and pepper.

Ensalada murciana: refreshing summer pleasure consisting of ripe tomatoes, strips of roasted bell pepper, onion, and capers, topped with pickled tuna.

Ensalada del mar y de la huerta: "salad from the sea and garden" with dried cod, tomatoes, roasted red bell pepper, capers, onion, and garlic.

Remojón de bacalao: fresh orange segments with broiled and soaked dried cod, onion, and olives, marinated with olive oil and sherry vinegar.

Ensalada mixta: mixed salad consisting of Romaine lettuce, tomatoes, onion, and olives.

MULBERRIES AND THE FEAR OF THUNDER

When a storm gathers and there is a peal of thunder, the silkworms in Murcia's Huerta are threatened with an inglorious end. According to an old myth they are immensely sensitive creatures who cannot bear any noise. Like the mulberry tree, the silkworm was brought to the country by the Arabs in the 9th century. Silk production immediately ensured modest prosperity and the Murcians treated their worms with the utmost care. In order to protect the animals from noise and vibrations, they were always put on the top story of a house with their mulberry frames. The *jota*, a country dance, was invented to protect against harmful thunder, and it would be accompanied by very loud singing in order to drown out the thunder from above. The relative prosperity brought about by the production of natural silk came to an abrupt end at the beginning of the 18th century. During the War of the Succession, Bishop Luis de Belluga ordered the dams, which had been constructed by the Moors, to be burst and flooded the land in order to halt the enemy. This also meant the end of numerous worm cultures. However, in a small way the people continued to make use of the mulberry tree and the silkworm: the black fruits were boiled to a tasty purée, and the larvae were pickled in wine vinegar. (The intestines, which are excellent for stitching up wounds, were removed first.) Today mulberries are generally just eaten fresh. The fruity *moras* not only look like blackberries, they also taste similar. They are ideally suited as a filling for fruit tarts and cookies; for making jam, jelly, juice, and a delicious fruit liqueur; and for custard-based desserts and ice cream.

Figs

The fig was always a controversial plant. To Christians it was explicitly called the Christian fig, whereas the prickly fruit of the opuntia cactus was called the Moor fig. The Arabs saw it similarly – only the other way round. The tree and fruit have been connected with sin since Biblical times. After all, Adam and Eve, once they became embarrassed by their nakedness, covered themselves up with fig leaves, and Judas even hanged himself on this type of tree. The branches of the fig tree reach out like countless arms, and in Spanish vernacular the fruit *(higo)* stands for the female genitals – probably because only the female tree can bear fruit. Every farmer knows that goats become restless in the shade of an *higuera*, and even insects are known to become love-stricken by the intoxicating aroma of the juicy fruit of the fig. The fig tree (lat. *Ficus carica*) belongs to the mulberry family. It originates from southwest Asia and arrived on the Iberian Peninsula with the arrival of the Romans. Today it is widespread throughout the Mediterranean countries. As the fig tree is particularly sensitive to the use of chemicals, it is usually grown naturally. However, sulfurization often takes place during processing.

Figs are available fresh or dried as *higos pasos*. The Spanish like to coat the latter with chocolate, which is delicious, or use them to make the famous fig bread *pan de higos*. The fruit is rich in various minerals, in particular potassium, calcium, and phosphorus. In addition figs, with their many small seeds, are useful in stimulate digestion.

Pan de higos
Fig bread

2¼ lbs/1 kg dried figs, chopped
1¼ cups/250 g chopped hazelnuts
1¼ cups/250 g chopped almonds
1 tsp cinnamon
2 tbsp sugar
1 tsp grated orange rind
1¾ oz/50 g coverture
2 tbsp aniseed brandy
2 tbsp toasted sesame seeds (optional)
40 shelled, blanched almond kernels

Mix the chopped figs well with the hazelnuts, almonds, cinnamon, sugar, and orange rind. Melt the chocolate in a *bain-marie*; then let it cool a little before working into the fig mixture. Add enough aniseed brandy to produce a slightly damp, but firm mixture. Divide the dough into 10 equal pieces, and roll out each piece to a thickness of about 2 inches/5 cm. If liked roll in the toasted sesame seeds, and finally decorate each piece with 4 almonds. Store in a cool place until required.

Figs are versatile: they can be eaten fresh or dried, and they go well with almonds.

Something substantial with wine

Throughout the millennia numerous peoples have left their mark on the cultural and culinary life of Murcia. So it is no surprise that a type of meat pie appears on Babylonian writing tablets from around 4000 BC, and that a very similar one can later be found again in Murcia. Today the spicy *pastel de carne* is considered a national dish of Murcia. An original variation is *pastel cierva*, a sweet and salty pie with chicken and sugar. Both meat pies go especially well with the region's powerful wines.

Pastel de carne
Meat pie

1 (10 oz/300 g) package of frozen
puff pastry
2 tbsp oil
Scant cup/200 g ground veal
2 lamb brains, or 1 calf brain, cut into
small pieces
2 oz/50 g chorizo sausage, diced
Generous 5 oz/150 g roast veal leftovers,
cut into small pieces
2 hard-cooked eggs, diced
2 eggs
Salt and pepper
Flour for the work surface
Egg yolk for brushing

Thaw the puff pastry thoroughly following the directions on the package.
Heat the oil and brown the ground meat until crumbly. Mix in the brains and fry briefly. Remove from the heat and leave to cool slightly.
Then transfer to a bowl and mix in the sausage, roast leftovers, diced and raw eggs. Season with salt and pepper. Roll the puff pastry out on a floured work surface. Rinse out a springform pan with cold water and line with half the puff pastry, easing the pastry up around the edges to cover the sides well. Fill with the meat mixture and smooth the top. Cut strips from the remaining puff pastry, stretching them lengthwise. Place the puff pastry strips on the pastry from the center outward forming a rosebud shape. Brush the pastry with egg yolk and then bake in a preheated oven at 345 °F/175 °C for approximately 30 minutes.

Until recently the hot and arid wine regions of Murcia produced wines with up to 16 percent alcohol. (In the background stands Jumilla Castle.)

Even Stone Age peoples cultivated grapes in the almost desert-like hinterland of Murcia. The resistant variety Monastrell grows very well here.

Monastrell wine

When a few years ago the trucks from Jumilla, Yecla, and Bullas thundered north at night during the harvest, the initiated knew: the wines of the neighboring region of La Mancha were to be given more body, color, and alcohol content with the help of Murcian Monastrell must.

Numerous archeological finds point to the fact that wines were cultivated and pressed in the Murcia region even during the Neolithic Age. In particular the undemanding and resistant Monastrell grape was grown. Wine from this grape cannot tolerate being stored in wooden barrels. It is a slightly sweet table wine which is best drunk young or used for blending. Until a few years ago Murcian wines could be characterized generally as robust, full-bodied reds with a high alcohol content (up to 16 percent) – they lacked a true fruity quality and aroma, generally due to their natural fermentation process achieved at high temperatures.

In the last few years, however, great efforts have been made to gain a place for Murcian wines on the European market and to adapt them to current tastes. Thanks to new methods, wine-producers in Jumilla and Yecla have succeeded in eliciting a still full-bodied, but now fruity, fresh, aromatic wine with a big nose from the Monastrell grape. Recently rosé and white wines have also been produced, but they only make up about 8 percent of production.

The **D.O. Jumilla** with around 160 square miles (42,000 hectares) of vineyards is not confined to the region of Murcia, but also includes six municipalities in the southeast of the province of Albacete (Castile-La Mancha). The pure Monastrell wines are cherry-colored with brick-red reflections. Today they have a surprisingly pleasant fruitiness and full body, as well as a certain silkiness. Furthermore, the raisin flavors so typical of Monastrell reveal a potential for producing sweet wines that until now has scarcely been exploited. The Garnacha grape gives Jumilla wines dryness and violet tones. Blending both Cabernet Sauvignon and Tempranillo has meant that Monastrell wines keep for significantly longer. In the last few years wine lovers have, therefore, enjoyed the first generation of high-quality, barrel-aged wines from Jumilla.

Furthermore small amounts of Cabernet Sauvignon have also been planted alongside the main varieties of Monastrell and

Murcian vintners were late to discover the potential of their wines and now also sell barrel-aged red wines. The Bodega San Isidro in the Jumilla region is one of the pioneers.

Garnacha in the **D.O. Yecla**. As the number one producer in the area, Bodegas Castaño produces fine wines. Beside the solid, wood-aged wines, the estate is also known for its fresh reds which are obtained by carbonic maceration (compare page 177). The white Merseguera and Verdil grapes, which are typical of the area, also have a role to play when it comes to wines of certified quality and origin. However, they only play a secondary role.

Wines from the **D.O. Bullas**, the largest wine area in the region, consist of 96 percent Monastrell grapes. The rosé wines are fruity and slightly sharp, the ruby-colored reds velvety and aromatic. It must be said that on the whole, Murcian wine-producers have adapted to the European market and the prevailing popular taste surprisingly quickly and well over the last few years. However, this has been at the expense of the specific character of the region's wines.

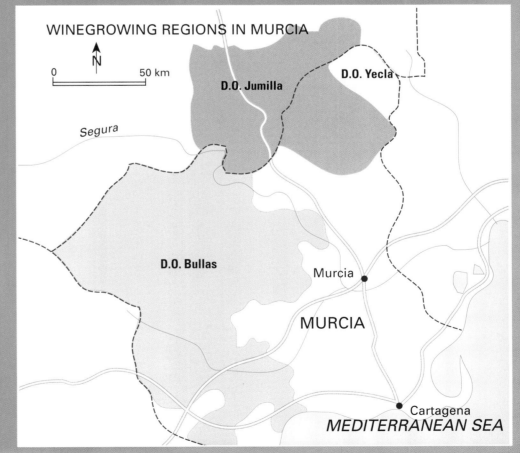

ANDALUCÍA

Harald Klöcker

ANDALUSIA

Between ritual and art: with the silver *venencia* the
vintner of an Andalusian bodega pours fine sherry into
a typical tall glass.

There is no landscape that could be called Andalusian, rather a variety of sensory stimuli extending to all four points of the compass without a break or monotony, and at the same time including all possible types of landscape and all forms of the transparency of a light that is only the same everywhere in one aspect: in its intensity.

As it did for the writer Antonio Muñoz Molina, Andalusia has always prompted flights of fancy from the world's poets, aesthetes, and masters of the art of living. It embodies the south, with its light, warmth, and passion. Andalusia is a region of changing landscapes and climatic zones: pine, cork, and holm oak woods alternate with dust-dry steppes and sand-dunes, while mountains like the Sierra de Grazalema rise up in the hinterland of the province of Cadiz, which receives more precipitation annually than any other region of Spain. It is this extreme diversity of landscapes, resulting from the different influences of the Atlantic, Mediterranean, and continental climates, that gives this region its charm. In the hinterland of the tourist conurbations and beyond the cities of Seville, Granada, Cordoba, and Jaén, Andalusia is characterized by huge expanses of agricultural land and vast natural areas. Indeed, approximately 20 percent of the total territory is now a conservation area.

The 800-year epoch of Moor and Arab rule left more of a mark on Andalusia's appearance than it did on any other Spanish region. The Arabs' advanced civilization can be seen in the architecture as well as in the irrigation system, crafts, music, and cuisine. Recipes that creatively combine meat or fish with fruits and herbs originate from the Arabs; furthermore, cooks from the East were experts at preparing highly imaginative sweet dishes. They brought figs, pomegranates, citrus fruits, and melons with them, and these sun-loving fruits still flourish on the Andalusian Mediterranean coast and in the Guadalquivir valley where an abundance of strawberries, prickly pears, peaches, cherries, and quince also grow.

Andalusia's cuisine lacks finesse, preferring to emphasize the solid basic taste of its produce – and here it has a whole variety to offer. This is due to the vastly different landscape and climatic zones: fish and seafood, exquisite ham and sausage produce, meat and many types of vegetables, as well as all possible variations of olives. Many of these very fine ingredients are best displayed in the form of tapas, those famously irresistible little tidbits that originate from Andalusia. Comined with a glass of sherry, the world-famous wine from the sunny region in the south of Spain, tapas are a delicious way to start an evening.

Santiago de Compostela
Vitoria-Gasteiz
León
Pamplona
Barcelona
Valladolid
Zaragoza
Madrid
Toledo
Valencia
Palma de Mallorca
Mérida
Ciudad Real
Murcia
Sevilla
Granada
Andalucía

Opposite: The Alhambra, the former palace of the Islamic rulers in Granada and an architectural gem. The Court of the Lions graces the sultan's private chambers.

Olive cultivation

Even during Roman times Andalusia exported olive oil to other Mediterranean countries, and the evidence lies buried in Rome: as the archeologist Heinrich Dressel discovered in 1872, the almost 165 foot (50 meter) high Monte Testaccio on the banks of the Tiber consists of the remains of old amphorae. Olive oil is supposed to have been transported in these from the Roman province of Baetica, present-day Andalusia, to the capital of the empire. There are apparently 40 million earthenware vessels on the "trash mountain," precisely labeled according to producer, production year, and the quality of the olive oil stored in them.

The olive tree is presumed to have arrived in the Mediterranean region from Asia Minor more than 3000 years ago. It was first cultivated in Greece and on Crete to produce the variety *Olea europaea*, which is well-known today. The Romans grew the olive tree throughout their provinces, including Andalusia, and used olive oil as an important commodity. Under Islamic rule, olive cultivation continued to flourish on the Iberian Peninsula and developed into a major branch of agriculture.

Today Spain is the largest producer of olive oil in Europe. Around 215 million olive trees grow over an area covering 7720 square miles (2 million hectares). More than 60 percent of this land is in Andalusia, particularly in the provinces of Jaén and Cordoba. Here the plantations stretch as far as the horizon – some monocultures with decades-old trees, as well as many new plantations supported by grants from the European Union. The most important variety of olive for oil in Jaén is the Picual. It occupies more than 90 percent of the area used for growing olives. In Cordoba, *Picuda* and *Hojiblanca* are also cultivated.

Three factors above all are decisive for producing the best cold-pressed olive oil: the care given to the trees throughout the year, proper harvesting, and processing the olives into oil as gentle as possible.

In traditional cultivation there are only about 80 trees on 2½ acres (1 hectare) so that each tree receives sufficient moisture and nutrients from the soil. Only horse manure is used as a fertilizer, watering is carried out sparingly, and machines are not used for harvesting. The traditional method of harvesting, by which men knock the olive branches with long sticks, is called *vareo*. The ripe fruit falls into nets which have been spread out under the trees. For very fine oils, the olives are picked individually by hand in order to ensure less damage to the fruit.

Olive trees are undemanding, requiring hardly anything. A poet even said that the Andalusians had assumed this characteristic from the ancient trees.

Although the soil in the Andalusian provinces of Jaén and Cordoba often receives no rain for months at a time, the olive trees here bear juicy fruit.

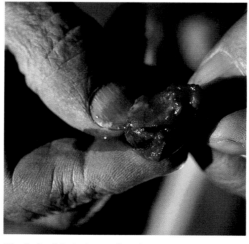

The flesh of fresh, intact olives has a clear, rich color (above). The oil mill belonging to the Núñez de Prado family business in the town of Baena is becoming an historic building (below).

Producers who grow, harvest, and produce the oil traditionally are increasingly subject to the standards of the Andalusian Committee for Ecological Agriculture. Their products are sold as organic olive oils and carry the organization's stamp of quality. Spanish environmentalists are fighting for subsidies from Brussels and seeking support not for a constantly increasing number of olive trees, but for ecological agriculture and the jobs linked to this.

Nevertheless, in the last few decades the modern growing method, which ensures higher yields for much less labor, has increased considerably. This method involves the trees being planted closer together and lopped in such a way that they do not grow too tall, but wider instead. They are then easier to harvest mechanically. These plantations in turn require more water and are more prone to plagues of insects. Chemical fertilizers are used instead of horse manure to help obtain high yields from the plants.

When the olives are ripe, between November and February, hundreds of pickers pour into the groves to bring the fruit down from the trees. Only fully ripe, undamaged olives are suitable for the very best oil. Split, unripe, or oxidized olives reduce the fruitiness of the oil by their bitterness. The olives should, therefore, be processed within 72 hours of being picked. In traditional businesses they are ground to a paste, together with the pit, using granite rollers. However, many companies today use more modern machines.

The highest quality olive oil is *flor de aceite* (flower of the oil). To obtain this fine juice the olive paste is neither centrifuged nor pressed. The oil that runs out of the olive paste on its own during the grinding process is simply collected. Flavors, vitamins, and unsaturated fatty acids are still retained to a large extent, although the yield is very small.

If normal cold-pressed olive oil is to be produced, the ground olive paste is hydraulically pressed between circular mats – once made from esparto grass, today they are usually plastic. Ultra-modern businesses also use electric centrifuges. However, this does not impair the quality of the oil. What is always important is that the excellent juice is obtained as gently as possible and without the influence of heat. High temperatures or solvents, as used in the production of refined oils, reduce the aroma, flavor, and nutrient content of olive oil. After pressing, some oils are filtered to give them a lighter, more transparent and more pleasing appearance. More and more companies, though, are leaving their oils naturally cloudy. Finally, the fresh olive oil is bottled mechanically and transported to the market as quickly as possible.

Traditionally, the olives are knocked out of the tree with sticks (main photograph). For very fine oils (small photograph) they are even hand-picked.

The freshly harvested olives are initially ground to a brownish paste between heavy granite rollers.

The paste now goes into a centrifuge. The oil is then extracted as the drum rotates very quickly.

The light olive oil can run out at the edge of the centrifuge; the olive marc is left inside the drum.

Before it is bottled, the fresh oil is stored for a short time in collecting tanks, or in large earthenware or stone containers.

Using olive oil

Olive oil is good for everything. It is used for frying eggs for breakfast, drizzling on toast, for cooking and frying, as well as for marinades, sauces, and salads. Vegetables, sausages, fish, or cheese can all be preserved in good olive oil, which also intensifies their natural flavor.

The right oil should be chosen for the purpose. Some oils are particularly fruity and sweet, others coarse and rustic. Some have a delicately bitter almond or nut flavor, while yet others smell slightly of bananas, lemons, or figs. As a rule, olives that are harvested early produce a sweeter, fruitier, and paler oil than late-harvested fruit. Unfiltered oils, usually more cloudy and greener, generally have a more intense flavor than the filtered oils. When buying olive oil, the acidity level gives an initial indication of the quality and flavor (see box left), but the final decision should always be made after smelling and tasting it.

The health benefits of cold-pressed olive oil over animal fat are undisputed. Olive oil contains a large amount of monounsaturated fatty acids, which assist the metabolism and can prevent high levels of cholesterol and therefore many heart and circulatory diseases. In addition, the vegetable dye and phenols protect the heart and vessels. Vitamin E is regarded as an extremely effective antioxidant and increases the immune system. Also, olive oil is easily digestible and even assists in curing stomach ulcers and various digestive problems.

Rubbed into the body, good olive oil relieves bronchitis, and helps to tone and freshen the skin, strengthening its defensive mechanisms. Hair packs containing olive oil and lemon vitalize the scalp and help strengthen the hair. Furthermore, anybody who is concerned about the well-being of their plants can also reach for the olive oil: a few drops rubbed on the leaves put an end to aphids.

Olive oil should, if possible, be used within a year of being produced as it starts to lose flavor and nutritional value with time. It should always be stored in a cool, dark place, preferably in dark glass or stoneware containers, as sunlight and heat reduce its keeping properties and destroy the oil's precious nutrients.

Olive oil qualities

The acidity level of an olive oil refers to the proportion of oleic acid, a monounsaturated fatty acid. This occurs through oxidation if the olives fall from the tree and burst open on the ground or if the fruit is stored too long before pressing. The lower the proportion of fatty acid, the better the oil. Since November 2003, all chemical parameters have to be listed on the bottles sold the EU. The most important qualities are:

Aceite de Oliva Virgen Extra (Extra Virgin Olive Oil): the highest quality grade with a great variety of tastes. This quality is guaranteed to be mechanically-pressed and must not exceed an acidity level of 0.8 (0,8 gram fatty acid per 100 grams oil).

Aceite de Oliva Virgen: mechanically-pressed oil. The acidity level may be a maximum of 2.0.

Aceite de Oliva: refined olive oil or a blend of refined and mechanically-pressed oil. This oil is comparatively cheap, and suitable for frying. The maximum acidity level is 1.0.

Left: Unfiltered cold-pressed olive oil is like balsam from the gods: it enhances almost any dish, is very healthy, and even improves skin and hair.

Spanish olive varieties for oil

Picual produces a markedly fruity oil that is reminiscent in fragrance and flavor of dried figs and peaches. It is particularly suitable for giving a touch of sophistication to fruit and sweet dishes, and goes well with thinly sliced oranges, flavored with thyme honey and cinnamon. Picual oil is often blended with Picuda or Hojiblanca.

Hojiblanca produces an elegant oil with sweet and bitter nuances. Its piquant character quickly disappears and leaves behind an aroma of herbs and blossom. It goes well with any fried dish, with braised dishes, and also in *gazpacho* and marinades for fish or meat.

Verdial comes mainly from small cooperatives in the Vélez-Málaga region and produces greeny-golden, very mild, fruity oils with a slight almond aroma. They are suitable for *gazpachos*, marinades, and gently steamed dishes.

Arbequina produces a pale yellow to greenish colour oil with a slightly bitter quality, a typical smell of ripe artichokes, and a light freshness. It is particularly suitable for marinated dishes and green salads. Oil from riper fruit is ideal for *alioli* and mayonnaise.

Empeltre mainly produces an oil ranging from pale yellow to old gold in color. It has a fruity, sometimes slightly sweet almond flavor as well as slight bitter flavors. It is suitable for salad dressings, marinades, and mayonnaise. A few drops of oil on sheep cheese give it a quite special quality.

Cornicabra produces a golden oil with greenish reflections, which tastes velvety, sweetish, and slightly bitter. It intensifies vegetable dishes and is also very suitable for mayonnaise and game.

SPANISH OLIVES FOR
OLIVE OIL

It is the variety that matters: as with wine, the choice of fruit determines the taste of the oil.

PRESERVING

The task of preserving food has existed since people first settled. With farming there was always more food available after the harvest or slaughter than could be eaten immediately. Furthermore, it was advisable to preserve food for leaner times.

One of the oldest methods of preservation, which was certainly discovered by chance, is **drying**. The principle is extremely simple: by inputting heat and removing water, mold and putrefactive bacteria are unable to form. In hot, dry regions this happens quite simply when the food is exposed to the sun, as is the case with the small red paprika pods that are dried and then used ground as a spice. Raisins and dried figs are also produced using this simple process. There are now also manufacturing plants in which foodstuffs are dried gently. For *bacalao*, the dried cod which is very popular with Spaniards, drying is combined with **salting** or **pickling**. As well as various types of fish, meat and vegetables too can also be preserved using salt, which was of course always readily available from the sea.

Lactic fermentation is another traditional method of preserving vegetables. The lactic acid bacteria contained naturally in vegetables convert carbohydrates, in particular fructose, into lactic acid. This, often strengthened by the addition of sodium chloride, prevents the growth of anything that will spoil the food.

Even the ancient Egyptians, Assyrians, and Babylonians knew the technique of **pickling in vinegar**. They realized that, with time, alcoholic drinks turned into vinegar and used it to prepare tart dishes. In addition, they used vinegar to preserve meat and vegetables. The Moors brought this technique to Spain where it was also adopted for fish, such as the popular anchovies in vinegar *(boquerones en vinagre)*. **Pickling in alcohol** made use of the germicidal effect of spirits in particular.

Thousands of years ago, the inhabitants of Mediterranean countries also discovered that food could be preserved by **pickling in oil**. Vegetables, fish, sausage, and cheese can be kept for a long time using this method, which intensifies their flavor, as is the case with goat cheese pickled in olive oil.

In the **smoking** process, fish or meat is preserved by smoke. Wood in the form of shavings, dust, and twigs is burned. The resulting smoke has a germicidal and desiccant effect. The flavor and smell of the produce can be influenced by the use of certain types of wood, herbs, and spices.

The techniques of **bottling** or **canning** are relatively recent preserving methods. Meat, vegetables, and fruit (with or without sugar) are preserved by heat sterilization in jars or cans. The activity of food pests can also be stopped by **freezing**. In the case of vegetables, they should be blanched briefly before freezing. All of these techniques are still employed today in Spain, and all over the world. Even though many modern homes have freezers for preserving foods for long periods, most kitchen shelves will hold canned soups, pickles and dried fruits.

Fruit, vegetables, tomato paste – a well-stocked larder should not be without jars containing the treasures of the field and garden that you have preserved yourself.

ACEITUNAS MACHACADAS
Pickled olives

2 ¼ lbs/1 kg fresh green olives
1 ¾ oz/50 g sodium bicarbonate
6 cloves of garlic, thinly sliced
2 tbsp dried oregano
A few sprigs of thyme
1 bay leaf
A few sprigs of fennel
⅛ tsp cumin
3 fresh red chili pods, seeded and cut into rings
⅓ cup/75 g salt
½ cup/125 ml wine vinegar

Wash the olives thoroughly. Crack each olive with a mallet or stone taking care not to damage the pit. Place the cracked olives either in a porcelain or glass container. Drain off the juice. Dissolve the sodium bicarbonate in 12 cups/ 3 liters water and soak the olives in this for 1 day. Then drain and soak the olives again in fresh cold water for another 2–3 days, remembering to change the water every 12 hours.

Drain the olives and leave to drip. Crush half the garlic with the herbs using a mortar and pestle. Place the olives, herb paste, garlic slices, and chili pods in layers in a porcelain or glass container. Dissolve the salt in the vinegar and add 3 cups/750 ml water. Pour the brine over the olives. Then weigh down the olives with a plate so that all the fruit is covered by the brine. Store in a cool place and leave to marinate for a minimum of 1 week.

Variation: Black olives must not be placed in caustic soda. Their bitterness is removed by placing them in salt water for 3 days, changing the water every 12 hours.

Right: Women sitting on the ground or at tables outside and cracking open olives are a common sight. A fine delicacy is made from the olives (below).

First the olives are cracked open one by one with a mallet, so that the flavors of the marinade can penetrate right inside.

Fresh olives contain an unpalatable bitterness. The fruit is, therefore, placed in a caustic soda solution for a while before being pickled.

As soon as the soda solution has been drained off, the olives are put in fresh, cold water for two or three days.

The water must be changed very frequently to rinse out most of the unpleasant bitterness present.

No olive marinade is complete without garlic. The cloves are crushed well using the mortar and pestle, then the spices are added.

Thyme, oregano, fennel, and cumin add flavor, while chili pods add the required sharpness.

FERIA IN SEVILLE

Seville in April… two weeks after Easter, when the bewitching fragrance of orange blossom hangs over the town like a soft mist, festivities take place round the clock for a week. The Sevillians abandon themselves to the merriment of their *Feria* with the same enthusiasm with which they repented and atoned during Easter week *(Semana Santa)*.

Hundreds of colorful huts *(casetas)* are crowded close together on the huge festival ground in the southern district of Los Remedios. Large groups of festival-goers make their way through the streets; music booms out; there is dancing on the stages. Women in gloriously colorful, spotted flamenco dresses, the one-time gipsy costume, sway and turn in time to the rhythm. The heels of their shoes tap on the wooden floor, nimble hands coax infectious rhythms out of wooden castanets. Every now and then, horses carrying magnificently dressed riders thunder through the crowd, causing the sand and wood shavings to swirl up. There is frenetic applause, and cheering.

The tradition of the *Feria* dates back to 1847; it was originally a corn and cattle market with an agricultural show. Over time this developed into a spring festival and today it is a mixture of a fair, dance festival, and entertainment – a wild spectacle for the senses.

The *Feria* turns night into day, offering sensations around the clock: bullfights and Sevillian dances, displays with horses and barouches, magnificently dressed people in typical Sevillian costumes. People from all walks of life, from manual workers to prominent figures from the world of politics, business, the church, and culture, come to see and be seen. However the individual groups often stay together in their huts: most of these are rented by family clans, sports clubs, or parties. Only those lucky enough to be given an invitation are admitted to "their" *caseta*.

Outside in the streets the smell of the horses mixes with the diverse aromas from hundreds of huts: barbecued meat and sardines, vegetables and herbs as well as candy and fragrant sherry. At the bars small fried fish are served, along with Gordales olives stuffed with almonds, small meat balls in a red bell pepper sauce, and grilled shrimp sprinkled with coarse-grain sea salt. The choice of excellent tapas is endless, and with them a great deal of wine is drunk. Red and white wines can be obtained here and there, but the Andalusians particularly enjoy a glass of dry sherry above all else. At every *Feria* an incredible several hundred thousand pints of Fino and Manzanilla sherry are consumed (see pages 438 ff).

Gipsies, still often outsiders in everyday Spanish life, are, however, the main attraction of the *Feria* with their colorful equestrian spectacles.

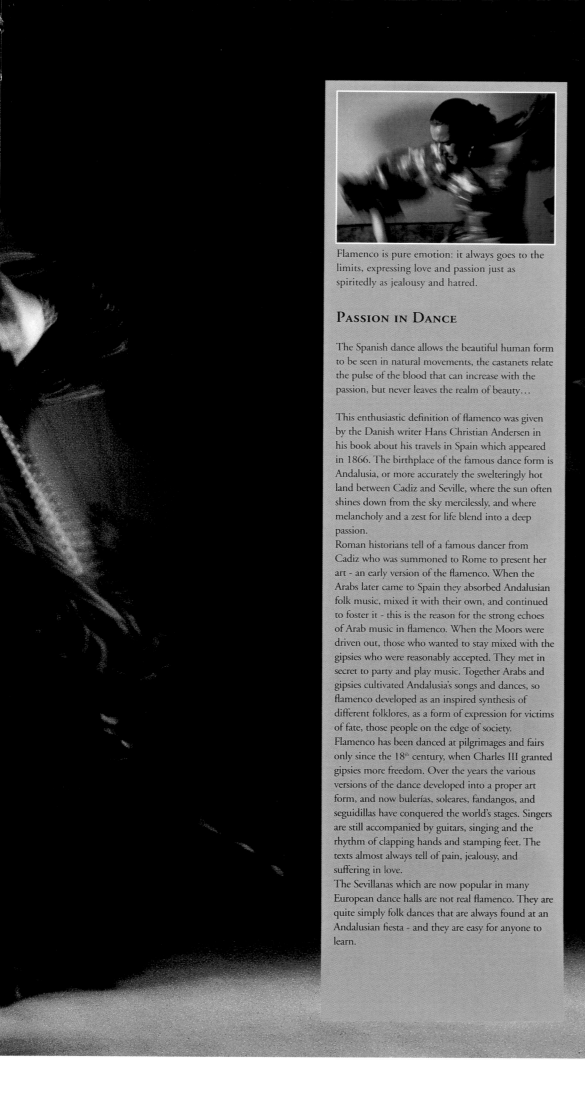

Flamenco is pure emotion: it always goes to the limits, expressing love and passion just as spiritedly as jealousy and hatred.

PASSION IN DANCE

The Spanish dance allows the beautiful human form to be seen in natural movements, the castanets relate the pulse of the blood that can increase with the passion, but never leaves the realm of beauty…

This enthusiastic definition of flamenco was given by the Danish writer Hans Christian Andersen in his book about his travels in Spain which appeared in 1866. The birthplace of the famous dance form is Andalusia, or more accurately the swelteringly hot land between Cadiz and Seville, where the sun often shines down from the sky mercilessly, and where melancholy and a zest for life blend into a deep passion.

Roman historians tell of a famous dancer from Cadiz who was summoned to Rome to present her art - an early version of the flamenco. When the Arabs later came to Spain they absorbed Andalusian folk music, mixed it with their own, and continued to foster it - this is the reason for the strong echoes of Arab music in flamenco. When the Moors were driven out, those who wanted to stay mixed with the gipsies who were reasonably accepted. They met in secret to party and play music. Together Arabs and gipsies cultivated Andalusia's songs and dances, so flamenco developed as an inspired synthesis of different folklores, as a form of expression for victims of fate, those people on the edge of society.

Flamenco has been danced at pilgrimages and fairs only since the 18th century, when Charles III granted gipsies more freedom. Over the years the various versions of the dance developed into a proper art form, and now bulerías, soleares, fandangos, and seguidillas have conquered the world's stages. Singers are still accompanied by guitars, singing and the rhythm of clapping hands and stamping feet. The texts almost always tell of pain, jealousy, and suffering in love.

The Sevillanas which are now popular in many European dance halls are not real flamenco. They are quite simply folk dances that are always found at an Andalusian fiesta - and they are easy for anyone to learn.

Flamenco is a very demanding art; Sevillanas, on the other hand, can be danced by anybody. The popular folk dance is celebrated at the *Feria*, in tents and outside.

The fiesta is thirsty work. The Andalusian rider drinks his wine straight from the *porrón*. The drinking vessel is then passed straight on to the next person.

Hunger comes in stages – and tapas are exactly what are needed. There are olives, shrimp, and many other tidbits practically everywhere at the *Feria*.

Gazpacho & Co.

"Del gazpacho no hay empacho", says a proverb: "You do not get an upset stomach from gazpacho." The cold vegetable soup *gazpacho andaluz* has conquered the world as a hearty, easily digestible snack that is a refreshment on hot summer days. Even in pre-Roman times shepherds feasted on the original version made from stale bread, garlic, vinegar, oil, and water. Later, farmers added vegetables to it to make it more substantial, and when working in the fields, they ate the gazpacho to satisfy their hunger, quench their thirst, and in scorching heat supply them with necessary salt and vitamins. The word *gazpacho* comes from the Latin *caspa* meaning "leftovers" or "little something." This is also how *gazpachos manchegos* from La Mancha are described, although they are made not from cold vegetables, but from small pieces of game, and are eaten hot (see page 327).

The base for a classic *gazpacho andaluz* is still the original mixture of bread, garlic, salt, vinegar, and oil. The latter should be of the very best quality – according to popular belief, "you cannot make a good gazpacho from poor vinegar and even poorer oil." Diced tomatoes, bell pepper, and cucumber are added. Earlier the whole mixture would be laboriously puréed with a mortar and pestle. Nowadays no-one is ashamed to use an electric blender to make the task a great deal easier.

To accompany the gazpacho, which is brought to the table well chilled, *tropezones*, small cubes of toasted bread, tomato, cucumber, bell pepper, onion, or hard-cooked egg are served in separate bowls. Each person puts whatever suits their taste on their soup plates.

A variation of gazpacho is *salmorejo cordobés* which contains just tomatoes rather than mixed vegetables, and is often supplemented with ham, tuna, or eggs. *Ajo blanco* (literally "white garlic"), a cold soup made from garlic, white bread, vinegar, oil, and where possible, tender, young almonds, comes from Malaga. In its home town *ajo blanco* is served with Moscatel grapes, raisins, or slices of apple. By contrast, *ajo colorado* (red garlic), a type of purée made from potatoes, tomatoes, bell peppers, onion, olive oil, garlic, and salt, is eaten warm. Traditionalists serve it with small corn cakes fried in oil.

White bread provides the calorie base for a *gazpacho andaluz*. Break it up roughly using your fingers.

Pour some water over the bread and leave it to soak while the other ingredients for this dish are being prepared.

First skin the tomatoes, then seed them. Peel the cucumber, then cut everything into large rough pieces.

It is not a gazpacho without plenty of garlic: peel the cloves and roughly dice them.

Modern equipment makes food preparation child's play: put all the diced vegetables in the blender.

Gazpacho would not be authentic if it did not contain green bell papers. Remove the seeds and dice the flesh into small pieces.

Gazpacho andaluz

2–3 slices of white bread
Generous 1 pound/500 g ripe tomatoes, skinned, seeded, and diced
1 cucumber, peeled, seeded, and diced
1 green bell pepper, seeded and diced
3–4 cloves of garlic, peeled and diced
½ cup/125 ml olive oil
Salt
2–3 tbsp wine vinegar or sherry vinegar

To garnish:
Cubes of white bread
Small cubes of tomato
Bell pepper, diced up small
Diced onion
Cubes of ham
Hard-cooked egg, diced up small

Left: Good olive oil puts the finishing touches to *gazpacho andaluz.* Everything is then puréed.
Above: *Ajo blanco* is often served with white grapes.

Roughly break up the white bread, and pour some water over; then leave to soak for at least 30 minutes. Put the tomatoes, cucumber, bell pepper, and garlic in a blender, then add the bread, and finally the oil, and purée the whole mixture. Add enough water as necessary to give the soup the required consistency. Then, if necessary, pass the soup through a fine sieve. Season with salt and vinegar. Place the gazpacho in the refrigerator for a minimum of 1 hour. Serve it very cold with separate bowls of white bread cubes, small pieces of bell pepper, diced onion, cubes of ham, and diced hard-cooked eggs, which each person mixes into their soup themselves.

AJO BLANCO
Cold garlic and almond soup

2 slices of toasted white Spanish bread
1 cup/150 g shelled almonds
3 cloves of garlic, peeled
½–1 tsp salt
8 tbsp olive oil
2–3 tbsp sherry vinegar
9 oz/250 g white, seedless grapes

Soak the white bread in some water for a few minutes. Purée the almonds with the garlic, some salt, and the drained bread in a blender. Gradually add the oil and finally the vinegar. Add some more water depending on the required consistency. Season the soup with salt and vinegar, and pass through a fine sieve. Pour into soup plates and garnish with the grapes.

423

THE POMEGRANATE

„When you eat the pomegranate, eat it with the fruit flesh as this tans the stomach, and each seed that is found in a person's stomach lights up his heart and silences the whispering devil for forty days." Abdullah Ibn Abbas, a cousin of the prophet Muhammad, found such sublime words at the beginning of the 7th century to describe the effects of the pomegranate. It is a fruit that was said, according to legend, to have been fertilized by a drop of water from paradise.

The Carthaginians are presumed to have brought the pomegranate bush, which originates from Asia, to the Iberian Peninsula 3000 years ago. Jews and Arabs cultivated it in Andalusia and even named a whole town after the fruit: *Gharnata*. This later became Granada, and today the pomegranate is the symbol of the city.

Both Jews and Muslims regarded the bright red pomegranate as the symbol of fertility and renewal. The Arabs used it to make drinks and to flavor meat dishes. The blossom of the bush was even thought to have a healing effect on bleeding gums. The fruit, which is surrounded by a tough skin, used to be immersed in hot tar and attached to a string. This was supposed to keep the center fresh and juicy for a long time. Pomegranates are not the most tidy of fruits to eat but their taste compensates for this!

Background: The harmony of Moorish architecture is displayed in the mosque at Cordoba.

THE ARABS' CULINARY LEGACY

As more of Spain was conquered by the Arabs in the 8th century, luxury arrived for the first time. Until then life had been hard for the native population of al-Andalus, as the Arabs called the conquered region. However, they first introduced public baths, dressed in sumptuous cloth, and smelt of ethereal oils. They left their mark in many aspects of life, on architectural forms, and brought with them their knowledge of medicine, weapons technology, and the manufacture of leather, ceramics, and silk. In particular, their cuisine served not only to satisfy hunger, but also to stimulate the taste buds, something which was particularly true of their wonderfully fancy sweet dishes.

In agriculture the Arabs introduced very highly developed irrigation systems and fertilizer methods. They also cultivated useful plants that were until then unknown on the Iberian Peninsula. They obtained rice, sugarcane, and eggplants from India through the Persians who already traded with India and China. They brought honeydew melons from Egypt, water melons from Africa, and figs from Constantinople. They spread Near Eastern citrus fruits, peaches and apricots, carob and quinces, almonds and pistachios as far as the Atlantic coast. Later, dates arrived from Iraq and coffee from the Yemen. Transporting foodstuffs over large distances required new preservation methods such as drying fruit and pickling in honey.

Herbs and spices also played an important role in the cuisine of al-Andalus. Particularly popular were basil, cumin, coriander, saffron, aniseed, mint, ginger, and jasmine, as well as almonds, pistachios, pine nuts, sesame, tamarind, and cinnamon.

Numerous words in the Spanish language serve as a reminder today that the cultivation of many foodstuffs on the Iberian Peninsula was introduced or perfected by the Arabs. These include above all those words that begin with the Arabic article *al-* or *a-* : *alcachofa* (artichoke), *albaricoque* (apricot), *almendra* (almond), *azafrán* (saffron), *azúcar* (sugar), *arroz* (rice), and *aceite* (oil). Other words such as *naranja* (orange), *berenjena* (eggplant), and *zanahoria* (carrot) also have Arabic roots.

As a source of protein the Arabs favored mutton and lamb as well as fish, and they also brought suitable methods of preparing these with them. They were inspired by Persian cooks and also Egyptian and Turkistan customs. They combined meat and fish dishes with fruit, spices, and herbs, and invented dishes such as tuna with sour cherries, dried cod with orange, mutton with apricots, or lamb with mint or cumin sauce. The Arabs also introduced the rice pudding with honey that is still highly popular in Spain today, as well as countless different types of almond pastries and other cookies, quince jam, and dates stuffed with nuts and almonds.

Although many cultural achievements from that period were forgotten when the Christians recaptured Spain, the art of making sweet dishes has remained. Catholic nuns in many convents still maintain this tradition to the present day (more about this, see page 446).

Spanish cuisine owes a large part of its riches to the Arabs. They brought rice and almonds, vegetables and fruit, as well as many herbs and spices.

Tuna

Tuna from the Andalusian Atlantic coast was a much sought catch and an extremely lucrative business even in Phoenician, Roman, and Arab times. At the time of the Arabs, men in watchtowers (atalayas) announced the arrival of large shoals of tuna so that the fishermen knew in which direction they should lay out the nets. The ships sailed toward the shoals, confronted them, and formed an almadraba, a tuna trap, with the nets. The fish got caught in the mesh and they were then easily able to be killed with poles. Back on land the fish were cut up, salted, and transported to the markets in wooden barrels.

Today the Spanish fishing fleet operates throughout the world. Tuna, which is processed in Andalusia, often comes from distant seas.

The Spaniards most value the long-fin tuna (lat. *Thunnus alalunga*). They call it *atún blanco* or even *bonito del norte*. It is fished off the Cantabrian coast in summer and can weigh more than 22 pounds (10 kilograms). Its pale flesh is almost white, moist, firm, and full of flavor. The filleted abdominal flesh (*ventrecha*, or in the Basque country *mendreska*) is considered a particular delicacy.

The yellow-fin tuna (lat. *Thunnus albacares*), called *atún claro* or *rabil* in Spain, is mainly caught in tropical seas, frequently off Ecuador. It is significantly

Atún (top) and *bonito*: the quality of the flesh of these two varieties of tuna is very different.

larger and heavier than the long-fin tuna. Its flesh is usually a pink color and not as aromatic, firm, and moist as that of the long-fin tuna.

The blue-fin tuna (lat. *Thunnus thynnus*) is called simply *atún* in Spain. It is found mainly in the Pacific and other tropical oceans and can weigh up to an amazing 44 pounds (20 kilograms). The reddish flesh is very oily and less muscular than that of other varieties of tuna. It is nowhere near on a par with the long-fin or even the yellow-fin tuna as regards flavor, tenderness, and moistness. The flesh of the blue-fin tuna is usually used to make *mojama* or it is sold in chunks in cans.

Mojama

On Spain's southwest coast it is hot, as well as being fairly windy and dry. This has two consequences for fishermen: a disadvantage is that fresh fish can go off quickly, but it also dries easily in the sun. What is more obvious than putting sea salt on fish from the Mediterranean and Atlantic and then hanging it in the sun to dry? Even the Arabs preserved fresh tuna in this way and called the result *musama* . Today the specialty is called *mojama* and is produced in particular along the Andalusian coast around Huelva, Cadiz, and Almería, as well as in Murcia and Valencia.

"In principle *mojama* can be produced from any variety of tuna," explains Carmelo Díaz Vázquez from Isla Cristina. "The smaller *bonito* is suitable and even mackerel. But blue-fin tuna has the best and largest fillets for this purpose. In addition you naturally have to have the right climate for *mojama* so that the fillets can dry thoroughly." The conditions on Huelva's Atlantic coast are, therefore, particularly ideal because a proper wind blows in this area almost all year round.

The expert cuts up the fresh tuna with a large, sharp knife for the purpose. The first specimens are quickly taken apart neatly and the pale red fillets removed. Then Carmelo washes them with water, and salts them, before leaving them to mature in salt for a few days. Then the fillets are washed thoroughly and hung up to dry. "And when they hang in the cool wind and dry slowly," the *mojama* man explains, "they shrink and darken until they are reddish brown, of a firm consistency, and dried through completely."

Carmelo has already expertly prepared a few slices of *mojama* as a snack – sliced so thinly that you can almost see through them. He marinates the slices in olive oil for an hour to make them more moist. He then toasts a few almonds on the stove and serves the marinated slices of *mojama* on a large plate accompanied by the toasted almonds. A light, fruity white wine from the Condado de Huelva is proffered with them.

In Alicante or Murcia *mojama* is often served cut into small pieces and then sprinkled in a salad – only just acceptable to connoisseurs given that the mild taste of the sea cannot take a great deal being added to it. Indeed, combinations with mayonnaise or particularly garlic sauce *(aioli)* are regarded as sacrilege by the initiated. In comparison, however, a little fine, cold-pressed olive oil is allowed: it makes the noble salted fish even more pleasant.

Fishing has been an important source of income for Andalusians in the coastal areas for centuries.

Some of the tuna for *mojama* comes from Andalusian waters, while some is imported from other seas.

After the fresh tuna has been neatly cut up and filleted, it is rubbed vigorously with coarse-grain sea salt.

The fish fillets are washed before the drying process. This removes any surplus salt.

During the drying process the tuna fillets shrink and develop the intense reddish brown color typical of *mojama*.

Finally the *mojama* is thoroughly cleaned once more and then packed. A large number are sold sealed in film.

The flesh of the blue-fin tuna is the most suitable for producing *mojama*.

The salted tuna fillets, air-dried in drying sheds (main photograph), are an exquisite delicacy. They are cut into very thin slices and usually eaten on their own (above).

FROM ANDALUSIAN SEAS

They are much too good for a lot of fat and a thick breadcrumb coating: *langostinos de Sanlúcar* and *gambas de Garrucha* are two of the gems of the Andalusian seas. Gourmets have to dig deep in their pockets for the jumbo shrimp from Sanlúcar de Barrameda on the Atlantic coast and the small, white shrimp from the Garrucha area in the Mediterranean province of Almería. A generous 2 pounds (1 kilogram) of the noble seafood can cost over US$50. They are so tender and delicate that they should only be steamed gently or prepared on the hot metal plate *(a la plancha)* so that the flavor is not adulterated. Otherwise, though, the Andalusians love their *fritos:* fish and seafood from the deep-fat fryer – as a tapa or main course. Sardines and anchovies, portions of shark or tuna, shrimp or crab are all suitable for deep-frying. Very small fried fish *(pescaitos)*, especially anchovies *(boquerones fritos)*, are particularly popular with the Andalusians, as are tiny fried squid *(puntillitas* or *chopitos)*.

Jumbo shrimp from Sanlúcar de Barrameda are among the stars of Andalusian seafood (above). Fish is often served deep-fried (main photograph).

Before being fried the fish can be tossed in a mixture of wheat flour, egg yolk, whisked egg white, and salt according to taste. If the batter becomes particularly thin, some compressed yeast and milk are added to the mixture. Very small fish are given a particularly spicy flavor if a dash of beer is poured over them just before cooking.

FROM THE SEA TO THE TABLE

BONITO CON ACEITUNAS Y ALCAPARRAS
Long-fin tuna with olives and capers

4 slices of fresh long-fin tuna, weighing about
7 oz/200 g each
½ cup/125 ml white wine
2 tbsp sherry vinegar
2 cloves of garlic, finely diced
1 bay leaf
2 sprigs of thyme
6 black peppercorns
Salt
Scant ½ cup/100 ml olive oil
1 large onion, cut into thin rings
7 oz/200 g pitted olives, diced
1 tbsp capers
Pepper
Oil for the baking pan

Wash and dry the tuna. Make a marinade from the white wine, vinegar, garlic, bay leaf, thyme, peppercorns, and a little salt. Place the fish in a dish and pour the marinade over; then marinate them for 1 to 2 hours.
Remove the tuna from the marinade and drain. Keep the marinade, removing the bay leaf and sprigs of thyme. Heat the olive oil and fry the onion rings in it until translucent (do not brown). Pour in the marinade and ½ cup/125 ml water. Add the olives and capers, and leave to reduce a little. Season with salt and pepper. Place the tuna slices in an oiled baking pan and pour the sauce over. Cook in a preheated oven at 390 °F/200 °C for about 20 minutes. Serve in the baking pan.

URTA A LA ROTEÑA
Rota-style dentex

4 dentex fillets, or gilthead bream fillets,
weighing about 7 oz/200 g each
Salt and pepper
Flour for tossing
5 tbsp olive oil
1 onion, finely diced
3 cloves of garlic, finely diced
2 small green bell peppers, seeded and
cut into pieces
3 ripe tomatoes, skinned and diced
1 bay leaf
2 sprigs of thyme
Salt and pepper
⅛ teaspoon cinnamon
1 cup/250 ml white wine

Wash the fish fillets and pat dry. Season with salt and pepper. Toss in flour, shaking off any surplus. Heat the olive oil and briefly brown fish on both sides. Remove from the pan and place side by side in a baking pan. Fry the onion and garlic in the oil until translucent. Add the bell pepper and fry briefly with the onion and garlic. Stir in the tomatoes and season with the bay leaf, thyme, salt, pepper, and cinnamon. Pour in the white wine and let the sauce thicken for 10 to 15 minutes. Then remove the bay leaf and sprigs of thyme, and pour the sauce over the fish. Cook in a preheated oven at 345 °F/ 175 °C for approximately 15 minutes. Serve in the baking pan itself.
Variation: The fish fillets can also be placed on top of slices of fried potato, covered with the sauce, and baked until cooked.

CAZUELA DE FIDEOS A LA MALAGUEÑA
Malaga noodle stew with clams

½ cup/125 ml olive oil
2 onions, finely diced
4 cloves of garlic, finely diced
2 large green bell peppers, seeded and
cut into strips
2 potatoes, cut into small pieces
3 ripe tomatoes, skinned and diced
Salt and pepper
A few saffron threads
Scant ½ cup/100 g ground almonds
1 cup/250 ml white wine
2 ¼ lbs/1 kg clams, cleaned
3 ½ oz/100 g Spanish fideos (noodles),
or thick vermicelli

Heat the oil in a deep pan, and fry the onions and garlic in it until translucent. Add the bell pepper and potatoes and braise for a while. Stir in the tomatoes and season with salt and pepper. Simmer the vegetables for 10 minutes. Crush the saffron with the ground almonds and some white wine using a mortar and pestle. Stir the paste and the remaining white wine into the vegetables. Add the clams and noodles, and pour in 1 cup/250 ml water. Simmer on a low heat for about 15 minutes, adding more water if necessary. Finally, season with salt and pepper before serving.

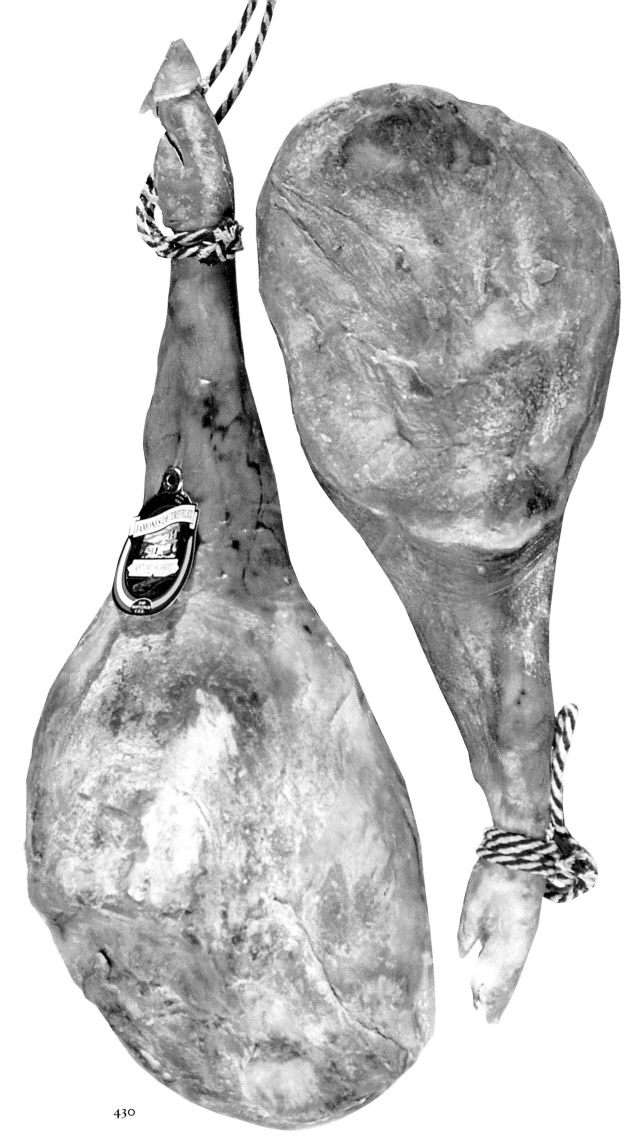

SOMETHING SUBSTANTIAL WITH MOUNTAIN HAM

HABAS CON JAMON
Young fava beans with ham

7 oz/200 g Serrano ham, cut into cubes
3 tbsp olive oil
1 onion, finely diced
2 cloves of garlic, finely diced
Generous 1 ½ lbs/750 g fava beans, shelled
Salt and pepper
1 tbsp chopped mint or parsley

Brown the ham in the olive oil; then remove from the pan and set aside. Fry the onion and garlic in the oil until translucent. Add the beans and pour on some water. Cook the beans on a medium heat for approximately 30 minutes. Shortly before the end of the cooking time, stir in the ham and reheat with the beans. Season with salt and pepper. As a final touch, sprinkle with chopped mint or parsley before taking to the table.

TRUCHAS RELLENAS DE JAMON
Trout stuffed with ham

4 trout, ready to use
Salt and pepper
1 tbsp almonds, roughly chopped
1 tbsp pitted green olives, roughly diced
1 shallot, finely diced
1 tbsp chopped parsley
4 thin slices Serrano ham, or other
air-cured ham
2 tbsp olive oil

Wash and dry the trout. Rub the inside and outside with salt and pepper. Mix together the almonds, olives, shallot, and parsley. Spread a quarter of the almond/olive mixture on each slice of ham. Roll up the ham and place in the abdominal cavity of the trout. Close the opening using wooden picks. Brush 4 sheets of aluminum foil with olive oil. Place a stuffed trout on each sheet and fold the foil over to cover the fish. Press the folds down firmly. Grill the trout in the foil on a hot rack for 10 minutes on each side. Before serving open the foil to let the steam escape and serve the fish in the foil.

Left: Air-cured haunch (*jamón*, left) and shoulder (*paleta*) of ham are both obtained from white pigs, but differ in size and taste.

Croquetas de jamon serrano
Croquettes with Serrano ham

9 oz/250 g Serrano ham
3 eggs
2 tbsp butter
3 tbsp flour
1½ cups/375 ml milk
Salt and pepper
⅛ tsp ground nutmeg
Flour for coating
1¾ cups/100 g breadcrumbs
Oil for frying

Cut the ham into very thin slices and mix with 1 egg and 1 egg yolk. Melt the butter in a pan and stir in the flour; then cook until pale yellow.

Pour in the milk, while stirring, and bring the mixture to a boil. Then cook on a low heat for 10 minutes, stirring constantly, until a thick Béchamel sauce forms. Remove from the heat and fold in the ham. Then season with salt, pepper, and nutmeg.

Beat the remaining egg with the egg white. Using a wet tablespoon, cut pieces off the mixture and form into little croquettes. Coat first in flour, then roll in the beaten egg, and finally in the breadcrumbs, ensuring they are covered. Fry in the oil in batches. Drain briefly on paper towels and serve very hot.

Jamon serrano from Trevelez

Air-cured ham from white pigs is produced in several Andalusian mountain regions. It is known as *jamón serrano* (or mountain ham) and is derived from the word *sierra*, or mountain range. The ham from Trevélez has the best reputation. The village lies on the southern slope of the Sierra Nevada and, at around 5575 feet (1700 meters) above sea level, it is Spain's highest. Almost all year round dry, cool winds blow through here, and the air is exceptionally clear and clean. Every year under these conditions thousands upon thousands of haunch and shoulder hams mature in the village's drying sheds *(secaderos)*. These were once aptly described by the Andalusian poet Pedro de Alarcón as *secaderos a la ventilación de la nieve*, with "snow ventilation." The end product of the procedure is the highly aromatic *Jamón de Trevélez*. Like every *jamón serrano*, this ham always comes from white pigs which are fattened intensively. After being slaughtered the haunches are salted with coarse-grain sea salt and then air-cured for at least 12 months. In some cases, the fine pieces of ham mature for 20 months, and in extreme cases for as long as 32 months. Shoulders of ham, which are matured in the same way, are called *paleta curada* or *paletilla curada*. They are somewhat smaller than the haunches (see photograph on opposite page).
Serrano hams from white pigs are a similar shape to a guitar. They are wide and plump. Hams from black Iberian pigs, on the other hand, are produced in a V-shape. They have a shape in fact a bit like a violin, and are thinner and longer (see also page 338 ff).
There are a total of about 1700 producers of *Serrano* ham in Spain. In 1990, 18 of the leading ones joined together to form the *Consorcio del Jamón Serrano Español*. Their produce must meet high quality standards before it is labeled with an "S" for *Serrano*: it must weigh at least 14 pounds (6.5 kilograms), and have been air-cured for at least nine months. Beside Trevélez, Teruel in Aragon and the provinces of Girona (Catalonia) and Soria (Castile-León) are well-known for their excellent *serrano* ham.

The climate in Andalusia's mountain regions, where snow remains well into spring, offers ideal conditions for the production of air-cured ham.

After the salt has been washed off, the ham is hung up in special drying huts. It matures here supplied with fresh mountain air.

Small holes appear where the punch was inserted. These are filled in with pork fat so that the delicate meat inside does not dry out.

For real *jamón serrano*, the ham from intensively fattened white pigs is used. The ham is first salted thoroughly with coarse-grain sea salt.

Serrano ham is air-cured for at least twelve months. Then the producer takes out some of the meat with a punch to check the quality.

Air-cured *jamón serrano* is cut into thin slices using a fine knife and often served as a tapa. However, it also goes well in the cooking pot.

Meat variations

Cordero a la moruna
Moorish style lamb
(Photograph right)

2 ¼ lbs/1 kg shoulder or leg of lamb
Salt and pepper
½ tsp cinnamon
½ tsp ground cumin
Scant ½ cup/100 ml olive oil
2 large onions, diced
2 cloves of garlic, diced
2 cups/500 ml stock
1 tbsp golden raisins, soaked in 2 tbsp sherry
1 tbsp almonds, roughly chopped

Wash the shoulder of lamb and pat dry. Then rub thoroughly with salt, pepper, cinnamon, and cumin. Heat the olive oil in a braising pan and fry the onions and garlic until they are translucent. Place the meat in the pan and brown well on all sides. Then pour in the stock and add enough water to just cover the meat. Braise, covered, on a medium heat for about 1 hour, adding more water if necessary. Shortly before the end of the cooking time, add the golden raisins and almonds, and season with salt and pepper.

Pinchos morunos
Moorish kebabs

1 ¼ lbs/600 g pork or lamb fillet
Scant ½ cup/100 ml olive oil
3 ½ tbsp dry sherry
1 tsp mild paprika
½ tsp hot paprika
½ tsp ground cumin
Salt and pepper

Cut the fillet into ¾–1¼ inch (2–3 cm) chunks. Make a marinade with the olive oil, sherry, and spices, and marinate the meat chunks in it for at least 2 hours.
Then take the meat chunks out of the marinade, and thread onto 4 kebab skewers. Broil under a medium heat for about 10 minutes, turning several times.

Pato a la jerezana
Jerez style duck

1 duck, weighing about 4 ½ lbs/2 kg, ready to use
Salt
4 tbsp olive oil
5¼ oz/150 g streaky bacon, cut into strips
2 onions, diced
2 cloves of garlic, diced
2 carrots, sliced
2 ripe tomatoes, skinned and cubed
7 oz/200 g pitted green olives
1 cup/250 ml stock
1 bouquet garni (parsley, thyme, oregano, bay leaf)
Pepper
2 cloves
½ cup/125 ml sherry

Wash the duck and pat dry; then cut into equal-sized portions. Rub thoroughly all over with salt and pepper. Heat the olive oil in a braising pan and brown the duck portions on all sides until nicely golden brown. Remove the portions and set them aside.
Fry the bacon, onions, and garlic in the oil until translucent. Add the carrots and fry briefly. Stir in the tomatoes and olives, and then pour in the stock. Add the bouquet garni and cloves. Bring to a boil and at that point return the duck portions to the pan. Braise, covered, for approximately 45 minutes. 5 minutes before the end of the cooking time, stir in the sherry and season the sauce with salt and pepper to taste.

Rabo de toro con ciruelas pasas
Oxtail with prunes

7 oz/200 g pitted dried prunes
2 ¼ lbs/1 kg oxtail, cut into pieces
1 onion, spiked with 1 bay leaf and 2 cloves
Salt and pepper
Flour for coating
½ cup/125 ml olive oil
4 ½ oz/125 g streaky bacon, cubed
2 onions, diced
3 cloves of garlic, diced
2 carrots, sliced
1 sprig each of thyme, oregano, and parsley
⅛ tsp ground cinnamon
⅛ tsp ground nutmeg
1 cup/250 ml white wine
Scant ¼ cup/50 g pine nuts

Soak the prunes in water overnight. Wash the oxtail. Put in a pan with some cold water, the spiked onion, and 1 tsp salt. Bring to a boil, then simmer for about 1 hour, skimming off the fat several times. Drain well and pat the pieces of meat dry. Season with salt and pepper, and coat with the flour.

Heat the olive oil in a braising pan and brown the meat well. Remove from the pan and set aside. Brown the bacon, onions, garlic, and carrots in the oil. Add the herbs, cinnamon, and nutmeg, and stir in the wine. Pour in enough water to just cover all the ingredients. Simmer on a medium heat for approximately 1 hour. Shortly before the end of the cooking time, stir in the prunes together with the pine nuts, and season with salt and pepper.

PERDICES RELLENAS A LA ANDALUZA
Andalusian style stuffed partridge

4 partridges, with giblets
3½ oz/100 g Serrano ham, cut into thin strips
3½ oz/100 g streaky bacon, cubed
4 salted anchovy fillets, finely diced
2 slices of white bread, cubed
2 tbsp chopped parsley
Salt
Pepper
3 ripe tomatoes, skinned and diced
2 carrots, thinly sliced
1 green bell pepper, seeded and diced
1 cup/250 ml stock
½ cup/125 ml sherry

Draw, wash, and dry the partridges thoroughly. Finely dice the giblets. Mix with the ham, bacon, anchovy fillets, white bread, and parsley. Season with salt and pepper. Stuff the partridges with the mixture and then close the opening with wooden picks.

Place the tomatoes, carrots, and bell pepper in a baking pan and lay the stuffed partridges on top. Pour in the stock with the sherry. Cook in a preheated oven at 390 °F/200 °C for about 1 hour. During this time baste the partridges several times with the stock. Serve in the baking pan. Fried potatoes go well with this.

ANDALUSIA'S FRUIT PARADISE

The name evokes a sense of the exotic: *Costa Tropical* is the name the Andalusians give to the area around the Mediterranean towns of Motril, Almuñécar, and Salobreña in the province of Granada. Huge mountain ranges protect this coastal plain from cold northerly winds, and the region is blessed with plenty of sunshine well into the winter. This is the reason why tropical fruits actually grow here. Beside sugarcane, which is used for local rum production, mangos and maracujas, papayas, medlars and limes, persimmons and avocados grow here. Growers on the Costa Tropical are even experimenting with litchis.

CHIRIMOYA

The chirimoya, a tropical fruit that has not yet become an established part of European fruit baskets, also grows in this region. Even attempts to describe the fruit's taste prove to be quite exotic: these range from a "mixture of pineapple, strawberries, and banana" to the "delicate temptation of raspberries and cream." The cherimoya (lat. *Annona cherimolia*) originates from the Latin American Andes, but has been indigenous to the permanently frost-free Costa Tropical and the Canary Islands for a long time. The greenish, scaly, tree fruit belongs to the group of tropical custard apple plants and is also called the custard apple. Its delicate skin conceals numerous large, black seeds in a sweet flesh. Few amounts of the 38,570 tons (35,000 tonnes) of chirimoya harvested from September onward every year are now sold on markets abrood. An extremely delicious fruity cherimoya liqueur is also produced in the Motril region.

PERSIMMON

During the winter months in Andalusia persimmons glow on leafless branches up to altitudes of 3280 feet (1000 meters). The bright orange fruits of the persimmon tree look a bit like large, somewhat pale tomatoes, but they are not botanically related to the member of the nightshade family from America. The persimmon tree is an ebony plant originally from China. It was first cultivated in Spain as an ornamental plant in parks and gardens. It was only at the beginning of the 1950s that the culinary qualities of the fruits were discovered. Today persimmons are grown particularly in the coastal regions of the province of Granada and in Valencia. Their taste is reminiscent of apricot, peach, and pear. A single persimmon provides half the daily requirement of vitamin A.

RAISINS FROM MALAGA

As early as the 18th century raisins from the mountainous hinterland of the province of Malaga were traded throughout Europe as an exquisite delicacy. Today more than 2600 small farmers in some 35 villages of the region produce approximately 2200 tons (2000 tonnes) of raisins every year. As they are truly *Pasas de Málaga*, the raisins are protected with an official stamp of quality (D.O.).

In the main, the grape variety Moscatel de Alejandría is used. After being picked in the months of August and September they are spread out on special drying areas (*paseros*), which are located on the southern slopes. The riper grapes are put at the edge as they dry to form raisins more quickly and in this way they are easier to collect. The grapes that are drying have to be frequently turned over by hand. If rain or fog is forecast, they are protected by being covered with tarpaulin. It takes until December or January for the grapes to be dried through evenly and to have become sufficiently dark in colour.

The best quality ones are the particularly large, evenly ripened raisins sold in whole bunches (*racimos*). Second best are the individual raisins. They are not picked from the stalks, but are carefully cut off with special scissors so that the fruit is not damaged. The best hand-sorted grades of grape are placed one by one in poplar-wood crates and covered with paper. This is how the produce arrives at the market.

Opposite: In Andalusia water melons grow just as well as many other fruits that adorn the market (above).

FRUITS FROM SPAIN

Spaniards can enjoy fruit from their own country all year round thanks to the varied climatic zones from the Pyrenees to the Canary Islands.

The apricot *(albaricoque)*, a legacy of the Arabs, is often used for fine jams.

The star fruit *(carambola)* grows mainly on the Canary Islands. It decorates any dessert.

Juicy cherries *(cerezas)* have made a name for the Valle de Jerte in Extremadura.

Raspberries *(frambuesas)* come increasingly from plantations.

The cherimoya originated in the Andes. It is consumed fresh or as a sweet liqueur.

Strawberries *(fresas)* ripen very early in Spain and are dispatched to Europe from Andalusia and other regions.

The prickly pear *(higo chumbo)* is the fruit of the *opuntia* cactus which comes from Latin America.

The persimmon *(kaki)* is very rich in vitamins A and C as well as calcium.

Kiwi fruits *(kiwis)* originated in New Zealand. They contain a lot of vitamin C.

The peach *(melocotón)* came from China and contains carotene.

The most important melon varieties are the Spanish melon (photograph), the *sandía* (water melon), and the *melón* (honeydew melon).

Pears *(peras)* are particularly popular in northern Spain, where they are often combined with meat.

The papaya *(papaya)* is particularly rich in enzymes which aid digestion (papain).

Plums *(ciruelas)* come in many colors and varieties. Most of them contain a lot of carotene.

Figs *(higos)* are mostly grown on the Mediterranean.

The mandarin *(mandarina)* came to Spain directly from China in the 19th century. It is mostly grown on the Mediterranean. New seedless varieties are continuing to gain more ground in the market.

The lime *(lima)* is slightly bitter and suitable for cocktails.

The lemon *(limón)* is popular in the kitchen, particularly for salads and fish marinades.

The guava *(guayaba)* is one of the exotic fruits that contain a lot of phosphorus as well as calcium.

The pomegranate *(granada)* arrived in the country with the Arabs. It has very tasty, bright red seeds.

The orange *(naranja)* is an export success, particularly for the Levante region in the south.

Nectarines *(nectarinas)* are sent to the Central European market in huge numbers.

The medlar *(níspero)* is regarded as a fruit that is very kind to the stomach and also aids digestion.

Quinces *(membrillos)* are mainly used to make quince jelly *(carne de membrillo)*.

The mango *(mango)* is the epitome of a tropical fruit and is extremely aromatic.

Many apple *(manzana)* varieties are grown, particularly in Catalonia and Asturia.

The pineapple *(piña)* has an extremely sweet flavor when picked ripe, and is rich in vitamin C.

Behind the unprepossessing skin of the passion fruit *(maracuyá)*, extremely tasty flesh is concealed.

The tasty pomelo *(pomelo)* is particularly suitable for fruit juices.

Sherry is made from the Palomino grape. Despite little rain this variety grows particularly well on the chalky soils around Jerez de la Frontera.

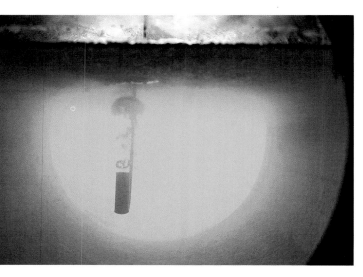

In many barrels a yeast layer *(flor)* forms on the surface of the wine. The wines with the best *flor* are converted into fino sherry.

When the sherry is to be tasted, the vintner takes a sample from the barrel with his *venencia*, a narrow, silver glass on a rod.

SHERRY

"If I had a thousand sons, the first human principle I would teach them should be, to forswear thin potations and to addict themselves to sack," enthuses the knight Falstaff in Shakespeare's play *Henry IV*. Wines have been cultivated in western Andalusia for 3000 years, although sherry was discovered only in the 13ᵗʰ or 14ᵗʰ century. At that time the Andalusian seafarers discovered on their travels that wine could be preserved for a long period by adding spirits. From this the first form of sherry was developed.

In 1587 Sir Francis Drake attacked Cadiz and is supposed to have taken 2900 butts of sherry which were being stored in the port and which were intended for the Spanish armada. From then on, British sailors regularly shipped sherry from Jerez de la Frontera to their homeland and made it very popular there. The town of Jerez was then called Xeris, a word which the English could not pronounce easily. Derived from the Arabic, it was pronounced *scherisch*, but the English simply called it *sherry,* which it has been called ever since.

Today only wine from the "Golden Triangle" of the towns of Jerez de la Frontera, Sanlúcar de Barrameda, and El Puerto de Santa María in the province of Cadiz may bear this name. The grapes grow on white, chalk-rich soils *(albarizas)* which are capable of storing every drop of water in this dry region. The typical grape variety for sherry is Palomino Fino, which is grown on some 94 percent of the total area. Pedro Ximénez and Moscatel add sweetness to the wine.

To produce sherry, Palomino must is first fermented to give a dry white wine. This is fortified to 15 or 16 percent with spirits and then put into oak barrels which are only filled to a good two-thirds. This allows optimum penetration of the moist, oxygen-rich Atlantic air. The wine spends its first year in the cool, damp atmosphere of the bodegas. Coarsely woven esparto grass mats cover the windows, letting in only a small amount of light and the moist Atlantic winds. After a few weeks in these special conditions a layer of white yeast, the so-called *flor* ("flower"), develops on the young wine. After six to ten months the vintner tastes the wine for the first time so that he can monitor its development. He takes a little wine from each barrel using his *venencia*, which is a narrow, silver glass on a rod. He then proceeds to check the color, clarity, smell, and taste of the wine. It is the composition of the cotton-white layer above all that determines what the wines will become. The vintner marks the result on the barrel in chalk.

Wines with particularly good *flor* become *fino*. The yeast layer continues to develop and protects the wine from oxidation. In addition, it gives this type of sherry its typical aroma and hint of slightly bitter almond.

Wines without flor are converted into *oloroso*. The alcohol content is fortified with the addition of more spirit up to 18 to 20 degrees. All the yeast dies, and so the wine matures when in contact with the oxygen in the air. With increasing age it takes on a dark color, and becomes more aromatic and full-bodied.

An *amontillado* develops from an aging fino, the yeast *flor* of which dies after some time. Then the wine continues to mature still under the influence of the air. In order to obtain sweet sherries, the sweet wines from the Pedro Ximénez or Moscatel grape are added either to an *oloroso* or an *amontillado*.

All traditional sherries typically undergo an aging process lasting for years under the *solera* system: at least three rows of barrels are stacked on top of each other; the barrels containing the oldest wines, the *soleras* (derived from *suelo*,

floor) are at the bottom. The vintner takes a certain amount of wine out of this *solera* at regular intervals. This is replaced by the same amount from the *criadera* above it, and this in turn is topped up from the next row. So all the rows are gradually transferred and the top one is made up with young wine. Over the years, the sherry from the top row of barrels moves down to the bottom one. In the process the wine matures as the younger qualities are gradually "married" with the older ones. The minimum aging time permitted for sherry is three years, but this is far exceeded by most of the *bodegas*. In the case of quite fine, old sherries the vintage of the original wine is stated on the label. You may, therefore, be lucky enough one day to be served an aged sherry whose *solera* began in the middle of the 19th century. Incredibly, a few drops of the fine stuff can, therefore, have been maturing for 150 years.

Right: Sherry needs a damp atmosphere to age in the barrel. The floors of the *bodegas* are therefore covered with sand and kept damp with water.

Sherry production is a creative process. The result is checked time and again, and the tools of the trade are reminiscent of artists' implements.

TYPES OF SHERRY

Fino
The aroma of the light, pale golden, dry sherry is shaped by the formation of the yeast *flor* on the surface of the wine in the barrel. Slight hints of almond are typical. The alcohol content is between 15.5 and 17 degrees. *Fino* is considered a classic apéritif wine and a light version has recently become available with an alcohol content of around 15 degrees. In Andalusia, *fino* is also drunk together with the meal.

Manzanilla
This light, pale, very dry *fino* is only allowed to come from Sanlúcar de Barrameda. The special microclimate right by the Atlantic means that the yeast layer, which protects the wine from oxidation and gives it a particularly fragrant aroma, "blooms" all year round. (In Jerez de la Frontera, in contrast, it blooms only in spring and fall.) This gives the *manzanilla* its typically dry and fragrant style, as well as its slightly salty taste and sea aromas.

Amontillado
If *fino* is left to mature long enough in the *solera* the *flor* yeast dies. The wine then oxidizes, subsequently becoming darker and more aromatic. *Amontillado* has an alcohol content of between 16 and 18 degrees and can be dry or medium dry. Its powerful nutty bouquet with a dry and mildly bitter taste is typical.

Oloroso
This is a dark, full-bodied sherry oxidized through the effect of oxygen in the air without yeast *flor*. It has powerful, sumptuous nutty aromas and often a slight residual sweetness. It can be either dry or medium dry and attains an alcohol content of between 18 and 20 degrees.

Pale Cream: What is understood by this is a *fino* from Palomino grapes to which grape must concentrate is added. This is what gives this sherry its typical sweetness.

Cream
This type of sherry is produced when sweet wine from Pedro Ximénez grapes is added to an *oloroso*. It is dark and aromatically sweet with a bright mahogany color.

Palo Cortado
This sherry, which is produced only in small quantities, lies between *amontillado* and *oloroso*. It ages without *flor*, is dark in color, and has an alcohol content of between 18 and 20 degrees.

Pedro Ximénez: This velvety sweet wine from the Pedro Ximénez grape has an alcohol content of around 17 degrees and a dark mahogany color. Raisin flavors are predominant.

Right: The various types of sherry are characterized by quite different colors.

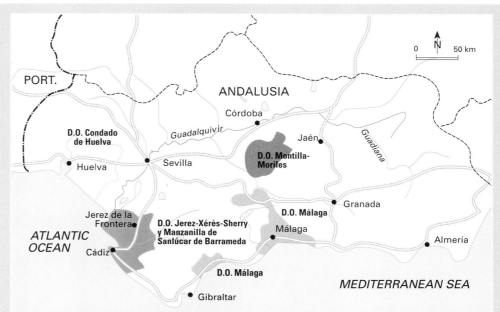

WINE-PRODUCING AREAS IN ANDALUSIA

D.O. Jerez-Xérès-Sherry y Manzanilla de Sanlúcar de Barrameda

The area covers just over 24,700 acres (10,000 hectares) in the Jerez de la Frontera, Sanlúcar de Barrameda, and El Puerto de Santa María triangle. The principal grape variety is the Palomino fino; Pedro Ximénez and Moscatel are also used. Sherry wine is chiefly produced here according to the *solera* process. Since 1990, there is an age certificate for this D.O., guaranteeing *Very Old Sherry (VOS)* to be at least 20 years old, an *Very Old Rare Sherry* to be at least 30 years old. Recently, several *bodegas* have decided to experiment with vintage wines as well as with several unfortified, light, pleasant white table wines from the Palomino grape.

D.O. Malaga

Vines were probably grown in the area around Malaga in 600 BC. There is clear evidence that they were cultivated during the Roman period and also later during Moorish rule. The Arabs called the sweet wine *Xarab almalaquí* (Malaga syrup). It was traded as a much sought specialty in Europe from the beginning of the 13th century, and as early as the late 15th century local wine-producers set up their own brotherhood to protect the exquisite product from inferior imitations. At the end of the 18th century Malaga wine was better known in Europe and overseas than that from Jerez. Production dropped considerably because of the mildew and phylloxera plagues at the end of the 19th century and the turmoil of the Spanish Civil War (1936–1939). Subsequently, sweet wines went more and more out of fashion and Malaga wine continued to lose its market shares. Now, however, demand for this reasonably sweet and always intense dessert wine is increasing again. The officially registered vineyards cover some 2225 acres (900 hectares) at present, from the mountainous hinterland down to Malaga's coast. The predominant grape variety is the Pedro Ximénez, but Malaga wines are also made from Moscatel or a blend of the two varieties. The must is usually fermented by small wine-producers at their vineyards.

The young wine is then taken to the larger aging cellars where it is mixed with spirit or thickened must *(arrope)*. Like sherry, it is then matured in the barrel by the *solera* process. Here, the Malaga wine gains significant color, aroma, intensity, and character. Classic Malaga wine matures in wooden barrels for at least two years and at the end displays touches of caramel, coffee, raisins, cocoa, nuts, and spices. The sweetest variant is described as *lágrima* (tear). It has a dark amber color and leaves a long, decidedly aromatic aftertaste. Beside the classic Malaga type, there are also today relatively dry variants which undergo a particularly long barrel-aging period and are similar in taste to an *oloroso* sherry.

D.O. Montilla-Moriles

This area with some 42 square miles (11,000 hectares) of vineyards lies in the south of the province of Cordoba. The predominant grape variety is the Pedro Ximénez which can withstand the region's heat better than the Palomino sherry grape. Apéritif wines with an alcohol content of between 15 and 18 degrees are produced using the *solera* process. The most famous are the young, hearty finos from Montilla-Moriles which are equal in every way to a sherry *fino*. Smaller amounts of *amontillados, olorosos,* and *palo cortados* are also produced. Even the substantial, sweet dessert wines from this region can count on a very large number of devotees.

D.O. Condado de Huelva

The area located in the province of Huelva on the Atlantic contains only 29 square miles (7500 hectares) of vineyards situated at between 164 and 656 feet (50 and 200 meters) above sea level. The principal grape variety here is the white Zalema. Palomino, Moscatel, and Listán grapes are also grown. Beside the classic fortified apéritif and dessert wines, the light, fresh white wines mainly pressed from the Zalema grape have recently become a real talking point.

Cooking with Sherry

Riñones al Jerez
Kidneys in sherry

2 calf's kidneys, weighing about
10 oz/300 g each
Salt
3 tbsp olive oil
1 onion, finely diced
2 cloves of garlic, finely diced
½ cup/125 ml dry sherry
1 cup/250 ml stock
Pepper
2 tbsp chopped parsley

Cut the calf's kidneys lengthwise, and then clean and wash well. Simmer in slightly salted water for 1–2 hours. Then dry well and cut into thin slices. Heat the olive oil and fry the onion and garlic until translucent. Add the kidneys and brown them briefly. Add the sherry and pour in the stock. Simmer, with the lid on, on a low heat for 5 minutes. Season the sauce with salt and pepper. Before serving sprinkle with the chopped parsley.

Almejas al Jerez
Clams in sherry

2¼ lbs/1 kg clams
2 tbsp olive oil
2 cloves of garlic, finely diced
1 cup/125 ml dry sherry
2 tbsp chopped parsley
Salt
Pepper

Wash the clams really thoroughly. Discard any that are already open.
Heat the olive oil in a pan and fry the garlic until pale yellow. Add the sherry and parsley, and season lightly with salt and pepper. Place the clams in the pan and cook, covered, for about 4 minutes, shaking the closed pan vigorously several times. Discard any clams that have not now opened after cooking. Serve the open clams either hot or cold in the cooking liquor.

When the onion and garlic have been cooked until translucent, add the sliced kidneys to the pan and brown briefly.

Pour the dry sherry over (right) and let it all simmer for a few minutes. Finally, add the chopped parsley (above).

Sherry vinegar

Everyone makes vinegar from what is to hand. No wonder, then, that the Germans use potatoes, the British malt, and the Japanese rice. Spain, on the other hand, with 3860 square miles (1 million hectares) of vineyards produces more wine vinegar than any other country in the world. "The better the wine, the better the vinegar," according to the old basic rule that every producer is familiar with. What ingredient is more suitable for good vinegar than sherry? Sherry vinegar is made from first-rate sherry wine. During a second fermentation process, acetic acid bacteria (lat. *Mycoderma aceti*) turn the wine into vinegar. This matures according to the *solera* process (see pages 438 f), in oak barrels in which sherry was previously stored. During this process, vinegars from different vintages are mixed gradually. The very best types mature in oak for 30, 50, or even 100 years, and so take on a profound flavor and a pleasantly soft quality. Furthermore, the vinegar becomes darker with a longer aging time. The color ranges from a light caramel to a deep crimson. Sherry vinegar, which is produced according to the traditional process laid down, has the protected designation of origin D.O. *(Denominación de Origen).*
In addition, there is a colorful variety of aromatic wine vinegars in Spain today which are mixed with rosemary, tarragon, or garlic. Raspberry vinegar is also popular, and recently gourmets have even been able to enjoy an aromatic, top-of-the-range vinegar with saffron.

Señor Lustau
Solera Gran Reserva
from Emilio Lustau

Cardenal Mendoza
Solera Gran Reserva
from Sánchez Romate

Carlos I
Solera Gran Reserva
from Pedro Domeq

X.O. Wisdom
Solera Gran Reserva
from Wisdom & Warter

Fernando de Castilla
Solera Gran Reserva from
Rey Fernando de Castilla

Gran Capitán
Solera Gran Reserva
from Bobadilla

Conde de Osborne
Solera Gran Reserva
from Osborne

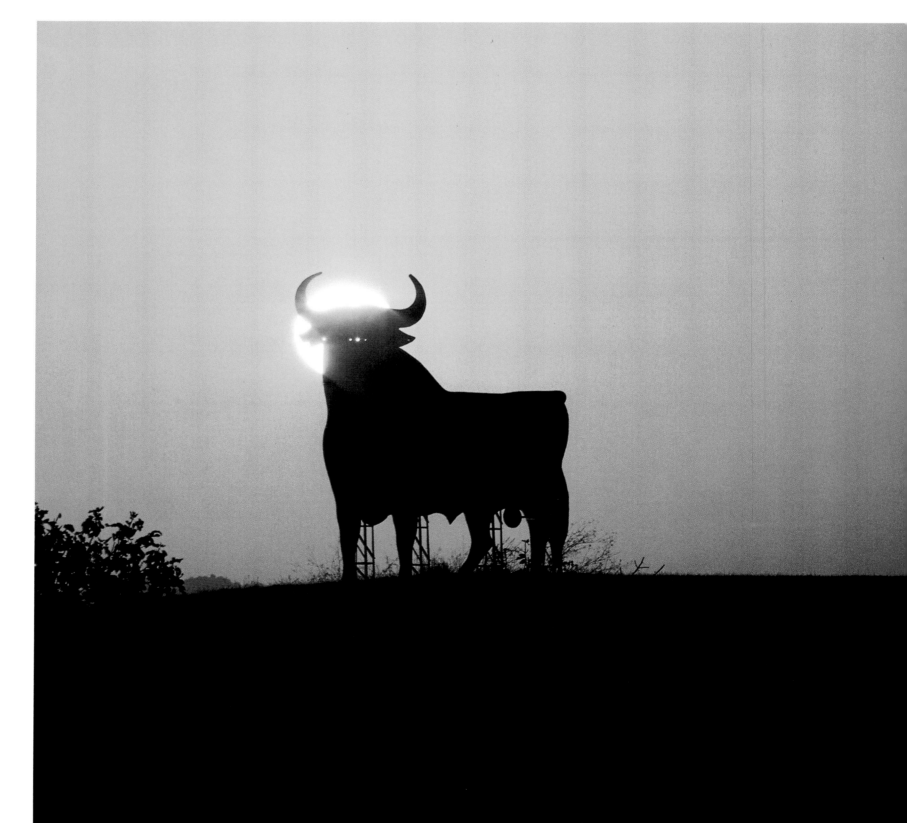

Lepanto
Solera Gran Reserva from
González Byass

Gran Duque de Alba
Solera Gran Reserva from
Williams & Humbert

Brandy de Jerez obtains its flavor and colors that range from pale golden through deep mahogany by maturing in used sherry barrels.

Left: The Osborne bull is a Spanish trademark. Accepted as a work of art, it is thus allowed to stand in a landscape that is otherwise advertising-free.

BRANDY DE JEREZ

As early as the 8th century, the Arabs brought stills *(alquitaras)* to Andalusia in order to turn wine from the Jerez region into high-proof alcohol. They mainly used it for perfumes and medicinal purposes. Centuries later, long after the Moors had been driven out of Spain, the alcohol was used in sherry production. In addition, the first producers began to ship large quantities to the Netherlands, where it was used to make liqueurs and spirits. It was not long before the wine distillates from Andalusia came to be called *holandas* after the main Dutch customers.

However, chance lent a helping hand to the birth of Spanish brandy. One fine day a Dutch customer, who had ordered wine alcohol from Jerez, is said to have canceled his order. What, then, was to be done with the precious stuff? Out of pure embarrassment it was poured into barrels in which sherry had previously been stored. Years went by and during this time the remaining stock was almost forgotten – and then one day it was sampled and the discovery was made that the maturing process in the sherry barrel had rendered the alcohol very aromatic, smooth, with a velvety texture. Brandy had been invented.

What was once produced by chance in the cellars of the "Golden Triangle" is today matured to an exquisite flavor, and exported throughout the world under a protected trademark: *Brandy de Jerez*. The classic production process has scarcely changed. First of all, light wines with an alcohol content of 10.5 to 13 degrees are pressed from white grapes. In the past Palomino, the native sherry grape, was usually used, but today the wine may also come from other Spanish quality wine regions. The majority comes from La Mancha, where it is distilled – often still in the traditional copper distillation equipment – to give a pale, transparent alcohol which even now is called *holanda*.

In order to develop the color, bouquet, and taste which allow it to bear the name *Brandy de Jerez*, the wine distillate must mature in old sherry barrels in bodegas in the sherry region. *Oloroso* barrels in particular give the brandy a distinctive flavor. Like sherry, *Brandy de Jerez* also ages according to the *solera* process (cf. pages 438 f.). At the end it has an alcohol content of 36 to 45 degrees and is sold in three degrees of maturity – depending on the length of time spent in the barrel:

Fine brandies were once made in this old distillery. Today, distilling usually takes place in modern plants, although the brandies still mature in the *bodegas*.

Old distilleries are still used only in very small family concerns. On the whole, this historic equipment has become just a museum piece.

Fine brandies of the *Solera Gran Reserva* type, which often mature in the barrel well in excess of ten years, are also put in expensive bottles, like this Lepanto.

- **Solera:** brandy that has matured in the barrel for at least six months, still relatively pale, winy, and light.
- **Solera Reserva:** distillate with a barrel-aging of at least 12 months, darker, more harmonious, and with more aromatic intensity.
- **Solera Gran Reserva:** highest grade, barrel-aged for at least 36 months.

The minimum legal aging times are often exceeded. A *Solera Gran Reserva* brandy frequently matures for 10 to 15 years or longer. This produces a brandy with an enormous concentration of flavor, smoothness, and complex taste with shades of mahogany wood, coffee, or chocolate.

Cortadillos de cidra: small lemon cakes

Torta de hoja: a puff pastry

Tocino de cielo: a type of custard made with egg yolk and sugar

Pastas de chocolate: chocolate cookies

Pastas de almendra: almond cookies

Canapés de almendra: crispy almond cookies

Canastillas: "baskets" with jelly and almonds

Clarisas: cookies from the Santa Clara convent

Mantecados and **polvorones:** delicate lardy cakes and shortbread

Yemas de almendra: confection made from egg yolk and almonds

HEAVENLY TEMPTATIONS

Some Christian nuns owe their sweet life to the Moslem Moors of all people, since it was they who brought the art of making confectionery to Spain. Even sinful wine played a role in the history of convent delicacies. Whipped egg whites were once used to clarify sherry and red wine. The wine producers traditionally gave the egg yolks that were left over to the convents as alms, and the nuns used them to make candy, which they then sold or gave to generous donors as a thank-you. As such benefactors and their donations became increasingly rare, the convents adapted and began to sell direct in order to earn their living.

Twelve Augustinian nuns still live in the San Leandro convent in Seville. They produce the famous *yemas*, an exquisite confection made from egg yolk, the recipe for which goes back to the 15th century, and which still today is in principle produced exactly as it was in the Middle Ages. The only innovations in the convent kitchen are a mixer and a special piece of equipment that separates the egg white from the yolk automatically.

The nuns from Santa Inés, on the other hand, specialize instead in pastries: lightly baked pastry balls made from flour, sugar, and sesame powder *(bollitos de Santa Inés)*; fine round, flat dough-cakes with sugar, aniseed, and a touch of olive oil *(tortas de aceite)*; small cakes *(cortadillos)* filled with candied lemon peel and pumpkin or apple jam; as well as delicate shortbread or lardy cakes with chocolate or almonds *(polvorones* and *mantecados).*

In a shop in the inner courtyard of the Santa Paula convent, the nuns sell exquisite fruit jams made from peach, quince, or orange, in addition to a pastry filled with pumpkin purée *(cabello de ángel)* and their best seller, a unique exquisite tomato jam.

In the surrounding province, too, convents sell homemade confectionery, like the Santa Clara convent in Alcalá de Guadaira and convents in Bormujos, Lebrija, Marchena, and Morón de la Frontera. In some orders the nuns are still not allowed to be seen by their visitors. Here a ring of a bell opens the door to the sweet paradise. In response to the bell a woman's voice is heard from behind a revolving wooden door (the traditional *torno)*, asking for the customer's order. The customer now gives the order and places the correct money, if possible, on the wooden turntable. Thereupon the invisible person inside turns the *torno* around. The customer takes the products requested, while on the other side the nun takes the money. Sometimes the nun behind the revolving partition greets locals with a softly spoken *"Deo gratias"* ("Thanks be to God"). The visitor then replies: *"Ave María purísima"* ("Hail, the most blessed Mary").

POLVORONES
Cinnamon cookies

4½ cups/500 g flour
¾ cup/200 g lard
1¾ cups/200 g confectioners' sugar
1 tbsp ground cinnamon
Juice and grated rind of 1 unwaxed lemon
Flour for the work surface
Confectioners' sugar for decorating

Sift the flour onto a baking sheet and lightly brown in a medium hot oven. Toss the flour several times so that it browns evenly; then remove from the oven and leave to cool.

Make a pile of the flour on the work surface and make a hollow in the middle. Place the lard, confectioners' sugar, cinnamon, lemon juice, and rind in the hollow, and using your hands quickly knead everything together to form a smooth dough. Roll this into a ball and wrap in aluminum foil; leave it to rest in the refrigerator for 1 hour.

Take out the chilled dough and roll it out on the floured work surface to the thickness of a finger. Using a small cake pan or a glass cut out rounds 1½–2 inches/4–5 cm in diameter. Line a baking sheet with baking parchment and place the cookies on it. Bake in a preheated oven at 345 °F/175 °C for about 25 minutes until golden brown. Leave the cookies on the baking sheet to cool and decorate with confectioners' sugar before serving.

MONASTERIO DE SANTA INES
Doña Maria Coronel, 5
Teléfono 422 31 45
SEVILLA

So that the nuns cannot be seen, they sell their sweet delicacies via a revolving door (*torno*, main photograph) in many convents. In Seville, though, there is even a special convent shop selling their products in the Plaza del Cabildo (above).

ISLAS CANARIAS

WULF ZITZELSBERGER

Canary Islands

Self-sufficiency is still the order of the day in the Canary Islands; many families keep one or two goats for milk, cheese, and meat.

There is an aura of mystery in the seven islands which make up the Canary Island archipelago. They are situated at what was once the edge of the known world, where the sun sinks into the sea, and where the Hesperides, or the daughters of Atlas, concealed their golden apples to prevent them being seized by thieves. They have inspired human beings to flights of fantasy since time immemorial: Plato saw in them fragments of the legendary lost continent of Atlantis; it was here that Homer's hero Odysseus was to sing the praises of the Elysian Fields; and the Greek philosopher Plutarch was to make the islands the home of the blessed ones, "an idle people, unaccustomed to work or toil," who were nurtured by the fertile soil.

The fascination exerted by the Canary Islands has endured, though it has to be said that the advertisements in travel brochures praise the beauty of the landscape with language which is far less poetic than that of the ancient Greeks. Although only a few hours' flight away from the continent of Europe, the climate is subtropical, thanks to the trade winds and the Canary Current, an offshoot of the Gulf Stream. The eastward islands of Lanzarote and Fuerteventura have endless sandy beaches and are dry and barren. Owing to their different geographical characteristics, Gran Canaria and the westward islands of Tenerife, La Palma, Gomera, and El Hierro enjoy more frequent rainfall; this has resulted in lush vegetation, especially on Tenerife and La Palma. The history of the archipelago, which was the home of ancient native tribes before the arrival of the Spaniards, is extremely diverse. Hailed as the gateway to the New World, a milestone for Columbus and the conquistadors, the islands later became wealthy as a result of the sugar and wine trade, and were tossed back and forth like a football between the world powers of England and Spain. At other times, though, they have suffered poverty and emigration.

Today the Canary Islands are for some people a symbol of mass tourism and concrete jungles, while others love the islands for their incomparable natural landscape and relaxed atmosphere. Tourism and country life are not mutually exclusive, however; there are still farmers, fishermen, and goatherds going about their work as their forefathers did. It soon becomes evident that culinary extravagance has no place here. The cuisine of the Canary Islands is plain and robust. Its main components include the following: substantial soups; lavish stews; roast meat with hot, spicy sauce; poached and broiled fish; sugary sweet desserts; and strong wines. And when Canary Islanders celebrate they display a side of their nature that they owe to their Caribbean compatriots in the New World – their fiery temperament.

Islas
Canarias

LA PALMA

Santa Cruz
de Tenerife

LANZAROTE

FUERTE-
VENTURA

LA GOMERA

TENERIFE

Las Palmas
de Gran Canaria

GRAN CANARIA

EL HIERRO

PORTUGAL

ESPAÑA

OCÉANO
ATLÁNTICO

Islas
Canarias

MARRUECOS

Opposite: The Canary Islands emerged from the sea; volcanoes thrust up from the Atlantic ocean bed. The volcanic soil is fertile, even where it appears barren.

Bananas

The contrast could not be greater. Just a few miles inland, behind a barrier of beaches and hotel complexes, are tropical green fields stretching out almost endlessly through the landscape of the western Canary Islands – nothing but banana plantations as far as the eye can see. Portuguese seafarers brought the banana, as it was called in West Africa, with them from Guinea. At first it was planted as an exotic ornamental shrub, and then at the beginning of the 16th century it was taken by the conquerors from the Canary Islands to the Caribbean and Mexico.

However, it was not until the second half of the 19th century that it was exploited economically, when shrewd English businessmen in Gran Canaria and Tenerife planted the dwarf banana imported from Indochina *(Musa cavendishii)*. This was so successful that the first freighters unloaded their delicate cargo in England in 1878. The export business was soon flourishing, and the banana, which the Spanish call *plátano* (a logical contraction of the Latin name *platanus orientalis*), has been the most important crop and the main commercial product of the archipelago for over a hundred years.

The best known varieties today include the dwarf banana, which is distinguished by its thin skin and extreme sweetness, and Williams, Johnson, and Gruesa Palmera, as well as a number of unnamed hybrids that are particularly robust and fast growing. No distinction is made between the different varieties for marketing purposes in the Canary Islands; the company logo of the producer or packing station is printed on the packing case, accompanied only by the few simple words *Plátanos de Canarias*.

A banana plant requires over 100 US gallons (400 liters) of water to ripen just 2 pounds (1 kilogram) of fruit. In the Canary Islands this can be achieved only by artificial irrigation. As a result of the high costs of water, fertilizer, and insecticides, as well as fierce international competition (see inset), it is becoming increasingly less profitable to grow bananas. The younger generation is being drawn into the tourist industry where wage prospects are better. However, those who wish to continue cultivating the land are trying to move away from monoculture by growing avocados, mangos, papayas, and flowers. It is unlikely that the Canary Islands banana will disappear completely; it still has a chance, provided that it is cultivated on a much smaller scale, in areas with an adequate water supply. And especially if new, robust, well-flavored varieties such as Gran Enano (Great Dwarf) are grown, the banana may fill a niche in the market for connoisseurs prepared to pay a higher price.

Politics and the banana

The Germans were fortunate enough in 1957 to be given the privilege of buying bananas as a duty-free exotic fruit by their Chancellor, Konrad Adenauer. Within a very short time the supermarkets had been flooded by cheap South American and Central American fruit from plantations belonging to the big multinationals. Germany soon had the highest per capita consumption of bananas in the whole of Europe, and consumption was given a further boost following German reunification in 1989.

The Canary Islands banana was unable to profit from this boom, however – it was far too expensive. So in 1992 the European Union, under pressure from its member countries Spain, France, Portugal, and Greece, fixed import quotas and minimum duties for the "dollar bananas." The expensive Canary Islands banana was at last given a chance against the "Chiquita," whose price was now artificially elevated. However, the multinational corporations viewed the European Union's import restrictions as a discriminatory act. As a result, the producers of the "Eurobanana" were charged with infringing international trading rights before the World Trade Organization (W.T.O.) by the United States, Ecuador, Guatemala, Mexico, and Honduras. This charge was upheld in the fall of 1997. In April 2001, the EU found an agreement with Ecuador and the United States to the effect that, by the end of 2005, the system of confingencies will be changed into a pure customs system. Within the EU, no customs will have to be paid for bananas from the Canary Islands, and they will remain to be subsidized in order to be able to compete with the „dollar bananas". But they really rely on the customers who need to be convinced that these small, freckly bananas can actually be much more tasty than the big, uniform fruit that bears no outer blemishes.

Background: the banana plantations of La Palma stretch right down to the sea, thanks to the fertile soil on this volcanic island.

1 Bananas are herbaceous perennials. They bear fruit only once, but grow extremely quickly.
2 It is possible to harvest only ten months after planting. This is heavy manual work, even today.

3 A cluster usually weighs 65–90 pounds (30–40 kilograms). It can weigh as much as 175 pounds (80 kilograms).
4 The delicate fruit is temporarily wrapped in order to prevent bruising during transport.

5 At the packing plant the bananas are unloaded and their quality is assessed by an expert.
6 Next the cluster of fruit *(piña)* is divided into individual bunches *(manos)*, since this makes the fruit easier to pack.

7 Before the bananas are packed and exported, they are thoroughly washed and disinfected.
8 Canary Islands bananas are exported as *Plátanos de Canarias*. They are still struggling for their market share.

Exotic fruits

Most of the exotic fruits piled into Spanish fruit baskets today were originally natives of the continents of South America, Africa, or Asia. Because of the subtropical climate, however, these fruits flourish in the Canary Islands or Andalusia to the extent that they are regarded as practically indigenous.

In addition to avocados, mangos, and papaya, other exotic fruits such as kiwi, prickly pear, pineapple, passion fruit *(maracujas)*, cherimoya (also called custard apple), cape gooseberry (also known as physalis), and guava are also grown (see photographs on pages 435 ff). A large proportion of these fruits is exported to other European countries.

Avocado
In the 15th century the conquerors of Mexico brought pits from the fruit of the avocado plant *(aguacate)* back to Spain for ornamental purposes. Commercial cultivation did not begin until after 1960. The high nutritional value of the fruit has also come to be appreciated due to its polyunsaturated fatty acids, proteins, vitamins, calcium, potassium, and iron.

Mango
From a distance it is possible to mistake a mango tree for an avocado tree, if it has been windswept and laid low by a storm. On closer inspection, however, the difference becomes apparent; the fruits of the mango tree hang in umbelliferous bunches, pulled down low by their own weight, from thin branches which are almost devoid of leaves. They vary in size, and their skin is slightly leathery and an iridescent green or reddish yellow. A native of India, this evergreen tree is cultivated in all tropical and subtropical countries and has been established in the Canary Islands for a long time. After a period of several years' growth, the first fruits with their fibrous, flattened pit and incomparable, exotic flavor finally ripen from a mass of blossom.

Papaya
The semi-woody papaya tree (in the background) is often planted alongside bananas, because it favors the same rich soils and sunny conditions. The papaya came originally from South America and grows very quickly to a height of between 10 and 20 feet (3 and 6 meters). The fruits, which can be round or oval in shape, grow directly beneath the crown of leaves and can weigh several pounds. The flesh of the fruit can be yellow or reddish orange. Served chilled and sprinkled with a few drops of orange or lemon juice, papaya is a refreshing pick-me-up particularly at breakfast time, and is very easily digested, since the fruit contains the digestive enzyme papain. Papaya is also suitable for making conserves and punches, and if the flesh is fairly firm, it can also be diced, then added to salads.

Prickly pear
The Spanish conquerors brought the prickly pear *(opuntia)* back with them from the New World as an ornamental plant. Its tasty fruits *(higos chumbos* or *tunas)* can be bought, fresh or dried, at any market in the Canary Islands. However, much more profitable is to use the plant as a host for the cochineal beetle, from which the highly sought carmine red food coloring is obtained. Originally it was Mexico, which used to export many tons to Europe, but around 1830, extensive fields of *opuntia* began to be planted in the Canary Islands. Cochineal production soon became the islands' main source of income, due to the enormous demand for the coloring in the textile industry. With the development of artificial aniline colorings around 1880, however, the market collapsed. Today cochineal is used only in the manufacture of lipsticks containing purely natural coloring and in some countries as a coloring in lemonade, apéritifs, candy, and silk.

SILK FROM LA PALMA

It was not just for its delicious fruit that the Spanish settlers brought the mulberry tree to La Palma in the 16th century. Its main function was to act as a host for the silkworm. In an imperial edict in 1538, Charles V placed silk production in La Palma under the protection of the Crown and exempted it from paying dues to the Church. Silk production rapidly developed into a thriving branch of the economy. Silk from La Palma was regarded as particularly fine and was exported to many European cities. Noblemen and rich tradesmen had fine robes made from it, frequently colored with the red dye of the cochineal beetle (see prickly pear, opposite). Silk production continued until the end of the 19th century, when 3000 looms were still in operation. After that the number of looms was reduced drastically with the advent of machinery. Even today, however, some families on La Palma are still skilled in the ancient craft.

Natural silk is produced by silkworms living on the branches of mulberry trees.

Cochineal beetles produce a red dye that is suitable for coloring spun silk.

The silk threads are then woven into the finest cloth using a hand loom.

PHYSALIS

This miracle of nature, which resembles a lantern, is also known as the cape gooseberry or ground cherry and is a member of the solanum family. It is a native of South America, but today it is grown mainly in Africa, Asia, and Australia, in addition to the Canary Islands. The tasty fruit, yellow to orange in color, is concealed inside a raffia-colored husk, which is the enlarged calyx. The berries should always be left in this husk until they are ready for eating, as this gives them the best protection. The flesh of the fruit has a slightly sour taste and contains tiny white edible seeds. It is rich in vitamins A, B_{12}, and C, and also contains the minerals calcium and iron.

Gofio is produced from maize, barley, and other types of grain. Impurities are removed by sieving.

The grains are then dry roasted. In earlier times this was done in the fields over an open fire (main photograph).

In order to roast the grains of corn evenly, they should be stirred and turned constantly in the pan.

Gofio

The sand-colored, raw mass of *gofio*, is a kind of whole-grain meal that is kneaded by hand into balls following the addition of liquid. It was regarded with contempt, if not downright disgust, by the Spanish conquerors in the Canary Islands. The natives of the Canary Islands were not familiar with the art of baking bread, having neither yeast nor walled ovens. In order to survive hard times, they used a simple method of processing harvested grain: they roasted clean corn in an earthenware dish over an open fire and then ground it by hand between stones. The resulting product, which resembled whole-grain meal, had liquid stirred into it, forming a paste that was then eaten.

The tradition of preparing *gofio* is a very old one and is based on historical connections between the original inhabitants of the Canary Islands and those of the Atlas mountains and the northern Sahara. Stories have been handed down the generations of voyages of discovery made by Mauretanian seafarers into the waters of the Canary Islands before the birth of Christ, and skills and customs probably found their way onto the islands together with the goods that were bartered.

The fact that *gofio* could be kept for long periods of time, and the ability to make even the poorest quality grain palatable by roasting it, were advantages appreciated by Stone Age hunters and gatherers. A calorific and filling dish, *gofio* remained for centuries the nutritional mainstay of the native islanders, and later also of Spanish agricultural laborers. Usually the whole-grain meal was simply mixed with water, pork fat, whey, or even wine, while chopped almonds and goat's milk were also added to the "luxury version."

Today, *gofio* is usually only to be found in rural households. In earlier times barley predominated, but the mills now grind mixtures of maize, wheat, rye, oats, and even rice. On restaurant menus, however, a search for *gofio* is usually in vain: restaurant owners are either too embarrassed to offer foreigners such an outmoded dish, or they want to spare the guest any culinary disappointment. In any event, a special request is necessary to obtain *gofio*, for example *gofio con chicharrones* (*gofio* with pork crackling) as a first course; *escaldón* (*gofio* mixed with a little broth) as an accompaniment to soup or a stew; or *gofio* with milk and honey as a dessert. While *gofio* enjoys great popularity among Canary Island traditionalists, doctors advise moderation; the high carbohydrate content and the fact that it is hard to digest are not in keeping with the modern trend toward lighter fare.

Poor man's bread

Until not so very long ago, farmers and agricultural workers in the Canary Islands were fortified principally by *gofio*, kneaded with a little liquid. In hard times, however – and there were plenty of these on the islands – the glutinous dough had to be stretched. If roasted and ground chickpeas were available to be added to the *gofio*, people still felt well fed. There were much worse times, though, when women were obliged to dig up bracken roots or collect lupine seeds in order to feed their families. The bracken roots were roasted and ground, then baked into round, flat cakes. This poor man's food was imaginatively named *pan de helecho*, or bracken bread. In order to make the seedpods of the wild lupine, a leguminous plant, at all palatable, they had to be placed in sacks and soaked for four or five days, either in running water or in the sea, to get rid of the bitter substances. Today the seeds of specially cultivated sweet lupines are nibbled as a snack (*chochos*) when drinking wine or beer. The seeds have to be prepared by soaking them in water for four or five days. They are then lightly boiled and stored in water. Before eating, the *chochos* are sprinkled with salt, and in rural areas it is still the custom to serve the seeds on vine or yam leaves.

After the roasted grains of corn had been milled, farmers out in the fields used to pour the fresh meal into a goatskin bag.

Usually a little water was added, but on high days and holidays, or if the farmer was prosperous, the liquid might be whey or even a drop of white wine.

Strong hands are needed to knead the *gofio* through the leather bag. The cornmeal and liquid combine in a homogenous mass.

The *gofio* is now ready to eat. It is either eaten cold from the bag or mixed with a little broth and then added to a soup or stew.

Ground *gofio* is also available packaged from health food stores.

THE CULINARY CONQUEST

In the 13th and 14th centuries the quest by Portuguese, Genoese, and Spanish seafarers for land and slaves from the Canary Islands brought to an end the peaceful life enjoyed by the natives. The conquest of the archipelago began in 1402 with the landing on Lanzarote of the Norman nobleman Jean de Béthencourt. The indigenous population of the Canary Islands put up a resistance for nearly a hundred years, until the islands were finally subjugated to the Spanish Crown following the conquest of Tenerife in 1496.

Christopher Columbus had discovered America in 1492, and the Canary Island ports rapidly became the most important point of departure for the royal fleet's voyages to the West Indies. Trade with America centered upon Santa Cruz de la Palma, which in just a few years became Spain's third largest port. Ships crossing the Atlantic put into port in the Canary Islands to pick up slaves, goods, food, and water, and on the return journey they carried cargoes of gold, silver, spices, and raw materials. In addition to the merchants, there were smugglers and adventurers from all over Europe who took part in both legal and illegal trade, creating enormous traffic in goods compared with the standards of the times. Trade was fueled by the constant stream of silver and gold that was pillaged and sent back to Spain by the Spanish *conquistadores* during their ransacking of South America.

They brought back more than riches, however; without the conquistadors, Europe would be a less colorful place today – and this applies even to the contents of our cooking pots. In addition to gold and silver, the Spanish conquerors brought back from Central and South America many culinary delights that have become an indispensable part of everyday life in modern Europe – potatoes and beans, tomatoes and avocados, papaya and passion fruit, maize, cocoa, and tobacco.

The Canary Islands have not always been blessed with such abundance. Periods of drought and famine repeatedly drove the population to try their luck abroad, with the result that past centuries saw wave after wave of emigration to Central and South America, mainly to Venezuela and Cuba. If an emigrant from the Canary Islands had made his fortune after years of hard work, he was often drawn to return to his homeland, taking with him a slice of Latin American culture – music and dance, food and drink, as a result of which the culinary exchange with Latin America has endured well into the 20th century.

Tomatoes are also a legacy from the islands' conquerors. The Canary Islands grow many tempting varieties; some the size of a man's fist for salads, some medium-size varieties for purées and soups, and tiny cherry tomatoes to tickle the palate. Tomatoes, or "apples of paradise," are grown in the open, either as bushes or staked, especially in southern Tenerife, Gran Canaria, and Fuerteventura. In many places they are also grown in enclosed conditions under plastic. Thanks to the subtropical climate they can be harvested all year round, for which the whole of Europe has reason to rejoice – many thousands of tons of sun-ripened fruit are exported to the mainland (for more about tomatoes, see pages 402 f).

TUBERS FROM THE CANARY ISLANDS

Sweet potatoes

The sweet potato has been in Europe for longer than the regular potato. It was also brought by the conquerors from Santo Domingo to the Canary Islands as long ago as the beginning of the 16th century, a good hundred years before the introduction of the tuber which is so popular today. The fruit, which has a high starch content, still remains the staple food of many South American Indian peoples.

The *boniato* or *batata*, as it is called in the Canary Islands, is also very popular. As well as being cultivated on a large scale, it is also planted in many private gardens – often alongside bananas. When ripe, tubers weighing up to about 4½ pounds (2 kilograms) can be harvested. With their firm flesh and yellow or orange color, *boniatos* go well in vegetable stews and provide an accompaniment to spicy dishes. In the Canary Islands they are also used as a sweet filling for pastries.

Yam

The yam *(ñame)* also thrives under the subtropical Canary Island sun. It was known in earlier times in China, India, Africa, and tropical America, where the sap from the plants was used as a preservative for meat and even as a tanning agent for fishing nets. As something of a botanical curiosity, the yam has strayed into the warm and humid northeastern area of La Palma and northern Tenerife. At the end of a ripening period lasting ten months it produces tubers weighing up to 11 pounds (5 kilograms) and measuring up to 16 inches (40 centimeters). Botanically, like the sweet potato, yams do not belong to the potato family. Boiled yams are often eaten as a sweet dish, preferably with sugar syrup. Those with more sophisticated tastes prepare a cream of yams, bananas, pineapple, and brown sugar, which is further enhanced, for the extravagant, by the addition of liqueur.

Mojo sauce requires red bell peppers, garlic, sea salt, and oil.

Soak the peppers and then place them in a blender.

Purée all the ingredients, except for the vinegar, which is added later.

The finished *mojo* is a spicy sauce that goes well with meat or potatoes.

The most popular sauces and dips are red and green *mojo* and the white cream cheese *almogrote*.

POTATOES

Geographical and climatic conditions in the Canary Islands permit the farmers, some of whom only grow potatoes, to bring in three harvests each year. On these predominantly agricultural smallholdings, varieties are grown to suit the diverse local soil conditions. The best known are *bonita, jaerla, margara, ortodate, cara,* and *negra (chiquita arraguda)*. At the end of the winter, when the previous year's crop is still being eaten in Central Europe, the Canary Islands supply the wholesale markets with the first new potatoes. However, in recent years their share of the export market has fallen; the Canary Islands are finding it difficult to compete with large agricultural concerns in other countries of the European Union, where water supplies and vast fields make production easier.

The potato is a legacy of the Incas. It was introduced to Europe in around 1550, brought back by the conquerors from the Andes. At first, it was cultivated in botanical gardens; recognition of the nutritional value did not come until later. Potato cultivation began in the Canary Islands in the 17th century, where according to Latin American tradition the tubers are called *papas*, by contrast with mainland Spain where they are called *patatas*.

Papas arrugadas – wrinkled, salt-encrusted potatoes that are served as an accompaniment to meat and fish dishes – are a specialty of Canary Island cuisine. The most suitable varieties are the very small ones such as the *papa negra* from Tenerife, the *bonita* from Gran Canaria, or the pink-colored, evenly sized small potatoes called *ojitos*. The recipe for these shriveled potatoes must have been born of necessity, since the inhabitants of the Canary Islands were once obliged to boil their potatoes in seawater as a result of fresh water shortages. They taste best broken into pieces with the fingers and dipped, in their skins, into the piquant sauce known as *mojo*.

PAPAS ARRUGADAS
Wrinkled potatoes

2¼ lbs/1 kg small quick-cooking potatoes
1-2 tbsp coarse sea salt

Wash the potatoes well and place them, in their skins, in a pan. Add water until the potatoes are just covered. Add the salt and boil the potatoes for about 20 minutes until cooked. Pour off the water. Return the potatoes in the pan to the stove and let the steam evaporate until a layer of salt has formed on the dry skins, shaking the pan several times. Serve immediately.

SAUCES AND DIPS

Mojos are sauces based on vinegar and oil that are served cold. Red and green *mojos* are encountered on all the islands, and there is a cheese dip that originates from La Gomera. The sauces are handed round separately with potatoes, meat, and fish. *Mojo colorado*, based on mild red Canary Island bell peppers, is transformed into piquant *mojo picón* by the addition of small hot peppers. There are also two kinds of green *mojo* – *mojo verde* with parsley and *mojo de cilantro* with fresh cilantro leaves. *Salsa almogrote* made with ripe goat cheese, sometimes also referred to as *mojo de queso*, goes well with *papas arrugadas* and is good spread on bread.

MOJO PICON
Hot red pepper sauce

4 dried red Canary Island bell peppers
¼ tsp cumin
2–4 cloves of garlic, halved
1–2 dried red chilies
½ tsp sea salt
1 cup/250 ml olive oil
Stale white bread
Vinegar to taste

Soften the dried red bell peppers in warm water for 15 minutes. Pour off the water and drain the peppers well. Grind the peppers, caraway, garlic, chilies, and sea salt to a fine paste in a blender. Add the olive oil gradually. Stir in a little water, or bread from which the crusts have been removed, to achieve the desired consistency. Add vinegar to taste. To store, pour into jars, cover with a little olive oil, and seal.

MOJO DE CILANTRO
Green sauce with cilantro

¼ tsp cumin
3–4 cloves of garlic, chopped
½–1 tsp sea salt
A bunch of fresh cilantro
¾ cup/200 ml olive oil
Freshly ground pepper
Vinegar to taste

Pound the cumin with the garlic and sea salt in a mortar and pestle or in a blender. Wash the cilantro and shake dry; remove the leaves from the stalks. Add the leaves to the mixture in the blender and gradually pour in the olive oil. Mix the ingredients well to form a fairly thick paste, adding a little water if necessary. Add pepper and vinegar to taste.

FISH FROM THE CANARY CURRENT

Without the Canary current and the trade winds, the Canary Island archipelago would be like a part of North Africa – dry as a desert, inhospitable, and unwelcoming. Lanzarote and Fuerteventura, which lie just off the African coast, give this sort of impression. However, the relatively cool ocean current around the Canary Islands, an offshoot of the Gulf Stream, ensures that most of the islands have a pleasant climate that is not too hot, either in summer or winter. Sunshine, water temperature, the current, and water that contains nitrates and phosphates and which is forced up to the surface from the depths of the ocean, all encourage the growth of plankton, which in turn is an essential link in the food chain for fish. The waters around the Canary Islands thus provide optimum conditions for an extraordinary variety of species – wreckfish, sea perch, and blue merlin are at home here, as are parrotfish, alfonsino, golden mackerel, sea eel, and moray. However, the fishing grounds, once so rich, have become increasingly depleted as a result of overfishing. Spanish, Portuguese, and Moroccan fishing fleets with their constantly modernized equipment have ensured bigger catches that do not allow the stocks the time they need to recover. The disputes in Brussels about fishing quotas demonstrate how fierce the competition has become, particularly between Spanish and Moroccan fishing fleets in the Canary Island fishing grounds.

As a result the selection of fish on restaurant menus in the Canary Islands has shrunk in recent years. Tuna fish, mackerel, and sardines are frequently on offer, while a parrotfish might occasionally stray onto the menu as *pescados del día* (fish of the day.) The Canary Islanders prefer to cook fish in succulent stews or simply *a la plancha*, on a hot griddle with oil, garlic and parsley. It is almost always accompanied by piquant green sauce *(mojo verde)* and wrinkled potatoes *(papas arrugadas)*. On St. Martin's Day, which falls on November 11, the dish traditionally served is crisp fried salt cod, or stockfish, with boiled sweet chestnuts or cooked bananas, frequently to the accompaniment of new wine.

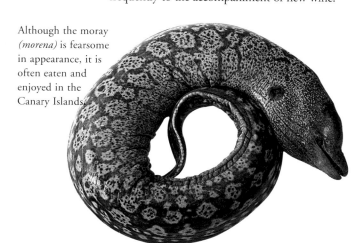

Although the moray *(morena)* is fearsome in appearance, it is often eaten and enjoyed in the Canary Islands.

The freshly caught fish must first be descaled with a wire brush. This is best done under running water, brushing from the tail end toward the head.

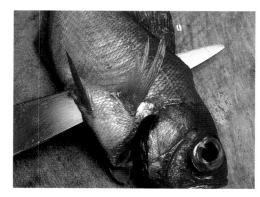

Next, slit the fish in half lengthwise. Either cut right through the backbone, or just cut through the rib bones and open the fish out flat.

In the Canary Islands the head is often left on the fish when it is cooked. When the fish is cut in half, therefore, the head is also cut through with a sharp knife.

First, the fish is fried with the cut side downward. Then turn it over (above) and cook the outside until it is nice and crisp (below).

LIMPETS

No sooner has the Atlantic receded a few yards on the ebb tide, exposing the damp cliffs, than entire families start to clamber between the slippery rocks, using sharp knives to loosen tasty limpets from their moorings. With their thick covering of green algae, these limpets have adapted themselves so well to their surroundings that it takes a practiced eye to spot them. Protected by their round or oval ridged limestone shell, they cling tightly to the stones. A certain amount of skill is needed to thread one's way barefoot between seaweed and shards of stone that are as sharp as glass, without slipping and losing all the seafood that has already been gathered. For people who live on the coast, searching for limpets at the water's edge is a favorite hobby; on good days a few pesetas can even be earned by selling the haul to nearby restaurants. The limpets, which are popular eaten as tapas, are extremely easy to prepare; they are often eaten accompanied by a piquant sauce:

LAPAS CON MOJO
Limpets in piquant sauce

7 cloves of garlic, chopped
1 tbsp chopped parsley
½ tsp sea salt
½ tsp cumin
½ cup/125 ml white wine
½ cup/125 ml olive oil
12 tbsp breadcrumbs
2¼ lbs/1 kg limpets in their shells,
ready for cooking

Crush the garlic with the parsley, salt, and cumin in a mortar and pestle. Gradually stir in the white wine and olive oil. Add enough breadcrumbs to make a stiff paste.
Arrange the limpets on a griddle or platter over a hot flame. Dot a small amount of the paste on each one. The limpets are ready as soon as they begin to loosen in their shells. Serve immediately while hot.

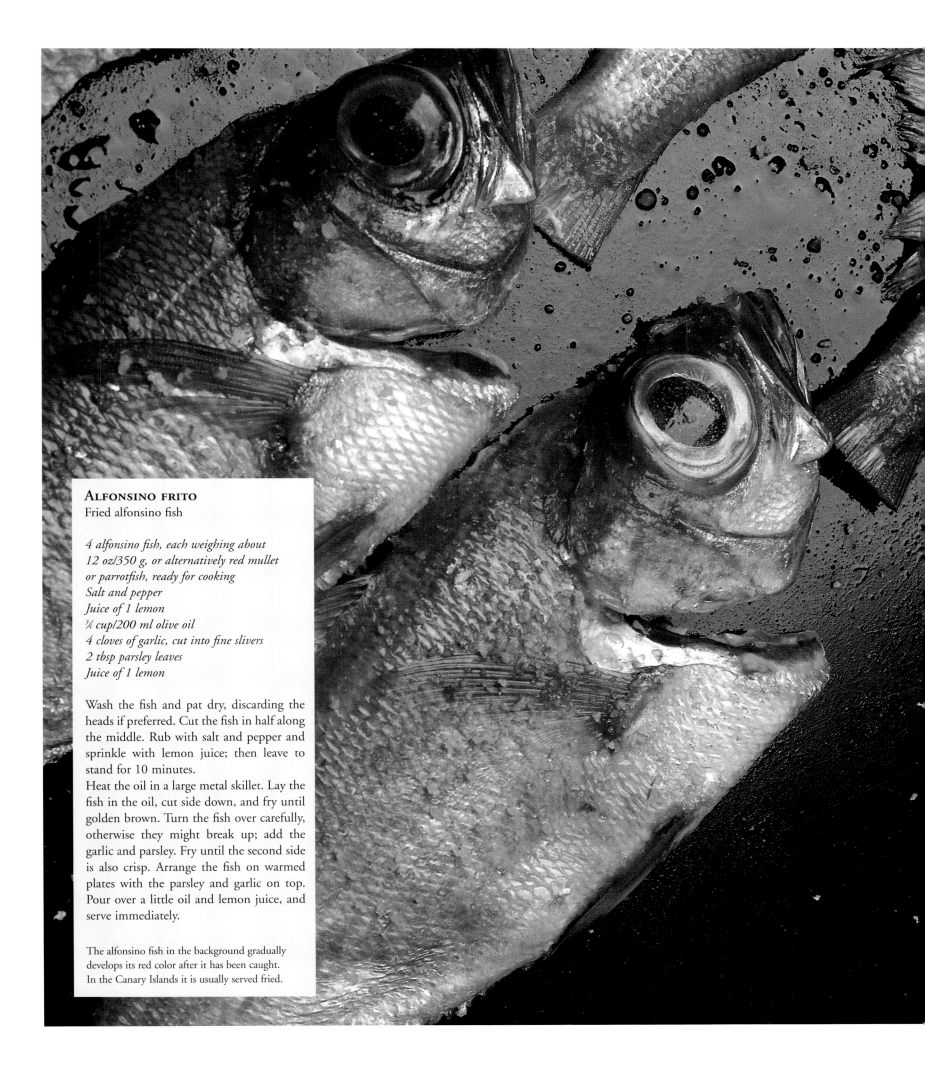

Alfonsino frito
Fried alfonsino fish

4 alfonsino fish, each weighing about
12 oz/350 g, or alternatively red mullet
or parrotfish, ready for cooking
Salt and pepper
Juice of 1 lemon
¾ cup/200 ml olive oil
4 cloves of garlic, cut into fine slivers
2 tbsp parsley leaves
Juice of 1 lemon

Wash the fish and pat dry, discarding the
heads if preferred. Cut the fish in half along
the middle. Rub with salt and pepper and
sprinkle with lemon juice; then leave to
stand for 10 minutes.
Heat the oil in a large metal skillet. Lay the
fish in the oil, cut side down, and fry until
golden brown. Turn the fish over carefully,
otherwise they might break up; add the
garlic and parsley. Fry until the second side
is also crisp. Arrange the fish on warmed
plates with the parsley and garlic on top.
Pour over a little oil and lemon juice, and
serve immediately.

The alfonsino fish in the background gradually
develops its red color after it has been caught.
In the Canary Islands it is usually served fried.

VEGETABLES

There is a popular saying among the Canary Islanders insisting "anything that tastes good must be ripe." Scarcely has one field been harvested than a new crop is being planted or sown. Growth is hardly ever interrupted as a result of the changing seasons in the Canary Islands; the rhythm of blossoming and ripening is affected only by irrigation. In order to afford some protection from excessively hot sunshine and dehydration, whole areas of land are covered in plastic netting and sheeting, under which grow lettuce, cucumbers, tomatoes, beans, peas, and often bananas as well. Many small farmers grow produce mainly for their own consumption and for sale in local markets and stores. Green and yellow pumpkins (*bubangos*), dark green chard, leeks, cabbage, fennel, red and green chili peppers, bell peppers, and white, red, green, and black beans, peas, maize, onions, garlic, spinach, radishes, chickpeas, lentils, – all grow in multicolored profusion.

The variety of vegetable pear known as *chayote*, a native of Latin America, is something of a curiosity in the Canary Islands. This climbing plant has large leaves and entwines itself around trees; when cooked, the pear-shaped, prickly fruit taste similar to zucchini. Stuffed with ground meat and herbs they are a real delicacy. Whether eaten alone in vegetarian dishes or in combination with various kinds of meat, especially pork and kid, all these vegetables go well together in tasty Canary Island stews.

Chayote or vegetable pear

There is hardly any type of vegetable that does not grow on the islands. Canary Island stews are just as colorful.

Various types of pumpkin are to be found in gardens in the Canary Islands (above). The substantial dish known as *puchero canario* also contains chickpeas, sweet potatoes, maize, cabbage, and leeks (main photograph), as well as two kinds of meat, bacon, and sausages.

Vegetables and Meat

Puchero canario
Canary Island stew

Scant 1 cup/200 g chickpeas
2 salt pork ribs
Generous 1 lb/500 g shin of beef
3½ oz/100 g smoked bacon
Salt
¼ tsp black peppercorns
1 onion, spiked with 2 cloves and 1 bay leaf
2 cloves of garlic
9 oz/250 g green beans
9 oz/250 g green pumpkin (flesh only)
9 oz/250 g yellow pumpkin (flesh only)
9 oz/250 g white cabbage
2 large sweet potatoes
2 fresh corn cobs
1 tomato
1 bouquet garni (parsley, cilantro, and oregano)
2 chorizo sausages

Soak the chickpeas overnight in plenty of water. Next day, drain the water from the chickpeas and place them in a net or muslin bag. In a large pan bring the pork ribs, beef, and bacon to a boil with 8 cups (2 liters) of water. Skim several times, then add the chickpeas together with a little salt; season with the peppercorns, spiked onion, and garlic. Cover and cook everything on a medium heat for approximately 1½ hours, adding a little more water if necessary. Then lift the meat and the chickpeas out of the stock and strain it into a second pan.

Clean the vegetables and cut into small pieces. Cook with the chickpeas and herbs in the stock until the vegetables are tender. Add the ribs, meat, and sausages just 10 minutes before the end of cooking time, and heat through in the soup.

Traditionally, the broth is served first with a little *gofio*; then the vegetables, meat, and sausages follow as a second course.

Potaje de berros
Watercress soup

1½ cups/200 g dried white beans
7 oz/200 g smoked bacon, diced
1 onion, finely chopped
2 cloves of garlic, finely chopped
2 ripe tomatoes, skinned and diced
Generous 1 lb/500 g potatoes, diced
Salt and pepper
⅛ tsp ground cumin
2 bunches of watercress
A few threads of saffron

Soak the beans overnight. Cook the bacon in a large pan until the fat runs. Add the onion and garlic and cook gently until soft and translucent. Then add the beans together with the water in which they have been soaked and simmer for about an hour. Stir in the tomatoes and potatoes, and season with salt, pepper, and cumin. Cook for about another 25 minutes until the ingredients are tender.

Wash and clean the watercress, removing any coarse stalks. Chop the watercress and stir into the soup with the saffron. Simmer for a few minutes; then season to taste and serve with green *mojo* or *gofio*.

Carajacas
Marinated liver

6 cloves of garlic, chopped
1 tbsp chopped parsley
1 tsp sea salt
½ cup/125 ml olive oil
½ cup/125 ml wine vinegar
1 tsp hot ground paprika
½ tsp oregano
½ tsp thyme
4 slices of ox liver, each weighing about 7 oz/200 g
Oil for frying
⅛ tsp cumin
Freshly ground pepper

To prepare the marinade, crush the garlic with the parsley and salt in a blender. Gradually add the olive oil, vinegar, ground paprika, oregano, and thyme. Wash the liver and pat dry; then lay in a porcelain or glass dish. Pour over the marinade mixture and turn the liver over in it several times. Cover and marinate overnight in the refrigerator. Heat some olive oil in a pan and fry the liver on both sides. When cooked, remove the liver from the pan and keep it warm. Stir the marinade into the juices in the pan and boil for a few moments to reduce and intensify. Season to taste with salt, pepper, and cumin. Serve the liver with the sauce, and with boiled potatoes as an accompaniment.

CARNIVAL TIME IN TENERIFE

The weight of the thousands of glass beads and sequins adorning the peacock costume of the *Reina*, or carnival queen, is almost too much for the delicate beauty wearing it. On the back of the peacock there is a quivering circle of shimmering feathers 3 feet (1 meter) high, cleverly supported by concealed fiberglass rods – a symbol of power and nobility. The carnival queen has been chosen and so the Tenerife carnival can begin.

The official program lasts for two weeks, with grandiose processions, street parties, music, and dancing. No expense is spared; bands from Cuba and Venezuela play fiery Latin American rhythms to which exotic-looking girls dance on magnificently decorated stages. Ceremony and scenery, brightly colored costumes and the traditional fancy dress are all a testament to the unfettered imagination. This is Mardi Gras in Tenerife, with its wild antics and inexhaustible pursuit of anarchy and ecstasy. It rivals the carnival in Rio de Janeiro. Nor is it all over by Ash Wednesday; in Tenerife the celebrations continue for another week, and as a kind of overture to the smaller carnival which follows *(carneval chico)*, the people participate in the ceremonial burial of a gigantic sardine *(entierro de la sardina)* on that day.

During the carnival season there is, of course, great feasting on these sensual, pleasure-loving islands. Dancing to salsa, merengue, and cumbia rhythms uses a lot of energy, and a great deal of strength is needed to be able to dance the night away. Besides, what life would be worth living without sweet things, especially at carnival time? Canary Islanders love them, without reservation, despite all dietary advice and doctor's orders. Sugar, honey, sugar cane syrup *(miel de caña)* and palm syrup *(miel de palma, see page 473)*, almonds, raisins, cinnamon, and aniseed are all used, in addition to lard, oil, and butter, to bake delicious crisp, golden yellow buns, cookies, and pies.

TRUCHAS DE NAVIDAD
Pies with sweet potato filling

For the pastry:
Generous 1 lb/500 g flour
½ cup/125 g lard
1 egg yolk
1 tsp sugar
A pinch of salt
1 cup/250 ml white wine

The carnival in Tenerife rivals that of Venice. For a whole week night is turned into day, and many people consider the carnival to be as spectacular as Mardi Gras in Rio.

In Tenerife the carnival lasts a week longer than anywhere else. The sardine's arrival signals the end of the carnival.

The ceremonial burial of the sardine *(entierro de la sardina)* is celebrated in Santa Cruz.

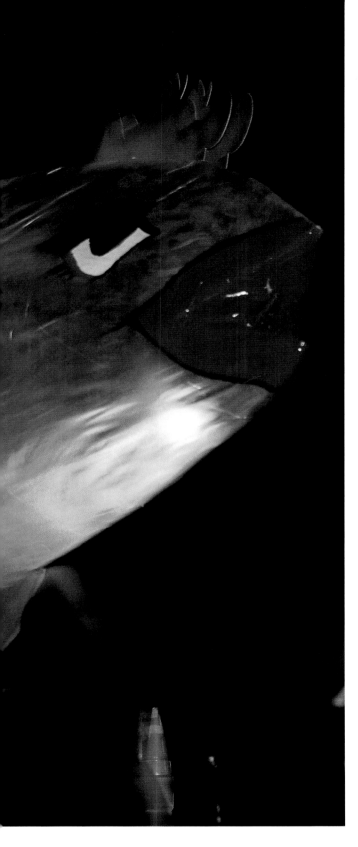

1 Almonds, blanched and ground, are needed to make *truchas de navidad* (literally "Christmas trout").
2 Make a paste from almonds, sweet potatoes, and spices as a filling for the pastry.
3 Place some filling on a round of pastry and fold it in half.

 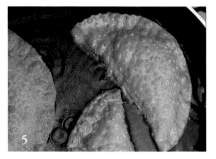 

4 Seal the edges of the semicircular pies with a fork. This looks attractive and keeps the filling inside.
5 Fry the *truchas* in hot oil. They should be crisp and a nice golden brown color.
6 *Truchas* taste even better sprinkled with confectioners' sugar – not just at carnival time or Christmas.

For the filling:
Generous 1 lb/500 g sweet potatoes
¾ cup/75 g ground almonds
⅛ tsp cinnamon
2 tbsp sugar
Rind of ½ lemon, grated
⅛ tsp ground aniseed

Flour for the work surface
Egg for glazing
Oil for frying
Confectioners' sugar to finish

Knead the flour, lard, egg yolk, sugar, salt, and wine together, adding enough water to make a smooth dough. Roll into a ball, cover and rest for 1 hour in the refrigerator.

To make the filling, peel and boil the sweet potatoes; then drain off the water and leave to cool for a few minutes. Press through a potato ricer and mix with the remaining ingredients.

Roll the dough out thinly on a floured work surface and stamp out rounds using a glass. Place 1 tablespoon of filling in the center of each and fold the pastry rounds in half, making sure the filling is covered. Brush the edges with egg and seal them using a fork to push down the dough.

Heat the oil in a pan or deep-frier (350 °F/ 175 °C) and fry the *truchas* in batches until they are a nice golden brown. Remove the *truchas* with a slotted spoon and leave to drain for a while on paper towels. Sprinkle with confectioners' sugar before serving.

BIENMESABE
Tasty almond cream

2 cups/200 g ground almonds
⅔ cup/175 g sugar
Rind of 1 lemon, grated
⅛ tsp ground cinnamon
3–4 egg yolks (depending on size), whisked

Roast the ground almonds in a dry pan until they are golden brown, but not too dark. Remove from the heat. Slowly dissolve the sugar in about 1⅔ cups (400 ml) water and bring to a boil to form a clear, thick syrup. Add the lemon rind, cinnamon, and roast almonds, stirring constantly and adding a little extra water if necessary. Remove from the heat, leave to cool for a few minutes and then fold in the egg yolks. Bring to a boil again; then pour into a glass dish and chill. Store in the refrigerator before serving.

When the sardine is dead, the carnival in Tenerife is at an end; all that remains is the ashes.

467

Keeping a goat ensures a daily supply of fresh milk, which is more digestible for humans than cow's milk. Canary Islands farmers turn a large proportion of goat's milk into cheese.

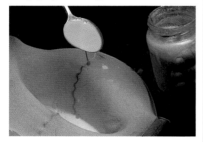

Rennet *(cuajo)* is used to curdle the fresh milk. This enzyme was once obtained from the stomachs of newly born animals, but artifical rennet is also used today.

The fresh milk is heated to about 104 °F (40 °C). Then the rennet is stirred in, and the mixture is left to stand until it is completely curdled.

The coagulation resulting from the addition of rennet causes the curds and whey to separate. The curd cheese is obtained by squeezing the jelly gently with the hands.

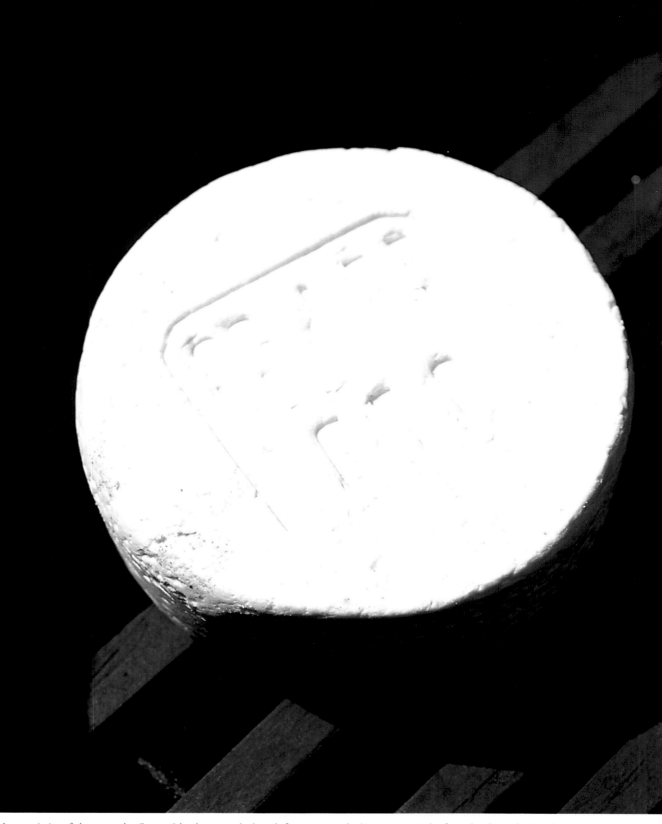

Many varieties of cheese on the Canary Islands are smoked; each farmer swears by his own particular formula when selecting the wood for the fire. Some use branches of a specific type of tree, while others use heather or vine wood. The cheese can also be lightly salted before smoking, or flavored with herbs, or rubbed with paprika pepper, which gives the rind a reddish color. A variety of different cheeses is thus created from a similar basic product.

Next the solids are poured into molds, and further gentle pressure is exerted to remove all the whey. Muslin cloths can also be used in this process.

While the remaining whey drips slowly from the molds, the cheese sets and gradually becomes firm. It is usually consumed as curd cheese.

Next the farmer puts his stamp on the curd cheese. This enhances its appearance and is also a legal requirement if the product is to be sold in a store.

The curd cheese can then be removed from the mold. It is now ready to eat, but many producers flavor it further by adding herbs or smoking it.

Goat cheese

The exodus from the countryside has not yet been halted in the Canary Islands. The young and the malcontent have moved away from the villages, leaving only elderly people. Although nobody today is obliged to endure the dreadful poverty experienced at the time of the mass emigration to South America, many families would not have potatoes or other vegetables, salad or fruit on the table were it not for the produce from their back yards. It is customary to keep a couple of goats, even though it becomes increasingly hard for old people to find food for these perpetually hungry animals, especially in summer. The goat in its stall signifies a little financial independence – milk and meat for the family's own consumption and cash in return for cheese sold.

Canary Island cheese is produced mainly on farms. Raw unpasteurized goat's milk is used for the most part, but it may also be combined with ewe's and cow's milk on some islands. Only a small part of the 13,200 tons (12,000 tonnes) of cheese produced annually in the Canary Islands is made in commercial dairy operations, which exasperates both bureaucrats and hygiene fanatics. As a result there has been no shortage of attempts in recent years to restrict private production of cheese using raw milk and to oblige farmers and goatherds to deliver goat's milk to central dairies for processing under totally hygienic conditions. This would be a great loss. Every farmer has his own recipe, and the products from two neighboring farms can taste completely different.

A goat's milk cheese from the Canary Islands is best enjoyed on its own without accompaniment. At most all it needs is a piece of farmhouse bread and some olives. It is used to make the popular cheese dip *almogrote*.

Queso majorero from Fuerteventura owes its name to the fact that the goats in the meadows graze largely on marjoram, imparting an outstanding flavor to the milk. The cheese is available in different stages of ripeness, and is sometimes also ripened with oil and paprika or even sometimes with *gofio*. *Majorero* cheese bears the official designation of origin *Denominación de origen (D.O.)*.

The amber-colored, spicy *queso herreño* from El Hierro is rubbed with paprika pepper and lightly smoked. It is held in high esteem on the other islands as a result of its delicate flavor. On La Gomera the farmers make a particularly strong, piquant cheese, which is smoked using heather, grapevines, or *tabaiba dulce*, which is a non-poisonous type of spurge. This cheese is particularly suitable for making the typical cheese spread *almogrote*, which is usually eaten on bread or with *papas arrugadas*.

Goat cheese from La Palma (*queso palmero*), which is often smoked with almond wood, pine needles, or dried *opuntia* leaves, is lightly salted before ripening. On the outside the cheese is slightly brown in color, while it is white to a pale yellow color on the inside. It has a mild flavor and tastes best eaten while it is fresh and still soft.

Picnics in the Canary Islands

Picnics need not always be on the beach. In recent years, resourceful independent tourists have discovered a new, charming activity on the Canary Island archipelago – hiking across the islands of the Atlantic. The diversity of the landscape, with its deserts of black lava, cool valleys, and evergreen forests of laurel, is a fascinating challenge for nature lovers, from the typical rambler to the ambitious mountaineer. Island-hopping is also an option, and there are four national parks in the Canary Islands: on Lanzarote the national park contains the Timanfaya volcanoes; the Tenerife national park has the volcano Teide and Las Cañadas; on Gomera there are the Garajonay cedar forests; and La Palma boasts the ancient crater Caldera de Taburiente. Farmers on the islands also act as tour guides, laying the picnic table with a spread of the delicious fare they produce. The management of the national parks has prudently established resting places in carefully chosen spots, where it is also possible to cook safely on open fires. *Mojo* is served with meat and substantial pepper sausages; juicy melons are eaten with salami and ham; and almonds, dried figs, and country wine accompany spicy goat cheese.

Right: The only other thing needed to accompany goat cheese, fresh figs, and homemade farmhouse bread, is a robust country wine.

WINE FROM THE VOLCANOES

Tastes change with the times, and this is also true of wine. For centuries the heavy, highly alcoholic Malvasía or Malmsey wine produced in the Canary Islands was the ultimate in luxury for the European aristocracy and the wealthy bourgeoisie. However, in the 18th century connoisseurs and wine lovers preferred wines from France and Portugal. Exports of wine from the Canary Islands all but ceased. In a few decades an entire wine-producing industry fell into decay: the area covered by vineyards was drastically reduced, and the grapes produced from those that remained were of poor quality. On Lanzarote, however, the tradition of Malmsey wine has survived. The El Grifo and Mozaga *bodegas* from the winegrowing district of La Geria, in the Yaiza and San Bartolomé region, produce Malvasías that are full of character. These are distinguished above all by their bouquet, which is reminiscent of muscat and apricots. Drunk as sweet and semisweet dessert wines, they are fruity and soft, and turn amber in color following a brief period of aging in wooden barrels. The straw-colored *secos*, which are the dry variants, have a fine bouquet and should be drunk as young as possible.

The key to the good wines produced on Lanzarote is the *modo lanzaroteño*, a method of cultivating dry fields that exists only on Lanzarote. Vines and fruit trees grow on this desert island, despite the fact that there is scarcely any rainfall. The secret lies in fragments of a type of dark-colored pumice stone known as lapilli, which fell onto the fields during volcanic eruptions and completely buried them. The lapilli cool down rapidly at night, which increases condensation in the layers of air near the ground. This results in a great deal of dew at night. The stones are porous and absorb the moisture greedily, and then release it to the plants. In the daytime they protect the soil beneath from the scorching rays of the sun and prevent the water from being evaporated by the hot wind. In order to expose the soil beneath the layer of lapilli so that the roots of the plants can reach it, craters about 3 feet (1 meter) deep are dug out, at the base of which the vines are planted. Then, to provide protection from the trade wind that blows constantly from the northeast, semicircular walls are built around the craters using lumps of lava. In this way a fine wine is produced under the most difficult climatic conditions.

Vines grown for winemaking on Lanzarote are protected in small craters, constructed from lapilli, or fragments of pumice stone, that are typical of the island.

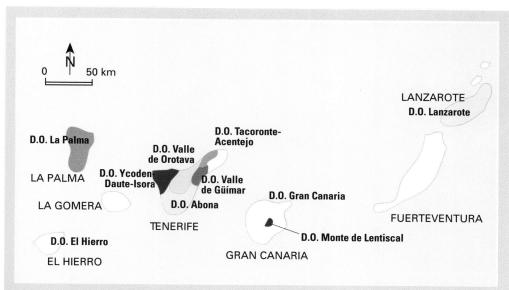

WINE-PRODUCING AREAS ON THE CANARIES

Tenerife

The principal grape varieties cultivated in the **D.O. Tacoronte-Acentejo** vineyard, are Listán Negro and Negramoll that make predominantly red wines, but also some rosés. The white wines are produced from Listán Blanco, Malvasía, Moscatel, and Verdello. The wine-producing area designated as **D.O. Ycoden-Daute-Isora** is renowned for its aromatic white wines. The preferred grape varieties grown here are Malvasía and Listán Blanco. Another ten white and seven red grape varieties are authorized here.

The **D.O. Abona** can pride itself on the highest mountain vineyards in Europe. Situated on the southern side of Tenerife, at up to 5250 feet (1600 meters), it mainly produces fresh white wines and juicy red wines of consistent quality.

In the **D.O. Valle de Güímar** the ancient vineyards ascend to a height approaching 5000 feet (1500 meters). The white wines made from the Listán Blanco grape, possess wonderful fruit combined with elegant softness. Red wines are also found in this D.O., but to a far lesser extent.

On the north coast of Tenerife, in the **D.O. Valle de la Orotava**, rounded, soft white wines and fruity red wines are produced from at least 990 acres (400 hectares) of vineyards. Included among the ten officially authorized main grape varieties are Pedro Ximénez, Listán Negro, and Negramoll.

Lanzarote

The **D.O. Lanzarote** district produces mostly white wines. The Malvasía grape dominates; Listán Blanco, Diego, and also the red variety Listán Negro are grown here.

La Palma

The modern bottling plants of the **D.O. La Palma** produce light, dry table wines, mostly made from Listán Blanco and Bujariego grapes; a red wine from Negramoll and Listán Negro; and, in deference to ancient tradition, dry and sweet wines from the Malvasía grape. In Mazo, on the eastern side of La Palma, a strong red wine is produced from the Negramoll grape.

Gran Canaria

The vineyards of **D.O. Gran Canaria**, a protected designation of origin since 2000, lie in hight of up to 5000 feet (1500 meters). The main grape varieties are red Negra Moll and white Malvasía. The dry white wines are light, with a tinge of herbs. The reds are usually young, light and balmy. D.O. Monte de Lentiscal covers the natural reserve of Tarifa with the Pico de Bandama crater. The volcanic soil yields grapes from the Listán Negro and Listán Blanco varieties. These mild and fruity wines have a rather simple structure. 90% of the wines produced are red, of which only a small amount is natured in casks.

El Hierro

D.O. El Hierro, situated on the smallest and driest of the Canary Islands, proudly offers twelve varieties of grape grown on less than 1235 acres (500 hectares). The traditional wines are made from blends, while the modern wines are

VINO DE TEA

Little has changed over the centuries in the wine cellars in the north of La Palma. The grapes are still trodden barefoot in huge tubs before the remaining juice is squeezed out in wooden presses. The must is fermented in wooden barrels that hold 105 US gallons (400 liters) and are known as *pipas*. The farmers are not particularly careful about how they handle the aging wine, adding rose leaves or peach leaves, or pouring a generous shot of marc into the barrel to arrest fermentation so that the wine does

not become too alcoholic. This is regarded here as a pardonable offence, since the wine is not bottled, but is intended only for consumption by family, friends, and acquaintances. It is very rare for a barrel of country wine of this kind to find its way into a restaurant. Visitors are offered a glass somewhat hesitantly, since this raw, light red wine has a character that does not appeal to everybody – it tastes strongly of resin. *Vino de tea* or Resina (it tastes not unlike Greek retsina) owes its flavor to being stored in barrels made from the fragrant heartwood *(tea)* of native Canary Island pine trees.

Sugarcane was a precious asset in the Canary Islands until the 16th century. Today *caña de azúcar* is only grown on a very small scale. Children enjoy licking pieces of sugar cane as a tasty treat, while adults distil the sap of the sugarcane plant to make rum with a high alcoholic content.

SPIRITS AND LIQUEURS

A true Canary Islander swears by the family recipe for homemade herb-flavored liqueur, which is used as a panacea for all manner of afflictions and is naturally drunk as a *digestivo*. A long tradition of *licores caseros*, homemade liqueurs, exists on the islands, for wherever wine and sugarcane are produced there is always a good supply of simple brandy. Marc distilled from grapeskins *(orujo* or *aguardiente)* is transformed by the addition of rosemary, mint, wormwood, cress, aniseed, cinnamon, lemon grass, and cloves into a drink that is aromatic and aids digestion.

The names given to these liqueurs and spirits and the recipes for them vary from island to island, as the ingredients depend upon local conditions. On Gran Canaria and La Palma, where sugarcane is still grown today, good rum is to be found. The natives like to drink it as *ron con miel* – rum with honey, sugar, and lemon juice; it is also known as *mejunje*, a name derived from the Arabic word *mechun* meaning "mixture." On Tenerife the preferred drink is *yerbilla*, which is rum with honey, enhanced by the addition of herbs, spices, and coffee beans. The name and recipe for this was brought back by Canary Islanders on their return from Cuba long ago. And on Lanzarote, social evenings are often rounded off with a *malvasía fin de fiesta,* which is made from dry Malmsey, sugar, eggs, and tea.

SUGAR AND RUM

With a simple swing of the machete, the 3-foot (1-meter) high plant is felled with a single stroke, just above soil level and close to the root, so that not one drop of the sweet, juicy sap is lost. Then the stalks are put to one side, and the farmer straightens up and reaches back to take yet another swing at another plant.

The rhythm of the sugarcane harvest continues to reverberate around the Canary Islands like an ancient ritual. It has never changed; no machine has ever relieved the farmer of the task. Sugarcane (caña) still grows on Gran Canaria and in the fertile, wet northeastern part of La Palma as it did in the time of the *Conquista*, hidden like small islands in the green sea of banana trees. However, only a few farmers now plant their fields with sugarcane, because the work is arduous and the profit gained, in view of the low prices, is small.

Five hundred years ago, when sugar still held the promise of a quick deal, African slaves labored for the plantation owners who had arrived on the islands as adventurers and profiteers. Having secured rights over land and water, they had made a fortune from the lucrative sugar trade. The well-known German commercial dynasty of

the Welsers in Augsburg owned their fields on La Palma. In those days sugar was still considered a valuable healer and fortifier, and was used as a medicine for all sorts of ailments. Only wealthy people could afford to use it for sweetening their food, since it had to be shipped at great expense from the Canary Islands to Europe. Trading in this fine commodity was very profitable for growers, traders, and ship owners.

Yet by the 16th century the boom was already at an end. High production costs resulting from artificial irrigation and fuel shortage, together with cheap competition from the Central American colonies, made it unprofitable to grow sugarcane on the Canary Islands. However, the islanders have continued to use the remaining sugarcane for the local production of rum. There are a few distilleries in San Andrés y Sauces on La Palma and in the north of Gran Canaria that produce very respectable rum – either a simple white spirit, or a golden brown version, aged in the barrel to produce exceedingly fine flavors (see photograph below).

Sap from sugarcane is also an essential ingredient in *miel de caña*, the syrup which is highly popular in the Canary Islands for baking and preparing the many sweet dishes.

SUGAR FROM THE TREETOPS

The men who harvest the raw material from which palm syrup *(miel de palma)* is produced have to climb right up into the crowns of the Canary Island palm trees. They use an axe to cut out the topmost palm branch, drawing up the sap inside the plant. The sap *(guarapo)* is collected by means of a piece of piping made from a reed in a bucket that the *guarapero* has secured with ropes in the top of the palm tree. The sap is later reduced by boiling to make palm syrup. This is used mainly to prepare sweet dishes, or it can simply be drizzled over pastries and desserts. It also tastes good with cheese or *gofio*. Palm syrup is said to have disinfectant properties and is used to treat throat infections and other inflammations of the mouth and pharynx.

Below: Rum produced in the Canary Islands is not exactly in a favorable position to compete with its famous Caribbean rivals. Yet Canary Island rum is definitely worth tasting. Producers on Gran Canaria and La Palma market rum of astonishing quality, including varieties that have been aged in the barrel.

The filler inside a cigar is made up of different qualities of tobacco according to taste.

The leaves are cut into small pieces using the *chaveta*. They are then laid on the leaf to be used as the wrapper.

The *tabacalero* rolls up the filler inside the binder, which is likewise selected to give the desired aroma.

Next, the unfinished cigars are pressed by placing them in wooden boxes inside mechanical presses.

Hand-rolled *puros* are the pride and joy of the cigar rollers and a source of great pleasure.

How the cigar arrived in Spain

Many of the conquerors of the New World claimed to have discovered tobacco. However, Christopher Columbus was without doubt the first European to encounter, on the islands he had discovered, Indians who walked around with a small glowing stick made of grasses, inhaling its smoke. He was to record the fact with amazement in his logbook. He also mentioned that the natives called the outer covering of these sticks *tabagos* and the grass they contained *cohiba*. The Mayas in Central America called the rolls of tobacco *jiq* or *ciq*, which evolved into *Ciq-Sigan*, from which the Spanish word *cigarro* was ultimately derived.

The conquerors brought the tobacco plant to Spain at the beginning of the 16th century, from where it spread throughout the world. Initially regarded as a botanical curiosity, tobacco was for a long time used as a medicinal herb, administered as snuff. It was some time before the custom of smoking tobacco in pipes became established. The development in Spain of a new method of drying and fermenting tobacco resulted in the creation of smooth wrappers to bind the filler (the tobacco inside the cigar), and it was only then that the new culture of tobacco smoking emerged.

The first Spanish cigars were produced in 1676 in Seville. The royal factories founded in 1731 in the Andalusian city played a decisive role in their popularization. At the peak of their success, around 1800, these operations employed thousands of workers who every day produced huge quantities of *puros*, or "pure ones," as cigars were called. Spain thus became the land of the cigar. Today around 40 million cigars are imported annually, and trade in Latin American cigars has become a very important commercial phenomenon.

The *tabacalero* does not need many tools; the most important is the tobacco knife or *chaveta*.

Smoke signals from La Palma

"When I light up a genuine *puro*, it brings back memories from the old days in Cuba – my grandfather with a cigar between his teeth, the wonderful aroma – *hombre*, that was really something!" Fernando Fernández who is eighty years old rolls his cigar critically between his fingers. He is an expert, having worked as a *tabacalero* all his life.

After Castro's revolution in Cuba he returned to La Palma and with very little money began manufacturing *puros* (pure ones), managing to support his family with his one-man business. Since then, however, times have become hard on La Palma, the only island in the archipelago where tobacco is grown and processed. Government bodies are promoting anti-smoking campaigns, young people prefer cigarettes, and the market for quality cigars is shrinking. There are still some traditional family businesses on La Palma, though, where the art of rolling cigars is being handed down from the older to the younger generation.

Cigar manufacture began on La Palma about a hundred years ago. At that time, when Spain was obliged to relinquish its South American colonies, many former emigrants returned to the Canary Islands with expertise acquired in the field of tobacco and cigar production. Tobacco was then cultivated intensively on La Palma and made into cigars in small workshops that were mostly family businesses. The quality of these cigars was so outstanding that they were comparable to Havana cigars. Exports to Europe, and especially to England, the Netherlands, and Scandinavia, brought a degree of prosperity to the villages, evidence of which can still be seen today in the weathered villas built in the Spanish colonial style.

The most aristocratic *puro* ever produced on La Palma was created as follows: the filler came from Breña Alta on the eastern side of the island, the binder from El Paso in the west, and the wrapper from plantations in the Caldera de Taburiente valley. However, those produced today are comparable, being also of excellent quality. The hand-rolled Corona, a Havana-type cigar, consists of a tobacco filler from La Palma, albeit wrapped in the finest leaves from Brazil or Sumatra.

And there is new hope for lovers of La Palma cigars – the European Union is planning to promote tobacco-growing in order to guarantee the future of a branch of the economy that is steeped in tradition, with its jobs and its trade mark *Puros hechos a mano en Canarias* (hand-made Canary Island cigars).

Finally the cigar is rolled in a wrapper. Only immaculate tobacco leaves are used for this.

Real dexterity and a feel for the cigar tip are required, especially to roll the ends of these fine cigars.

Next the ends of the wrapper are affixed using a special glue which is made from plants.

475

Cuban cigars

The most famous cigars in the world come from Cuba. The smoking of Havana cigars is a way of life that is no longer confined to circles of older men; these aromatic cigars appeal to younger men as well, and it is also becoming increasingly common to see women lighting up a Havana – with good reason.

The extraordinary complexity of Cuban cigars is primarily due to the good soil and ideal growing conditions for tobacco plants in the province of Pinar del Río, west of Havana. This is the sole factor that makes such a difference, and consequently it is impossible to find cigars with a flavor comparable to that of a true Havana anywhere else.

Tobacco was already being grown in the west of Cuba by the native islanders. In 1541 a Spaniard opened the island's first cigar factory, but it was in the first half of the 19th century that most of the great brand names came into existence, such as Partagás, H. Upmann, La Corona, Por Larrañaga, Punch, Bolívar, Romeo y Julieta, and Hoya de Monterrey.

The manufacture of premium quality cigars is an art, even more so than wine production, since it has been impossible to introduce machinery. From the careful choice of seedlings, via picking, leaf selection, drying, fermenting, sorting, and mixing, to the rolling and packing of the cigar, everything is done by hand – *hecho a mano.*

The Cohiba is the most expensive of all Havana cigars. It was Fidel Castro himself who gave the order in 1967 for the creation of a cigar of the finest quality, using the best mixture of tobacco. For many years Cohiba cigars were reserved for diplomats and important state visitors. Since the best tobacco leaves in Cuba were kept back for Cohiba production, the world-famous high priest of cigar manufacture from Geneva, Zino Davidoff, withdrew from Cuba in protest at this action. His company now manufactures cigars in the Dominican Republic and in Honduras.

The highly prized Cohibas have also been exported since 1982, initially in Lancero, Corona, Especial, and Panatella format. The Espléndido, Robusto, and Exquisito formats completed the "Línea Clásica" range in 1989. In 1992 – 500 years after the discovery of Cuba by Columbus – the Siglo I, II, III, IV, and V formats (*siglo* means century) were added to the new Cohiba range, "La Línea 1492." As before, only the very best tobacco is used in these top quality cigars, and only the best cigar makers in Cuba have the honor of hand-rolling Cohibas. Comprehensive quality testing involves checks carried out by professional testers *(catadores)* of a fifth of the day's production. Now nearly 3.5 million Cohibas are sold every year, or approximately 1 percent of all the cigars rolled in Cuba.

Choosing and smoking cigars

When buying cigars it is perfectly acceptable to open the box and handle the fine items inside. The wrapper should be neither too heavily ribbed, nor too pale, nor should it be marked. In order to establish whether a cigar has been properly stored, all that is required is to squeeze it carefully and lightly at the end where it will be lit. If it is elastic, first yielding and then springing quickly back into its original round shape, it contains the correct amount of moisture. If on the other hand it stays flattened, then the dealer is storing his cigars under excessively humid conditions. If the cigar is inelastic and does not yield very much at all, then it is too dry. A faint white or greenish dust on the surface, however, is not a bad sign (or mildew!). On the contrary, the deposit shows that the cigar is "living," for a little albumen is secreted naturally from the leaves at the precise point in time when the tobacco plant would have been due to flower. This can simply be wiped off.

At home, cigars are best stored in a humidor, a box made from hardwood or high-grade acrylic in which the moisture level remains constant. The temperature should be between 64 and 68 °F (18 and 20 °C) with a humidity of between 65 and 75 percent.

Time and patience are needed to enjoy smoking a cigar. First of all, the round end of the cigar is cut using a cigar cutter. Then it is lit using a gas lighter, cedarwood spill, or long match. The cigar should not touch the flame, but should be turned slowly above it until it is burning evenly. Only then does one take the first pull. The cigar should be smoked slowly, so that the wrapper does not become hot. A connoisseur never inhales, incidentally, in order not to lose the fine aroma. As the tobacco burns, the ash produced cools and protects the burning end, and therefore should not be removed too soon – once every four or five minutes is sufficient for a high-quality cigar. The ash should not be knocked off, but instead should be stroked off against the side of the ashtray. Uneven burning indicates that the cigar has been too loosely rolled. If the cigar should go out, it can be relit, provided that no more than half of it has been smoked.

Above: **standard formats for Havana cigars**

1	Demi-Tasse	4 inches/102 mm	30
2	Panetella	4 inches/114 mm	26
3	Robusto	5 inches/127 mm	50
4	Pyramid/Torpedo	6⅛ inches/156 mm	52
5	Small Corona	5 inches/127 mm	42
6	Corona	5½ inches/140 mm	42
7	Large Corona	6 inches/152 mm	42
8	Churchill	7 inches/178 mm	47
9	Especial	7½ inches/191 mm	38
10	Double Corona	7⅞ inches/200 mm	49

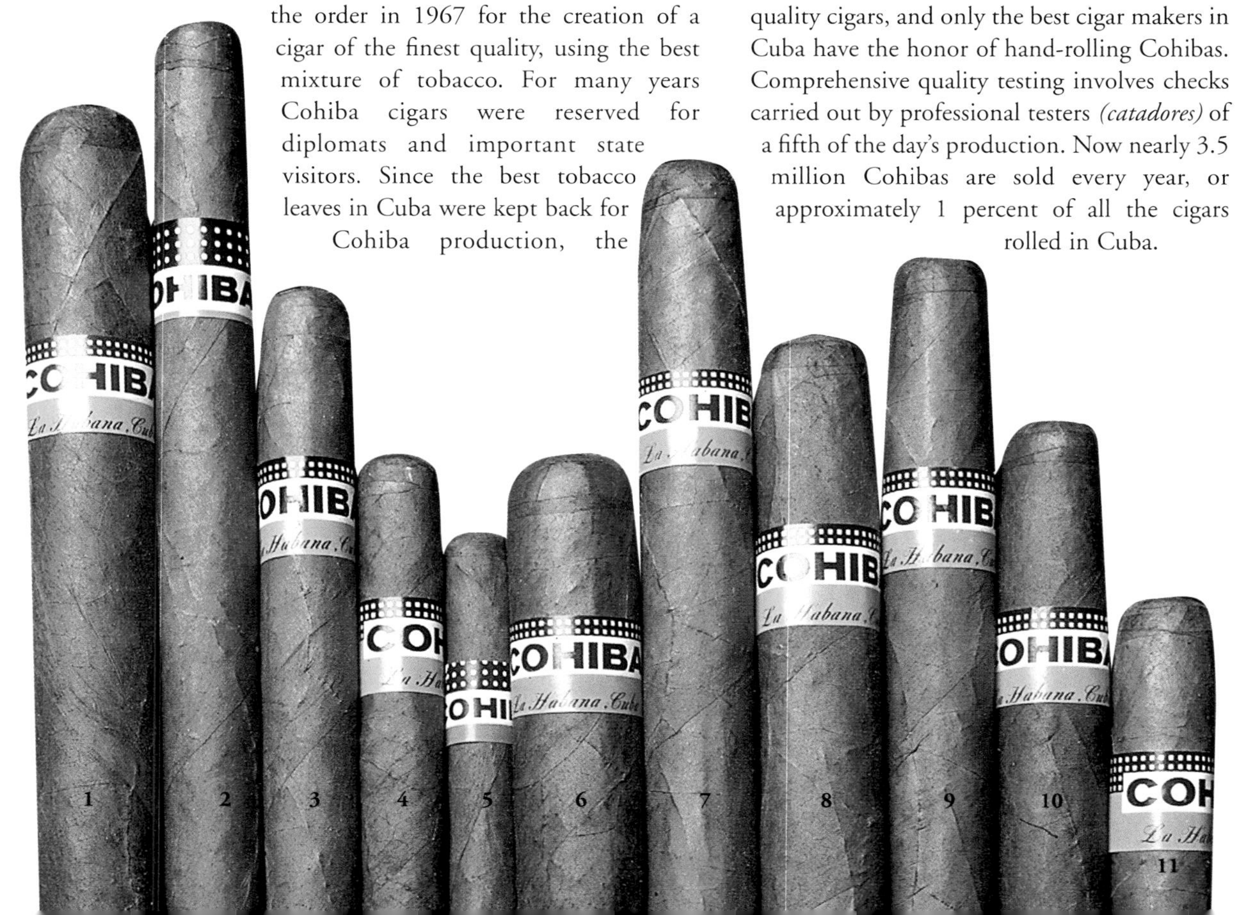

Left: **formats for Cohiba cigars**

1	Espléndido	7 inches/178 mm	47
2	Lancero	7½ inches/191 mm	38
3	Corona Especial	6 inches/152 mm	38
4	Exquisito	5 inches/127 mm	36
5	Panatella	4½ inches/114 mm	26
6	Robusto	5 inches/127 mm	50
7	Siglo V	6¾ inches/171 mm	43
8	Siglo IV	5⅝ inches/142 mm	46
9	Siglo III	6 inches/152 mm	42
10	Siglo II	5 inches/127 mm	42
11	Siglo I	4 inches/102 mm	40

Length and thickness of a cigar is measured in inches (1 inch = about 25.4 millimeters). The diameter is indicated by a ring measurement (see right column) based on units of $\frac{1}{64}$ of an inch. Thus a cigar with a ring measurement of 50 has a diameter of $\frac{50}{64}$ of an inch.

BRAND NAMES AND COLOR

Cohiba
This is the ultimate in Havana cigars. It has a moderately strong to strong aroma.

Partagás
Connoisseurs are divided; those who do not swear by Cohiba often claim this brand to be the best. It is of course a matter of taste. The company, which dates back to the time when the Cuban cigar industry was founded, manufactures over 30 different formats. The Large Corona *Presidente*, a cigar well worth trying from the Robusto *Series D No. 4,* is particularly strong. The showpiece cigar from this manufacturer is the Double Corona *Lusitania.*

Hoyo de Monterrey
Among the top Cuban cigars, the traditional Robusto *Epicure No. 2* rivals those from Partagás. The very mild *Doble Corona* is also highly recommended.

Montecristo
The *"A"* format of this brand, which is possibly the most famous brand of Havana cigars, is the flagship of the Cuban cigar industry. Retailing at over US$ 45 for a single cigar, this Especial, which is over 9 inches (23 centimeters) in length, also has the ultimate in price tags. The Torpedo *No. 2* is also recommended.

H. Upmann
H. Upmann was a German banker, who emigrated to Cuba in the 19th century. He was initially producing cigars exclusively for business associates until after some time he decided to devote himself entirely to cigar manufacture. The most famous of his products is the heavyweight Churchill format, *Sir Winston.*

Romeo y Julieta
This is one of the oldest and most famous brands in the cigar world. Connoisseurs praise its delicate aroma. For experienced smokers the *Cazadores* is worth trying, but be warned – owing to the quantity of smoke produced and the intense smell, this Gran Corona should be smoked in the open air.

Saint Luis Rey
Only the best tobaccos are used to make this cigar from the legendary Vuelta Abajo tobacco growing area. Most formats strike a perfect balance between mildness and strength. The Double Corona *Prominente* is especially worth trying and is a close rival of the top Pártagas cigar, the *Lusitania.*

Vegas Robainas
This is the youngest of all the Havana cigar brands; it is manufactured in five formats, including Robusto and Torpedo. Even the experts are as yet unable to predict how the brand will develop; ultimately cigars, like fine wines, need long periods of aging to enable them to develop their subtle character.

Other important brands are **Punch**, whose *Punch Punch* cigar is earthy and strong, and **Bolívar**, with its Lonsdale format *Immensas* cigar. The cigars from **El Rey del Mundo** are relatively light, and therefore well suited to novices. Among the light, rather sweet specimens are the elegant cigars from **Sancho Panza**, for instance the surprisingly mild *Torpedo Belicoso.*

It should also be noted that the color of a cigar does not provide the key to its taste and strength. These are primarily determined by the quality of the filler and the binder, to which the wrapper then adds fine nuances. A cigar that looks black on the outside, therefore, need not necessarily be heavier than one with a blond wrapper. Havanas are available in the following colors:
• *clarísimo* (green)
• *claro* (all the light, golden brown tones)
• *colorado* (reddish brown)
• *maduro* (all the brown tones)
• *negro* or *oscuro* (blackish brown)
These can be further divided into subcategories.

Glossary

a la brasa: charcoal grilled

a la marinera: cooked mariner-style (with white wine, onions, and tomatoes)

a la parilla: broiled

a la plancha: broiled on a (metal) hot plate (usually fish, seafood, meat)

aderezar/aliñar: to season or dress (salad)

adobo: see escabeche

ahumado: smoked

al ajillo: fried with garlic

al horno: roasted or baked in the oven

almuerzo: brunch, hearty second breakfast

al pil-pil: (fish) sautéd slowly in oil with garlic, shaking the pan constantly so that the gelatine in the fish combines with the oil to form a jelly-like sauce

al vapor: steamed

alimento(s): food

aliño: dressing, seasoning

arroz/arroces: rice/rice dishes

asado: roast meat, roasted

aves: poultry

bien hecho: well cooked (meat)

blanquear: to blanch or pre-cook in boiling water (vegetables)

caldereta/caldeirada: stew, prepared with fish and/or seafood, or with meat (usually lamb or goat) depending on the region

caldo: clear broth

caña: small beer from the cask

carne/carnes: meat (dishes)

caza: game, game dishes

cena: evening meal (usually substantial)

cocido: thick stew, usually based on pulses and meat

cocina casera: good home cooking, plain fare

comida: meal, dinner, lunch

crustáceos: crustaceans

degustación: tasting or sampling of food or drink

desalar: to remove the salt from a foodstuff that has been preserved in salt by soaking it in water (e.g. salt cod or salt meat)

desayuno: breakfast

descamar: descale (fish)

desgrasar: to remove fat (usually from soups or sauces, by skimming the cold fat from the surface)

despepitar: to remove the seeds or stones from fruit or vegetables

dorado: browned, fried golden yellow

dulce: sweet

engrasar: to grease with butter, oil or lard, e.g. a baking pan or baking sheet

ensalada: salad

entradas/entremeses: starters, hors d'œuvres

escabeche/adobe: marinade based on vinegar, oil, and spices

escalfar/pochar: to poach, or cook carefully in water below boiling point (e.g. eggs)

estofado: braised, pot-roasted

fondo: juices remaining in pan after cooking meat or fish, usually used as a base for sauce

frito: fried in oil; fish and seafood are often coated in egg and flour before frying

frutas: fruit

glasear: to glaze, or coat with sugar or jam

gratinado: cooked au gratin, given a crisp topping by cooking under fierce heat (with the addition of cheese or breadcrumbs)

guarnición: garnish

guisado: braised, fried and then cooked in liquid

huevos: eggs

ingredientes: ingredients

en su jugo: in its own juices

ligado: thickened, bound with cream, egg yolk, or butter

mariscos: shellfish

merienda: afternoon snack

mortero: mortar, usually used for crushing spices, garlic, or herbs

olla, puchero: stew (also cooking pot)

pan: bread

en papillote: cooked in foil

pastelería: pastries

pescado: fish

plato: plate, dish, course

postre: sweet course, dessert

potaje: soup (usually thick)

pote: stew

queso: cheese

quitar las espinas: to fillet (fish)

rebozar: to roll in breadcrumbs, to coat ingredients (e.g. meat, fish, vegetables, eggs) in flour, egg, and breadcrumbs before frying

rehogar: to sauté, toss in oil

relleno: stuffed

salmorejo: marinade of oil, vinegar, salt, and pepper

salpimentar: to season with salt and pepper

salteado: sautéd

segundo (plato): second course, main course

solomillo: sirloin, fillet

sopa: soup

suprema: boneless fillet of fish or meat

tapas: canapés, small piquant hors d'oeuvres (hot or cold)

tostado: toasted, browned (usually bread)

verduras/hortalizas: vegetables

vino tinto/blanco: red/white wine

Credits and Copyright

BIBLIOGRAPHY

Academia Española de Gastronomía: El café en la cocina moderna. Barcelona 1996

Alegría, Francisco Abad / Ruiz Ruiz, María Rosario: Nuestras verduras. Pamplona 1990

Amate, Pablo: Embutidos. Madrid 1992

de Amezúa, Clara María G. / Arenillas, Ángeles / Capel, José Carlos: From Spain with Olive Oil. Madrid 1988

Amigos da cociña galega (Ed.): Amigos de la cocina gallega. Santiago de Compostela n.d.

Andrews, Colman: Cocina Catalana. Barcelona 1989

Apicius, Caius: Frutas. Madrid 1992

Aris, Pepita: Die ländliche Küche Spaniens. Augsburg 1996

Azpiazu, Iñigo: La Cocina Española. Barcelona 1991

Bach, Sibylle: Spanische Hausmannskost. Munich 1984

Baur, Eva Gesine / Seifert, Anuschka: Der Reichtum der einfachen Küche – Spanien. Munich 1997

Beltrán Martínez, Antonio / Porquet Gombau, José Manuel: Gastronomía Aragonesa. Zaragoza 1994

Berasategui, Joaquín: Cocina vasca. Oiartzun 1994

Bettónica, Luis: Cocina regional española. Barcelona 1981

de Bobadilla, Vicente Fernández: Brandy de Jerez. Madrid 1994

Caballero Bonald, Manuel: Brevario del vino. Madrid 1988

Cabo, Roberto: Reiseführer Natur – Spanien. Munich 1995

Canut, Eric / Navarro, Francesc: Catálogo de Quesos de España, Ministerio de Agricultura y Pesca. Madrid 1990

Capel, José Carlos: Aceite de Oliva. Madrid 1992

Capel, José Carlos: El pan. Barcelona 1991

Capel, José Carlos: Manual del pescado. n.p. 1995

de Cervantes Saavedra, Miguel: The Adventures of Don Quixote, trans. John M. Cohen, paperback reprint edition (June 1988), Penguin USA

Ciurana i Galceran, Jaume: Els Vins de Catalunya. Generalitat de Catalunya, Departament d'Agricultura, Ramaderia i Pesca. Barcelona 1979

Club G (Grupo Gourmets, Ed.): Weinführer '97. Madrid 1997

Confederación Empresarios de Hostelería y Turismo de Aragón: Guía Gastronómica de Aragón. Huesca 1989

Costa Clavel, Xavier: Ganz Santiago. Barcelona 1989

Davidson, Alan / Knox, Charlotte: Fische & Meeresfrüchte. Munich 1991

Delgado, Carlòs: El libro del vino. Madrid 1985

Delgado, Carlos: Diccionario de gastronomía. Madrid 1996

Departament de Comerç, Consum i Turisme / Institut Català de la Vinya i el Vi (Ed.): The Wine and Cava Route in Catalonia. Barcelona 1995

Díaz, Lorenzo: La cocina del Quijote. Madrid 1997

Domingo, Xavier: El Sabor de España. Barcelona 1992

Domínguez Barberá, Martí: Els nostres menjars. Paterna 1979

Dumas, Alejandro: Cocina española (Ed. Juderías, Alfredo). Madrid 1982

Echeverría, Ignacio / López de Lamadrid, Claudio / von Berenberg, Heinrich (Ed.): Spanische Reise. Berlin 1987

Equipo de expertos Cocinova (Ed.): Cómo cocinar los caracoles. Barcelona 1992

Equipo de expertos Cocinova (Ed.): Pescados y mariscos. Barcelona 1991

Fàbrega, Jaume: El llibre del peix. Barcelona 1996

Fernández de Alperi, Sofía: Cocina y gastonomía de Castilla y León. Madrid 1995

Galiana, Ismael: Los 50 mejores recetas de la cocina de Murcia. Murcia 1995

García, María Luisa: El arte de cocinar, Vol. 1 and 2. Madrid 1987

García, María Luisa: Platos típicos de Asturias. Gijón 1993

García del Cerro, Carlos / Arroyo González, Manuel: La cocina del queso español. Madrid 1990

Garnweidner, Edmund: GU Naturführer Pilze. Munich 1987

Garrido, Carlos: Mallorca Mágica, Palma de Mallorca, 1988

Gómez González, Eduardo: Cocina riojana. n.p. 1995

Gómez Roth, Adelaido: Gastronomía Regional Murciana. Murcia n.d.

González del Peral, Antonio: De caza y de cocina. Madrid 1996

González Sevilla, Emilia: El fogón del pobre. Barcelona 1996

Grewe, Rudolf (Ed.), Llibre de Sent Soví (Receptari de Cuina). Barcelona 1979

Haberkamp de Antón, Gisela: Eßdolmetscher Spanien. Munich 1991

Hausch, Bruno / Hudgins, Sharon / Messer, Christine: Spanien - Küche, Land und Menschen. Weil der Stadt 1991

Hemingway, Ernest: The Sun Also Rises, Macmillan Publishing Company, 1995

Herbers, Klaus (Ed.): Der Jakobsweg. Tübingen 1991

Herce Garraleta, Francisco Javier / Ramírez Martínez José Manuel: La Gastronomía en La Rioja. Logroño 1981

Hilgard, Peter: Der maurische Traum. Kassel 1997

Iglesias, Pilar: El libro del tomate. Madrid 1990

Jover, Lluïsa: Cuina Llaminera. Barcelona 1996

Junta de Castilla y León (Ed.): Gastronomía de Castilla y León. Valladolid, n.d.

Laux, Hans E.: Setas. Barcelona 1993

López Fernández, José: La naranja. Composición y cualidades. Valencia 1985

López Palazon, José: El almendro y su cultivo. Madrid 1972

Luard, Elisabeth: The La Ina Book of Tapas. Cambridge 1989

Luján, Néstor: Como Piñones Mondados. Barcelona 1994

Luján, Néstor: Diccionari Luján de Gastronomia Catalana. Barcelona, 1990

Luján, Néstor: Pequeña historia de los canelones, in: 100 Recetas de Canelones. Rubí 1990

Luján, Néstor: Die sieben Tode des Grafen Villamediana, Munich 1989

Luján, Néstor y Tin: La cuina moderna a Catalunya. Madrid 1991

Luján, Néstor und Tin: Spanien - Eine kulinarische Reise durch die Regionen. Munich 1991

Luján, Nestor / Perucho, Juan: El libro de la cocina española. Barcelona 1970

Lladonosa i Giró, Josep: El gran llibre de la cuina catalana. Barcelona 1991

Mapelli López, Enrique: Varia noticia del buen comer andaluz. Malaga, n.d.

March, Lourdes: La cocina mediterranea. Madrid 1988

March, Lourdes: El libro de la paella y los arroces. Madrid 1985

March, Lourdes / Ríos, Alicia: El libro del aceite y la aceituna. Madrid 1989

Martín Iniesta, Fernando: Antología de la gastronomía madrileña. n.p. 1994

Martínez Llopis, Manuel: La cocina de las aves de caza. Madrid 1996

Martínez Llopis, Manuel / Irizar, Luis: Las cocinas de España. Madrid 1994

Martínez Llopis, Manuel: Historia de la gastronomia española. Madrid 1989

Marvin, Garry: Bullfight. Oxford 1988

Mendel, Janet: Cooking in Spain. Malaga 1992

Méndez Riestra, Eduardo: Cocinar en Asturias. Gijón 1994

Méndez Riestra, Eduardo: Guía Gastronómica de Asturias. Oviedo 1994

Méndez Riestra, Eduardo: La Hora de Comer. Oviedo 1995

Mestayer de Echagüe, María: La cocina completa. Madrid 1994

Mestayer de Echagüe, María: Confitería y repostería. Madrid 1993

Michael, Edmund / Henning, Bruno / Kreisel, Hanns: Handbuch für Pilzfreunde. Jena 1978

Millo, Lorenzo: Cocina Valenciana. León 1995

Ministerio de Agricultura y Pesca: Catálogo de Embutidos y Jamones Curados de España. Madrid 1983

Navarro Garrido, Andrés: Quesos Artesanos de Asturias. Gijón 1994

Nogués de Lecuona, Rosario: España plato a plato. Madrid 1991

Nola, Rupert de: Libre del coch. Ed. Veronika Leimgruber. Barcelona 1982

Nonell, Carmen: Cerámica y alfarería populares de España. León n.d.

Ohne Autor: Guía Gastronómica del País Vasco. San Sebastián 1995

Ohne Autor: Murcia. Calidad en su mesa. Murcia 1992

Ortega, Inés: El libro de las carnes. Madrid 1994

Ortega, Inés: El libro de los pollos, las gallinas, el pato y la perdiz. Madrid 1987

Ortega, Inés: El libro de las verduras y las ensaladas. Madrid 1990

Ortega, Simone: Quesos españoles. Madrid 1987

Ortega, Simone: Tabla de quesos españoles. Madrid 1983

Paczensky, von, Gert / Dünnebier, Anne: Leere Töpfe, volle Töpfe. Die Kulturgeschichte des Essens und Trinkens. Munich 1994

Palacios Sánchez, Juan Manuel: Historia del vino de Rioja. n.p. 1991

Paradores de Turismo de España (Ed.): Cocina tradicional en Paradores - Aragón y La Rioja. Madrid 1996

Pardo Bazán, Emilia: Das Gut von Ulloa, Düsseldorf 1946

Parra, Andreu: Todo sobre el Cava. Madrid 1994

Peñín, José: Los mejores vinos y destilados. Madrid 1995

Pérez, Dionisio: La Cocina Clásica Española. Huesca 1994

Els Professionals, Federació Catalana de Gremis de Pastisseria: Pastisseria. Barcelona 1993

Read, Jan: Sherry and the Sherry Bodegas. London 1988

Read, Jan: Spaniens Weine 1997/98. Bern 1997

Riera, Ignasi: Diccionario de cocina. Barcelona 1993

Rigau, Alejo: El cultivo del almendro. Barcelona 1975

Rodríguez Pérez, Juan Alberto: Flora exótica en las Islas Canarias. León 1987

Rollhäuser, Lorenz: Toros, Toreros. Reinbek 1990

Rosales de Molino, Cornelia: Spanien (»Küchen der Welt« series). Munich 1993

Salcedo Hierro, Miguel: La Cocina Andaluza. Sevilla 1995

Sánchez Araña, Vicente: Cocina canaria. León 1993

San Valentín, Luis: La cocina castellano-leonesa. Madrid 1995

Sarobe Pueyo, Víctor Manuel: La cocina popular navarra. Pamplona 1995

Sauleda, Jorge: The Wines of Navarra. Pamplona 1989

Sauleda Parés, Jorge: Pacharán navarro. Pamplona 1994

Schauhoff, Frank / Oliver, Tonina: Zu Gast auf Mallorca. Cologne 1993

Strosetzki, Christoph (Ed.): Spanien erzählt. Frankfurt 1991

Sueiro, Jorge-Víctor: El libro del marisco. Madrid 1990

Teubner, Christian (Ed.): Das große Buch des Meeresfrüchte. Munich 1996

Teubner, Christian (Ed.): Das große Buch vom Fisch. Munich 1995

Toharia, Manuel: El libro de las setas. Madrid 1991

Torrado, Llorenç: Els embutits a Catalunya. Barcelona 1985

Torres Rojas, María Angustias: Las fiestas en la cocina. Madrid 1991

Vázquez Montalbán, Manuel: L'Art del Menjar a Catalunya. Barcelona 1988

Vázquez Montalbán, Manuel: Contra los Gourmets. Barcelona 1990

Vázquez Montalbán, Manuel: Las recetas de Carvalho. Barcelona 1990

Vega, Luis Antonio de: Viaje por las cocinas de España. Madrid 1969

Vélez, Carmen: El libro de los pescados. Madrid 1987

Vives Molins, Josep: El Llibre de les Neules i dels Torrons. Barcelona 1991

Vossen, Rüdiger: Töpferei in Spanien. Hamb. Museum für Völkerkunde und Vorgeschichte. Hamburg, 1972

Xunta de Galicia (Ed.): Guía para a indentificación dos mariscos en Galicia. Santiago de Compostela 1995

Zapata, Antonio: Vivir para comer en Almería. Almería 1993

Zarzalejos Nieto, María del Carmen: La Cocina del Camino de Santiago. Madrid 1993

ACKNOWLEDGEMENTS

The publishers would like to express their thanks to everyone who has given their kind support and assistance, including those individuals and institutions who are not known to the publishers by name, but who have contributed to the project.

Special thanks are due to Rafael Martinez, who inspired our enthusiasm for Spanish cookery and without whom this book would not have been written.

Juan Carlos Sanz and all his colleagues in the trade department at the Spanish general consulate in Düsseldorf, for tireless assistance in our research
Dr. Isabel Sánchez Gil of the Spanish tourist office in Düsseldorf, and the Spanish tourist office in Munich, for research, logistics, and travel
David Schwarzwälder, Salamanca, for acting as a consultant on wines
Ruth Eberhard Correia, Lisbon, for obtaining photographs
Claudia Bettray for assistance with co-ordination
Karin Hertzer and Annette Rehrl, both of Munich, for editorial assistance
Gloria Pérez, Munich, for help with the recipes
Birgit Beyer, Cologne, for help with the layout
Regine Ermert, Cologne, for help with the layout
The Trutter family, who gave the editor constant encouragement

Catalonia
Montse Alcina, Barcelona
Distribucions Avinova, Sr. Capdevilla, Barcelona
Susana Barquin, Institut Català de la Vinya i el Vino, Barcelona
Teia Casacuberta, Barcelona
José Casellas Sala, Berga
Cafetería El Cisne, Platja d'Oro
Departament d'Agricultura, Ramaderia i Pesca, Generalitat de Catalunya, Barcelona
Fleca Balmes, Eduard Crespo, Barcelona
Juan-Carlos Galdámez, Barcelona
Gertraud Gromes-Schmid and Dr. Johannes Schmid, Esplugues
Xarcuteria Martí, Vic
Cristina Martínez Sánchez, Barcelona
Restaurant Mas dels Arcs, Antoni Izquierdo, Palamos
Restaurant Nymphenburger Hof, Munich
Pep Palau, Restaurant La Rectoría D'Oris, Oris
Jordi Parramón, Vic
Mantequerías Puig S.L., Barcelona
Ines Roca, Barcelona
Jaume Roig Sabaté, Restaurant Pitarra, Barcelona
Restaurant Sala, Miquel Marquez Moya, Berga
Anuschka Seifert-Gabel, Barcelona
Josep Solá, Barcelona
Hotel Balneario Vichy Catalán

Balearic Islands
Pedro Barbadillo, Palma de Majorca
Can Matarino, Sóller
Gabriela Cifuentes, ICEX, Palma de Majorca
Restaurante Es Cranc, Sr. José Garriga, Fornells/Menorca
Bartomeu Deyà, Foment de Turisme, Palma de Majorca
Caty Juan de Corral, Palma de Majorca
José Antonio Olives Orfil, Mahón
Pedro Quetglás, Conselleria de Agricultura, Palma de Majorca
Consejo Regulador de la Sobrassada de Majorca, Antonia Torres Oliver, Palma de Majorca
Xoriguer, Mahón

Aragon
Adico S.L., José Miguel Martínez, Zaragoza
Pastelería Ascaso, Zaragoza

Bodega-Licorería Barbacil, Sr. Juan Barbacil, Zaragoza
Bodegas Bordeje, Sr. Fernando Bordeje, Ainzón
Horno Artesano, Fraga
Miguel Lorente, Zaragoza
Julian Montal, Restaurante Montal, Zaragoza
Bodega Pirineos S.A., Barbastro
Victor Prats, Bar Prats, Campo
Eberio Rubio, Campo
La Tabla Nueva, Luis Ferer, Huesca
Restaurante Venta del Sotón, Marcelo Pesajovich, Esquedras
Bodega del Vero, Barbastro

Navarra
Cámara de Comercio, Conchi Biurrún and Virginia, Pamplona
Colmado Chirinta, Pamplona
Bodegas Guelbenzu, Ricardo Guelbenzu, Cascante
Bodegas Irache, Ayegui
Larra, Burgui
Bodegas Magaña, Barillas
Martiko, Luis Aoiz, Pamplona
Monasterio de Leyre, Padre Germán Santa María, Yesa
El Navarrico, José Pedro Safedo, San Adrián
Consejo Regulador de Pacharán, María Eugenia López, Pamplona

La Rioja
Bodegas Bretón, Rodolfo Labastida, Logroño
Pabo Calvo, ICEX trade department, Düsseldorf
Cosecheros Alaveses, Juan Carlos Carlos de Lacalle, Laguardia
Grupo de Criadores y Exportadores de Vinos de Rioja, Tom Perry, Logroño
Felix Losada, Dr. Muth PR, Hamburg
Bodegas de la Marquesa, Juan Pablo de Simón, Villanueva del Ebro
Obrador de Pastelería, Manolo Iturbe, Logroño
Bodegas Paternina, Haro
Bodegas La Rioja Alta, Javier Amescua and Marta Enciso, Haro
Quesos San Román, San Román
Tonelería Mecánica Riojana, Francisco Vásquez, Logroño

Basque Country
Bodegas Amestoy, José Antonio Amestoy, Getaria
Bretxa 2000, Luis Enrique Hernández, San Sebastián
Casa del Bacalao, Bilbao
Restaurante Ganbarra, Donostia-San Sebastián
Confituras Goya, Sr. Ramón, Vitoria-Gasteiz
Santuario de Arantzazu, Nicolas Segurola, Oñate
Merca Bilbao, Basauri
Pasteleria Otaegui, Maria Otaegui, San Sebastián
Consejo Regulador de Txacolí, Ruth Mozo, Getaria
Restaurante Urola, San Sebastián

Cantabria
José Castañeda Venero, Valdaliga
La Gancuenca, Teresa Martín Real, Roiz-Valdaliga
Hotel del Oso, Salud Briz, Cosgaya
Restaurante El Pescador, San Vicente de la Barquera
Joaquín Samperio Sañudo, Casón de la Marquesa, Las Fraguas
Viaval Conservas, Lamadrid

Asturias
Agromar, Armando Barrio Acebal, Gijón
Leticia Blanco, Gijón
Consejo Regulador D.O. Cabrales, Carreña de Cabrales
Carniceria Diaz, Arriondas
Joaquín Crespe Solares and Alicia Peón Solares, Villaviciosa
Sidra Fontcueva, Luis Fontcueva Vega, Sariego
Javier Artime Gonzales, Gijón
Pasteleria Niza, Oviedo

Galicia
Restaurante Alvariñas, Jaime Alvariñas Vicente, Combarro
Amegrove, O Grove
Restaurante Bitadorna, Chus Castro, A Guarda

Fernando Blas, Hotel-Restaurante Pousada O'Almacén, Cervo
La Casa de los Quesos, Carmen Blanco Campos, Santiago de Compostela
Restaurante El Castillo, M. Gomez Carpintero, Vigo
Emilia Castro Roboredo, Ordenes
Charol, Casa de la Queimada, Vigo
Cooperativa Arzuana, E. Monte Vaziño, Arzúa
Restaurante El Coral, A Coruña
Cruceros Rías Bajas, José Manuel Alvares Domínguez, O Grove
Cuevas y Cia S.A., Manuel de las Cuevas Fraga, Ourense
Restaurante Paco Feixó, Paco Feixó, Praia de Compostela
Angulas del Miño, Benítez Fernández S.L., Goian, Tui
Consejo Regulador de Orujo, Ourense
Francisco Esteban Palomo, Santiago de Compostela
Manuel J. Pol Cruces, Santiago de Compostela
Confitería Vilas, Carlos Vilas Vidal, Noia
Restaurante Vilas, Santiago de Compostela

Castile-León
Bodegas Antaño, Rueda
Asador Mauro, Peñafiel
Restaurante El Bodegón, Salamanca
Restaurante El Candil, Salamanca
Colmado Delabuelo, Astorga
Mariano García, Valladolid
Sonia Ortega and Bettina Krücken, ICEX Madrid
Jamones Joselito, Guijuelo
Confitería Pablo Rodríguez, Salamanca
Hnos. Rodríguez Bellido, Pozaldez
Victor and Margarita Salvador, Restaurante Chez Victor, Salamanca
Salchicherías Sandoval, Santiago García Rivero, Salamanca
Restaurante Valencia, José Luis Valencia, Salamanca
María Villalba, Salamanca
Bodegas Vinos de León, Armunia
Barbara Wehowsky, ICEX trade department, Düsseldorf

Madrid
La Boutique del Pan, Clara Orio
Restaurante La Bola, Agustín Verdasco del Hoyo
José Carlos Capel
Cervecería Alemana
Librería Clarín, María Carmen
Bar El Chicote
Café Gijón, Manuel Mesa Viso
Restaurante La Hoja, Paco Rodríguez Fuertes
Bettina Krücken, ICEX
Cafetería José Luis
Cervecería Naturbier
Restaurante El Olivo, Jean Pierre Vandelle
Stop Madrid
Tahona San Onofre, Daniel Guerrero López

Castile-La Mancha
Bodegas Miguel Calatayud, Valdepeñas
Ayuntamiento de Consuegra, Ramón Fernández, Consuegra
Ferajos Capital, Carlos Iran Fernández, Las Pedroñeras
Apoloño García Moreno, Consuegra
José Luis González, Consejería de Agricultura y Medio Ambiente, Junta de Castilla-La Mancha, Toledo
Gonzalfar, Ramón Gonzáles Nieto, Castellar de Santiago
Cristina Martínez and Francisco Menéndez, Depto. de prensa, ICEX, Madrid
S.A.T. La Plata, Andrés de la Plata, Villanova de Bogas
Gregorio Muñoz Martínez, Puertollano
Dionisos de Nova, Valdepeñas
Restaurante El Pincelín, Pedro Blanco Ruano, Almansa
Bodegas Felix Solis, Toas Pérez Clemente, Valdepeñas
Restaurante La Venta del Quijote, Puerto Lápice

Extremadura
Restaurante Atrio, Toño Pérez and José Polo, Cáceres
Restaurante El Convento, José Picado Carillo, Valencia de Alcántara

Corchos y Tapones Geval, Matías Berzas Rodríguez, Valencia de Alcántara
Bodegas Inviosa, Piedad Fernández Paredes, Almendralejo
Charcutería Maria Isabel, Valencia de Alcántara
Juan Romero, Depto. de Comercialización de Productos Agrarios, Badajoz
Carnicería, Juan Fransisco Paniagua Sánchez, Valencia de Alcántara
Unión de Productores de Pimentón, Jesus María Fernández Manzano, Jaraiz de la Vera
Julio Yuste, Cofradía Gastronómica de Extremadura, Badajoz

Valencia
José Fco. Arcis Martínez, Coop. Hortifruticola, Benifayó
Bodega Redonda, Utiel
Cohoca, Benifayó
Arroz DACSA, Paco Martí, Almassera
Restaurante L'Estimat, Baltasar Gil, Playa de las Arenas
Restaurante Galbis, Juan Carlos Galbis, L'Alcudia
Bernd Knöller, Restaurante Angel Azul, Valencia
Turrones El Lobo, Jijona
Frutos Secos Mañan, Antonio Sánchez, Pinosa
Merca Valencia, Gregorio López Moraleda, Valencia
Ayuntamiento de Murrla, Juan Giner Mulet, Murrla
Gerhardt Papenfuss, Wolfratshausen
Riera Orxater, Alboraya

Murcia
Luis Aronis, Konservenfabrik Hero, Alcantarillo
Salazones Garre, Felipe Garre Martínez, San Pedro del Pinatar
Ramón Gómez Martínez, Lo Pagán-Pinatar
Adelaido Gómez Roth, Murcia
Museo del Vino, Juan Carcelen, Jumilla
María Roth Hummer, Murcia
Salinera Española, S.A., San Pedro del Pinatar
Bodegas San Isidro, Jumilla
Churrería Sota, Jumilla
Restaurante Venezuela, Anastasio Giménez Delgado and José Antonio Giménez Hernández, Lo Pagan-Pinatar

Andalusia
Antonia Alivares, Vélez-Blanco
Antonio Alvarez, Sergio Alvarez Peres, Trevélez
Martín Dorado, Miguel Martín Dorado, Isla Cristina
González Byass, Jerez de la Frontera
Horno de San Buenaventura, Seville
Julia López de Sagredo, Almería
Núñez de Prado, Paco Iván Núñez de Prado, Baena
La Orza, Encurtidos vegetales del Guadajoz, Baena
Frutería Peñasco, José Herrera Sánchez, Seville
Antonio Pérez Moreno, Seville
Ginés Rodríguez Campos, Vélez-Blanco
José Luis Roiz Rangel, Seville
El Torno, Sebastiana Alvarez Martín, Seville
Bartolomé Vergara, Fedejerez, Jerez de la Frontera
Antonio Zapata, Almería

Canary Islands
Matilde Arroyo, Los Llanos de Aridane
Cejas, Lorenzo Fernandes, San Andrés y Sauces
Pedro Gómez Pede, El Paso
Hanspeter Heckel, Munich, consultant on cigars
Bodegas Llanovid, Fuencaliente
Juan Gilberto Martín Bentangu, El Paso
María Isabel Méndez Pino, El Paso
R. Enrique Naumann, El Paso
Antonio Orribo Alonso, Santa Cruz de la Palma
Bertila Pérez González, El Paso
Restaurante Playamont, Tazacorte
Azariel Rodríguez García, El Paso
Carmen Rosa Rodríguez Rodríguez, Los Llanos de Aridane
Supermercado San Martín, Antonio Miguel Martín Martín, El Paso
Compañia Transmediterránea, Antonio Sosa Rodríguez, Santa Cruz de la Palma

Index of Photographs

All photographs by:
Günter Beer, Barcelona

With the exception of:

AKG Archiv für Kunst und Geschichte, Berlin:
Page 100, top; page 126; page 298/299; page 316/317 (background); page 352/353 (background); page 458/459 (woodcut)

Bagyi, Franz, Weil der Stadt:
Page 323 (wild boar)

Botanik Bildarchiv Laux, Biberach an der Riß: Page 168, top

© Herrera, Mariano, Barcelona:
Page 373, top and bottom

© ICEX, Madrid: Page 137 (all grapes); photo: Antonio De Bevuto: p. 37, centre; page 99; photo: Felix Lorrio: page 98, left; page 170; page 244 (Rubia Gallega); page 245 (Retinta, Moruña de Salamanca, Avilena Negra)

© Kern, Thorsten, Köln:
Page 377 (parrot fish)

© Könemann Verlagsgesellschaft mbH, Köln:
Photo: food photograph on page 400, top (background); photo: Fuis & Büschel GbR/Büschel page 204, bottom right (inset); page 240 (inset, right); page 241 (carp, tench, pike); photo: Ruprecht Stempell page 36; page 70 (fennel); page 71, bottom; page 110; page 116 (onion, spinach); page 121 (chicken, goose); page 146 (wine-tasting); page 157, top; page 241 (trout); page 368, top; page 369 (background and inset); page 385 (medlar); page 404 (lollo rosso, lollo biondo, batavia, oakleaf lettuce); page 435 (custard apple, persimmon, raisins); page 436 (star fruit, apricot, peach); page 437 (plum, passion fruit, lime, nectarine); page 455 (physalis);

Marek, Erich, VS Schwenningen: Page 323 (stag, deer);

Museu Etnogràfic de Ripoll: Photo: Miquel Parés page 348 (inset);

© OKAPIA, Frankfurt a.M.:
Photo: Roland Birke page 115, top;
photo: Michel Brosselin page 121 (pigeon);
photo: Manfred Danegger page 121 (pheasant);
photo: Eric Kamp/Phototake page 121 (turkey);
photo: Robert Maier page 121 (quail);
photo: G. Synatzschke page 121 (woodcock);
photo: Andreas Hartl page 213 (salmon);
photo: G. Büttner/Naturbild page 307 (aniseed plant);
photo: Manfred Danegger page 323 (hare);
photo: Cyril Ruoso/BIOS page 323 (rabbit);
photo: Winfried Wisniewski page 323 (Iberian wild mountain goat);

Oroñoz, Madrid: Page 124, left (inset); page 190 (background);

Otto, Christoph, Berlin: Page 232, top left, bottom left, and right, page 232/233 (background);

Soltmann, Luis J., Lanzarote: Page 462, below left (limpets);

Spanish Tourist Office, Munich: Photo: González Grande page 29, bottom, right; photo: Foat page 171, top; photo: F. Ontañon page 228 (inset); page 268; page 269; photo: Massats page 275 (inset); photo: De La Puente page 280 (Saint Teresa); photo: Ramon G. Lopez Alonso page 330 (inset); photo: Kramer page 396 (background); page 397, top and bottom; photo: Pepe Parras page 420 (inset); photo: A. Garrido page 470/471;

Vedella dels Pirineus Catalans, Berga: Page 245 (inset, left);

© White Star, Hamburg: Photo: G. P. Reichelt page 121 (duck); photo: Jörg Steinert page 309 (Bar Bolero); photo: Monika Gumm page 396 (inset);

Wildlife, Hamburg: Photo: D. Harms page 265; photo: D. Usher page 353 inset

RECIPE INDEX
Recipes with illustrations have page number in bold type

483

RECIPE INDEX

Recipes with illustrations have page number in bold type

General Index

Illustrations have page numbers in bold